MW00624523

IN HARM'S WAY

IN HARM'S WAY

The Pornography Civil Rights Hearings

EDITED BY

Catharine A. MacKinnon

AND

Andrea Dworkin

HARVARD UNIVERSITY PRESS

Cambridge, Massachusetts

London, England

1997

Copyright © 1997 by Catharine A. MacKinnon and Andrea Dworkin
"The Roar on the Other Side of Silence" by Catharine A. MacKinnon
copyright © 1997 by Catharine A. MacKinnon
"Suffering and Speech" by Andrea Dworkin copyright © 1997 by Andrea Dworkin
All rights reserved
Printed in the United States of America

Library of Congress Cataloging-in-Publication Data

In harm's way : the pornography civil rights hearings / edited by
Catharine A. MacKinnon and Andrea Dworkin.
p.   cm.
Includes index.
ISBN 0-674-44578-3 (cloth : alk. paper).
ISBN 0-674-44579-1 (pbk. : alk. paper).
1. Obscenity (Law)—United States.
2. Pornography—United States.
3. Women—Legal status, laws, etc.—United States.
I. MacKinnon, Catharine A. II. Dworkin, Andrea.
KF9444.I54   1998
345.73'0274—dc21   97-30374

To Valerie Harper, Steve Jevning, and Therese Stanton

—*Andrea Dworkin*

To Linda Boreman, Charlee Hoyt, and Annie McCombs

—*Catharine A. MacKinnon*

To the memory of Ruth Christenson

—*Andrea Dworkin and Catharine A. MacKinnon*

Acknowledgments

The women and men who testified at the hearings, whose voices speak from these pages, and the gifted organizers in each city, who brought it all into public light, have our gratitude. What they did made our work possible. Of the many who worked so hard and gave so much, those whose contributions are especially memorable are Meg Baldwin, Jeanne Barkey, Karen E. Davis, Charlee Hoyt, Steve Jevning, Dorchen Leidholdt, Annie McCombs, Sharon Sayles-Belton, Therese Stanton, Diane Stoltenberg, John Stoltenberg, Van White, Gail Abarbanel, Sandy Mullins, Myra Riddell, Betty Rosenstein, Beulah Coughenour, Deborah Daniels, Steve Goldsmith, William Hudnut, Rhea Becker, Gail Dines, Lierre Keith, Amy Elman, and Barbara Findlen.

Without Valerie Harper's timely intervention, there would be no record of the Minneapolis hearings. David Satz's computerized version allowed the Minneapolis hearings to be passed hand to hand in photocopy for many years. Rhea Becker, Ann Russo, and Lierre Keith saved the Massachusetts hearings from probable oblivion. Sarah Zeller and Emily M. Lindell helped locate documents. Rita Rendell's skillful and tireless assistance made this volume possible. The proofreading of Kaethe Hoffer, with the help of Pamela Shifman and Leslie Bell, and of Christopher N. Kendall and Lila Lee, made it more accurate. We take responsibility for the contents.

Lindsay Waters at Harvard University Press published these hearings, ending almost fifteen years of their effective suppression. We thank him wholeheartedly.

Note on the Editing

These hearings are based on transcripts of oral testimony. The Minneapolis hearings were transcribed live by a court reporter, Kimberley Kramer of Janet Shaddix, Inc. The Indianapolis hearings were transcribed from an official but incomplete videotape. The Los Angeles and Massachusetts hearings were transcribed from audio tapes. Ellipses mark removal of anything that was said. Brackets indicate any other editorial alteration, such as correction, substitution, or addition. Editorial comment is confined to footnotes.

We intend these hearings to be as complete and accurate a record of what was said as possible. The excised material consists of some small talk, pleasantries, arrangements (for instance, scheduling), and legislative minutiae that is frankly incoherent when written down. Exhibits and written submissions, by contrast, are highly selected. Exhibits are renumbered consecutively, with original numbers or letters in brackets. Books, letters, and briefs, originally submitted whole, are excerpted. Internal citations in documents are not updated. For reasons of space, since Catharine MacKinnon spoke in all four hearings, much of her Indianapolis testimony (on the Minneapolis hearings and specific proposed amendments) is removed, as is testimony by Deborah Daniels that duplicated information testified to elsewhere. Not a word of testimony by opponents to the ordinances has been cut.

All survivors who testified were fully identified to the bodies before whom they spoke, unless they state otherwise on the record. For this volume, each survivor chose an identification. Those who could not be relocated to make this choice are identified by their initials. Some proper names had to be transcribed phonetically and have not been able to be further verified, despite our efforts. We apologize to anyone whose name is misspelled.

Contents

INTRODUCTIONS

The Roar on the Other Side of Silence

Catharine A. MacKinnon

Women speak in public for the first time in history of the harms done to them through pornography in the hearings collected in this volume. Their first-person accounts stand against the pervasive sexual violation of women and children that is allowed to be done in private and is not allowed to be criticized in public. Their publication, which comes almost fifteen years[1] after the first hearing was held, ends the exclusion from the public record of the information they contain on the way pornography works in social reality. Now ended is the censorship of these facts and voices from a debate on the social and cultural role of pornography that has gone on as if it could go on without them.

Until these hearings took place, pornography and its apologists largely set the terms of public discussion over pornography's role in social life. Public, available, effectively legal, pornography has stature: it is visible, credible, and legitimated. At the same time, its influence and damaging effects are denied as nonexistent, indeterminate, or merely academic, contrary to all the evidence. Its victims have had no stature at all. The hearings changed the terms of this discussion by opening a space to speak

---

1. Everywoman published only the Minneapolis hearings, and those only in Britain, in 1988. *Pornography and Sexual Violence: Evidence of the Links* (Everywoman, 1988). Everywoman noted in its introduction, "[p]ublication of this material . . . is an historic event because strenuous efforts have been made . . . to persuade a publisher in the United States to make them publicly available. It has proved impossible to persuade any publisher, in the very country where pornography is itself protected as 'freedom of speech,' to risk any association with evidence about its harmful effects on society—and especially on women and children. This is one of many indications that in the United States, freedom of speech is available only to the assailants and not to the victims. The power and wealth of the pornography industry, and interconnections with 'respectable' publishing, distribution, and sales outlets, mean the power to censor those who do not participate, do not agree with what is being said, and seek to expose the harm they are doing" (p. 1).

for the real authorities on pornography: the casualties of its making and use. Against a background of claims that the victims and the harms done to them do not exist, must not be believed, and should not be given a legal hearing, the harms of pornography stood exposed and took shape as potential legal injuries. These hearings were the moment when the voices of those victimized through pornography broke the public surface. Their publication gives the public unmediated and unrestricted access to this direct evidence for the first time. The authority of their experience makes the harm of pornography undeniable: it harmed them.

In late 1983, legislators in Minneapolis initiated this process[2] by employing Andrea Dworkin and me to write a law for the city that we had conceived on pornography as a human rights violation. Other jurisdictions followed, including Indianapolis, Los Angeles County, and the Commonwealth of Massachusetts,[3] each seeking to adapt our civil rights approach to local concerns. All these laws recognized the concrete violations of civil rights done through pornography as practices of sex discrimination[4] and gave the survivors access to civil court for relief through a law they could use themselves. The hearings that resulted from the introduction of the legislation gave pornography's survivors a forum, an audience, and a concrete opportunity to affect their world. Grasping the real chance that rights might be given to them, seeing that their participation could make a difference to the conditions of their lives, these women and men became prepared to run the risks of this political expression. The consequences anticipated at that time included public humiliation and shame, shunning and ostracism, loss of employment, threats, harassment, and physical assault.

2. As with all social movements, the process began substantially earlier with the women's movement as a whole, and more particularly with the feminist movement against pornography, "Take Back the Night" demonstrations and rallies, Women Against Pornography in New York City, and formatively with Andrea Dworkin's pathbreaking *Pornography: Men Possessing Women* (G. P. Putnam's Sons, 1981).

3. The ordinance has been actively considered in many other jurisdictions in the United States and was introduced before legislative bodies in Germany, Sweden, and the Philippines. No Canadian legislature or court has considered the civil rights ordinance. The Supreme Court of Canada upheld Canada's pre-existing *criminal obscenity* law on the constitutional ground that pornography harms women and equality. *R. v. Butler,* [1992] 1 S.C.R. 452 (S.C.C.). Widely circulated false reports of the role of *Butler* in customs seizures of gay and lesbian pornography in Canada, and an analysis of the contribution of the civil rights approach to pornography to promoting gay liberation, are discussed in Christopher N. Kendall, "Gay Male Pornography After Little Sisters Book and Art Emporium: A Call for Gay Male Cooperation in the Struggle for Sex Equality," 12 *Wisconsin Women's Law Journal* 21 (1997).

4. We also worked with the cities and citizens of Bellingham, Washington, and Cambridge, Massachusetts, to pass these ordinances by referendum on direct vote of the people. The ordi-

The act of introducing the antipornography civil rights ordinances into the legislative arena gave pornography's victims back some measure of the dignity and hope that the pornography, with its pervasive social and legal support, takes away. The ordinances, in formulating pornography's harms as human rights deprivations, captured a denigrated reality of women's experience in a legal form that affirmed that to be treated in these ways violates a human being; it does not simply reveal and define what a woman is. As ending these violations and holding their perpetrators accountable became imaginable for the first time, and women participated directly in making the rules that govern their lives, the disgrace of being socially female—fit only for sexual use, unfit for human life—was exposed as a pimp's invention. In these hearings, women were citizens.

The first-person testimony, contextualized by expert witnesses as representative rather than unique or isolated, documented the material harm pornography does in the real world, showing the view that pornography is harmless fantasy to be as false as it is clichéd. Women used for sex so that pornography can be made of them against their will—from Linda "Lovelace"[5] forced to fellate men so *Deep Throat* could be made to a young girl sold as sex to *Hustler*'s "Beaverhunt"[6] to Valerie Harper's face on another woman's naked body on a T-shirt[7]—refute the assumption promoted by the pornography industry that women are in pornography because they want to be there. The information provided by these witnesses also underlines the simplest fact of the visual materials: to be made, the acts in them had to be *done to someone*. A few who have escaped the sex factories describe the forms of force required.

Woman after woman used by consumers of pornography recounts its causal role in her sexual violation by a man close to her. A husband forces pornography on his wife and uses it to pressure her into sex acts she does not want.[8] A father threatens his children with pornography so they will keep silent about what he shows them is being done, audibly, to their mother at night.[9] A brother holds up pornography magazines as

nance in Bellingham passed with 62% of the vote. The ordinance in Cambridge failed to pass but received 42% of the vote. A bastardized version was introduced in Suffolk County, New York, which we helped to defeat.

5. Testimony of Linda Marchiano, Minneapolis Hearings, pp. 60–65.
6. Letter of Women Against Pornography, Minneapolis Hearings, pp. 131–133.
7. Letter from Valerie Harper, Minneapolis Hearings, pp. 140–142.
8. Testimony of R. M. M., Minneapolis Hearings, pp. 108–112.
9. Testimony of S. G., Minneapolis Hearings, pp. 145–147.

his friends gang-rape his sister, making her assume the poses in the materials, turning her as they turn the pages.[10] A woman's boyfriend becomes aroused by watching other women being used in pornography and forces sexual access.[11] A gay man inflicts the abusive sex learned through using pornography on his male lover, who tolerates it because he learned from pornography that a man's violence is the price of his love.[12]

Although intimate settings provide privileged access for these acts, such violations occur throughout social life. White male motorists, spewing racist bile, rape a Native American woman at a highway rest stop in reenactment of a pornographic video game.[13] Working men plaster women's crotches on the walls of workplaces.[14] Therapists force pornography on clients.[15] Pimps use pornography to train and trap child prostitutes.[16] Men who buy and use women and children for sex bring pornography to show those prostituted what the men want them to do.[17] Pornography is made of prostituted children to threaten them with exposure to keep them in prostitution.[18] Serial sexual murderers use pornography to prepare and impel them to rape and kill.[19]

Grounded in these realities, the ordinance that produced and resulted from the hearings provides civil access to court to prove the abuse and the role of pornography in it in each situation. The ordinance, with local variations, provides a cause of action to individuals who are coerced into pornography, forced to consume pornography, defamed by being used in pornography without consent, assaulted due to specific pornography, or subordinated as a member of a sex-based group through traffic in pornography as legally defined.[20] The chance to prove in court the harmful role of pornography in each situation is what pornography's victims have sought. This, to date, is what they have been denied.

The opponents of the civil rights laws against pornography are amply represented in the hearings. They did not openly defend pornography as

10. The details of this account were provided at the press conference on July 25, 1984, by the young woman whose statement appears on p. 265.
11. Testimony of N. C., Minneapolis Hearings, pp. 106–107.
12. Testimony of G. C., Minneapolis Hearings, pp. 107–108.
13. Testimony of Carole laFavor, Minneapolis Hearings, pp. 147–149.
14. Testimony of J. B., Minneapolis Hearings, pp. 121–124.
15. Minneapolis Exhibit 11, Letter of Marvin Lewis, p. 227.
16. Testimony of T. S., Minneapolis Hearings, pp. 114–120.
17. Ibid.
18. Ibid.
19. Minneapolis Exhibit 16, pp. 230–232.
20. The ordinances appear in the Appendices beginning on p. 426.

such,[21] or address the harms the witnesses document even to deny them. They treat the survivors as if they are not there or do not matter. That those victimized by pornography are lying or expendable is the upshot of the First Amendment defense of pornography that the opponents do present, proceeding as if the "speech" of violation matters over the violation of the violated. Some opponents adopt the view that any factual disputes over the harm should not be resolved in court—in other words, that whatever harm may exist can be debated so long as the debate is endless, but the harm can never be stopped. As the Massachusetts hearing shows, the issue of whether pornography is harmful matters to pornography's defenders only as long as it is considered impossible to demonstrate that harm. Once it is judicially established that pornography does the harms made actionable in this law—as it was established in the litigation on the ordinance in 1985[22]—the ordinance's opponents lose interest in the question.

Addressed not at all by the opposition in the hearings is whether or not the practices of pornography made actionable by the ordinance are properly conceptualized as sex-based discrimination. Like the conclusion that pornography causes harm, the conclusion on the nature of that harm is based on evidence, on fact; these hearings provide those facts. As an analytic matter, although many people are shown to be victimized, actually and potentially, if even one woman, man, or child is victimized *because of their sex*, as a member of a group defined by sex, that person is

21. Increasingly, since then, they do. *Sex Exposed: Sexuality and the Pornography Debates*, ed. Lynne Segal and Mary McIntosh (Virago Press, 1992); Nadine Strossen, *Defending Pornography: Free Speech, Sex, and the Fight for Women's Rights* (Scribner, 1995); Wendy McElroy, *XXX: A Woman's Right to Pornography* (St. Martin's Press, 1995).

22. American Booksellers v. Hudnut, 771 F.2d 323, 328 (7th Cir. 1985). "Therefore we accept the premises of this legislation. Depictions of subordination tend to perpetuate subordination. The subordinate status of women in turn leads to affront and lower pay at work, insult and injury at home, battery and rape on the streets." See the Appendix on pp. 465–482 for the full text of this opinion. Given that Judge Easterbrook strongly concludes that pornography as defined does the harms the ordinance makes actionable, some statements in its footnote 2 (see Appendix, p. 481) have generated confusion. Contrary to footnote 2, the empirical studies on the effects of exposure to pornography do not "conflict"; the older studies have merely been superseded, as often happens when science progresses. The legislative record in turn did not "conflict" either. The legislative record before the Seventh Circuit contained only empirical studies and victims' testimony documenting harm. There were no empirical studies that showed no harm. Legal briefs before the Seventh Circuit by ordinance opponents *did* contain in their arguments references to prior governmental bodies elsewhere that, based on the superseded empirical studies and no testimony by victims, had concluded that the empirical record on harm was divided. This, however, presented no conflict in the legislative facts of record. Further contrary to the suggestion implicit in footnote 2, no court is constrained to conclude that a

discriminated against on the basis of sex; those who testified to their experiences in the hearings incontestably were hurt as members of their gender. Their specifically, differentially, and uncontestedly sex-based injuries ground the state's interest in equality that is vindicated by the ordinance.

The hearings show the ordinance in practice: it produced them. The hearings also present case after case of precisely the kinds of evidence the ordinance would introduce into court if it were enacted into law. These are the people who need to use it, who have nothing to use without it. The hearings empowered individuals to speak in public, provided a forum for them to confront their abusers, to prove their violations, and to secure accountability and relief, as the ordinance would in court. The hearings present witnesses to acts of abuse and injury—acts, not ideas, like those acts the ordinance would redress in court. In the hearings, the industry of exploitation and violence that produced these acts is connected inextricably with them, as it would also have to be in civil court proceedings. The hearings challenged the same concentration of nongovernmental power that the ordinance would challenge in court, empowering the government no more than the hearings did. The hearings used the legislative process for the ends to which it is given to citizens to use, as the ordinance would use the civil judicial process to its designed purposes of conflict resolution and rectification of injury. As the ordinance would in court, the hearings brought pornography out of a half-lit underground into the public light of day. The hearings freed previously suppressed speech. So would the ordinance. Neither the ordinance nor the hearings have anything in common with censorship.[23]

Until the publication of this volume, the public discussion of pornography has been impoverished and deprived by often inaccurate or incom-

---

legislature's factual record adequately supports its legislation if that record is not strong enough. That is, there was no empirical conflict of legislative fact before the Seventh Circuit on the question of harm, and the Seventh Circuit was not compelled to find that Indianapolis was permitted to legislate on the basis of the facts it had.

23. The hearings also show some differences among the ordinances in specific localities, distinctions that have been previously obscured. Unlike the Minneapolis ordinance, the Indianapolis ordinance requires that violence be shown or done for the materials to be actionable (see p. 444, defense to trafficking claim that materials are only subsection (6) of definition). The Massachusetts ordinance effectively limits its trafficking provision to visual materials (see p. 460). Both of these features were thought by politicians to make the bills more acceptable to the ordinance's opposition, but they made no difference at all. The judge who invalidated the Indianapolis ordinance did not even notice that it was limited to violence, and the Massachusetts ordinance was just as politically untouchable as if it had also made words-only materials actionable.

plete reports of victims' accounts and experts' views.[24] Media reports of victims' testimony at the time of the hearings themselves were often cursory, distorted, or nonexistent. Some reports by journalists covering the Minneapolis hearings were rewritten by editors to conform the testimony to the story of pornography's harmlessness that they wanted told.[25] Of this process, one Minneapolis reporter assigned to cover those hearings told me, in reference to the reports she filed, "I have never been so censored in my life." Thus weakened, the victim testimony became easier to stigmatize as emotional and to dismiss as exceptional. Its representativeness has been further undermined by selective or misleading reports of expert testimony on scientific studies. This body of scholarship predicts that the precise kinds of consequences *will* happen from exposure to pornography that the survivors report *did* happen in their own experience. In making the whole record available, this book shows these two kinds of evidence documenting the same harm in two different ways.

This volume contributes other neglected or otherwise inaccessible information to the public discussion over the civil rights ordinance against

24. Notable examples can be found in accounts of the Indianapolis hearings in Donald Alexander Downs, *The New Politics of Pornography* (University of Chicago Press, 1989) ("Downs"), which was not based on a transcript, but on a document footnoted by him as "Administration Committee Notes." Errors resulted. For example, Edward Donnerstein's appearance before the Council was not, as Downs asserts, a "surprise move" (Downs, p. 123). It had been clearly announced before by Deborah Daniels. See Indianapolis Hearings, p. 283. Downs states further: "As at Minneapolis, MacKinnon questioned Donnerstein, eliciting testimony on his research to support her legal points" (Downs, p. 123). I was not present when Donnerstein testified in Indianapolis. The ordinance's proponents did not manipulate these events, as Downs implies. Downs did. Presumably, the publication of these hearings makes distortions like these less possible. It should be noted that the official videotape on which the transcript of the Indianapolis hearings in this volume is based was incomplete when received. Attempts to locate sources for the hearings beyond the partial videotape proved fruitless. Asked for the source documents he referenced, Downs said he no longer had them (Letter of Donald A. Downs to author, July 19, 1996). John Wood and Sheila Seuss Kennedy, asked for written copies of their testimony, said they could not find them. The Records office at the City-County Council in Indianapolis said they keep official documents for seven years only, which is legally standard. Media sources who videotaped the hearings independently said they did not keep the tapes.

25. Altering the record to weaken the case on causality is illustrated by comparing two editions of the first national story *The New York Times* ran covering the Minneapolis hearings. One included in its report of the testimony of R. M. her direct how-to causal sentence: "When he convinced me to be bound, when he finally convinced me to do it, he read in a magazine how to tie the knots." "Minneapolis Rights Attack on Pornography Weighed," *The New York Times,* Sunday, December 18, 1983, p. 22. A different edition of *the same article,* headlined "Minneapolis Asked to Attack Pornography as Rights Issue," omitted *only this sentence,* leaving the witness with only her testimony stating by simile a weaker relation between using pornography and his actions: "My husband would read the pornography like it was a textbook." Sunday, December 18, 1983, p. 44.

pornography. For example, the allegation that opposing points of view were excluded from the hearings by the bills' proponents[26] is refuted by the hearings on their face. Opponent after opponent of the civil rights of women, mostly liberals, parade through these pages, testifying ad nauseam. The hearings also go some distance toward refuting the now ubiquitous fabrication that locates the engine of the civil rights antipornography ordinances in an "unusual coalition of radical feminists and conservative women politicians."[27] This invention originated in a false report in *The New York Times* that Charlee Hoyt, one of the bill's original sponsors in Minneapolis, opposed the Equal Rights Amendment. The *Times* published a correction affirming Hoyt's constant support of ERA, but the lie about the ordinance's alliance with the right stuck, always changing ground but always growing.[28] The same *Times* article stated that the Indianapolis ordinance was passed with "the support of the Rev. Greg Dixon, a former Moral Majority official," who "packed Council hearings to lobby for passage of the proposed ordinance."[29] Neither Rev. Dixon nor his followers appear to have spoken at the Indianapolis hearings. Enough votes for passage (the bill passed 24 to 5) existed prior to the meeting at which these individuals sat in the audience. No one has said that Rev. Dixon or his group had any other contact with the process. Thus it was that the outcome of a legislative vote came to be attributed to the presence of some who came to watch as others cast it.

Taint through innuendo has substituted for fact and analysis in much reporting and discussion of the ordinance. As the hearings document, of all the sponsors of the bill in all the cities in which it has been introduced, only one—Beulah Coughenour of Indianapolis—has been conservative. Work on one bill with an independent individual is hardly an alliance with a political wing.[30] And exactly what is sinister about women uniting

26. For example, Wendy McElroy, *XXX: A Woman's Right to Pornography* (St. Martin's Press, 1995) states: "Dworkin and MacKinnon orchestrated the public hearings at which the ordinance was aired. They called only the witnesses they wished to hear from" (p. 92). In Minneapolis, Andrea Dworkin and I were hired as expert consultants to present relevant witnesses. As the transcript shows, we did not control who was called or who was allowed to speak. Everywhere, the hearings were public. Notably, Wendy McElroy was listed third of those who were to speak against the ordinance at the Los Angeles hearing, but she did not present herself to speak.

27. E. R. Shipp, "A Feminist Offensive Against Exploitation," *The New York Times,* June 10, 1984, sec. 4, p. 2.

28. Minus the claim about Charlee Hoyt and plus many additional false or misleading details, essentially the same "report" was recycled six months later in Lisa Duggan, "Censorship in the Name of Feminism," *Village Voice*, October 16, 1984, p. 13, as if it were news.

29. *The New York Times,* note 27 above.

30. Beulah Coughenour was chosen by Mayor William Hudnut to shepherd the bill through

with women across conventional political lines against a form of abuse whose politics are sexual has remained unspecified by the critics.

The hearings correct such widely distorted facts simply by showing the sponsors and supporters of the ordinance in action, illustrating its progressive politics. The ordinance's two original sponsors in Minneapolis appear: Van White, a liberal Democratic African American man, and Charlee Hoyt, a liberal Republican white woman. (Sharon Sayles Belton, the Democratic African American woman who is now mayor of Minneapolis, sponsored the reintroduced ordinance after the first veto.) The grass-roots groups who inspired the Minneapolis ordinance by requesting help in their fight against pornographers' invasion of their neighborhoods testify in support of it. These same groups later supported the Indianapolis ordinance when it was challenged in court.[31] Battered women's groups, rape crisis center workers and advocates, organizations of survivors of sexual abuse in childhood, and groups of former prostitutes present unanimous evidence from their experience in favor of the ordinance. They, too, supported it against later legal challenge.[32] The large, ethnically diverse Los Angeles County Commission on Women that sponsored and supported the ordinance chaired the hearings there.

The progression of hearings reveals that opposition to the ordinance became better organized over time, its strategy refined. In the Los Angeles hearing on April 22, 1985, in which the pro-pimp lobby remained as always centered in the American Civil Liberties Union, the woman card was first played. There, a tiny, noisy elite of women who defend pornography professionally contrast with survivor after survivor whom they talk past and disregard—a division of a few women from all women subsequently magnified by a gleeful press. There, women's material interest in pornography was presented as divided: if it hurts some women,

---

the process largely on the basis of her political skills, which were exceptional. She also chaired the Administration Committee, through which the bill had to pass in order to be voted on by the City-County Council.

31. Brief of the Neighborhood Pornography Task Force, *Amicus Curiae,* in Support of Appellant, American Booksellers v. Hudnut (No. 84-3147), 771 F.2d 323 (7th Cir. 1985).

32. Brief *Amici Curiae* of Women Against Pornography et al., American Booksellers Association, Inc. v. Hudnut (Docket No. 84-3147), 771 F.2d 323 (7th Cir. 1985) (brief for groups including The Minnesota Coalition for Battered Women, "a coalition of fifty-three local, regional, and state-wide organizations that provide services and advocacy to battered women and their families"); Brief of *Amici Curiae* Trudee Able-Peterson, WHISPER et al. in support of Defendant and Intervenor-Defendants, Village Books v. City of Bellingham, No. C88-1470D Memorandum and Order (D. Wash., Feb. 9, 1989) (unpublished) (brief of organizations of and for formerly prostituted women); Memorandum of *Amici Curiae* Institute for Youth Advocacy, Voices in Action, et al., Village Books v. City of Bellingham, No. C88-1470D Memorandum and Order (D. Wash., Feb. 9, 1989) (unpublished) (brief on harms of pornography to children).

other women love it, and stopping it hurts women more.[33] Women against women subsequently became the pornographers' tactic of choice, as if women's oppression by pornography had been argued to be biological, as if biological females saying they were not hurt by it undercut that case. This choice of strategy was revealed in the orchestration of the ordinance referendum battle in Cambridge, Massachusetts, in November 1985, in which the ordinance narrowly lost, and even more graphically in evidence in the Boston, Massachusetts, hearing of March 1992. In Boston, speaking almost entirely through female mouthpieces, the corporate interests of the entertainment industry came out of the woodwork for the first time weighing in on the side of the pornography industry, arraying abstraction after evasion after obfuscation after self-interested, profit-oriented rationalization against survivors' simple, direct accounts of the role of pornography in their abuse.[34] Much of the media persistently position women against women in their coverage, employing the pornographers' strategy in the way they report events and frame issues for public discussion. Corrective letters showing wide solidarity among women on the ordinance are routinely not published.[35]

These hearings took place in public and on the record. The witnesses, unless they say otherwise, were fully identified to the governmental bodies before whom they testified. Some of the consequences to them show why it has taken so long and has been so hard to make this information public, and prefigure the onslaught that followed. Some of those who spoke in Minneapolis were hounded and punished for what they said. One woman's testimony was published by *Penthouse Forum* without her knowledge or permission, selling her assault for sexual use. A copy of *Penthouse*'s pages with "We're going to get you, squaw" scrawled across it in red appeared in her mailbox. A dead rabbit appeared there a few

---

33. That this was a concerted strategic decision is clear from the fact that the FACT brief, adopting this same tactic, was filed on April 8, 1985. See Nan D. Hunter and Sylvia A. Law, Brief *Amici Curiae* of Feminist Anti-Censorship Taskforce, et al., 21 *University of Michigan Journal of Law Reform* 69 (1987/1988).

34. In contrast, many Hollywood actors, producers, and directors had actively lobbied for the passage of the Minneapolis ordinance, and some supported the Los Angeles one.

35. *Time* magazine, for one example, refused to publish the following letter signed by Gloria Steinem, Kate Millett, Alice Walker, Susan Brownmiller, Diana E. H. Russell, and Robin Morgan: "The reasons feminists oppose pornography as a practice of sex discrimination [were] invisible in your story (*Sex-busters*, July 14, 1985). We oppose the harm pornography does to those who are coerced to make it, forced to consume it, defamed through involuntary appearances in it, assaulted because of it, and targeted for abuse and exploitation through its eight billion dollar a year traffic. When pornography's victims—mostly women and children—are believed, its harm is amply documented. Unlike the right wing's approaches, the civil rights

days later; she was telephoned repeatedly by a man who appeared to be watching her in her home. Another witness was subsequently telephoned night after night at her unlisted telephone number: "The calls are not simply harassing phone calls. It is like someone is reading something out of the pornography books . . . we can't get away from it."[36] These are techniques of terror.

By bringing forward festering human pain that had been denied, the hearings unleashed an explosion of reports by women and men desperate for help. A local organizing group formed after the Minneapolis hearing was deluged with them. Women told "about the time their boyfriend urinated on them while using pornography depicting 'golden showers.'"[37] Rape victims reported that "their attacker took pictures during the rape and that she's afraid he is going to sell and distribute them."[38] The group reported that "we have received a call from a man in Fort Collins, Colorado, terrified because a group of men were holding him captive and making pornography with him. He has called and sent us the pornography in hopes that it could be used as evidence, that the whip lashes would prove that he was forced."[39] Some groups held more hearings. The National Organization for Women hosted testimony on pornography across the nation.[40]

The Minneapolis hearings, circulated in photocopied transcript hand to hand, had a substantial impact on consciousness, politics, scholarship, theory, and policy.[41] At the federal level, the first explosion of public-

---

approach to pornography was created to permit the injured access to court to try to prove that pornography *did* harm them in these ways. Inflicting such devastation on human beings is no one's civil liberty." This unanimity was particularly remarkable in light of Kate Millett's signature on the FACT brief, although many who signed the FACT brief seem not to have read it.

36. Task Force Hearing on Ordinances to Add Pornography as Discrimination Against Women, June 7, 1984, p. 81 (Testimony of E. M.). This Task Force was set up by Mayor Fraser to look responsive after his second ordinance veto. Nothing came of it.

37. Task Force Hearings on Ordinances to Add Pornography as Discrimination Against Women, June 7, 1984, p. 45 (Testimony of Therese Stanton).

38. Ibid.

39. Ibid., p. 46.

40. NOW Hearings on Pornography, Materials on the Personal Testimony of NOW Activists on Pornography (Lois Reckitt, Twiss Butler, and Melanie Gilbert, eds.), National Organization for Women, Inc., May 23, 1986. NOW also adopted a national resolution that pornography violates the civil rights of women and children and testified against pornography in Congress. NOW Resolution of June 1984 National Conference; Testimony of the National Organization for Women, presented by Judy Goldsmith, President, on the Impact of Pornography on Women before the Subcommittee on Juvenile Justice, Committee on the Judiciary (September 12, 1984). It has done little to nothing to implement this position since.

41. See, for example, Diana E. H. Russell, "Pornography and Rape: A Causal Model," 9

ity surrounding the Minneapolis hearings revived a long-moribund proposal for a new national commission on pornography. Attorney General William French Smith created the Attorney General's Commission on Obscenity and Pornography and selected its members. The prior Commission on Obscenity and Pornography in 1970, appointed by President Nixon, had exonerated "obscenity" and "erotica" of a role in "crime," looking at no violent materials and looking for only violent effects.[42] The President's Commission heard from not a single direct victim—offended moralists are not victims—and considered only evidence from "experts," meaning academics, on the question of harm. Understanding that asking the wrong questions of the wrong people might have produced the wrong answers, the Attorney General's Commission took extensive testimony from scores of survivors of all kinds of real abuse and investigated the effects of violent as well as nonviolent sexual materials. In other words, it investigated what those on the receiving end were in a position to know about the materials that are actually made and marketed by the pornography industry and consumed by its users. This commission was later named "the Meese Commission" by a hostile press in order to discredit it by association with an almost universally despised man who did announce the inquiry's formation but did not originate it and did virtually nothing with its results.

The *Final Report* of the Attorney General's Commission, which repeatedly footnoted the Minneapolis hearings, substantially adopted the civil rights approach in its approach, findings, and recommendations. The report included an entire chapter on harm to "performers"—of all survivors, the most ignored and, when noticed, blamed. It found that "the harms at which the ordinance is aimed are real and the need for a

Political Psychology 1, 41–73 (1988); Gloria Cowan, Carole Lee, Daniella Levy, and Debra Snyder, "Dominance and Inequality in X-Rated Videocassettes," 12 *Psychology of Women Quarterly* 299–311 (1988); Wendy Stock, "The Effects of Pornography on Women," in Laura Lederer and Richard Delgado, eds., *The Price We Pay,* pp. 80–88 (Hill and Wang, 1995); James Check and Ted Guloien, "Reported Proclivity for Coercive Sex Following Repeated Exposure to Sexually Violent Pornography, Nonviolent Dehumanizing Pornography, and Erotica," in D. Zillmann and J. Bryant, eds., *Pornography: Research Advances and Policy Considerations* (Erlbaum, 1989); E. Sommers and James Check, "An Empirical Investigation of the Role of Pornography in the Verbal and Physical Abuse of Women," 2 *Violence and Victims* 189–209 (1987); Catherine Itzin, ed., *Pornography: Women, Violence and Civil Liberties* (Oxford University Press, 1992); Andrea Dworkin, "Against the Male Flood: Censorship, Pornography, and Equality," 8 *Harvard Women's Law Journal* 1 (1985); Catharine A. MacKinnon, *Only Words* (Harvard University Press, 1993).

42. Commission on Obscenity and Pornography, *The Report of the Commission on Obscenity and Pornography* (Government Printing Office, 1970).

remedy for those harms is pressing."[43] It concluded that "civil and other remedies ought to be available to those who have been in some way injured in the process of producing these materials."[44] It endorsed a limited concept of civil remedies.[45] It found that the civil rights approach "is the only legal tool suggested to the Commission which is specifically designed to provide direct relief to the victims of the injuries so exhaustively documented in our hearings throughout the country."[46] The Commission also agreed that pornography, as made actionable in the ordinance, "constitutes a practice of discrimination on the basis of sex."[47] In an embrace of the ordinance's specific causes of action as well as its approach, the Commission recommended that Congress "consider legislation affording protection to those individuals whose civil rights have been violated by the production or distribution of pornography . . . At a minimum, claims could be provided against trafficking, coercion, forced viewing, defamation, and assault, reaching the industry as necessary to remedy these abuses."[48] Unable to find constitutional a legal definition of pornography that did not duplicate the existing obscenity definition, the Commission nonetheless found itself "in substantial agreement with the motivations behind the ordinance, and with the goals it represents."[49]

43. Attorney General's Commission on Pornography, *Final Report* (U.S. Department of Justice, July 1986) (hereafter cited as *Final Report*), p. 393.

44. *Final Report*, p. 396. The Commission also said that no remedy could reach coerced materials that were not also legally obscene (p. 396)—an incoherent, unprincipled, and legally unsupported restriction on relief for proven injury.

45. *Final Report*, pp. 393–395.

46. *Final Report*, p. 749. New Zealand's *Pornography: Report of the Ministerial Committee of Inquiry* (January 1989) adopted the ordinance's definition of pornography for its own investigation, on p. 28, and called the ordinance "a brilliant strategy for expunging pornography from the face of any society that might adopt it" (p. 152). It recommended that the Human Rights Commission Act be reviewed and "that pornography be considered a practice of sex discrimination which can be expressly identified" by the Act (p. 155). The Human Rights Commission of New Zealand, before the Committee, recommended that the coercion, forcing, assault, and defamation provisions be added to the causes for complaint under the Act (p. 153).

47. *Final Report*, p. 756.

48. Ibid. Accordingly, Carole Vance's claim, in reference to Andrea Dworkin's and my work, that the Commission "decisively rejected their remedies" and that "the Commission's Report summarily rejected Minneapolis style ordinances" is false. Carole S. Vance, "Negotiating Sex and Gender in the Attorney General's Commission on Pornography," in *Sex Exposed: Sexuality and the Pornography Debates*, ed. Lynne Segal and Mary McIntosh (Virago Press, 1992), p. 37. Her charge that we publicly misrepresented the Commission's results when we said it supported our approach—"Even more startling were MacKinnon's and Dworkin's statements to the press that the Commission 'has recommended to Congress the civil rights legislation women have sought,'" p. 38—is defamatory as well as false.

49. *Final Report*, p. 393.

In the years soon following the Commission's Report, parts of the ordinance were introduced as bills in Congress. Senator Arlen Specter introduced a version of the ordinance's coercion provision as the Pornography Victims' Protection Act, making the coercion of an adult or the use of a child to make pornography civilly actionable.[50] Senator Mitch McConnell introduced a rendition of the ordinance's assault provision as the Pornography Victims' Compensation Act, creating a civil action for assault or murder caused by pornography.[51] Most stunningly, Congress in 1994 adopted the Violence Against Women Act, providing a federal civil remedy for gender-based acts of violence such as rape and battering.[52] In so doing, Congress made legally real its understanding that sexual violation is a practice of sex discrimination, the legal approach that the antipornography civil rights ordinance pioneered in legislative form.

More broadly, the exposure of pornography's harms has moved the ground under social theory across a wide range of issues. The place of sex in speech, including literature and art, and its role in social action has been thrown open to reconsideration, historically and in the present. The implications of visual and verbal presentation and representation for the creation and distribution of social power—the relation between the way people are imaged and imagined to the ways they are treated—are being rethought. The buying and selling of human flesh in the form of pornography has given scholarship on slavery a new dimension. More has been learned about the place of sexuality in ideology and about the importance of sexual pleasure to the exercise of dominant power. The hearings are fertile ground for analyzing the role of visceral belief in inequality and inferiority in practical systems of discrimination, and of the role of denial of inequality in maintaining that inequality. The cultural legitima-

---

50. 98th Cong. 2d Sess., S13191–13193, S. 3063 (October 3, 1984) and S13838–S13839 (October 9, 1984); S. 1187 (1985), 99th Cong. 1st Sess., S6853–6855 Cong. Rec. (May 22, 1985). The bill proposed to "allow victims of child pornography and adults who are coerced, intimidated, or fraudulently induced into posing or performing in pornography to institute Federal civil actions against producers and distributors." S6853 Cong. Rec. (May 22, 1985).

51. Originally S. 1226, the McConnell bill gave a civil right of action to victims of sexual crimes against pornographers if the victims could prove that "sexually explicit materials" influenced or incited the assault. 101st Cong. 1st Sess., S7281–S7283 Cong. Rec. (June 22, 1989). In 1991, as S. 1521, the bill addressed "obscene materials and child pornography" instead. Its purpose was to require that those who trafficked such material "be jointly and severally liable for all damages resulting from any sexual offense that was foreseeably caused, in substantial part, by the sexual offender's exposure to the obscene material or child pornography." S. 1521, 102d Cong. 1st Sess. (July 22, 1991), Sec. 2(b).

52. 108 Stat. 1796 (1994). In one early case, the performer La Toya Jackson sued her former husband under the VAWA for systematically beating her until she performed for *Playboy* and

tion of sexual force, including permission for and exoneration of rape and transformation of sexual abuse into sexual pleasure and identity, is being newly interrogated. New human rights theories are being built to respond to the human rights violations unearthed. As events that have been hidden come to light, the formerly unseen appears to determine more and more of the seen. The repercussions for theory, the requisite changes in thinking on all levels of society, have only begun to be felt.

For those who survived pornography, the hearings were like coming up for air. Now the water has closed over their heads once again. The ordinance is not law anywhere. Mayor Donald Fraser of Minneapolis vetoed it twice after passage by two different city councils. Minneapolis has dithered and done nothing to this day. The Indianapolis ordinance was declared unconstitutional by the Court of Appeals for the Seventh Circuit in a decision that inverted First Amendment law, saying that the harm of pornography only proved the importance of protecting it as speech, and reduced equality rights, by comparison, to a constitutional nullity.[53] The U.S. Supreme Court summarily affirmed this result without hearing arguments, reading briefs, or issuing an opinion,[54] using a now largely obsolete legal device for upholding a ruling without expressing a view on its reasoning.[55] Although the Seventh Circuit decision is wrong in law,[56] and the summary affirmance of it need not necessarily bind sub-

---

other pornography. Complaint, Jackson v. Gordon, D. Nevada, Case No. CV S 00563 DWH (RJJ).

53. American Booksellers v. Hudnut, 771 F.2d 323 (7th Cir. 1985).

54. Hudnut v. American Booksellers, 106 S. Ct. 1172 (1986) (affirming without opinion). For the dissent see Appendix, p. 482.

55. Robert L. Stern, Eugene Gressman, Stephen M. Shapiro, and Kenneth S. Geller, *Supreme Court Practice*, 7th ed. (BNA, 1993), pp. 264–268.

56. In January 1984, Constitutional scholar Laurence Tribe wrote Minneapolis City Council President Alice W. Rainville "to express dissent and dismay at Mayor Donald Fraser's veto of your ordinance to define pornography as a violation of civil rights . . . While many hard questions of conflicting rights will face any court that confronts challenges to the ordinance, as drafted it rests on a rationale that closely parallels many previously accepted exceptions to justly stringent First Amendment guarantees. While remaining uncertain myself as to the ultimate outcome of a judicial test, I urge you not to allow an executive to prevent the courts from adjudicating what may eventually be found to be the first sensible approach to an area which has vexed some of the best legal minds for decades." (Letter of Laurence Tribe to The Honorable Alice W. Rainville, January 8, 1984.) See also Catharine A. MacKinnon, *Only Words* (Harvard University Press, 1993); Cass R. Sunstein, "Pornography and the First Amendment," 1986 *Duke L. J.* 589 (1986); Frank I. Michelman, "Conceptions of Democracy in American Constitutional Argument: The Case of Pornography Regulation," 56 *Tennessee Law Review* 291 (1989); Owen M. Fiss, "Freedom and Feminism," 80 *The Georgetown Law Journal* 2041 (1992).

sequent courts, the ordinance passed in Bellingham, Washington, by public referendum was invalidated by a federal court there, citing the Indianapolis decision as controlling.[57] The Los Angeles ordinance was narrowly
defeated, 3 to 2, in a vote delayed in order to be as inconspicuous as possible. The Massachusetts ordinance was maneuvered behind the scenes
out of coming to a vote at all. Senators Specter and McConnell compro-
mised their bills fundamentally.[58] Neither bill—for all the purported political expediency of their sponsors in gutting them as tools against the
pornography industry—passed or even made it out of committee.

The victims have been betrayed. To adapt George Eliot's words, "that
roar which lies on the other side of silence"[59] about sexual violation in
the ordinary lives of women was heard in these hearings. Now society
knows what is being done to the victims and has decided to turn away,
close its mind, and, "well wadded with stupidity,"[60] go back to masturbating to the violation of their human rights. The debate over pornography that was reconfigured by the survivors' testimony to make harm
to women indispensable to the discussion has increasingly regressed to
its old right/left morality/freedom rut, making sexual violence against
women once again irrelevant and invisible.[61] Politicians are too cowed by
the media even to introduce the bill. Truth be told, for survivor and
expert both, it has become more difficult than it was before to speak out
against pornography, as those in these hearings did. The consequences
are now known to include professional shunning and blacklisting, attacks on employment and publishing, deprivation of research and grant
funding, public demonization, litigation and threats of litigation, and

---

57. Village Books et al. v. City of Bellingham, C88-1470D (W.D. Wash, 1989).

58. Senator Specter, under intense pressure from liberals, exempted traffickers in coerced
adult materials. Senator McConnell, under pressure from across the political spectrum, adopted
the obscenity definition for the materials his bill covered. Senator Specter's bill thus left the
material incentive for coercion into pornography squarely in place, permitting pornographers to
coerce women into sex for pornography and run with the products and profits. He was told this.
Senator McConnell's bill was rendered useless for victims because the legal definition of obscenity makes harm to victims irrelevant and is nearly impossible to prove. He was told this.

59. "If we had a keen vision and feeling of all ordinary human life, it would be like hearing
the grass grow and the squirrel's heart beat, and we should die of that roar which lies on the
other side of silence. As it is, the quickest of us walk about well wadded with stupidity." George
Eliot, *Middlemarch* (Bantam Books, 1985 ed. [from 1874 ed.]), p. 177.

60. Ibid.

61. See Catharine A. MacKinnon, "Pornography Left and Right," 30 *Harvard Civil Rights-
Civil Liberties Law Review* 143 (1995); Andrea Dworkin, "Woman-Hating Right and Left," in
The Sexual Liberals and the Attack on Feminism, ed. Dorchen Leidholdt and Janice G. Ray-
mond (Pergamon, 1990), p. 28.

physical assault.[62] The holy rage of the pornographers at being publicly exposed, legalized through ACLU lawyers at every bend in the road and accompanied by the relentless beat of media lies, has made aggression against pornography's critics normative and routine, fighting back unseemly, seemingly impossible. The silencing is intentional, and it is effective. In this atmosphere, few stand up and say what they know.

The concerted attacks on anyone who dares to give even a respectful hearing to the critique of pornography from this point of view has been reminiscent of the left's vicious treatment of so-called "premature antifascists" during the period of the Hitler-Stalin pact, or of those who questioned Stalin including after the Moscow Trials. In the establishment today, support or at least tolerance for pornography, if slightly shaken,

62. To document specifically most instances of the treatment that forms the basis for this and the next paragraphs would further target those subjected to it. Below are just a few examples that can be mentioned.

The Attorney General's Commission on Pornography was sued as a whole, and its members individually, on the basis of a letter sent by the Executive Director asking distributors of adult magazines whether they were selling pornography. Penthouse International, Ltd. v. Meese et al., 939 F.2d 1011 (1991). The fact that the case was thrown out on appeal as baseless did not prevent it from operating as an instrument of intimidation and silencing of the commissioners.

Al Goldstein, editor of SCREW, a pornography magazine, sued Women Against Pornography and Frances Patai, an individual member of WAP, for libel for Patai's statement on WCBS-TV that SCREW "champion[ed] abuse of children." Goldstein said he did not champion or defend abuse of children. Goldstein and Milky Way Productions, Inc. et al. v. Patai and Women Against Pornography, Summons and Complaint (Supreme Court of the State of New York, County of New York, October 10, 1984). The defendants produced extensive examples of eroticization of incest and other sexual use of children in SCREW magazine over time. Having seriously damaged those sued, the case was settled.

Marty Rimm, undergraduate author of a sound and methodologically creative study, "Marketing Pornography on the Information Superhighway," 83 Georgetown Law Journal 1849 (1995), described accurately the pornography that is available on computer networks and measured patterns of its actual use. He found the simple truth of pornography's content and use, for example, that the more violating the materials are to women, the more popular they are. Once some of his findings were given visibility and credibility in a Time magazine cover story, he was hounded, harassed, and probed by journalists and attacked in Playboy; excoriated as a censor and subjected to an intense rumor campaign of vilification on the Internet; likely deprived of a scholarship offer for graduate school at MIT; canceled before a Congressional committee, where he was to testify; and threatened with the loss of his degree by his sponsoring institution, Carnegie Mellon University, which convened a formal inquiry into bogus charges that went on for years, although he was eventually cleared of all the serious charges. His initially sought book proposal, an analysis of the approximately 85% of his data that was not discussed in the article, suddenly could not find a publisher. No lawyer could be found to defend his academic freedom.

Shots were fired into the windows of the office of Organizing Against Pornography in Minneapolis when the ordinance was pending there.

Andrea Dworkin and I have each been attacked in most of the ways described in this and subsequent paragraphs, and in others as well. Andrea Dworkin discusses some of her experiences in Letters from a War Zone (E. P. Dutton, 1988).

remains an article of faith among liberals and libertarians alike. The liberal establishment is its chief bastion but the right is actively complicit, its moralistic decency crusades and useless obscenity laws protecting pornography while pretending to stop it, contributing its share of judicial and other misogynists to the ranks of pornography's defenders, forever defending private concentrations of power and mistaking money for speech.

Against this united front, many a well-placed and secure professional, upon taking a rather obvious position against exploitation and abuse, or upon simply describing what is in the pornography or in the research on its effects, has been startled to be screamed at by formerly rational colleagues, savaged by hostile mail (sometimes widely electronically disseminated), defamed by attacks on professional competence, subjected to false rumors, ostracized instead of respected, libeled in and out of pornography, sued for speech by those who say they oppose suits for speech, and investigated by journalists and committees—not to mention blandishments of money from pornographers, eviction from homes, and threats against families. Most fold. With intellectuals intimidated, what chance do prostituted women and raped children have?

In the defense of pornography against the ordinance—the first effective threat to its existence—the outline of a distinctive power bloc has become discernible in the shadows of American politics. Cutting across left and right, uniting sectors of journalism, entertainment, and publishing with organized crime, sprawling into parts of the academy and the legal profession, this configuration has emerged to act as a concerted political force. Driven by sex and money, its power is largely hidden and institutionally without limits. Most of those who could credibly criticize it either become part of it or collaborate through silence. No political or legal organ is yet designed or equipped to counter it. Existing structural restraints on excess power—such as the government's checks and balances—are not designed to counter social combinations like this one. In western democracies, only governmental power is formally controlled, as

---

Exploring the attacks on Martin Garbus, a well-known defender of rights of free speech, for the sin of suing the press for a plaintiff in a libel case, *The New Yorker* said this: "Robert Sack, who represents the *Wall Street Journal*, likens First Amendment law to a religion. 'Switching sides,' he concludes, 'is close to apostasy.'" Reflecting the pressure brought on him, Garbus was also quoted as saying: "I've told my colleagues within the First Amendment world that I would *never* take another plaintiff's case." *The New Yorker* author commented, "[u]ndoubtedly, membership in the club does have its privileges . . ." Susie Linfeld, "Exile on Centre Street," *The New Yorker,* March 11, 1996, pp. 40, 42.

if the government is the only entity that can cohere power or abuse it. Private in the sense of nongovernmental in origin, this bloc uses government (such as First Amendment adjudications) as just one tool, wielding less visibly against dissenters a clout similar to the government's clout in the McCarthy era.

Politicians who live and die by spin and image grovel before this machine. Law has been largely impotent in the face of it and lacks the will and resources to resist it. Indeed, law has largely been created by it, the reality perceptions entrenched through the machine's distinctively deployed weapons of sex, money, and reputation being largely indelible and impervious to contrary proof. Academic institutions are often found cowering before it and have ceded to it much of their role of credentialing the intelligentsia. Its concerted power defines what is taken as reality and aims to destroy those who challenge or deviate. Almost no one stands up to it. Those who testified in these hearings did.

One incident exposed the workings of this *de facto* machine accidentally. In 1986, a leaked memo from the public relations firm of Gray & Company proposed a press campaign for the Media Coalition, the group of trade publishers and distributors, including some pornographers, that is substantially funded by *Penthouse*[63] and was behind the litigation against the ordinance in Indianapolis and Bellingham. Gray & Company proposed to "discredit the Commission on Pornography" and stop "self-styled anti-pornography crusaders" from creating "a climate of public hostility toward selected publications."[64] They got the contract, which budgeted about a million dollars to pursue their recommended lines of attack. As reflected in the press this campaign produced, this planned onslaught focused on two items of disinformation contained in the proposal. The first is that there is no evidence that pornography does harm. In their euphemistic PR language, "there is no factual or scientific basis for the exaggerated and unfounded allegations that sexually-oriented content in contemporary media is in any way a cause of violent or criminal behavior."[65] The second is that the campaign to stop pornography "is being orchestrated by a group of religious extremists."[66] The mainstream media slavishly published *as news* the spewings of the

---

63. Susan B. Trento, *The Power House* (St. Martin's Press, 1992), p. 192.
64. Letter from Steve Johnson to John M. Harrington, June 5, 1986, pp. 2, 1.
65. Ibid., p. 4.
66. Ibid.

groups fronting this strategy, establishing both lies as conventional wisdom.

The false statement that scientific evidence on the harmful effects of exposure to pornography is mixed or inconclusive is now repeated like a mantra, even in court. It has become the official story, the baseline, the pre-established position against which others are evaluated, the standard against which deviations must defend themselves, the common sense view that needs no source and has none, the canard that individuals widely believe as if they had done the research themselves. Few read the scholarly literature or believe they need to. No amount of evidence to the contrary—and evidence to the contrary is all there is—is credible against the simple reassertion of what was believed, without evidence, to begin with. Associating all work against pornography with widely reviled extremists of the religious and political right—without regard for the lack of factual basis for this guilt by association—is similarly impervious to contrary proof and produces a self-righteous witch-hunt mentality. Individuals strategically singled out as threatening to the financial health of Gray & Company's "selected publications" are also used in pornography,[67] this cabal's ultimate weapon. Such attack-pornography potently and pervasively targets sexualized hostility at pornography's critics and destroys their status as credible speakers who have anything of value to say. The effect of lowering the human status of the critics can be relied upon to be discounted as having occurred by the norms of public discourse, which pervasively pretend that what is done in pornography occurs off stage in some twilight zone—coming from nowhere, meaning nothing, going noplace.

If this cabal acts in planned and organized ways at times, usually its common misogyny and attachment to pornography are themselves the conspiracy. The legitimate media act in their own perceived self-interest when they defend pornography, making common cause with mass sexual exploitation by calling pornography "speech." They seem to think that

67. *Hustler* Magazine has often attacked critics of pornography in their "Asshole of the Month" feature. Peggy Ault, Dorchen Leidholdt, and Andrea Dworkin sued them for libel. Ault v. *Hustler* Magazine, Inc., 860 F.2d 877 (9th Cir. 1988); Leidholdt v. L.F.P. Inc., 860 F.2d 890 (9th Cir. 1988); Dworkin v. *Hustler* Magazine Inc., 867 F.2d 1188 (9th Cir. 1989). All three cases were held legally insufficient before reaching the facts, holding in essence that pornography is unreal, hence not factual in nature, hence protected opinion. Both Gloria Steinem and Susan Brownmiller were used in pornography by *Hustler*. See Brief of *Amici Curiae* in Support of Plaintiff-Appellant, Dworkin v. *Hustler* Magazine Inc., 867 F.2d 1188 (9th Cir. 1989) (App. No. 87-6393) (pornography of both women in appendix). Andrea Dworkin and I have been used in visual pornography.

any restraint on pornography is a restraint on journalism. Their mistaken view that mainstream media and pornography are indistinguishable—the ordinance's definition of pornography distinguishes them, as does every pornography outlet in the world—pervasively distorts factual and legal reporting.[68] The resulting tilt is inescapable and uncorrectable; other than one's own experience to the contrary, which this process makes marginal, readers have no access to other information. That mainstream journalists tend to see their own power at stake in the legal treatment of pornography is particularly worth noting because they are not pornographers.

Sometimes the ax being ground is close to home, such as for journalists to whom Linda "Lovelace" was pimped when in captivity.[69] Those who used her sexually have a specific stake in not believing that she was coerced to perform for the pornography film *Deep Throat*. They remain at large, mostly unidentified and writing. How often pornographer-manipulated news stories are concretely bought and planted can only be imagined, but how difficult can privileged access be for the pornographers and their point of view, given that they are often dealing with their own customers? Under these conditions, with access to information owned and controlled for content, with sex and money as potent motivators, the availability of unmediated original materials such as these hearings—these documents against the deluge—is as precious as it is rare.

You hold in your hands the samizdat of a resistance to a sexual fascism of everyday life—a regime so pervasive, so ordinary, so normalized, so established, so condoned, that there is no underground from which to fight it or in which to get away from it. The hearings are the only source on the way pornography concretely works in everyday life that has seen the public light of day. And they may be the last. Every day the pornography industry gets bigger and penetrates more deeply and broadly into social life, conditioning mass sexual responses to make fortunes for men and to end lives and life chances for women and children. Pornography's up-front surrogates swallow more public space daily, shaping standards of literature and art. The age of first pornography consumption is young, and the age of the average rapist is ever younger.[70] The acceptable level of

68. This is particularly apparent in reports of rapes and sexual murders (in which the presence of pornography is usually just left out, particularly of national coverage), on child pornography, and on the technological frontiers of the pornographers' coveted new markets, such as computer networks.
69. Linda Lovelace and Mike McGrady, *Ordeal* (Citadel Press, 1980), pp. 177–179.
70. James V. P. Check and D. K. Maxwell, "Pornography and Pro-Rape Attitudes in Chil-

sexual force climbs ever higher, women's real status drops ever lower. No law is effective against the industry, the materials, or the acts. Because the aggressors have won, it is hard to believe that they are wrong. When women can assert human rights against them, through a law they can use themselves, women will have a right to a place in the world.[71]

dren," paper delivered at 25th International Congress of Psychology, Brussels, July 19–24, 1992. Check and Maxwell found, in a survey of 276 grade 9 students in Canada, that 9 out of 10 boys and 6 out of 10 girls had viewed video pornography. The mean age of first exposure was just under 12 years of age. Boys who were frequent consumers of pornography and/or reported learning useful information about sex from pornography were more accepting of rape myths and violence against women. Forty-three percent of the boys in one or both of these categories agreed that it was "at least maybe OK" to force a girl to have sexual intercourse "if she gets him sexually excited."

Examination of the Department of Justice's *Uniform Crime Reports* from 1991 to 1995 shows a steady increase in the double digits in the number of arrests for sex crimes reportedly committed by perpetrators under 18 years of age up to 1993, then a small decrease thereafter. FBI, U.S. Department of Justice, *Uniform Crime Reports for the United States*, 1991, 1992, 1993, 1994, 1995. Closer scrutiny of the affected groups, beyond simply reported crime, suggests that sexual assaults are increasingly being committed by younger and younger perpetrators. Melinda Henneberger, "Now Sex and Violence Link at an Earlier Age," *The New York Times,* July 4, 1993, sec. 4, p. 6, col. 4; Claudia Morain, "When Children Molest Children," *San Francisco Chronicle,* May 4, 1994, p. F7. "The 'portrait' of the American sex offender increasingly 'bears the face' of a juvenile." Sander Rothchild, "Beyond Incarceration: Juvenile Sex Offender Treatment Programs Offer Youths a Second Chance," 4 *Journal of Law and Policy* 719 (1996). In the same publication, see a report of a 1992 study at the University of New Hampshire's Family Research Laboratory concluding that "forty-one percent of sexual asaults on children ages 10 to 16 were done by other children," p. 720.

71. This passage was inspired by Louis Begley, "At Age 12, A Life Begins," *New York Times Magazine,* May 7, 1995, p. 101: "Hitler was dead and the 10 days of miracles had begun . . . finally I could believe the Germans had been wrong. I had not, after all, been marked at birth as unfit to live. My disgrace was not inside me; it was their invention. I had the right to a place in the world."

Suffering and Speech

Andrea Dworkin

In these hearings—Minneapolis in 1983 to Massachusetts in 1992—
women testify about being hurt in and by pornography. This hurt includes every kind of sexual exploitation and abuse. The hearings are road
maps of injury, made graphic through the speech of those who had their
legs spread, their hands tied, their mouths gagged. These hearings and
the political organizing that went into creating them pushed silence off
the women in these pages—they stood up and spoke. But while some
legislators listened—and while other hurt women, still silent, hoped—society at large pretty much turned its back on the suffering caused by
pornography and refused to consider honorable and equitable remedies.
These hearings also contain all the familiar leftist arguments for pornography: it is free speech or free sexuality in a free marketplace of ideas.
Only when women's bodies are being sold for profit do leftists claim to
cherish the free market. The protectors of pornography have arguments
and principles; the status quo supports the validity and legitimacy of
their world view. Their arguments and principles help to continue pornography's current status as constitutionally protected commerce in
women and maintain the colonialization of women's bodies for male
pleasure.

Listening to the arguments for pornography is like listening to the
refrain of a song one can sing in one's sleep. Listening to the victims, on
the other hand, requires patience and rigor; it requires the courage to
take in what they have to say—to feel even a tiny measure of what they
have endured. Many women try to distance themselves from the shame
and squalor of sexualized violation—and refuse to empathize with hurt
women. They especially do not want the hurt to be public; they reject
what they consider a politics of victimization. In reality, they are rejecting

the facts of women's lives, often including their own, and a politics of resistance to male power over women.

I come from a generation of women who did not have feminism. I was born in 1946 and graduated from high school in 1964. Women were invisible in history and culture, literature and politics, art and athletics. The best way to see a woman protagonist would have been to go to a play by Euripides. After the Greeks, it was all downhill. I found myself on the political Left because of the issues I cared about as a child: prejudice against blacks, including de jure segregation in the South and apartheid in South Africa; abortion and contraception, both of which were then criminal in the United States; anti-Semitism, from pogrom to Holocaust, all of which my family, mostly dead, had experienced; the rights of the working man, because my father, who was pro-union, worked in a post office as well as being a teacher; literacy and access to books; poverty; peace in the face of nuclear threat and the Cold War; and I liked Lenny Bruce, Bessie Smith, and jazz. My concerns had to do with human suffering—I was against it—and social fairness—I was for it. This may sound simplistic, but concentrating on suffering and fairness is an exacting and difficult discipline. For me, these were urgent and troubling issues of conscience, not ideology. I never took a stand based on what is now called theory, although I did read Marx and Engels, Bakunin, Kropotkin, Prudhomme, Henry David Thoreau, and even Ernesto Che Guevara's *Guerilla Warfare,* which, in high school, along with *Catcher in the Rye,* I studied and adored. There weren't any mountains where I lived in New Jersey, but I practiced possible assault strategies on the first shopping mall built in the United States, just blocks from my parents' home. My understanding of politics has always been concrete: humans are being hurt; here are actions that must be taken and institutions that must be changed. And I read to learn: more about suffering, more about fairness. As with many of my generation, maybe all, the Vietnam War was the defining event of my young adult life. I was against it. I fought against it from 1965, when I was arrested at a sit-in at the United States Mission to the United Nations, until April 1975 when it ended.

It has been a devastation to me to see the U.S. Left's disregard for women and women's rights over the last twenty-five years: a nearly absolute indifference to our suffering and an unapologetic disdain for what is fair. In the 1960s many women my age lived as militant left-wing radicals or flower children or both; but by 1970 some began to apply to women the standards of justice applied to other disempowered groups. On the

Left women were used as menial labor, and our sexual availability was taken for granted. Fighting for others, some of us learned to fight for ourselves. Radical feminism emerged from the Left and brought left-wing values of equality to women. The Left opposed feminists every step of the way—and not just because the boys were losing cheap labor and cheap lays. They were blind to injustice against women: injustice that had their names on it. The Left especially opposed emerging consciousness and activism regarding rape, wife-abuse, incest, pornography, and prostitution. In the early 1970s, rape became a cutting-edge issue. The organized Left opposed prosecuting rapists without fear or favor because bogus charges of rape had been used to persecute black men. Convicting white men who raped did not seem to the men on the Left a fair move—one that would change everyone's perception of rape and of black men. Redefining rape from the point of view of the victims was taken to be vindictive and mean. Men of the Left wanted female voices on rape silenced. In the mid-1970s, battery became a cutting-edge issue. Left-wing lawyers conjured up the specter of the "knock on the door," police-state entry into the home that is, after all, a man's castle. They wanted the voices of beaten women and feminist advocates silenced. Rather than face the suffering of the victims, they became militant on the due-process rights of the perpetrators. A few years later, incest became a cutting-edge issue. The Left denied its existence while protecting the sexualization of children under the rubric of free sexuality for children. The Left simply denied the harm done to children by pedophiles, rapists, sadists, and pornographers, any of whom might be strangers or acquaintances or family. Efforts to protect children from sexual abuse and exploitation were characterized as a tyranny of the repressed. The Left wanted the voices of adult survivors silenced and refused to listen to child victims without a mountain of independent corroboration. In the late 1970s, pornography became a cutting-edge issue. The Left took the position that pornography was liberated sexuality and that those opposing it were right-wing collaborators. A free-speech absolutism, which in earlier years the Left abhorred with respect to racism, became the Left's über-principle. When prostitution and the trafficking in women globally became cutting-edge issues in the mid-1980s, the Left suddenly honored money, contracts, and exploited labor—as if it were the dream of all girls to suck cocks for a few bucks.

This chronology of issues is only approximate, because victims, survivors, and organizers worked on all these issues (always with opposition from the Left) before the larger public became aware of them. For instance, the first antipornography demonstration by feminists was in 1970 in New York City: a sit-in to denounce both the low pay of women workers at Grove Press and its publishing of pornography. Barney Rossett, owner of Grove, condemned the sit-in as a CIA plot. The charge of right-wing collaboration was born then. Earlier, in 1968 and 1969, there had been protests against the Miss America Pageant: protests against objectifying and dehumanizing women through sexual voyeurism. In the public's perception, one issue followed on the heels of another, often supplanting attention paid to the prior agitation; but for feminists who worked against violence against women, the 1970s and 1980s were two decades of constantly expanding knowledge, all related through speak-outs, consciousness-raising, books, conferences, demonstrations, marches, civil disobedience, lobbying, drafting legislation, and building women's studies departments. It started with rape, what is now called "stranger rape." But once women began to understand rape, to unravel the lies about it (legal and vulgar), each of the other issues began to show through what had been a lead barrier of obfuscation, denial, indifference, and outright cruelty. These issues were all connected, intertwined; in any given woman's life, they intersected in complex ways.

The Left has pretty much failed in its efforts to block feminist work against rape, wife-abuse, and incest, but it has been more successful in protecting pornography and prostitution. Every conceivable effort has been made to silence women who have been hurt in or by pornography: they are slandered, stigmatized, stalked, and shunned. Similarly, survivors of prostitution are expected to disappear into that thin gray line between night and day, not living or dead: touched too much inside; dirty vaginas, dirty mouths; not citizens, not like us, not of us; nothing to say. The men who rape or batter or incestuously rape or sexually abuse children or make pornography out of women and children or use pornography made of women or children or use prostitutes or pimp prostitutes always have something to say. On the Left, these men are deemed to have ideas; their experience is respected—the more low-down, dirty, or violent, the better; they are crowned as liberators, rhetorically worshiped as freedom-fighters—each woman or girl used (plugged or boned or whatever the current hostile slang is) representing a triumph over repression or suppression or oppression; in fact, a triumph of expression.

In addition to romanticizing forced sex and celebrating sexual exploitation, the Left has joined the Right in defending the culture of dead white men: protecting it from criticism or change; keeping it inviolate, immune from contamination by creative persons not dead or white or male. The culture of dead white men, built on the bodies of silenced women and colonialized people of color, has become a weapon to keep living women of all races silent. Like a private club that keeps out all but an elite few, art and books especially are used to tell the emerging women—emerging not only from silence but often enough from hell— that they are not good enough or important enough or worthy enough to be listened to. The proof of their insignificance is in their suffering: having been raped or beaten or prostituted. Was Aristotle? Was Descartes? Why listen to women who are more pleasing laid out flat, legs spread, than standing up, talking back, talking real? Why should the men of liberation interrupt the liberatory act itself to listen to the person whose hole he was sticking it in? And if I were to say that hole is not empty space waiting to be filled by anyone or anything, what would my authority be? How do I know? But he knows—every "he" knows.

The books I read growing up—the books of dead white men, or near dead, the men living but remote by virtue of their own presumed superiority to women—did not, could not, tell me about the suffering of women or what it would take to make society fair for women. I read the men of conscience—but Camus did not consider these questions, nor did Sartre or Whitman or Shelley or Lord Byron. I read the men of suffering—Dostoevsky, Proust, Rimbaud—but they were silent on the suffering of women. The things I wanted in life were in the realm of men, of culture: to write books, to be politically engaged; to strategize against injustice, to expose it; to break down institutions that supported suffering—laws, manners, habits, threat of force or threat of the mob or threat of prison or threat of exile. I simply did not understand that girls in my generation were excluded by definition from doing virtually everything I wanted to do. The exclusion was egregious; but so was the consequence of not identifying the excluded group by name—women. I empathized with every group I knew to be excluded and I knew them by name: blacks, the poor, exploited workers. But men were the real people; women did not exist in consciousness. Men were actors on the stage of history, doers in the culture of intellect and creativity. Women were absent; and it is impossible to empathize with a vacuum, a blank space, a nonentity. There was no injustice in this invisibility; it was the nature of women to be absent from action. There was no political conception that women were excluded, thus disenfranchised, socially stigmatized, politically powerless—only that women had a different, opposite function to men, a preordained, predetermined purpose that precluded heroism and originality. History, culture, justice were not our province; romance was, marriage was, babies were. In truth, one's body got touched and pushed into and hit and knocked around by men who had a birthright to invade using force, which was taken to be a measure of desire: and one rooted for the invader, the action hero, and disavowed her, the culpable victim. Wanting to be the hero, a girl did not recognize rape as rape even when it happened: she'd stumble around hurt and confused, trying to forget. Wanting to be human, even when one was pushed down and pushed over and drilled into, one did not recognize the generic nature of the event. Any such recognition would strip one's life of dignity and individuality; one would lose all credibility, even in one's own mind. Wanting to love, even when treated with contempt wrapped in seduction and condescension, one could not draw a line, even around one's own body, because he, not she, was the significant person, the one who acted, the line drawer: the real person. Girls wanted so much, not knowing they wanted the impossible: to move in a real world of action and accomplishment; to be someone individual and unique; to act on one's own feelings, not to have to wait passively until a boy felt something so that one might react—he turns on the switch and then the current flows; which switch will he flick? One had appetites and ambitions, talents and desires, capacities and potential, drive and vision, questions and curiosity. Almost inevitably in my generation, girls were raped in response to assertions of self: being in a proscribed place; being alone; being outside; being inside; showing affection or interest or delight; asserting ambition—intellectual, creative, athletic: every act was a provocation, and eventually a man punished one for wanting either something or anything.

It was the biblical god of the Old Testament who said that knowledge and sex were synonyms and made knowledge a male domain: he knew her. She knew nothing and ate the apple from the Tree of Knowledge because she was pliable and weak; she got expelled from the Garden, her home, and got pregnant and multiplied, her labor painful and bloody to punish her for daring to want to know, or for daring to act—to pick an apple. There is no divinely inspired paradigm for a woman's wanting to know without her also deserving and getting punishment: not, at least, in the Judeo-Christian world. The punishment is against her body: taking it, using it, entering it, causing her pain, her will irrelevant. The punisher has power and gets pleasure, his recompense for being mortal. The girl, erased and mute in the culture originating in that old book, increasingly becomes invisible and silent to herself. The ambitions die. The dreams die. The adventurer, the explorer, the creator in her dies. She becomes whatever her body means to men. Her mind is hurt by rape and other physical assault to her body; it fades and shrinks and seeks silence as refuge; it becomes the prison cell inside her. Rape and physical assault damage the mind; and rape is concrete and consistent, mandated by the man's ownership of the woman and by her separate destiny, her bloody, painful destiny. Every invasion of the body is marked in the brain: contusions, abrasions, cuts, swellings, bleeding, mutilation, breaking, burning. Each capacity of the brain—memory, imagination, intellect, creation, consciousness itself—is distressed and deformed, distorted by the sexualized physical injuries that girls and women sustain. No matter how much we are undressed, the shadow of unexplained, undeserved pain covers us with shame and despair. All around us there are other women, seemingly not hurt, making small talk, acting normal, which means happy, not discontent, certainly not devastated. Girls are still being socialized not to identify with—feel empathy for—other females: she got hurt because she did x, y, z—I didn't, so I didn't get hurt; she's at fault, I'm not; the punishment fits her crime; blame her, exonerate him. This continuing, culturally applauded socialization of women not to empathize with other women is a malignant part of the culture of men, dead white ones or not. Women are perceived to be appalling failures when we are sad. Women are pathetic when we are angry. Women are ridiculous when we are militant. Women are unpleasant when we are bitter, no matter what the cause. Women are deranged when women want justice. Women are man-haters when women want accountability and respect from men. Women are trash when women let men do what men want. Women are shrews or puritans when we do not.

We learn—still, now, despite the gains of feminism—not to call attention to ourselves, only to the signets of our conformity: the sexualized conventions of grooming. We cover over being the victims of sexual abuse, because otherwise we are exposed in poses and positions and with bruises that excite some men or many men or nearly all men or the next man. Each abuser makes his cut, adds his mark, his smell, his ejaculate, his contempt, his destruction, to the social identity of a woman exposed. She is in the male mind—the minds of men—as the spread-out thing, or the bruised and brazen thing, or the serially fucked thing. She's rarely more than a picture in his mind anyway: spread ejaculate on her and she's a dirtier picture.

In 1972 I came back to the United States after five years in Amsterdam, four of which I spent doing time as the battered wife of a tormenter, a torturer even Amnesty International would hesitate to approach. In the year before I came back—a year of being stalked, a year of running, hiding, being homeless, having nothing—I began to ask questions about women: why women were treated with contempt, violence; why no one cared or intervened or helped even a little. When I was battered, virtually every person whom I asked for help the many times I tried unsuccessfully to run away told me I provoked the violence, that it was my fault, that I liked it (even though I was running from it). My friends were all leftists who cared about human rights—about suffering and fairness. Only one was honest when I asked her why she wouldn't help me: I'm afraid he'll hurt me, she said. Only feminists did not back off; only feminists cared about how badly I had been hurt; only feminists did not think that whatever he, the mad dog, did, I deserved or craved—or that it was his right.

Back in the United States in November 1972, I started working with antiwar groups again. I found my former allies indifferent to violence against women—and these were mostly pacifists. Organizationally, Left groups embraced the idea of "strong chicks" (in the parlance of the time) but repudiated a politics of anathematizing violence against women. Feminists in the United States had been organizing speak-outs and consciousness-raising groups since at least 1970; rape had emerged as a political issue. The Left ignored, trivialized, and opposed the new movement; and feminists did the work of creating a real political home for women, a social place out in the open in which the suffering of women counted and fairness toward women was a goal of social policy, not just noblesse oblige on the part of individual men.

The accomplishment of the women's movement in this regard was staggering. Silence—a heavy tombstone over each woman's hurt body and torn heart—was broken; one could hear the concrete crack, splintering, breaking open, crevices becoming gorges. Women talked: this happened to me. The stories were similar even as the women were different. The rapes were similar even as the rapists were different. The devaluing through insult and overbearing arrogance and vulgar assumptions of an innate superiority was the same, no matter what the social or economic status of the woman appeared to be. The rapists were men who crawled through locked windows and skylights or emerged at night from dark bushes or alleys; the rapists were teachers and neighbors and friends; the rapists were daddy or daddy's best buddy or step-daddy or uncle or brother or brother's best friend. Only the victims were able to articulate the elements of the crime. Only the victims knew who the rapist was, what he said, what he did, how he did it, and what it meant: what the act expressed. (Rape is a very expressive act.) U.S. laws on rape, originating in English common law, made assumptions about women that disguised and protected both rape and the rapist. Those laws assumed that women would lie: accusations of rape were construed to be vengeful lies by an angry slut or spurned lover. Rape itself was seen as a crime against men if it was seen as a crime at all: a husband was injured in his conjugal rights if his wife—loyal and not adulterous—was violated; a father's rights over his unmarried virgin daughter became worthless when she was ruined and despoiled. The crime was not against the rape victim but against her male owner. If the male owner raped her, it was not rape. Only when women said what happened to them when they were forced was rape properly defined, understood, and prosecuted.

The Left and the Right have consistently had different positions on rape; but neither has acknowledged rape from the point of view of the women who experienced it. Both the Left and the Right denounced rape with varying degrees of outrage, but the Left saw most rape as free sex saturated with desire and the Right characterized rape as deviant and rare. Rape in marriage was legal; this was not an issue for Left or Right. The Left, which wanted to bring down power, hierarchies, and despotism, did not have a problem with forced sex—with its gender-based power, hierarchy, or despotism. I left the Left, although, really, the Left left the Left by betraying women, who were suffering and needed fairness in law, social policy, money, culture, speech, media, politics, and governance. The Left moved rightward when it abandoned women to rape, battery, incest, pornography, and prostitution. As with many women, for me equality became the heart of a living political quest to end the suffering caused by sexual abuse and exploitation through finding fairness. In betraying women, the Left sold itself out; and it is correct to say, I think, that the demands of feminism have caused a political realignment in the United States in which the recognized political continuum moves from Right to further Right to armed and murderous Right. Far to the left, off the mainstream continuum—at least as currently articulated in popular discourse—are women whose politics are animated by a commitment to listening to those who have been hurt and finding remedies that are fair.

The fact is that the speech of the socially worthless, the sexually stigmatized, is hard to hear even when the victims shout. Rapists and pimps talk louder, their speech amplified by the money behind the words they use. Rapists and pimps, representing the interests of normal men, some of whom rape, some of whom buy, seem to have the law of gravity on their side: they reify the status quo, which is what gives them credibility, legitimacy, and authority. They sound coherent. No matter what lie they tell, it passes for truth, because the hatred of women underlying the lie is an accepted hatred, a shared and unchallenged set of prejudiced assumptions. The woman who has been raped or pimped has to convince a hearer to listen because she counts. But she does not count unless she can make herself count, unless she can change the direction of gravity—turn the status quo, even momentarily, not just upside down but also inside out. She needs the women's movement; she needs courage; she needs stubbornness; she needs to want justice. It is fine for her to hate those who ripped into her if hate keeps her willing to talk, unwilling to let silence bury her again. She must dare to remember what she prefers to forget; and then she must stand fast on the sickening memory, which tries to drown her. She must stand right there. Any healed wound she must reopen, must tear away scar tissue and scabs to see what's underneath: ripping off her own skin, she sees the color of her own blood. She has to use her body to remember and he's on her and in her again; and this she must endure in order to speak. She has to be able to relive pain and humiliation: however shy, however modest, however unhappy to do so, she has to articulate violation, communicate dread, explicate sadism, remember the hate he had for her, which motivated him, and not die from that hate or the memory of it. Then he—rapist or pimp or buyer—says something, anything, and she is drowning again, back under, invisible, silent, worthless, except for whatever he gets out of her—pleasure or power or money. He always has a revered principle on which to hang his prick: free speech or free sex in the free market.

He has a constitutional right to express himself, and if his art requires that she be the canvas, so what? If he's an engraver and her skin is his surface, so what? If he wants to sculpt her to death or twist her body until it breaks where he turns her, so what? He's a citizen; she's a cunt. The Constitution protects him. All's right with the world.

Then there is the right to sex, which is implicitly his, since he gets what he wants: law, justice, honor, and feminist agitation notwithstanding. If it gives him sexual pleasure, getting in his way is mean and petty. If it hurts her, so what? If it insults or dehumanizes her, so what? If—in order for her to be available—she needs to be fucked as a child, trained, seasoned, so what? And if she screams, and he gets off on it, so what? If she tears—her rectum, her vagina, her throat—and he likes it, so what? If she bleeds—well, bitches bleed; so what?

The free market is where she is bartered, bought, and sold. It is often euphemistically called a marketplace of ideas, but only his ideas have value, especially his ideas, put into practice, of how to sell her. She is meat in his marketplace; he is the butcher who wields the knife to get the right cut; and he communicates through the cutting, then the display of the body parts. She is worth more in pieces than she ever was whole. The pimps' motive is twofold: money and pleasure. The user does what he wants, calls it what he likes. Everyone wants to be him—to be the user, not the used. This is a political point: what once was the Left wants to be the user, does not want to be anywhere but on top of the used; and some so-called feminists want to be the user, not to be under, not to be the condemned, the injured. Each time a victim is looked at, a man gets hard; the brave "women-aren't-victims" girls want to be allies of the users, not of the used. It was ignorance to disassociate oneself from the raped be-fore raped women articulated what rape is and means; it is malice, cow-ardice, and venality to disassociate oneself from the raped now—after the raped have made rape socially real. The same is true for battery, incest, prostitution; the same for pornography, made from the raw mate-rial of women's bodies, used against women's bodies, the production and the use designed to control, dehumanize, humiliate, injure, and subordi-nate: push down, push under, make lower, make less, render inferior.

I am asking you to listen in these hearings to those who have been hurt—and to care. I have always thought that conscience meant bear-ing witness to injustice and standing with the powerless. I still think that. I have always thought that equality meant an antagonism to exploiters. I still think that. I used to think that the Left was the side that valued those dehumanized by hate. I don't think that anymore—unless feminists fighting pornography and the global trafficking in women are the rem-nant, the last living leftists: facing the new millennium in opposition to the biggest trafficking in human beings this planet has yet seen. All the power is on the other side: all the money, media, current law, unexam-ined assumptions about speech, sex, women; all the fetishized sex that depends on dominance and submission as a dynamic and the objectifica-tion of women as a fundamental element of pleasure. There is nothing wrong with selling objects, generally speaking, provided the labor of human beings is not exploited to make the desired profit; but it is always and without exception a vicious practice to buy and sell human beings, which we are—which women are—no matter how used or raped or prostituted or incested or beaten we have been; no matter how shamed or humiliated by the overt sadism of some and the brutal indifference of the rest. You need to listen. You need to know. You need to care about the suffering pornography causes and be willing to decide what is fair.

THE HEARINGS

The Minneapolis Hearings

GOVERNMENT OPERATIONS COMMITTEE
SESSION I: MONDAY, DECEMBER 12, 1983, 1:30 P.M.

Government Operations Committee:
Van F. White, Chairman
Walter Dziedzic
Patrick Daugherty
Sally Howard
Charlee Hoyt

CHAIRMAN VAN WHITE: Having a quorum, the Government Operations Committee will come to order. One of the things that I would like to ask is that when there is a person who is presenting whatever they have of material in terms of verbalization, that there be no other comments because we do have a court reporter here who is taking it and when one or two or three people are talking, she can't get it down. So do it one at a time and let there be no other comments. This is not a debate, this is a public hearing. We are going to hear and receive the comments both pro and con from the audience. The persons that are now about to take over will make their presentations, they will make their comments, their slide presentations, and after that we will go into public comments. It is in three stages. Today we go at 1:30 until 4:00 o'clock and we will reconvene at 5:00 o'clock and continue on, God willing, it will be over by at least 7:00 or 8:00 o'clock. Tomorrow we have a 5:00 o'clock public hearing, the same continued public hearing. I would ask that the persons who are going to make comments and make presentations use the microphone at the very end of that table so that the television cameras can zoom in on you and do their thing. Okay. Now, starting out, those that wish to speak, the sign-up sheet is right at that table *(indicating)*.

Does anyone wish to sign up to speak? How many people in the audience are going to speak? Okay, we will allow three to four minutes in your speaking. We will try to hold it down because there are quite a few people who are going to speak. Number one on the agenda is Dr. Edward Donnerstein.

ALLEN HYATT: Excuse me, may I speak before we get into Professor Donnerstein?

CHAIRMAN WHITE: Go ahead, City Attorney.

HYATT: I am Allen Hyatt, Assistant City Attorney for Minneapolis and I am assigned to this committee. Prior to the starting of testimony, we are going to hear from Professors Catharine MacKinnon, I believe, and Andrea Dworkin, both who are under contract to the City Council to develop an ordinance relating the violation of women's rights in regard to pornography to civil rights. And they have been asked by our City Council to develop that ordinance, they have done so, proposed ordinances before this committee and we will now hear from Professor MacKinnon. Before we do that I would like to give you background. She is a Professor of Law at the University of Minnesota. She has, with Ms. Dworkin, conducted a course this year on pornography, particularly its effects on women, particularly the violent aspects of pornography. [She is] eminently well qualified to speak on this topic and that is why we have contracted with her to do so. Professor MacKinnon.

CATHARINE MacKINNON: As the committee knows, Andrea Dworkin and I are here today to discuss with you the proposed ordinance which we have drafted together under contract with the City to define pornography as what it is, that is to say, as a violation of the civil rights of women. We are proposing for your consideration a statutory scheme that will situate pornography as a central practice in the inequality of the sexes, in specific, as a practice that is central to the subordination of women.

This statute's principle arises under the Fourteenth Amendment, which guarantees equality and freedom from discrimination to all citizens, including on the basis of sex. The concept of the systematic relegation of a group of people to inferiority because of a condition of birth, that that idea should be, that those practices should be, illegal—that idea is not novel in the context of the Fourteenth Amendment.

The understanding and the evidence which we will present to you today to support defining pornography as a practice of discrimination on the basis of sex *is* a new idea. I will be submitting to you, as soon as I am finished with this statement, a copy of my book, which is a book about sex discrimination which made the argument that defined sexual harassment as a form of discrimination on the basis of sex on the basis of a similar view, that is, the same view of sex discrimination that underlies this ordinance.

In this hearing we are going to show the harm of pornography to women: what it takes to make it, particularly how it is used on people, from the coercion into making it to the effects of men consuming it, which they act out on women, to the trafficking that provides both the motivation and the access, to the harm of forcing it on someone to attempt to get them to perform sexual acts that they have no desire to perform, to seasoning children and prostitutes and wives and girlfriends so that they will be more compliant sexually, so that they will become debased and lacking in self-respect and lacking in existence and ideas of their own, to more direct assaults, stimulated, made desirable, and made legitimate and made sexy by pornography.

We plan to show why and how and in what sexual violence has become fun and sexy and entertaining and feminine and liberating and a definition of love.

In particular, we want to show how the concept of pornography conditions and determines the way in which men actually treat women. Also the way men actually treat men and children.

We will show the ways that this abuse goes on in public as well as in private environments, and we will show that this is central to the way in which women remain second-class citizens in those environments, despite all our efforts to change that status.

We will document this on a national scale and in particular, replicate and show how everything that can be shown on a national scale is occurring now in the City of Minneapolis.

We will then argue that pornography has everything to do with why public policies against some of the deepest injuries and injustices against women—that is to say sexual violence including rape, sexual harassment, battery, and prostitution—systematically have consistently failed women, and we will argue why it is this ordinance will protect them.

The purpose of this hearing is principally factual. We think that we have found a large part of the way that women have been kept silent for a very long time, and that is that pornography silences women. This hearing, this opportunity for our speech, is precious and rare and unprecedented. That we can speak to our real injuries in a public forum is the kind of opportunity without which, before now, the guarantees of the

First Amendment have not been useful to us. And they have not worked for us. What I am saying is, if pornography silences women, if it has already accomplished that silence, the First Amendment which prohibits the way that the state can silence people is not useful to us.

When I say that the purpose of this hearing is factual, what I mean is that we will provide a factual basis for a legally sufficient sex discrimination statute, both in terms of the Fourteenth Amendment requirements and also to survive defenses that might be raised against it under the First Amendment. It is designed in both of those ways.

The primary purpose of the hearing, as I am understanding it now then, is not to advance legal arguments about why the statute withstands attack under the First Amendment, although we believe that it will, and I will be happy to respond to any questions that you have about that. But the primary purpose is to provide a factual basis so that it can withstand the defenses that most probably will be raised by principally the pornographers under the First Amendment.

Now, if asked, I am happy to address all—

COUNCILMEMBER WALTER DZIEDZIC: Mr. Chairman, as one of the five committee members here, I will tell you why I think we are having a public hearing. That is to gather input from the public about the issue so this committee could gather the input and we could go to the Council with a rational and intelligent suggestion on the issue. That is why we are having a public hearing.

MacKINNON: Absolutely, that is exactly our purpose. And that, in particular, I think it is crucial that the people who are here to speak can be able to speak. I am not going to advance a lot of legal arguments to the hearing. The purpose is factual and the people should be able to speak.

CHAIRMAN WHITE: That is on the onset what I was saying. We are here to receive and listen. If there is any written documentation I would like that to be passed up to the committee clerk so it goes into the record. I have some here too that I will give you.

But secondly, I would like to say I recognize the fact that there's going to be consensus which will bring about applause. I would ask that you would cease on that, because it will slow down the process. It takes away from the presenters in terms of what they are trying to say, and it prolongs the hearing. So I will ask you to please not applaud whether you agree or disagree with a certain presenter.

MacKINNON: I will also submit to you a copy of my book and my vita, in that I am here as an expert consultant. Andrea Dworkin will make brief comments and then we will begin the testimony.

CHAIRMAN WHITE: Yes. What I am going to do is that you will make your presentation and then what I would like, since I don't have the knowledge of the three presenters that will be coming before us, I would like you, Professor MacKinnon, to introduce them and then we will continue.

ANDREA DWORKIN: I would just like to situate the amendment that we have drafted in the context of international law. And, in particular, in the context of the United Nations Convention on the Elimination of All Forms of Discrimination against Women, from which I would like to now read briefly. Article 2 states, "States parties condemn discrimination against women in all its forms, agree to pursue by all appropriate means and without delay a policy of eliminating discrimination against women and, to this end, undertake to embody the principle of the equality of men and women in their national constitutions or other appropriate legislation if not yet incorporated therein and to ensure, through law and other appropriate means, the practical realization of this principle. To adopt appropriate legislative and other measures, including sanctions where appropriate, prohibiting all discrimination against women. And protect the legal rights of women on an equal basis with men." And it goes on in that vein, which I think is clear.

Article 6 specifically states, "States parties shall take all appropriate measures, including legislation, to suppress all forms of traffic in women and exploitation of prostitution of women."

Now, I want to make clear the dimensions of the problem that we are talking about. Pornography is part of the traffic in women. In this country it is a seven billion dollar industry that buys and sells women's bodies. I am going to put into evidence two pieces of literature. One is a magazine article from the magazine *Aegis,* called "The Political Economy of Pornography," that describes the actual economic dimensions of the industry. And I quote from the article, "If all of this material were produced by a single corporation, 'Pornography, Incorporated' at seven billion dollars a year would be the fortieth largest company on the Fortune 500, as large as Xerox, RCA, or Bethlehem Steel." In addition, I would like to suggest that pornography is an industry based entirely on the domination of women by men and that this description of the material now available is accurate from the same article, "At least 25 percent of all the heterosexual material sold in Washington's 'adult' bookstores, for example, depicts explicit violence against women—torture of all kinds, whipping, beating, mutilation, rape, and murder. Not all the violence is vicarious; the stores also stock everything from whips and chains to twelve inch spiked plastic penises, so that the customers can participate directly. The hard-core material has become increasingly sadomasochistic during the past few years, but even the basic soft-core presentation of unequal, one-sided nudity (vulnerable, exposed women with fully clothed or unseen men) conveys a very clear message of male sexual dominance. Such one-sided nudity is commonly used by men to dominate and humiliate other males in prisons and military training, and has the same psychological effect when applied overwhelmingly to women in culturewide media like soft-core pornography."

In other words, we are dealing with an endemic and systematic dominance of men over women. That is the subordination we are trying to address.

I would also like to submit into evidence a copy of my book, which is a description of the actual content in the pornography that is being produced at this time.

I thank you very much for this time, and we will now advance with the testimony.

CHAIRMAN WHITE: I would like to state with these presentations, you have an hour each. I read that to mean that within this time frame from 1:30 to 4:00 o'clock that this will be cut down. You will not speak for one hour each.

MacKINNON: No. The understanding is that that is the amount of time given to each of those experts. They will speak in some cases only for, say, 15 minutes, and then there will be questions from the Council, in some cases questions to us in an attempt to clarify the relation between their testimony and this ordinance.

DZIEDZIC: Chairman, just so there is no misunderstanding, we have twelve.

MacKINNON: That is this evening.

DZIEDZIC: We have ten other people that wish to speak.

COUNCILMEMBER CHARLEE HOYT: That is tonight.

DZIEDZIC: Sorry, that is tonight.

MacKINNON: Dr. Donnerstein, are you ready? Dr. Donnerstein, if you could begin by identifying yourself and I will submit your vita.

EDWARD DONNERSTEIN: I wonder, can I be heard in the back of the room without a mike? Can you hear me?

My name is Ed Donnerstein, D-o-n-n-e-r-s-t-e-i-n. I am a psychologist at the Center for Communication Research at the University of Wisconsin, Madison, 200 miles south and a bit warmer.

What I want to present into evidence is an outline of some of the major topics I wish to cover with some of the major references in scientific literature [Exh. 1], also allowing some space for notes by the City Council, and four major book chapters, discussing overviews of the major research of the last ten years on the effects, particularly the effects of sexual violence or aggressive pornography or pornography in general, and the effects it has on attitudes towards women about rape and aggressive behavior. There are essentially six topics, really five, I would like to cover [Exh. 2] and it is going to be a little difficult, I think, given the slide projector, but I will try and I hope the gentlemen and the women on the City Council will see them. I apologize to members of the audience who can't.

The six topics are as follows, in terms of dealing with the relationship with sexual violence in the mass media on attitudes on rape and attitudes on aggression. Number one, what are the images and secondly, is there an increase in the media. The answer is going to be a definite yes, and I will give some brief descriptions very shortly.

Secondly, what are the effects of this type of material on a number of things. One, what are the effects of sexual violent images or aggressive pornography on sexual arousal in rapists, known criminal offenders, and, more importantly, quote unquote normals. I will describe what I mean by that shortly.

Thirdly, what are the effects of this type of material on rape-related attitudes—the attitudes meaning myths about rape stereotypes, willingness for a person to say they would commit a rape and attitudes in general about women.

And [fourth], what are the effects of this type of material on aggressive behavior, primarily aggressive behavior against women in a laboratory type situation which is, of course, the only place one could conduct such a research.

[Fifth], what is the relative contribution of sexual and violent contents of the material. I think what the research tends to indicate, this is not an issue of quote unquote sexual explicitness or nudity. It is a question of how women are portrayed, particularly women as victims which we are really talking about.

Finally, what are the effects of massive long-term exposure to this type of material.

Let me make a preface here. We are going to be talking about, initially, short-term exposure in a research context. Short-term is five or ten minutes of exposure, primarily to very normal types of male subjects. I think you will see, even with that, some fairly dramatic type of results.

When we get to long-term exposure, I think you will see the effects are even stronger, particularly with the types of material which have no physical violent content, that is, the straight type of pornographic or erotic material. So keep in mind a number of things. One, when I mention in this research that there are no effects in the short term for erotica, we are talking about material made by myself or other colleagues, material which is sexually explicit and does not show power orientation between males and females.

When we talk about aggressive pornography, we are talking about material in which women are abused physically and in which there are acts of rape, mutilation, or other types of physical aggression. We will talk about the long-term effects of this type of material.

Number one, what are the images? Let me give you examples of what we are talking about. We have what is classified as obviously nothing to do with pornography at all, to the hard-core effects. We have three or four images which will suffice.

(Slide show being shown.)

DONNERSTEIN: This, I think, has nothing to do with pornography, but I think the message is very clear. We find it as a common scenario in most of the common material. This is a slide of a woman who is tied up, bound, black and blue. It is nothing more than an advertisement for a Rolling Stones album cover. I think it is interesting, the woman is saying a scenario we find in a great deal of pornography: "I am black and blue from the Rolling Stones and I love it." Violence is a sexual turn-on—that is the message which consistently comes through in this type of material. And what we are going to say is that, without question, that has very, very strong effects, particularly on adolescent males and males who are beginning to form certain types of stereotypes about human sexuality, about rape and violence.

The next slide I call subtle. It might be my own desensitization. I think it represents the over-the-counter magazine, *Hustler,* which depicts violent types of images against women. I think it deserves no other comment, but it is a subtle image compared to the types of graphic violation we will get to very soon.

This gets a little closer to the hard-core market. I should admit that every one of these slides I have, you can find in almost every city. In fact, the next slide you don't have to go to an adult bookstore to find. I am not sure you have to find this in an adult bookstore either. I think it gets a little more toward the violence.

The next slide I have [is] a blank. I show it to only demonstrate the excessive types of sex against women. Until we started on a recent science foundation project, I found this is not excessive. I think a number of people will find it a bit difficult to look at. I don't mean it to offend anyone. I don't mean it to show anger to anybody. I think you have to have some ideas about the type of material we are talking about when we talk about aggressive pornography. This type of material is readily available. I present it to show that the research will show inclusively that many healthy males become sexually aroused to this type of image.

Now, the question is what are the effects of this type of material. Like we just saw, the first question is, what are the effects on sexual arousal and there are a number of reasons why I would like to discuss that.

I have a quote up there from Neil Malamuth who is at UCLA and basically what he says, I can't read the quote, I am going to have to paraphrase it. Basically what Malamuth says [is] that if individuals become sexually aroused—which is a very positive state, we are not saying there is anything wrong with sexual arousal—if they become aroused from scenes of rape in the media, in pornography—that is, number one, do they become sexually aroused? Would they go ahead and make the attribution that if they engaged in such behavior it would be a sexually arousing experience? Those are a number of conceptual leaps.

First of all, you have to determine whether or not quote unquote normal healthy males could conceivably become sexually aroused to brutality, scenes of rape, scenes of mutilation.

Secondly, even if they did, would they go ahead and make the attribution that, number one, I would like to engage in such behavior and secondly, if I so did, it would not only be sexually arousing for the victim, which in fact it usually is shown that way, that it would also be sexually arousing for myself.

Let's ask the first question: is the material sexually arousing, and who is it sexually arousing to? Most of the early research dealt with the effects of this on a rapist. It was widely assumed that rapists would be sexually aroused by images of rape in the media. If you look at the graph up in the front, you see an example of a rapist and the nonrapist population. Rapists were shown films which depicted rape or films of mutually consenting intercourse. A group of nonrapists were shown similar types of materials. When and what the researchers did was look at sexual arousal, penile tumescence in males. Basically what they found is that rapists do in fact become very sexually aroused to violent images, images of women being aggressed against in the sexual context. The assumption, however, was that normal males, not convicted of a sexual crime, do not show the same type of reactions. The assumption is that normals would not become sexually aroused to this type of material.

A few years ago Neil Malamuth at UCLA conducted a large amount of studies, by the way I am mentioning one percent of the research in this area to get through it, but Malamuth found if you take normal males and present them with a scene of rape from pornography, but you present them with the common type of scenario which is a woman enjoying being raped, when a woman is violated, aggressed against, she becomes sexually aroused. What Malamuth found—one, normal, healthy males also became sexually aroused when they viewed that type of image. If you present them with a highly explicit erotic film, they become sexually aroused. If you present them with a scene in which a woman is raped but doesn't become sexually aroused, the majority of males would not become sexually aroused. But most normal males, when you present them with a scene of rape and the only differences between the scene on the left and the other scene is right at the end of the rape, even though the violence is the same, the victim shows sexual arousal—which, again, is a common type of scenario one finds in the material—you find normal males becoming sexually aroused to these type[s] of images.

Let's go on for a second. Malamuth has found, as have we and other researchers, that is, a scale called the Rape Myth Acceptance scale . . . touches many of the common types of myths which individuals hold about rape: any woman who hitchhikes deserves to get raped, women unconsciously set up situations which force rape on them, women enjoy being raped, women who wear provocative clothing are putting themselves in a place to get raped. These are common myths held by rapists. It is held as an instrument to determine if treatment for a rapist was satisfactory.

What you find is that after only ten minutes of exposure to aggressive pornography, particularly material in which women are shown being aggressed against, you find male subjects are much more willing to accept these particular types of myths. In fact, this particular slide again shows a good example of that.

Male subjects or female subjects were shown a sexually violent film in which a woman is raped and gets turned on to the rape. After they had seen this film a week later, they are more accepting of these types of myths and more accepting on an Acceptance of Interpersonal Violence scale. That scale has items [such] as: it is justified to hit your wife or spouse, the only way to turn a woman on is through force, and that women find aggressiveness a sexual turn-on. You find, after exposure of this type of material, more acceptance of these types of myths.

Another interesting thing, if you look at Neil Malamuth's research, you also find some other changes in attitude. This particular study showed that if male subjects were presented with a rape depiction, that is aggressive pornography, that is, if a woman shows a positive reaction—I apologize for having to use that term, it is a term that is used meaning that the victim in the scene becomes sexually aroused—you find again that normal, healthy male subjects say the following. If asked "What percentage of women do you know who enjoy being raped?"—think about the question for a second, think about the context of how this research is done—you find normal males, after five minutes of exposure to pornography, say 25 percent of the women they know would enjoy being raped.

Secondly, what percentage of women do you know who enjoy being aggressively forced into sexual intercourse? Again, we are not talking about rapists, not talking about sexual deviants, [we are] talking about normal, healthy male college students at Manitoba, UCLA, Blooming-ton, and other places. [They say] 30 percent of the women they know would enjoy being aggressively forced into sexual intercourse.

The most important question of all is questions that ask subjects, after [being] exposed to this material: "what is the likelihood that you would commit a rape if I guarantee that you won't be caught." Think about that for a second. You are asking a normal, healthy male, "would you commit a rape after exposure to this type of material?" And on a five point scale, you find that after exposure to sexually violent images, particularly when those sexual violent images depict women enjoying rape, up to 57 per-cent of those males indicate some likelihood they would commit a rape if not caught.

In fact, in the general population, as it turns out, anywhere between 25 and 30 percent of normal, healthy males indicate some willingness they would commit a rape. And, in fact, if you look at those individuals, and I think it is important to do so very quickly, you find a number of interest-ing things about them. Again, this is the normal distribution of at least male college students.

One, they believe other men would rape if not caught. They identify with the rapist, basically meaning, if you put them in a situation which involves a rape, there is a good likelihood they would never convict the rapist. They believe that, one, rape victims cause their own assaults, two, derive pleasure from their assaults. It is associated with rape, with aggression against women.

More important than that, if you take the 25 or 30 percent, we are not talking about a small minority, but a large percentage of people. Particularly when you think about the amount of people that might see any particular film, even if it is only one percent, we are talking about an incredible amount of potential harm to women. Twenty-five to thirty percent, if you take these individuals, and if you look at the bottom graph that measures sexual arousal, the likelihood to rape people, meaning those are males, that 25 percent indicate that they would commit a rape. Basically you find those particular males, again normal males in the population, not rapists convicted or sentenced in any way, those particular males are sexually aroused to all types of rape images. They are sexually aroused to rape images which give, the images, that is, women enjoy[ing] being raped. More importantly, that they are sexually aroused to the graphic forms of violence against women. Even if it doesn't show these quote unquote positive reactions.

In fact, if you take a good close look at that bottom graph, you find that those 25 to 30 percent of the male population are much more sexually aroused to that scene of rape than they are to erotic types of material. Furthermore, if you ask these males, would they find committing a rape sexually arousing, the answer is yes.

Now, what does this say about sexual arousal and attitudes? It says, number one, there is a substantial amount of normal, healthy males who can become sexually aroused to violent images, particularly in which the woman is shown to experience pleasure—again, the common scenario. More important than that, there was at least 25 percent of the male population who would commit a rape if not caught. We are not saying they would in fact commit a rape, except there is a high correlation between items which I have just talked about and the use of actual physical force admitted by these individuals. And in fact, if you use the same scales on known offenders, you would find the same data.

I am not going to make that leap that this would predict actual rape. It predicts attitudes about rapes by offenders, that 25–30 percent are aroused to all forms of sexual violence against women, not only finding it arousing, but are willing to admit they will commit that type of act because it would be arousing for them.

Secondly, what type of an effect does this type of material have on aggressive behavior against women? There is a lot of research that shows if you expose male subjects to specifically violent erotica, you find increases in violent behavior. Let me give a quick example. This is a study in which male subjects saw [a] neutral type of films, erotic films that we constructed, or a standard type of aggressive film in which a woman is raped. In one condition, she shows a great deal of pleasure from getting raped. In another we had to construct ourselves, there was a negative ending. The interesting thing is, the scene was identical. You are showing normal males a violent type of scene. And if you look at the bottom data, how many women did suffer when male subjects saw the women enjoying the rape? She enjoyed it less. She enjoyed it more when there was more done. If the woman was raped but there was a positive reaction at the end, she is seen as being more responsible for what happened. There is no difference between the positive and the negative ending of those films. The violence against the woman, the pain and suffering, the brutality is identical. The only thing is, one takes on the common pornographic scenario that violence is a turn-on to the victim. What do males do, normal males? They see less violence. In fact, after exposure to that type of material—by the way if you take the same males, sit them in a room an hour later and ask them to think of something sexually arousing and write it down as soon as they become sexually aroused and write down what they are thinking about, what do you think their passages are? They are scenes of rape. That is what is becoming sexually arousing for them: violence. There is nothing wrong with sexual arousal. The problem is its juxtaposition with violence.

What happens after a few conditioning trials is, as soon as you begin to remove the sexual content and leave the brutality and the violence, what do you find? Sexual arousal. In fact, in Abel's research at New York University, you can predict how violent a rapist is in terms of, did they in fact mutilate and murder the victim, in terms of how sexually aroused they are, not to scenes of sex but to scenes of simply violence against women.

In our research, we are not talking about rapists. We are talking about normal, healthy, young males. What happens in terms of aggressive behavior? You find, for instance, that the erotic films have no effect. Again, when I talk about erotica, I am talking about films we put together ourselves. They show sexual explicitness, no power, anything of that nature. When male subjects are angered and exposed to a scene of rape, whether it has a positive or negative ending, as you can see from the dotted line on the top, they are aggressive against the female. If you show them a violent scene in which there is a positive ending, in which they have not been angered, they are less aggressive against females.

Let me point out, I have been in the area of aggression for years. Those of us who have worked in media violence or television will say one thing: it is almost impossible to find individuals becoming aggressive when they see violent films unless they have been angered or predisposed. Here we have a group of subjects who are not angered or predisposed. Yet after seeing several types of sexually violent material, particularly the common scenario in which women enjoyed being brutalized, enjoyed being raped, you get increases in aggressive behavior. Keep in mind throughout all of this—I think it will be more clear shortly—we are not dealing with hostile people. We are not dealing with a prison population of sex offenders. We are dealing with normal, healthy males.

By the way, I don't mean to complicate things, my professional remarks always come out in some of this. That is a little more complicated graph than it should be, but I present it mainly because of a number of things. Somebody asked me, I think in a news conference, about objectivity. The best way to show objectivity is by replication of other people. A lot of the research I have been talking about has been done by mainly other people. I will talk about my research shortly.

This shows, if you can measure sexual arousal to sexual images and measure people's attitudes about rape you can predict aggressive behavior with women, weeks and even months later. That is what it shows. And what we know is that this type of material does lead to sexual arousal, and it does lead to changes in attitudes. Once you have found those, you can predict aggressive behavior.

We are not talking about correlations where we get into chicken/egg problems of which came first. We are talking about causality. The ability, at least [in] this research, to take certain types of images, expose people to those images and make a prediction independent of their background, independent of their past viewing habits, independent of their initial hostility and make quite accurate predictions of potential aggressive behavior. We have obviously come a long way, at least as researchers. I think it suggests quite strongly there are strong relationships between the material and subsequent aggression.

In fact, good colleagues of mine would argue that the relationship between particularly sexually violent images in the media and subsequent aggression and changes in or toward callous attitudes toward women is much stronger statistically than the relationship between smoking and cancer, mainly because most of that research is correlational. This is not.

Another question: what are we really talking about? Are we talking about the effects of sexual explicitness or the effects of violence against women? We are talking about the effects of violence against women, at least in the research we have been doing. Let me briefly mention one study in which we went ahead and took normal males. They saw a sexually explicit film, a film which depicted violence against women or a film which only presented violence against women. Besides looking at aggressive behavior, we asked the subjects' feelings about rape and if they would have used force to have sexual acts against women or if they would have raped a woman if not caught. At the bottom, there is erotic material. You find that both the aggressive erotic and aggressive films increased attitudes about rape in a negative direction. And, in fact, 50 percent of our subjects said they would not commit a rape if not caught, if they saw just the aggressive film. It is not so much the sexual content, it is however the role of the women in the film. However, many subjects, when they see a woman aggressed against, will see sexual content.

If you look at the aggressive behavior, you find the same thing. The erotic film in and of itself—that is a film that ends with intercourse between sexually consenting adults—it does not lead to violence. The aggressive film does, whether or not the people are angered or not angered, and so does the aggressive erotic film.

Let me end up talking, in the last couple of minutes, about the long-term research. Researchers like myself and Neil Malamuth at UCLA are looking at massive long-term exposure to this material. Some interesting things occur. If you expose male subjects to six weeks' worth of standard hard-core pornography which does not contain overtly physical violence in it, you find changes in attitudes towards women. They become more calloused towards women. You find a trivialization towards rape, which means after six weeks of exposure, male subjects are less likely to convict for a rape, less likely to give a harsh sentence to a rapist if in fact convicted.

In our own research we are looking at the same thing. Let me point out one thing. We use in our research very normal people. I keep stressing that because it is very, very important. What we are doing is exposing hundreds and hundreds of males and now females to a six-week diet of sexually violent films, R-rated or X-rated or explicit X-rated films. We preselect these people on a number of tests to make sure they are not hostile, anxious or psychotic.

Let me point out, the National Institute of Mental Health and the National Science Foundation and our own subjects committee will not allow us to take hostile males and expose them to this type of material because of the risk to the community. They obviously know something some of us do not.

What we do is take these males and we prescreen them. That represents—and I again apologize [for] getting so technical. I want to point out how normal those males are. That is a straight line on top which represents our population. The line underneath represents the males we chose. As you see, they are below the mean. More than that, this is a scale that runs from one to four. A score of one means you possess some of these traits. As you can see, our chosen people possess none of the traits. They are so normal, incredibly normal, that there is no risk. This works against us in what we are doing.

These males are then shown a number of films. Let me give you the names, okay? They are porn, they see R-rated films: *I Spit On Your Grave, Maniac, Toolbox Murders, Vice Squad, Texas Chainsaw Massacre,* and others.

The X-violent are commercially released films. They have scenes of overtly physical violence. They are: *Captain Lust, Defiance of Good, Sex Wish, Easy, Dirty Western.*

The X-rated films, the violence in them, if there is, is not seen by the subjects. Such films are: *Health Spa, Debbie Does Dallas, Other Side of Julie.* They see them over a two-week period.

Let me, by the way, if I can, read the one quote. I think it is important. This comes from a video cassette. Here is the advertisement for one of our R-rated films. "See blood thirsty butchers, killer thrillers, crazed cannibals, zonked zombies, mutilating maniacs, hemoglobin horrors, plasmatic perverts, and sadistic slayers slash, strangle, mangle, and mutilate bare-breasted beauties in bondage!" Unfortunately, there is truth in advertising. That is what you get. I think one should keep in mind, this material is for a young audience. This is for fifteen, sixteen-year-olds rather than those that are eighteen. We study eighteen-year-olds.

Some examples. This material is classic. Women are killed in sexual ways, in the bathtub or shower, as in *Psycho*-gone-astray films. Things have gotten explicit. Every time a woman is killed, it has a sexual overtone—it is to get the audience sexually aroused—and juxtaposition with sexual forms of violence. Of course, the classic, *Texas Chainsaw*—let me give you an example from one of these. This comes from *Tool Box Murders.* Basically, in this scene we have an erotic bathtub scene. A woman in the bathtub massaging herself. There is a beautiful song, *Pretty Lady.* It is a nice country western song that comes on. In two minutes the psychotic killer comes in. The woman notices him. He is carrying a long, what is called a nail gun, it drives nails through walls, a power nail gun. The music stops. He chases her around the room and, in fact, again, it exemplifies the typical type of scenario. When men are killed they are killed swiftly, no sexual overtones. When women are killed, it is dragged out indefinitely. He shoots her through the stomach with the nail gun. She falls across a chair. He then comes up to her and the song *Pretty Lady* comes back on as it did when she was taking the shower, or excuse me, in the bathtub. He puts the nail gun to her forehead and blows her brains out.

Again, I think we have got to think about the audience watching this film. It is a young audience. There is nothing wrong with the bathtub scene, there is nothing wrong with sexual explicitness. What is wrong is, it's incredible, it is in juxtaposition with some of the [most] graphic violence available. And yes, young males will become sexually aroused with the images. If you remove the sexual context, unfortunately they will become aroused to the violence.

After subjects and since—by the way, I have colleagues here who are lawyers. After they had watched two weeks of the films, they are brought to our law school and they see a documentary of rape, State of Wisconsin versus David Tyler. It is a reenactment of a real rape trial. They sit in the trial as jurors. We were not interested in the rape behavior, we were interested in the men's thoughts on violence with women and how they view women. I think what you will see is desensitization. This is our victim. During the testimony, into the trial, a physician who attended to the victim presents into evidence a picture of the victim after she was raped and this is passed out, by the way, to these male jurors. Again, two weeks after exposure to this type of material, what do we find?

Basically, what they show is the same thing. Let me go through quickly. Here are the subjects' moods on a daily basis. You see over a time less depressed, less annoyed or bothered by forms of graphic violence. If you ask them about particular perceptions of violence, if you look at the same films from day one to day five, if it is one week or two weeks, they see less blood and gore, and less violent scenes. Over time they find the material more humorous, they are less depressed, they enjoy the material more and are less upset. You also find the same things for the X-violent films— those are X-rated in which the main scene is women being raped, women being bound, hung, aggressed against in general. You find that subjects find less violence, as time goes on, against women in these films over repeated exposure. They are just as sexually aroused over this, however,

[as] to the material. Sexual arousal does not decrease. They feel much less likely to censor the material, they are less offended by the material, they see this [as] less graphic and less gory, they look away less. What that means on the first day when they see women being raped and aggressed against, it bothers them. By day five, it does not bother them at all. In fact, they enjoy it.

If we look again, how upset? They were less upset and less [depressed], and they found the material makes a great deal of sense and was more meaningful by the end of the week. I am not sure what is exactly meaningful. If we look at how offensive the material is, it is much more offensive on day one than day five. The violent material was very degrading on day one, much less degrading on day five. If we look as time went on, they found it less and less degrading, until the fifth day. There is a reason for that. We happen to tell them we will show them a double feature and we don't do that. They find the material less degrading with time.

We have a film called *Vice Squad*. If subjects saw that film on day one, on day one they see a lot of scenes of rape. On day four, nothing has changed in the film, they see half the amount of rape, they become desensitized to what rape and violence is. This represents their recollections to the one and a half hour rape trial. We are a long way from completely analyzing this data.

On the last day we bring in a control group of subjects who have never seen the films. We ask how injured the woman was. Subjects who have seen violent material or X-rated material see less injury to a rape victim than people who haven't seen these films. Furthermore, they consider the woman to be more worthless than any of them who have not seen this material. There are a number of other correlations which I am going to summarize because of time.

Basically what happens is, the less violence the subjects see, the less sexually aroused they are and less bothered by the material after one or two weeks of exposure, the more they say the woman is responsible for her rape, the less likely to convict the rapist. The less injury they see on the part of the victim, the more worthless they see the individual.

Let me make a 30-second closing statement. What does all the research say? Well, compared I think to 1968, when we had the Pornography Commission,[1] I think it says many different things.

1. See The Report of the Commission on Obscenity and Pornography (1970).

One, the material has changed quite drastically. Secondly, the research techniques we have as researchers have also changed. I think we are asking many different questions today than years ago. Unfortunately, I think it shows that short-term exposure to very normal, sociable, intellectual young males is going to have an effect. It is either going to reinforce already existing predispositions about rape in women and maintain these callous types of attitudes or, worse than that, in fact, change them in a very negative direction. And that is the majority of the subjects. Unfortunately, there is out there a small percentage—and I hate to use the word small, about 30 percent is obviously not a majority, but I think it represents an incredible minority—who are so influenced by this material that it becomes the ultimate sexual turn-on. Individuals are becoming sexually aroused to the trivialization, the degradation, and the use of women.

The data—I think it speaks for itself. I am not a lawyer. I am not an advocate. I am unfortunately an ivory tower professor that does his research. I think the data is a little too clear, not only from myself but dozens of professors across the country. I doubt that anybody disputes the data. There are effects. Thank you.

CHAIRMAN WHITE: I feel that I would like to ask you a question. In terms of your research, [are] the typicals of your research beginning to reach out not only to women showing this love affair with violence, is it not pointing also to men and children? I just ask you that question. In other words, is it affecting men?

DONNERSTEIN: In fact, our research [looks] only at the effects it has on [men.] A number of my graduate students who are women are now conducting research, independent of myself, on the effects which this material has on women and the effects are more dramatic. Our issue is how it affects men, not only in terms of how it affects their aggressive behavior. We can't expose the material to them and see if they go out and commit a rape. We are much more interested in effect: how it affects our attitudes, attitudes about women, attitudes with human sexuality, our attitudes about violence in general. And the issue of desensitization [to] violence is not new. There are thousands and thousands of studies. We can't show them violence. It [wouldn't] purge all this aggressive energy. There is no research in the academic community which supports that. There never has been and there never will be. It is a theoretical issue. I am not just talking about my research, by the way, we are talking about thousands upon thousands of studies. Theoretically, if it is men leading to desensitization against men, or violence against children, or violence against women, the same thing is going to occur.

More important than that, I think, we have got to realize it, if you assume that your child can learn from Sesame Street how to count one, two, three, four, five, believe me, they can learn how to pick up a gun and also learn attitudes. I think the concern should be what attitudes are they learning about male/female relations. Unfortunately, their attitudes are influenced with too much degradation and violence.

MacKINNON: I have a couple of questions. Dr. Donnerstein, could you explain why it is that your research comes to conclusions that are so different than the conclusions of the Commission on Obscenity and Pornography in 1970?

DONNERSTEIN: Ms. MacKinnon, it is not my research, it is everybody's. But the material has changed. The Pornography Commission made a concerted effort not to deal with violence images. In fact, there were a couple of studies that eroticism leads to aggression. That doesn't come through in a final report. You have to read the technical reports to get that. They made a concerted effort to get away from violence. They are asking questions we don't ask today. They were looking at short-term effects. You are not going to find people's attitudes changing over night. It is going to take a long time.

What the research is doing today, thanks to the national support from Mental Health and the [National] Science Foundation, is to allow researchers to look at pornography which is drastically different, and allow us to look at it with long-term type of exposure. I think, for the most part, that is why the results are different.

Let me comment, Professor MacKinnon. Many of the people who were on the Commission that did the research, they have also changed their mind.

MacKINNON: Could you also describe just very briefly what you are seeing, how do you characterize the long term effects of the X-only?

DONNERSTEIN: One of the problems, I think, in our own naiveté is, we thought nonviolent X-rated material would lead to aggression with five minutes of exposure. The material presents more subtler types of images which are going to work at stereotypes and certain myths about women. What we find as soon as you get into long-term exposure to this material, you begin to get these types of changes. You may not necessarily get definite relations to aggressive behavior, because that is going to be a little longer to do. I think eventually we are going to get there.

You get increases in sexual stereotypes and pretty much exactly the same things in terms of the attitudes that you get with the violent material. The only difference is the immediate increase in aggression. That is really where the differences occur.

MacKINNON: And is your research the first research to complete this study of long-term effects of this kind of material?

DONNERSTEIN: Well, I think both ours—

MacKINNON: Particularly X?

DONNERSTEIN: Zillmann has, but that was reported a few years ago. Basically the research by Zillmann stated that exposure did produce arousal. Unfortunately, when you show them a scene of rape, they became sexually aroused. There was some selective exposure.

Basically, when they looked at attitudes, it was the attitudes that were changing over the long run in a very subtle way. We can't expect, as we did with the violent material which is so graphic, to get an immediate effect. What we are finding is, the longer exposure, you begin to get subtle changes in attitudes toward women.

Let me bring this up. Zillmann happens to use the Sex Callousness scale. The Commission found with one hour of exposure, there were no changes in sexually-calloused attitudes, the same as violence. Those sexually-calloused attitudes are correlated with violence, if you read the scale. With six weeks of exposure, when you have the funds to do the research, you in fact find an increase on the part of males of sexually-calloused type of attitudes.

CHAIRMAN WHITE: I want to thank you for your presentation. You articulated it well. You have a vast reservoir of research to share with this Committee and with the audience.

MacKINNON: Andrea Dworkin has one question.

DWORKIN: I would like Dr. Donnerstein to address the fact that there have been a lot of general studies of violence in the media and I would like to know if it is proper to say, from what you have told us here, that the study of the impact of pornography is very specific and concrete in ways that are distinguishable from the general environment?

DONNERSTEIN: In fact, the effects are much stronger and occur much more rapidly. I think the interesting thing is, if you take a look at the research and really talk about hundreds and hundreds of studies—I present[ed] them into evidence, a number of chapters which have all these bibliographies—there is an incredible amount of consensus across populations and measures and studies. That I think is interesting because in the media violence area we have some ambiguity and the relationships are statistically not as strong as they are here. So yes, I agree with you.

DWORKIN: Thank you.

MacKINNON: Thank you, Dr. Donnerstein.

CHAIRMAN WHITE: Thank you very much. I hope you can stick around and listen to others.

MacKINNON: Next is Linda Marchiano.

CHAIRMAN WHITE: All right. Now prior to Ms. Marchiano's speaking, I would ask there be no discussions during this, because once again to reiterate, the stenographer is taking down testimony. You now have the floor, if you wish to begin.

MacKINNON: We are trying to arrange so that you can see the witness. Go ahead.

CHAIRMAN WHITE: Give your name and spelling for the stenographer.

LINDA MARCHIANO: I feel I should introduce myself and tell you why I feel I am qualified to speak out against pornography. My name today is Linda Marchiano. Linda Lovelace was the name I bore during a two and a half year period of imprisonment. For those of you who don't know the name, Linda Lovelace was the victim of this so-called victimless crime.

Used and abused by Mr. Traynor, her captor, she was forced through physical, mental, and sexual abuse and often at gunpoint and threats of her life to be involved in pornography. Linda Lovelace was not a willing participant but became the sex freak of the '70s.

It all began in 1971. I was recuperating from a near-fatal car accident at my parents' home in Florida. A girlfriend of mine came to visit me with a person by the name of Mr. Charles Traynor. He came off as a considerate gentleman, asking us what we would like to do and how we would like to spend the afternoon and opening doors and lighting cigarettes and all so-called manners of society.

Needless to say, I was impressed and started to date him. I was not getting along with my own parents. I was twenty-one and resented being told to be home at 11:00 o'clock and to call and say where I was and to call and give the phone number and address where I would be.

Here comes the biggest mistake of my life. Seeing how upset I was with my home life, Mr. Traynor offered me his assistance. He said I could come and live at his home in Miami. The relationship was platonic, which was fine with me. My plan was to recuperate and then go back to New York and live. I thought then he was being kind and a nice friend. Today I know why the relationship was platonic. He was incapable of a sexual act without inflicting some type of pain or degradation upon a human being.

When I decided to head back north and informed Mr. Traynor of my intention, that was when I met the real Mr. Traynor, and my two and a half years of imprisonment began. He began a complete turnaround and beat me up physically and began the mental abuse. From that day forward, my hell began.

I literally became a prisoner. I was not allowed out of his sight, not even to use the bathroom. Why, you may ask? Because there was a window in the bathroom. When speaking to either of my friends or parents, he was on the extension with a .45 automatic 8 shot pointed at me. I was beaten physically and suffered mental abuse each and every day thereafter.

In my book *Ordeal*,[2] an autobiography, I go into greater detail of the monstrosity I was put through, from prostitution to porno films to celebrity satisfier. The things that he used to get me involved in pornography went from a .45 automatic 8 shot and M-16 semi-automatic machine gun to threats on the lives of my family. I have seen the kind of people involved in pornography and how they will use anyone to get what they want.

So many people ask me, why didn't you escape? Well, I did. I'm here today. I did try during the two and a half years to escape on three separate occasions. The first and second time I was caught and suffered a brutal beating and an awful sexual abuse as punishment. The third time I was at my parents' home and Mr. Traynor threatened to kill my parents. I said, "No, you won't. My father is here in the other room." And he said, "I will kill him and each and every member of your family." Just then my nephew came in through the kitchen door to the living room. He pulled out the .45 and said he would shoot him if I didn't leave immediately. I did.

Some of you might say I was foolish. But I'm not the kind of person who could live the rest of my life knowing that another human being had died because of me.

The name, Linda Lovelace, gave me a great deal of courage and notoriety. Had Linda Boreman[3] been shot dead in a hotel room, no questions asked. If Linda Lovelace was shot dead in Los Angeles, questions would have been asked. After three unsuccessful attempts at escaping, I realized

2. Linda Lovelace and Mike McGrady, *Ordeal* (Citadel Press, 1980).
3. This is the birth name of the witness.

I had to take my time and plan it well. It took six months of preparation to convince Mr. Traynor to allow me out of his sight for 15 minutes. I had to tell him he was right, a woman's body was to be used to make money, that porno was great, that beating people was the right thing to do. Fortunately for me, after I acquired my 15 minutes out of his presence, I also had someone that wanted to help me.

I tried to tell my story several times. Once to a reporter, Vernon Scott, who works for the UPI. He said he couldn't print it. Again on the Regis Philbin Show, and when I started to explain what happened to me, that I was beaten and forced into it, he laughed. Also at a grand jury hearing in California after they had watched a porno film, they asked me why I did it. I said, "Because a gun was being pointed at me," and they just said "Oh." But no charges were ever filed.

I also called the Beverly Hills Police Department on my final escape, and I told them that Mr. Traynor was walking around looking for me with an M-16. When they first told me that they couldn't become involved in domestic affairs, I accepted that, and asked them and told them that he was illegally possessing these weapons, and they simply told me to call back when he was in the room.

During the filming of *Deep Throat,* actually after the first day, I suffered a brutal beating in my room for smiling on the set. It was a hotel room and the whole crew was in one room. There was at least 20 people partying, music going, laughing, and having a good time. Mr. Traynor started to bounce me off the walls. I figured out of 20 people, there might be one human being that would do something to help me and I was screaming for help, I was being beaten, I was being kicked around and, again, bounced off of walls. And all of a sudden the room next door became very quiet. Nobody, not one person came to help me.

The greatest complaint the next day is the fact that there was bruises on my body. So many people say that, in *Deep Throat,* I have a smile on my face, and I look as though I am really enjoying myself. No one ever asked me how those bruises got on my body.

Mr. Traynor stopped searching for me because he acquired Marilyn Chambers, who I believe is also being held against her will. A reporter from a Philadelphia newspaper did an interview. His name is Larry Fields. During the course of the interview, Ms. Chambers asked for permission to go to the bathroom and he refused it. Mr. Fields objected and said, why don't you let the poor girl go to the bathroom, she is about to go on stage? And he came back with, "I don't tell you how to write your newspaper, don't tell me how to treat my broads."

I have also been in touch with a girl who was with Mr. Traynor two months prior to getting me, who was put through a similar situation but not as strong. And as it stands today, she still fears for her life and the life of her family. Personally, I think it is time that the legal system in this country realize that one, you can't be held prisoner for two and a half years and the next day trust the society which has caused your pain, and resume the life you once called yours. It takes time to overcome the total dehumanization which you have been through.

It is time for something to be done about the civil rights of the victims and not criminals—the victims being women. But realize, please, it is not just the women who are victims but also children, men and our society.

CHAIRMAN WHITE: Thank you for your testimony, Ms. Marchiano. I would like to say, because of time again, there are those who are a little irate that they are here thinking that they would have the opportunity to participate in this public hearing by getting in a comment. So I think we are going to have to be expeditious in terms of questions and answers, we should move this right along so we give people who are here this morning, who will not have the opportunity this evening, to have their day to speak. So would you begin?

DWORKIN: Thank you, I will try to do that. Ms. Marchiano, I have to ask you some questions that are difficult for me to ask and I apologize to you for asking them. It is important that we get the answers. Could you describe for us the first time that Mr. Traynor prostituted you?

MARCHIANO: It happened in Florida. I had thought we were going to visit a friend of his, and we pulled up to a Holiday Inn. So my second reaction was a buffet, I thought we were going to lunch. And he took me up to a room, and there was five men in the room, and [he] told me that I was there to satisfy each and every one of them. And I said that I wouldn't do it, so what he did is he took me into this little dressing area and he told me that if I didn't do it, that he would shoot me. And I said, you won't shoot me, there is five men in this room. You just won't do it, somebody will say something and do something. And he just laughed hysterically. He said that my body would be found and I would be another prostitute who was shot in her hotel room or something like that, and that none of the men would do anything. They would just laugh.

During this event, I started to cry, and while these five men were doing whatever they wanted to do, and it was really a pitiful scene because here I was—they knew I wasn't into it. One of the men complained and asked for his money back because I was crying and I wasn't the super freak that Mr. Traynor usually brought around. And he was given back his money. And the other four men proceeded to do what they wanted to do, through my tears and all.

DWORKIN: Thank you, Ms. Marchiano. One of the major themes in pornography is that women are portrayed having intercourse of—doing various—

COUNCILMEMBER PATRICK DAUGHERTY: Could you speak into the mike, ma'am?

DWORKIN: One of the situations that is commonly portrayed in pornography is women being—women having sexual intercourse and doing various sex acts with animals. You were forced to make such a film. Could you describe for us the situation in which you were forced to make this film?

DAUGHERTY: Would you like to respond?

MARCHIANO: Yes, I think it is important that everyone understands.

Prior to that film being made, about a week, Mr. Traynor suggested the thought that I do films with a D-O-G, and I told him that I wouldn't do it. I suffered a brutal beating. He claims he suffered embarrassment because I wouldn't do it.

We then went to another porno studio, one of the sleaziest ones I have ever seen, and then this guy walked in with his animal, and I again started crying. I started crying. I said, I am not going to do this, and they were all very persistent, the two men involved in making the pornographic film and Mr. Traynor himself. And I started to leave and go outside of the room where they make these films, and when I turned around there was all of a sudden a gun displayed on the desk and having seen the coarseness and the callousness of the people involved in pornography, I knew that I would have been shot and killed. Needless to say, the film was shot and still is one of the hardest ones for me to deal with today.

DWORKIN: Thank you. I am sorry but this is something that I had to ask. There was one other incident that you described in your book *Ordeal* that involved Mr. Hefner, Hugh Hefner at the Playboy Mansion, that was about the same theme. Would you tell us briefly about that?

MARCHIANO: Yes. Well, we first met Mr. Hefner. Mr. Traynor and him sat around discussing what they could do with me, all kinds of different atrocities. And it seemed that Mr. Hefner and Mr. Traynor both enjoyed seeing a woman being used by an animal. And so Mr. Hefner had Mr. Traynor's dog flown in from Florida to the L. A. Mansion. And one evening they decided that it was time and they had one of the security guards bring the animal down to Mr. Hefner's bathhouse and fortunately, during my two and a half years in imprisonment, there was a girl that tried to help me in her own sort of way. She told me the tricks to avoid that kind of a situation, and I did what I could to avoid it, but Mr. Traynor and Mr. Hefner were both very disappointed.

DWORKIN: Thank you. Would you explain to us how it was that Mr. Traynor taught you to do what is now known popularly in this culture, because of the movie *Deep Throat,* as the sex act of deep-throating?

MARCHIANO: Well, he used hypnotism. He told me that it would overcome the natural reflexes in your throat that would prevent you from gagging, and it was through hypnotism that I was able, I guess, to accomplish the feat, I guess you could say.

DWORKIN: So that hypnotism was added to the prostitution?

MARCHIANO: Yes, it was.

DWORKIN: My final question is this: some people may think that you could have gotten away, for instance, when Mr. Traynor was sleeping. Could you explain to us why that was impossible?

MARCHIANO: Well, at night what he would do is put his body over my body so that, if I did try to get up, he would wake up. And he was a very light sleeper. If I did attempt to move or roll over in my sleep, he would awaken.

DWORKIN: Thank you very much.

MacKINNON: How do you feel about the existence of the film *Deep Throat* and its continually being shown?

MARCHIANO: I feel very hurt and very disappointed in my society and my country for allowing the fact that I was raped, I was beaten, I was put through two and a half years of what I was put through. And it's taken me almost ten years to overcome the damage that he caused. And the fact that this film is still being shown and that my three children will one day walk down the street and see their mother being abused, it makes me angry, makes me sad. Virtually every time someone watches that film, they are watching me being raped.

DAUGHERTY: All right. Catharine, do you have another witness?

MacKINNON: We were going to allow the space for a member of the public who was given the wrong information. She is not part of what we were going to proceed with. We thought it was best to be more brief with Ms. Marchiano so that this woman could speak.

We have a couple of documents to submit.

DWORKIN: May we do that first?

MacKINNON: We will submit these and then this woman can speak.

DAUGHERTY: Thank you, Mrs. Marchiano, for showing up.

MARCHIANO: Thank you. I would like to say, thank you for everybody who made it possible for me to be here tonight. I want to speak out for what happened to me and for other members in our society. I feel that it is important that victims have a chance today in our society. And I also want to say that my children thank you.

DWORKIN: I would like to just put into evidence, in support of Linda's testimony, we will be providing you with a copy of her book *Ordeal*, which tells the facts. We are also providing you with a copy of her lie detector test that bears out the truth of everything that she has said to you today. [Exh. 3]

In addition, I would like to read a letter by Dr. Kathleen Barry who is a Professor of Sociology, and who is an author of the book *Female Sexual Slavery*. We will also put this into evidence. [Exh. 4]

"In this memo I intend to identify the practices related to pornography which constitute a violation of woman's civil rights, and in accordance with the International Declaration of Human Rights, they constitute a violation of woman's human rights. As I have already conducted, reported and published the research" in this book—she goes on to say that she is not going to reiterate all of the conclusions.

Number one, pornography is used by pimps as part of the illegal act of procuring and attempting to induce young girls and women into prostitution. By presenting young women and girls with pornography which fraudulently represents actually painful sexual practices and acts as pleasing and gratifying to the female represented in the pornography, the pimp attempts to convince young and vulnerable (usually homeless) young women to prostitute themselves for him. Pornography plays a large role in the deception that is necessary to put naive young women into prostitution.

When a young girl or woman is procured, pornography is often used as part of the seasoning and blackmail strategies which will force her into prostitution. Prior to being "turned out" to prostitution, many pimps "season" or break down their victims through sessions of rape and other forms of sexual abuse. Sometimes these sessions are photographed or filmed and used in a variety of ways which include personal pleasure of the pimp and his friends, blackmailing the victim by threatening to send them to her family, and selling them to pornographers for mass production.

This constitutes the use of pornography as a form of torture and the marketing of actual torture sessions in the form of film and pictures as a pleasure commodity.

Pornography is a form of prostitution and consequently pornographers are pimps. There have been several court cases upholding the convictions of pornographers as pimps for having been supported off the earnings of prostitutes.

That is a small portion of Kathleen Barry's letter, which I will submit with her book.

I would also like to read just two paragraphs to you from the U.N. report on the suppression of the traffic in persons and the exploitation of the prostitution of others.[4] I will also put this into evidence.

4. Report of Mr. Jean Fernand-Laurent, Special Rapporteur on the suppression of the traffic in persons and the exploitation of the prostitution of others, "Activities for the Advancement of Women: Equality, Development and Peace," Economic and Social Council, United Nations, Item 12 of provisional agenda, 1st Sess. 1983, paras. 18–23:

18. Like slavery in the usual sense, prostitution has an economic aspect. While being a cultural phenomenon rooted in the masculine and feminine images given currency by society, it is a market and indeed a very lucrative one. The merchandise involved is men's pleasure, or their image of pleasure. This merchandise is unfortunately supplied by physical intimacy with women or children. Thus, the alienation of the person is here more far-reaching than in slavery in its usual sense, where what is alienated is working strength, not intimacy.

19. The market is created by demand, which is met by supply. The demand comes from the client, who could also be called the "prostitutor." The supply is provided by the prostitute. This is the simplest but also the rarest example. In most cases (8 or 9 times out of 10, according to observers, at least in Europe), a third person comes into the picture, perhaps the most important; this is the organizer and exploiter of the market—in other words, the procurer in his various guises: go-between or recruiter, pimp, owner of a house of prostitution, "massage parlour" or bar, or provider of a hotel room or studio. The procurer is usually a professional, involved to some extent in the world of crime. When it comes to children, it can be an older child who runs a "racket."

20. In the industrialized market-economy States, a concern not to hamper trade allows an overt market for eroticism and pornography to develop alongside the discreet prostitution market. The two complement and reinforce each other. The streets on which the sex shops are located are those where prostitution is heaviest.

21. Of the three partners in the three-way relationship—client, prostitute and procurer—least is known about the first mentioned. Since there are no laws or regulations that either punish or restrict *the client,* he can remain anonymous. . . . One can only suppose that his desires and his behaviour stem from the image that society gives him of his virility and from the conception which he has of women's duty being to serve his pleasure. Military service and the media no doubt play a decisive role here. . . .

22. More is known about *the prostitute,* because she is monitored by social workers and has often been described in literature. Moreover, in recent times, several former prostitutes have given autobiographical accounts of their prostitution experiences. Today, therefore, we know what brings a woman to the point of becoming a prostitute. Economic hardship is the main reason, but it is not enough; not all poor women become prostitutes; in addition to poverty,

CHAIRMAN WHITE: Ms. Dworkin, I would like to—I hate to continually talk all the time, if you could just submit them for the record. The media, if they wish them, they can get them from the committee clerk and so we can move right along.

DWORKIN: Thank you. There is one other point I want to make. I won't read the whole letter. I will tell you we have a letter here from a New York crisis worker about the increased existence of rape of the throat since the distribution of the movie *Deep Throat*. And in addition the increased use of cameras in actual rape situations. [Exh. 5]

CHAIRMAN WHITE: We are going to move quite quickly now. Ms. Marchiano, I want to thank you for coming to testify.

MARCHIANO: Thank you very much.

CHAIRMAN WHITE: We have Dr. Pauline Bart, who will utilize as little of the time that has been allotted to her, if she can make it precise as possible, I would appreciate that. We do have speakers and it is rather long. We will give people an opportunity to speak for three minutes. We have a young lady out here with a baby. I would like her to go first after Mrs. Bart. Dr. Bart is a Professor of Sociology, Abraham Lincoln Medical Center, University of Illinois, Chicago. . . .

DR. PAULINE BART: I have spent the last twenty years studying gender, studying what happens to women and what happens to men and women and children, because of the problem of gender inequality in this country. Beginning with depressed middle-aged women, Portnoy's mothers, what gynecologists say about women in their textbooks, and abortion.

---

there must be a loss of respect for moral strictures, an emotional frustration (rejection of parents or by parents, desertion by a husband or by a lover), and a lack of outside assistance or a refusal to use it when it is available. Statistically, most prostitutes have been raised in broken families; a large number of them have been the victims of rape or incest. . . . In the quite rare cases where the prostitute comes from an affluent family, she is motivated by a desire to challenge conventional morality combined with an excessive interest in money and the satisfactions it can provide. . . . More basically, a woman of any social level can fall into prostitution as she would fall into alcoholism or drug abuse, or as she would commit suicide: through grief, loneliness, boredom or despair. Then again it can happen in the case of addicts that prostitution seems to be the only means of obtaining drugs. In short, it could be said of most women prostitutes that they have moved from a marginal situation into another even more marginal state.

23. At any rate, even when prostitution seems to have been chosen freely, it is actually the result of coercion. That was the gist of the testimony given to the Congress of Nice on 8 September 1981 by three "collectives" of women prostitutes from two major developed countries: "As prostitutes, we are well aware that *all* prostitution is forced prostitution. Whether we are forced to become prostitutes by lack of money or by housing or unemployment problems, or to escape from a family situation of rape or violence (which is often the case with very young prostitutes), or by a procurer, we would not lead the 'life' if we were in a position to leave it."

For the past ten years I have been studying rape and rape avoidance. This was a study funded by the National Institute of Mental Health. In the course of focusing on rape and the injury it causes, I, as other researchers in sexual assault such as Dr. Russell and Dr. Scully,[5] realized that we had to learn about pornography for reasons I will discuss below.

I must say that it is a pleasure to be in the Minneapolis/St. Paul area, which has in so many ways led the way in having data-based public policy on preventing child sexual assault, on battery, the study on arresting the batterers, having the first women's shelters in this country. I hope fervently that will follow with pornography. My pleasure is increased by the knowledge that my city celebrated Hugh Hefner Day last week.

My presentation will deal with the following themes: pornography as harm to women, including its use to socialize men in gender and inequality, very briefly critiques of studies which purport to show that pornography is harmless, and the study of audience response to a film about pornography, data which clearly indicates that women believe pornography injures us as a class.

When I first came to the University of Illinois Medical School and I sat in on a sex education class, I learned that they were, and I saw that they were, being shown pornography to desensitize what they might hear about in their practice. I know there are some of you that [think that physicians] are insensitive enough as it is. And, of course, most of us are aware that as part of medical school education . . . physicians were shown pornographic slides intermixed with the ordinary anatomy slides to liven up the lectures. Professor Myra Marx Ferree at the University of Connecticut told me, and I then called her on December 6th to get words that I could use for you, that when they went around to the various dorms to tell them the relationship between pornography and violence against women, particularly rape, . . . one of the male students made an argument that pornography was not harmful. In fact, they were interested in getting the porno films on campus at the beginning of the fall semester, because the freshmen guys did not know how to relate to women, and you have to show them. And they said that, you know, Professor Ferree was talking about the relationship between pornography to bad things. You're talking about relationships to normal men, not to rape. It is really about normal sex. So I think that the use of this as a teaching device should be something we should investigate.

5. Diana E. H. Russell, Professor Emeritus, Mills College; Diana Scully, Professor, Virginia Commonwealth University.

A recent study by Strauss and Baron, University of New Hampshire, [studied the] relationship between the sales of sex magazines and the rate of rapes reported to police from the crime reports, and they found that "pornography induces attitudes that increase the likelihood of rape." The correlation in '79 was .63 and the correlation in 1980 was .58. For those of you who are familiar with the social science literature, these are substantially high correlations.

The work [of] Zillmann, who had been mentioned before, showed that explicit sexual behavior films shown to students over an extended period showed that, at the end they—the ones who saw the films—were more hostile to the women's movement, that is to the equality of women, and suggested lower sentences for rapists than those who saw neutral films, or saw half neutral films and half sexually-explicit films.

Diana Russell, who I mentioned before, in her random sample of women in San Francisco found that 10 percent said "yes" when she asked them, "have you ever been upset by anyone trying to get you to do what they have seen in pornographic pictures, movies, or books?" Now, maybe they were wrong, and the guys didn't get the idea from pornography. On the other hand, similarly maybe they were asked to do things that they did not *know* came from pornography. So the 10 percent figure is one we can become comfortable with.

Let me tell you some of the things that they had been asked to do because of pornographic pictures, and this was by their husbands and boyfriends. And on the basis of some prior research I did, I can tell you that research done by people we trust, excuse me, that sexual assault done by people whom you trust is worse than sexual assault done by a stranger. Your trust, your judgment, everything about you is violated more than if you have the kind of rape that everybody would agree is a rape.

Miss A: Urinating in someone's mouth.

Miss B: It was a three-girls-and-him situation. We had sex. I was really young—like fourteen.

Miss C: He was a lover. He'd go to porno movies, then he'd come home and say, "I saw this in a movie. Let's try it." I felt really exploited, like I was being put in a mold.

Miss D: I was staying at this guy's house. He tried to make me have oral sex with him. He said he'd seen far-out stuff in movies, and that it would be fun to mentally and physically torture a woman.

Miss E: It was physical slapping and hitting. It wasn't a turn-on; it was more a feeling of being used as an object. What was most upsetting was that he thought it would be a turn-on.

Miss F: He'd read something in a pornographic book, and then he wanted to live it out. It was too violent for me to do something like that. It was basically getting dressed up and spanking. Him spanking me. I refused to do it.

Miss G: He forced me to have oral sex with him when I had no desire to do it.

Miss H: This couple who had just read a porno book wanted to try the groupie number with four people. They tried to persuade my boyfriend to persuade me. They were running around naked, and I felt really uncomfortable.

Miss I: It was S and M stuff. I was asked if I would participate in being beaten up. It was a proposition, it never happened. I didn't like the idea of it.

Interviewer: Did anything else upset you?

Miss I: Anal intercourse. I have been asked to do that, but I don't enjoy it at all. I have had to do it, very occasionally.

Miss J: My husband enjoys pornographic movies. He tries to get me to do things he finds exciting in movies. They include twosomes and threesomes. I always refuse. Also, I was always upset with his ideas about putting objects in my vagina, until I learned this is not as deviant as I used to think. He used to force me or put whatever he enjoyed into me.

Miss K: He forced me to go down on him. He said he'd been going to porno movies. He'd seen this and wanted me to do it. He also wanted to pour champagne on my vagina. I got beat up because I didn't want to do it. He pulled my hair and slapped me around. After that I went ahead and did it, but there was no feeling in it.

Miss L: I was newly divorced when this date talked about S and M and I said, "You've got to be nuts. Learning to experience pleasure through pain. But it's your pleasure and my pain." I was very upset. The whole idea that someone thought I would want to sacrifice myself and have pain and bruises. It's a sick mentality. This was when I first realized there were many men out there who believe this.

Miss M: Anal sex. First he attempted gentle persuasion, I guess. He was somebody I'd been dating a while and we'd gone to bed a few times. Once he tried to persuade [me] to go along with anal sex, first verbally, then by touching me. When I said, "No," he did it anyway—much to my pain. It hurt like hell.

Miss N: This guy had seen a movie where a woman was being made love to by dogs. He suggested that some of his friends had a dog and we should have a party and set the dog loose on the women. He wanted me to put a muzzle on the dog and put some sort of stuff on my vagina so that the dog would lick there.

Miss O: My old man and I went to a show that had lots of tying up and anal intercourse. We came home and proceeded to make love. He went out and got two belts. He tied my feet together with one, and with the other he kind of beat me. I was in the spirit, I went along with it. But when he tried to penetrate me anally, I couldn't take it, it was too painful. I managed to convey to him verbally to quit it. He did stop, but not soon enough to suit me. Then one time, he branded me. I still have a scar on my butt. He put a little wax initial thing on a hot plate and then stuck it on my ass when I was unaware.

Miss P: My boyfriend and I saw a movie in which there was masochism. After that he wanted to gag me and tie me up. He was stoned, I was not. I was really shocked at his behavior. I was nervous and uptight. He literally tried to force me, after gagging me first. He snuck up behind me with a scarf. He was hurting me with it and I started getting upset. Then I realized it wasn't a joke. He grabbed me and shook me by my shoulders and brought out some ropes, and told me to relax, and that I would enjoy it. Then he started putting me down about my feelings about sex, and my inhibitedness. I started crying and struggling with him, got loose, and kicked him in the testicles, which forced him down on the couch. I ran out of the house. Next day he called and apologized, but that was the end of him.

As may be clear from some of the quotations cited, there was often insufficient probing by the interviewers to determine the exact nature of the unwanted sexual experience. That is, the number of clear-cut cases reported is likely to be a considerable understatement. And we can't, of course, prove by this that the pornography caused this kind of behavior, but it is like the relationship, in this case, the correlation, between smoking and cancer. I would suggest that these women, as well as the women in my study that I will talk to you about, may well [experience] what is called Post Traumatic Stress Syndrome in the diagnostic and statistical manner which we are veterans in the cases of, which we are very familiar with. They have nightmares, loss of appetite, the kind of things that women who are [injured] have experienced, and it goes on for a long time. Let me talk a little bit about the women in my study, and then I will talk about the attitudes in response to Linda Lovelace's story.

I spoke to forty-three women who had been raped. Many of the men denied that what they were doing was raping. One man said, "I am not raping you, you are raping me." And another said, "You entered this place of your own free will." And one man said, "There is no such thing as rape." Now, sociologists, you know, use big words to explain things, and the word we use is neutralization. It is used to justify the kind of behavior originally that was enjoyed by juvenile delinquents, and it involves denial of responsibility and denial of injury.

Now, denial of injury was the most common rationale the men used. Let me tell you what the women told us that the rapist said: "You are going to enjoy this" as he raped her at knifepoint. "I know you won't mind what I do to you," as he was displaying a gun. "I don't want to rape you, I just want to screw," as he locked her in his room penetrating her anus and vagina with his fingers. "You know there is no such thing as a rape, a man is doing a woman a favor." This is a man who had conned a woman into his apartment and forced her to have oral sex and masturbate him. "You are going to feel good, I am going to penetrate you," said a cab driver viciously trying to rape his passenger. Said he "wanted to make love" but if she did not cooperate, he would kill her. This was said by a naked man, holding a knife, mounted on a sleeping woman. He left saying, "Here I was trying to be nice." He also said that he was shy and it was too bad that they had to meet this way. And the last quote is "You will feel better when I am inside you."

Now, men aren't born believing this. They have to learn it someplace, and I maintain that one of the ways they learn it is through pornography. The women told me that frequently they were asked or demanded to state how much they were enjoying the rapes and *that* was harder for them to do than the act, than experiencing the actual rape.

One of my friends was raped with a gun to her head and her rapist insisted that she have an orgasm. He then wanted her to have another orgasm and then backed down. He said, well, she might be a little tired from the first one. As if rape itself isn't enough of an injury, these women were further injured by the lie which academics call ideology. That women enjoy forced sex and enjoy forced pain—and this is the ideology that is presented in pornography. That is one of the reasons that I got into studying pornography.

The third part of the study that I am going to report, third study, has to do with audience research on "Not a Love Story." Before I do so, I want to simply briefly recapitulate what Professor Donnerstein said about the [1970 President's] Commission Report.

There were two [reports] that came out the same time, one on violence and one on pornography. The one on violence was based on ordinary learning theory, which is a substantial theoretical perspective inside psychology. And the theory is, the more you see, the more you do. The one on pornography, however, came out with a different explanation, the catharsis model, which was, the more you see, the less you do. And as we have been so eloquently spoken to, there is absolutely no data for the last analysis.

I have written a paper which I think has been submitted to you called "Dirty Books, Dirty Films, and Dirty Data" that addresses the issue. And all I can say is that if any of my students ever did any research as shocking as that research which has been so quickly picked up and put into textbooks and is still there—you ask people what they think and do, where they learn that pornography was harmless—I would feel that I had failed as a teacher. If indeed it were true that the catharsis model is successful, then since we have had a proliferation of pornography, we should have a diminution of sexual assault and rape, and that is certainly not the case.

I did the only study, to my knowledge, that has been done on a more or less national audience. That is, I didn't use students in my class and I didn't call a group together. I studied people who went to see "Not a Love Story," a film about pornography. The ads just said "a film about pornography." Word got out that it was an antipornography film, but not everyone who came to see the film came thinking that. I did not have a random sample, and I certainly would not claim that I had a random sample. However, that in a sense strengthens my findings, because the sample was biased in exactly the way that would be associated with people who would be pro-pornography. They were young and they were well educated compared with the general population. And we know from prior research that this group generally has a more permissive attitude towards pornography.

I read this in *The New York Times* yesterday. They apparently removed from the park a bronze entitled "Playmates" showing three boys gazing at a centerfold of a *Playboy* magazine. In the centerfold was a black view—excuse me, a back view, also a black view—of a woman wearing a scanty negligee. There was opposition on some part of the communities and kids were seen giggling about it. And the sculptor said, "Actually the piece was not designed to have kids elbow each other and giggle. It was to have adults reminisce a bit about this stage of their development." I suggest that it did not allow the women to reminisce a bit about our development.

Okay. What I want to basically tell you, and the rest of the stuff is submitted, will be submitted, is that what I have found in [studying] "Not a Love Story."[6] . . . [It studies] the audience over a month period. My findings were that men and women have very different attitudes towards pornography. Men didn't like it very much and women hated it. There were particular differences on two issues. One was that pornography has—the question was: Do you think pornography has its place? Women and men really split, with most women saying no, it didn't. They strongly disagree. Seventy-two percent disagreed strongly.

On the question of rape, some of the increase in the rate of rape can be attributed to pornography, 81 percent of the women agreed and 51 percent of the men agreed.

The [Society for the] Scientific Study of Sex has changed. When I showed the film "Not a Love Story" and had a panel with Donnerstein, Malamuth, Stock, and Abel, even in this group I found there were similar differences between males and females. There were 40 percent of the men strongly agreeing that there was a place for pornography but only 11.5 percent of the females agreeing. [Exh. 6]

I will just close with a poem, because I think it is the poets that get at the essence of our experience, not the academics. It is a poem called "Homage to Virginia Woolf," who as you recall walked into the river and drowned.

> I am thinking of a woman
> who walked into the waters of a river
> with stones in her pockets.
> I am thinking of the waters of the rivers of my life.
> I am thinking of the stones
> in my pockets.
> All women are born with stones in our pockets.
> Empty them, empty them, empty them,
> swim.[7]

---

6. The research to which Dr. Bart refers was subsequently published in Pauline Bart, Linda Freeman, and Peter Kimball, "The Different Worlds of Women and Men: Attitudes Toward Pornography and Responses to *Not a Love Story*—a Film about Pornography," *Women's Studies International Forum* 301 (1985).

7. Anonymous, *off our backs* (February 2, 1997).

I hope that the Minneapolis City Council helps us take out the stones which pornography has in our pockets, and take them out so that we can all swim.

DAUGHERTY: Pauline, one second.

MacKINNON: I think for the sake of time, Chairman, in order to preserve as much time as possible to the public, I won't ask for any other questions.

I will submit one document, which is a letter from a doctor who recently went to a medical school and found pornography still being used in the training of gynecologists in sex education, to document that it is still going on. Thank you.

CHAIRMAN WHITE: I want to thank you. I was out of the room but I will tell you and the audience that there are speakers in all the other rooms. We are not slighting anyone when we are running back and forth. It is now public hearing time and there is a lady here with her child who wishes to speak. And what is her name, Jane Strauss. I would like to say three to four minutes in your presentations so that we can move right along, we are getting close to the time that we are supposed to be breaking, we may have to go over a little bit.

If you will begin by giving your name and address to the stenographer and to the committee clerk.

JANE STRAUSS: First of all, thank you very much, Mr. White, for making this possible. We were a little confused about times here and the baby is getting a little restless.

I am Jane Strauss, S-t-r-a-u-s-s. I live at 3120 Third Avenue South. I am coming here with two concerns, and I will try and be as brief as possible.

The first concern is, I am a parent trying to raise a child in South Minneapolis. Just recently, well, at the present time the place where we live is within five blocks of two pornography stores and two health clubs, 24-hour girls in lingerie. I have some concerns from that standpoint. I have some concerns in that my husband and I own some legitimate bookstores in which a small, very small percentage of what we carry, which is asked for by some of our customers, is things which might be considered to be pornography under this ordinance. And I have some concerns with regard to that, with regard to small business people who are trying to survive as compared to the Alexanders who make their living exclusively from the pornography, degradation of men, women, and children.

I have read over the proposed ordinance several times. I have shown it to my spouse who, say what you will, he appears to be a man, but who is an attorney by training, and to several other attorneys whom I know, some of whom are women. One of my concerns is that this deals only with pornography per se. One of the major concerns that I see is the presence of prostitution and, yes, pornography may encourage that. There is no direct provision with regard to the presence of prostitution in this. I am concerned about that, I am concerned about probable discriminatory stuff. The definition which is given in the ordinance points to degrading pictures of women. It is women in this and women in that. We have here men, seen in *Buns,* available in B. Dalton or lots of other places. We have gay-oriented pornography. I find this offensive. It is not covered. We have *Playgirl.* That is men. My God, I don't think it is that great. It is stuff that is commonly available. It is stuff that you can get at the local magazine wholesaler, at the local book wholesaler in this town.

I also have some concerns that violence is no less violent because it is violence against men. That focusing on a male crotch as an essence of that person is not less demeaning than focusing on a female crotch or breasts. I have some concerns about that.

The second thing—another thing I have a concern about is that no distinction is made between a full-line bookstore or convenience store that has *Playboy* and *Penthouse,* maybe, and an operation like that owned by the Alexander Brothers, [in] which their primary purpose is peddling pornography. I think there is a distinction in kind of those two. You may disagree, but this is my concern.

Another concern that I have is that, for example, if three out of 20,000 titles are offensive to somebody in a full-line bookstore, the person who owns that bookstore is still liable to suit. From a purely practical viewpoint, it is not physically possible to read absolutely everything that you stock in that store. I will show you. These are romance novels. The current trend in category romance novels is for increasingly graphic things. Many who are thinking women would find those quite offensive. I do. On the other hand, there are women who buy and devour three or four a week and this is the market at which these are aimed—young women, sixteen to forty, or sixteen to thirty-five, many of whom are housewives and things like that. I don't just think it is real appropriate.

I am concerned that this could possibly open the way for a large number of suits at personal expense against general bookstores for a very small percentage of what they stock, rather than against those people who make their living primarily selling pornography—who are, I might add, better able to defend themselves and better able to afford an attorney than the independent bookseller is.

I don't know how many of you know about the bookselling business.

It has a small margin of profit. It is hard to make a living by a legitimate bookstore.

I am concerned that if a number of the cases go to court, it is not likely to help the calendars in court. I don't know that this has been properly addressed. I am concerned that it appears that written suits need to be about specific books or magazines. What happens if one of these pornography bookstores had thousands of titles? Do you have to sue over each title individually? It seems unwieldy to me. It seems difficult to enforce.

I have another concern on the statute of limitations. To give you an example, the statute of limitations on medical malpractice, including assault by a physician, is two years. I do not think that it is appropriate to have a longer statute of limitations on the crime of peddling pornography than of the crime of physically assaulting a woman. I was assaulted by a psychologist. When I fought back, I was told by an attorney, when I got up enough nerve to sue for malpractice, too bad, it was two and a half years ago. You have no cause of action.

I also have some concerns that in addressing movies, again I don't know, and I wonder, I ask for your, you know, whatever, for your enlightenment, what the effect will be on R-rated movies, which I may or may not choose to see, which do run in the downtown houses. There doesn't seem to be any distinction drawn between those and the specialty pornography houses. I am concerned about the lack of distinctions in this legislation.

Finally, I consider this a good start, perhaps meaningless, it seems to me the city has abrogated its police power to be forcing women to spend their own money in order to live in safety, in order to keep themselves from being harassed in walking by the places. I have a problem. I like to put the baby in a baby buggy and go down to Sears. I have to pass a number of these places, and I am not ready for the harassment outside. The City Council would say, yes, women, we give you the right to get the money to bring suit yourselves. We are not able to do anything for you.

I grew up outside of Boston. I have some questions as to why [the] combat zone seems to work there. They are under the same Constitution as we are, last I heard, and yet for whatever reason, it has not been applied here.

And in conclusion, I would like to encourage the Committee and the entire Council to consider carefully some of these questions I have raised. To consider very carefully the wording in this, so when you pass something relating to pornography, and hopefully relating to prostitution as well as pornography, that you will pass something that will have teeth and not force the victims to come up with the money to defend themselves. Thank you.

CHAIRMAN WHITE: Thank you very much.

MacKINNON: Could you stay so you could respond?

You know I may not address everything, you did a lot. As to what you say, the discriminatory stuff and the things you say would not be covered. The intention of this ordinance is to cover, as pornography, one, women, because that is where the strongest data is as to the relationship between women in pornography and concrete harms and abuses towards women, but also as to cover, as pornography, men, children, and transsexuals when they are used in the place of women.

STRAUSS: Okay, I think it should be made a little clearer.

MacKINNON: And we accept your saying that it should be a little clearer. In fact, I accept that. I will do that.

STRAUSS: Very good, thank you.

MacKINNON: The second question that you made as to the difficulty of the legitimate booksellers making a living, part of the hope here is that by allowing people to sue, principally women, traffickers in pornography, that there will be an alteration in the competitive atmosphere. That is the view. In other words, that women know how hard it is to bring suits that will stick, and we all know who the traffickers of pornography are in the city. And what we are thinking is that it is important that there not be exceptions, so that pornography can always be available even if because it is only sold in small quantities. In other words, it is just as harmful if you get it at the town grocery store or at a store like yours. If one gets it from there, then it is just as harmful in grocery stores as it is if it was bought in the emporium bought by the Alexanders.

STRAUSS: I would like to address it briefly. I don't know if you are familiar with the current thing in category romances. Frankly, I find those highly offensive and yet there is a very large—those of us who own stores and make our livings from them would very much like to not have to carry this, but there are a large number of women in South Minneapolis who have very little in the way of brain and like this garbage. I can tell you how many we sell.

CHAIRMAN WHITE: This is not a debate. This is a public hearing.

STRAUSS: Yes.

CHAIRMAN WHITE: I have initiated your concerns. There has been a response of what?

STRAUSS: I am responding to her that we wish we had a guaranteed income. We do have a large number of customers who are regular customers who we can't afford to lose who like this kind of category romance and we can't afford not to carry them.

CHAIRMAN WHITE: We are not going to go into debate, from now on we are going to hear public testimony that will be put in the record and we will not—except from the committee members, if they wish to ask a question. But have no responses. I want to thank you.

STRAUSS: I wish to thank you and I wish to thank those of you who were respectable and those of you who were not, I wish to—

CHAIRMAN WHITE: Let's go on.

Richard Alberta, you have the floor, three or four minutes.

RICHARD ALBERTA: Richard Alberta, I live at 4617 East 36th Street. I am a freelance editor for a private journal here in town.

In less than two weeks, I have heard three different explanations on the research on pornography and violence. Dr. Elizabeth Rice Allgeier, I sent that testimony to the council last week, said we lack conclusive evidence regarding this issue. Professor MacKinnon said there is a concreteness between exposure and violence. And scientific works on the subject seldom, if ever, use the word causality but rather talk about correlations or results of studies. Which suggests, in other words, different people look at the same data and come up with different conclusions. Today is a perfect time to clear up some of those conflicting conclusions. Now, most of the conflicts deal with words, two words in particular, attitudes and aggression. So, I have organized the conclusions within the scope of these two words.

Number one, aggressive pornography and attitudes. The Malamuth and Donnerstein study of 1982 listed studies regarding this but studies with conflicting results. On the one hand, Malamuth and Check suggested that exposure to films of films showing "aggressive sexuality as having positive consequences tended to increase acceptance of male rape myths." On the other hand, another study, Malamuth et al., 1970 found no evidence of changes in attitudes. So one study says yes, another study says no.

On the second and last point, aggressive pornography and aggression, in the laboratory when a female researcher angered a male, the aggressive pornography increased his aggression towards her. However, aggressive nonpornographic exposures also increased aggressivity toward female victims.

With regard to the last category of studies, this question has been asked: How do these effects go to outside nonlaboratory conditions? Malamuth and Donnerstein, alluded to before, said "while laboratory experiments provide a useful framework for determining whether aggressive pornography can affect aggressive tendencies, there is a need at this point to examine the extent to which such stimuli actually exert and impact in naturalistic settings."

Parenthetically I might add that although we have been told the [quantity] of pornography is increasing and this increase should result in more violence in women, the incidents of rape in Minneapolis have not been increasing since 1973. In fact, in 1981—between '81 and '82 there was a 7.3 percent decrease in rape in Minneapolis. So this is a complex issue as well as an emotional issue. For the benefit of the Council members and audience today, I hope that some of these complexities can be addressed here today.

CHAIRMAN WHITE: Thank you.

Is there anyone that can't be here before 5:00 that wishes to speak? We do have a break scheduled. Is there anyone that can't come at 5:00 and continue the testimony?

MacKINNON: The dozen people on the list can all come at 5:00.

CHAIRMAN WHITE: They can?

MacKINNON: They can and they will be there.

HOYT: Mr. Chairman?

CHAIRMAN WHITE: Yes, Councilman Hoyt?

HOYT: If there is no one signed up on the list—as long as there is no one signed on this list, who indicated that they can't be here at 5:00, I think the whole audience and the committee might be able to stand the break that we have scheduled. So I would move that we recess until 5:00.

CHAIRMAN WHITE: On the motion, all those in favor say aye.

THE COMMITTEE: Aye.

(Hearing recessed until 5:00 in the evening of Monday, December 12, 1983.)

SESSION II: MONDAY, DECEMBER 12, 1983, 5:00 P.M.

CHAIRMAN WHITE: Who will speak here?

COMMISSIONER TOM BEAVER: I think all of us will.

CHAIRMAN WHITE: Since there are four of you and I notice three on this list, who else?

HYATT: We are also expecting Cliff Greene. He will be in shortly. He is an attorney. He has extensive knowledge in the area of civil rights.

BEAVER: And Sharon Warwick may not be on that list that you have in front of you.

CHAIRMAN WHITE: She is not on here.

COMMISSIONER SHARON WARWICK: I was on the other list.

CHAIRMAN WHITE: What other list?

WARWICK: The Civil Rights Commissioner's.

CHAIRMAN WHITE: We need a quorum. Will you please come in Councilmember Howard or Daugherty or Dziedzic. The quorum being present, we will reconvene the hearing on the Pornography Ordinance.

COUNCILMEMBER SALLY HOWARD: Chairman White?

CHAIRMAN WHITE: Councilmember Howard?

HOWARD: I would like to announce, before the public hearing was called a couple of months ago, I agreed to give a speech at the League of Women Voters Meeting at 7:00. It is not because I am not interested. It is because I can't cancel out on a different speech.

CHAIRMAN WHITE: Okay. We have members of the Civil Rights Commission here who are with us. I am going to allow them to speak briefly with their tentative statements. They will also have an ample opportunity in two days to prepare their concerns or agreements on the ordinance. And at this time, I will allow them to participate.

Whomever wishes to go first.

BEAVER: I am Tom Beaver, Chairman of the Civil Rights Commission. We, as a Commission, have not had an opportunity as a Commission to fully discuss and talk about this ordinance in a Commission meeting. So as of today, we are unable as a Commission to give you a yes or a no on this issue of our support.

We have some very serious questions. One, how is this going to affect our department and our resources to implement other aspects of the civil rights ordinances. And before I can give you a yes or no on the support, we need to have a meeting and we have successfully arranged a meeting between the makers and your consultants which will take place. And after that meeting, we will be making a prepared text to let you know of our support or nonsupport. It would be unfair to tell you yes or no on our support tonight.

We would like to let you know that we do have some concerns and we will talk those out with your consultants, and with Charlee Hoyt on Wednesday, when we meet with everyone. I sense in the conversations that I have had with other members, the support is not full and complete for this amendment, and I think that it might be because of some lack of knowledge on our part on what this amendment is going to do and how it is going to operate.

Until that meeting, until we get our questions answered, we will hold off on formal testimony for you and present it at other hearings. Other members of the Commission have things to tell you and some of their concerns, and I will let them go ahead and explain their testimony.

HOYT: Chairman White?

CHAIRMAN WHITE: Councilman Hoyt?

HOYT: I appreciate the fact that the Chairman is making it possible for a meeting of the Commission to take place. It is my understanding that when our meeting was set up last week with the Executive Director of the Civil Rights Department, I made an automatic assumption that that also meant the Commissioners, and I found out right away that it didn't. And it was hard to call you at 9:00 o'clock and say, would you like to come to a meeting at 10:00 o'clock. I did call Mr. Beaver. It is a misunderstanding on my part. They would have had full access earlier.

CHAIRMAN WHITE: Okay. I would ask you to be as brief as you possibly can because we do have some that have waited over to get whatever they wish into the public hearing setting.

You may go ahead with someone, whoever wishes to go.

WARWICK: I am Sharon Warwick, Commissioner of Minnesota Commission on Civil Rights. I have a few problems with this. First of all, I would like to say that I am against pornography, since over half the proposed zones are in the area where I live and my friends live and where we shop and do business. I am very much concerned with what is going to happen within the city. I am not going to speak to the First Amendment rights. I think there are a lot of other people who can speak to those issues better than I can.

I have a problem with the ordinance and how it is written. I feel it is somewhat discriminatory, particularly with part *g* which defines the word pornography. I don't believe that it should be exclusive to women. I am also very much concerned about how this ordinance will be enforced, and the fact that we will need more staff, concerned about whether or not people realize that it is going to involve a lot more staffing for the department. I think there is a misconception, perhaps, that this ordinance will close the bookstores. I am not sure that that would happen.

I am also concerned about the time that has been spent on this ordinance. As the Commission, we have not been approached at all regarding this ordinance, and I find that rather troublesome when in fact we are the people who are to be concerned with civil rights in the city. And it was almost a surprise when we received the ordinance in the mail. We had naturally read about it in the media, but no one had ever contacted us regarding the ordinance itself.

I am not sure that this particular ordinance belongs with civil rights. I think that there might be other forums that would deal better with pornography than the Civil Rights Commission. I would like the City Council to consider that carefully.

Again, I am concerned about the time. I hope that we don't rush into something. I think this does need more study and I am concerned that the full council should get time to study all of the testimony that is taken here today. I guess I might like to suggest tabling the matter, if it should come to that point, and give us time to work with it and to talk it over more. Thank you.

RICK OSBORNE: Mr. Chairman, my name is Rick Osborne. I am also on the Civil Rights Commission. I won't promise to be brief, and I hope the Chair will indulge me because you have heard a lot of testimony this afternoon. And I believe that, because this is an issue that is so new to the city, having just surfaced publicly some five weeks ago, and which potentially involves cost to the city of thousands of dollars to prosecute and enforcement costs, assuming that it is passed and upheld on the part of the Commission, that you will give me a few minutes to discuss with you my concerns.

CHAIRMAN WHITE: Mr. Osborne, I don't want to be capricious. I would like you to limit your remarks to three or four minutes.

OSBORNE: I am on the general speakers' list. If I don't make it now, I will talk then too.

CHAIRMAN WHITE: You are not going to double up on me like that.

OSBORNE: Okay, I will try and make it quick, Mr. Chairman.

I should point out to the [Committee] that I don't speak on behalf of the Commission. This is my own opinion. The same goes as Assistant Criminal County Attorney in the Criminal Unit and the Appeals Unit. I have had experience as a counselor for the runaways for victims of pimps. I have some experience and expertise in those fields.

My underlying personal commitment is fighting discrimination against women and all the groups protected in our ordinance. My philosophy is that no matter how noble and good that end is, we must use means to fight and accomplish it that are fair and just and, most important, legal. And I don't believe this ordinance meets any of those criteria.

One of the consultants who worked on the preparation of this ordinance said in her introduction today, "The First Amendment is not useful to us." Unfortunately, Mr. Chairman, it is that attitude that has been prevalent on the part of our country's history. Who would deny freedom of speech, freedom of the press, and freedom of religion[?] The First Amendment was designed to be inconvenient to people who would suppress public debate in the country. So, I don't have much sympathy of the drafter because she has that opinion. This Committee must not allow legal objections to be ignored by the simple assertion of some that this hearing is merely to find facts. I have specific objections to the proposal itself.

First, semantic objections. The phrase "graphically depicted" is legally meaningless and this is a dilemma that you as a Committee have to recognize in that language. I feel that phrase is so overbroad so that the following articles will be banned because they are sexually explicit and subordinate women. I am going to use a definition of sexually explicit as something on a person's face, that refers to their sex. Subordinate refers to a lesser position, either physically or power. And graphically depicted merely means expressed or obvious. If that very admittedly broad definition is used, it could be used to cause the following to be banned.

HOYT: One second. Be aware that it is simply not that paragraph. It is that paragraph plus one of the nine references that follows it. So in the ordinance, it would not apply if it were simply the one without the others.

OSBORNE: I understand that, but that is the initial threshold requirement. The matter must meet that definition before it can consider the others.

HOYT: It has to have one of the other nine with it.

OSBORNE: I understand that.

HOYT: It can't stand alone.

OSBORNE: I understand. With that understanding I suggest that is—it is possible that somebody can try and bring an action against the Commission for the following materials: from Geoffrey Chaucer, *The Wife of Bath's Tale,* "He took his wife in his arms and kissed her, overcome with joy. Thereafter she obeyed him in everything that might add to his bliss, and thus they lived for the rest of their lives in perfect happiness." It is sexual, it refers to her as a wife, as a woman, that is explicit. It obviously refers to her explicit capacity. She is definitely subordinate. Bear in mind it refers to the woman being subordinate because she has to obey the man, and which of the other nine criteria does it need? By someone's definition that she is being treated as an object, a thing, or a commodity, it might mean that she is being presented in a posture of sexual submission because we don't know what he meant, Geoffrey Chaucer means, when she is overcome with joy. The problem is, we don't know if that material is going to be covered by this ordinance. That is taking a broad definition.

What if you narrowly define sexually explicit subordination of women as it has to display genitalia or some sexual act, as we understand it. Then I would suggest that the following material, which is objectionable to me and I am sure many of the people that are backing the ordinance, would not be banned. First, the cover of *Hustler* magazine which shows a pair of presumably women's legs in a meat grinder, this would not be banned because there is no display of sexual genitalia. We don't know if those legs are women. The album cover with a woman's black and blue body of bruises would not be covered, as I understand it, there was no show of sexual acts and—

CHAIRMAN WHITE: Let me say this. First of all, as I asked earlier on, this is not a debate and your comments, whether you agree or disagree is not necessary. This is input. This is going into a document. This is very serious business. He is stating an objection to it, possible objection. There will be those that will speak in the affirmative for what has been stated that he objects to. Let us not get into a hair-raising aspect here. This is not a circus. We will let everyone say what they have to say and get it over with.

Go ahead.

OSBORNE: Finally, I would suggest that if a narrow definition of that phrase is adopted, that any item in which the woman is physically above, especially a man in the process of committing a sex act, would be bannable under that ordinance. I don't think that that is desirable. Because I also have here, and I will give it to the Committee, a photograph which appears in this week's article of *Newsweek* magazine. It is a classical statue in which breasts of the woman are displayed and genitalia of the man are displayed. The man is physically in the position of preeminence over the woman in this statue, and I suggest that that would be banned, and I don't think that this Committee wants to get into the position of doing that. I would submit this to the Committee for whatever weight you want to give it.

Now, the whole problem with the definition being vague is from the merchants' point of view. You heard from a young woman who runs a legitimate bookstore. She has materials she didn't know would be covered or not. The merchant is faced with a choice, either he or she has to guess that a book or magazine that is being sold in that bookstore is going to fit the broad definition and therefore, get rid of it, or they can take the risk that it would not fit a narrow definition and sell it and run the risk of prosecution. It is exactly that choice that a merchant has to make.

The First Amendment is designed to protect that chilling effect of uncertainty because a rational prudent business person is not going to carry the item and it won't be available.

I have one final legal objection to this, Mr. Chairman, and that is that this particular ordinance just plain is not needed. We have civil remedies for the victims of assault in the form of court actions for assault and battery. If someone such as Ms. Marchiano was, appears, in movies and she doesn't want to be in movies, she can bring an action in defamation of character or privacies. We have nuisance laws that govern a business that harasses passers-by. They can be shut down if we have the will to enforce them. They are on the books.

We have zoning laws, which doesn't get rid of pornography. To begin with, at least you will allow the First Amendment to come into effect. There are criminal statutes, my office prosecutes sexual assaults. One of my most—one is when I prosecute sex offenders, they are hideous crimes. We can use the laws on the books to take care of them. Thank you, Mr. Chairman.

HOYT: I appreciate your concerns. Perhaps if we added the word genitalia we could make it so that it is definite. I hope you will take some advantage of being able to press that in the meeting that you are all going to have, to find out if it does. And I plan, if at all possible, I plan to be there.

I caution you one thing. That is, almost every past civil rights ordinance that I have seen has had people in opposition saying the laws were already on the books that could be used. I can appreciate your concern. I would not want to have culture accused of being pornographic, and I believe you will have an opportunity to probe that in depth.

And again, my personal apologies. It was my ignorance of not knowing that the Civil Rights Commission should be there when the Director was, or you would have had that opportunity prior to public hearing time.

OSBORNE: Councilmember, I appreciate that. I guess my position would be even if the definition is drafted more narrowly, I, as a Commission member who will be sitting on at the complaint hearings for this, don't want to be in the position of a community hearing censor. It is impossible for any of us, no matter how far it is drafted, to separate out what is bannable and what is art. The Supreme Court has consistently said that.

CHAIRMAN WHITE: This is strictly for a public hearing.

Ms. Laurence?

COMMISSIONER WANDA LAURENCE: My name is Wanda Laurence. I am with the Civil Rights Commission. I am speaking on my personal opinion, and I am kind of uncomfortable with testifying because of the fact that I have a very close friend that was raped. And the man said, when he admitted the fact that he did rape this friend of mine, that he had just come from a pornographic movie. And I am giving this testimony as my own personal opinion, not necessarily the views of the Commissioner or anybody else in my neighborhood or the audience.

I live in a neighborhood that is very, very much inundated with bookstores and theaters that show porno movies or which is usually advertised as porno movies or porno books. Because of the fact that I sit on the Commission, I feel like I have a right to testify just as much as you people do. Also because of the fact that I am on the Commission, I want to make sure that the way it is written, the ordinance, something, is written that will not be challenged in court, [and] that it will ban or greatly reduce the amount of pornography that is happening not only in my neighborhood but in other areas. Because I really feel that it not only adversely affects and attacks and dramatizes the life of a woman, it affects youth, it affects men, it affects everybody in some way or another. It affects a person regardless of age. There is a lot of child pornography, there is a lot of pornography that affects women, and I think the majority right now that I have been made aware of, that has been what people complained about, is the fact that it affects women more than it affects most of the other people. Right now I tend to agree with that.

But I find a problem with reading this thing as to whether we can implement it monetarywise. I think that the way it is presently written, it will be challenged in court by the people that have a lot of money to be able to afford to take it into court. And a lot of it adversely affects [us] whether we have been attacked or not. And I think that adversely affects us, this porno stuff, and most of us I daresay in this room can't afford financially to take anybody to court that shows this kind of stuff, sells this kind of stuff or whatever. We just can't afford it. Grassroots people especially can't afford it.

Most of these places are located in areas that are in grassroots or places where a lot of grassroots people go. It happens to be that that is where most of the people have put these things and allowed a license to occur. Most of these places are in the neighborhood that I live in and I am really, really opposed to them being there. First Amendment right or any other amendment right, I am opposed to them being there.

I know it is adversely affecting my neighbors who are renting. I speak for a lot of people in my neighborhood. They can rent a lot of the facilities there because of the fact that there is so much porno in our area. People are afraid of being hassled when they are waiting for the bus, and a lot of places where they are waiting for the bus is right outside of these places. I really, really resent that the bus stop is there. For those that want to patronize the place, if they want to patronize the place, that is fine. I resent them being in my neighborhood, a good share of them.

Also, I am opposed to the fact that Charlee [Hoyt], she explained, but people were calling me and asking me my views as to how the Civil Rights Commission would handle this type of a thing when I hadn't even received a copy of it yet. I just want to voice my frustration with that.

And as far as the ordinance, I would like to not only see some form to ban this, and especially the effects that it has about women. I would like to see an ordinance change occur where these all aren't located in one area. And from what I have been told, they are going to be located in either downtown or else in commercial areas. And I live not too far from Lake Street which means we would probably get more than we already have. I don't know where they are going to put it. I am afraid that every time someone vacates, they are going to put it there.

One of the people that lives next door to me recently said that she—

CHAIRMAN WHITE: Can you wind it up?

LAURENCE: One of the people that lives next door to me said that her sister was raped and that they recently arrested the person that did it. I live not too far from where [the] person that committed the crime lives. It is getting so that I am afraid, and a lot of people that I have talked to from various parts of the city are afraid to even go out at night.

I believe the way it is written now, some form has to be drafted up, written, that can pass without a phenomenal court battle, that will not only help women so they can feel safe out there, but help other people that have to put up with this pornography stuff.

CHAIRMAN WHITE: Okay.

COMMISSIONER CLIFFORD GREENE: Members of the Council, my name is Clifford Greene. I am in my second term as a Civil Rights Commissioner. I will try and be as brief. I understand the Chairman does not want to get into a great deal of substantive debate. I will merely raise the concerns that entered my mind upon reviewing this ordinance when I did receive it.

I appreciate [Councilmember] Hoyt's comments that the exclusion of input from the Civil Rights Commission was not intentional. I look forward to meeting with the officers of the ordinance. I think we might have some constructive input for all of you later in the week.

I am an attorney and I represent municipalities other than the City of Minneapolis and have drafted and interpreted local obscenity laws. I am also an adjunct professor of law and teach a civil rights course at William Mitchell, serving as a full-time law professor there two years ago.

I make my comments mindful of the evils of obscenity and pornography and also the concern about the need to balance the First Amendment rights. As an individual member of the Commission, my concerns are primarily that I would be asked to adjudicate disputes that exist in coming under this discrimination ordinance. I am very, very careful, as are all of the members of the Commission, to apply the law in a consistent manner so people know what the standards are.

As I read the ordinance, the standards are not self-explanatory to me. I look forward to talking with Professor MacKinnon and her colleagues regarding the intention of the drafters of the ordinance, so perhaps we might be able to find some language that would give those who have to adjudicate these disputes, as well as people subject to them, an indication exactly what the standards of liability would be.

I give an example of the concern I have, without resolving it here. We can discuss it later. That is a situation where there is a book containing a character where there is a prostitute and, for one reason or another, enjoys being so. The prostitute character may or may not reflect the opinion of the author that prostitution is good, bad, or indifferent but may, in fact, be a character in the book to generate thought about a particular issue, perhaps even the issue of discrimination against women in our society. I am concerned that I will be asked to interpret the intent of the author, is this character truly expressing an idea or attitude towards women that is harmful and discriminatory. So, I am concerned about how to deal with that kind of problem and troubled by the possibility that I may be asked to construe these kinds of dilemmas. And I ask for guidance from the authors of the bill regarding what they had in mind.

In addition, I do have some questions about whether or not the standards as written are constitutional. As currently written my impression, and I state only an impression because I do not purport to be an expert on obscenity, is that they probably are not, but they might become so. And I would be very interested in hearing the strategies that Professor MacKinnon has in mind for defending those particular ordinances from the attacks that will inevitably occur. They will occur. If the attackers are successful, they will get attorney fees under the Civil Rights Act. Therefore, I think we should anticipate a costly battle but be ready to defend one in case it occurs. In particular, my concern is about how the regulation of pornography will enable us to reach types of expression that is not considered obscene under Federal definitions of obscenity.

The courts have allowed us to regulate obscenity, to ban it, criminalize it, zone it, whatever. It is my understanding, and perhaps I misunderstand, that the intent of this legislation is to allow us to create a cause of action for expression that may not be obscene but is harmful because it is pornographic. I would like to understand how this particular approach to the regulation of pornography would be constitutional whereas other approaches to widening the definition of obscenity are not.

I am concerned also about the impact of this proposal on the current operations and objectives of the current Civil Rights Commission. We have been very busy. We take our mandate seriously to make sure that all citizens of the City of Minneapolis have an opportunity to raise their concerns, be they legitimate conflicts, perceived conflicts, or whatever regarding discrimination in housing and in a variety of other activities. I want to know what the impact of our involvement as a Commission will be on other very important activities, such as our efforts to assure affirmative action and our efforts to assure that housing is made available to all and that none of the protected classes receives any less attention because of our ability to now deal with the new issue.

Another concern that I would like to discuss with the authors of the legislation is why this legislation is aimed at the local level. I am aware and have previously assembled the multitude of obscenity laws that are enacted by the federal and state authorities and that are on the books. I wonder whether the intentions of this legislation is to say these agencies will not enforce those laws or saying that these laws are inadequate. It seems to me that there are some tremendous advantages to forcing obscenity laws via state and federal legislation because they can cross jurisdictional lines. They can deal with issues such as the making of pornographic movies which may not be made in our particular city.

And finally, I would like to understand what the supporters of the legislation hope this legislation will accomplish. It is very important that we not create unrealistic expectations. If the purpose of this particular legislation is to assure that we do not have certain types of pornography exhibited or made available to children or others, I would like to understand that. If the purpose, however, is the expectation that this ordinance will do away with adult, I use the term loosely, bookstores, I think that expectation is unfounded. I think that, fortunately or unfortunately, depending on what your reading pleasure may be, that the adult bookstores are not going to be closed by this ordinance. We are required item by item to take a look at particular materials.

So those are the five concerns that I have, that I hope we have a chance to discuss. And I know I for one will attempt to be as helpful and as receptive and as willing to learn this area as I will be willing to contribute.

HOYT: Mr. Chairman?

CHAIRMAN WHITE: Alderman Hoyt?

HOYT: I will leave most of those for when you have the meeting. However, being one of the major authors, I will tell you it is in Minneapolis for the same reason that we seem to have had a sexual preference [law], which is not at state levels or other levels. It is here not at the choice of the consultants we have hired, but at the request of the committee, who in an open public hearing was considering a zoning ordinance on bookstores. Her testimony concerned civil rights of women and, at that point, the committee requested our City Attorney to talk with the people that we have now hired as our consultants, to help us construct that ordinance. So, it is in Minneapolis at the choice of Minneapolis and at the choice of this committee, which said we would like to pursue this and to look into it.

I am sure you can go into more depth when you get in to your meeting specifically. But do be aware someone did not bring this, other than this committee asked for it, and we fortunately have some consultants around.

CHAIRMAN WHITE: I would like to hitchhike on what Councilmember Hoyt has said. That is the reason it is before this committee. In zoning and planning they came in with the possible zoning in various aspects of the city, leaving out some. There was a cry throughout the best part of the cities that had those points or sites designated as being the recipient of pornography.

One of the things that everyone here has to understand, the victims are crying out, "what about us?" whether it is burglary or whether it is rape, whether it is any kind of act that violates the human aspects of our society. They are saying, "what about us?" And what they are asking is justice for all.

OSBORNE: Chairman White, in my case I missed a point that I wanted to bring to the Council's attention. Many of the underlying sentiments that I am hearing on behalf of the proponents of this proposal are that the attitudes that are infused in our culture, that men have perpetuated violence against women, I don't disagree with that at all. What I would draw to the Committee's attention is that the same sort of attitudes of silence and hatred and empathy have been fused in our culture against gay and lesbian people as well. I don't want the source of that hatred propaganda by evangelists, I don't want that banned by the marketplace either. I want the Committee to know that.

CHAIRMAN WHITE: Okay, thank you. We will now continue on with the— would you take your conversations in the hallway, please, if necessary. We are going to take this yellow sheet, it only has a few more on it. I will allow them three minutes and then we will go to the proposed sheet of those that wish to speak.

So would you give your name?

TIM CAMPBELL: Thank you, Mr. Chairman. My name is Tim Campbell. I am here to testify today as a member of the gay male community. I believe that what should be significant to the public and to the City Council and to the Commission as they consider this type of ordinance is that the gay male community has been systematically a target for sexual assault as women have been.

I testify today as a gay rights activist who sat in a cell block for fourteen days with four rapists in this very building. I have been the victim of sexual assault three times at the hands of men and once at the hands of women. There is a sexist bias that says the act of violence perpetrated against men is not sexual assault. I beg to differ with that sexist thinking.

In the course of twelve years working full time as a counselor, a comforter, a theoretician and an activist, for twelve years we have worked from the theory that what is going on at the University of Minnesota is the most effective cure for sexual ignorance and for the violence that results from sexual repression, sexual frustration and sexual ignorance.

As much as I empathize with Linda Lovelace, I believe that this ordinance will be more dangerous than helpful to Linda Lovelace and her kind. Linda Marchiano, victimized under the name of Linda Lovelace, came to the name of freedom under the name of Linda Marchiano and a new body of language.

Basically you heard a lot of testimony this afternoon that amounts to telling you that things lose shock value after you repeat them a number of times. I am here to tell you, any drag queen could have told you that. Sure, the more times you see a rape on TV, the less shock value it will have. That doesn't prove anything.

Basically we agree on goals. I would like to see queer bashing stopped. I would like to see sexual assault against women stopped. I fear, however, this ordinance will only increase the amount of weirdo pornography coming out from the makers. In the last twelve years there has been a change in the production of gay pornography. In early 1970 it was difficult to find anything but really sleazy, shoddy looking models and a whole lot of abusive stuff in gay male pornography. With the movement towards liberation and greater access and larger market, normal adult males consenting in adult sex, there is more of it than there was in 1970.

In the recent couple of years, a negative reaction to the current drive against pornography, violence in pornography, have what I consider an artificial production of "we will show you," thumb [your] noses type of pornography, like the cover of *Hustler* that shows the woman going through the meat grinder or the woman's legs going through the meat grinder. I believe that is temporary. I have great confidence in the long run that, as you heard today, these women want to use this ordinance to stop things like the sexuality seminars that are going through and Bart testified that is what she would like to stop. That is what she testified. She objected that medical students were seeing things they called pornography.

I can't tell what will be pornography by reading the ordinance proposed. I can assure you I can find four paragraphs in the ordinance to bring suit against the Bible. Cinderella is a myth that would not pass the test. In fact, I defy, I invite the City Council members to sit down now and write a three-sentence story involving a woman and sex that would pass the test of this ordinance. I don't think you would be able to write anything.

So, I would ask you, one, I believe that this ordinance as proposed is a threat to civil rights. Others pointed out that it is blatantly sexist. It is un-American, it is fascist, it is antisexual and it is antiheterosexual. Basically, the missionary position is no longer acceptable storytelling. The only thing you can do is Jack met Jill, maybe, and neither one pursued the other one, and they lived happily ever after, is the only love story you could write now. I would ask the Council to send it back and put this kind of litigation somewhere else. Don't erode the concept of civil rights with this concept.

ROBERT HALFHILL: My name is Robert Halfhill and I live at 125 Oak Grove, Apartment 45. I am opposed to the ordinance also as a gay activist. I will comment first on the ordinance.

It states that pornography shall include the sexually explicit subordination of women, graphically depicted, whether in words or in pictures in conjunction with one or more of the following. And then one is, women are presented as sexual objects, things, or commodities. That might seem to be a very narrow definition as came out of this hearing today. It turns out that even though members of this antipornography movement will deny that they are against erotica, when it actually comes down to examples, anything that is sexually explicit is viewing women as sexual objects, or commodities, and so forth.

We had someone testify to the calendars of nude males coming out. She also said gay pornography is offensive to her and she also referred to romance novels which some people might consider pornography. Just the fact that "one or more of the following" would mean that this ordinance would cover anything sexually explicit.

But I am more concerned with the following. This movement against pornographic bookstores has had a terrible effect on the gay community. There have been three thousand arrests, according to the Twin Cities readers of gay and adult bookstores, under the liberal administration. And every time we go in to talk and complain to the Police Chief about it, he says, "I am getting it from the other side."

So the point I am making is that this movement against the bookstores has been one of the factors, perhaps not the only one, one of the factors that led to the arrest of three thousand gay men with the police brutality and insult of police and so forth. One example. We had one police officer, and this will have to be a sexually explicit quote, we had a police officer beat a gay up and he said, "You mother-fucking faggot, if I ever see you around here again, they will find you in the river and your own mother won't be able to recognize you." What I am here to announce publicly, if this movement doesn't stop the arrest of gay men, we are going to have to retaliate in some way. It is just as easy for us to picket the pornography on U of M campus as it is for women to picket pornographic bookstores. If it doesn't stop, that is what we are going to have to do.

HOYT: Mr. Chairman?

CHAIRMAN WHITE: Councilmember Hoyt?

HOYT: Could I first reiterate to the audience, one of the best things we have in our society is the right of people to testify before their government and make their feelings known. No one should be put down for expressing their thoughts and their views before this Committee, and I would appreciate it if we could honor that.

EUGENE CONWAY: I am Eugene Conway, Senior. I am the state president of Morality in Media in Minnesota, Incorporated. We are the state affiliate of the national organization of Morality in Media. I had to leave early and I just got back and I don't know a lot of the things that have transpired.

But our organization is the organization that brought out the minority report of the Presidential Commission and also that was taken in the place of the majority report. Our state organization is 100 percent in favor of this ordinance. We have a few questions about the problems that might come up later on with regard to the constitutionality of the ordinance, but we are generally—in fact, we are in favor of the ordinance.[8]

Sitting here this afternoon, one thing I would like to bring out, we have a long legal constitutional history of obscenity and pornography in this country. In 1957 the *Roth* decision of the Supreme Court stated very categorically that obscenity is not free speech. Now, this is aimed not only at women but men and every person in society. Those of you that are active in this movement also know that in 1973 the *Miller* decision of the Supreme Court gave us about seven or eight activities that may be obscene.

The other point I would like to bring out, it was mentioned several times, is we don't have a definition of obscenity. For those of you that follow this closely, I am sure you know the three-prong test of obscenity that was brought out in the *Roth* decision and reaffirmed again in the *Miller* decision. Obscenities are actions, words, or shows, depictions, descriptions of activities, from the *Roth* and reaffirmed by the *Miller* decision, which would, taken as a whole, appeal to the interest in sex. This is the first standard, the first prong [of the] test of obscenity.

The second is that the obscene activities, whatever they might be, must be patently offensive, as we know meaning very evident[ly] that way. One of the justices didn't know how to define it but "I know it when I see it."

8. His organization later withdrew this support at an unrecorded session.

The third prong [of the] test is that, taken as a whole, that these activities must lack those four famous values: literary value, artistic value, political value, and scientific value. We also know from *Roth* and *Miller* that none of us in ourselves can decide what is obscene. That must be done by our peers in a—by a jury from the jurisdiction.

I would also like to point out one other fact which is very heartening. That was recently, two months ago, the President set up a coordinator, Mr. Boch, to coordinate customs in the FBI and post offices in enforcing all of our Federal laws.

I would like to, as a citizen, maybe ask one question, maybe to Mr. Hyatt or to Professor MacKinnon. We have had a lot of experience in this area. How do you feel that ordinance can cope with the city ordinance, the interpretation of *Miller* through the *Wilke* decision and the Supreme Court decision. How do you feel your ordinance will relate to these? Thank you.

CHAIRMAN WHITE: Mr. Hyatt, you can do that in a written answer.

MacKINNON: I will be happy to do that.

CHAIRMAN WHITE: Okay.

THERESA McDERMOTT: My name is Theresa McDermott, M-c-D-e-r-m-o-t-t. I live [in] downtown Minneapolis.

CHAIRMAN WHITE: Three minutes, please.

McDERMOTT: All right. I am a peace activist. I think these hearings were very revealing today for the state of our society. We have a Civil Rights Commission that didn't take the trouble to come to this morning's hearings that were upon a very serious matter. They say they have so many other things to do. We are 51 percent of the population. You have rape, abduction, imprisonment, the maiming of our women, if that isn't bad enough, the pollution of the minds of the men of our society. What is this society going to come to when they can't see the differences between pornography and a love story, between erotica, nudity, sexuality, and by far deviant behavior which is punishing us because we don't have the political power to fight you?

How many women sit in the Senate of the United States? How many women ever have? We are 51 percent of the population, I will repeat once more. We are now talking of the possibility of a black man being President in the United States. Black men, I suppose since blacks are 10 percent of the population, are five percent.

We as 51 percent of the population are sick and tired of walking down the street and seeing our names and our faces and our bodies defamed and depicted in this way. The title on your little piece of paper for your citizens to see says "Government Operations Committee." We want to be a part of the government and we want to have some right to define what we are.

The definitions made in literature, as someone pointed out, some ten or fifteen years ago in *Sexual Politics*[9]—if you haven't read it I suggest you do—the way we are defined is, as in literature, it is everywhere and done all by men. Just in the last ten or fifteen years have we had the ability to do it ourselves.

We want the filthy bookstores out. We want the freedom to walk in the streets. We brought you men into your lives, and every one of you has a mother and a daughter and a sister, and where would you be without us? We don't do this to you, and we demand that you stop doing this to us.

CHAIRMAN WHITE: The Chair would like—I notice that the hands were pointing this way. And the Chair, being a male person, I would like to let everyone know that I haven't participated in that kind of activities that you wish to abolish. And I also want to say I recognize the fact that over the years in the history of this United States that the course of civil rights is very difficult to come by. There are now cries that are coming from women of color saying, "what about us?" So you better recognize that those that are the majority of women, that women of color are beginning to say "what about us." Go ahead.

DZIEDZIC: I would like to say, starting January 2nd or 3rd, whatever date Council takes effect, there will be seven women on the Council, which is a majority.

HOYT: Mr. Chairman?

CHAIRMAN WHITE: Yes, go ahead, Alderman Hoyt.

HOYT: I would like to point out that we all recognize that this is strictly not [a] male/female division in society—that there are many, many men who definitely do support the equal rights of women and the recognition of their civil rights.

PAUL PRICE: My name is Paul Price. I live at 2707 Garfield Avenue South and I will speak very briefly.

I have a loosely informed background, however, I think one that is personally well thought out and rather conscious. I find that, in particular, in the list of nine points whereby this proposed ordinance action accusing pornography and the violation of civil rights, in particular number one, is very ambiguous. And I think it can be easily substantiated through any discussion you have on a very well practical level as to the

9. Kate Millett, *Sexual Politics* (Doubleday, 1969).

definition of those terms. And I fear, because of the ambiguity, as other speakers have mentioned, the possibility of great harassment due to a very wide perception of just what it takes to be a negative sexual object. And thus, you must then be concerned with the recipients of that type of harassment.

I am trying very hard to be an artist. And I would find myself somewhat ill at ease with the selection of material that may come to my mind. I think that relates also to the points that Dr. Donnerstein earlier this afternoon was addressing and describing, his research concerning the crux of his studies, using, as he defined it, sexually explicit aggressive pornography and that concerning activity between consenting adults. I don't find—as he strove for, I believe, in his research, he set that distinction forward. I don't find that forwardness here. With clarity, as one of the members on the Civil Rights Commission addressed, the clarity of the chilling effects.

I would also like to inquire, as it is my very uninformed understanding of the laws in society. It is my belief there are activities that humans involve themselves with in varying levels of abuse, in varying levels of the way their behavior affects other people. I think in following the logic of this, I as a resident living next to a bar or a liquor store, might legitimately follow the points of this ordinance and ask that the City Council provide for me the means to sue the purveyor of some alcoholic beverage as their drunken behavior somehow violated my civil rights. I would like to inquire, this is part of what I think or how the area will begin to broaden itself out, and I would hope that that will be addressed because I think statistically even a stronger case could be put forward as the presence of alcohol in our society is on a much more destructive force as I think most everyone in the psych. therapy could let you know. With the presence of automobiles, all are activities which do indeed violate people's civil rights in pursuit of happiness.

Thank you very much.

COUNCILMEMBER WALTER ROCKENSTEIN: Mr. Chairman, there is a dramshop act where a person who has been served too much alcohol, and they hit you, and the owner of and purveyor of the goods can be sued. It is a good analogy in this case.

STEVE CARLSON: My name is Steve Carlson. I am from Minneapolis. I am not a member of the gay community, but I sympathize and wish to protect the people and civil rights [of] the gay community. I have often said that.

I am very sorry to see the conflict that politics are generating. I hope that we can overcome that here. I will not appeal to any interest or hatred for one class of people against another, justly or unjustly, because I understand, and I am not preaching, but I understand that love is the most powerful force which is operating in this society right now. I hope that it is operating right here in this room today. It hurts me to see all of this hatred.

I was here this afternoon. What I saw moved me very deeply, as I am sure it did everybody in this room. I have no doubt that at this time that everybody in this room wants very much to stop the kind of activity which we were advised of. I have no doubt that we all want to work together to use the law to further the sanctity of human life. And I don't mean any religious or ideological overtones by saying that. I mean it very simply, it is not cool, it is not in any way hip going around beating off, mutilating women, or subjecting them to this. And anybody who starts talking about the First Amendment and being glad that it allows the feeling that somehow it is proper protection, I believe they do not understand the law.

Let me get to the point. The point is, we have a job to do. I am proud to be here in this room with these people, and these people who I am very glad to meet, and I hope I can align myself with.

The lawyer over here, the one on the end of the Civil Rights Commission, brought up some very helpful input as well as did the person from the media on [morality]. There has been a lot of progress, as we have learned today and know already on obscenity. We should proceed on the local level. We should proceed immediately to protect the life and well-being of the women and others when they are victims of pornography. We should act as far as we can within what the law has already provided. Protections against obscenity, you can even ban it. Obviously that we have come this far today. It shows we are mindful of protecting that.

The new area that has come up today is violence against women. We must—we had a psychologist who presented new painful but startling and provocative research and some findings. I wish that all of us would act together to put into effect what we have come to know through this research, through the advent of women's studies at the University which indicates a great deal of hope in this process, in this society, to be concerned about and appreciate the contributions of women's rights. It has brought to us its knowledge. We must extend beyond the obscenity into the evidence. We have to protect property, personal well-being of women, and that is why I hope that we will get down to work. I thank you.

CHAIRMAN WHITE: Now we have had some requests of personal testimony that has been on the agenda for quite some time, and I would like to allow those persons who are about to begin to speak to utilize their three minutes and move on. If there is any questions from the Committee, I would hope you would hold it brief.

They will be excused from giving their address because of some of the degradation that they have suffered. And we don't want you to know where they live and so forth and so on.

So if the first person to speak is here, Cheryl Champion, R. M.?

DWORKIN: Mr. Chairman, the people who are going to speak to the actual ways in which pornography has been used against them would very much appreciate being able to sit up here.

MS. M.: My name is R. M. and I live in the 9th Ward. I am going to talk about being raped and how pornography was involved in that rape.

HOYT: R., could you pull it a little closer?

MS. M.: When I was thirteen, I was camping with the Girl Scouts in Northern Wisconsin. It was ten years ago in November. I was walking through the forest outside of the camp in midafternoon and came upon three deer hunters who were reading magazines and talking and joking around.

I turned to walk away and one of the men yelled, "There is a live one." And I thought they meant a deer, and so I ducked and tried to run away. I realized that there wasn't any deer in sight and that they meant me. And I started running and they ran away—they ran after me. I tripped, the forest was covered with pine needles and leaves and they caught me. And I told them that I would go away, to leave me alone, please.

And they said, "You are not going anywhere" and forced me to get up and pulled my hair and started looking at me up and down, calling me a little Godiva—I had long hair then—a golden girl, and making jokes.

They told me to take my clothes off and I did. It was very cold. It was November. I took my clothes off, and they told me to lie down and the first man started. They told me not to say anything, that if I made a sound that they would kill me, they would blow my head off.

MacKINNON: Were they armed?

MS. M.: Yes. All three of them had hunting rifles. They—two men held their guns at my head and the first man hit my breast with his rifle, and they continued to laugh.

And then the first man raped me. And when he was finished, they started making jokes about how I was a virgin and I didn't know how they knew I was a virgin, but they did. And they made jokes about this, and jokes about how they could have used something like this when they were in boot camp, and made jokes about being in the military.

The second man then raped me. None of the men attempted to kiss me or touch my breasts. They simply wanted to have intercourse. When the second man was finished, the third man was not able to get an erection and they, the other men, told me to give him a blow job, and I didn't know what a blow job was.

The third man forced his penis into my mouth and told me to do it and I didn't know how to do it. I did not know what I was supposed to be doing. He started swearing at me and calling me a bitch and a slut and that I better do it right and that I wasn't even trying. Then he started getting very angry and one of the men pulled the trigger on his gun, so I tried harder.

Then when he had an erection, he raped me. They continued to make jokes about how lucky they were to have found me when they did, and they made jokes about being a virgin. They started kicking leaves and pine needles on me and kicking me and told me that if I wanted more, that I could come back the next day.

Then they started walking away and I put my clothes back on and it was not far from where they had set up their camp, and I looked down and saw that they had been reading pornographic magazines. They were magazines with nude women on the covers.

I went back to the camp—well, first I got my clothes back on and walked a fair amount away, and then I broke down and cried under a tree and decided what I needed to do. And I went back to the camp and I didn't tell anyone that I had been raped. I went to the bathroom and saw that I had bled on my underwear, so I assumed that I had gotten my period. I did not know that virgins bleed. I didn't find that out until a few years later.

I didn't seek any medical help. I didn't tell anyone that I was raped until I was 20 years old.

DWORKIN: Had you seen pornography before?

MS. M.: Yes.

DWORKIN: Could you say how?

MS. M.: My father and my older brothers all had pornography. They kept it under their mattresses and under their beds. I had looked at the pornography that was in my home when I was growing up. When I was a young child I assumed that that is how it would look when I grew up.

DWORKIN: So you recognized the magazines as being basically the same kinds of magazines that you had seen in your home?

MS. M.: Absolutely.

MacKINNON: What do you remember about what you were thinking they would do to you at the time?

MS. M.: When I was being raped, I thought they were going to kill me. I assumed I wasn't going to live through that, that this was what they were going to do to me before they killed me.

HYATT: Excuse me, what went through your mind when you decided not to report this?

MS. M.: Well, in retrospect I realized that I felt like I needed some control over what had just happened, that I didn't feel like I could tolerate anyone and having them think it was my fault or blaming me or not understanding. And to have no control over who had that information once I told someone, knowing that my mother would most likely tell a great deal of people and I would have no control over that information.

MacKINNON: We are finished.

CHAIRMAN WHITE: Okay, thank you. I recognize that was difficult with all the ears that were here, for you to sit here and make that kind of statement. Thank you. I will probably say this to them all. It takes a lot of guts.

E. M.: . . . I live in the 10th Ward.

CHAIRMAN WHITE: Will you bring the mike up?

E. M.: Okay.

I am afraid to be here. I am also afraid not to be here. In thinking about coming here today to speak, I realized that my life would be in danger. As a woman of color these dangers seem many and great—an absolute loss of credibility and respect, wrath and disgust, potential violence both verbal and physical, and ridicule and harassment, to name a few. I also realized the dangers to my life if I did not come. These dangers being complacency, letting go of my rage and terror about pornography and its impact on my life, accepting that the shame is mine, accepting that I am the slut and the whore that deserved what was done to me, believing that I am useable. I have no illusions about men not seeing me as a slut. They do. They see all women as sex itself, even the ones they venerate. But I also want to say to you that I have no illusions about my refusal to accept that I am and must always be these things.

I want to tell you how pornography has affected my life, how I am fighting self-loathing, disgust and shame, how I am fighting at the beginning, and how I am fighting tearing out my skin.

The first thing I want to talk about happened when I was three years old. When I was three, I was sexually abused by a fourteen-year-old neighbor boy. I would tell you it seems really bizarre to me to use the word "boy," because the only memory I have of this person is as a three-year-old. And as a three-year-old, he seemed like a really big man.

I was told by him and some other neighborhood kids, which also included his sisters, that we would be playing a secret game. They told me that it was safe and that they had played it before and that I had nothing to be afraid of. What this game consisted of was each child going into a tool shed with this guy. When my turn came, I didn't want to go in because I was scared. It was dark in there and it was dirty. There were cobwebs and there was this giant pitchfork.

One of the kids pushed me inside and shut the door. Then this boy grabbed me and he pulled down my shorts and sexually abused me. In short, he finger-fucked me and he made me masturbate him. I was really terrified. I thought I was in hell, and I was also in a lot of pain. I started crying really hard and he finally let me go, but I was told that if I told anyone, I wouldn't be believed, that it was all my fault and that I would be punished. He also told me that he would hurt me again if I told anyone.

His sister told me that this game he had learned from his dirty books. I knew that he had these dirty books because I had seen him with them.

The second incident I want to talk about occurred eight years ago, and I want you to know that for the past several weeks I have been living in hell because for the first time I am remembering this. And, for me, this memory is my first experience with it.

About eight years ago, I went to a friend of mine's house for dinner. She was living with what I call her pimp friend, most people would call him her boyfriend. Some male friends of hers—of theirs—came by, and she went out to the store to get something that they had forgotten for dinner. While she was gone, someone poured me some wine, and after she came back I drank it. She came back, I started feeling really dizzy and disconnected, and I wanted to go home. They kept telling me to stay, that I could sleep there. Everyone was laughing at me. I found out later that I had been drugged.

What I remember is this. I am on the couch and everyone is looking at me, laughing. They are talking about—they started talking about taking pictures of me. I am not sure they took pictures. I passed out. I do remember flashing lights and what I do know is that they made and they sold pornography.

What I remember next is being on the stage of this club where my friend strips. I want you to know that I use this term "friend" not with a whole lot of sincerity. I knew it was this club where she stripped because I had been there before. I had tried previously to understand and to accept what it was she was doing, and so I had gone there with her and her parents.

I remember being on the stage, and there were two men that were holding me up and they were taking off my clothes. A third man was sexually fondling me. I saw a lot of faces in the audience that were laughing and men were waving money. One of them shoved it in my stomach and essentially punched me. I kept wondering how it was possible that they couldn't see that I didn't want to be there, that I wasn't there willingly. I am not sure what else happened. I have real bad feelings about what may have happened. Somehow, I don't know how, I got to a pay phone and I called this friend of mine who came and took me home.

You are probably wondering, have I told anyone about this. As to the incident with my friend, no, I didn't report it to the police. How do you report something you don't remember? Even when you remember, if you are a woman, even if you do remember, you are not believed. Even if you have bruises, you are bleeding, or whatever. I didn't remember anything, and what could I have reported?

And I didn't tell anyone about the sexual abuse when I was three because I was terrified and I was real ashamed. And also because I didn't have any words to describe it. I didn't tell anyone about that for 24 years. I confronted my friend about the incident, and she told me that it was all my imagination. I told her I didn't have an imagination and I was trying to find one. She laughed. I asked her why I had been found naked, passed out by the phone, if it wasn't true and she told me that was a joke.

Like I said before, I don't know if any of those men fucked me. I do know that that boy fucked me. I know that, in both instances, I was violated, and I am not alone in these experiences. There are thousands of women and girls who are forced and coerced into accommodating men's degrading sexual pleasures.

Now you tell me that pornography doesn't hurt women, doesn't violate us, does not use and abuse us, does not instigate and inspire the abuse of women. And when I say women, I include children, in particular girls. I don't understand how anyone can believe it is harmless. I don't understand how anyone can call this fantasy, a deflection of aggression against women. I don't understand how anyone can say that this is speech when actual live women are being brutalized.

On the other hand, I can understand it because it is men who are saying this. It is the pornographers who create it, who get the money from it, who get erections from it, and society shuns this. I want to stop this for me, for all women and for all girls. There are men here, and we have heard from some of them, who say that pornography has to exist because they have a right to it, its pleasure, its so-called political message. I disagree and I want you to consider this when you make your decision about these amendments. At what cost does this have to exist? Surely not at all costs, surely not at the cost of any woman or girl's life and integrity.

I am going to urge you for once to look at pornography for what it really is, a violation of women's civil rights, and I want you to take action to stop it.

CHAIRMAN WHITE: Thank you, Ms. M.

MS. C.: My name is [N. C.] and I live in Ward 14. I would really like to thank [E.] for saying what she said.

I am also afraid to be here and afraid not to be here. What brought me here is that I know a lot of women who have stories to tell about how pornography has hurt them and how they are trying to recover from the destruction it has brought into their lives, and that can't be here because they are still working through a lot of that pain. This for me is also a way of purging my own shame about this. I would also like to preface what I am going to say by saying that in my testimony here, I say fuck three times because I believe in calling something what it is.

I was twenty-one years old at the time. It was 1980 in March or April. I did have a sexual relationship with this man for about a year. He had gone to a stag party. This particular evening I was home alone in my apartment. He called me on the telephone and he said that he had seen several short pornographic films and that he felt very horny. Although he did make some general comments about the content of these films, I do not remember what they were at this time specifically. So he asked if he could come over specifically to have sex with me. I said yes, because at that time I felt obligated as a girlfriend to satisfy him. I also felt that the refusal would be indicative of sexual quote unquote hang-ups on my part and that I was not quote unquote liberal enough.

When he arrived, he informed me that the other men at the party were envious that he had a girlfriend to fuck. They wanted to fuck too after watching the pornography. He informed me of this as he was taking his coat off. He then took off the rest of his clothes and had me perform fellatio on him. I did not do this of my own volition. He put his genitals in my face and he said, "Take it all." Then he fucked me on the couch in the living room. All this took about five minutes. And when he was finished he dressed and went back to the party. I felt ashamed and numb, and I also felt very used.

This encounter differed from others previous. It was much quicker, it was somewhat rougher, and he was not aware of me as a person. There was no foreplay. It is my opinion that his viewing of the pornography served as foreplay for him.

There were no lasting detrimental effects on me from this experience alone. It was simply an intensification of the ordinary treatment I received from him. It [was ordinary]—something I feel worth noting—and this usual treatment did result in feelings of low self-esteem, depression, confusion and a lot of shame.

I do not have any knowledge of him purchasing any pornography at any time in the relationship. I know that the friends he got together with twice a week, they had it in their homes. He was exposed to it regularly.

I feel what I have to say here is important because I feel what he did, he went to this party, saw pornography, got an erection, got me to inflict his erection on. There is a direct causal relationship there. Thank you very much.

MR. C.: My name is G. C. I live in the 9th Ward. I strongly support the proposed ordinance on pornography. I am going to tell you how pornography affected my life. Obscene is not the word for pornography. Pornography is dangerous. I was battered by my first lover, and the pornography each of us used condoned the violence.

When I was younger, I was exposed to heterosexual pornography, including *Playboy, Penthouse, Oui,* and other magazines. It was one of the places that I learned about sex, and it showed me that sex was violence. What I saw there was a specific relationship between men and women. The woman was to be used, objectified, humiliated, and hurt. The man was in a superior position, a position to be violent. In pornography I learned that what it meant to be sexual with a man or to be loved by a man was to accept his violence. When my lover was violent, I was taught that the violence was normal. I accepted the violence, which I did not like, and it was some time before I left the relationship.

My ex-lover used pornography. One of his first contacts with other men were in gay pornography theaters. He used pornographic magazines before I met him. He started wanting to look at pornography together. I believe that the pornography influenced his behavior. As our relationship progressed, it became violent. He threatened me with a knife, forced sex on me, and battered me on different occasions. The heterosexual pornography that I had been exposed to was one thing that convinced me that this kind of treatment was normal. The battering was one of the most profoundly destructive experiences of my life. Pornography has showed me that a man's love was violent and to be close to my ex-lover I had to accept his violence.

There is a lot of sexual violence in the gay community, and pornography condones it. I was with my ex-lover after he had been raped by a casual sex partner, and my ex said that rape was just a risk you had to take. I was with a friend after he had been violently raped by his boyfriend, and his boyfriend did not understand that violence and force was not supposed to be a part of sex. The objectification and the violent themes in pornography promote and increase these kinds of violence.

I understand pornography to be a force in creating violence in the gay community. I was battered by my ex-lover who used pornography. The pornography, straight and gay, I had been exposed to, helped convince me that I had to accept his violence, and helped keep me in that destructive relationship.

Pornography is harmful and I want something to be done. The proposed ordinance provides concrete measures for action.

R. M. M.: My name is R. M. M. I live in St. Paul. I am here today to share with you some of the ways in which the presence of pornography is directly related to physical, sexual, and psychological abuse in my life.

My first introduction, before I began in the game of art or more directly under the guise of art, my earlier recollection is of my boyfriend and he was an art student. We were sitting together, I seventeen, he nineteen. He showed me art books and also books, magazines of pornography. And as he was showing me these works, he was doing critique of women's bodies, of their facial expression, of parts of their bodies and of their dress. Following this was a critique of my too athletic, too muscular body. I was seventeen. It was very devastating to me that my body was being torn apart in this way.

Within a year, my boyfriend had a photography assignment, and he came home from school and asked me if I would help him with his assignment. When I asked him what it was, he said it was a photography assignment where he had to photograph a series of pictures in which he had to use a woman. He said the woman had to be naked and said he thought that I would want to help him do this. When I objected to doing this, he told me, he came up with the reply, "You don't want me to see another woman naked, do you? You never know what could happen, and I really thought you would want to help me." He said he had the perfect site, it would only take a few minutes.

The next—I was home from school with the German measles at the time—the next day he picked me up. We went to the perfect site. It was an abandoned bus in an overgrown field. When we got there he asked me, he told me, to take off my clothes and to pose in various positions, either draped over the corroded, rusty seats or in positions where I acted as if I was running towards the door. And then he asked me to put my body in contorted different positions, draped down the stairs of the bus, and they were quite jagged, and at that moment I realized that we were depicting a murder. I became very terrified and scared and I was really cold. I told him I didn't want to do this and that I wanted to go home and that I was really scared.

While we were doing this, I would like to backtrack for a minute. I wasn't achieving the right facial expressions for the pictures. So he started telling me stories that depicted pursuits during rape so that I would have the right expressions on my face like the women in the magazines. I remember being very distant from him and just wanting to get home. I remember being very scared.

When he had his next assignment, this was about a year later, and it was casting bodies in plaster. At the time, I told him that I would prefer if he hired models to do this. On one occasion, I flew out to see him at college and he said that there were several positions that he couldn't get the models, that he was paying to model, in, either because the plaster was too heavy or because the women would start fainting. When you put plaster on your body, it sets up, it draws the blood to the skin and the more area it covers on your body, the more blood is drawn to your skin. You become dizzy and nauseous and sick to your stomach and finally faint. I tried to explain this to him because I was a pre-med student at the time, and he said if you would just try to help me with these, he said, you know, my work is being shown in the current art shows and it would be a good [exhibit] and I would like if you could help me create these artistic pieces.

So I told him that I would try. The first few attempts, I failed. He was very disappointed. I failed under the weight and under the heat of the plaster. He wanted me to be in poses where I had to hold my hands up over my head and they would be numb and they would fall. He eventually tied my hands over my head. Finally he succeeded. He ended up getting a plaster cast of my body.

MacKINNON: Do you recall if you did faint at that point or not?

R. M. M.: I remember I was fainting as he was pulling the cast off my body. And he said, it is not quite set yet, hold on, see if you can hold onto it for a little longer. At that point I think I had been holding the pose for about 40 minutes. After this he switched to watercolors.

At the time, when I was twenty-one, I graduated from college. I was thinking about going to medical school, and I wasn't receiving a lot of support at that time for that decision. Women weren't supposed to do that, was the message I was getting.

At that time, I married this man, and for the next two years we mainly pursued our careers. During the second year of our marriage, he started reading more and more pornography. He started out reading *Playboy* and started picking up magazines like *Penthouse* and *Forum,* and as I would come home [for] dinner—come home from work and fix dinner— he would read excerpts from the magazines. Some of them were articles and some of them were letters to the editor ranging from group sex, wife swapping, anal intercourse, and bondage, to mention a few. I was really repulsed at the things he was reading me and I was really in disbelief. I kept saying, people are just making these things up for this magazine, I don't believe it. He bought more and more magazines to prove to me that people weren't making it up, that all of these people were saying how wonderful these things were.

About this time, when we went out we started meeting his friends at wet T-shirt contests, amateur strip nights or elsewhere—we would meet together as a group—or pornographic adult theaters or live sex shows. Initially I started arguing that the women on stage looked very devastated, like they were disgusted and hated it. I felt devastated and disgusted watching it. I was told by those men, if I wasn't as smart as I was, and if I would be more sexually liberated and more sexy, that I would get along a lot better in the world, and that they and a lot of other men would like me more.

About this time, I started feeling very terrified. I realized that this wasn't a joke any more: that this was something that he was really serious about. I called my mother and I told her that there were things happening in my marriage around sex that I really didn't like, and she told me that divorce was something that she didn't want in our family, and it was very disgraceful, and she knew how competent I was and she said, I know you can hang in there and give it your best.

About this time, to kind of numb myself, I remember that there was a lot more drinking with my husband and I and with our friends. When people would come over to dinner, there was a lot of alcohol consumed, he would bring out a drinking and stripping game. After the game began, he started to ask the people to live out the various different scenarios that he had been reading to me in the magazines. A few times, the people participated in this. A couple times I stayed. Once I left.

Following this, we would have incredible arguments with each other. I would tell him I loved him, I only wanted to love him, I wanted to be a good wife, I wanted our marriage to work, but I didn't want to be with these other people. It was he I wanted to be with, and no one else. He told me if I loved him I would do this. And that, as I could see from the things that he read me in the magazines initially, a lot of times women didn't like it, but if I tried it enough I would probably like it, and I would learn to like it. And he would read me stories where women learned to like it.

During this time once when I was asleep at night and a friend of his was over, he asked the friend—he set up with a friend to come into our room and sleep with us. I woke up finding this friend in bed with us. Once he realized that I was not a willing participant in this experience, he apologized to me and said he was sorry and he left.

To prevent more of these group situations, which I found very humiliating and very destructive to my self-esteem and my feeling of self-worth as a person, to prevent these I agreed with him to act out in privacy a lot of those scenarios that he read to me, a lot of them depicting bondage and different sexual acts that I found very humiliating.

About this time when things were getting really terrible and I was feeling very suicidal and very worthless as a person, at that time any dreams that I had of a career in medicine were just totally washed away. I could not think of myself any more as a human being.

Because of his job, we were transferred overseas. When we got to overseas, the pornography that he was reading and that his friends were reading was much more violent than the pornography that he had been reading to me at home. He started taking me to sex shows where there were women and animals, especially snakes. He started taking me to sex shows where the women were called "banana lady shows." We went to sex shows where men were participating in the sex acts with women on the stage.

About this time, he started having to go away a lot and I was left alone. I started studying karate over there, and I also started feeling again like I had some kind of control over my body. And I started really feeling in touch with the fact that I was a person. I started traveling. I did a lot of traveling by myself and I started feeling more and more courageous. I went to the Philippines on one of my last visits overseas and I was there for three weeks. During the time that I was there I was staying mainly at a Navy base. Outside of that Navy base the prostitution was very visible and very explicit. Everywhere you went there were men hiring prostitutes. Those were the only women that I saw there. I was one of the few American women.

One night when I was in one of the pornographic institutions, I was sitting with a couple of people that I had known, watching the women on stage and watching the different transactions and the sales of the women and the different acts go on, and I realized that my life wasn't any different than these women except that it was done in the name of marriage. I could see how I was being seasoned to the use of pornography and I could see what was coming next. I could see more violence, and I could see more humiliation, and I knew at that point I was either going to die from it, I was going to kill myself, or I was going to leave. And I was feeling strong enough that I left.

I spent the next few years of my life, through the help of therapy, education and friends, healing myself. I would like to forget that the woman's story is me, but I know those memories and those scars will remain. Pornography is not a fantasy. It was my life, reality. It involved abuse to my body to create it.

If what I said today can help prevent one woman from experiencing what I experienced, the pain that I was involved in, it is worth it. Thank you.

DWORKIN: I would like to ask you just a couple of questions. How old were you when you left [the] marriage?

R. M. M.: I was 25 when I left, and my divorce papers came through when I was 26.

DWORKIN: How old are you now?

R. M. M.: I am 29.

DWORKIN: I just want to ask you about when you were married and when you were still in the States. Did your husband talk to you about making films and making the kinds of things that he was seeing with you as a participant?

R. M. M.: Yes, he did. Both when we would go to the amateur nights, he would try to get me up on stage and I refused to do that, and then when he would read through the magazines, one of the things that became a theme for a while in the magazines were husbands trafficking their wives, having sex with a friend or some man. And there would be—I remember various stories, one was about a woman in a cabin and it was all staged— how the man would be hiding, how the husband would be hiding to photograph his wife, and he tried to get me to do that several times.

DWORKIN: During the period of time, were you actually raped in your marriage?

R. M. M.: Yes, I was. I actually refer to my whole marriage as marital rape. But specifically at the time, what I was considering rape was several times, especially following the incidents where he asked our friends to come to bed with us after I was already asleep, following that time he felt that it was his privilege to, when I was sleeping, if he felt at all sexually turned on or in the need to be gratified, to rape me in my sleep. Most of the times I would wake up. Sometimes I would just keep my eyes closed and try to tolerate it.

DWORKIN: So this could happen to you any time when you were sleeping?

R. M. M.: Yes, it could happen to me any time when I was asleep. And several times when I confronted him on this he said if I refused to have him do this, then he had to masturbate. And as I know from his religious background, that was a sin.

DWORKIN: When you were actually living in the Orient, you said that the porn[ography] was very much more violent. Could you describe to us what was actually in it [that was different from] what you had seen before?

R. M. M.: Okay. The pornography had mostly Oriental women in it and black women in it and it depicted women as animals and had women having sex with animals in it. It was women in cages. There were a lot of whips. I guess some of them is what they call S and M pornography. Women were led around with collars. They showed women being penetrated anally. They showed more gang rapes. It was more abusive in that the women were not portrayed as these glamorous perfect women, what I had seen before. They were portrayed more as slaves.

MacKINNON: Could you describe in a couple of words what you see to be the relationship between the pornography and the things that your husband asked you to do?

R. M. M.: He would read from the pornography like a textbook, like a journal. In fact, when he asked me to be bound, when he finally convinced me to do it, he read in the magazine how to tie the knots, and how to bind me in a way that I couldn't get out. And most of the scenes that we—most of the scenes where I had to dress up or go through different fantasies—were the exact scenes that he had read in the magazines.

MacKINNON: Did your husband remarry?

R. M. M.: He remarried within the year that we got divorced to a woman that was almost ten years younger than he was. And at the time I had seen him to finalize things on our divorce and get some of my last possessions, he showed me pictures of her and said, "Do you want to see what she looks like?" They were pictures of her naked and in pornographic poses.

MacKINNON: Thank you.

DWORKIN: Thank you.

CHAIRMAN WHITE: Thank you.

T. S.: My name is T. S. I live in the 7th Ward. Before I start, I just want to say what is happening right now is very incredible to me, and I know it is very hard for everyone in this room to be here and to be listening to these horror stories. And I hope that people stay with their full concentration for the rest of the evening.

I am speaking for a group of women. We all live in Minneapolis and we all are former prostitutes. All of us feel very strongly about the relationship between pornography and prostitution. Many of us wanted to testify at this hearing but are unable because of the consequences of being identified as a former whore. This is absolutely incredible to me that prostitution is seen as a victimless activity, and that many women are rightly terrified of breaking their silence, fearing harassment to themselves and families and loss of their jobs.

We have started to meet together to make sense of the abuse we have experienced in prostitution and how pornography endorses and legitimizes that abuse. These are some of our stories. The following has all happened to real women who are the exception because they have survived both pornography and prostitution. We are all living in Minneapolis and all of these events happened in Minneapolis. And as we sit here, this abuse is happening right now in the city tonight.

One of the very first commonalities we discovered as a group: we were all introduced to prostitution through pornography. There were no exceptions in our group, and we were all under eighteen.

Pornography was our textbook. We learned the tricks of the trade by men exposing us to pornography and us trying to mimic what we saw. I could not stress enough what a huge influence we feel this was. Somehow it was okay. These pictures were real men and women who appeared to be happy consenting adults, engaged in human sexuality.

Before I go on—one might make the assumption that if a woman got involved with pornography and prostitution after she was eighteen, that she is a willing participant. And since the women I speak for were all underage when they began, it is easier to see them as victims. Personally, I feel this to be very dangerous. By talking to women who got involved with prostitution and pornography in their early twenties, the powerlessness and victimization they described and experienced is the same that younger women and children feel.

Here are specific stories we have shared about how pornography encouraged and taught us and how it was used to brutalize and terrorize us as women.

One of us had the experience of being paid by a client to go to a house located in the 6th Ward. When she got there, she found a group of physically disabled men and a group of physically abled men. Everyone was watching pornographic films—movies of men fucking women, women doing oral sex on men, and women being penetrated by animals. The movies were played continuously.

The able-bodied men were joking and making comments like, "That's how real men do it," instructing the handicapped men, teasing them that if they watched enough of these movies they would be able to perform normally. There were constant remarks made about what normal male sexual experience was. Then the disabled men were undressed by the abled men and the woman was forced to engage sexually with the disabled men. There were two weapons in the room. The woman refused and she was forced, held down by the physically abled men. Everyone watched and the movies kept going. There were various physical deformities, amputees, paraplegics. Some were able to perform. Some weren't.

After this, the able-bodied men said they were going to show the handicapped men how "real men" do it. They forced the woman to enact simultaneously with the movie. In the movie at this point a group of men were urinating on a naked woman. All the men in the room were able to perform this task, so they all started urinating on the woman who was now naked. Then the able-bodied men had sex with the woman while the disabled men watched.

Another story is, a woman met a man in a hotel room in the 5th Ward. When she got there she was tied up while sitting on a chair nude. She was gagged and left alone in the dark for what she believed to be an hour. The man returned with two other men. They burned her with cigarettes and attached nipple clips to her breasts. They had many S and M magazines with them and showed her many pictures of women appearing to consent, enjoy, and encourage this abuse. She was held for twelve hours, continuously raped and beaten. She was paid $50 or about $2.33 per hour.

Men would constantly want to do what they have seen in pornography. If pornography was not actually in the room with the client, there would be constant reference. One example is that a woman was in a room with two clients, one man told the other that he had seen some pictures of women who had shaved their pubic hair and that it had turned him on. They then proceeded with a jackknife to remove the woman's pubic hairs, plucking and burning what the knife missed. They made comments of how her hairless vagina reminded them of their young daughters' genitals. They then, of course, engaged in intercourse.

Women were forced constantly to enact specific scenes that men had witnessed in pornography. They would direct women to copy postures and poses of things they had seen in magazines and then they would take their own pictures of the women.

One man paid a woman in the 6th Ward $35 to recruit another woman so he could direct them in a lesbian scenario he had seen in a movie. She was supposed to recruit the other woman for him. When *Deep Throat* was released, we experienced men joking and demanding oral sex.

It is very amazing to me what happens when a group of ex-prostitutes get together in one room and tell stories. One of the things we discovered was that the men we had serviced were very powerful men in this community. Especially interesting to us are the amounts of men involved in the media in this community that use prostitutes and pornography. These are the same men that perpetuate the myth that Minneapolis is a clean city with exceptional morals and a high quality of life.

In closing, I would like to say that, in my experience, there was not one situation where a client was *not* using pornography while he was using me, or that he had not just watched pornography, or that it was[n't] verbally referred to, and directed me to pornography.

I know that this is a very complicated issue. I am asking you to recognize the pure simplicity of it. Men witness the abuse of women in pornography constantly, and if they can't engage in that behavior with their wives, girlfriends, or children, they force a whore to do it. My wish is that you could see with my eyes just for a day how clear the relationship is between pornography and the systematic abuse of women.

I would also like to say that I'm petrified and scared for young women today. I believe the pornography that is published today is more brutal and dangerous than when I was involved. And because I understand clearly the direct relationship between the material and the abuse of women, I am very terrified of the consequences of what that means. I worry about how this will affect your daughters, who I know will be victims in one way or another to this pornography. I also worry about the prostitutes on the street who are currently being used by the porno-graphic industry. I know that we are helping them tonight by speaking out and voicing our outrage and by saying that as adults who believe in human rights and human intimacy, that pornography is absolutely not acceptable to us.

The other thing I just need to stress is that every single thing you see in pornography is happening to a real woman right now. There is no way out of that connection, and that we are all responsible for knowing and having that information.

I also have a couple written testimonies of women who were not able to speak tonight for the reasons I already gave.

This is a story of a woman who works at the University of Minnesota and could not speak for herself. She was involved in prostitution between 1970 and 1974.

I remember a house on Second Avenue South, near 22nd Street which I was asked to go to by a trick. He told me that I would be able to make a lot of money there. It turned out to be the same house that my pimp had been urging me to go to where he told me young pretty girls could go and get tied up, beaten and burned with cigarettes, and earn $500 for a short half hour's work. I had steadily refused to go, but when my pimp found out that I had been invited, so to speak, I had to go there.

The woman who ran the place actually lived there with her children. She kept a room upstairs for the tricks to use. It had a projector to show porn films and there was stacks of pornographic material in the room. The tricks would go in there, look at the porn to get psyched up and then the girl would be sent into the room. The youngest girl I know about who went there was only 13.

When I went into that room, the trick said that I was almost too old, but he was pleased with me because I looked young. He stripped me, tied me up, spread-eagled, on the bed so that I could not move and then began to caress me very gently. Then, when he thought that I was relaxed, he squeezed my nipple really hard. I did not react. He held up a porn magazine with a picture of a beaten woman and said, "I want you to look like that. I want you to hurt." He then began beating me, and when I didn't cry fast enough, he lit a cigarette and held it right above my breast for a long time before he burned me. I told him that as God was my witness, he had better kill me or untie me right now, because if he didn't, I would turn him in to the police and that I would call his wife and tell his family about him. He believed me and let me go. But I know that this house continued to provide that service for those who could pay.

When I worked at massage studios, the owners had subscriptions to *Playboy, Penthouse, Penthouse Forum* and the like. These magazines were arranged in the waiting area of most of the massage places which I worked in. If a girl was not inside with a trick, she was expected to sit out front with the men who were waiting or who were undecided and to look at the magazines with them in order to get them titillated. The men would ask me questions like, "Do you really like it when more than one man fucks you?" "Do you really like to suck men off, like this hot little number who wrote the letter to the Forum?" et cetera. They used the soft porn to help them work up the courage to try the acts described in the magazine with the prostitutes at the massage studio. At one point, I was on the company payrolls of a couple well-known businesses in Minneapolis. One of these companies, an insurance firm, kept an apartment in Edina which was used as a place to entertain big clients when they came to town. The place was very expensively furnished, had parquet oak floors, a well-stocked bar, and in the closets, stacks of pornographic films and magazines and pictures, as well as lingerie for the women to wear. When I was there, what usually happened was that the man in Minneapolis who was in charge of "entertainment" would invite some local associates who wanted to have a good time along with any visiting big shots who needed or wanted to be entertained by the apartment. The men would usually get there first, and start drinking and watching porn movies. Then three or four women, always a lesser number than the number of men present, would arrive. They would ask us to get into the lingerie and maybe show another film or bring out pictures. And then the intercourse would start, all in one room, so that some men were watching. This was all straight sex and the men were never coercive, but I got paid extra money if I could find prostitutes who were willing to have anal sex or who were willing to perform oral sex on another woman in front of the men. These slightly deviant acts were depicted in the films and photos in that apartment. Although I don't know one way or the other, I have no reason not to believe that this apartment still exists today.

This is another story of a woman who is currently working downtown in Minneapolis.

I was the main woman of a pimp who filmed sexual acts almost every night in our home. The dope man, who supplied us with cocaine for free in exchange for these arranged orgies, was a really freaky man who would do anything. They arranged to have women, who I assumed were forced to be there, have sex with dogs and filmed those acts. There were stacks of films all over the house, which my pimp used to blackmail people with.

One morning I came downstairs in time to see a very young girl run naked out of the house. I found her friend, also naked, tied up in the closet. The one who ran away, after being forced to perform sexually all night, went to the police. I don't know what my pimp did with the other girl. I do know that he kidnapped them and felt safe, because they were foreign and alone. The girl came back with the police, but nothing ever happened. My pimp continued to make films of people doing every kind of sex act in the living room of our home. He was never involved in the acts; he got off on watching.

The other thing, very briefly, that I need to address tonight, and some other women have addressed it, is the specific abuse of women of color in our community, specifically black women and the Native American women living here. There is a Native woman, Carole laFavor, who will testify tomorrow night, who six months ago was brutally raped and beaten. And the men that attacked and raped her were making continuous comments about Custer's Last Stand, which is a video thing about these men chasing a "squaw" and they do things to her. They said, "this is better than Custer's Last Stand," "let's try the chase scene in Custer's Last Stand."

I want people to know that there is pornography dealing with color, and that is happening in our community right now. That is all I have, unless there is questions.

DWORKIN: Ms. S., may I ask you a question? You talked about how all of the women that you were meeting with and talking with were introduced into prostitution somehow with pornography.

T. S.: Yes.

DWORKIN: Could you describe that a little more and talk about the relationship between the pornography shown and pictures actually taken of the young women that it was being shown to?

T. S.: How it was introduced was that young women would be picked up on the street, off the street, and everyone's first experience was always the same, which was that the man would show either magazines or take you to a movie and then afterwards instruct her to act in the way that the magazines or the films had depicted. Usually after, I call it a training period, what would happen then is that these men or different men would set up scenarios of usually more than one woman to very, very specifically copy and reproduce scenes that were portrayed in magazines and books that they had witnessed. And then they would make their own movies using home video equipment and also Polaroid cameras and they would all collect their own library of pornography involving these women.

DWORKIN: Thank you.

MacKINNON: Thank you.

COUNCILWOMAN BARBARA CARLSON: I have a question of Mrs. [*sic*] MacKinnon and some of the people that have talked, and I would like to preface my question by thanking the people that have shared their stories tonight. I know it was extremely painful for them, for me, for the women to share their stories.

The statement is I have gone through somewhat the catharsis that the women have gone through in my bout with alcoholism. I have shared many of the same things in the first step, in group treatment, and I have heard some references to drinking and use of alcohol and I am presuming the use of drugs in some of these stories.

And my question of you—and I am not going to be able to stay for the rest of the testimony, I have a meeting—but my question to you and the women and men that shared their stories is, how much alcoholism or alcohol and drugs are relevant in the stories?

DWORKIN: Thank you for the question. It is a very, very good one. The answer is that the abuse of drugs and alcohol is absolutely systematically present through almost all of these stories. And that there is a cynical and purposeful use of both drugs and alcohol by pimps on women, both to produce the material, that is the pornography, and to keep women in prostitution.

CARLSON: My question to you though is one of, could it be the use of chemicals, drugs, or alcohol that has caused some of these problems, rather than pornography?

T. S.: What I know about that is, there is a group of Christian men who actually use pornography and prostitutes in this town, and they are totally against the use of alcohol, and they manage to do just fine.

DZIEDZIC: I will announce that the next speaker will be J. B., followed by Shannon McCarthy Bicha.

MacKINNON: What I would like to also say, Councilmember Carlson, is that while the use of drugs and of alcohol are part of the systematic pattern of abuse, it isn't the same thing to say that those things cause that abuse. In other words, we are making the argument that pornography motivates it, inspires it, leads people to believe that it is justified, that it makes it profitable, and that it also—it basically defines it as something that is okay to do. Once it is defined as something that is okay to do, it is okay to abuse these women in these ways, then anything that is abusive to women becomes okay to do, and drugs and alcohol are those things. Do you see what I am saying?

CARLSON: What I am hearing you say is that the pornography is the beginning?

DWORKIN: All of the stories that you have heard are representative of a thousand more stories and some of them involve direct drugging. And we are not talking about people, about women who are choosing to drink, although in some cases, for instance the testimony of R. M., drinking was a part of her lifestyle, and it was a part of being able to endure the abuse. I think it is important to understand the different situations in which drinking and drugs are used. But the constant in all of the situations is the pornography.

MacKINNON: Also, the men are not doing what they are doing to the women because of alcohol and drugs. The data that we had earlier on today showed a direct causal relationship between pornography and aggression towards women.

E. M.: My name is E. M. I talked earlier. What I want to say to you is that what I am hearing is a tendency, and I find that real dangerous, to say that these people were drinking or were on drugs, and so therefore, we attribute it to that. And that really frightens me because in my situation, I was in a normal social situation. I had gone to dinner. No one was drinking. I was on my second glass of wine as were the other people. Some of them were only on their first. What I know is that this was something that was planned and there is no way that any of—that I can attribute any of what happened to me to my being drunk, or any of these men being drunk, because they weren't.

MS. B.: I am J. B. I live in St. Paul right now. I used to be a resident of Minneapolis. I am simply going to relate what happened to me about four years ago on the job. I, for the past six years, have been in training to be a plumber. And about four years ago I got stuck on a job that was almost completed but not quite. I don't know if you understand construction set-ups, but generally in the winter, certain trades will get together and have a little shack inside of a building where they will eat lunch and have coffee and everything else.

When I got on the job, three of the trades had set up a nice little shack and had lunch there. And it was a real shock when I walked in, because three of the four walls in the room were completely decorated with pictures out of various magazines, *Hustler, Playboy, Penthouse, Oui,* all of those. Some of them I would have considered regular pinups, but some of them were very, very explicit, showing women with their legs spread wide and men and women performing sex acts and women in bondage. It was very uncomfortable for me to go down there and have dinner and lunch with about twenty men, and here is me facing all these pictures and hearing all these men talking about all the wonderful things they did on the weekend with all of these women.

I put up with it for about a week, and it finally got to the point where I could no longer tolerate sitting there and realizing that all of these men were there. I felt totally naked in front of these men. The only thing they talked about during lunch period was women—their old ladies, their girlfriends, and all their conquests of the weekend.

I got to the point where I couldn't put up with it any more. And being one of the only two women on the job, and being rather new at it and not knowing that I had any alternatives, I got pissed off one day and ripped all the pictures off the wall. Well, it turned out to be a real unpopular move to do. I came back in at lunch time and half the pictures were back up again. They pulled them out of boxes and stuck them on the wall and proceeded to call me names, and just basically call me names or otherwise ignore me.

MacKINNON: Do you recall what names they called you?

MS. B.: There was one electrician that had it in for me. He always said, "Hey, bitch" or some other term that didn't really sit with me too well. It was very, very hostile.

So after lunch, I went back in and took them all down again, and I came back the next morning and some of them were back up again. At that point I decided that I no longer wanted to eat with these men, and I began to eat my lunch at other places in the building and was totally boycotted at work. The men wouldn't talk to me. I mean I was treated like I had just done something terrible.

Just by happenstance on that weekend, I was at a meeting and was relating my story to some women, and one of them happened to be a woman who worked for the Affirmative Rights Office in Minneapolis. She said we can help you out. It was an affirmative action job. It was getting federal funds. And she organized three other women and herself to make an unannounced inspection and they did that. And I said, I don't want them to know that I had anything to do with this because I am scared. And they came and took note of all the pictures that were up—I hadn't tampered with them any more. They were all on the walls. They wrote letters to each of the companies involved.

And during this time, at some point when I was at work, this one electrician was extremely angry at me. I have no proof that this man did this, but I came out of work one day, my car door was bashed in. It wasn't parked anywhere near where any other car would have hit it. It was bashed in in a place that wasn't logical to be hit by another car. I have no proof that this man did it, but I had a sneaky suspicion on that. He was removed from the job, subsequently.

After the LEAP offices and state had written letters to send out to these various employers, my boss, the man who owned the company, called me up one day and said, "Look, I heard you are having a little trouble down there. Why don't you just kind of calm down a little bit? Don't make such a mess. We don't need any trouble down there. Just calm down, just ignore it." I said, "Hey, I can't ignore it. I don't have to, I can't, it is already done." A couple days later they got the letter and they were told that this did not comply with the action guidelines. In the meantime, I had asked for a transfer and my transfer came through, which was very fortunate but—

MacKINNON: What part in your transfer did this pornography play?

MS. B.: It came a lot faster, is what happened. They decided I was making too much trouble and had to get me out of there.

MacKINNON: Was it where you wanted to transfer to?

MS. B.: No. I had requested that much earlier and had been waiting on it. But it was really uncomfortable. I felt no support from the men, none of the men at all. In fact, I approached my boss one time and said, "I don't like these things," and he said, "I can't do anything about it. These men do what they want to do." And I said, "Piss on it, I will do what I want to do."

It would have been nice if I would have known that there was some action I could have taken, knowing I didn't want those pictures there, or not knowing that I could have taken them down, shots of women's genitals.

MacKINNON: Do you have any idea, just to enlighten it for all of us, what their stake in it was, why they kept putting it up over and over?

MS. B.: I, for a long time and, you know, this might not be right, but this has been my sense. I mean, I have encountered pretty much hostility in the last six years being the only woman on the job doing men's work. On that particular job, I was a legal threat because I had replaced one of the other men who was causing trouble, who was one of the good old boys. And I think they were doubly angry at me on that job and they wanted to get rid of me.

CHAIRMAN WHITE: I think we will now take a short recess, be back in 10 minutes.

(Short recess.)

CHAIRMAN WHITE: We will resume the public hearing. There is a time certain at 9:00 o'clock. If there are people who have added their names since the last time, I don't know who came up and got this, but they have added their names. So I would like the people to utilize the three minutes, because the other persons that testified gave stories of their lives that were rather horrendous, and we gave them a little more than the time that should have been allotted. But we are after 8:00 o'clock now, so we will move right along.

We have Shannon McCarthy Bicha. Did I say that correctly?

SHANNON McCARTHY BICHA: I won't correct you. I prefer to have it said the way it was. That is fine.

I am a resident of St. Paul, and I have been throughout the majority of my life. What I would like to provide you first is a personal history of where I have been.

I have lived in St. Paul the majority of my life, excluding five years. And during those five years—it was more than five years, it was eight years—during four years of which I went to the University of Minnesota in Duluth, and the remaining four years I lived in Toronto, Ontario in Canada. What I learned during those eight years was very difficult. I was away from St. Paul. I knew my city very well before I went to the University of Minnesota, Duluth. And when I came back from Canada in 1978, I felt I still knew my city, even though I was away from St. Paul.

My husband and me moved close to Dale Street and University, which is located close to quite a lot of pornography places, the Faust Theater, the Flick and the other is called the Belmont Club. I remember when I was a little girl on Sunday we would drive by the Belmont Club. I would say, what is the Belmont Club, and my father would say, it is nothing that would interest you, Shannon. And still being a young girl, I didn't care much if my dad said, you are not concerned.

What happened, I went to the local high school, I went to St. Agnes High School, which is located only four blocks from those three pornography shops. And at that time the Faust Theater and the Flick were not in operation, so the Belmont was still a pretty silent place, and everyone who lived in that neighborhood felt rather protected and secure from being subjected to sexual harassment and violence as a result of pornography.

What happened is that my husband and I moved into the residence in 1981, and at that time I was exposed to sexual harassment that I never knew existed. What I would like to discuss are three of the types of sexual harassments that I had to face within two years. For myself it was disgusting, it was very frightening, and I really don't think that I have any way to work around it, and that's the strongest fear that I have at this point.

I would like to speak on behalf of the other people who live in my residence because we all, to a large degree, feel that we are invisible, silent people. Our neighborhood is very working class, a lot of the people don't have 9:00 to 5:00 jobs. They are working in the afternoon or afternoon shifts. We are the type of people who like to have our voices heard. We don't have political power. We don't have money. We are barely making it day to day. When it comes to having people hear us speak, we don't feel we are heard. The police that are working in our neighborhood are upset with the Faust and the Flick because a man can pay a quarter and go and see a quarter show, and all he has to do is pay two dollars and he can have a female completely nude do all the dancing for him in three minutes.

The police have gone to the Flick and tried to bust it time and time again. Finally the police in our residence have said, forget it, we are giving up, nothing has been done. We are not going in there and taking the chance of having our heads blown off. Us, the people that live in the neighborhood, we have to fear that day in and day out, especially the women.

Just last week, I had an exceptionally horrifying situation when my husband was not home and a man tried to get into my house by both the front and the back door. He wouldn't leave. He continued to knock. He was trying to get the door open. And it was so serious in the sense that the police even tried to get him, but at the same time too, they didn't make the attempt. What this boils down to is that the police have come to the end of the rope with my neighborhood. They feel that they can only do so much and consequently, they are not giving the same protection and same security which they did for other neighborhoods. I empathize with them, there are a number of good people that don't live in our residence but happen to be at the porno shops, and they subject the police to constant harassment. They subject them to the fear of physical abuse and, consequently, the police are in a position where they are stepping back. But the people who are paying the price are myself and my neighbors.

What I said before was that within two years I had been subjected to sexual harassment. It all started in 1981 when I moved—my husband and I moved in. At that time, I was pregnant, and I was walking just to the Country Club Store across the street, but I was in the vicinity of the Belmont Club, the Faust, and the Flick. And a middle-aged man, white, he had on a business suit, was crossing the street, same as myself. Right off he asked me if I was a prostitute. We were crossing University Avenue. I was shocked. I wanted to get away from him as fast as I could, but at the same time I was seven months pregnant and I couldn't run. The best I could do is walk and ignore the man. I came home and I was shaking like a leaf with my husband. He was so disgusted because there was not a damn thing he could do. He has to hope to hell that his wife is going to be able to live a somewhat normal life.

Then it happened again where I was going to Wendy's Hamburger Shop. Instead of asking me if I was a prostitute, he asked me how much I cost. You are just in a position when you think, when is this going to stop? Is it because I live close to these pornography shops that this continues to happen?

The third time that it did happen to me, I am very firmly convinced that it has a very strong significant high correlation with the pornography. The third time it was another work, another businessman, but at this time the man was around the age of 50. Rather than ask me if I was a prostitute or how much I cost, he walked right up to me and said, "You are the dancer from the Belmont, aren't you? I saw you a couple nights ago. You really did a good job." You don't know what to say. I am in that position where I am so thoroughly frightened, I am shaking in my shoes. At the same time, I am so disgusted, I would like to be able to tell him how I feel. I can't do that, especially living so close. My fear is that this man is going to be very disgusted with my comment and he can follow me right home.

I have a daughter who is two years old, and there are many mothers, many parents who live in my neighborhood. The average number of children per block on my block is at least fifteen kids, and those I am referring to are infants all the way through eighteen-year-old children. And we all have to face that constant fear. What is it going to be like when my daughter is old enough that she can walk and go to the stores? How often can I tell her, don't go there, that is a bad place for you to go? All the parents feel that way but at the same time we feel powerless. We don't feel that we have the voice, and we don't feel that people will listen to us because we are working class. It is a very sad situation.

The last thing that happened to me puts me in a position. I have epilepsy. I have a physical disability whereby I am partially conscious during the seizures. As a result of that, I can look very quote unquote normal in the sense that I hear a person to a certain extent, but I can't comprehend what the person is saying to me. I can see things but that doesn't mean I am going to be able to do the correct thing, in the sense of seeing a green light and walking with a green light. I might see the light but go ahead and walk, even if it is yellow or red.

The last time it happened, I was in the bus shelter, it was raining, and I decided I was going to take my chance and sit there rather than being wet and going to work. As a result of that, two men saw me, this is—everything occurred during the daylight, nothing has happened at night, which is more difficult to deal with. In the evening I can't even walk out of my house, with this happening during the day. A man came on one side of the bus shelter and a man on the other side. I was inside. They came into the shelter at the same time and talked to me as if they had known me. I didn't know who the men were. And automatically I have that fear—I was in front of the Belmont Club—that these men are going to interpret me as being a prostitute or a dancer, and it boiled down to them asking me if I was a prostitute. With it happening three times before and one more time, I just got to the point where I was going to try my chance and shock these men as best as I could, and I played as if I was mentally retarded. It was a sad case to go through. They both saw me as being the person I am now.

I totally ignored them. I didn't respond to anything they were saying. They continued talking and finally one of the men said, "Do you happen to know what the time is?" It's just crazy, the only thing I could do was to say, "Well, I really don't have a watch on now but I think it is about 11:00." (Using slurred speech.) It frightened the men. It put goose bumps on me because I think this is what I have to do in my own neighborhood to protect myself. And these men walked away from me. They didn't want any contact with me at all, because I played the role of a woman who was mentally retarded.

It is a sad case when the police have approached my neighbors and myself and they said, "The best recourse you have and your husband have and your children is to get up and move." Why should I have to move from my neighborhood when this is all I can afford? This is the very best type of structure that my husband and I ever are going to gain. At the same time, the police are at the point where they are ready to give up. At the same time, they are explaining to us, "We really empathize for you, but get up and get out, that is your best result, that is your best recourse." And that is why I wanted to come tonight, because I know the concept of pornography is associated with the First Amendment in regards to freedom of speech. In my life nothing compares to the freedom of equality, the freedom of not feeling fear and being sexually harassed, the possibility of being sexually raped, the possibility of sexual abuse in another form of rape. I would give my freedom of speech up in two seconds flat if I knew myself as well as my daughter as well as my husband and all of my neighbors didn't have to face the garbage that results from the Faust, the Flick, and the Belmont Club.

That is why I hope everyone that is here tonight will take a strong look at this. I have invited many people who have supported pornography to come to my neighborhood and live there for a week, and I will walk you all past the Belmont Club, Faust, and Flick. I will give you a tour. You can see what it is like. You can bring your children and bring your wife and anybody else who supports pornography. You move into my neighborhood and I will move into yours. It chokes me up, because you have the power, I don't.

I have worked with cases of women who have been sexually harassed. I have worked with young mothers who are single as a result of rape. They have children physically handicapped because of it. The children are going to have to grow up facing the result that they are a by-product of rape. These young women who were exposed to pornography from day one, they are accustomed with all the pornography magazines. *Hustler* is nothing to them. The *Playboy* is like *Time* and *Newsweek,* they are so adjusted to this psychologically because it's been rammed down their throats. They have had no alternatives.

And all of you have a very strong say in what can happen in Minneapolis as well as St. Paul, and I really hope you do something about it. It has got to stop. There has got to be a time where a woman as well as a father can have the opportunity to say, hey, we live in America. We have the opportunity to be treated just as equal as everyone else, unaware of money, and unaware of status and accreditation. Everyone should be treated equal. I would like to end there. Thank you very much.

CHAIRMAN WHITE: Thank you for coming from our sister city. It just goes to show it is not just on one block or one street.

MacKINNON: I believe that Steve Jevning is going to speak for the neighborhood group.

DZIEDZIC: Chairman White?

CHAIRMAN WHITE: Yes, Councilman Dziedzic?

DZIEDZIC: I was disappointed to hear that the police told someone in the neighborhood to move. That is really a poor indication on whether or not the police can control a situation in a neighborhood. I am sorry to hear that goes on in St. Paul. I think we could put a stop to that kind of rhetoric in Minneapolis.

Whenever you hear that, the way to answer is to tell the police officers that their hands aren't tied, and they have every right to enforce the laws to make that a safer neighborhood. If they don't, their boss should come and see the Council and there should be steps taken. I am not talking about just this issue. When a police officer tells you that, he is saying he can't do his job, is what he is saying.

STEVE JEVNING: Mr. Dziedzic, Mr. Chairman, Members of the Committee, my name is Steve Jevning. I represent the Neighborhood Pornography Task Force. The Task Force is really the most recent organized group of a number of concerned citizens in South Central Minneapolis who have rallied around the issue of fighting pornography for a number of years. The Task Force members are for the most part made up of residents of the Powderhorn Park and several neighborhoods of Central Minneapolis who happen to have a number of adult entertainment establishments within their city-designated boundaries.

I would like to start my comments tonight, and I will indeed keep them brief, by telling all of you that I feel privileged as a white, Anglo-Saxon Protestant male to exercise my First Amendment right to speak in favor of the proposed civil rights amendment that would guarantee Fourteenth Amendment rights for all members of this community, particularly women who are underrepresented at the least, and abused, raped, and killed at the worst. I have spoken before this Council Committee and other committees of the City Council about the need for the City of

Minneapolis to take steps that would indicate not only to the women, the men, and the children of this community how important they are in the eyes of political leaders, community leaders, but also to take a step that would indicate to this society as a whole that in at least one tiny city, village, whatever, there are people, men and women elected to represent their constituents who are committed to support the rights of everyone. To exist day to day in this society with reduced levels of anxiety, fear, so that they too can feel as comfortable and as privileged as I do as a white Anglo-Saxon Protestant male, to do the things that they should all be able to do—to live a peaceful life, to live an important life, and to contribute in ways that make this society a better place to live for this generation, for the people who are here today, for the people who are yet unborn, so that one day people can look back upon the actions that this Council will hopefully take, and say that here was a group of people who identified an overlooked problem, an overlooked ill of society. But they realized the significance of that tiny overlooked problem as being extremely representative of the overriding inequities that exist, continue to exist, and in fact, flourish today.

Pornography is a very graphic representation of the sexual inequalities and the conflicts between power and powerlessness that exist in this city and this state and in this country. And I urge you to put aside some of the questions which you are finding difficult to answer and take a bold step and allow the answers to be formulated by those people who are not as courageous as you have been. Thank you.

CHAIRMAN WHITE: The Chair would like to say this to you, Steve. It does my heart good to hear a younger person talking about the camaraderie amongst people, whether he is white, Anglo-Saxon, Protestant or if he is Afro-American or whatever, but as a human being, because this did exist here in this city, and there are those of you that know that, and people did not lock their doors, women were not afraid to walk the streets, the crime that we have in our communities that transcends all of the things that we talked about here today did not exist here in this city as rapidly as it is today. And hopefully, what you are saying, that with the help of all others, we can buy us a society back as much as possible, reach into the past and bring forth that which is good and make it applicable, and do it again in our society today and in the future.

MacKINNON: Chairman White, might I be able to be permitted to read a letter which is written by Women Against Pornography, which is the foremost group working against pornography in this country. I think it will give a national perspective to everything that was stated here locally. I would appreciate the permission for me to read this letter. I think it will take two minutes.

CHAIRMAN WHITE: Two minutes.

MacKINNON: All right.

Dear Councilmembers: The steering committee of Women Against Pornography would like to convey to the Minneapolis City Council its strong support for the proposed amendment to Title 7, which would enable women to sue persons trafficking in pornography. We believe that this amendment is urgently needed, and we call upon the members of the Minneapolis City Council to support its passage.

Women Against Pornography is a New York City-based feminist organization with a national membership of 7,000 women and men. We believe that pornography perpetuates a system in which women are regarded as subhuman beings who seek out and deserve humiliation, ridicule, and abuse. Since our inception in 1979, we have been fighting pornography through a diverse program of education and activism. We have held public forums, lectured at over 500 high schools and colleges, organized boycotts, and sponsored demonstrations and marches. Although we have made considerable progress in raising public consciousness about the misogynistic and sexually violent nature of pornography and have had tangible victories stopping sexually degrading ad campaigns, we have met with little success in our attempt to curb the growth and the abuses of the pornography industry. Our fight against that industry makes David's battle with Goliath seem like a contest between equals: the feminist anti-pornography movement, composed largely of volunteers and funded primarily by individual donations, is up against a seven-billion-dollar-a-year industry with roots in both respectable corporations and organized crime.

Although our work has not curbed the power and influence of the pornography industry, it has made us acutely aware of the magnitude and severity of the harm done to girls and women by pornography. We have received phone calls from women who have been sexually abused by men who used pornography as the script for their assaults. We have received calls and letters from women whose employers and coworkers have used pornography to harass and intimidate them. We have heard from wives whose husbands have pressured them to act out their favorite pornographic scenarios. Our storefront office in the Times Square pornography district has been visited by women who reported being coerced to perform degrading public sex acts in order to keep their jobs in a nearby pornography emporium. We organized a speakout in which dozens of women testified about the ways in which pornography has impaired their sense of self, self-esteem, sexuality, and relationships. (The tapes of this event are herewith.) Recently, we received a phone call from a mother whose 14-year-old daughter was being recruited for *Hustler Magazine*'s "Beaver Hunt" by a pair of 14-year-old boys emulating *Hustler* publisher Larry Flynt. . . .

We have learned that women are hurt by pornography and hurt badly. Up to this point, however, there has been nothing we could do to help women victimized by pornography take action against those who victimized them. The proposed amendment to Title 7 would provide us with the means to help these women receive justice. It would be a tremendous step toward ensuring that women are regarded and treated as citizens equal to men, deserving of the same civil rights and human dignity.

Our organization has long been reluctant to endorse laws against pornography because most such legislation has been written in terms of obscenity and has thus failed to address the real harm caused by pornography—its physical, psychological and social injury to women. In addition, we have been concerned that legislation against obscenity might be used to censor women and members of other oppressed groups. We have also declined to support zoning laws, which usually are designed to protect property values rather than the rights and welfare of women. The only piece of legislation we have endorsed has been a section of New York State's penal law that prohibited the production, distribution, and/or display of certain clearly specified sexual performances by a child under sixteen, without couching the prohibition in terms of obscenity. (This law was first struck down by the New York Court of Appeals and later upheld unanimously by the United States Supreme Court.)

Because the proposed amendment to Title 7 is directed not against obscenity but against discrimination on the basis of sex and because it is concerned neither with "prurient interests" nor with property values but instead with the abuse and subordination of women, we feel confident in giving it our whole hearted support. Moreover, because the amendment's definition of pornography is so specific and narrow and because it so accurately describes the pornography we have seen, we believe that it could not be applied to material other than pornography.

We understand that legislation like the proposed amendment would not end our work or the need for feminist groups fighting pornography. Advertising images, which are saturated with pornographic values, would not be affected by this ordinance. Nevertheless, we are convinced that this legislation will equip us with an invaluable new tool with which to challenge the practice of the pornographers.

For more information about our organization's analysis of pornography, see the script to our slide show (attached). Key passages are marked in blue ink.

In closing, we would like to express our gratitude to the Minneapolis City Council for developing and supporting this groundbreaking legislation. Such support indicates a rare commitment to the rights and welfare of women. We hope that the Minneapolis City Council and this proposed amendment will serve as models for city and state governments throughout the country. Sincerely yours, the entire steering committee.

DWORKIN: Mr. Chairman, I am not going to try to read a whole letter— [Exh. 8]

CHAIRMAN WHITE: Wait a minute, no. Some of the Council members are going to have to go, and if you can submit that letter, these people have got their names here and it is getting close to 9:00 o'clock. We will try and get as many of you as we can. If we don't reach you at 9:00 o'clock, then hopefully you can come back tomorrow at 5:00. Please do that.

DZIEDZIC: Mr. Chairman, I am sorry I couldn't attend the whole meeting this afternoon. We had an intergovernmental meeting and we had a press conference on the "I" Team. Right now at the Government Center across the street there is a hearing going on with problems in northeast Minneapolis. I will have to excuse myself and go over there. There are three events planned tomorrow evening, and all of those events start at 5:00 o'clock. I will come tomorrow and stay as long as I can. I would like to know the intention on what the time frame is on the vote from you.

CHAIRMAN WHITE: The intent of the time frame?

DZIEDZIC: Yes.

CHAIRMAN WHITE: Hopefully, at the end of the public hearing tomorrow we can take a vote.

DZIEDZIC: I was wondering about the objection from the Civil Rights Commission that we table this to look at the ordinance.

HOYT: We will have had their letter by Friday, so if it goes the other way, that can be taken into consideration.

DZIEDZIC: I will repeat my intent to not have it go to Council on Friday, that the Civil Rights Commission be given the opportunity to look at it, repair any damage that was done with them as far as this body not going through the proper channels. I have heard a lot of testimony today. I have been sensitized by what I have heard. I can recall issues in the past, I have heard issues in the past, and recall becoming sensitized with the events as they occurred. With color breaking into baseball in 1948, having witnessed different singular schools become coeducational, one of them being the college that I attended. And I remember a letter that I received from that college that was asking for input from alumni. And I wrote back. With a wife and three daughters, you figure out how I would have voted, or what my input would be as it relates to changing St. Thomas College to a coeducational college.

I think the main thrust of the ordinance—I think we are going to have some difficulty, as Alderman Rockenstein said today. This is probably the first day of a ten-year battle, like our fight for civil rights is still going on. I think that the basis of what we are trying to do is have some input. I don't think you are talking about just pornography. I think you are talking about the whole printed media and some of them which have been legitimized, *Playboy* and some of those magazines, have some of the best ratings. I think that when you—please don't be a high school audience.

UNIDENTIFIED SPEAKER: Don't be a high school speaker. Are you testifying, sir? Is he testifying? You are wasting time.

CHAIRMAN WHITE: It is all right. He is on the Committee.

DZIEDZIC: I think the whole motion picture industry will have some sort of a fight of what we are trying to do here. I think all of those things should be taken into consideration. That is why I think we shouldn't vote on Friday.

There have been nasty people out there today. I will tell you right to your face.

UNIDENTIFIED SPEAKER: It takes one to know one.

CHAIRMAN WHITE: Would you go ahead.

M. M. D.: My name is M. M. D. I live in the 6th Ward. I am not going to speak about the ordinance. I am going to speak about my life also.

I was at the demonstration on Lake Street and Chicago Avenue a week and a half ago along with a number of other women who went into the porn shop and movie theater there. I looked, glancing really, at the images on the shelves and on the screen and, even in the midst of the large and angry powerful group of women, I was afraid. Two days later, having failed my attempts to keep those images away from me—

I was sexually abused in my family. I don't know if the man that abused me uses pornography, but looking at the women in those pictures, I saw myself at fourteen, at fifteen, at sixteen. I felt the weight of that man's body, the pain, the disgust.

I am angered now and horrified. You see so clearly that I was used as if I was a disposable image. I am also angered and horrified to find that such limited exposure to pornography called up the memories and the behavior patterns of my victimization so profoundly. I don't need studies and statistics to tell me that there is a relationship between pornography and real violence against women. My body remembers.

JAMES H. KOPLIN: My name is Jim Koplin. I live at [address deleted]. I will speak of the ordinance under discussion as an individual, not representing any organization. I am not a lawyer, but I have been bothered by discussions of pornography as a First Amendment issue. The move to change the base of the civil rights area strikes me as an important tactic. My remarks aren't legalistic, they are general issues.

I am a gay man. I want to talk mainly to my gay brothers. We can easily find ourselves in ambivalent positions in where the distribution of pornography is. For some gay communities, adult bookstores are main outlets for pornography material. They are—in fact, they serve as a meeting place and as a place to be sexual together. In a society of loving someone and being sexual with someone of the same sex, this can have severe negative consequences. Gay men have had to develop signals in order to recognize each other and cultivate places where we can feel relatively safe. Adult bookstores have come to be part of that picture. So I do not take lightly that such places will be lost to the gay community when the stores of pornography, this porn ordinance of pornography comes to be successful.

I would ask gay men to accept the teachership of women, to listen carefully to the points raised by women during these hearings. I have tried to do that here and on other contacts, and my personal conclusion is that gay men should accept the inconvenience of the world without adult bookstores in order to promote the survival of women which is very much threatened by any situation that promotes pornography. And that is my main point.

I want to add something, looking toward the long range. Ordinances like this are important, but in my judgment, pornography will only truly disappear from a society when all people are able to express their sexuality freely and openly, or when the space now occupied by pornography is empty or perhaps better than that, be filled with eroticization of positive values, like justice and respect. We are so far from that now that it is almost impossible to even imagine what this might be like.

I do have flashes of this vision now and again. I suspect all of you have such moments as well. My intuition tells me that gay men and progressive women are allies in elaborating this vision. I don't mean to exclude anyone but both of these groups are defined by outside values. Frequently these visions come from outsiders.

So my hope is that we can work together in the short term and in the long term, rather than end up in whatever positions, divided positions. That is my hope. We are a long way from realizing that. I am committed to realizing that hope. [These are the] kinds of thoughts that let me come here to ask our Council members to vote in favor of the ordinance. Thank you.

CHAIRMAN WHITE: C. B.

MS. B.: I am C. B. [spelling name deleted]. I am the outreach advocate for a group called PRIDE.[10] PRIDE is a self-help group for women who are or have been involved in the behavior of prostitution. PRIDE is sponsored by the Minneapolis Family and Children's Services. As the outreach advocate, I would like to support the amending of the civil rights ordinance and turn your attention to Section 5 number 2 specifically.

I was involved in the behavior of prostitution for a period of three years. Since then, I have been involved with the PRIDE group for a year and a half. In my own experience, and in working with women, I have become aware of the prevailing attitude that women who have been involved in prostitution are somehow exempt from coercion. Therefore, I would like to emphasize the importance of the inclusion of Section 5, number 2, letters aa through mm, as a part of this ordinance.[11]

The same societal attitudes which support pornography also support prostitution. By allowing pornography to continue, our society is condoning and supporting the degradation of all women. Thank you.

CHAIRMAN WHITE: The next speaker.

NAOMI SCHEMAN: My name is Naomi Scheman, S-c-h-e-m-a-n. I live in Ward 6. I am an Associate Professor of Philosophy and Director of Un-

10. PRIDE no longer speaks of "the behavior of prostitution," as if the women are freely acting rather than being acted upon. PRIDE now refers to prostituted women, like all battered women, in terms that make clear that they are being violated, exploited, and abused—in their case, by tricks and pimps. This change was made when survivors took control of the politics and definition of the organization from therapists.

11. As passed, this section of the Indianapolis ordinance on facts which alone do not negate a finding of coercion is Section 4 (m)(2)(i)–(xiii). See Appendix, pp. 442–443.

dergraduate Studies in Women's Studies at the University of Minnesota. I teach "Feminist Criticism of Concepts of the Self." I have taught it two or three times a year. This is my fifth year.

It is very clear to me in teaching that course what the connection is between pornography and freedom of speech, because over and over and over again in that class I have the students in that class discuss with me the experience that we have all had here this evening. That is, women finding their voices, finding the ability to speak—often for the first time—and identifying what it is in their lives, what the forces are in the society that have kept them silent for so long, that have forcibly kept them silent, that have chased any possible words out of their heads, that have given no ground to stand on and no voice to speak with. They speak within that class, and within that class we learn how to speak the truth to each other. We learn how to hear it, learn how to articulate it, learn how to be clear about it.

The question is: what do we do when we go out of that class? What do we do when we go out of that class into that world that tells us that we are imagining it, we are making it up, that they are not like that, that these things did not happen to us, or if they did there is nothing so terribly wrong. That is, we go back to the world that is structured by pornography and we lose our voices.

I believed every time I taught that class, there is a problem with what to say to those women, what to suggest. With the anger they feel, they often turn into depression. They often retreat back into silence. They express the anger to those who are closest to them. Sometimes they deserve it and sometimes they don't. But there has been, as of yet, no way of moving into the public world, moving into the society, moving into the world as structured and defined by the law—which matters because, in our society's terms, it tells us what is most real, what is most taken seriously, what most matters. There has been no way of moving back into that world and speaking the truth and expecting to be heard, of having that anger, of carrying one's voice outside of that classroom, outside of small groups and friends into the world and having it taken seriously.

It has been different teaching that class this quarter. I have been able to say: they are listening. There is an ordinance here, there is something that could become part of the law of the city in which we live, that will enable us to speak the truth, that will enable us to be empowered. That will not empower the City of Minneapolis, that will not empower the police of

Minneapolis, that will empower women to speak the truth and know that there is a space in this society—not just in isolated classrooms or friendship groups or support groups—for that truth to be heard, taken seriously, believed, and acted on. And it has been a different experience in teaching that course. I have been able to say to them, it is not your own private anger any more. It is being listened to, taken seriously.

I am going to teach that course again in the summer. I don't want to have to go into that class saying, well, they listened for a while. When it came to having the courage to provide the space for women, to listen, when it finally came to that they didn't come through, and there still is no room in this society for your voice to be heard. I don't want to have to do that.

CHAIRMAN WHITE: Carrie Rickard?

CARRIE RICKARD: My name is R-i-c-k-a-r-d. I am on the staff of Women's Health Care Associates, a private clinic in south Minneapolis. Our services include those of an obstetrics gynecologist, certified nurse, midwives, and nurse practitioner. Many of the women that come to our clinic have been sexually abused.

Dr. Patsy Parker, obstetrician and gynecologist in our office, estimates that over 50 percent, over 100 of the women that she sees, have told her of past or of continuing sexual abuse. The emotional pain caused by the sexual abuse of these and of all women makes any promotion of that abuse intolerable and a violation in and of itself. Pornography and the legality of pornography suggests that the violent subjugation of women is okay. For that reason, everybody at Women's Health Care Associates supports this Chair's amendment to ratify this ordinance.

CHAIRMAN WHITE: It is now that hour. Those that added their names later on this evening, if you would possibly come back we will begin at 5:00 tomorrow evening, and hopefully you will be—well, you will be the first ones on the agenda to speak. So with that—

UNIDENTIFIED SPEAKER: Are you going to vote on Friday?

CHAIRMAN WHITE: I beg your pardon?

UNIDENTIFIED SPEAKER: The City Council?

CHAIRMAN WHITE: The City Council will, after the Committee meeting tomorrow, we will vote whether to send it on to the City Council or not.

UNIDENTIFIED SPEAKER: But will they vote on Friday if you vote to send it on?

CHAIRMAN WHITE: If we move it out of Committee, it will be before the Council on Friday.

UNIDENTIFIED SPEAKER: What time would it be?

HOYT: Mr. Chairman?

CHAIRMAN WHITE: Alderman Hoyt.

HOYT: It was given its first reading and referred. It then has the public hearing. The Committee then takes an action and that action, is either to vote it forward at the meeting or postpone it and go at a later meeting to collect more data, or to send it forward with a recommendation for denial. That action is then forwarded to the Minneapolis City Council. They can agree with what the Committee has said, they can reverse what the Committee has said, or they can hold it on the Council floor in search of further action. Once they take an action on to the Minneapolis City Council, it is then referred to the Mayor of the City of Minneapolis, who has five working days in which to make a decision of whether to sign it, let it pass without signature, or to veto it. If it is vetoed, it comes back to the Minneapolis City Council for a decision of whether or not to override.

Be aware that in the city of Minneapolis, all public speaking and testimony is done in Committee. In the Minneapolis City Council meeting, the only people who speak are the Councilmembers themselves.

CHAIRMAN WHITE: Very well done, Councilmember Hoyt. I think that what I am hearing—I am glad to spell it out—what I am hearing is, there will be a vote Friday and that what—

UNIDENTIFIED SPEAKER: And what time will it be?

CHAIRMAN WHITE: Well—

UNIDENTIFIED SPEAKER: We would like to be here.

CHAIRMAN WHITE: You understand that she said you can't speak, but you can participate. You can sit.

UNIDENTIFIED SPEAKER: Right. So we want to know what time.

CHAIRMAN WHITE: Council starts at 9:30.

UNIDENTIFIED SPEAKER: 9:30 A.M.?

HOYT: Council starts at 9:30 A.M. generally with 200 items on the agenda. It depends how much debating we have to do.

CHAIRMAN WHITE: Now, this can go forward to postpone until a further Council meeting before the end of the year, until then, because we do have a problem seriously with the Civil Rights Commission not being notified of their part in it. So we may have to pass it out of Committee, dependent upon the Civil Rights, having the meeting with them and having the information before Friday.

HOYT: Adjourned until 5:00 tomorrow?

CHAIRMAN WHITE: Adjourned until 5:00 tomorrow.

(Hearing adjourned until 5:00 in the afternoon of Tuesday, December 13, 1983.)

SESSION III: TUESDAY, DECEMBER 13, 1983, 5:00 P.M.

CHAIRMAN WHITE: The subcommittee of the Government Operations of Health and Social Services will come to order. There is a Ways and Means meeting in the other room across the hall that has two of our members of our Committee. And when they get through, they will come over here. But the Ways and Means and Budget is a very important aspect of the city government.

I would like to begin this meeting with an honor that I was a recipient of. Valerie Harper, those of you know her as Rhoda, she gave me a long distance phone call, and I talked to her for about 20 minutes. And she told me she had sent a letter in strong support, and she is going to get other support from other actresses and other people who live in Hollywood, to send telegrams and mail to me as Chairman of the Government Operations. And the letter I have before me, since Professor MacKinnon has amazed me ever since I heard her in Zoning and Planning, I would like you to read this letter from Valerie Harper.

MacKINNON: Well, I was inspired by Andrea Dworkin when I was in the Zoning Committee. I was inspired by Andrea Dworkin, so would you like to read it? *(indicates no)*

> To the City Council of the City of Minneapolis: It is a pleasure and a privilege to participate in this hearing, even if only by letter. I want to acknowledge the City Council and everyone involved in these discussions for collectively taking such an historic and beneficial step.
>
> The damage that pornography has done and continues to do to every woman, child, and man in our society is of such enormous proportion as to be practically immeasurable. The pornographic and untrue image of human beings abounds. Because we are living within such an image, it is sometimes difficult to see and painful to confront. But we must . . . as you are in these hearings. Extensive research inalterably proves the connection, both direct and indirect, of pornography to violence, assaults and crimes against women (and children and men as well). I am therefore thankful for the opportunity to share my personal experience of pornography with this assembly.
>
> Approximately six years ago, on an evening when I was about to film a

segment of "Rhoda," the CBS series in which I played the title role, I was presented with a gift by three co-workers. I opened the package to find a framed likeness of myself that measured about eight inches by ten inches. It was not a photograph but rather a sketch and the face was absolutely recognizable as me. It was a full length figure, naked except for high heeled shoes and stockings, taking off a shirt. Never in my life had I posed for any photograph, drawing, or painting remotely similar to this image. The people giving me this laughed, thought it was funny, thought I would find it funny, and truly meant no harm—they are all talented, intelligent, nice people, an indication of the extent of the pornographic mind set we all suffer under. I felt upset, ripped-off, diminished, insulted, abused, hurt, furious and powerless. All of which I concealed from my friends by smiling and saying "Where did you get this?" (For the moment I thought they had had it made up by the art department at the studio.) "From a magazine," was the answer. Added to the aforementioned reactions was horror! I thought, "this has been published! It is publicly available for anyone to see and assume I may have posed for it."

I curtailed my honest reaction because in a few minutes we would all have to begin filming our show—which we did. They thinking it had been a fun joke, me in a great deal of pain and distress.

Subsequently I saw the same drawing in a magazine, I believe was called *Chic*. In one corner was a short rhyme or limerick alluding to Rhoda although not using the name Valerie Harper. However, a short time later, I was told about an advertisement in *Hustler* magazine which I saw. It was for T-shirts called *Shock Tops* that people could send away for. The buyer had their choice of seven famous women pictured in the nude; all of our full names were listed and, of course, choice of color of T-shirt. I was appalled and angry and had meetings with a lawyer regarding what action I should take. All my then advisors, this attorney, my personal manager (regarding career) and my business manager (regarding accounting and finances) advised strongly against taking any action whatsoever. They all concurred that it would be extremely costly and would draw attention to and sell more of the shirts.

I retained another lawyer who in several phone calls seemed to scare the magazine sufficiently as to discontinue the advertisement. He checked the magazine the following issue and the ad was not there. From there I dropped the whole matter, hoping it was over but feeling quite incomplete and unsatisfied about it.

As a young dancer-actress-singer in New York City, I experienced first-hand (and have heard countless accounts from many other women in these fields and modeling) continual attempts to convince, that pornography, photography, films, et cetera were a stepping stone to stardom. Young people and children are particularly vulnerable to this kind of enticement in New York City and Los Angeles as they are show business centers. A common statement was, and may still be, "Marilyn Monroe did that calendar and look what she became."

Also, during the audition process, actresses, singers, dancers, models are extremely vulnerable. I know of instances when women have entered the audition room to find the man who would be giving the job completely nude. Point blank proposals of sexual service as part of getting the job are extremely common.

A real fear now exists in terms of the horror of snuff movies, films in which women's *actual* murders have been recorded and then presented as pornographic entertainment. The audition process in unscrupulous hands can put the job applicant at tremendous risk.

A detective in NYC [New York City] cited a case to me of a pornography ring in Manhattan that enticed young models to an office supposedly for a job interview. Once there the young women were attacked, subdued by beating or drugs and then photographed in hideous pornographic poses, tied, tortured, bound to trees in sexual union with animals, several men and on and on. When they came to or were released, it was with the warning that if they contacted the police all the Polaroid shots of them would be sent to their parents, places of business, schools and so forth.

The police officer told me it wasn't until scores of women were so victimized in this manner that one finally took it to the authorities. This group had been doing millions of dollars worth of business. I have been working with the Rape Treatment Center of Santa Monica Hospital for almost five years now (adjacent to LA area). It is the opinion of the staff there that rape, sexual and physical assaults on women and children are definitely linked to pornography, as a particular climate is created by its use, acceptability, and encouragement. More and more brutal and sadistically violent attacks are occurring with alarming frequency—as are attacks and sexual assaults on children (often within their own families).

It would be a *massive* move in the right direction to create in the law a recourse for victims and future victims, a deterrent to current and would-be pornographers and a new context within which human beings could live their lives. A context of support, sharing, love and contribution to one another—true partnership on our planet. Thank you.

—Valerie Harper

DWORKIN: Mr. Chairman, may I put into evidence, I won't read it, it is a letter. "To whom it may concern" by Jaime Lyn Bauer, who talks about her own exploitation by pornography. [Exh. 9]

CHAIRMAN WHITE: Yes, just put it into the record. But I am also aware that Valerie Harper sent you the T-shirt, but we won't show that.

Now, to reiterate my discretion, I would like to limit the speakers to three minutes. I am going to allow Bill Neiman of the Hennepin County Attorney's Office to speak because of his having to get out of here for some reason he didn't explain to me. But I am certain that it is important. Bill Neiman, would you come and speak briefly?

BILL NEIMAN: Thank you. Bill Neiman, Assistant County Attorney in the Hennepin County Attorney's Office. And I appreciate being taken out of order. The reason is, I have to get back home to take care of my children.

CHAIRMAN WHITE: Okay, I didn't know that.

NEIMAN: The reason I was asked by Councilmember Hoyt to speak today regarding the subject is because I have been in the Hennepin County Attorney's Office for five years and on the team of attorneys who prosecute all sexual assault cases and child abuse cases at Hennepin County.

In brief, the background, our office did support and did draft the bill which was passed a year ago that makes virtually all forms of child pornography a felony. Now, in terms of the relationship between pornography and sexual assault and child abuse, what I am best equipped to talk to you about is what I have seen as prosecutor, having reviewed hundreds, certainly a hundred or more cases involving sexual assault of adults or the sexual abuse of children.

Now, I should emphasize, and this is important to understand, that generally speaking with pornography, materials are seized or found at the time of the arrest or shortly after the arrest. It is not with a purpose. That is, the police are not looking for those materials, so that when I talk about the numbers I am about to speak of, I say that with the understanding that I have little doubt that if the police, in each case where they suspected sexual assault, looked for material of this type, if they did, they would find a much greater number than are found. I say that because quite a number are found without any special effort being made to look for pornographic materials.

Now, in cases involving adults, primarily women—that is women, female victims—pornographic materials are often found. I would not say in a majority of cases, but a substantial percent of cases, those materials are found in or near where the person lives or, say, the motor vehicle which was used to transport the assailant to the place of the sexual assault.

We do see, with children, a much greater use in pornographic materials. I would say that in the cases that I had—that I have had, and I have had many of them—that pornographic materials are found, if not in a majority of cases, very close to the majority of cases, found in the home of the person who is sexually abusing the children, and often there are very substantial numbers of pornographic materials. These pornographic materials are both adult and children.

Now, an example, and I could give you many examples, an example of a recent case I had—or I have, actually—where such materials were being used. Just for the Committee's information, this young girl was raped, I believe, by her stepfather, a live-in boyfriend. And one of the things that he did as part of the sexual assault of the girl is, he would sit on the toilet undressed, and she would be undressed in the bathroom, and he would have her, while undressed, hold up, for example, the centerfold of a magazine that depicted a naked woman or whatever. And while she was holding this and standing naked herself, he would masturbate himself. And this use is not extraordinary. It is no more bizarre or less bizarre a use of pornographic material than we have seen. So I think it is fair to say, from the point of view of the Hennepin County Attorney's Office, that we have found pornography to be used very substantially where children are the victims and substantially where adults are the victims. Thank you.

DWORKIN: May I ask you one question?

CHAIRMAN WHITE: I wanted to ask one too.

DWORKIN: I am sorry. Please.

CHAIRMAN WHITE: Under Section One, 139.10 in the ending sentence of that paragraph it reads, "Such discriminatory practices degrade individuals, foster intolerance and hate, and create and intensify unemployment, substandard housing, under-education, ill health, lawlessness and poverty, thereby injuring the public welfare." As an attorney dealing with all of those things, what does that sentence say to you?

NEIMAN: In terms of pornography, well, my personal belief is that pornography does cause people to act out criminally, sexually, criminally in a sexual fashion, sometimes in a physical aggressive fashion. My personal belief is that there is a relationship. I don't have scientific evidence of that, but I have simply seen too many cases to believe otherwise. That is how I would read that sentence and it is hard—as stated, it is hard to describe something which has that terrible impact as anything other than discriminatory, when the impact it has on the victims is as great as it is.

CHAIRMAN WHITE: Thank you.

MacKINNON: Would you say it is against the public welfare?

NEIMAN: I would say that given what happens to the victims in these cases, especially the child victims that are most often, if not destroyed, partially ruined for life, that if it had that effect on one victim, it would have a terrible effect. I think it has that effect on hundreds of children.

MacKINNON: Have you found the taking of pictures to be part of these things you see?

NEIMAN: We have seen—

MacKINNON: In the course of your work?

NEIMAN: Yes, I have. And others in the office have prosecuted these cases. Frankly, I think there is much more of it than we have had the good fortune to discover. And in fact, our office is presently trying to develop a somewhat more sophisticated approach to locating, arresting, and prosecuting pornographers. The persons that we have found, we have prosecuted, and I believe they have been involved sexually with the children. My personal belief is that, although we have had some success, there is much more out there that we haven't been able to locate or find, as [it is] a sophisticated offense and it is difficult to get to the perpetrator. Thank you.

CHAIRMAN WHITE: Thank you very much.

The next speaker, and please, we would like to get out of here. I know how you feel, but we don't have the time that I would like to have here this evening. So if you would hold your statements to four minutes, as closely as possible to it, I would appreciate it. The next speaker would be Wanda Richardson.

MacKINNON: S. G., I believe would be first if she is here. And then Carole laFavor and then Carol Ann.

MS. G.: Before I begin, I have to say that I am unable to state what my relationship is to the people I am going to talk about, because many of them are still victims whose lives are in danger.

For the majority of my life, I lived with a divorced woman and her children in the house that she owned. Her ex-husband also lived in the house we lived in. He would not leave. He threatened to kill the woman if she ever tried to get help in getting him away from her and out of her house.

Over a period of eighteen years, the woman was regularly raped by this man. He would bring pornographic magazines, books, and paraphernalia into the bedroom with him and tell her that if she did not perform the sexual acts that were being done in the "dirty" books and magazines, he would beat and kill her. I know about this because my bedroom was right next to hers. I could hear everything they said. I could hear her screams and cries. In addition, since I did most of the cleaning in the house, I would often come across the books, magazines, and paraphernalia that were in the bedroom and other rooms of the house. The magazines had pictures of mostly women and children and some men. Eventually, the woman admitted to me that her ex-husband did in fact use pornographic materials to terrorize and rape her.

Not only did I suffer through the torture of listening to the rapes and tortures of a woman, but I could see what grotesque acts this man was performing on her from the pictures in the pornographic materials. I was also able to see the systematic destruction of a human being taking place before my eyes.

At the time I lived with the woman, I was completely helpless, powerless in regard to helping this woman and her children in getting away from this man. I was told by the man that if I ever told anyone about the things that he did, or if I ever tried to run away, that he would beat me, that he would break and cut off my arms and legs, that he would cut up my face so that no man would ever want to look at me, that he would kill me, and that he would make me sorry that I ever told on him. During the time that I was held captive by that man, I was physically and psychologically abused by him. I was whipped with belts and electrical cords. I was beat with pieces of wood. I was usually forced to pull my pants down before I was to be beaten. I was touched and grabbed where I did not want him to touch me. I was also locked into dark closets and the basement for many hours at a time. And I was often not allowed to speak or cry.

The things that this man did to me were also done to the children of the woman, except that they suffered from even worse abuse. I believe that part of the psychological abuse I suffered from was from the pornographic materials that the man used in his terrorization of us. I knew that if he wanted to, he could do more of the things that were being done in those magazines to me. When he looked at the magazines, he would make hateful, obscene, violent remarks about women in general and about me. I was told that because I am female, I am here to be used and abused by him and that because he is male, he is the master and I am his slave. I was terrorized into keeping silent, and it wasn't until three years after escaping from him that I was psychologically and emotionally strong enough to tell anyone what had happened to me.

I am not saying that pornography caused that man to do those things to me and to other women and children. I am saying that pornography is an extension of the violence and hatred against women that already exists in this society. To get rid of pornography is to get rid of part of the violence against women that permeates this society. Pornography makes a mockery of the torture, beatings, rapes, mutilations, degradations and killings that I and other women have suffered from—all for men's sexual gratification.

Every time I walk into a neighborhood grocery store or drug store I am reminded that if I don't watch my step, do what I'm told, keep silent or stay in my place, that I could end up like one of the women in that pornographic material being sold in those stores.

I believe what those magazines say because it has happened to me.

The last statement that I have to make is a political one. If someone wants to study the condition of women in this society, all that person has to do is to view a pornographic book, magazine, or movie. Pornography is an example of a picture, of a diagram with instructions of how to degrade a woman. It is a blueprint of the state of women's conditions in the society. Pornography tells the truth about women's conditions. But pornography lies about how we think and feel about our condition.

MacKINNON: Chairman White, a woman named A. W. got in touch with me this morning, and I would like to submit her written statement. Perhaps it would be better if I didn't read it and put it in. It is a statement with detail, and just like the statement that was just made. [Exh. 10]

CHAIRMAN WHITE: As I said last night, it takes quite a bit to sit and stand, as last night, before all the eyes and ears that are looking and let forth, and let it all hang out, and tell what happened to someone. It is something I will never forget.

Carole laFavor, please?

CAROLE LAFAVOR: First I want to thank my friends for coming to support me today. It's scary to stand before you and talk of something so painful. It helps me having women on the Council. It makes it a little easier. I wish more of you were people of color.

I would like to direct my story, even though he is not here, to Mark Kaplan,[12] because I am from his ward. He represents many women of

---

12. Councilmember Mark Kaplan.

color, and by his vote on this ordinance he can give us a safer community in which to live.

When I was first asked to testify, I resisted some, because the memories are so painful and so recent. I am here because of my four-year-old daughter and other Indian children. I want them to grow up in a more healthful and loving society.

I was attacked by two white men, and from the beginning they let me know they hated my people, even though it was obvious from their remarks they knew very little about us. And they let me know that the rape of a "squaw" by white men was practically honored by white society. In fact, it has been made into a video game called "Custer's Last Stand." And that's what they screamed in my face as they threw me to the ground, "This is more fun than Custer's Last Stand." They held me down and as one was running the tip of his knife across my face and throat he said, "Do you want to play Custer's Last Stand? It's great. You lose, but you don't care, do you? You like a little pain, don't you, squaw?" They both laughed and then he said, "There is a lot of cock in Custer's Last Stand. You should be grateful, squaw, that all-American boys like us want you. Maybe we will tie you to a tree and start a fire around you." They made other comments—"the only good Indian is a dead Indian," "a squaw out alone deserves to be raped"—words that still terrorize me today.

It may surprise you to hear stories that connect pornography and white men raping women of color. It doesn't surprise me. I think pornography, racism, and rape are perfect partners. They all rely on hate. They all reduce a living person to an object. A society that sells books, movies, and video games like "Custer's Last Stand" on its street corners gives white men permission to do what they did to me. Like they said, I'm scum. It is a game to track me down, rape, and torture me.

So I bring my screams of that night here to you today, hoping that they will help you decide to stand against the dehumanization and violence of pornography. I would like to end with a poem that I wrote about my nightmares after my attack.

> I used to welcome the first shadows of night
>   as they slid along the edge of day.
> The thunderbird closing her eyes slowly,
>   softly pulling us all into the beauty of the darkness
> and the dream.

Now the shadows hide danger and hatred.
The thunderbird screams her warning
 of the terror of the darkness and the nightmare.
The hoop of the universe is broken.
Sacred eagle feathers are strewn on the ground
 where they throw me, naked, to play out "Custer's Last Stand."
Knives slash red streaks.
Mean, twisted faces, large rough hands, swirl and chase me through
 the darkness.
I struggle awake just as the owl calls my name.

DWORKIN: Mr. Chairman, just for the record, I just want to say that the actual name of the video game which portrays the rape that was described here, and that was actually lived through, is "Custer's Revenge."

CHAIRMAN WHITE: Cheryl Champion, are you here?

MacKINNON: Mr. Chairman, she is coming in a car. She is trying to get a ride. She may be a little bit late. We should just proceed.

CHAIRMAN WHITE: Then Wanda Richardson.

WANDA RICHARDSON: I work at Harriet Tubman Women's Shelter. I was asked to speak about the connection that we see at the shelter between pornography and violence against women. What I would like to say is not [only] my own thoughts and experience, it is also that of many other women both working at the shelter and women who have come to the shelter.

The first thing that I would like to say is that there is a very similar status between women who are battered and women in pornography. Battered women are reduced to being physical objects. They are no longer people, they have no rights, they have no dignity. They are just objects and things. Women in pornography are also reduced to the level of objects and things. They don't exist as human beings but they are merely there to satisfy a man's desire.

In the case of battering, we see women existing as something men have there to vent their feelings on. In pornography, they are there supposedly for sexual desire. Pornography is a classic example of the objectification of women. We see results of that every day at our shelter.

I would say that, in many cases, a lot of violence that we see really has nothing to do with sex or anger or anything else. It really is just a power relationship where there is a great deal of inequality between men and women, and men are just using that to their advantage to carry those things out. There is a lot of sex and violence, both in battering situations and in pornography. If you look at a lot of pornography, it shows women being beaten, humiliated, tied up. It shows women tied and stabbed, poked, prodded and abused by devices, assaulted by several men or animals, and many ugly and degrading things. When you see a woman being battered, you see a lot of the same ugliness and violence at the same time. Not only do they portray women as liking and deserving this sexual abuse, it shows them as enjoying it, deserving it. And that is what one of the great myths of battery is, is that women deserve to be battered and that they enjoy it. If they didn't like it, they wouldn't stay.

Men look at women in pornography magazines. They say the same things about them—they like it, they enjoy it. The women coming to the shelter say over and over again the men say that to them—you enjoy this, you deserve it. Men look at pornography and they observe that message—the women liking and deserving that treatment. They act it out on specific women, usually their girlfriends and wives, sometimes anonymous, like a rape on the street. What they are doing are acting out the messages that women are not human beings, they are objects.

There is many specific cases that I could cite. I don't want to go into it now. I would like to say we have many, many examples of women coming to the shelter who have cases of combined sexual and physical assault where the violence and the sex is intertwined, but you can't tell the difference—closely intertwined. They are a target not only for violence but also seen as sexually appealing. And a lot of times this is acted out at home where men will beat a woman and find that very sexually arousing. Many of the women come and say that immediately after battering, or shortly thereafter, the man wants sex and they said, how could he want me after he has done this to me, how could he expect me to not be upset, like nothing has happened. And to them, nothing has happened. To the woman it has been a degrading experience, and to the man it has been sexually exciting.

If you look at any pornographic magazine, you will see the answer to those questions that the women are asking. We had two recent cases that I would like to cite, one in which a woman was taken repeatedly by her boyfriend to the Rialto Theater and made to watch "X" rated movies. And then he would take her home and force her to act out with him these movies. Of course, a lot of these movies contain extreme violence. After one of these episodes, she ended up in the hospital. That is how she came to our shelter.

In another case, a woman was imprisoned in the house by her husband. He had a video cassette recorder and he would bring home pornographic movies and tie her to a chair and force her to act out what they were seeing on the screen. Of course, she was eventually severely injured and, again, came to our shelter. These are just two examples. They are not by any means unusual ones. These things happen all the time.

The effects on the women of this kind of abuse—of course, there is the physical abuse which we see and deal with every day. But there is a tremendous amount of emotional abuse, mental abuse, that is, they are degraded and humiliated by the pornography and the violence. There is a tremendous loss of self-esteem and self-worth. A lot of times that is what they feel like: that is all they are worth. They are only bodies and they don't deserve anything better than that treatment. They have no rights or respect either from others or from themselves.

I would also like to point out that a lot of this information that we have gotten from women of the shelter has not been looked for. We don't have specific questions on our intakes about sexual abuse and violence. Most of this comes out during the discussion that we have when the woman first comes. And as we have seen it over and over again, the women saying the same things, where you have many separate incidents itself, but a lot of similar occurrences. You start seeing a pattern, and you start saying, where is this pattern coming from?

Well, it is coming from socialization from cultural images. And the strongest influence that we have been able to find on this type of treatment of women is pornography. Many of the women said that pornography is around their house. They say, he has been to the theaters, he does this and he does that and he sees these things. He comes home and he acts it out on me, or he makes me act it out also. We think that pornography is probably the most extreme example of anti-women socialization that men receive in this society. We don't believe that men are born to be sexually and physically abusive to women. They learn this. And the main place they learn this is through pornography. We see the victims of this every day.

I would like to finish up by saying that because we have seen so much of this and it does seem to be increasing, that we are going to be adding questions on our intake to try and document the connection between pornography and violence. We are going to try to be collecting some data, hopefully, that will be helpful for proceedings such as this. Thank you.

CHAIRMAN WHITE: Thank you. I can understand, but please try to hold it to four minutes. We have got so many people. Four minutes, please.

SHARON RICE VAUGHN: My name is Sharon Rice Vaughn and I work at the Minnesota Coalition for Battered Women which is in St. Paul. I would like to read testimony from Donna Dunn from Rochester. Have you called her name? She says that the storm started there this morning, and that she was all dressed in her dress with her testimony and couldn't get here because of the snow. Would that be all right? I would like to start with that and finish with mine.

CHAIRMAN WHITE: Okay. Do this as expeditiously as you can.

RICE VAUGHN: Yes, I will. And I will identify Donna Dunn. Donna Dunn works at Women's Shelter, Incorporated in Rochester, Minnesota. She is also a member of the Board of Directors of the Minnesota Coalition for Battered Women.

This is Donna's statement:

> I am taking part in today's testimony regarding pornography in order to bring you some information about how pornography has contributed to the abuse of some women we have come in contact with at Women's Shelter in Rochester. Women's Shelter is a home for battered women and their children. Women's Shelter has operated as a shelter for five years. In that time over 800 women have stayed with us. An additional 500 women contact the shelter each year in need of assistance, advocacy, and/or support.
>
> Our experience in working with battered women has led us to a clear understanding of the way our society supports, allows and even encourages male violence against women. The incapacity to identify women as valuable, contributing members of American society [along with] the continuing insistence on identifying and validating women in terms of their relationships or service to men, contributes to the extreme isolation of all women, particularly battered women.
>
> In [our] experience we are finally beginning to create an atmosphere in which battered women can identify, talk about, and seek help [and] support in escaping abuse and violence. While broken bones, concussions, broken teeth, ripped out hair and beatings that render women unconscious are now frequently shared stories from battered women, sexual assault within sexual relationships remains all too frequently behind the veil of privacy—a sense of privacy that is a result of a society in which a woman learns from birth that her body is not her own and that her sense of worth is defined by those who would use her body.

Historically, women have been denied their own sexuality and along with that the right to make decisions about how they are used sexually. This lack of decision making power combined with society's victimization of the woman who is sexually assaulted creates a sense of shame, of guilt, of dirtiness that disallows her to speak of the sexual assault even within the safe atmosphere of the Shelter.

Particulars about the use of pornography and its perpetuation of abuse are not a part of our regular data collection. However, we at Women's Shelter, Inc. know it to be a fact that pornography contributes to the battering of women and children.

While doing our intake procedure and in the ongoing close contact with shelter advocates, pornography is frequently stated as a hobby of the abuser. We would like to give you three examples of how pornography encouraged the ongoing beatings and rape of women we know.

Number one, one woman known to us related that her spouse always had a number of pornographic magazines around the house. The final episode that resulted in ending the marriage was his acting out a scene from one of the magazines. She was forcibly stripped, bound and gagged. And with help from her husband, she was raped by a German Shepherd. His second wife became known to us when she sought out support because of the magazines and bondage equipment she discovered in their home.

Number two, another woman spoke of her husband's obsession with tying women up. She said he had rape and bondage magazines all over the house. She discovered two suitcases full of Barbie dolls with ropes tied on their arms and legs and with tape across their mouths. She added, "He used to tie me up and he tried those things on me." But she also stated that she had not recognized this as sexual abuse. This statement from her reinforces our earlier contention that she did not have the freedom to identify sexual assault because she felt no ownership of her own body.

Number three, *Penthouse* and *Hustler* were always a part of the literature in the third woman's home. Occasionally her spouse would add *Cheri, Oui, Swedish Erotica* to the collection. His favorite form of abuse was bondage. He enjoyed playing what he called a game of whipping and slavery. She knows that what he did to her was directly related to articles about bondage and sex lays which he read. He wanted to involve a second woman, her friend, in the scenarios. Her refusal to comply with his demands resulted in her being violently anally assaulted. She stated, "Even if he had not gotten these specific ideas from the magazines, the magazines reinforced his attitude about women and his attitude that he could do what he wanted with me."

Our experience at Women's Shelter indicates and even demands that we as a society recognize and be accountable for the very specific ways in which individual women are hurt and the role that pornography plays in that hurt. It is because of that obvious connection that I submit this testimony to you.

I would like to say, from working in two shelters and working with the Coalition for a total of eleven years, that Wanda said for all of us, I think, a lot of things that I won't repeat. But I think I can add to them.

One thing that battered women and women of—victims of pornography—have in common is an irony. Battered women and women that are victims of pornography are invisible in this culture. This ordinance is the beginning of defining their visibility, and it is extremely important that it pass, and it does not go nearly far enough. Battered women, until about ten years ago, were invisible. They were told to turn the other cheek. They went through the revolving door of emergency rooms. Nobody wanted to help them, and that is the classic way of creating a victimless crime. You don't even have a victim. She is so invisible she doesn't exist. When a woman is blamed for the assault that is done to her, she does not exist. She is invisible in the society. That is something that has begun to change. It hasn't changed nearly enough. Women do have options. If a woman is invisible as a victim of a crime, she has nowhere to go. She literally has no options. This ordinance is the beginning of options, and it is small.

Another thing that women have in common—those who are battered and victims of pornography—they are part of an epidemic. That is an irony of their visibility. They are not victims of social psychopathic deviants. There is an epidemic of . . . battering of women. Battery happens in the home. It is private. Battering is sanctified pornography. Battering happens behind the lace curtain of the sacred home, and it is a form of pornography and an act of pornography.

There are 40,000 women in Minnesota who are estimated by the Department of Corrections to be 40,000 incidents of battering of women per year, which is an underestimation. And ten years ago, there were none. It wasn't even a category of crime. The FBI has called battering the nation's most underreported crime. It estimates, which is an underestimate, that a woman is beaten every eighteen seconds. What we know about the epidemic of pornography is that it is a seven-billion-dollar industry in this country. The entire national, federal, AFDC budget is eight billion dollars. Pornography is one billion below that. Both involve women who are hurt in every way. They are hurt psychologically, they are hurt physically, and they are hurt sexually. And the combination of what it does to a woman is that, as women have said who talk to shelter residents, that they don't even define it as rape. If you ask a woman has she been raped, in an intake, she says no. If you ask her if sex is forced on her, she says yeah, of course it has. I mean, that is where we are. We don't even have a definition of what has happened to women.

I would like to urge you to pass the ordinance, and I thank you for holding this testimony. You realize what you have done. You have opened this floodgate of women. [You] have been here to listen to them. And every woman has a story to tell.

CHAIRMAN WHITE: You most certainly are correct. The floodgates are open. You should see my desk. Barbara Chester?

BARBARA CHESTER: I am here to speak for some of those women that have stories and can't be here to tell them.

Presently, I am the Director of the Rape and Sexual Assault Center in Hennepin County. Pornography, like rape, is not about sex but about control, hostility and violence. I have read in some of our papers that there has been suggested that there is no connection between pornography and sexual violence because there has never been a case on record of a man walking into an adult bookstore and exiting ten minutes later to pounce on a victim. I would agree, and add that since our first big study on rape back in 1971, we know that rape is a planned act, rape is not an act of impulse. It is an act that is well-nurtured in our society.

Rape is a social disease that is born in an environment that links sex with violence and humiliation. For two years, I ran a group with another woman at one of the men's correctional facilities in Minnesota. All of these men, almost all of these men, were violent offenders and had committed rape. Although . . . in twelve years, only one was in prison for rape. One man in our group admitted to raping over 100 women, I might say bragged about raping over 100 women. He also admitted masturbating to hard-core pornography before his crimes. Almost every one of the men in the group admitted to masturbating to fantasies of violence. And most of them acted out this violence against women or children.

Let us use our common sense for a moment. When two things are linked by something visual, we associate the two. When this association is reinforced, it is likely to become a repeated behavior. Some of them say it is a catharsis—if they look at pictures of women being slashed and humiliated, then they won't have to do this in real life, parents beating children and/or child abuse. Yet no one would suggest that we all look at films of parents beating children in order to end child abuse, or to watch films of Blacks, Indians, and Hispanics being handcuffed and humiliated in order to end racism. There is no reason, then, to suspect that pictures of bound and mutilated women will decrease misogyny. Indeed, as many offenders in my experience have noted, masturbating to fantasies of these images is extremely reinforcing and in many cases led to their acts of sexual violence.

We have seen cases at our own and other rape centers in Minnesota, cases like one involving a mentally handicapped woman being taken to an apartment, handcuffed to a steam pipe, having food shoved into her vagina while dogs licked it out to the amusement of the spectator. Cases like the woman who was tied by her heels and suspended upside down and forced to perform oral intercourse with her husband, who later raped her in the bathroom after urinating and defecating on her. Cases like the man who never had intercourse with his wife unless it was in front of other men he brought home from the local bar. I wonder where these ideas came from?

Many of us reacted with shock and horror to the gang rape of a woman on a pool table in a bar in New Bedford in March of 1983, while bystanders cheered and applauded. Yet in the January issue of *Hustler,* a layout appeared of this exact scenario, a woman spread-eagled on a pool table being gang-raped. I wonder if any of the participants in New Bedford two months later were readers of *Hustler.*

Permission to violate, once given, cannot be constrained. There is no such thing as "slightly violated" or "a little bit raped," because sexual violence is a continuum, not a hierarchy. Pornography is the permission and direction and rehearsal for sexual violence. It is the rape of our fantasy lives and, ultimately, the rape of our bodies.

MacKINNON: I have a letter from Marvin Lewis, to the City Council, who is bringing cases for women against psychotherapists who abuse their authority. I know we also have a statement by a woman who works with prostitutes stating that many girls and young women are directed into pornography and making a movie by being threatened with physical harms. And the pictures are being taken and told they are for private use and later are sold. [Exh. 11; Exh. 12]

DWORKIN: We also have a letter from Dr. Phyllis Chesler who is a psychotherapist who describes in detail the effects of pornography on women's self-esteem, and who believes that pornography leads to chronic depression, self-hatred, and other extremely damaging psychological states. [Exh. 13] And also a letter from Family and Children's Services here in Minneapolis, Minnesota. Specifically about pornographic abuse of women in psychotherapy by psychotherapists, the uses of women in pornography to exploit women. [Exh. 14]

CHAIRMAN WHITE: Let the record show these. Okay. Am I saying this correctly? The next speaker is Daryl Dahlheimer. I hope I am saying it correctly.

DARYL DAHLHEIMER: You are. Well, I think I have a lot to say that is similar. I will try to skip over the parts that are repetitive. I do wish to say—and I am not embarrassed to be repetitive—that we have been silent too long on the issue. I am pleased we are spending a lot of time on the particular issue. As you announced, my name is Daryl Dahlheimer and I am going to try to talk about the connection of sexual violence and some of the offenders I work with, and pornography.

My background is a psychotherapist who has worked with both victims and perpetrators of sexual violence. I spent the past two years working with male felons in an alternative-to-prison treatment program in Hennepin County, approximately half of whom are sex offenders. I can't claim to hold any definitive or rigorous scientific data on the subject.

I tried hard to answer the following questions in my practice. First, what changes are necessary in the offenders' values and beliefs in order to assure that he will not revictimize someone? And secondly, what factors contribute to sexually violent behavior? I would like to share some of my conclusions so far.

CHAIRMAN WHITE: Excuse me, could you lift that up a little more?

DAHLHEIMER: Before I start, I want to state several understandings so that we have common definitions. My understanding of sexual violence, with many forms, ranges from rape in marriage to sexual assault on the streets to incest in families. And the common ground of all of these is that sexual violence is prevalent in each of its forms, and is fundamentally assaultive, not sexual, with women being the primary target and women, excuse me, and men virtually having cornered the market on who is the aggressor.

The second understanding is that pornography is also prevalent, in both written and picture form, and is distinguishable from erotica or sex education material in that it specifically involves the demeaning or degrading representation of women, men, or children.

With that in mind, I'd like to tell you what I have learned in working with sex offenders. First, sexual violence is not the work of the insane or the inhuman. The rapist or molester is always seen as a stranger, working in alleys and schoolyards, not as one of our own. This, I believe, blurs the truth that sexual violence is learned behavior and that we are all capable of it, given the proper training, distortions, and permissions. In a study of motives of men who rape, Nicholas Groth, one of the leading researchers in the area, identified that 95 percent of rapes fall into patterns of anger in which sexuality becomes a hostile act, or power in which sexuality becomes an expression of conquest. I want to stress hostility and conquest are the primary motivations in 95 percent of the rapes studied.

Consider the following verbatim statements by several rapists who Groth interviewed: "I wanted to knock the woman off her pedestal, and I felt rape was the worst thing I could do to her." "She wanted it. She was asking for it." "She just said 'no' so I wouldn't think she was easy." I wish to state that we are witnessing violent acts, but often women are pictured smiling, enjoying it. There are statements accompanying these pictures and articles to the [effect] that women are supposedly wishing to give in. So I wish to, you know, call your attention to the fact that in terms of their own motives, there are some connections between the pornography and what is going on with these offenders.

Secondly, sexual beliefs of men who are sexually violent tend to be the following: women are perceived as seductive, manipulating, powerful. Men are dichotomized into strong or weak, "studs" or "queers." He sees his task as one of conquering women and competing with men. A sexual encounter for him is getting something rather than sharing something. And I think if you take a look at the pretty graphic representations of what is mentioned, of what goes on in pornographic literature and images, I think you will see similar images between pornography and the basis of and outlooks of these offenders. Which brings me to my final point. I want to help you understand some of the mechanisms by which pornography may end up reinforcing sexual violence or creating sexual violence.

First is the fact that the sex offenders, it is well documented, tend to view others—other people, particularly women—more as objects or obstacles than as individuals. This is part of their belief system that separates these people from their humanity and treats them as objects. It is no secret that pornography can be objectification of women's bodies and women's sexualities. In that particular way it may be a reinforcement tool.

Second, we know in the psychotherapy field that imagination and visual imagery are powerful tools for shaping human behavior. It is no secret that violent images have led to increased violence in people, and violent images and pornography may give them rationales, minimizing the pain, projection of blame, and other distortions along with the image.

The third is that we recognize as a society the importance of prohibiting hate-material toward minority groups. Given the fact that violent behavior has been shown to lead to imitative results after exposure to violence on TV, I think this mechanism may work for the offenders.

It feels crazy to many of us working in therapy with offenders and victims that society is so silent on what looks to us like a clear link between written and visual images of victimization and acts of victimization. In both my professional capacity and as a resident of Minneapolis, I am grateful to this committee for taking steps to end this silence. Thank you.

CHAIRMAN WHITE: Those of you who do have notes, if you do read from them, please leave them with the City Clerk.

MacKINNON: Mr. Chairman, I would like to submit some additional documentation on the exact points that were made by Mr. Dahlheimer. One is from a book called *The Rapist File*. It is interviews with rapists as they discussed, as did Mr. Dahlheimer, the use that the rapists themselves report making of pornography. [Exh. 15]

And I would also like to submit an interview excerpt written in the form of a book about Ted Bundy, the mass murderer of women—interviews with him, sections from that book. He said, this is the interviewer, he states, "'Victims, you indicated that they would be symbols and images. But I'm not really sure. Images of what? And Ted exclaimed, "Of women. I mean, of the idealized woman. What else can I say?"' The interviewer, "A stereotype?" This is Bundy, "No, they wouldn't be stereotypes necessarily. But they would be reasonable facsimiles to women as a class. A class not of women per se, but a class that has almost been created through the mythology of women and how they are used as objects." This is the basis on which he chose which women to kill. [Exh. 16]

CHAIRMAN WHITE: Okay.

MacKINNON: I would also like to submit a report from the—it's an ongoing criminal case from which I have removed the names. I do have the names. I have the name of the one victim who is not a minor. I don't have the victims who are minors. It describes a young woman who was abducted by a man who branded her and who burned her viciously, and a

number of other monstrosities. The same man is being—is also simultaneously being—tried for the abuse of several minors in which his modus
operandi appears to be, from the allegations in the complaint, that he
would pick up young girls, show them pornographic movies, keep them
prisoners for several days up to a week or whenever they could escape,
during which time they were tortured, raped, et cetera. So I am submitting those two complaints with all of their numbers on them, but with the
names of the individuals removed by me. [Exh. 17]

CHAIRMAN WHITE: Let the record show. Is that last one you read from, is
this something within the State of Minnesota?

DWORKIN: Yes.

MacKINNON: Yes. This last—the ones with the names deleted—I believe it
is, Chairman White. It is the State of Minnesota, [as] the papers do
reflect. Everything is on the papers except the names of the individuals.

CHAIRMAN WHITE: Bill Seals.

BILL SEALS: Good evening, my name is Bill Seals. I am the Director of
Sexual Assault Services at the Center for Behavior Therapy in Minneapolis. I have worked with hundreds of sex offenders over the past ten years.

Unfortunately, the relationship between pornography and sexual assault gets mixed reviews in the literature. My experience has been that
pornography is often used by sex offenders as a stimulus to their sexually
acting out. The sexual insecurity of sex offenders is reinforced by porn.
Quite often sex offenders will use porn because they think of it as being
safe. They live vicariously through the pictures. Eventually, that is not
satisfying enough and they end up acting out sexually.

I believe we would have sex offenders even if we didn't have porn. I
also believe that we must make safeguards and take the measures which
are necessary to minimize sexual assault. Knowing that I was going to
appear here, I asked thirty-seven sex offenders of various types of sexual
assault how many of them had actually used pornography prior to their
sexually acting out. And of the thirty-seven, thirty-five of them stated
that they had at one time or another. Not all the time, at one time or
another.

Whenever we read about another sexual assault case in the paper, we
instinctively react with rage. We cry out for stronger prison terms. Seldom, however, do we ask why? Seldom do we look at the causes. Perhaps
if we take a look at those causes, which include pornography, we might
find that we have more control over preventing sexual assault than we
think.

The relationship between pornography and sexual assault does exist. If some therapists believe that pornography is a positive influence in treating sexual dysfunction, then I suggest those therapists become a little more creative in their therapeutic approach.

All sex offenders have a warped perception of women. Let's not continue to reinforce this belief by selling the tools of sexual assault. Usually, I'm a First Amendment freak. But if I have to choose between defending the First Amendment and protecting the rights of women and children, I am going to choose the latter every time.

CHAIRMAN WHITE: Cheryl Champion.

CHERYL CHAMPION: Thank you.

My name is Cheryl Champion. I have worked in the field of sexual abuse for twelve years, from 1971 to 1983. Since 1975, I have worked in Minnesota. I have chosen to work in Minnesota because we have some of the best laws in the United States for working in the field of sexual abuse if you intend to do anything about it. I have been involved with the Minnesota Coalition of Sexual Assault programs which represented thirty-seven statewide programs and have been a member of the Board of Directors of the National Coalition Against Sexual Assault, representing programming across the United States. I have lectured on many of the issues relating to sexual abuse, most recently, the relationship between pornography and sexual violence, so it is most appropriate that I was asked to testify today. I am willing to tell you what I have personally observed in my clinical work with the victims and offenders involved in sexually violent crimes.

I am currently employed by Washington County Human Services, Inc., as part of their Sexual Abuse Unit. My colleagues and I are responsible for a multifaceted program that provides 24-hour crisis intervention and advocacy to victims, individual therapy and support group counseling to victims and their families, and an intervention program for juvenile sex offenders, and a treatment program for families involved in the behavior of incest. I do this to acquaint you with my experience in the field, so that you can understand what I have to say.

CHAIRMAN WHITE: Excuse me, you said also families who are involved in incest?

CHAMPION: Yes.

CHAIRMAN WHITE: Okay.

CHAMPION: I would first like to comment on the incidents in which we have seen a direct relationship between pornography and the crime. Although I am opposed to telling horror stories, I think this is a time and place where this is appropriate. I can tell you about a young married woman who we saw whose husband had the house so filled with his collections of pornography, she was too embarrassed to allow her in-laws or her family to come in. She finally came to us for help when she was left hanging upside down in the bedroom, even though the baby was crying and in need of nursing.

The second case I will tell you about is about the kidnap of two young junior high school women in my county who were kidnapped on their way home from school and taken out into the woods and held captive over night by a young man who had constructed a very interesting tree fort in which he had papered the walls with pornography, and spent two hours assaulting these two fourteen-year-old girls following illustrations from the pornographic magazines that he had collected.

The third one I will tell you about is a gang of juveniles who papered the attic to their parents' garage with pornographic magazines. They kidnapped an eight-year-old neighborhood girl and gang-raped her.

They are not pleasant stories. They are not the only stories we hear. I do not tell them to horrify people, but to state that pornography is clearly connected with sexual assaults that we work with. It is not uncommon for our victims to speak of the pornography involved in their assaults when giving testimony to law enforcement and in the court and in processing the incident in their therapy with us. I am continually amazed that when we have public hearings like this, no one bothers to ask the real experts. That is, the street cops. They should contact Chief Bouza's investigators and find out just how much pornography they collect and catalogue every time they get a search warrant and investigate the residence of some sexual offenders.

The second point is the prevalency of pornography amongst our offenders. Because ours is an outpatient facility, the offenders we are seeing come to us while they still live in the community. We are very careful not to treat offenders that we judge to be at risk to the community, that they would act out again. We are seeing the most, if you will, innocuous members of the offending community. The more dangerous are referred to locked inpatient facilities such as Lino Lakes and St. Peter's Criminal Hospital. Even the exposers who are guilty of visual rape in that they never physically touch their victims, to the more disturbed juvenile offenders or the incest offenders who have violated their own children, are heavily connected to pornography. Each of these individuals has an ac-

tive fantasy life involving the use of pornographic materials for masturbation, fantasy contemplation, and eventual acting out of their scenarios
on their victims.

One of the underlying philosophical [tenets] of our program is for all
offenders in treatment to clean out their homes, garages, cars, and offices
of pornographic materials. We are quite clear about not rationalizing the
content—everything: pin-ups, books, magazines, TV cassettes and films.
They must also contract with us not to use porn during their treatment
with us. There is active discussion in groups and individual therapies
about the inappropriate nature of pornographic material. Those people
who violate the rule are subject to group criticism and a decision by the
treatment facility whether or not they will continue that treatment and
[revoke] their probation.

Several things are clear from our work with offenders and pornographic materials. First, that porn takes over their lives to the exclusion
of any other entertainment material. Some of these people have collected
such a mass of pornographic material, their garages and basements are
full and they can't park their cars in the garage. It is an obsessive relationship that they have with pornography. The second is that it is a relief, a
validating statement to the families of these offenders, when we encourage them to clean out these collections. In some way, the family has
suspected all along that the porn had some connection to the inappropriate sexual behavior.

The behavioral impact of pornography can be summarized so: first of
all, that all of our offenders show that they were exposed to and involved
with pornography at a very early age.

Two, that their secretive collections are significantly higher than those
we find in other populations of adolescents.

Three, when more appropriate sexual education materials are available, juveniles do not seem to need pornographic materials.

Four, that most of our offenders in psychological testing seem predisposed to violent acting out behavior. The question then becomes, would
they have chosen violent sexual acting out without the influence of porn?
I am not willing to make a statement about that, because we have not
done research that would stand up in the community.

And five, we use porn as a tool for redefining sexual behavior and
orientation. It is clear to us that it does influence behavior. Sexual gratification from porn is a strong reinforcer. We do much work to redirect
fantasy and gratification to more appropriate, less violent, object-ori-

ented self-gratification, and so we are using porn as a way to hold up something that is negative to these men and teach them how to redirect their fantasies and their lives and their tempers.

The final argument that I want to make is that I believe it is a very sexist issue that those defenders of pornography will say to you that porn is a portrayal of normal violent nature of men's sexuality. That is the most sexist statement, and that says something also about men, if we are to believe that men all have a violent expression of their sexuality.

The second thing I want to talk about is the saturation issue. We will find that term in the literature is very clear, if you are a reader of pornography. I have had to because of my work, that over the last twelve years pornography has become more and more violent, that the themes in it have become more and more explicit. It is, in a sense, as if we can't get enough of it, and so once you have seen one murder, not so explicitly, you need to have more and more portrayed realistically. You will find that people become saturated, and those juveniles you see starting out with low levels of magazines that simply portray nudity, quickly move on to those how-to-rape-and-murder magazines that are published.

The third point that I want to ask is whether or not it is that difficult for us to recognize hate. If you will flip through any of these magazines, you will notice that the central themes are racist in many of the portrayals that are of women. And the actors, who are [put there by] pornographers, there tends to be a difference, in that often the person is portrayed as a Black person or an Oriental person or an ethnic member of a group. You will also notice that besides being racist, there are a lot of themes of violence such as Nazi prison camps, people who are held against their will and held powerless. It is a literature of hate, and that is not very hard to understand if you were to look at it.

The fourth thing I want to say, [is] that I have seen a percentage growth and a change in the people who are my victims. Twelve years ago when I did this work, most of the people I dealt with, it looked like the women in this room. They were white and middle-class and fairly well educated. That has changed. The majority of the victims I see now are children. The other change I have noticed is there was a percentage increase in what I call child pornography. The explicit portrayal of children being sexual with each other or adults. I think I can directly correlate that with the increase in the number of child victims I see.

The fifth thing I would say, is whether or not porn causes violent acts to be perpetrated against women is not really the question. Porn is already a violent act against women. It is our mothers, our daughters, our sisters, and our wives that are for sale for pocket change at the news stands in this country.

The last thing I would like to say, is that porn does not exist in isolation. It is not just in sleazy neighborhoods. You need to know that the gang rape in the bar in Massachusetts which gained so much notoriety was portrayed many months earlier in one of the top selling magazines in this country as a pornographic picture outline.

The central division is between the sense of rape as an act of hostility and violence, as women see and know and experience it, and rape as an erotic act, as fantasized by men and practiced by some. That is a direct quote from a feminist writer who I think elucidates it very clearly.

In closing, I want to commend this public body for having the courage to hear this sort of testimony and encourage you to maintain your convictions in the face of those who would see this as no threat to our community. I would urge you to vote for the safety and dignity of your citizens, those you are elected to represent. Thank you.

CHAIRMAN WHITE: Ms. Champion, are there other reports from police, say in Washington County, that show when they do arrests in homes, what kind of material—

CHAMPION: Yes.

CHAIRMAN WHITE: Do you have—are there persons that could come and speak, right here in this department?

CHAMPION: Would you like me to leave a list of names or—

CHAIRMAN WHITE: Yes, I would.

CHAMPION: Okay.

CHAIRMAN WHITE: Okay, the next speaker.

GARY KAPLAN: Gary Kaplan. I have not really prepared anything to say. I am the Executive Director of Alpha Human Services, which is an inpatient treatment program for sex offenders. It's the only community-based inpatient program specifically for sex offenders in the country. There is a handful of inpatient programs, although most are within some type of institution.

I am also the Director of Outpatient Treatment Programming for Sex Offenders and a licensed psychologist. I have a private practice. As part of my private practice, I do a great deal of court-ordered psychological evaluations. I am currently, for instance, doing five court-ordered psychological evaluations that are on my calendar already.

I don't have a prepared speech. On the other hand, I have a number of years of experience with criminal sex offenders, probably about ten. I was an adviser to the only private psychologist with male sex offenders for a period of five years. I would like to say a few things about my observations. Unfortunately, all of us that are here that are working with criminal sex offenders lack hard data to say exactly what percentage of sex offenders are linked in some way to pornography. Yet most of my colleagues, I think, feel as I do: that clinically our impression is that there is a substantial role that pornography plays. Certainly with virtually all sexually-obsessed or preoccupied individuals that we see, whether committing sex crimes or not, pornography seems to be a pretty major role.

I have heard a number of people talk and it really is true. I always get the police reports and everything else when I am doing a court order. And over and over again I end up seeing they, with a search warrant, pulled out boxes of pornography. I am doing a court-ordered psychological evaluation for Scott County right now—normally, I have two actually in progress at the same time—and pornography played a role in that, showing pornographic materials to fifteen-year-old girls and getting them drugged in exchange for allowing them to engage in sexual conduct.

CHAIRMAN WHITE: Sir, are they movies or magazines or what?

KAPLAN: In this particular incident, they were videotapes. The psychological evaluation I just finished for Hennepin County, for Judge Schiefelbein, actually they were magazines, boxes of magazines and videotapes. Incidentally, that evaluation just went in the mail yesterday. It is really recent. The sex offender had been arrested in an adult bookstore for soliciting sex. He was anally penetrating his son, twelve-year-old son, with his penis and also a son, fifteen years old, from another marriage.

Another way that we see pornography being used in the commission of crimes is showing them to kids. I remember an interesting case in which an ice cream man, a Good Humor man, always kept an open magazine by him as he drove along, and the kids would look at it. And he would use that as some kind of a manipulative technique to involve the people into talking about sex or getting interested in sex, as a comment: have you ever seen anything like this before, or have you ever done anything like this previously. So, you know, there is certainly a number of ways that pornographic materials are used. You know, written pornography is just as troublesome, . . . if not more so, and it would be a lot easier for us in doing treatment with people if pornographic materials weren't around. But in a lot of respects, the written pornographic materials are as troublesome as those that are graphic or pictorial.

We recently—by the way, in our programs we don't allow any porno-graphic materials whatsoever. To my knowledge, most of the other pro-grams, of which there are two other inpatient programs in Minnesota—the treatment program in Lino Lakes and one down in St. Peter—to my knowledge, I can't say for sure, they don't allow pornographic materials to be used. At least, I am sure they discourage the use of pornographic materials.

At any rate, we recently found a fellow reading a book. But it is illegal taking pictures of or soliciting one under the age of eighteen, you know, for the purpose of engaging in obscene works. It is illegal, but it does not seem to be difficult for sex offenders to become aroused simply by read-ing photographically-detailed stories about deviant sexual behavior or child molesting or something like that.

MacKINNON: Mr. Kaplan, could you say, from your clinical experience, do you see any relationship—that you have observed—between what the people you treat choose to look at, in terms of pornography, and what they actually do?

KAPLAN: Yes. And I have said that a number of times to different audi-ences. You can't say that, if you find an individual who, let's say, has pornographic materials depicting children, you know, I can't say with certainty that that person is going to engage in that behavior, but I can certainly talk in terms of probabilities. And I feel that there is an in-creased possibility that, in fact, that individual can be seen at some time in the future to engage in that activity. Of course, common sense will tell you, you know, people read pornographic materials for the most part to attain some type of sexual arousal or sexual feelings. And so, common sense would suggest that somebody wants to look at pictures involving children engaging in some kind of sexual behavior and that, at least to him, that that sexual fantasy represents the hope for reality.

Maybe I should mention a little bit about that role. There are two schools of thought, that in fact deviant sexual fantasy is an outlet, or enforcer. For those of us, certainly my colleagues—I have been doing this for ten years—there is absolutely no doubt in my mind that masturbation to deviant sexual fantasy reinforces and increases the probability that that behavior will recur, as opposed to decreasing, as it would [if it] became an outlet.

I remember many years ago, we really may have been the first to take that position, and I don't know of too many treatment programs that are still encouraging people to masturbate to deviant fantasy. So, if you look at sexual fantasy as a hope for reality, if you look at masturbation or climax as a reinforcer—it hardly could be considered punishment—you can see what we are doing is, we are pairing deviant sexuality with pleasurable sexual feelings, which is problematic.

Offenders have an attachment between a particular sexual stimuli, a deviant sexual stimuli or activity, and pleasurable sexual feelings. And an analogy is that many men or women may find that they become sexually aroused when they go out with somebody that wears a certain type of perfume, or they smell a certain type of perfume, and without a doubt you can usually trace that, and there is some positive early sexual experiences or encounters with someone who, say for a woman, someone who she really cared about and felt very good about with a particular cologne that that man wore. And there is a condition[ing], [a] kind of attachment.

Of course, that is our concern with pornographic materials, because they are used as a stimulant. And what it does is, it pairs positive sexual feelings with deviant stimuli, and particularly with those who are somewhat backward sexually or at a young age and they are just learning.

MacKINNON: In deviance, do you include something like battery or rape?

KAPLAN: Well, a sexual behavior—

MacKINNON: We are trying to be brief here. I don't mean for you to go on.

KAPLAN: In diagnosing sexual deviance, look at the target of sexual behavior. The type of rape is a certain way of deviant type of sexual behavior, or you look at the motive of sexual behavior.

MacKINNON: Thank you.

CHAIRMAN WHITE: Thank you.

KAPLAN: I don't think I was through.

CHAIRMAN WHITE: I am glad she said it, because it was coming.

KAPLAN: Well, I support the ordinance. I can't say whether it is going to have a preventative effect. I do know that [it] will make my life a whole lot easier in treating sex offenders. Criminal sex offenders will go to great lengths to get pornographic materials. If they are not accessible, it would make my life a lot easier.

CHAIRMAN WHITE: Thank you.

Nancy Steele.

NANCY STEELE: Thank you.

For twelve years, I have worked in prisons in Colorado and Minnesota, providing direct clinical treatment services to men convicted of sex offenses, rape, incest, and child molesting. For years, I've heard them talk in depth about their feelings about themselves, their crimes and their sexuality. These are my own personal professional opinions I have formed in listening to them over the years on the relationship between their crimes and pornography. I also want to say that some of my opinions are based on research that I did for my doctorate.

At that time, I was trying to research fantasy. This is a nonpublished dissertation. I started out with that new idea of catharsis. And I used violent offenders and nonviolent offenders in a fairly complicated design. And the net result showed the opposite of what I had predicted, and was [in]consistent with all the other literature and research I had read for my dissertation, that the angry fantasies increased anger in the offenders. What was of particular importance was that it increased it most in the most violent offenders, the most sadistic offenders.[13]

What I want to say about a sex offender, and what I have learned about them, is that they are a long time in the making. It doesn't happen suddenly with no cause. There are always long-standing background reasons for their crimes and generally triggers in their current emotional environment that bring about the crimes. Pornography is both a cause and an effect of their emotional problems and very frequently plays a major part in their assaults on women and children. They generally will increase their consumption of pornography prior to sex offenses. They will get very specific ideas in reading pornography of exactly what they will do in their crimes, to whom they will do it in their crimes.

Certain types of them live years of their life in a fantasy world, isolated from real human relationships. They don't have emotional pairing relationships with other people, they don't have positive messages and values of sexuality, they don't see sexuality as a loving expression of things. What they see in their homes, and what they read, and what they hear in the media, is what they tend to believe about sexuality.

One man said to me just last week in group—he had been molesting his daughter over and over and over, and he knew it was wrong, and he felt terrible and hated himself. But, he said, I read about it in a magazine, I read how the children really like this, how they want their fathers to

13. Nancy Steele's study of convicted violent offenders found that fantasy did not reduce anger or the expression of aggression, contrary to the predictions of the psychoanalytic literature. None of the behavioral studies discussed on which the empirical hypothesis of the cathartic effect of fantasy was based specifically studied the effects of exposure to violent *sexual* materials on anger or aggression. Nancy Martin Steele, "The Role of Fantasy in the Reduction of Anger in Three Types of Convicted Offenders," Ph.D. diss., Ohio State University (1973).

abuse them. I knew it wasn't right, but it gave me the excuse I needed to keep on doing it. They [turn] to pornography as a way to sort of satiate an appetite that grows in themselves. It doesn't satiate them. It is like drinking salt water. The more they drink, the more they need, the more they have to seek to get what they believe they deserve.

For very lonely, very disturbed, angry men, pornography is a way in which they practice their crimes of sexual assault. They read stories, watch movies, and masturbate to angry destructive stories of rape and degradation. Over and over, they pair their fantasies with masturbation, ejaculation, and sexual release. Through a very basic conditioning process, their sexual response becomes conditioned to anger, violence, and shame. Some reach the point where they cannot feel sexual feelings in a loving and respectful context with women they care about. Fantasy is not harmless for many people. Certainly not all, but for many people, fantasy leads to action.

I do not believe that pornography would make abusers out of most men. Most men are as disgusted by sadistic pornography as most women are. We have to recognize that there are all too many men who live very lonely, unhappy lives, and for whom pornography is like a loaded gun. There are also a lot of adolescent girls and boys who are very curious about sexuality who are willing to try dangerous or forbidden things, and they too are vulnerable to the ideas, messages, and feelings in pornography.

So, we have to ask ourselves as a society: just what values do we believe in? What message do we want to give to people about violence and sexuality? Why are we condoning and in some ways supporting the very sick destructive proliferation of materials that can only harm other human beings?

I don't believe that the offender is here today that I had asked to come. He may have had trouble with the weather. Is he here? No, I guess not.

HOYT: I would like to ask you a question, based on your professional life. Is it fair to say that the men you work with use violent pornographic materials as they are feeling these feelings of anger and frustration and self-loathing? Because, you know it is awfully hard to separate out erotic material.

STEELE: Right.

HOYT: I mean, it isn't hard for me. I know what I think is erotic, and I know what I think is dangerous, because a woman in a sexual pose who is there without any whips and chains is erotic. Somebody tied to a bed with blood running out of their nose and mouth is violent. I was wondering, did you ever get into what kinds, I would guess it would be violent stuff?

STEELE: For the violent rapist, they tend to use violent material. Child molesters use child pornography. I am not against erotic or sexual literature. We use it to condition child molesters to be turned on by adult sexuality. I am against sexuality which is portrayed in a degrading or violent context.

HOYT: Thank you.

CHAIRMAN WHITE: Now, the next speaker is Michael O'Brien. Are there people in the hall? If they are, have them come in, especially if they are speakers.

Michael O'Brien?

UNIDENTIFIED SPEAKER: He is not in the hall.

CHAIRMAN WHITE: Not in the hall. Okay.

RICHELLE LEE: I am Richelle Lee. I work with sex offenders. I work with the State of Minnesota Department of Corrections, in Oak Park Heights currently, and I also worked at Lino Lakes for one year. I recently have been establishing a sex offender program at Oak Park Heights. I have also worked extensively with victims in sexual family abuse.

Basically I would validate the rest of the comments made by other sex offender therapists. So I will keep myself brief for your benefit and mine.

I have yet to work with an offender that does not use pornography. I have had a number of offenders who made the statement that pornography, they believe for themselves, was directly responsible for where they got their ideas—very early in their lives they were exposed to pornography—and that these messages and images about women, about what sexuality is, this is where they got their education. And they believe that that exposure early in their life had a direct effect upon them as to why they then acted out later on.

Offenders that I work with in the Department of Corrections said the pornography is for sale, insofar as *Playboy, Penthouse, Screw* magazine and other contraband magazines that are sold by the prison itself in the commissary. I think the sale of pornography right there happens to condone it. Our society is condoning those images and messages about women.

I spend hours in groups a day with men discussing their attitudes about women, their beliefs about sexuality. They, in fact, fit stereotypically with those images of women, that they like to be raped, that they like to be beaten. They are very open about that. They find it difficult to change those ideas and opinions. After spending hours in a group, they go back to their cells where they read the magazines and have the pin-ups on the walls.

I think the sale of pornography, at least from my perspective, has increased [to] where any grocery store I walk in, any gas station I walk in, is selling those magazines. There is something terribly wrong with the fact that our bodies can be sold as a commodity on any shelf, that most of the magazines, I know in one store I visit quite regularly, are on the bottom shelf where any child—even though there are plastic covers on those—any child can see those.

The incest women that I work with report that they were shown pictures of pornography by their uncles or fathers or aggressors to show them how it was done—that this is in fact what they were about, what they were for, and that this is okay.

Basically, I will just validate the rest of what has been said, and I think that the overuse of pornography, and the frequent selling of it, and the readily availableness of it is—let's not have it. Thank you.

CHAIRMAN WHITE: I thank you for making it brief, because there are quite a few people who have signed up, some who signed up last night that didn't get a chance to speak and also are here again tonight. But, we will get to you.

Paul Gerber from the Hennepin County Bureau of Criminal Apprehension?

DWORKIN: He doesn't seem to be here.

CHAIRMAN WHITE: Okay. Charlotte Kasl?

CHARLOTTE KASL: I am Charlotte Kasl. I am a therapist in private practice. I work with adult women survivors of sexual abuse as well as children of these survivors and the families. I also come from a—I have been doing therapy for about seven years with the victims and survivors.

I want to make two points. Basically I want to connect pornography as sexual addiction, and I want to connect sexual addiction to childhood sexual abuse. I also want to say I am just terrified talking here. I don't know when I have been so scared speaking about something as this issue. I think it is loaded emotionally. It is hard to stay focused on the issues. I hear about it so much because I work with abuse.

It has been my experience that pornography is an integral part of sexual addiction, and sexual addiction is an integral part of child abuse. And as these are addictions, they follow a course of escalation. They follow a course of compulsion. They are out of control. The addict using pornography is on a spiral, on a course that is getting worse that leads to escalation of the sexual acting out, whether it be peeping Tom, whether it be molesting children, exposing himself and so forth. I think by opening up this issue about pornography and sexuality and sexual addiction, we are going to open up the whole area around child abuse and around the way we need to redefine what is sexual instead of what is violence.

All children who live in the home—this is my opinion—all children who live in the home of a sexual addict at some level become victims of that addiction. And that person does not have to bring pornography home for that to happen. The energy that person carries, the fantasies, the thoughts, the way they talk and look at their female children, communicates something about this child to their bodies. Young girls talk about, "I couldn't stand it when my father touched me. There was something wrong." Some direct connections I have talked about with clients, and they said they were glad to have the stories here. They felt it was so important.

One example, for instance, was a young girl. By the age of four, she saw her parents sitting on the couch together reading pornographic magazines. When she tried to go join them, they were laughing and happy. She said it was the only time she saw her father's eyes light up. He felt alive. When she would try to read, they said no, no, which was confusing because they seemed happy reading this. By five years old, this young woman, at that time a young girl, would bring boys from the neighborhood, draw off her clothes the way she had seen in the magazines, and let herself be abused sexually. This is by five years old. This woman has gone through a great deal of work. She was alcoholic, very ill. She is now a student. She is now working through these things in therapy and is recovering, but she had never herself made the connection to the pornography. All she felt about herself [was], she was crazy, she was sick. How at five years old could I have been doing this? Pornography in the home is insidious. Girls pick up the message, they act it out, they don't know why they feel suicidal and crazy. I have seen this many, many times.

Another example I would like to share with you was a little boy I worked with whose father was preoccupied with pornography and had a house full of it. The little boy was known at school as the kisser. He would jump at girls, grab them, and kiss them. He was already developing an abuser mentality by the age of six. This happens to children, again, without them knowing it. He wanted to be like his father. That is what his father liked. He was doing what every child will do. It models for children that sexuality has power and that women are basically pieces of meat.

A third example was in a very abusive violent family where the father had read a great deal of pornography. It was kept in his room and the children knew it was there. He beat his children a lot, his daughters particularly. The girls used to sneak in when the parents were gone, read the pornography. They became addicted to it. It was their only escape, as it had been their father's escape. The woman that reported it—today at thirty—is addicted to pornography, has yet to have intimate sexual relationships or free herself from the connection of silence and sexuality. I think the growing use of twelve-step groups for sexual addicts and co-addicts in the city of Minneapolis will say that the awareness here is growing extremely quickly, and we have a lot to be proud of, that we are opening up the issues.

Another woman with a battering father, she saw her father read a great deal of pornography. She came away imprinted in her mind that all her father was interested in was sex, which generalized too that all men must always be interested in sex and no men can be trusted. When she was around them, she thought, what is my father thinking of me. In both these cases, the fathers were silent with the daughters. I believe a lot of battering of young girls has to do with sexual feelings, much of what comes every time in families where there was pornography. The father feels sexual towards his daughter, wants to repress that, and instead of taking responsibility for his addiction, which is out of his control, beats his daughter. It is connected many times. I have had fathers open up to this when they come to family therapy and talk about it.

Myself, I was in therapy some years back. I walked into a drug store and saw my therapist reading a pornographic magazine. I actually froze in my tracks. I felt so abused. In therapy with this man I always thought, "what is he thinking of me, what is he thinking when he sees my body?" I know the feelings I had, were those [the] children had. This was a trusted person I put my faith into, and I never could get past it. And I, at that time, didn't know enough or didn't have the feeling to speak, just as a child doesn't know enough to speak. They don't have the ability. They believe whatever goes on at home must be normal. These things are imprinted to children. They are dangerous to children.

The last example is going into a local grocery store there to return grapefruit. There was in the back room a picture of a naked woman from the back with a little diagram saying rump, ribs, shoulder, like they do with cows. I was upset. The first time I saw it, I couldn't talk. I came back later, walked in and saw it again. I was incredibly amazed that the store could have this. This is damaging. I said to the man, "I find this offensive, returning white grapefruit for pink ones and standing here with my daughter, that my daughter is a piece of meat, and her mother is a piece of meat." He finally took it down.

The fact is that we need to wake people up. I think Minneapolis has an incredible opportunity to put themselves on the map as a very strong forerunner in these liberties for women and making us feel free, to make us not feel we are violated and not see ourselves as meat.

CHAIRMAN WHITE: Thank you.

MacKINNON: Chairman White, I would like to submit a couple documents now from Minneapolis that are in the same vein as the testimony that was just given. I will not read them.

CHAIRMAN WHITE: Thank you.

MacKINNON: The first is from the Family Nurturing Center. I will note, in it, children are exposed to pornography, and this can include child pornography and adult pornography. Even the exposure in that way leads to people responding in later life, at that time, as if they were actual incest victims. [Exh. 18]

I am also submitting a letter to the City Council from the Kiel Clinics in Minneapolis talking about the use of pornography in the abuse of children and adult women. [Exh. 19] And a letter from VOICE, Incorporated, which is a national organization for victims of incest, to the City Council talking about the place of pornography in incest. [Exh. 20] And all of these letters are expressing support for this ordinance.

CHAIRMAN WHITE: Okay. Joan Weber?

Sue Santa?

SUE SANTA: I am Sue Santa. I work with a local nonprofit private organization in Minneapolis called Minneapolis Youth Division. My position there is outreach worker working exclusively with adolescent females involved in prostitution. Over the course of the years, six years that I have been there, I noticed a direct correlation between pornography and prostitution with my clients. I can say almost categorically never have I had a client who has not been exposed to prostitution through pornography in one way or the other. For some young women, that means that they are shown pornography—either films, videotapes, or pictures—as, this is how you do it, almost as a training manual in how to perform acts of prostitution.

CHAIRMAN WHITE: Excuse me. You are saying they are pimps training them with those kinds of messages?

SANTA: That is correct.

In addition, out on the street when a young woman is plying her trade, as it were, many of her tricks or customers will come up to her with little pieces of paper, pictures that were torn from a magazine and say: I want this. As one client put it, it is like a mail order catalogue of sex acts, and that is what she is expected to perform.

Another way that pornography plays a part in the lives of my clients is that as young women, very young women, some as young as eleven, they want the good things that are to be had in the United States. They want the kinds of things that they see on TV, and they see taking part in nude modeling, taking part in movies—pornographic movies—as a way to be a star, get to Hollywood. Now, this may seem foolish to those of you who are adults and say ha ha, we know that is wrong. We are talking about children who are very naive and are told that Marilyn Monroe made it this way, Brooke Shields made a movie about *Pretty Baby*. You have been there baby, you can do it.

Another aspect that plays a big part in my work with my clients is that, on many occasions, my clients are multi-, many-, rape victims. These rapes are often either taped or have photographs taken of the event. The young woman, when she tries to escape or leaves, is told that either she continues in her involvement in prostitution or those pictures will be sent to her parents, will be sent to the juvenile court, will be used against her. And out of fear, she will continue her involvement in prostitution.

On several occasions, not many but on several occasions, these young women have found that later that their pictures have been published in pornographic magazines without their knowledge and consent. This is very traumatic, especially when I have been working hard with this young woman to make things in her life better. She is involved in the straight lifestyle and finds out there are published pictures of her engaged in various sex acts.

I would like to close with a comment of one of my clients who heard I was going to be here tonight who said, "It is about time that those folks figured out what is going on." Thank you.

SHERRY ARNDT: My name is Sherry Arndt, and I am a moderator and trainer with the Illusion Theater here in Minneapolis. The Illusion Theater is a theater based in Minneapolis which has, since 1977, had a child sexual abuse prevention program as part of its theater.

Many people, I think, are probably aware of our existence and some of the work that we do. We perform two plays, one called *Touch,* which is for elementary students and helps explain to children what the difference is between good and bad touch, and what they can do when they are confused by touch. Our second play is called *No Easy Answers,* and it is for a teenage audience and helps—it covers the material presented in *Touch,* and enlarges on that to cover as well as images in advertising, sexual decisionmaking, acquaintance rape and incest, and other pertinent information that is interesting to teen-agers.

We also do numerous workshops for parents, community groups, and professional groups on the area of child sexual abuse prevention. We have performed in over thirty-five states to over 280,000 people.

My only background is as a public health nurse. I worked for eleven years in public school systems, nine of those years serving as a founder and representative on our county's child abuse team.

Our two plays are based on research done in the Minneapolis public schools with school children. They are based [on], and also use, the actual comments of children in the plays as well as comments from victims, comments from offenders, and some of the actors who corroborated . . . the plays' own experiences.

And in a recently published major study of child sexual abuse by David Finkelhor, who is a major researcher, in a major study published, one of the reasons that children gave for why they did not report that they had been sexually abused was that they were confused by the offender's insistence that the sexual behavior was normal and that other people liked the activity.

One of the most common ways that offenders do convince children . . . that the sex is normal and pleasurable, or should be pleasurable, is through showing them pornographic pictures of other children engaged in sex acts, looking as though they enjoy it. This is also one of the main ways that offenders coerce children into posing for pornographic photographs, is by showing them other pictures of other children and saying, "Well, everybody else likes it. There must be something wrong with you if you don't find this pleasant," and "Gee, you know you liked it the last time we were together." Offenders are very seductive with children.

In all of our work—and as I said, we travel extensively—we see over and over again a confusion that exists between what is okay and what is not okay in the whole area of sex, between what is sexuality and what is violence. This confusion is brought about in large part by pornography as well as other images in our culture that confuse us about what we are supposed to be like, and what other people are like, and how we are supposed to act. In fact, this is so pervasive that I think the influence of pornography has seeped into other written material that most of us don't consider pornography.

I brought with me a couple of examples of that: the December issue of *Harper's Bazaar,* which shows an eight-year-old girl in a perfume ad. She is dressed seductively. The photograph has made sure that her nipples are exposed. Part of the copy in this article is "Jasmine and Gardenia for seduction, with just a hint of innocence. Dreams of far away places synonymous with elegance, the height of confident femininity." I think it is not difficult for any of us to see the influence of pornography in this magazine article. I also have another article from the December issue of *Vogue,* which shows a photograph of a woman elegantly dressed in evening wear, fondling a naked, about fourteen-year-old boy. The caption on this is, "Age makes no difference." Neither magazine would probably be identified by most of us as pornographic.

So much confusion exists in our culture about the differences between sexuality and violence that we are currently working on a third dramatic piece that will be for adult audiences, and it will specifically focus on the confusion between sexuality and violence that exists in our culture. When society sanctions violence, especially violent use of sex against women and children, this attitude and resulting behavior begin to be defined as normal and natural. I think we have heard testimony to that over and over again today. I don't think I need to give any examples of that here.

When healthy sexual attitudes are prohibited by society, they begin to be defined as unnormal and unnatural. Sexuality and violence are used in our culture to the point that they are not separated in our minds, nor are they separated in our behaviors.

It is my position that we must separate sexuality and violence. This ordinance certainly speaks toward a good beginning to do that. We must accept the normality of sexuality and the seeking of pleasure or we will see increase in individual and group violence. Thank you.

CHAIRMAN WHITE: Thank you. Christopher Street representative?

MacKINNON: I think they said they were unable to make it.

CHAIRMAN WHITE: Okay. Sue Schafer?

SUE SCHAFER: My name is Sue Schafer. I am a psychologist in private practice. And over the last eight years, I would say at least half of my clients have been physically or sexually abused. I just arrived, and I don't have the history to know what has been addressed. The point I would like to make is similar to the previous speaker, Sue Santa, who talked about how pornography is used as training guides. While Sue talked about how the underworld often uses it to solicit young ladies for prostitution, I would like to talk about how pornography is used by acquaintances or family members, again as guidelines or as recipe books.

CHAIRMAN WHITE: It seems to me since 1:30 of yesterday that I have been hearing more and more, it seems to be that the family structure is a part of the problem. And could you speak to that?

SCHAFER: Well, I think the example that I am planning to use may address that. I would like to state three present or near-present cases that I am working with, where family members or acquaintances have used pornography as recipe books. Presently or recently I have worked with clients who have been sodomized by broom handles, forced to have sex with over twenty dogs in the back seat of their car, tied up and then electrocuted on their genitals. These are children or in the ages of fourteen to eighteen, all of whom I could have found a direct impact by pornography, either where the perpetrator has read the manuals and manuscripts at night and used these as recipe books by day, or had the pornography present at the time of the sexual violence. And so, as the previous speaker talked about, the importance of separating sex and violence, I recognize. I think any step to take or eliminate pornography would be a step in the direction of separating out sex and violence.

Another further complication I see in working with the clients, as children—once these children grow up into adults, there becomes a tremendous link between sex and violence, so much so that in their mind that sadomasochistic behaviors are something they fight, oftentimes on a daily basis. For these children that grow up and become adults, oftentimes sex becomes impossible without some form of self-mutilation or violence. So while it is directly connected with their adult sexual activity, it is also connected in a general sense with self-mutilating types of behaviors that continue. Thank you.

CHAIRMAN WHITE: Thank you very much.

MacKINNON: Chairman White, I would like to submit a few documents at this time.

CHAIRMAN WHITE: Okay.

MacKINNON: I would also offer a brief interpretation of the evidence, in answer to your question. Perhaps one way to think about what we have heard about family is that we have illustrated that the family is no exception to the abuses that exist of women and children throughout this society. The documents I would like to submit, the first three are by writers, each of whom has submitted a statement to the Minneapolis City Council on the occasion of the consideration of this ordinance. They are all writers in the area of incest and child abuse.

The first is by Trudee Able-Peterson, who wrote the book *Children of the Evening,* which is looking at child prostitution in America. [Exh. 21]

The second is by Katherine Brady, who wrote the book *Father's Days.* And she brings up a statement about her own particular experience of incest and how pornography plays in that, as well as other accounts from her knowledge of the subject. [Exh. 22]

The third is a letter from Louise Armstrong, who wrote the book *Kiss Daddy Goodnight,* a speakout on incest. [Exh. 23] She wrote a letter and extensive statement to the Minneapolis City Council connecting her research on incest with pornography.

A fourth letter to the Minneapolis City Council comes from Incest Survivors Resource Network International from New York who "enthusiastically endorses your efforts in bringing the relationship of incest and pornography to a public forum." [Exh. 24]

CHAIRMAN WHITE: Let the record show.

Floyd Winecoff?

MacKINNON: He is unable to come.

CHAIRMAN WHITE: Michael Laslett?

MICHAEL LASLETT: My name is Michael Laslett. Before I read my own statement, I would like to read a statement of a psychologist by the name of Floyd Winecoff, who was unable to be here this evening. He has been working with men for many years. The title of his statement is "Pornography and its Effects on Men."

My expertise in addressing this subject comes from a 10-year psychotherapy practice specializing in services for men. My practice has included over the years an ongoing treatment group for men who are physically, verbally, or sexually abusive. I have repeatedly found a direct link between pornography and attitudes towards women as objects that contribute to the ongoing crime of violence against women.

The myth about pornography is that it frees the libido and gives men an outlet for sexual expression which liberates mind and body. This is truly myth. I have found that pornography not only does not liberate men, but on the contrary becomes a source of bondage. Men masturbate to pornography only to become addicted to the fantasy. There is no liberation for men in pornography. Pornography becomes a source of addiction much like alcohol. There is temporary relief. It is mood altering. And it is reinforcing, i.e. "you want more" because "you got relief." It is this reinforcing characteristic that leads men to want the experience which they have in photographic fantasy to happen in "real" life.

An endless search ensues to capture the docile woman of fantasy in total real life availability. The more hopeless it is to find this sort of woman, the more desperate becomes the interaction between men and the women they pursue.

The problem arises when real women do not like being dominated, controlled, and "made love to" on one-sided terms. When women assert themselves, men experience a loss of the feeling of being in control. Violence occurs in men when their own personal concept of "masculinity" is challenged. A man who is already addicted to the feeling of needing to have sex, and the fantasy of being in control, becomes desperate in his behavior when confronted by a woman who doesn't want what's being given out.

Women lose, and men lose too. Women lose, of course, because they are the object of this abusive pursuit. Men lose because they never experience true intimacy that comes from letting down and opening up with someone. Many men let down and open up when there is a threat of losing the relationship; but violence is a more common occurrence.

There is no social communion in domination and control. By nature we are social beings, and as such require true social interaction for well-beingness. Without such social communion, there exists only isolation and desperation.

Pornography portrays a fantasy of social communion, but in reality it contributes to the desperation that leads men to abusiveness. There is no difference between the person who will lie, steal, cheat, or kill in order to get the drug or chemical of addicted choice. Pornography is the chemical of sexual addiction.

And my own statement. I have been raised and socialized in a pornographic society. Pornographic images of women have surrounded and bombarded me throughout my life—images which depict women primarily as sexual objects available to me at any time, as sexually submissive, as meaning yes even when they say no, as always wanting sex, and as finding abuse sexually enjoyable.

Everywhere I go, I carry a pornographic notion of what an "attractive" woman is, what she looks like, how she acts, what she says, and so on. I have been infected with pornographic, sexist, and blatantly oppressive expectations of women as friends, co-workers, passers-by, lovers. My sexism, however, is not a haphazard occurrence. I am the result of a systematic socialization process which trains all men to oppress women, because it is in the interests of men as the economic, political, sexual, and cultural rulers of this society to keep women down. Pornography is a crucial tool in the maintenance of male power.

While consolidating this male supremacist system, pornography also directly harms men as individuals. For most of my life, I accepted pornographic definitions of women—how large were their breasts, their buttocks, their waist. I was only attracted to women who met very narrow standards, and my sense of self-worth depended, in large part, on how many such women were interested in me. But pornography portrays women as insatiable. So while, for the good of my self-image and my status in the eyes of my male friends, I wanted as many women as possible to be attracted to me, I was also terrified of being sexually inadequate.

Even after I became aware of my sexism and its link to pornography, I couldn't simply shed a lifetime of socialization. I couldn't escape the perceptions of women I had been taught. I began to hate myself for being sexist and for finding pornography arousing.

For years, I couldn't interact with a woman without feeling that I was oppressing her, especially if I found her attractive. Since physical love-making is one of the most intimate forms of interaction, and since it has been so twisted and mutilated by pornography, I couldn't sleep with a woman without feeling that I was oppressing her because my attraction for her had been influenced by pornography. I am still struggling with these feelings today.

Women are assaulted daily by and because of pornography, and my life and sexuality have been warped and distorted by it. Countering these effects of patriarchy will be a lifetime endeavor. I urge you to pass this legislation to help us in the task of dismantling our crippling pornographic images. Let us work so that women will be less oppressed, that men will be less well-trained to oppress them, and that women and men will be free to live healthier and more equal lives. Thank you.

DWORKIN: May I please put these documents into evidence. I am sorry that Chairman White isn't here. He has been expressing a desire to have confirmed his perception that pornography does hurt men in a very serious way. And we would like to end by submitting a part of a book by an author named Timothy Beneke on rape, which documents the relationship between pornography and men's attitudes on rape. [Exh. 25] And in addition, a letter from an individual named Jim Lovestar who talks about how he feels that pornography has hurt him as a man because it has genuinely decreased his intimacies. And he is from Minneapolis. [Exh. 26]

And I would also like to submit into evidence a letter from John Stoltenberg, who is originally from Minneapolis, who is not living here now. He is the Chair of the Antipornography Task Group of the National Organization for Men. And that group sponsors this ordinance. And Mr. Stoltenberg has had a lot of experience doing workshops on pornography with men, and men find it to be extremely disorienting and disruptive to their social learning behavior, and I think that he is representing a political opposition among men to the existence of pornography. So I submit this letter also. [Exh. 27] Thank you.

HOYT: Ms. Dworkin, I will tell you that we do have microphones, we do have speaker boxes back in our offices. And from time to time, as you see committee members getting up and leaving, they are not out of hearing of the hearing going on. And Chairman White, I am sure, is listening.

DWORKIN: Thank you. I was concerned only because the Chairman, I think, has been very clear about his own feelings in that direction and in the course of these hearings.

DAUGHERTY: Anything further? We will move on to Omar Johnson.

HOYT: Mr. Chairman?

DAUGHERTY: Go ahead, Charlee.

HOYT: I will go ahead. I would like to reiterate the statement—the longer we are here, the tireder we seem to become—as we hear all testimony tonight, either in agreement or in opposition of your feelings, I ask that you give all credence—inasmuch, don't hiss, don't boo. Please let people have their say.

DAUGHERTY: All right. Mr. Johnson, proceed. Give your name and address.

OMAR JOHNSON: Omar Johnson, 1920 Third Avenue South, Apartment 21. And I'm going to be talking about myself.

I was raised in Ecuador on a mission compound. The school library was well-censored. My sexual life began quite late. In fact, I was a junior at Dartmouth College before I even masturbated. The procedure, I remember, was self-conscious, primitive, even silly. But at the moment of orgasm, there was an image. I saw a green, grassy knoll out of which popped a white rabbit and it looked at me quizzically, then bounded away, cotton tail flipping through the foliage. It's an image that will always stay with me: the fertility of the rabbit, the continuing virginity of the whiteness, nothing ever lost that cannot be regained, and the green, green earth all around.

Of course, this poetry didn't last too long. I had a friend down the hall that introduced me to another bunny. It was so legitimate—an interview with Jimmy Carter and everything. The pictures gave me a feeling somewhere between queasiness and arousal. I didn't know what to do or think about them. But the section where readers write in to the editor detailing their exploits solved that problem. I was a very quick study. I mean, I had already internalized messages suggesting that women were second-class creatures. I mean, I lived in a society that had applauded me when I knocked someone out on the football field and then wandered around in a daze myself for a couple of minutes. Violence as pleasure was something I already knew. This was just another context. By the end of the year I was stringing together long involved fantasies where women did what I wanted and loved me for it.

Then—I am out of college now—I met and got involved with a real woman. She was very special in that she did not have the capacity to seem simpler than she was. It was I who would have to learn to live with and love her complexity. It has not been easy. She is very sensitive to what she calls "connectedness." I could not manage it. Trying hard to do right by her, I failed miserably, got frustrated, used to storm out of the house yelling, "What more can I give?" I have never been physically violent with her, but there have been occasions when I was so enraged at my inability to love—and I think that is an important connection—that I got angry at her, and then I found myself in an adult bookstore reading my fantasies. As I said before, women felt fear, and pleasure, and fulfillment, according to my whim.

But all this time—perhaps because I remembered the beauty and creativity of my first sexual image, which I found very ludicrous at the time. By the way, I knew her way with sex and with love was what I wanted. My point is, that if women in a society filled by pornography must be wary for their physical selves, a man, even a man of good intentions, must be wary for his mind. My spill into pornography felt like a congenital weakness, like getting a hernia. Perhaps it is only a cultural weakness. The point is, for me, having porn around was like the freedom to fall into a trap that I have been a long time climbing out of.

I would like, very much, to get back to following the rabbit of my own dreaming. I do not want to be a mechanical goose-stepping follower of the *Playboy* bunny, because that is what I think it is. Porn makes me feel goose bumps as well as erections. These are the experiments a master race perpetuates on those slated for extinction.

Now, the woman I live with is Jewish. She makes me think about the connection. She was very afraid after the brutal rape and beating a couple of weeks ago which happened a couple blocks from our apartment. She tried to joke about arming herself with a frying pan and was comfortable with organizing a frying pan brigade. But it was no good. She was still afraid. And just as a well-meaning German was afraid in 1933, I am also very much afraid. Thank you.

CAROL ANN: My name is Carol Ann.

CHAIRMAN WHITE: Excuse me, before you begin, did we get documentation of Mr. Johnson's notes? You may go ahead.

CAROL ANN: I am speaking as a resident of Minneapolis. I have lived in Minneapolis for approximately twenty-eight years and about twenty of those have been within a six-block radius of the Lake Street area. I am presently living in the Chicago/Lake area, less than a half a block from the Rialto Theater and the bookstore.

As a child, when I was growing up, I experienced some good things on Lake Street. I don't know if anybody can remember. I used to go roller-skating on Dupont and Lake, movies at the American and Vogue—I am just shaking—theaters at Lyndale and Lake, and the hobby shop and pet shop at Bryant and Lake.

Also in my past, I was raped by my father for over a year from six to seven years old, and I witnessed the beatings of my mother through my entire childhood, through my teenage years. Also I saw the pornography literature—paperback books, black and white magazines—in my father's bedroom through the entire time of my childhood and into my teenage years until I left. I didn't know that that sexual abuse and physical abuse was wrong. I found that out about two and a half years ago, and I have been working on it ever since. The only thing that I did know, or that I felt, was that it was my fault. My struggle to stay alive is my process which I call reclaiming myself, not living out the shame.

Daily when I walk out of my house, and I would see the doors open as usual and business as usual at the Rialto Theater and the bookstore, and I go into the Marlin Gas Station to get bus change, and in front of me displayed in *Hustler* magazine, "Hustler Rejects," depicting a naked woman stuffed into a garbage can, legs hanging out and dismembered body parts stuffed behind her. What I see is that women's bodies are rejected, it is okay to be dismembered, and they belong in a garbage can. It says to me that physical and sexual violence is okay, acceptable, in demand, and paid for. That the rape of a six-year-old girl is okay and acceptable. I also see pornography as relying on mass production and marketing. And I see its main motive as providing sensory stimulation and gratification through extreme sexual violence, mutilation, and finally death of women and children's bodies.

This incident of my rape is but a part of the entire oppression. In the midst of this social decay that confronts each of us here, I believe there is a strong resistance growing. No longer do I need to seek recognition through the rape of my body, but that I rid myself of the fear that silences me to repossess myself. What is deadly to me is the masses which rely on this form of violent visual expression to base their daily interaction with me as a woman.

And I publicly protest the pornography in my neighborhood and the Chicago/Lake area. And I am glad that I am able to speak here, and I support this ordinance. Thank you.

CHAIRMAN WHITE: Is Joan Gilbertson in here?

JOAN GILBERTSON: My name is Joan Gilbertson. I live at [address deleted] in close proximity to the Chicago/Lake district. I am here to say, for the Powderhorn Park Association, [of] which I am a member, supports this ordinance wholeheartedly. We encourage you to pass this ordinance. Thank you.

CHAIRMAN WHITE: Thank you. Due to the snow, there was someone that was late.

KATHLEEN McKAY: My name is Kathleen McKay. I am a licensed psychologist in the State of Minnesota and I am Administrator of Sagaris, a Mental Health Center for women located in South Minneapolis, for nine and a half years.

I am speaking from my experience and that of my colleagues, psychologists and psychiatrists. We see women who voluntarily seek assistance for life's problems, relationships, parenting, career issues, and so on, and they range in age generally from 23 to 63.

I can say without exaggeration that every woman we have seen over the last nine and a half years has sustained damage living in a milieu which systematically presumes and teaches that women's bodies are available for the titillation of the public. The degradation and shame spoken about by Linda Marchiano is something all women know about: catcalls on the street, topless girls on a marquee, rapes, rapes and more rapes. Part of what I do with women in therapy must be to teach them how to compensate for this, how to live in an oppressive punishing culture that does not teach, and barely allows, women to take pride in their own bodies and in themselves.

United States Supreme Court Justice William O. Douglas, during the abortion debates some time ago, wrote a brief piece relating to the right of privacy, and I quote mostly from him. He talks about the customary presumption in a free society and the freedom to walk, freedom to stroll or even loaf without being harassed. Pornography is one of the most powerful teaching aids in the socialization and training of both girls and boys, and adult women and men. The consistent and persistent presentation of women as victims is training in the notion that women are available for use, abuse, degradation, shame, and disgust. My guarantees and promises as a citizen of the United States and resident of Minneapolis dictate that I should be able to walk or stroll in my town, even Hennepin Avenue and designated Lake Street corners, without having pornographic expressions screaming shame and humiliation at me. This does offend my civil rights as they are promised to me.

I want to express my appreciation and that of my colleagues at Sagaris to Ms. MacKinnon and Dworkin for their drafting of this ordinance, once again putting Minneapolis on the map as a first in progressive legislation. Also our appreciation to Alderman Hoyt and Van White for their understanding of the issue and sponsorship of this ordinance. I urge, may I say plead with you, to seriously consider this ordinance and get a workable law for Minneapolis. Thank you very much.

CHAIRMAN WHITE: Thank you. Dick Marple?

DICK MARPLE: I am speaking as a citizen of Minneapolis. I am not affiliated with any groups and wasn't a scheduled speaker or anything like that. I have some problems with the ordinance. I think a number of the points defining what pornography is are vague and fail to distinguish between violent pornography, which I find generally reprehensible, and general erotic expression which I find enjoyable, and I think it is my right as a citizen of the United States. Particularly the subheadings on the definition that I think are quite vague are numbers one, five, six, and seven. I fail to see how a jury or a judge would be able to determine "whether women are presented as whores by nature." I don't know what that means. It is a nice slogan. I don't think it is a legally significant term.

I think "women presented as sexual objects," I think in any professional encounter both, regardless of their gender, may be sexual objects to each other, and I see that as a legitimate form of sexual expression. I am unclear on number five. What is the "posture of sexual submission," if this has to do with the positioning of the bodies, or who is involved? I think that is pretty vague. And I am not sure about number six, which refers to women being reduced to these body parts. My main concern with this is that in attempting to eliminate pornography, [in silencing] pornography in Minneapolis, we may be stepping on legitimate rights of expression and people's right to enjoy themselves in a nonoffensive way. I am also appalled in a civil rights ordinance at the sexist language. It says the sexuality of women. There is no mention of children or men, and I don't believe that they should be relegated to second-class citizenship.

I would also like to say that [if] we have a civil rights ordinance trying to discourage presenting women as whores by nature, then I believe that men have a civil right not to be presented as rapists by nature. And I have read books by feminists in which they apparently describe men this way. And I believe that if you will not accept the predecessor of this law, that men act out according to descriptions or portrayals, then I question some of these writers who portray men as rapists by nature. Perhaps they just assign them to silence, or telling them, this is what you are, you might as well do it. I think that is sick.

I am a clerk at the Minneapolis Public Library. I do not speak for the Public Library. I speak as a concerned employee. And the bottom half of my sentence is that I don't see the distinctions between violent pornography and erotic material. I believe that the library can be in deep trouble if individuals are allowed to censor the material that is in the library, which would include art books, romances which are written by and for women, such instructive material as the Bible, lives of saints, tracts and feminist matters.

I am also concerned—I am concerned that there may be restrictions, at least threatened lawsuits, against news agencies who may, depending on your definition of the word graphic, when they describe a sex crime. The possibility of someone thinking the civil rights were violated might bring a lawsuit against a newspaper for reporting this. That defeats the purpose. I might also point out that if this bill had been passed before 1969, we may never have known about My Lai Massacre in Vietnam, because some of the photographs that we used to report this would have been considered pornographic and unlawful under this ordinance.

My concern with the subheading of section four, number one, which deals directly with public libraries is, they have to determine open display of pornography. We have heard a woman describe *Vogue* magazine, *Harper's Bazaar,* as having pornographic images in it. I don't believe the library has the funds to defend each and every item they have.

HOYT: Mr. Chairman, I am sorry for interrupting. I would like to call your attention in the ordinance on the second page, under the discrimination of trafficking in pornography, number one, which says, "City, state and federally funded libraries or private and public university and college libraries in which pornography is available for study shall not be construed to be trafficking in pornography but open display of pornography in said places is sex discrimination."

MARPLE: Is open display circulating a copy of a book that is on a shelf so someone can see the cover? That is not very clear to me.

HOYT: I wanted to make sure—

MARPLE: I have been stewing about it for five days. I also question section seven which is on the back page of the ordinance in which it refers to assault and battery due to pornography. Any person, which I think should be used in the previous section in pornography instead of women, who is assaulted or battered in a way that is directly caused by specific pornography, has a claim, et cetera. If you refer to an act as having been directly caused by a specific piece of pornography, are you not absolving the perpetrator from guilt?

HYATT: Would you move back?

MARPLE: Are you not absolving the perpetrator from guilt as a result of pornography? You are denying this person free will, and therefore I wonder if he can be [prosecuted]? I think the most dangerous part of the ordinance—

MacKINNON: I am sorry, I really missed what you said about assault and battery. What was the initial criticism?

MARPLE: I objected to the phrase "directly caused by specific pornography," because to me it seems to remove responsibility.

MacKINNON: That isn't what I meant. What I didn't understand is—I will tell you what I seem to understand from what you said before. That there was something wrong in saying "man, child or transsexual"?

MARPLE: Yeah. I was referring back to the section that defines pornography. I think a "person" or "human being" would cover all categories.

MacKINNON: Obviously you are saying that, to you, it would be an improvement to state that in that summary form, rather than the specific categories of persons?

MARPLE: Yeah, I think so. I think that would cover everybody. And I think in the definition under the ordinance using the word women—instead of people, or men, children, transsexual, anybody else you want to include—seems discriminatory in a civil rights ordinance. I think there should be as much concern against violence for women and children and men as there is for women.

HOYT: Are you aware, the reason there is a civil rights ordinance is because it is women who have been, as a class, placed in this subordination, second-class position, and that is why it is a civil rights issue? That is why it says women so often. Children are mentioned here and not mentioned elsewhere, because there are already laws on the books about child pornography.

MARPLE: Okay. I appreciate that. I still think men have the right also.

My major concern—and I am ready to close—is that the basic rights of expression in this country, I believe, are fundamental, and I think that this ordinance prohibits more than it [in]tends to prohibit. And I find it very difficult to accept that a writer or an artist can be prohibited from expressing himself or herself. I might add that books, organized opinions that are done with the intention of putting out abuses and injustices, would likewise be prohibited by this ordinance. And also I question if this ordinance were passed and lawsuits were taking place, whether other groups might not say that they have civil rights that are being violated by other things, such as I have an 87-year-old grandmother who is very religious and who I am sure thinks it is a crime against nature just even thinking about two women having sex together. And I wonder if she would have walked by the Amazon Bookstore or any place else, if her civil rights would not be violated.

CHAIRMAN WHITE: Is that all you have?

MARPLE: That is all.

CHAIRMAN WHITE: Thank you.

HYATT: Are you an attorney in a lawsuit?

MARPLE: No, I am not. I am a law clerk at the library.

JAN SPRING: Hello. I am Jan Spring. I live at [address deleted], which is half a block away from the nearest pornography theater. And, I have to say, I feel particularly privileged to speak following Mr. Marple. He addressed several of the items that I would like to address. Particularly the question of free speech and so forth which has always been brought up whenever feminists raised questions about pornography.

I believe that in this ordinance, for the first time, we have a way of dealing with pornography which doesn't get us into that problem. Up until this time, sexually explicit and abusive materials were dealt with in terms of obscenity. What obscenity means to me is that sex is dirty, that my body is dirty because it is associated with sex, and that I should be ashamed, and that any place, any bookstore or other thing that displays women's bodies or, you know, deals in sex at all, should be relegated to certain neighborhoods which are undesirable, such as my neighborhood, or such as neighborhoods in which poor men and women live, or in such neighborhoods [in] which people of color live.

In this ordinance, a distinction between simply sexual or erotic materials [is] not addressed by the ordinance and therefore, not prohibited, and materials which are designed to harm women to keep us in a state of submission, to keep us afraid—that latter group of materials is prohibited, and it doesn't depend on the neighborhood. The neighborhood I live in has been apparently for a long time considered a neighborhood where pornography is permitted. That does not go by zoning, and does not go by neighborhoods, and it is important that it not be permitted in somebody else's neighborhood.

Now I am speaking as a private citizen, although I have worked with sexually assaulted and battered women and I am a therapist. I have lived in Minneapolis for about four and a half years, and I have chosen to live in the Powderhorn neighborhood all that time, which means that for four and a half years, not every day but many days, I have stood on the bus corner in front of whatever happened to be the local closest porn shop, waiting for a bus. And I would walk by it on my way home, so that I am not able to forget about the existence of pornography.

Currently, I have two daughters, and when they want to walk to the drugstore or to the grocery store—both of which are in walking distance and easy for them to get to—they walk by the Avalon Theater. They probably walk by that theater once or twice a day. I wonder what it does to their minds. I don't know. I spoke to my daughter. I called her to wish her a happy birthday, and I asked her if anything had ever happened there. She said no, nothing particularly had ever happened there. But I worry about my daughters because they have to go by this place.

I worry about them when they have to go out to play with the other kids in the neighborhood, because most of the kids in the neighborhood are boys, and they are subject to the influence of pornography, which says to them that women and girls are objects and less than human, and because those boys have demonstrated that, because I don't live with a man, they think that my particular house is an okay house to vandalize, and my guests are okay to harass, and that it is okay for them to come and break into my house just for fun to scare my daughters. This happened. It is on the police report. And, you know, when I spoke to the parents about it, that is what the boys said: it was just for fun.

So what porn means to me, is that I can't forget that—what society thinks of me—which is that I am an object. I am a sex object. I am not a human being. If I ever get raped walking down a street, it will be my fault because I was alone.

My daughters are growing up in a society which demeans them as less than human. Their father has pornography in his home. I discovered it and was very shocked, and I was very afraid, and I can't do anything about it except to be afraid and wait and watch. And so, for me, listening to the stories that I heard earlier this evening, I felt very privileged, because I haven't been raped by anybody since I was a kid, you know. I haven't been raped silently by a stranger. My daughters have not been raped, and I hope they will not be. I have taken them to a self-defense class.

Yet, this is the kind of effect that pornography has on me. That I am constantly informed that it is okay to beat women, and it is okay to rape women, and women like being subjected to violence. And every time I step outside of my door, and every time I stay inside my house, I know that I may be the victim of violence against me, whether it be an obscene phone call or physical attack. And all I have to say applies not only to that porn which depicts violent acts. I feel the same about pornography which merely shows women's genitals without the rest of their bodies. I have not seen anything depicting men's genitals with the rest of their bodies missing. Thank you.

DAUGHERTY: Thank you. Next we have William Prock, 818 Southeast Seventh Street.

WILLIAM PROCK: That is correct. I am employed by the city of Minneapolis. I am the investigation manager for the Minneapolis Department of Civil Rights. I am not presenting a series of comments or position statements for the Department. I am aware that our Executive Director,

George Caldwell, has certain questions and certain disagreements with me. I am aware that other people on our staff have other concerns, other questions, and we may or may not be in agreement.

What I would like to present is not to talk about sexual abuse, pornography per se. I would like to talk about the proposal before the Commission in the context of the civil rights statutes and in particular in relationship to the Minneapolis civil rights ordinance. Some of these concerns were heard yesterday, and I anticipate a good session tomorrow afternoon, when I understand we are making a presentation to the Department.

The nation and the City of Minneapolis have a long history of concern for the rights of their citizens. These rights are embodied in the Constitution of the United States and the fifty states themselves. Unfortunately, we do not have the same history in ensuring that all citizens receive the opportunity to exercise those constitutionally guaranteed rights.

These constitutionally guaranteed rights are inherent in us as human citizens of the United States. As such, they are moral imperatives to all persons within the country. The concept of human rights is a moral, ethical, and some would say religious concept. However, human rights and civil rights are not one and the same. While human rights carry a moral imperative, civil rights are those ensured by statute, statutes enacted in a limited fashion, to render real concepts embodied in the Constitution. Statutory civil rights, particularly those which resulted from the struggle exemplified by Dr. Martin Luther King, Jr., were enacted to provide a means of redress for the denial of rights embodied in the statutes themselves. These rights all dealt with some aspect of life, the denial of which could produce some identifiable and concrete personal loss to the individual, such as denial of a job, housing, the inability to obtain credit, inability to purchase a meal in a place of one's choice, inability to attend a movie theater, use a washroom, ride a bus, obtain an education and a myriad of other concrete harms.

Thus, civil rights statutes have in common the need to identify a specific identifiable and compensable harm to the individual in order to be able [to] invoke their protections. Further, each statute requires that a person claiming to be aggrieved be a member of a specifically identified protected class, race, sex, color, affectional preference, et cetera. It is my opinion that the City of Minneapolis has one of the best-drafted and comprehensive civil rights statutes in the country.

However, under the proposal before the Committee today, the concept of protected class is turned on its ear. We are no longer looking at a status characteristic of an individual in order to obtain access to the laws' protection. Rather, we are dealing with an individual's behavior, the behavior of some other individual, or a graphic representation of behavior as the definitional basis for a new protected class. While this may be legitimate, it is a new and untried legal approach and deserves, at minimum, the due deliberation given to all previous substantive amendments to the ordinance. I cite in particular the deliberation and time spent by City Council on those amendments that added affectional preference as a protected class in 1982 and permitted families with children to bring actions to the Civil Rights Department in the area of housing discrimination.

There are some specific concerns I have that result not in objections to the ordinance per se, but as questions that I think the Council should consider in its deliberations. And I will do these by section. Section 2 (b)(1), this section provides that [victims of] pornography is another protected class, upon which a claim of employment, housing, and other forms of discrimination can be brought. And as such I believe—

DAUGHERTY: Just a minute, what page are you on?

PROCK: This is the first page, Section 2 (b)(1).

DAUGHERTY: Go ahead.

PROCK: This section, I believe, adds little or nothing in the way of further protection for women that already exists in the ordinance.

MacKINNON: Mr. Prock, is sexual harassment a status characteristic?

PROCK: No, it is not.

MacKINNON: It is there.

PROCK: It is a behavior that is directed—it is an obnoxious behavior. I understand that the pornography section is a theoretical extension of sexual harassment theory, as interpreted through Title VII and through the courts. Sexual harassment itself as under Section 7 is gender-free.

Okay. I don't want to debate, because what I would like to do is raise the concerns and the Council will deal with them. Some of them, I believe, will have policy implications for the Council.

Section 3 (gg), pornography is so defined that a judgment of what is within that definition is either extremely broad and very easy, or extremely difficult, meaning that it is very narrow, with the potential for page by page and paragraph by paragraph analysis being required, and to the extreme requiring a percentage content rule to determine the inclusion or exclusion. This places a tremendous burden with the individuals charged with making those judgments. I believe in most cases the people making the judgments would be my staff in the Civil Rights Department. This is a burden that the City Council would not want to give to anyone without the proper legal counseling and background.

Section 4 (l), this defines what consists of trafficking in pornography. Prosecution under this section does not, as it is currently written and I interpret it, require any individual to come forward alleging concrete, identifiable and compensable harm under the law, as civil rights statutes have been construed. The mere fact of production, regardless of the circumstances of that production, becomes a cause of action. The same would hold true for the sale, exhibition, or distribution. No one need come forward and allege personal harm. This seems nothing more than an open attempt at ultimate censorship.

HOYT: May I ask a question here?

PROCK: Yes, ma'am.

HOYT: What we are trying to say is that the existence of the material as described here is the harm.

PROCK: I understand.

HOYT: Do you understand that?

PROCK: Yes, I understand that. I think the implication is that, as I read it, it is a risk. I am not saying that this is gospel in any way. As I read it, the risk is that the mere sale, display, et cetera, would constitute a violation and would allow possibly the City Attorney's Office, my director, myself, any of my staff people essentially file the charge on sale, out it goes.

HOYT: That is right.

PROCK: I am not sure that that will stand up.

HOYT: Doesn't that make your job easier?

PROCK: Unfortunately, it might make it much more difficult. I think it might make it much more difficult. I don't know. These are concerns that I have.

I do believe, however, that the theory embodied in this particular section—and that is a body of literature and pictures or whatever, that deliberately and purposefully and with malice degrades and places into second-class citizenship a segment of our society—[that] this is a rather dangerous theory. Under this theory, it could be extended to the production, distribution, sale, or exhibition of literature produced by, in some cases, the Anti-Defamation League of the B'nai B'rith, because it could in times degrade and put in second-class status non-Jewish citizens. Or it could be extended to permit the banning of publications for the National

States Rights Party by directly and purposefully being aimed at perpetuating the second-class citizens of all racial minorities, particularly black people. This is one of J. B. Stoner's publications. It could be interpreted to ban, should the theory hold, publications of the Black Panther Party, if it ever comes back into the forefront, which are at times very degrading to whites. In other instances it could in fact be extended to ban some of the publications of the American Civil Liberties Union, which in most cases do not reflect the opinions of the majority of Americans.

HOYT: Could you tell me where in here that the material has to reflect the opinion of the majority of the Americans?

PROCK: I am not saying it is.

HOYT: It was under my impression that the definition of pornography did not refer to the opinion of the majority of Americans.

PROCK: That is correct. What I am trying to point out—

HOYT: You seem to be going down a track that was not directed at what was written in this ordinance. Are you saying this ordinance, you fear the passage of this ordinance would bring people to want to pass other—

PROCK: I think that is a risk that is inherent in the theory that is embodied in the trafficking section. While these last may seem farfetched and impossible, the theory underlying the trafficking provision is the basis for such outlandish possibilities.

Within the governmental library exemption is a puzzling inconsistency. It is assumed that when pornography is sold over the counter, controlled or free, it is being purveyed and purchased for less than noble purposes. However, when it is lent by or used within a public library, it is for research purposes, and the damage it commits upon its reader somehow seems to miraculously disappear. If pornography is damaging and dangerous, it is so whether obtained from a magazine rack or a public library.

MacKINNON: If we eliminated that section, what would you then say?

PROCK: I don't know. I would have to take a look at that in context with the rest of this. Further, the open display of pornography is defined as sex discrimination when the library does the displaying, thus making the libraries subject to suits by citizens of the City of Minneapolis, alleging sex discrimination, not trafficking, but invoking pain and suffering and punitive damages and other compensative awards for damages.

Section 5 (m)(1), this provides for a five-year statute of limitations in the bringing of a discrimination suit under this proposal. This is more closely allied to statutes of limitation for criminal actions. The remainder of the prohibited acts in the existing ordinance require action to be brought within six months. Is it proper to single out one form of discrimination, within a single statute, as being deserving [of] a longer statute of limitations than all others? I merely offer this for Council's consideration, as all other forms of prohibited discrimination are considered equally bad under the law.

Finally, I must say I have other reservations about this statute, particularly with Section 7 (o) which grants the Civil Rights Department investigative authority over acts of discrimination that are part and parcel of criminal activity. Currently, the existing ordinance, under Section 141.90, prohibits the Department from issuing a complaint or hearing any matter when the alleged discrimination is part of or arises out of an incident or occurrence which in itself could give rise to a criminal prosecution for the violation of any state statute other than the state act against discrimination.

As Aldermen White and Daugherty and Howard are aware, the repeal of this provision occupied much time for the Council and the Civil Rights Commission for several years. Ultimately, it was deemed by the Council that the exemption should remain in the ordinance. My question is now, has the Council changed its mind and does it now desire the Civil Rights Department to investigate discrimination that is entwined with criminal activity, or does the Council desire to retain the prohibition that was put in the ordinance at least ten years ago and reaffirmed in 1982?

Ultimately, I fully support the effort for providing an administrative—at low or no cost—enforcement mechanism for women who have suffered harm at the hands of pimps, pornographers, rapists, and et cetera. Too often, I believe, women can't pursue legitimate claims that would result in punishment of a person who used them as sexual objects, solely because they are women, due to the prohibitive costs of such actions. I only believe that the current proposal will not achieve that end, and if carried forward without due diligence for legal precedents and inconsistency with legal theory, it stands the risk of taking the effort back beyond ground zero.

I simply ask the Council to study this matter with the same thoroughness it studied the original Minneapolis civil rights ordinance and all the substantive amendments that have since been enacted.

DWORKIN: May I ask one question? It is a real question.

CHAIRMAN WHITE: Let's not—

DWORKIN: It is not a debating question.

CHAIRMAN WHITE: Quickly, so we can get as many to speak.

DWORKIN: Mr. Prock, I certainly look forward to our conversation time. I want to tell you that. I want to know what you describe as the concrete harms, the harms that the civil rights law is to address, and I would like you to say whether or not you consider the loss of your right to your own body as a concrete harm?

PROCK: Conceptually, yes. Legally, I don't know.

DWORKIN: And your life?

PROCK: Yes, it is covered under the civil rights statute.

CHAIRMAN WHITE: Those that are still remaining to speak, I'm going to have to cut you down to just quickly. If you have got something to submit, please submit it so that we can get out of here at 9:00 o'clock.

How many of you are still left here? Okay. You go, please.

TRINA PORTE: My name is Trina Porte [address deleted].

I have not yet been raped. At least, I have not been physically forced to have sex with men, which is not to say I have not been emotionally and psychologically coerced into having sex with men. I have. But that is not why I am speaking now.

I am speaking as someone who carefully listened to the testimony all yesterday afternoon and evening and I was astonished by all the people, who were mostly men, who said that they object to this ordinance because it might actually do something. Because it might affect some examples of pornography, as here very specifically defined. They felt that we should be satisfied with laws as they now exist. Laws written by and for men's use, for the protection of their speech, actions, and/or livelihood.

Yes, this ordinance might actually allow people to do something to address—and maybe provide a means of redress for—some of the unending violence done to women, children, and anyone else who has a case, as defined very specifically in this ordinance.

That is why this ordinance needs to be passed: because it might just possibly do something to alleviate some of the violence that each and every woman must live with, every day of her life, just because she was born a woman.

CHAIRMAN WHITE: I want to thank all of you.

HOYT: Chairman White?

CHAIRMAN WHITE: Alderman Hoyt?

HOYT: I would like to put one more thing in our records that I asked to be brought. As you know, we have in our Crime Prevention Department the ability to get sites, specific locations. And just one day I gave them the addresses of the bookstores that traffic in pornography, and the movie houses in Minneapolis, some of them. And I asked them to run a site, specifically within one mile, since last June, of the number of instances that we have had crimes that have occurred around those locations.

I also fed into it a location of a family movie theater which is 3800 42nd Avenue South, the Riverview Terrace. And we found that 424 Hennepin and 624 Hennepin were so close that it was run as 500 Hennepin Avenue and there were 566 crimes; 1111 Hennepin Avenue, there were 694; Franklin and 10th Avenue, within one mile, there were 894; 401 East Hennepin was 178; 2938 Lyndale Avenue South was 557; 409 West Broadway was 365; 345 East Lake Street was 810; 1500 East Lake was 656; 741 East Lake Street was 873. My momentary control—and we can run it on the other theaters—of 3800 42nd Avenue South, was 69.

CHAIRMAN WHITE: These are criminal acts against persons or—

HOYT: Against persons of assault, aggravated, simple assault, rape, indecent exposure, the sex crimes as they are put into our computers. And I would like to enter this on the record. Thank you.

DWORKIN: I have one final thing to put into evidence, and it is a telegram from Gloria Steinem who says: "As someone who looks to Minnesota for national leadership in social policy, I urge you to amend Title VII by including pornography as a form of sex discrimination. Your leadership is as historically important here as in making clear that rape is violence, not sexual expression, or that sexual harassment is a major form of sexual discrimination." I will not read the rest of the telegram, but I will enter this into evidence right now. [Exh. 28] Thank you.

CHAIRMAN WHITE: We are going to hear—

MacKINNON: Karen Kurtz says she wishes to testify.

CHAIRMAN WHITE: She wishes to testify. Please make it brief.

KAREN KURTZ: My name is Karen Kurtz. First of all, I want to thank those Council members who are staying here and listening to all of us. I appreciate the time you are putting in. I also want to say that I think it is . . . outrageous that more of the Council did not consider these hearings a high enough priority to be here.

Originally, I chose not to speak at this hearing, but to submit written testimony instead. After last night's hearing, I've changed my mind for two reasons. After some of the testimony, specifically that of the Civil Rights Commissioner's, I'm fearful that this ordinance will be postponed and then pushed aside. I don't want to be a part of the group that throws up their hands and says there's nothing that can be done, or we're already doing all we can.

Something else occurred to me last night. I have been sexually abused in one form or another since I was thirteen. I am now twenty-six. That's half of my life, and that's too long for me.

This statement that was originally submitted as written testimony is addressed to the Government Operations Committee.

> I am writing to express my support for passage of the proposed amendment to the civil rights ordinance recognizing pornography as sex discrimination against women. I do believe there is a strong connection between the use and existence of pornography and violence against women. This belief comes not from scientific studies, but from my personal experiences.
>
> As an adolescent, I was sexually molested in my own home by a family member who regularly used pornographic materials. I have been threatened at knifepoint by a stranger in an attempted rape. I have been physically and verbally harassed on the street, in other public places, and over the telephone at all hours of the night. I have experienced and continue to experience the humiliation, degradation, and shame that these acts were meant to instill in me.
>
> I believe that the only difference between my experiences and pornography was the absence or presence of a camera. This connection became clear to me when I saw a documentary about pornography called *Not a Love Story*. I realized that I was any one of the women in the film, at least in the eyes of those men who have abused me. I saw myself through the abusers' eyes and I felt dirty and disgusting, like a piece of meat. It was the same shame and humiliation as in the other experiences. It didn't matter that it was only a movie.
>
> The message that pornography carries is clear to me. There is no place in our society where it is safe to be a woman—not in our homes, not in the streets, not even within our families. Pornography promotes and creates the conditions that make it dangerous to be a woman.
>
> I don't believe that it has to be this way. I hope this committee will strongly support these proposed amendments. Recognizing pornography as sex discrimination against women is the first step in some day making it safe to be a woman in our society. Thank you.

CHAIRMAN WHITE: I would like to thank all of you who also sat through and listened. It has been quite an experience. I have had quite a few experiences in my life that I will never forget. I have been here some time on this earth. This is one of those experiences that will live with me until I shuffle off.[14] I want to thank you once again for coming out, and we will do whatever we can possibly do, those of us that are here. This is part of the Committee.

And for those of you who don't know, Councilmember Sally Howard had to leave and Councilmember Charlee Hoyt is here at my right, and at my extreme right is Councilmember Daugherty, Pat Daugherty. Hopefully together we can gather enough votes to get it through the Council. We are not going to promise you except one thing—and I think I am speaking for all of us—that we will do our very, very best to get this ordinance through this Council. Thank you very much.

HOYT: Mr. Chairman, may we move this ordinance for a special meeting on Thursday for discussion and Committee as to the action, tomorrow?

CHAIRMAN WHITE: You make that a motion.

HOYT: I would like to move that.

CHAIRMAN WHITE: Thursday morning. Time?

HOYT: 9:00, 9:30.

CHAIRMAN WHITE: 9:15.

HOYT: So that the reason we will move it to a special meeting at 9:15 on Thursday, so that there will be an opportunity for the Civil Rights Commission to have a chance to talk with and give us their suggestions. We would like to ask if our consultants can be present at our meeting on Thursday, and any other alderman that wants to come.

DAUGHERTY: I think we should ask the City Attorney also.

MacKINNON: Allen Hyatt also.

CHAIRMAN WHITE: On the motion, the motion is to move—

HOYT: To move the ordinance to a special meeting Thursday at 9:15.

CHAIRMAN WHITE: 9:15. All in favor say aye.

COMMITTEE MEMBERS: Aye.

CHAIRMAN WHITE: Opposed?

(No response.)

MacKINNON: I would appreciate a statement from you on the record that everyone that signed up and who requested to speak at this hearing was allowed to speak. And that the hearings were brought to a close at a point at which no person indicated they further wished to speak.

CHAIRMAN WHITE: Let the record so show.

14. Chairman White died on July 14, 1993, at age 68.

MacKINNON: Thank you, Chairman.

HOYT: I would also like to say I appreciate the fact that the consultants which the City Attorney's Office hired to construct and put together a public hearing which would give us the legal base we needed, and allowed the input from all sectors of Minneapolis, have done so. And I would like to publicly thank them and the City Attorney's Office and Al Hyatt who has worked very hard to bring us this far. Thank you.

(Hearing concluded.)

Minneapolis: Exhibits

Exhibit 1 [7]: Studies Submitted to the Minneapolis City Council, December 12, 1983, on the Effects of Pornography [Donnerstein]

Edward Donnerstein. *Pornography: Its Effect on Violence Against Women.*

Dolf Zillmann and Jennings Bryant. *Effects of Massive Exposure to Pornography.*

John H. Court. *Sex and Violence: A Ripple Effect.*

Mary P. Koss. *Sexually Aggressive Men: Empirical Findings and Theoretical Implications.*

Neil M. Malamuth. *Aggression Against Women: Cultural and Individual.*

Edward Donnerstein. *Overview and Summary of Research Project on Massive Exposure to Mass Media Violence for Commercially Released R and X Rated Films.*

Neil M. Malamuth. *Rape Proclivity Among Males.*

Neil M. Malamuth. *Factors Associated with Rape as Predictors of Laboratory Aggression Against Women.*

Neil M. Malamuth, Maggie Heim, and Seymour Feshbach. *Sexual Responsiveness of College Students to Rape Depictions: Inhibitory and Disinhibitory Effects.*

John Briere and Neil M. Malamuth. *Self-Reported Likelihood of Sexually Aggressive Behavior: Attitudinal versus Sexual Explanations.*

Jacqueline D. Goodchilds and Gail L. Zellman. *Communication and Sexual Aggression in Adolescent Relationships.*

Exhibit 2 [8]: Issues Related to Sexual Violence in the Mass Media [Donnerstein]

1. *What are the issues? Is there an increase?*
   Dietz (1982): *Amer. J. Psychiatry*
   Malamuth and Spinner (1980): *J. Sex Research*
   Smith (1974): *J. Communication*

2. *Are there effects on*
   A. *Sexual arousal?*
           In rapist:
           In normals:
   Malamuth (1981): *J. Social Issues*
   Abel et al. (1977): *Archives of General Psychiatry*
   Malamuth et al. (1980): *J. Per. and Social Psychology*
   Malamuth and Donnerstein (1982): *Advances in Exp. Social Psychology*

   B. *Rape-related attitudes?*
   Malamuth (1981): *J. Social Issues*
   Malamuth (1984): *Pornography and Sexual Aggression*
   Malamuth and Check (1982): *J. Research in Personality*
   Donnerstein (1984): *Porn[ography] and Sexual Aggression*

   C. *Aggression toward women?*
   Donnerstein (1980): *N.Y. Academy of Science*
   Donnerstein (1983): *Aggression: Theoretical and Empirical Reviews*
   Malamuth (1983): *J. Per. and Social Psychology*

3. *What is the relative contribution of sexual and violent content?*
   Donnerstein (1984): *Pornography and Sexual Aggression*
   Donnerstein and Penrod (1983) NSF 82-16772 Grant
   Donnerstein and Linz (1984): *Psychology Today*

4. *What are the effects of massive long-term exposure?*
   Zillmann and Bryant (1982): *J. Communication*
   Linz and Donnerstein (1984): *Public Communication and Behavior*

Donnerstein and Linz (1984): *Psychology Today*
Donnerstein and Linz (1984): *J. Applied Social
    Psychology*

5. *Where do we go from here?*
    A. *Ways to mitigate the effects*

    B. *Future research*

Exhibit 3 [10]: Nat Laurendi, Polygraph Examination of Linda Lovelace, November 8, 1979

During September 26, 1979, writer was contacted by Mr. Jeff Waller of the above firm, relative to giving a polygraph (Lie Detection) examination to Linda Lovelace in connection with her forthcoming book.

Writer was later contacted by Mr. Curto of the above firm about scheduling and to discuss the areas of inquiry on the polygraph with Mr. Mike McGrady, the author of the book "Ordeal."

Subsequently Mr. Mike McGrady came to this office and supplied writer with galleys of a book entitled "Ordeal" published by Citadel Press, Secaucus, New Jersey (Lyle Stewart, Inc.), 120 Enterprise Avenue, Secaucus, New Jersey.

In addition to the galleys, Mr. McGrady supplied writer with a list of 114 questions regarding the subject matter in the book. There were additional questions to be asked by the publisher.

Writer and Mr. McGrady discussed the general area and background of critical questions to be asked during the polygraph test. Writer read the galleys and reviewed the questions supplied.

On Friday, October 26, 1979, Linda Lovelace came to this office for a Polygraph examination with Mr. Victor J. Yannacone, Jr., Attorney of Yannacone & Yannacone P.C., 35 Baker Street, Patchogue, L.I., N.Y.

Before the examination Linda Lovelace signed two copies of a form stating she was taking the test voluntarily. The examination commenced at 3:07 P.M. and terminated at 4:44 P.M. Mr. McGrady and Mr. Yannacone were outside the polygraph examination room during the administration of the test.

A 4 pen stoelting 22695 desk model polygraph was used. The mixed control question type procedure was utilized including a numerical stimulation and a "silent answer test."

Pre-Polygraph Test Interview

During the pre-Polygraph test interview Subject stated she was born January 10, 1949, in the Bronx.

Linda Lovelace gave background information about herself and her previous life style. She is presently married and has one son.

Phase I

The following pertinent test questions were asked while Subject was attached to the polygraph during this phase.

Polygraph Test

QUESTION:	ANSWER:
4. DID THE THING YOU DESCRIBED IN "ORDEAL" REALLY HAPPEN TO YOU?	YES.
6. DID YOU SEE SAMMY DAVIS JR. GO DOWN ON CHUCK TRAYNOR?	YES.
8. WERE YOU FORCED BY CHUCK TRAYNOR TO HAVE SEX WITH FIVE GUYS IN CORAL GABLES IN 1971?	YES.
10. DID YOU GO DOWN ON LOU PERRINO IN HIS OFFICE IN NEW YORK?	YES.
12. DID YOU EVER HAVE SEX GAMES WITH PHILLIP J. MANDINA IN FLORIDA?	YES.

Analysis and Comments:

There were no emotional reactions indicative of deception to the above pertinent test questions and it is my professional OPINION that Subject's answers to the above questions were truthful.

Phase II

On Saturday, October 27, 1979, Linda Lovelace returned to this office for a continuation of the polygraph examination.

Before the examination Linda Lovelace signed two copies of a form again stating she was taking the test voluntarily. The examination commenced at 1 P.M. and terminated at 3:50 P.M.

During this phase other areas of her life were discussed with Linda Lovelace and the following critical questions were asked while Subject was attached to the polygraph.

Polygraph Test

QUESTION:	ANSWER:
4. TO YOUR KNOWLEDGE DID DR. GROSS OF MIAMI INSERT SILICONE INTO YOUR BREASTS?	YES.
6. DID ARTHUR MARKS TELL YOU AT ONE TIME TO GET READY FOR THE "FUCKING AND SUCKING SCENES"?	YES.
8. DID BOB PHILLIPS LIE DURING THE TRIAL OF CHUCK AND BOB INGELSBY IN FLORIDA?	YES.
10. IS IT A FACT THAT DURING YOUR TIME WITH CHUCK TRAYNOR YOU FEARED FOR YOUR LIFE IF YOU TRIED TO GET AWAY?	YES.

Analysis and Comments:

There were no emotional reactions indicative of deception to the above pertinent test questions and it is my professional OPINION that Subject's answers to the above questions were truthful.

Phase III

During the pre-test interview and while in the process of formulating the questions to be asked on the polygraph for this phase, Subject broke down and cried.

After a rest period the interview continued and the activities of Linda were discussed. After gaining her composure the following pertinent test questions were asked while she was attached to the polygraph.

Polygraph Test

QUESTION:	ANSWER:
4. DID BOB WOLF DIRECT YOU IN A MOVIE WHERE YOU HAD SEX WITH A DOG?	
6. DID HUGH HEFNER WANT TO SEE YOU HAVE SEX WITH CHUCK'S DOG NAMED "RUFUS"?	
8. DID YOU TELL ME THE TRUTH ABOUT THE TWO DOGS?	

Analysis and Comments:

This was a Silent Answer Test where Subject was instructed to answer to herself.

There were no emotional reactions indicative to deception to questions #6 and #8.

When Subject was asked during the first run of the Silent Answer Test #4 "DID BOB WOLF DIRECT YOU IN A MOVIE WHERE YOU HAD SEX WITH A DOG?" there were highly emotional reactions following that question specifically a blood pressure rise, sweat gland activity and in the breathing patterns.

During the asking of that question (#4) with verbal response by Linda Lovelace a second time, there were strong reactions in both pneumographic reading tracings and a violent and dramatic blood pressure rise to that question. Subject was crying and holding back tears.

It is my professional OPINION that Subject was answering truthful to questions #6 and #8. Because of the violent and dramatic reaction to question #4 which was followed by Subject crying, no opinion could be given.

However, writer is convinced that Subject was not attempting deception. Since she broke down and cried writer did not deem it proper or wise to re-examine her further on the polygraph. This phase terminated at 2:30 P.M.

Interrogation Phase

After a short rest period the interview continued without Miss Lovelace being attached to the polygraph. This time the questions supplied by Mike McGrady and the publisher were reviewed. All the questions outlined in that question sheet were asked of Linda Lovelace.

The only area where Subject had any problem was with a question which dealt with whether or not Chuck Traynor ever had sex, oral or otherwise, with Altovise Davis. Subject stated she wasn't sure since she did not see them.

During this phase of the questioning Subject again broke down and cried and after a short rest period the interrogation recommenced.

Analysis and Comments:

Based upon the information supplied, the galleys of "ORDEAL" with Mike McGrady, Citadel Press, Secaucus, N.J., the pre-Polygraph test interviews prior to each phase of each test, the analysis of the emotional reactions on the polygraph to the above critical questions and post-test conversation and interrogation of Subject, it is my professional OPINION that Subject's answers to the above critical questions were truthful.

The question "DID BOB WOLF DIRECT YOU IN A MOVIE WHERE YOU HAD SEX WITH A DOG?" aroused violent and dramatic reactions. Therefore, no opinion could be given and writer did not desire to put her through another ordeal.

1. Did your mother beat you when you were a child?
2. Did your mother hit you with a broomstick?
3. Did you ask your mother what "fuck" meant and did you get hit for asking?
4. Were you known as a straight-arrow during your school days?
5. Did you always have great respect for the institution of marriage?
6. Did your father ever come home drunk?
7. Did your mother ever go after him with a butcher knife in her hand?
8. When you were in Florida, after your accident, would your mother hit you when you came home late?
9. Did Chuck Traynor run a house of prostitution—a string of prostitutes?
10. The first night with Chuck Traynor: did he not have a full erection?
11. That same night—did he ask you to suck him?
12. Did Chuck Traynor hypnotize you?
13. Did the barmaids at Chuck's bar go topless?
14. Did you see the barmaids in an orgy?
15. Did Chuck Traynor urge you to help run a prostitution business?
16. When you refused to do this, did Chuck hit you?
17. Did beating you seem to excite Chuck sexually?
18. Did Chuck tell you to stop talking with your mother?
19. Did Chuck Traynor have a .45 caliber pistol?
20. Did Chuck have a semi-automatic machine gun?
21. When Chuck took you to the Holiday Inn, did he have five men waiting to have sex with you?
22. Did Chuck force you to have sex with them?
    Did you have sex with them of your own free will?

23. Did Chuck point a gun at you and threaten to kill you if you didn't have sex with them?
24. Was the Holiday Inn scene true as you described it?
25. Did Chuck then make you have sex with men for money?
26. Did he beat you from time to time?
27. Did Chuck Traynor keep the money that you made? Did you keep a percentage of the money you earned as a hooker?
28. Did Chuck give you the least attractive customers?
29. Did Chuck bring you to a pornographic photographer named Leonard Campagno, or Lenny Camp?
30. Did this photographer take pictures of you with another naked female model?
31. Did he take pictures of you with a dildo?
32. Did you enjoy working as a hooker? Did you experience orgasm when working as a hooker?
33. Did Chuck teach you how to relax your throat muscles?
34. Did Phil Mandina know who "Mister X" was? Did he speak with "Mister X" about the trial?
35. During one of your escape attempts, did another hooker turn you over to Chuck?
36. Did Chuck invent the story about the sky-diving club? Did Mandina know it was a lie?
37. Did Bob Phillips perjure himself at the trial?
38. Did you pay for Chuck's defense? Did Mandina get to handle your case in New York?
39. Did you want to marry Chuck Traynor? Did Chuck marry you so that you couldn't testify against him?
40. Did you say no, you wouldn't marry him?
41. Did he beat you the night before you were married?
42. Did you call your parents immediately after the wedding ceremony?
43. Did you have sex with Chuck's cousin's husband while Chuck was working with sheetrock?
44. Did your sister Jean see the pictures of you and Cricket?
45. Did your mother permit Chuck to come over to the house when you were trying to escape?
46. Did Chuck threaten to shoot your sister's son if you wouldn't go back with him?

47. When you were out with others, would Chuck tell you not to speak?
48. Did you have to ask Chuck's permission to go to the bathroom?
49. Did Chuck and Mandina brag about their hypnotizing prowess?
50. Did Chuck give you a post-hypnotic suggestion to undress and have sex with Mandina's girl friend, Barbara?
51. Did Barbara say that Phil Mandina wanted her to deep-throat him?
52. Did Chuck and Mandina have a contest to see which one could bring a woman to orgasm first?
53. Did you and Barbara have a similar contest with the two men?
54. Did you have oral sex with Phil Mandina?
55. Did Chuck ever ask you to put cinnamon candies in your vagina while you were driving?
56. Did Chuck ask you to proposition salesmen in stores?
57. Did Chuck threaten you by saying you were going to have sex with donkeys in Juarez?
58. Did you have a job interview with Xaviera Hollander?
59. Did Bob Wolf direct you in a movie where the actors urinated on each other?
60. Did Bob Wolf direct you in a movie where you had sex with a dog?
61. Did you say that you would not have sex with a dog?
62. Did Chuck threaten to kill you if you didn't make the movie?
63. Did you see a gun on the set of the dog movie?
64. Did you make 8-millimeter pornographic movies with Gerard Damiano?
65. Did Harry Reems want to arrange pornographic film work for you?
66. Was your total pay for "Deep Throat" $1200? Did Chuck keep the money?
67. Did Chuck tell you to have oral sex with Lou Peraino?
68. Did you perform oral sex on Lou Peraino several times?
69. After the first day of filming "Deep Throat" did Chuck beat you viciously?
70. Did the movie crew members hear the beating? Did you cry out for help?
71. Did Gerard Damiano notice the bruises?

72. Would Chuck ask hitch-hikers if they wanted to be hookers?

73. Did Chuck's mother say she had been friendly with mobsters? Did she call herself a "flower lady"? Did she say her store was a "front"?

74. When you escaped to Patsy's house, did Chuck threaten to kill you?

75. Did Chuck sometimes make you expose yourself in restaurants? In cars?

76. Did Chuck ever insert a garden hose in your rectum and turn on the water?

77. Did Chuck force you to greet your parents while you were naked?

78. Did Michelle poke you with a hot hair-dryer?

79. Did Michelle insert a dildo in your rectum?

80. Did Michelle seem to lose control of herself?

81. Did the Florida proctologist treat you in exchange for sexual favors?

82. Did a Doctor Gross illegally insert silicone into your breasts?

83. Did Chuck bring home a dog named Rufus?

84. Before your interviews, did Chuck tell you what answers you should give?

85. Did Chuck offer Al Goldstein oral sex from you?

86. Did Hugh Hefner say he liked the movie you made with a dog?

87. Did Hefner tell Chuck that he had many animal movies?

88. Did Hefner have Rufus shipped in from Florida and did he then put the dog in his own kennel?

89. Did Shel Silverstein discuss making a country-and-western album with you?

90. In *Deep Throat, Part Two* did you perform oral sex for the cameras?

91. Were you and Chuck and Andrea True involved in sexual acts together?

92. Did Andrea True introduce you to a top executive at Pinnacle Books? Did Andrea True say this was one of her clients?

93. Did Hugh Hefner urge you to have sex with a girl named Lila at an orgy?

94. Did Hefner want to see you have sex with the dog named Rufus? Was he there when this was attempted?

95. Did Sammy Davis Jr. tell you that he considered sexual intercourse to be infidelity—but oral sex to be okay?

96. Did Chuck have sex with Altovise?
97. Did Sammy Davis Jr. talk about tying you down on a bed?
98. Did you and Altovise have sex while Chuck and Sammy watched?
99. Did Sammy ever express an interest in marrying you?
100. Did you see Sammy Davis Jr. commit an act of oral sex on Chuck Traynor?
101. Did Buck Henry and Milos Forman ever discuss making a movie with you?
102. Did Chuck hit you when you were rehearsing for your stage act?
103. When you escaped from Chuck, did he come looking for you with a gun?
104. Did David Winters tell you he was millions of dollars in debt?
105. When you first wrote "The Intimate Diary of Linda Lovelace" with Mel Mandel, did the publisher complain about the lack of sex?
106. Did David Winters say you should tell a little bit of the truth now and the full story later on?

Exhibit 4 [12]: Letter of Kathleen L. Barry, Ph.D., sociologist, Brandeis University, November 15, 1983

In this memo I intend to identify the practices related to pornography which constitute a violation of woman's civil rights, and in accordance with the International Declaration of Human Rights, they constitute a violation of woman's human rights. As I have already conducted, reported and published the research which documents these practices as slavery (see *Female Sexual Slavery,* Prentice-Hall, 1979) and in view of the United Nations report of March 1983 of a survey conducted by Jean Fernand-Laurent for the Economic and Social Council which has reached similar conclusions, I shall not provide the supporting documentation here as it can be found in those works. As a result of my research I have found that

(1) Pornography is used by pimps as a part of the illegal [act] of procuring and attempting to induce young girls and women into prostitution. By presenting young women and girls with pornography which fraudulently represents actually painful sexual practices and acts as pleasing and gratifying to the female represented in the pornography, the pimp attempts to convince young and vulnerable (usually homeless)

young women to prostitute themselves for him. Pornography plays a large role in the deception that is necessary to put naive young women into prostitution.

(2) When a young girl or woman is procured, pornography is often used as part of the seasoning and blackmail strategies which will force her into prostitution. Prior to being "turned out" to prostitution, many pimps "season" or break down their victims through sessions of rape and other forms of sexual abuse. Sometimes these sessions are photographed or filmed and used in a variety of ways which include personal pleasure of the pimp and his friends, blackmailing the victim by threatening to send them to her family, and selling them to pornographers for mass production. This constitutes the use of pornography as a form of torture and the marketing of actual torture sessions in the form of film and pictures as a pleasure commodity.

(3) Pornography is a form of prostitution and consequently pornographers are pimps. There have been several court cases upholding the convictions of pornographers as pimps for having been supported off the earnings of prostitutes. My research has supported these legal findings to the extent that those who traffic women (and children, boys and girls) into prostitution also traffic them into pornography. It is a myth to assume that the "porn star" is someone other than a woman in prostitution and one who is most likely under the control of pimps who are either the pornographers or who contract their prostitute's "services" to the pornographers for a price. Consequently pornography performance is only one of the acts of prostitution required of the women involved in it.

I have kept my observations here within the limits of my empirical research. Obviously the use of pornography as a violation of woman's civil rights extends far beyond this which I have also written and commented on elsewhere.

Exhibit 5 [13]: Letter of Flora Colao, C.S.W., November 10, 1983

I have been working with sexual assault survivors since 1975. I am founder of the St. Vincent's Hospital Rape Crisis Program in New York City, a member of New York Women Against Rape and Co-Director of the Children's Creative Safety Program at the Safety and Fitness Exchange (SAFE Inc.) in New York City. I am writing to offer evidence, based on case histories of individuals and families I have worked with, as to how pornography directly affects the sexual victimization of women and children.

1. The use of cameras in rapes:

An increasing number of women I have counseled have reported to me that while they were being attacked by one man, they were filmed and/or photographed by another. In two incidents the women were told, "We can make real money if we kill you because then it will be a 'snuff' film." In other incidents the women were shown the Polaroid pictures and asked, "Do you want to report this? They'll have to show these pictures to everybody if you do, the police, lawyers, judge and jury will see them." Many of these women were too frightened to report these incidents to the police. Of the women I am still in contact with, several have stated that each time they think about the pictures, they wonder if they were sold. They continue to suffer chronic fear and anxiety.

2. The increased number of throat rapes:

I have been alarmed by the increasing numbers of women and gay men who have reported to me that they have been throat raped. In one such incident the woman reported hearing one of her attackers state, "I'll 'Deep throat' her" before losing consciousness. Gay men have reported similar assaults. It is important to note, however, that although we know about most of the murders that include sexual assaults, we don't know how many were caused by the victims suffocating during a throat rape.

3. The use of adult pornography to coerce children into sexually abusive relationships:

In this type of situation, a child is shown adult pornography, asked if s/he is allowed by parents to view such materials and then sexually assaulted. The child is then told that if s/he tells, the offender will tell that s/he looked at the materials. In the case cited in my book (pg. 38, *Your Children Should Know* by Flora Colao and Tamar Mosansky, © 1983 Bobbs Merrill Co., Inc.) after one child disclosed, twenty-two came forward including that child's younger sister. I have worked with increasing numbers of children both male and female who were coerced in this way.

Exhibit 6 [17]: P. Bart, Data on "Not a Love Story," Audience Research*

*This research was subsequently published in Pauline Bart, Linda Freeman, and Peter Kimball, "The Different Worlds of Women and Men: Attitudes toward Pornography and Responses to *Not a Love Story*—a Film about Pornography," 8 *Women's Studies International Forum* 301 (1985).

STATEMENT: PORNOGRAPHY HAS ITS PLACE

Female
Responses:

	AGREE		DISAGREE	
	29%		72%	
Strongly Agree	Moderately Agree	Moderately Disagree	Strongly Disagree
5%	24%	24%	48%

Male
Responses:

	AGREE		DISAGREE	
	61%		39%	
Strongly Agree	Moderately Agree	Moderately Disagree	Strongly Disagree
23%	38%	20%	19%

STATEMENT: MY GUT ANTI-PORN FEELINGS WERE VALIDATED

Female
Responses:

	AGREE		DISAGREE	
	82%		18%	
Strongly Agree	Moderately Agree	Moderately Disagree	Strongly Disagree
54%	28%	12%	6%

Male
Responses:

	AGREE		DISAGREE	
	59%		41%	
Strongly Agree	Moderately Agree	Moderately Disagree	Strongly Disagree
26%	33%	26%	15%

STATEMENT: THE FILM SHOWS HOW PORNOGRAPHY IS AN
EXPRESSION OF ANGER AND HATE AGAINST WOMEN

Female
Responses:

	AGREE		DISAGREE	
	88%		12%	
Strongly	Moderately		Moderately	Strongly
Agree	Agree		Disagree	Disagree
57%	31%		8%	4%

Male
Responses:

	AGREE		DISAGREE	
	73%		26%	
Strongly	Moderately		Moderately	Strongly
Agree	Agree		Disagree	Disagree
33%	40%		18%	8%

STATEMENT: NOBODY'S HURT BY PORNOGRAPHY

Female
Responses:

	AGREE		DISAGREE	
	4%		96%	
Strongly	Moderately		Moderately	Strongly
Agree	Agree		Disagree	Disagree
2%	2%		11%	85%

Male
Responses:

	AGREE		DISAGREE	
	13%		87%	
Strongly	Moderately		Moderately	Strongly
Agree	Agree		Disagree	Disagree
3%	10%		31%	56%

STATEMENT: THE FILM SHOWED PORNOGRAPHY AS A SYMPTOM OF A LARGER SOCIAL PROBLEM—MAKING OBJECTS OUT OF WOMEN AND SOMETIMES MEN

Female
Responses:

	AGREE		DISAGREE	
	92%		9%	
Strongly Agree	Moderately Agree		Moderately Disagree	Strongly Disagree
70%	22%		4%	5%

Male
Responses:

	AGREE		DISAGREE	
	86%		15%	
Strongly Agree	Moderately Agree		Moderately Disagree	Strongly Disagree
52%	34%		10%	5%

STATEMENT: I FOUND A FEW OF THE PICTURES EROTICALLY APPEALING

Female
Responses:

	AGREE		DISAGREE	
	41%		60%	
Strongly Agree	Moderately Agree		Moderately Disagree	Strongly Disagree
10%	31%		22%	38%

Male
Responses:

	AGREE		DISAGREE	
	62%		37%	
Strongly Agree	Moderately Agree		Moderately Disagree	Strongly Disagree
16%	46%		22%	15%

STATEMENT: AN IDEA CAN'T BE CALLED BAD IF
EVERYONE INVOLVED WANTS IT

Female
Responses:

	AGREE		DISAGREE	
	11%		88%	
Strongly Agree	Moderately Agree		Moderately Disagree	Strongly Disagree
3%	8%		22%	66%

Male
Responses:

	AGREE		DISAGREE	
	23%		77%	
Strongly Agree	Moderately Agree		Moderately Disagree	Strongly Disagree
10%	13%		25%	52%

STATEMENT: MOST PORNOGRAPHY EXPRESSES
GOOD SEX WITH LOVE

Female
Responses:

	AGREE		DISAGREE	
	1%		99%	
Strongly Agree	Moderately Agree		Moderately Disagree	Strongly Disagree
0%	1%		6%	93%

Male
Responses:

	AGREE		DISAGREE	
	5%		95%	
Strongly Agree	Moderately Agree		Moderately Disagree	Strongly Disagree
1%	4%		19%	76%

STATEMENT: SOME OF THE INCREASE IN THE RATE OF RAPE
CAN BE ATTRIBUTED TO PORNOGRAPHY

Female
Responses:

	AGREE		DISAGREE	
	81%		19%	
	Strongly Agree	Moderately Agree	Moderately Disagree	Strongly Disagree
	35%	46%	13%	6%

Male
Responses:

	AGREE		DISAGREE	
	51%		50%	
	Strongly Agree	Moderately Agree	Moderately Disagree	Strongly Disagree
	16%	35%	31%	19%

I HAVE SEEN . . .

	FEMALES	MALES
LOTS OF PORNOGRAPHY:	8%	16%
SOME PORNOGRAPHY:	76%	80.5%
NO PORNOGRAPHY:	16%	3.5%

Exhibit 7 [21]: Letter of Michelle Harrison, M.D., December 9, 1983

This letter is in reference to concerns expressed regarding the use and effect of pornography within the medical community. I am a family physician with training in both psychiatry and obstetrics and gynecology, and the author of *A Woman in Residence* (Random House 1982, Penguin 1983), and *Self-Help for Premenstrual Syndrome* (Matrix 1982). My CV is attached.

The pornographic view of women is one that is prevalent within the medical community unfortunately. This is expressed by the kinds of jokes that are made about women and their bodies, especially when they are under anesthesia and undergoing surgical procedures. This view includes seeing women as not worthy of respect and also seeing them primarily in terms of their sexual functioning.

Several years ago when I was teaching at the Rutgers medical school there was a week long sexuality program planned annually for students. The first day of this program consisted of all-day viewing of porno-graphic movies. The intent was to "de-sensitize" the students to sex. What it did in effect was to communicate a view of sex as being porno-graphic. For women in the audience, it was embarrassing and in some ways humiliating to see other women portrayed as they were on the screen.

We have come a long way in how we allowed racial minorities to be viewed and yet this awareness and consciousness has not spread to how women are treated in media. We are long past the time when we expect a roomful of Black people to sit and watch movies of Black people being presented in any of the stereotypic ways that degrade them. We also do not consider that viewing such films would be useful to anyone in understanding rights of these people but would rather assume the con-trary. There is no doubt that violence in imagery promotes violence to-ward people and there cannot be any doubt that a pornographic view of women promotes that view as a general way of seeing women.

I commend the Minneapolis City Council even for considering this issue and sincerely hope that your decisions will be those that add to the civil rights due to women.

Exhibit 8 [31]: Letter of Robin Morgan, December 5, 1983

The City Council
Minneapolis, Minnesota

Dear People:

This is written in support of the proposed legislation before the Coun-cil which would include pornography as a practice discriminatory against and degrading/endangering to the civil rights of female citizens of your city.

In twenty years as a writer, activist, and lecturer on women's rights in this country and internationally, I have heard literally numberless testimonials from individual women and women's groups (in this country and abroad) about the deleterious effects of pornography on their own and other women's lives, both in the public and private realms. Publicly, it is of course at best, degrading and at worst physically sickening and endangering to be forced to purchase one's morning newspaper from a kiosk, store, or stand where one is surrounded by brutalizing and graphic depictions of female human beings; the "man-on-the-street" comments which such displays both evoke and reflect are a source of enormous anxiety to all women—ranging from the adrenaline of distaste evoked in the woman-target all the way to the adrenaline evoked by real fear of real action (street rape, harassment, etc.) often following up on the menacing comment. Privately, literally hundreds of women have mentioned to me the anger and despair they feel when their husbands, lovers, or other male partners press upon them specific sexual acts which these men learned from pornographic materials—acts of bestiality, sodomy, "swinging," forced group sex, etc. The men feel such pressure on women is acceptable because pornography is acceptable, and pornography was the so-called "educational" source.

I assume you already are in possession of and/or will hear testimony about the recent bias-free studies which *do* in fact show that there are causal effects between the proliferation of pornography and the rising tide of violence against women in this country. The experiments and studies done by Dr. Edward Donnerstein (U. of Wisc.), and Drs. Check and Malamud [sic] (Winnipeg) utterly refute the "porn as a harmless outlet for sexual aggression" theory promulgated by pornographers. In addition, the work of Dr. Natalie Shainess (psychiatrist of New York) and Dr. Frank Osanka [sic] (psychologist and child-abuse specialist, Chicago) show that convicted rapists who, even five to seven years ago, expressed remorse about their acts of violence, recently show no such remorse and often cite as a reason for guiltlessness that "everyone knows women want to be raped; all the porn stuff proves that." Furthermore, Dr. Richard Gelles, probably the nation's foremost expert on domestic violence, has written and spoken publicly on the correlations which exist between pornography, abusive sexual demands made on women in the home, and domestic violence against both women and children. Dr. Gelles, based at the University of Rhode Island, has written many scholarly books on the subject of family violence and has been a government advisor on the subject.

I would remind the Council, as well, that stacks of pornographic books, magazines, and other such material were found in the commune of Charles Manson and in the apartment of Richard Berkowitz, the notorious "Son of Sam" convicted murderer; both men targeted women as their special victims.

Perhaps it is academic to add that pornography is demeaning to male sexuality as well as to female; it trains young males and encourages in older males the worst attitudes about sexuality in general and about female human beings in particular; it ill prepares men for encountering genuine female sexuality, or even for encountering aggression-free, mutually satisfying, affectionate relationships at all. Even so, this severe damage done to male citizens still is not comparable to the disastrous effects pornography has on female citizens—it literally endangers women's "lives, liberties, and sacred honor" as Constitutionally protected citizens.

As a writer, I am extremely concerned about the proper defense of civil liberties and freedom of the press. This issue, in particular as it comes before your distinguished Council, fortunately endangers and infringes on none of those rights to publish, print, etc. On the contrary, your vitally important decision to act on behalf of female citizens and children—as well as on behalf of a humane male vision of sexuality—would protect and defend citizens' civil liberties, freedom of movement, and safety of environment both at home and in public areas.

The most recent and most responsible scientific findings and evidence urge your passing of this Code of Ordinances Amendment. The Constitution of the United States in its stated protection of the rights of citizens urges your passing this Amendment. Women, not only in Minneapolis but in the country at large, urge your passing of this Amendment, for our sake, for the sake of our men and of our children, and for the sake of a sane vision of humane and amicable, tender, and healthy sexuality in our culture, free from the propaganda of violence and degradation.

Let me add my own individual voice to this chorus: I urge the passage of the Amendment, and congratulate you on considering passage, and on having hearings to deliberate the matter. I look forward to what I deeply hope will be a courageous and just decision on behalf of truly humane values and on behalf of the majority of this nation's citizens—women.

Respectfully yours,
Robin Morgan

Exhibit 9 [34]: Letter of Jaime Lyn Bauer

To Whom It May Concern:

In 1971, I shot some *test* pictures for Dwight Hooker that were submitted to Playboy. I was never paid for that shooting nor do I remember signing a release for them.

On the basis of those pictures they flew me into Chicago to shoot the centerfold, but after 3 days, because of personal problems the photographer was having, they sent me back to L.A. & put me on hold—the session being incomplete. For those 3 days they paid me $750.00 holding fee. I was not to do any nude work not even cosmetic commercials such as for soap where I would "appear" nude. After a year of turning down other jobs they said, "Sorry, we don't care to use you after all."

Exactly 10 years later after becoming a "star" or "celebrity" or "name," they published one of the *test* pictures of me in the Jan. 1981 issue along with about 8 other stars.

One of the other women ran into the hairdressing room wanting to show off her picture & asked if I had seen mine yet. I told her I didn't know what she was talking about. She then showed me my picture completely nude & hers & the other stars who were only partially nude. They had just shot theirs 3 months before & of course had been paid for it. Playboy never approached me & asked me to shoot with them they simply pulled my picture from some old file. They also never paid me. (They didn't use a picture from 3 day shoot.)

The press went wild & I was judged not only by them but by my peers & the public. If Playboy had asked me to do even the partially nude pictures I would have refused. I'm a wife & the mother of 2 children now, an actress not a model. The press was very critical & also very interested. How could a Christian pose for a nude picture—how much was I paid? I related my story & fortunately a couple of reporters checked. Playboy wouldn't discuss it & one of them was even hung up on so my story was confirmed. *Who would want to be judged 10 yrs later for the mistakes they made in their early 20's?*

There was another incident. Another photographer shot test pictures that were submitted to "Oui." Again I sign no release. They wanted me for a layout on the basis of the test pictures, but at the same time I had got my first contract for a show which made me a star. I didn't need the money anymore so I turned them down. About 3 yrs ago the photographer apparently sold my test pictures to Hustler Magazine. Again no release & no payment.

I was deeply embarrassed, but fortunately at the time I did nudes they were simply beautiful pictures of women who were undressed. There was no sexuality involved. No vampy half clothed or touching one's self, pictures. In fact my nude career was over for that reason. I refused when one photographer asked me to touch myself. Nude pictures were changing.

I have never sued or asked for payment for either publishing. I am deeply religious now & about 6 yrs ago I put it all into the Lord's hands. Scripture does not really support suing & payment would have been giving my approval or agreement to something which was unjust, hurt-ful, unethical & illegal, not to mention irresponsible.

Please excuse this paper & long hand, but I'm at work & doing my best to get this off to you before court convenes.

I pray that I have been of help.

Respectfully yours,
Jaime Lyn Bauer

P.S. I lost a couple of jobs because the producers & sponsors didn't want that kind of girl on their shows. I was even canceled from a charity ben-efit for crippled children. That hurt the most. I cannot explain to every-one who knows, that they were shot 10 yrs ago. Many people think I just did them. I also can't explain, I didn't do it to show off my body or sexu-ality. I was a model, a mannequin.

Things have changed & swiftly in this country. There is a perversion vulgarity & obscenity seen on many levels today in all circles.

Exhibit 10 [36]: Memo of A. W., December 13, 1983

TO: Alderman Hoyt, City Hall, Minneapolis, Minnesota
FROM: A. W., Minneapolis, Minnesota
SUBJECT: Personal Input for City Hall Meeting, 5:00 P.M. Today

I request that this letter be read at the City Hall meeting December 13th, 1983 in hopes that it will be another voice added to I am sure the thou-sands of others who have experienced abuse emotionally and physically because of the neglectful handling of pornography at all levels . . . I have been the victim of such abuse. I *refuse* to accept discrimination in *any way* . . . IT IS TIME FOR CHANGING THE ATTITUDES TOWARDS PEOPLE . . . NOT JUST WOMEN . . . ALL DISCRIMINARY ATTITUDES. . . .

I offer my support and helping hand to Linda Lovelace who had the guts and the love of her fellow-person in mind to speak-out and tell the horrible before, during and after-effects of pornography. . . .

My marriage was ruined, even many friendships were directly ruined, hopefully soon not my child because of pornography. . . . My ex-husband viewed this material is [*sic*] incredible quantities. He has seen *Deep-Throat.* We had pornographic and of course those supposed "harmless" girly magazines everywhere in our home. Our vanity was stacked full, there were stacks behind our toilet, there were boxes in the attic, the basement, under the bed in the den, in a hug [*sic*] vacuum cleaner box (two stacks deep) in the den closet. I would throw them out, do anything to get rid of them, but he would buy more. . . . The suggestions of horrible sex acts with family and friends by my ex-husband totally disgusted me. His wanting to act out stories he had read frightened me. He would do it anyway no matter what I said. Using objects. He tried things I have never heard before until I found out where he was getting these ideas— from the magazines that make us out to be objects. This pornography had pictures of severed limbs and other parts of the anatomy, actual rape scenes showing the woman supposedly showing pleasure in the act, discrimination tones involving other races, abusive degrading language, use of dildos on women and men, girls who I would dare say had to be under age although I can't prove, (or insinuating relations with a girl of a very young age).

This discriminatory material also almost ruined my life. Along with this garbage comes garbage—prostitution, drugs, stealing, blackmail, and even murder. What the public sees on the surface is nothing compared to the undertones this material represents. . . . My intent is not that of revenge but to put a stop to the blindness of our family, friends, and the laws of the damaging effect[s]. . . .

I was told by Family Court Services that "if incest has not occurred, it will." And, yet because I *can't get supervised visitation until* my ex-husband has completed some type of treatment, I am being forced to "wait until it happens," and in fact FCS recommended to the court that visitation be increased because at one point they found all that I had said too much for them to accept and that I was only on a revenge trip. I now sit back and keep a watchful eye hoping my little girl will be safe with this person. . . . [P]lease don't wait for the statistics to worsen—for every untreated victim comes many others.

. . . [T]here are just too many of us out here for you to ignore NOW.

A. W.

Exhibit 11 [43]: Letter of Marvin E. Lewis, Esq., December 7, 1983

[Expressing support for the proposed ordinance because of his experience of] approximately seven cases in my office alone, where Board Certified psychiatrists, clinical psychologists and therapists have used their patients for their own gratification. It would appear that these doctors, under the guise of therapeutic treatment, are taking advantage of patients who have subservient tendencies in order to completely dominate them sexually. This includes embarrassment and humiliation which ends up with the complete destruction of the ego and self-regard and finally, the patient is completely destroyed mentally and establishes suicidal tendencies.

. . . [In one situation] a Board Certified psychiatrist, with a good reputation, had bought seductive costumes for his patient to wear and handcuffed her, spanked her and photographed her with her privates exposed—all under the guise of treatment. . . .

Exhibit 12 [42]: Letter of Jann Fredrickson Ramus, M.S.W., Minneapolis Youth Diversion Program, December 13, 1983

In my work with prostitutes, I have found pornography to be harmful to women. Many girls and young women are tricked into pornography by (1) believing they are making a movie (2) being threatened with physical harm and (3) pictures being taken and told they are for private use and later are sold. . . .

Exhibit 13 [44]: Letter of Phyllis Chesler, Ph.D., December 7, 1983

Based on fourteen years of clinical research and clinical practice, (1969–Present, 1983), I have found that pornography significantly adds to women's psychological stress. After the sexual abuse, repression, and segregation of female children, pornographic literature, images, and practices, contributes to the abuse of adult women and female children.

In my professional opinion, pornography, together with certain other practices, contributes to women's masochism, chronic depression, anxiety and lowered self-esteem. For example, most women continually compare themselves with tyrannizing images of beauty. Pornographic images and expectations then turns what they feel about themselves, into a deeper self-hatred, and into greater attempts to please men, in order to be loved, in order to avoid being seen as truly "ugly."

Pornography, in addition to certain other practices, is potentially involved in female problems such as frigidity or dysmenorrhea.

In my professional opinion, what women learn from observing pornography directly, or from relating to men who observe pornography directly, is tolerance for physical, sexual and emotional abuse at male hands. This, in turn, leads to the suppression of anger, and its consequent self-destructive behavior among women.

Pornography also hampers men's abilities to relate in intimate and nourishing ways, particularly when they marry and create a family. For example, as I wrote in my book, *About Men*, pornography falsely promises men an endless supply of available women. Pornography falsely promises men that no male-male competition or rivalry exists for male access to "available" women. Pornography falsely promises and sets a standard for men of constant and easily achieved erections. Pornography falsely promises men sexual and psychological pleasure as a result of force, sadism, selfishness, or money.

To the extent to which men believe such lies—to that extent are men divided against themselves, against their wives, and against women whom they may love or live with.

Pornographic images are unbalanced by an equal input of non-pornographic images of love, lovemaking, or sexuality. This ordinance will give women and men the unprecedented ability to lead their private lives without being psychologically impaired by false and damaging images. I strongly support this ordinance.

Exhibit 14 [45]: Letter of Ellen T. Luepker, M.S.W., A.C.S.W., Family and Children's Service, December 12, 1983

[Luepker has worked with clients sexually abused in psychiatry for three years. Most are women.]

Our research shows that all of these women felt that "something was wrong" in their therapists' using sexual involvement as a therapeutic technique, but did not trust their common sense. . . . [T]his kind of bizarre situation occurs in a society in which the societal norms support degradation of women. This theory also explains the unfortunate acceptance of this kind of power abuse, despite women's inner warnings that such exploitation is not in their best interest.

Based upon these clinical experiences and impressions, I believe that we should do whatever is possible to change societal norms from viewing sexual exploitation of women as "normal." . . . [The ordinance] could be a small but crucial step toward changing some extremely destructive societal norms that support insidious kinds of abuses such as I have mentioned above.

Exhibit 15 [47]: Les Sussman and Sally Bordwell, *The Rapist File* (New York: Chelsea House, 1981)

This book consists of interviews with convicted rapists.

One named "Kasim" stated:

"You should concentrate on what brings about rape . . . Rape is a sexual and violent act. If you were sexually oriented in this society and then turned to something violent—this is where you get your rapist from. He's constantly being fed. That's why I don't go to a lot of them movies. One week they may show nothing but X-rated films—nothing but sex, people in bed. I don't call that sex. That's a complete distortion . . . Then the next week they go to a Superfly film full of murder and a little more sex. The next scene is more murder. That's an orientation . . . then, you got yourself a rapist . . . He does the same thing as in the movies." (pp. 84–85)

One rapist named "Zeke" said:

"What are your masturbatory fantasies?" Sally asks.

He fiddles with the ashtray. "I think of how I would do it with these women. Would I tie her up? And being that I'm looking at these magazines with sadomasochism, bondage, I believe that's my thing . . . I'm not coming back in here. I have a plan. As I said, I ran a photography and filmmaking studio. I'm going into pornography. I'll probably deal with sadomasochism and rape . . . This is my first time [in prison,] and for me to come back again it would have to be for murder." (p. 42)

A dialogue with a rapist named "Julio":

"Did you always get into bondage when you raped?" I ask.
He smiles broadly. "No, not always. In fact, I just got that out of *Penthouse* magazine. I never knew about that until I read that magazine." (p. 48). . . .
Sally asks if Julio believes all women have secret rape fantasies.
He grins at the question. "That's true, in my opinion. This is personal, a product of my own experience. Today even more so because society is so highly sexed. Everywhere you go there's pornography. The mentality of the young is being infested by so much pornography." (p. 52) . . .
"Bondage was as far as you went?"
"Yeah, and I learned that from *Playboy* magazine." (p. 56)

One anonymous rapist wrote:

". . . I thought it was pretty nice to be able to see my sisters and mother around the house . . . At those times my mind would fanticize [*sic*] to the point of things that I thought were only in Playboys and things, like taking my sister or even my mother." (p. 210)

Exhibit 16 [48]: Steven G. Michaud and Hugh Aynesworth, *The Only Living Witness: A True Account of Homicidal Insanity* (Simon and Schuster, 1983)

[A note by the editors]

This book on the serial sexual murderer Ted Bundy is based principally on interviews conducted with him in prison between 1978 and 1983. Bundy initiated the contact with the writers through Michaud's agent: "She told me that Ted Bundy, the noted alleged murderer, wanted to tell his story in a book." (p. 8). Michaud notes in his prologue: "[H]e knew that nothing he could say and no fact we could disclose would prevent the state from electrocuting him, appeals notwithstanding, probably within the next five years." (p. 10). Bundy was executed by the state in 1989.

The authors state that, at a time in 1969, before Bundy had ever had sex with anyone, when his only crimes were petty theft to support his image: "from what he later told us at the prison, it is certain that by this stage he had a strong appetite for violent pornography." (p. 65).

Ted Bundy followed the lead of these interviewers in creating a third person—referred to as "this person" or "the individual" or "he"—through whom he was able to reflect upon his background, development, murders, and attachment to pornography.

> His [Bundy's] first substantive remarks were on the roles of sex and violence in the development of the psychopath. "This condition," he explained, "is not immediately seen by the individual or identified as a serious problem. It sort of manifests itself in an interest concerning sexual behavior, sexual images. It might simply be an attraction such as *Playboy,* or a host of other normal, healthy sexual stimuli that are found in the environment. But this interest, for some unknown reason, becomes geared towards matters of a sexual nature that involve violence. I cannot emphasize enough the gradual development of this. It is not short-term."
>
> He told me that long before there was a need to kill there were juvenile fantasies fed by photos of women in skin magazines . . . He was transfixed by the sight of women's bodies on provocative display. He told me, too, of the protokiller watching X-rated movies and searching out the more violent police dramas on television. Ted said "this person" would carry home some pornographic book, read it, then shred it in anger, self-disgust, and fear of discovery. . . .
>
> "Maybe he focused on pornography as a vicarious way of experiencing what his peers were experiencing in reality," Ted opined, trying to sound reflective. "Then he got sucked into the more sinister doctrines that are implicit in pornography—the use, the abuse, the possession of women as objects." . . .
>
> Bundy explained that "he was not imagining himself actively doing these things, but he found gratification in reading about others so engaged. Eventually, the interest would become so demanding for new material that it could only be catered by what he could find in the so-called dirty book stores. . . . it does offer variety, and a certain percentage of it is devoted toward literature that explores situations where a man, in the context of

sexual encounter, in one way or another engages in some sort of violence toward a woman, or the victim. There are, of course, a whole host of substitutions that could come under that particular heading. Your girlfriend, your wife, a stranger, children—whatever—a whole host of victims are found in this kind of literature. And in this kind of literature, they are treated as victims." (pp. 104–105).

In one interrogation by police, which they counted on being picked up by a surreptitious bug that malfunctioned, the authors state that Bundy "admitt[ed] his voyeurism, a taste for pornography, and . . . what he called 'my problem.'" (p. 244). The authors also observe that Bundy "retained through life his preadolescent concept of females—remote and unreal, objects of perfection as he saw them on television and magazines; it was small step thence to viewing them as objects for exploitation and abuse once he began reading pornography." (p. 309).

Exhibit 17 [49]: State v. [defendant], SJI's Complaint #27-11-X-001435, Hennepin County District Court, October 7, 1983

COMPLAINT

The Complainant, being duly sworn, makes complaint to the above-named Court and states that there is probable cause to believe that the Defendant committed the following offense(s). The complainant states that the following facts establish PROBABLE CAUSE:

Complainant, JOHN SEARLES, is a Lieutenant with the Minneapolis Police Department, Family Violence Division, and in that capacity has investigated this matter by reviewing the reports of fellow officers and by personally interviewing the victim herein.

Complainant has learned from [L], who is 19 years old, date of birth 1/24/64, that she has known the defendant, . . ., date of birth 5/7/52, for approximately nine months and [he] was at one time her boyfriend. She indicated that she and the defendant had been living together in Des Moines, Iowa, [she] had left the defendant at the end of August, 1983, and had returned to Minneapolis, in order to break off the relationship. She stated that she had received a letter from the defendant stating that he had left town and that her clothes were at [T]'s apartment, . . . W. 26th

Street, . . ., Minneapolis, Hennepin County, Minnesota. On 9/7/83 she went over to the apartment in order to retrieve her clothes. [T] answered the door and assured her that the defendant had left two days earlier. [T] told her the clothes were in the closet and when she opened the closet the defendant jumped out and pulled her into the bathroom by holding onto her neck. The defendant then pulled out a knife and threatened her in the face and said, "If I can't have you, no one else will and I am going to slash up your neck." The defendant then lit a gas light torch and put a hanger that had been bent into a "B" into the flame. When it was hot he put the "B" end of the hanger on her neck and held it there. He then threatened her again with the knife and told her he was going to cut her up and burn her face up and that she wasn't going to get out of there without being "all fucked up." He also threatened to kill her. He then re-heated the hanger, came at her with it, trying to burn her face but she put her arms up to protect herself and was burned instead on her right arm. At that point she heard a knock at the apartment door. [T]'s mother came into the bedroom and the defendant took [L] into the bedroom and made her swear on a bible that she would never leave him again. She then was taken by the defendant to a cab waiting at the street. The defendant told her he had a knife in his pocket and that he'd cut her up if she tried anything. The defendant then told the cab driver to take them to . . . - 3rd Avenue South, Minneapolis, Hennepin County, Minnesota, which is the residence of the defendant's mother. [L] said the defendant's mother saw her neck and asked her what had happened but that she said nothing because she was frightened of the defendant. That night the defendant took her upstairs to the bedroom where the defendant told her to take her pants off. She did so because she said she was frightened. The defendant then took her top and bra off and then had sexual intercourse with her by placing his penis into her vagina. She then turned over and acted like she was sleeping for the rest of the night. The next day she and the defendant continued to stay at his mother's house. At about 2:00 p.m., the defendant wanted some cigarettes. She asked the defendant's mother if the two of them could walk to the store together to get them. The defendant and his mother agreed, and she and his mother walked to the 7-11 at 36th and Nicollet. On the way, [L] told the defendant's mother that she was really afraid the defendant would kill her and his mother replied that he wasn't crazy. When [L] got to 36th and Nicollet she got on a bus and left.

The defendant is presently in custody on criminal sexual conduct charges involving minor teenage girls. The victim has further told complainant that she is extremely scared of the defendant.

COUNT I: KIDNAPPING
Minn. Stat. 1983, 609.25, Subd. 1(2); 2(2); 607.11
Penalty: 1 yr. 1 day–40 and/or $40,000

That on or between the 7th and 8th day of September, 1983, in Hennepin County, [T], using a dangerous weapon within the meaning of 609.11, removed [L] from one place to another without her consent in order to facilitate the commission of a felony or flight thereafter.

COUNT II: ASSAULT IN THE SECOND DEGREE
Minn. Stat. 1983, 609.222, 609.11
Penalty: 1 year 1 day–5 years and/or $10,000

That on or between the 7th and 8th day of September, 1983, in Hennepin County, [T], using a dangerous weapon within the meaning of 609.11, assaulted [L] without inflicting great bodily harm, by branding her on the neck with a red-hot hanger, burned her on the arm and tried to burn her face.

COUNT III: CRIMINAL SEXUAL CONDUCT IN THE FIRST DEGREE
Minn. Stat. 1983, 609.342(c)
Penalty: 0–20 years and/or $35,000

That on or between the 7th and 8th day of September, 1983, in Hennepin County, [T], engaged in sexual penetration with [L], and circumstances existing at the time of the act caused [L] to have a reasonable fear of imminent great bodily harm to herself or another.

COMPLAINT

The Complainant, being duly sworn, makes complaint to the above-named Court and states that there is probable cause to believe that the Defendant committed the following offense(s). The complainant states that the following facts establish PROBABLE CAUSE:

Complainant, JOHN SEARLES, is a Lieutenant with the Minneapolis

Police Department, Family Violence Division, and in that capacity has investigated this matter by reviewing the reports of fellow officers and by personally interviewing the victim and witnesses herein.

Complainant has learned from [M], date of birth 9-23-68, the victim herein, that on March 6, 1983, when she was 14 years old she had run away from home and stayed with a friend for two nights. At that point, her father picked her up and took her home where upon she ran away again and called the defendant, [ ], date of birth 5-7-52, whose name and phone number she had gotten from a friend. She stated that when she called the defendant he stated he would pick her up, along with her sister, [ ], and a friend, [ ]. The defendant did pick up all three of them and took them to his apartment at [ ] Pleasant Avenue South, # [ ], Minneapolis, Hennepin County, Minnesota. [M] stated this was the first time she had ever met the defendant. At the defendant's apartment she was offered drugs by the defendant and she smoked some marijuana and took some speed. She also watched pornographic movies. Then she went into the defendant's bedroom to sleep because that was where he had told her to sleep. The defendant also told her that she couldn't sleep in his bed with her clothes on and so she removed her clothing and went to sleep. At some point that night she awoke and found that the defendant was laying on top of her and was having intercourse with her by placing his penis in her vagina. She stated she did not push him off because she was scared. She said she knew he was 30 years old. She stated that she told him she was 14 years old.

The defendant is presently in custody on similar charges involving other minor girls.

She stated that in Jan. of 83, she was in a group home and that she ran from the group home about the 14th of Jan. For the first 3 weeks, she stayed with friends in Brooklyn Center and Richfield. About the middle of March, she was walking in the area of Lake & Bloomington, hitchhiking and was picked up by a B/M driving a small red car. This B/M offered to let her stay at his apt. if she wanted to. She accepted and was taken to [ ] Pleasant Ave. So., # [ ], and the B/M introduced himself as being [ ]. She stayed with [ ] for approx. a week and a half. He gave her Speed, Marijuana and alcohol and they viewed porno films. While there, she slept with him in the bedroom. He did not make any sexual advances toward her until approx. 1 week after she moved in. One night, he stated that he was going to have sex with her and she stated that she was scared and did not resist and he had sexual intercourse with her. He did not threaten her, but she was afraid that he would harm her if she did not comply. The day after he had intercourse with her, she left, and did not go back.

While she was in the apt. for the week prior to the rape, she observed Mr. [ ] buying what she thought was stolen merchandise from people who came to the door.

On 3-18-83, at 1545 hrs., [ ], DOB. 9-29-66, 16 yrs., was interviewed in the FVD and a statement was taken. She confirmed that her sister and [ ] were picked up by [ ] and taken to his apt. She also stated that while there, she drank alcoholic beverages and witnessed the smoking of marijuana and the taking of pills in the form of Speed. She further stated that her sister went into the bedroom with [ ], and that he did not force her to do so. She does not know what transpired in the bedroom between them, but the next morning, her sister told her that [ ] had screwed her. [ ] also told her that he had had intercourse with her sister. She did not witness any type of violent behavior on [ ]'s part and further stated that her sister exaggerates a lot and that she does not tell the truth at times. It appeared thru the entire interview that [ ] was very protective of [ ] and it was felt that she would warn him at the first opportunity she got.

On 3-21-83, at 1230 hrs., a search warrant was executed at [ ]'s apt. in the presence of Mr. [ ]. Nothing of evidentuary [sic] value was found. Some items were confiscated and later released to Mr. [ ].

Contacted Mr. [ ] and he advised me that his daughter [ ] had been placed for long-term treatment at Fairview Hospital. It was decided to wait until her release to pursue any possible prosecution in this case.

CASE CONTINUED—OPEN.

Exhibit 18 [55]: Letter of Marcia Kading, Special Projects Coordinator, Family Nurturing Center, December 8, 1983

In 1974, Southside Family Nurturing Center pioneered the first program in the State of Minnesota for exclusive treatment of child abuse and neglect involving both parents and children. The programs of Southside Family Nurturing Center are designed to reduce the incidence of child abuse in families referred to the Center by Hennepin County Protective Services. The referred families have been identified as needing treatment in order to break the intergenerational cycle of child abuse and neglect.

I have been at Southside for seven years. My first year was spent as a teacher in the therapeutic nursery school, I then developed and implemented the Infant-Toddler program. Along with being the coordinator of the Infant-Toddler program, I was also a family worker. I was the primary worker for six families at a time. It was in this capacity that I became aware of the dynamics that take place when a woman is exposed to pornography as a child and adolescent.

We do not customarily ask about pornography on our intakes. As I became more involved with one of my clients, she began to tell me about what happened to her in her household. Her father had consistently showed her pictures of nude women, saying how he was attracted to them, using explicit language. He very often went to bars and picked up women and came back and told her all about his experiences. He also kept an arsenal of guns in his house.

This woman was very confused about why her behavior was so much like a victim of incest. She had three children with three different fathers, she got involved with abusive men who used her sexually. After talking about her background with myself and an incest therapist, she came to realize that what she was experiencing was common to victims of incest. This had happened even though her father had never touched her.

In talking to the staff, we came up with several other families in which pornography went hand in hand with abusive behavior. There is a definite link between the two, they are both harmful and destructive. It is because of this fact that I support the amendment to Title 7, Chapters 139 and 141 of the Minneapolis Code of Ordinances relating to civil rights.

Exhibit 19 [53]: Letter of Sandra Hewitt, Ph.D., The Kiel Clinics, December 9, 1983

I am a Licensed Consulting Psychologist working in the area of child sexual abuse, an area in which I have worked intensively for the last three years and broadly for the last eight years. About 70–80 percent of my client load at this present time is composed of sexually abused children ranging from preschool to school age children and adolescents. About one year ago, a conversation with Paul Gerber from the Bureau of Criminal Apprehension alerted me to that fact that many children have been exposed to pornography as part of their sexual abuse. At that time, on my case load, I indeed had a couple of children, 2 preschoolers and 1 school age child, who displayed this very strong interest in pictures of naked children and naked adults. Having heard this from Paul it seemed suddenly quite clear to me that these children may have experienced exposure to pornography in the course of their abuse. When I went back and checked with my clients, they indeed confirmed this. Since that time, I have been routinely checking with the children I see and I find that about 30 percent of my client load have been exposed to pornography at some time during their abuse history. This is most important to know because it certainly affects their presentation in treatment as they express a strong interest in any material which tends to shock and alienate adults.

In my office I have a number of small figures from plasticine clay which various children have made over the past three to four years when they've been in treatment with me. I use these figures as a way of "normalizing" the sexual abuse experience for new children or new clients that I'm seeing. I often say to them, "This figure was made by a child about your age and this is what happened to him/her." In the same way that I normalize the sexual abuse experience for children so I feel offenders normalize the abuse they do by showing a child a picture. "A picture is worth a thousand words," and for a young child it is much easier to show them what to do rather than tell them what to do. The nature of young children is to be dependent on the adults in their environment and when a trusted adult shows a child pictures of things children can do, they usually trust them and comply.

As a working professional in this area, I would very strongly support any measure you might consider which would curtail the use of pornography.

Exhibit 20 [54]: Letter of d.c., VOICE, Inc., December 5, 1983

. . . VOICE is a national network of incest survivors. For the last four years, we have communicated with thousands of sister survivors from all across the country. Whenever the subject of pornography comes up in correspondence or discussions, it is almost universally acknowledged that the perpetrator used either magazines or photographs that portrayed the sexual subjugation of women in their attempt to justify their actions against their daughters. . . . [M]ost women who are involved in pornography were themselves sexually victimized as children. Please help us—the victims and mothers of victims—to break the cycle of betrayal to which pornography so significantly contributes.

Exhibit 21 [58]: Letter of Trudee Able-Peterson, December 1, 1983

Recently, while lecturing on the issue of sexual exploitation/victimization of children, in a small Wisconsin town, a judge posed the following question: "Ms. Peterson, how would you counsel a twelve and a nine year old boy who, simultaneously, anally and vaginally raped a three year old girl, and when asked in court, why they did this, they responded, 'it's okay, we saw it in Hustler magazine.'?"

To those of us across the country who work with sexually abused children, it is common knowledge that adult pornography is often used to introduce children to this warped sexuality and then they are encouraged, coerced, or forced to simulate these sexual positions.

Pornography is object sexuality. It is arms, legs, breasts, genitals—disconnected parts. When men and women view the body as parts, and not as a whole, it is extremely dangerous to our potential growth and evolvement.

Because of this "object attitude," people can no longer respect their own bodies, or others' bodies. This becomes really evident when we note the rise of sado-masochistic "scenes" in pornographic magazines and movies. If it is just arms, legs, breasts, genitals, and not a person connected to them as a whole or a complete entity, it becomes "okay" to beat, mutilate, and tie up those parts.

Whatever is reflected in adult pornography affects us and our attitudes about our own sexual selves and certainly reaches down and influences our children about their own bodies.

While we continue to make the "Playboy Empire" wealthy, calling it "harmless soft porn," we forget that in the jokes, cartoons, and stories of Playboy, men are challenged to be superstuds who never respect or care for the women they have sex with. If a man isn't "knocking off a *piece*," any *piece*, as many *pieces* as possible, he is portrayed as an unmanly sap, someone to be ridiculed by his fellow men.

Playboy ran one *cartoon* of a little girl getting dressed and saying derisively to an old man in a robe, "and you call *that* being molested!" The old man standing there looking very inept and foolish, INADE-QUATE.

This *cartoon* accuses the little girl of being the seducer, and gives her all the power, and believe me, a 10-year-old girl who attempts suicide, sometimes successfully, rather than sleep with Dad or Uncle again, *has no power.*

I have worked in the field of sexually abused children for eight years. I have been a sexually abused child. I have been behind the porn camera. It has affected my whole life; my self-image, my sexuality, my relationships, my body, my mind, and, last but not least Professor, my heart.

Exhibit 22 [59]: Letter of Katherine Brady, November 29, 1983

My father incestuously molested me for a period of ten years when I was ages 8 to 18. During the early stages of the molestation, some of the things he used to coerce me into having sex with him were pornographic materials. In the beginning, the pornography materials were man-made oil paintings which he had taken from the inmates at two of the state institutions at which he worked in the capacity of corrections officer (Central State Hospital, Waupun, Wisconsin), and training officer (Reformatory for Boys, Green Bay, Wisconsin).

When I was age 10, he verbally told me about pornography and then sneaked it to me for explanation when my mother was at work and when he had sent my little brother off to play. Like most small children, I was naturally curious about what seemed to be an intriguing part of life, especially because my father seemed so excited when he talked about the pornography with me. When he showed me the paintings for the first time, this is how it went:

> "I confiscated these," he said, relishing the use of this official word. "Took 'em away from the boys at the Reformatory."
>
> As I sat down on the bed, he spread out the pictures so that I could see them. They showed men and naked women and animals in all sorts of sexual positions with each other. Looking at them, I felt a rush spread through my body, and once again the cycle was set in motion: intense sexual desire, total revulsion, increasing excitement, abandonment of reason, surge of climax, sense of sin and guilt and shame of it all, resolve to forget it until next time. (excerpted from *Father's Days*)

No one knew better about my developing curiosity of sexual matters than my father. My body developed early—in the sixth grade. I menstruated in grade school. Once pubescent, he escalated the genital molestation and by that time, his use of pornography had "sexually nurtured" (subtle coercion) me into submission. Because I was afraid of his physical power and verbal authority, it never occurred to me to challenge his use of pornography. It scared me, it confused me and yet it excited me and I felt trapped. My only escape was to send my mind off, a habit which has taken years to correct. I became, in essence, trained to respond to the porn for the sexual satisfaction of my father.

During the years of the intense genital molestation and entrapment in incest perpetrated by my father, and at a time when most other fathers in families such as ours (middle-class, Midwestern, protestant (methodist)) were teaching their children about life from the principles set forth in The Holy Bible, my father introduced magazines such as *Playboy* and *Hustler* in addition to the prisoners' man-made pornography, so that I would, as my father put it, "Be prepared for sex in life."

Over the last 10 years as I have spoken out across this nation as a survivor of incest turned child-abuse-prevention activist, and as I have counseled countless women, men and children about their own sexual victimization, I have learned that the use of pornography in the perpetration of sex crimes is alarmingly common. I can't speak for that legion of victims, but I can say that, for me, the use of pornography in the early stages of the fondling and set up of incest and then during the long-term genital molestation period has caused me over *30 years* of sexual anguish, the break up of my ten-year marriage to my high school sweetheart—the father of my two daughters, the loss of emotional support from my family and extended family, and, of course, the loss of any natural relationship with my father. In addition, I've spent (and my father has spent) hundreds of thousands of dollars in various therapies to patch up the damages of incest in our family. The use of pornographic materials tended to give me a negative image of myself as a female. It made me think of my body as an object for sexual abuse which caused (sadly) the deterioration of what could have been a joyous emotional and sexual relationship with my now ex-husband.

In closing, I really do think that the early and continual use of pornography by my father when he was perpetrating incest, became an integral part of the crime of incest and is comparable to the sexual excitement and thus added thrust manifested by the use of pornography of the pedophile/pederast who is attracted to the sexual powerlessness of children regardless of age and gender, and who is unable to control his sexual drives. To date, there is no cure for this type of sex offender. One of the few experimental programs (Columbia University, New York City) to control the sex drive of the rapist, incest perpetrator and basic child molester has introduced a drug (Depo-Provera) and it controls sex drive. In addition, the doctors administering that program have barred the use of pornography materials as they have learned from research data that pornography encourages the sex drive of sex offenders like my father.

Thank you for your work to prevent the use of pornography to discriminate against people who are coerced and nurtured and/or trained to respond to the stimuli that pornography presents.

Please let me know if there is further information—or testimony—that I can present.

Exhibit 23 [60]: Letter of Louise Armstrong, December 8, 1983

Attached is my statement regarding pornography and child sexual abuse, derived from my research.

I hope it proves helpful to the Council in its final considered determination.

Statement on Pornography and Child Sexual Abuse

I am the author of *Kiss Daddy Goodnight: A Speakout on Incest* (Hawthorn, 1978; Pocket Books, 1979). This was the first book to document—to listen to and validate—the experience of women who had been repeatedly molested as young children by fathers and stepfathers.

Apart from giving a voice to the millions of women of all generations in current American society who were sexually exploited as children within the family, the book has been widely used by mental health professionals—both those working with incest survivors, and those working to "sensitize" offenders (meaning to re-socialize them to see women and children, their victims, as humans).

Additionally, I have done articles on child sexual abuse for major magazines. I have spoken at sexual abuse conferences, at women's law conferences, was a keynote speaker at the 1980 National Women's Studies Association conference; and have lectured at colleges and universities around the country (including the delivery of the 1981 Bernice M. Wright Lecture at Syracuse University).

I contributed a chapter ("The Cradle of Sexual Politics: Incest") to the volume, *Women's Sexual Experiences: Explorations of the Dark Continent* (part of the series, Women in Context: Development and Stresses), Martha Kirkpatrick M.D., editor.

My recent book *The Home Front: Notes from the Family War Zone* (McGraw-Hill, Inc., 1983) is a continuation and expansion of my original research. It is the first synthesis of all disciplines (sociology, psychology, history, law, political science), their view and their response to the recent "discovery" of crimes in the home: paternal child molestation, wife battering, child abuse.

Additionally, I chair the Family Violence/Incest Committee under the National Women's Health Network.

During the seven years of my research in the area of paternal child molestation and other crimes against women and children in the family, I have spoken with thousands of women who were molested as children by fathers and stepfathers. I have read widely in the sociological, legal, and historical material pertinent to these abuses. And I have spoken with most (indeed, possibly all) of the leading experts in this area.

There is certainly no consensus that pornography *causes* paternal child molestation across the board: few would claim that if you eradicated child pornography, you would eliminate child sexual abuse.

There is evidence, however, of a direct linkage in an as yet unquantified number of cases.

The linkage is to both publicly available, printed and filmed, pornographic materials, and to privately circulated, "home-made" pornographic pictures of child-victims.

Several psychiatric experts I've spoken with recently, including child sexual abuse expert Dr. Roland Summit, Harbor General Hospital, Torrance, California, have referred to the growing incidence (that is, the greater number of cases coming to their attention) of men making private sexual-pornographic use of their children, exchanging and selling the photographs (and sometimes the children).

Within the last month, I have heard from a woman whose former husband was, as her four-year-old son testified, molesting the child during visitation, photographing him in pornographic poses, and sharing both the child and the pictures with friends.

And I've heard from a Connecticut lawyer about a case she had where the woman had re-married a well-to-do man. She'd brought two young girls to the marriage, and he two young boys. One morning, she went to his briefcase in search of two tax forms she knew she had to sign. In it, she found a pack of pornographic pictures of the girls.

The case of Annabelle (see attached chapter) is far from unique. It falls into a category which Dr. Summit and JoAnn Kryso call "Perverse Incest" or "Pornographic Incest," as they say, "in the absence of any better superlatives to describe kinky, unfettered lechery. These cases become more bizarre, more frankly erotic, more flagrantly manipulative and destructive than those in earlier categories. Many of them have a kind of self-conscious, sex-scene quality in which the individual seems to be trying to set up rituals to fulfill a variety of forbidden fantaises [sic]. . . .

"This group is called pornographic because of an apparent need to go beyond limits of socially acceptable sexual practice [sic] to explore whatever is most forbidden. Furthermore, the participants may want to record their achievements and to see themselves putting the fantasies into action: diaries, secret confessions and Polaroid photographs seem to heighten their excitement.

"Here the activity with children is contrived to gratify perverse needs and the rationalization evolves as a denial of guilt. Here the child is an accessory of the adult"—in what the authors describe as "lurid parodies of adult sexual function."

These "lurid parodies" are the very stuffs [sic] of commercial pornography—adult pornography, as well as child pornography.

Although child pornography is illegal, it remains available. And any diminished availability is more than compensated for by the proliferation of homemade pornography. And by the rampant infantilization of women in adult pornography—their graphic representation as child-like, in pigtails, with lollipops.

The Brooke Shields-ing of children and the infantilization of adult women in pornography—from that which is raw and violent, to that which is "soft core" and in the major media—are not anomalous as they might seem. They both represent the permission for men to exploit women and children.

That Dr. Summit and JoAnn Kryso, in the paper quoted from above, slip into speaking of going "beyond limits of socially acceptable social practice" in a paper called "Sexual Abuse of Children: A Clinical Spectrum" (*American Journal of Orthopsychiatry*, April, 1978), suggests the appalling reality of the risk children—girl children most especially—are born into in this country.

It is a reality for which pornography represents the green light, and signifies the chest-thumping boast.

Whether or not pornography is causative of real abuse practices, it is fully and profoundly *supportive* of them, as the recent rash of public rapes of women with the full and hearty support and assent of numerous male onlookers attests to. Pornography "de-sensitizes" men to the real and gross violation of a human being involved. It violates the civil rights of those its advocacy places at serious risk.

Much is currently being written about our inability to differentiate the images we are subjected to from reality. A recent piece by Barbara Goldsmith in *The New York Times* (12/4/83) quotes social historian Daniel J. Boorstin, writing in 1962 of "what then seemed a distant threat": "We risk being the first people in history to have been able to make their illusions so vivid, so persuasive, so realistic, that they can live in them." Although Goldsmith is writing on "The Meaning of Celebrity," her basic thesis—which is that images in our culture can override ethics, and throw exotic lawlessness and cruelty up to whet the public appetite (and so start a fad of gourmet abuse)—holds true for the image-power of pornography as well.

Goldsmith quotes George Gerbner, dean of the University of Pennsylvania's Annenberg School of Communications. He "estimates that by the time a typical American child reaches adulthood, he or she will have absorbed more thn [*sic*] 30,000 electronic 'stories.'["] These have, he suggests, replaced the socializing role of the pre-industrial church in creating "a cultural mythology" that establishes the norm of approved behavior and belief. [ ] No one has yet totted up the number of hours the typical American has spent absorbing pornographic images of women and children, both hard-core and soft. Perhaps someone should. For a person living, say on the west side of Greenwich Village in Manhattan, and working in, say, the Daily News Building on East 42nd Street, taking any form of surface transportation (bus, taxi, limousine) would provide you with between one hour and two hours of sexual victimization "rads" a day.

Pornography on cable should improve the dosage for every citizen.

I did not specifically direct my research to the role of pornography in child sexual abuse. Because that is true, it strikes me as more significant that I hear about its role as frequently as I do.

What is key to the issue is that *permission,* societal permission, is at the core of real paternal child molestation; and at the core of most marital and stranger rape.

Pornography is a blatant and powerful manifestation of that permission.

It gives the public stamp of approval to the degradation, objectification and exploitation of the two social groups whose victimization it lustily portrays and heartily endorses—in ever-escalating degrees of violence and contempt.

Repealing this permission by enfranchising those victimized—granting them the civil rights of citizenship in America—would represent extraordinary progress and social change toward the equal rights and equal protection under the law which the Constitution and the Bill of Rights attempt to guarantee.

Because we have donned a moral cloak of *apparent* outrage following the recent "discovery" of widespread child sexual exploitation in the home, let me briefly give evidence of the permission. (Further documentation can be found in *The Home Front*.)

Let's turn, almost at random, to one of the country's most respected psychiatrists, Dr. Joseph Rheingold, of Harvard University, with claim to 2,500 cases. In 1967, he published a book titled, *The Mother, Anxiety and Death*. The book focussed on destructive/seductive mothers. But he diverted from this focus to say, "The father is seductive too (of the daughter, very rarely the son), but the clinical evidence indicates that seduction of the girl is without significant pathogenic effect, even where it involves actual incest. It is the father's indifference to her femininity or his surreptitious interest that is detrimental to the girl's self-concept and the reason for strong protest against him later in life."

Note the—not only permission—but prescription for real-life, actual sexual exploitation of girl-children here, so as to ward off any strong protest against the father later in life.

In light of this, it is no less than wondrous that some people object to pornography because children get hold of it.

The permission to sexually abuse, exploit, and do violence to, women and children, is a historical one. Pornography, too, was, historically, available. Now, however, it has greater prevalence and greater power: it threatens to irradiate the public, and alter even what moral genetic structure we may have had.

What distance is there between the depiction of children "begging" for sex in pornographic display, and Maggie's father (in *Kiss Daddy Goodnight*) saying to then-three-year-old Maggie, "Tell me you like it. No, tell me you really like it. No, tell me like you mean it"?

What distance between the cartoon in *Playboy* showing an adult male in the bathroom doorway and a small girl adjusting her clothing and saying, "Is that what you call child molestation?"—and the North American Man-Boy Love Association (NAMBLA) seeking the "liberty" to legally exploit children sexually because the kids have a right to it?

Or between the Rene Guyon Society with its slogan, "Sex by eight or else it's too late"—and the millions of fathers and stepfathers across the centuries who have ordered, and are today ordering, their children into sexual servitude with the words, "It's natural." And, not infrequently, in my listening experience, adding, "I saw it in a magazine."

The major effort of therapeutic programs for rapists and child molesters is "sensitization": the effort to personify, to de-objectify, in these men's minds, their victims.

Psychologist Jonathan Ross, co-director of the Forensic Mental Health Center in New London, Connecticut, which treats child molesters, says, "These guys are responding to a blanket permission[.] Kids are sexual[.] There's nothing wrong with it."

Then, I ask him, is that therapy you're doing in your treatment? Isn't it re-socializing?

"Yes. These guys perceive the kids as objects. As *theirs*. Permission for this is everywhere in society. Kids are sexual. It's OK."

I ask, But then aren't you really re-socializing guys to a society which doesn't exist yet?

He agrees.

Pornography is a heavy duty, all-pervasive part of that permission. And for the most part it carries the extra-heavy-duty, sin-free sugar coating that the women and child victims are really loving every minute of it.

Bridgeport, Connecticut, attorney Cecilia Rosenberg is a member of the Masters Panel for Family Court, and has a degree in psychiatric social work. She says there's so much child molestation, "there's enough of it to be routine. It is something fathers feel they have a right to do. The underlying assumption is that females and children are available to them. If they don't use them sexually, it's an act of forbearance."

Pornography is the billboard on which that permission is posted across the United States of America.

When you abolish slavery, give blacks the vote, provide equal employment opportunity, give them access to the courts when they are depicted in gross ways, or slurred or slandered, you do not eliminate racism. You do however publicly and societally disavow it as socially acceptable. You empower its victims to seek remedy within the law: to go to America, as American citizens, for justice.

Women and children—two-thirds of America—should, it seems to me, have the same citizenship and civil rights when demeaned, outraged, and made increasingly vulnerable by increasingly available, and increasingly vitriolic and violent pornography.

Exhibit 24 [61]: Letter of Anne-Marie Eriksson, NYC Probation Officer, and Erik A. Eriksson, Lt. Col. USAF (Ret.), Incest Survivors Resource Network International, December 7, 1983

It seems unlikely that someone with a satisfying sexual life would want pornography. This raises the question of who uses pornography. Many incest victims have difficulty establishing a satisfactory sexual relationship with a peer. Many of the male incest victims, out of loneliness, turn to masturbation. For many of these, pornography appears to fill the need for masturbation fantasies. The industry also grinds up immature incest victims of both sexes and stuffs them into the sausage skins of pornographic films. Most pornographers are themselves incapable of maintaining relationships and a logical hypothesis is that many of them may be incest victims themselves.

Isn't it about time that we stopped the endless cycle of child sexual abuse? Everybody must reach out to both male and female victims of child sexual abuse and offer intervention.

Our group enthusiastically endorses your efforts in bringing the relationship of incest and pornography to a public forum.

Exhibit 25 [64]: Timothy Beneke, *Men on Rape: What They Have to Say about Sexual Violence* (New York: St. Martin's Press, 1982)

This book contains interviews with men discussing rape and sexuality. One, Jay, says this:

"In *Playboy* you see all these beautiful women who look so sexy and they'll be giving you all these looks like they want to have sex so bad; but then in reality you know that except for a few nymphomaniacs, they're doing it for the money; so I hate them for being used and for using their bodies in that way." (p. 44)

A convicted rapist, Chuck, is described by the author as follows:

At twenty, after two painful years of marriage, he separated from his wife and daughter, and felt enormous rage toward women for a year. One night while high on alcohol, pot, heroin, and downers, he went into a porno-graphic bookstore and watched a twenty-five-cent peep show that por-trayed a man raping a woman. That night he attempted his first rape. Within ten days he had attempted three, succeeded in one and was con-templating a fourth. (p. 71)

Chuck himself says this:

"One night about a year after I split from my wife, I was out partyin' and drinkin' and smokin' pot. I'd shot up some heroin and done some downers and I went to a porno bookstore, put a quarter in a slot, and saw this porn movie. It was just a guy coming up from behind a girl and attacking her and raping her. That's when I started having rape fantasies. When I seen that movie, it was like somebody lit a fuse from my childhood on up. When that fuse got to the porn movie, I exploded. I just went for it, went out and raped. It was like a little voice saying, 'it's all right, it's all right, go ahead and rape and get your revenge; you'll never get caught. Go out and rip off some girls. It's all right; they even make movies of it.' The movie was just like a big picture stand with words on it saying go out and do it, everybody's doin' it, even the movies. So I just went out that night and started lookin'." (pp. 73–74)

In response to being asked "If there had been no pornographic movies showing rape, would you have raped?" Chuck answers:

"I think I would've hurt a woman in a different way physically. If I wouldn't have committed rape I'd be in prison for murder right now, because it was goin' that way. I would've killed my next victim or the one after that . . . Pornographic movies have a lot to do with rape . . . Specials are okay because they can tell what can happen in rape, but a TV movie, a porn movie, or a regular movie about rape—they should ban them. You look at these movies and think, 'Wow, I wonder what it would be like to go out and rape somebody!' I heard stories in the hospital of people saying society must condone it—they have it on TV and movies. I know five or six guys who saw pictures of rape in a dirty book and believed it was all right to go out and rape; just still snapshots and that justified it to them. It said, okay, go out and rape because it's in a dirty book; there's nothing wrong with it. That goes for child molesting, too." (p. 79)

Exhibit 26 [65]: Letter of Jim Lovestar, December 6, [1983]

I have some feelings and opinions about pornography that I would like [to] express here. I'm certain that a great deal of information will be presented regarding the victimization of women thru [sic] pornography. I expect, too, that those presenting that testimony would be, appropriately, women.

I'd like to speak to the ways pornography harms me as a man. At its fundamental level pornography is lies about my sexuality. My sexual relationships with women are based on respect, trust, and love as best as I can feel & express those. The absence of these elements in pornography creates an incomplete and untrue portrayal of sexuality. It has given me and countless other men an education about sexual relations that is lacking in some essential components. I resent the existence of such misleading material.

Given that this presents an incomplete portrayal of sexual relations, it is presented in such a way that takes gross disadvantage of men's vulnerability. Men who take joy and celebration in their sexuality don't frequent X-rated stores. Men seek this outlet in a state of fear, shame, and powerlessness. They find a counterfeit and temporary sense of power and control. We (I've been there) are offered temporary respite, tho [sic] not comfort, from our pain. Our pain & humanity are ignored, even denied. All that counts is that we are male and can afford the price of this ersatz pleasure. Men who fear to look a woman in the eye can see images of the feared party in states of degradation. Men ashamed of their gender and sexuality can witness scenes of men who appear not [to] experience these feelings. Someone makes money off the suffering and loneliness of men who deserve recognition of their state from themselves as well as from the men and women. Pornography has no winners—women are abused and portrayed as powerless for the eyes of men who feel abused and powerless. I support any effort to challenge the system that this represents and submit that pornography hurts everyone and we all have a stake in its demise.

Exhibit 27 [66]: Letter of John Stoltenberg, M.Div., M.F.A., Chair, Antipornography Task Group, National Organization for Men, December 1, 1983

I am writing to you in support of the proposed ordinance concerning pornography as it affects the civil rights of women.

As chair of the antipornography task group of the National Organization for Men, I have had occasion to conduct workshops with men that deal with men's attitudes toward various forms of pornography. I have observed a rather clear pattern of recognition among men in these workshops that the commercial depictions and use of women in pornographic magazines and films do in fact have the effect of making women seem subservient, inferior, degraded, and enjoying pain and humiliation. However much these men report having some history of sexual arousal in relation to such material (and I have observed these histories to vary greatly), I find a pattern of quite candid acknowledgment that such pornographic treatments of women are without any question expressions of violence, power, hostility and aggression against women.

I have also found that many men report some degree of anger at their own recognition of how their own sexuality has been manipulated and shaped by pornography.

From the context of my experience talking with men in depth and at length about their perceptions of what pornography is about, I believe I can testify that a significant number of men when speaking honestly about themselves and their feelings would acknowledge that much pornography is indeed an expression of a will to power over women and that in its debasement of women it feels like debasement of men as well.

I applaud your landmark approach to this issue. I think you have found precisely the way to define what is hurtful in pornography and how a community can begin to heal and redress that great harm.

Exhibit 28 [78]: Telegram of Gloria Steinem, December 11, 1983

As someone who looks to Minnesota for national leadership in social policy I urge you to amend Title VII by including pornography as a form of sex discrimination. Your leadership is as historically important here as in making clear that rape is violence not sexual expression or that sexual harassment is a major form of sex discrimination. It is demonstrable

that pornography teaches and legitimizes the violence, torture, humiliation and inferiority of women. It is demonstrable that women have been
harassed and terrorized out of jobs, neighborhoods, union membership,
and educational programs through purposeful pornographic displays.
This ordinance does not constitute prior restraint but does allow citizens
to bring their grievances before the court. It could also be a valuable
parallel for constitutional redress of grievances of blacks and other racial
groups who have been harassed out of jobs and neighborhoods by the
literature of racial violence. Constitutional authorities have long made
clear that states and municipalities must be the laboratories for social
experimentation. This is a rare opportunity for Minneapolis to continue
a traditional path to progress.

Minneapolis: Memo on Proposed Ordinance on Pornography, December 26, 1983

TO: Minneapolis City Council
FROM: Catharine A. MacKinnon and Andrea Dworkin
RE: Proposed Ordinance on Pornography
DATE: 26 December 1983

Several of you have suggested to us that a short paper addressing some frequently asked questions would be helpful. Here we briefly discuss what this ordinance is trying to do, how it would work, why it is different from past approaches, and we assess supposed obstacles.

1. What this ordinance is trying to do

This ordinance defines pornography for what it is. Its central feature is that it subordinates women through sex. The influence of pornography on men who rule societies, and thus on the development of misogynist social institutions, can be traced back through feudalism, but it is only through relatively recent technology that the social environment has been glutted with pornography so that it hurts women openly, publicly, and with social legitimacy. This same pervasiveness and open availability have also made it possible to understand and document the effects of pornography, hence its place in the institutionalization of second class citizenship for women, for the first time in history.

The use of women in pornography and the impact of pornography on women's status and treatment is the primary focus of this ordinance. Pornography promotes environmental terrorism and private abuse of women and girls and, to a lesser extent, men and boys and transsexuals. Society's efforts toward the civil and sexual equality of women and men

253

are severely hampered—frankly, nearly destroyed—by the success of pornography. Most frequently, the pornography promotes rape, pain, humiliation and inferiority as experiences that are sexually pleasing to all women because we are women. The studies show that it is not atypical for men to believe and act on the pornography. Each time men are sexually aroused by pornography—the sexually explicit subordination of women—they learn to connect women's sexual pleasure to abuse and women's sexual nature to inferiority. They learn this in their bodies, not just their minds, so that it becomes a physical, seemingly natural, response. When real women claim not to want inequality or force, they are not credible compared with the continually sexually available "real women" in pornography. These men are the same normal men who make decisions that control much of women's lives and opportunities at every level of society. Until women achieve equal power with men, such men are in a position to control women's employment, educational advancement, social status and credibility in the media, on paper, on the street, in meetings, in court, in their own homes, and in public office. The fact that some women have successfully fought some of this discrimination does not prove it does not exist; it proves that victories, like the victory this ordinance would be, can be won.

In the hearings, we learned that it takes coercion to make pornography—for instance, *Deep Throat,* the highest grossing film ever.[1] We learned that pornography is forced on women and children and that frequently the women and children are then raped or forced to do what is in the pornography. We learned that pornography is used in sexual assaults and to plan the sexual assaults. We learned that exposure to pornography increases male aggression toward women and leads men to see women as things, less than human, and wanting and liking rape and torture and humiliation. We also learned that pornography has been used to, and has the effect of, terrorizing women in their homes, in their neighborhoods, and in their places of work. We learned that pornography is used in relationships that range from the intimate to the anonymous in ways that give women no choice about seeing the pornography or doing the sex.

---

1. It is, of course, difficult to document the profits of organized crime precisely. However, *Deep Throat* ended the 1970s "with an estimated gross income of six hundred million dollars from paying customers for the film itself." Gloria Steinem, "The Real Linda Lovelace," *Outrageous Acts and Everyday Rebellions* (Holt, Rinehart, & Winston, 1983), p. 243. This figure does not include videocassette or other spin-off product profits.

The purpose of the ordinance is to make available an effective remedy to those who choose to use it, so that women need no longer be paralyzed or passive or held back by the lack of a legitimate avenue for redress in the face of pornography—the systematic discrimination, the condoned brutality, and the glorified debasement that defines the condition of an entire group of people.

2. How the ordinance would work

Like any other law that prohibits discrimination, this law would make available the administrative apparatus of the Human Rights Commission and the courts to adjudicate complaints. Once the law goes into effect, a person who has been coerced into a pornographic performance, had pornography forced on them, or has been assaulted or physically attacked or injured in a way directly caused by a specific piece of pornography could choose to complain to the Commission or go directly to court. Any woman can also complain against traffickers in pornography. Because the data from the hearings show that pornography increases male aggression against women, the public availability of the pornography, as defined in the ordinance, is in and of itself a violation of women's rights to equal personhood and citizenship. The systematic sexual subordination of the pornography *is* the injury under this section of the act.

The Commission or the court would then see if the pornography complained of meets the definition of pornography in the statute. The definition of pornography in the statute states exactly what pornography is and does. It describes exactly the trafficking in women engaged in by the pornographers, which ranges from dehumanizing women as sexual things and commodities to torturing and maiming women as sexual acts. The dehumanization is fundamental to the subordination and the precondition for the more explicit violence. It is tempting to consider proceeding one step at a time, disallowing the explicit violence while allowing the dehumanization, objectification, and submission. This would leave the *inequality* intact. Such an approach would not go to the heart of this form of subordination. It would also draw a legal line that would take immense resources to adjudicate because it is not a line that can be drawn because it is not a line that is drawn in the pornography.

The definition includes everything that is pornography and does not include anything that is not. It does not include sex education, for instance, or erotica, which is sexually explicit sex premised on equality. Any law can be abused. Cynical attempts to undermine this law may center on attempts to apply it to materials and acts for which it was not intended. The pornographers have a lot of money and power at stake in making this law look bad. We believe that the Commission and the courts are as reliable instruments for distinguishing frivolous abuses from bona fide injuries in these cases as they are in any other kind of discrimination case.

The most legally likely place for issues other than sex discrimination to arise—issues such as the First Amendment—is as a defense. When sued under this ordinance, the pornographers are likely to say that it violates their First Amendment rights. The point here is that customarily people have to have a legal injury before they can sue. They can not customarily sue a law-making body just because it has passed a civil law that they do not like or agree with or think *might* be applied to them. People activate civil claims by alleging that someone else hurt them in a way the law recognizes. This means that other legal issues, such as the First Amendment, are most likely to be raised as defenses by pornographers against those who complain or sue them for injuries, rather than as a basis for a direct suit against anyone. Once an action commences against a respondent, they can seek to involve the city or the agency and/or to challenge the ordinance on its face. We discuss why we think that such uses of the First Amendment may not prevail in section 4.

3. Why this approach is better than past approaches

The major distinction between the civil rights approach to pornography and past approaches to all the problems of sexual inequality it involves is that this is the first time the legal concept of the injury is the same as the real social injury pornography does. Obscenity laws, besides allowing inconsistent, ill-conceived or politically motivated criminal prosecutions, created a lot of confusion about pornography by misidentifying the harm. Many people mistake obscenity for pornography. Obscenity is a criminal legal term. One possible root meaning of the word "obscene" is the ancient Greek for "off stage"—in effect, that which should not be shown, especially in the theatre for aesthetic reasons. This suggests that the injury of obscenity has to do with what is publicly viewed; the injury of pornography is what is done, whether it is public or private. Another possible and more likely root meaning of the word "obscene" is the Latin for "against filth": Is a given work "filth" and are we, the people, against it. Obscenity is not a synonym for pornography in this meaning either. Obscenity is a social value judgment. Pornography is concrete. Its root meaning is "the graphic depiction of whores." Everybody may have an idea of what is or is not obscene, especially given the myriad inconsistent legal definitions over the last 200 years. Pornography is specific, concrete, and, as we have said, about the sexually explicit subordination of women. In pornography, women are graphically depicted as whores by nature, that is, defined by our status as sexual chattel. Because the definition in the ordinance is concrete, specific, narrow, and describes what is actually there, it is not vague, not overly broad, not about ideas that some people think are good or bad, moral or immoral, normal or abnormal, natural or unnatural, nor does the ordinance suggest, as obscenity law does, that women's bodies are dirty or sex is dirty. A final distinction between obscenity and pornography is crucial. Courts have been hampered in enforcing obscenity laws because there was no evidence of the harm obscenity does to match the scope of the laws enacted. The harm of obscenity could not be documented or measured because it did not exist. Evidence from the hearings provided evidence for the harm of pornography because it identified the harm that pornography actually does: to the status and treatment of women.

The proposed ordinance differs from past approaches by going significantly beyond any existing law that regulates acts committed against women. Now, before this law, people who are coerced into pornography have no effective way to reach the pornography made by coercing them. The profit incentive to coercing more and more women remains. If they complain, they are not believed, in part because pornography in general convinces people that women love doing it and in part because the specific pornography they are forced to make is often convincing in depicting their simulated enjoyment. Now, before this law, when women are sexually assaulted, because the society is saturated by pornography, they are unlikely to be believed in court and are continually asked pornographic questions like, did you like it? Now, before this law, child pornography is a crime in Minnesota but forcing pornography on children is not. Often, adult pornography in which women are infantilized is used. Such pornography continues to target children for sexual assault, even if the models have actually aged one day beyond their minority.

Unlike all other previous approaches to the growing social problem of pornography, including zoning laws which have at times hurt poor and working-class neighborhoods or segregated women out of whole sections of cities, this law stands against the real traffic in real women. It is a civil law *against* pornography, but it is also *for* the equality of the sexes, women's rights, and the integrity and dignity of all persons regardless of sex. And it will *do* something: empower people and call into question the legal immunity of the exploiters for the first time.

4. *Assessment of supposed obstacles*

Nothing exactly like this law has ever been tried, so it can not be said conclusively that it will or will not work or will or will not be constitutionally upheld. Because it is part of the civil code, not the criminal code, there will be no state ban or police enforcement. Because it is not an obscenity law, nothing ever done under obscenity law strictly controls the interpretation of this law, although prior case law may indicate judicial attitudes toward some of the issues involved. The First Amendment right to speech has never been absolute. In the one case where the Supreme Court has balanced a municipal sex discrimination ordinance prohibiting sex segregation in advertising against the First Amendment, the ordinance won (1973). More recently, the Supreme Court, recognizing child pornography to be a form of child abuse, allowed states to make it a crime. The harm that the child pornography industry did to children allowed something that is speech (not obscenity) to be illegal consistent with the First Amendment. (The ACLU defended child pornography as speech throughout the litigation.) Our hearings show a similar level of harm done to women in adult pornography, as well as the integral role adult pornography plays in child abuse. The pornographers have relied for their impunity upon the indistinguishability of what they push from any other form of expression. This proposed ordinance draws a line that distinguishes them. The pornographers have convinced many that their freedom is everyone's freedom, obscuring what this statute is based on: the freedom of the pornographers enforces the subordination of women.

The First Amendment mainly prohibits state acts that interfere with speech. But there is an affirmative, if less prominent, side to the First Amendment that would allow the silence of women because of discrimination to be taken into the balance. The fairness doctrine in broadcasting, for example, recognizes that government sometimes has an obligation to help make access to speech available on an equal basis. The First Amendment's goals are furthered by restricting the speech of some so that others might have access to it. Pornography directly contributes to a silencing of women that is socially pervasive. The First Amendment is undermined when women are kept from having access to the social preconditions to exercise the rights the First Amendment guarantees from infringement by states. Equal access to the means of speech, which pornography discriminatorily denies to women sexually and socially, is a First Amendment goal that is furthered by this law.

The civil rights approach, unlike morals legislation and police power, is strengthened by the support of legal concepts outside the First Amendment, namely equal protection (the Fourteenth Amendment) and anti-discrimination law. That the systematic relegation of an entire group of people to inferiority because of a condition of birth should be illegal is not a new idea. This ordinance to further the equality of the sexes embodies an interest particularly appropriate for that level of representative government closest to the people.

Minneapolis: Press Conference, July 25, 1984

Press Release

For immediate release: July 25, 1984
Contact: Cheryl Champion
[phone number deleted]

There will be a press conference on Wednesday, July 25, 3:00 P.M., at the Minnesota Press Club. It has been called by women whose lives have been directly damaged by pornography and who have been waiting, out of the public eye, hoping to be able to bring complaints under an amendment to the Civil Rights Code.

Now, we feel it is time to make a public statement, encouraging the City Council to override the Mayor's veto.

There is a cost to waiting—waiting for a decision in a significantly different lawsuit in Indianapolis. The cost of waiting is more and more damaged lives, our lives, and the lives of countless other women, children, and men. It seems absurd to us to consider the possibility of having to spend money to defend the law more important than human lives.

Two sample paragraphs from one of the statements follow:

When I grew up, I had a relationship with a man who had posters from *Penthouse* and other pornography on the walls of his room. He raped me there, although I didn't call it rape at the time. I would say, "I don't want to." He would say, "Oh yes you do." He had a warped view of sexuality, of how women and men act. I came to see myself alone as worthless, as a commodity.

Earlier this year I had a job at a company which uses women in ads to sell its products. They had a lot of porn around. Men had centerfolds on their office walls. I was continually sexually harassed there. Men would call me "legs" or "honey" or "baby" or "sweetie"—never my name. I talked to the manager about the harassment three times in all. The more I resisted, the worse it got. Finally, I quit because a man grabbed me and the manager only reprimanded him.

We have invited three people to join us. Council Member Sharon Sayles Belton has been asked to make a statement about how an override of the Mayor's veto would affect situations like the one involving Vanessa Williams.

Cheryl Champion, from Sexual Assault Services at Washington County Human Services, has worked with victims of sexual assault for many years. She will speak about the deep connection of pornography with all forms of sexual abuse.

Attorney Catharine MacKinnon will join us to clarify the legal implications of our experiences and the importance of the amendment to the Civil Rights Ordinance.

Statement of Cheryl Champion

Good Afternoon.

We have called this press conference to make an appeal to the city council members of Minneapolis to override the Mayor's veto and make the Pornography Ordinance Law.

Who We Are

You will hear from each of us individually. We ask that you be respectful of the courage it requires to make this kind of public testimony. Some of us will be familiar to you, others of us will attempt to remain anonymous. Each time we have met with the press, women have come forward to speak with strength about the harm done to us. Women will continue to come forward. We are not members of some lunatic fringe, we are members of [the] community, citizens in good standing.

Format

We will each speak individually, at the end, some of us will leave and some of us will remain to answer questions. We ask that you hold your questions until the end.

Statement

I am not here to talk about myself, but to give credibility to my statement, I will tell you, my name is Cheryl Champion, I have worked in the field of sexual abuse for 14 years. Since 1975, I have worked in Minnesota. The Minnesota Coalition of Sexual Assault Programs, of which I am a member, represents 37 statewide programs. I have also been a member of the Board of Directors of the National Coalition Against Sexual Assault, a coalition of programs from across the United States. But [I'm] choosing to speak instead for the women unable to be here today.

I am here representing 14 years of work in the anti-rape movement, a movement created by voiceless, anonymous women. Women who fought, organized, [lobbied] and in some cases, gave their lives to fight against sexual abuse.

Pornography does not exist in isolation. This is not an issue of special interest for a small minority group. The sadistic violence and sexual enslavement we speak of is not isolated or remote—it is real. It is in the stories of the battered wives, molested children and raped women that happen everyday. It is precisely because this sexual violence is so immediate in our lives, we have been fighting for our survival, there has been no time to address this cause until now.

It is evident that pornography could not be the product of a non sexist culture where women are acknowledged as fully valuable human persons. In a non sexist culture it would be shocking and intolerable to the community to view these images of women. In ours it is commonplace.

We will know that we are free when pornography no longer exists. As long as it does exist we must understand that "we are the women in it," used by the same people, subject to the same devaluation.

Porn and prostitution will be the last to fall. There are rape crisis centers, there are battered women's shelters, there are incest treatment programs. As disbelieved as rape victims, incest victims and battered women were in the past, so are the prostitutes and pornographed models now[a]days. Women in pornography do not see a society that will stand behind them, individuals who will help them. They are the last group of powerless women.

Statement of Rev. Susan Wilhelm

I am Rev. Susan Wilhelm. I had not realized the extent of the harm pornography has done to me until this past winter, when I was working on a photo-montage of kinds of pornography for an educational forum. I came across a picture of a position . . . my ex-husband had insisted we try. When we did, I hemorrhaged for three days. My bruised cervix is still a problem after 10 years.

My father had used pornography like *Argosy, True, Saga, Stag,* and *Cavalier.* They are adventure stories, different from the slicks. No one claims they are intellectual magazines. I was not supposed to, but I read them. There was either the short dumpy fishwife with her hair in curlers or the beautiful sexy available creatures. The short dumpy ones were sexually used, too, but the man does not really enjoy them. That was my education on what women were like.

Most of my sex life with my ex-husband was very abusive. He had a lot of pornography around the house, both the slicks and the hard core. He went to Rochester [Minn.] to buy it. It made him expect that I would want to do crazy things. He kept saying our sex life was, and I was, dull, blah, unfun. When we were first married, he did not use pornography and did not drink. He started drinking first. But the sex became especially abusive after he started using pornography. He got his ideas from it. Having sex how he wanted it was nonnegotiable.

He had a fetish about hating pubic hair. He used to shave his and mine. Once he slipped and slit my clitoris. He claimed it was an accident. If he decided I liked something, he would try to kill it, like dogs we had. I am convinced he tried to kill me more than once. There are also more subtle ways of killing the spirit.

He exposed me to the pornography, too. Once we saw an X-rated film that showed anal intercourse. After that, he pressed me to try it. I agreed to once, but found the experience very painful. He kept trying periodically. He told me my vagina had become as sloppy as an old sow's and he could not get pleasure any other way. He also used to pinch and bite me. When I said "it hurts," he would say, "no, it doesn't." I became numb. I lost track of my own feelings. One time, he said in reference to himself sexually, "it's supposed to hurt." Something started to change for me then.

The mayor claims to be concerned about the cost of a court test of the civil rights ordinance. But what about the cost of the human lives that are harmed and need years of therapy to heal? We, the victims, are paying with our lives. We should have some place to go to complain about how the pornography is part of making our husbands into rapists.

Statement of Peggy

My name is Peggy.

Starting at age 4, old Mr. Edwards up the street used pornography to entice me into taking baths so he could watch, had me wearing his wife[']s clothes and eventually having oral sex and being penetrated by him. This went on for five years. He used the pornography to show me how to be—and what to do—until I didn't see anything wrong—with anything he did to me—or had me do to him. I became addicted to sex as a way of getting through life. I also drank a lot. My first marriage was purely sexual. I put up with more pornography because I thought—it would secure my marriage—but it destroyed it. The man I lived with last used pornography books to sexually arouse my son so he could molest him—and my son and his friends used pornography to molest my daughter—to experiment on her sexually—using the pornographic books as teaching guides. What was done to all of us physically is one thing—but you can also be crucified in your brain.

I never realized the whole pattern until the last two years. I have never been able to complete an education, or hold a steady job, I've had two children out of wedlock, and spent most of my life until recently on AFDC and in bars. I wonder what my life would have been, if what happened with the pornography hadn't happened. Or—if there had been a way to do something about it.

You talk about cost—

I'd like to know how much it has cost the state to support myself and children, the county to prosecute the man who assaulted my children, and for all these years of therapy for all of us, to try to undo what the pornography did.

Anyone who is worried about the cost of letting women fight pornography, or who wonders what there is to lose in waiting a few more years to let it start here, should think about how much of this we can afford, and who's paying for it.

Statement of Ms. J. (age 15)

I'm 15 and in the 9th grade in high school and many of the boys' lockers have porno pictures hanging in them. Many of my friends and I have been attacked in and out of our homes with the use of pornography. Covering the porn material won't protect children. Adults buy porn and either use it to abuse us, or leave it around for others to victimize us with it.

We feel betrayed by Barbra Carlson who only wants to hold our hands instead of doing something to help us.

We want the city council to answer our question:

What is more important, money or people's lives?

Statement of Ms. P.

I grew up in a middle class neighborhood, attended church every week and everyone knew my father as a public high school teacher. He has numerous teaching awards and was a church deacon. I saw a different side of my father, he called it his play-time. I didn't know why I posed nude with my sister, but by age eight I was forced into my first pornographic movie.

I can still picture the set, bright cameras, and the director yelling for me to look more seductive. My dad gave me advice when I didn't want to touch the boy's penis. "Just pretend his body is your daddy's," he said kissing me on the lips.

At home I was raped nightly. He'd get me a glass of water, wait till my mom was asleep and then force his penis into my mouth and vagina. After he finished I'd hide under the covers and listen as he entered my sister's room.

As he rose in the pornography business his temper flared. The movies were becoming bigger productions and he was now a director. Once I was placed in a scene with thirty other children. The sex finale had us all line up for an anal sex. I couldn't stop crying as the boy's penis tore into me. My father stopped the scene, and dragged me down into a basement room. He locked the metal door and began beating me. He ripped off my clothes, and I felt relieved that he'd only rape me. Then I saw the knife. Instead of cutting my throat he thrusted it into my vagina. I don't remember the sound of my screams, but when he had finished blood covered the floor.

He wiped off the knife, and went back upstairs. He and a set man returned, wrapped me in blankets, and brought me to his private doctor's office. My vagina was stitched up in a clean white room, with precision to prevent scarring. The doctor smiled a lot, told jokes and acted as if nothing was unusual about my situation. I was home in my bed by the next morning.

His temper and cumulative violence convinced me that something was wrong. I'd never been told that little girls didn't star in pornographic movies and weren't supposed to be raped by their father. His pressure to be secretive alerted me, but his violence kept me quiet.

The last stage of my father's abuse involves prostitution. By fifteen young girls are considered too old for child pornography. By then my father had his own production company and needed young women to please his clients. Sometimes I'd be placed in Hilton hotel rooms, but usually in his special bedroom suite, inside the studio. The first time I was tied up and drugged with sedatives administered by injection. The client came in, and raped me, a glassy eyed fifteen-year-old. Soon I didn't need to be drugged. I knew the score, either make the client happy or not see another morning. His clients appeared to be mob related, drug dealers and even public officials all investing in his pornographic movies.

My father's production company was a five story building complete with screening room, offices and various studios. Three or four movies were being made at the same time. Life inside the studio meant cocaine covered tables, studio people armed with guns, and hidden cameras in every room. I tried running away, attempted suicide, but never considered telling on my father. He gave me constant reminders of his power, but this one time convinced me I'd never escape.

He led me into one of his sound proof offices. I saw two men being held by my dad's security. My father explained that they were informers and pulled out a revolver. He shot them in the chest, and they fell to the carpet. "No one betrays me," was all he said, and then his men took out the bodies.

I was three when my father began sexually abusing me. I lived through fifteen years of pornography and three years of prostitution. I escaped because I lived a double life, at home I was a normal middle class child expected to attend college. The prostitutes you see on the street are the children who couldn't escape and didn't live double lives. Over seventy percent of all prostitutes are incest victims. The prostitute is an abused child who found her life at home so dangerous that she turns to the streets and stays there. She lives on the streets past her eighteenth birthday and suddenly she is the criminal. Instead of arresting the incest victim why doesn't the law arrest the real criminals, the pimps and clients that continue the abuse the victim faced in her home.

These children who didn't escape also need our protection and help. The prostitutes shouldn't be arrested, they're only trying to survive in an abusive world. Instead of placing them in jail, educate and train the women in constructive skills, making them accessible to other employment. Therapy should also be offered, they will get off the streets faster when they realize life doesn't always have to be abusive. Over seventy percent of the prostitutes come from similar backgrounds to mine. If I had not been raised in a double life, in the suburbs and not attended college, the police may have arrested me by now.

All adult survivors need access to free therapy programs. Incest survivors have to talk and work through all their years of abuse if they want to lead a normal life. Adult survivors are often not believed by their families, friends and the police. The victim only [h]as her word against the abuser. The abuser is seen as the minister, teacher, or respected professional, not as a rapist or pornographer. Free therapy clinics in every town, would give the victims the courage and validation needed to confront their abusers. Then they need laws to prosecute and bring their abuser to justice. The statu[t]e of limitations is limited to a few years after the victim is eighteen or remembers through therapy. A victim in therapy is reliving every time she was beaten and raped. Therapy of this kind takes years not months, and even longer to find the courage to face her abuser in court. There shouldn't be a statu[t]e of limitations on cases of child abuse. This statu[t]e only limits the rights of the abuse, while keeping pornographers and rapists accessible to children.

We can make changes to protect future children from being abused. In kindergarten and nursery schools information programs on abuse should be mandatory. Therapists would travel around school systems telling children that what's happening to them at home is wrong. One on one, these therapists could gain the child's trust, and teach them it's okay to tell someone about the abuse. These programs should continue throughout a child's education to save children who are abused at a later age.

Then a protection agency is required. An agency that treats the child as an individual, not part of her abusive family. No child will tell on a parent, if she'll have to return to that home. Agencies can't rely on family therapy, two years of therapy doesn't guarantee a rapist will stop attacking his child.

I'm giving testimony tonight because my story is not unique. One third of all girls, and one seventh of all boys are sexually abused before the age of eighteen. Rational treatment programs for abused children and adult survivors, the ending of statu[t]e of limitations, and realistic protection laws will make the difference for all the children[']s survival. My father has a new baby girl, and I'm fighting to find evidence and prevent her abuse. She and other children will suffer my childhood unless these changes are made.

The Indianapolis Hearing

INDIANAPOLIS CITY-COUNTY COUNCIL
ADMINISTRATION COMMITTEE
APRIL 16, 1984, 4 P.M.

BEULAH COUGHENOUR, CHAIRWOMAN: . . . Committee of the Council here today to consider an amendment to Chapter XVI of the Code, Human Relations and Equal Opportunity. We have with us several people to give expert testimony today. We will hear expert testimony, first we will have the pro, then we will have the expert con testimony and then we will open it to members of the public who have signed in. On the time for those members of the public, we will probably limit this to three minutes each in interest of the length of the meeting.

At this time I would like to introduce Ms. MacKinnon, Catharine MacKinnon. . . . We welcome Ms. MacKinnon to our committee and would like her to come forward and give the basis for this amendment. She has defined the legal argument for sexual harassment as a legal claim for sex discrimination, so she is well qualified today to speak to us concerning the ordinance in our amendment. Thank you. Ms. MacKinnon.

CATHARINE MacKINNON: Thank you, Councilmember.

I am extremely honored to be here in Indianapolis, in a place that takes seriously the rights of women and the rights of all people sufficient to consider that pornography should be defined as a violation of your civil rights code.

I am going to be speaking in general about the view both of sex discrimination and of the First Amendment with which this proposal is consistent. I will begin by submitting for more extended consideration by the Council a transcript of the factual hearings that were held in Minneapolis in support of a similar ordinance. . . .

This ordinance that we have proposed defines pornography as the sexually explicit subordination of women, graphically depicted, whether

269

in pictures or in words, that also includes one of a number of other characteristics. I will first talk about the provision's use of "sexually explicit" and "subordination of women," and then discuss the other characteristics.

"Sexually explicit" is a term that has a legal history. It is not a term that allows for the sex that is presented to be implied or left implicit or something that the viewer might think was sex. It has to be express. . . . A normal meaning of the term subordination has to do with being placed in a position of inferiority or loss of power. It is a way of being denigrated or demeaned. The "subordination of women" is an active term in this law. It is not "all depictions of" or "discussions of" or "advocacy of" the subordination of women. To be covered, they would have to [be] in fact the subordination of women. The element of subordination, embodying as it does a concept of force or placing someone down or in a lower status, is what is central to the way this is a discrimination law. It is a law that is addressed to the specific situation of the inequality of the sexes and the way . . . pornography as we define it makes the inequality of the sexes sexual, the way that it makes sexy, the way that it eroticizes putting women in an inferior position.

The list that we then add, which must also be present, is a series of specific items which must be in the pornography in order for it to produce the discriminatory and violent effects that it has. The "we" in this description that I have been saying is me and Andrea Dworkin. We are the co-authors of this approach and of this ordinance.

Each item in the definition . . . is supported by both research data of one sort or another—either laboratory, social or clinical, in fact in all cases, all laboratory, social data or clinical data—as well as by testimony from individuals, some of whom will be here to talk to you and others of whom testified before the Minneapolis City Council, and their comments are in the transcript. . . .

The combination of sexually explicit with the subordination of women makes this law not what lawyers may tell you it is . . . merely a content regulation. It makes it instead something that is more like other [restrictions] that have been held to be legal under the First Amendment. It's a message-medium combination. It combines what it includes, what it says, with a way of saying it that produces specific harms. . . . But anyone who says this is merely a content regulation is talking about it as if all it is, is the sub-parts of it. The list of specific covered things, with the sexually explicit subordination of women, is something that it is doing, not just what it says.

Other things that the law is not—it is not a criminal law. Classically, it is not censorship or a ban in a way that the state, that is the government, is involved actively in [taking] actions to enforce it. It is a civil rights law, a law that allows those people who have been harmed by this violation to bring actions against the people who have done that harm, including, in this case, the people who profit from it.

It is not a prior restraint, . . . a law that allows [materials] to be prevented from being seen before there's any legal action. It would allow anything to be acted against only after there had been a legal action to determine that this is in fact something that comes under the law.

It also doesn't have a single thing to do with offensiveness. Somebody can be real offended by something and if it isn't described by this statute, they can't do anything about it under this statute. They can also not be offended by it, and they won't be the people to bring an action under this law probably. You could think that this, in fact, is something that is covered by this law and not be offended by it. In other words, it doesn't have anything to do with subjective feeling. What the materials either are or are not, is described by this definition and the feelings are not central to it. . . .

What I now want to discuss is the way in which this law makes visible a conflict of rights between the equality rights that are guaranteed, particularly to women, but to all people to be free from discrimination on the basis of sex, and the rights that are guaranteed under the First Amendment but are particularly available, in this case, to pornographers as well as to sellers and distributors to argue that their First Amendment rights are at stake here. The way this particular issue, I think, is most likely to be approached judicially is for the Supreme Court to assess the rights of women, who argue that our lives and our opportunities including our freedom of speech and action, are constrained and, in many cases, made impossible, flat out precluded, by the pornography, that that will be balanced against those who argue that the pornography is harmless, or that it is partly harmful but not harmful enough, or that it is more important . . . to preserve this pornography as this law defines it, than it is to do anything about whatever harms it may cause.

Now, predicting how the court will cast this balance, first I will say that anyone who tells you that this ordinance is blatantly unconstitutional is giving you something more like a personal preference rather than a legal analysis. . . . This ordinance has never been considered by the Supreme Court, and no ordinance that is very much like it has ever been considered by the Supreme Court—except in one case in which a sex discrimination ordinance, a local ordinance that restricted sex segregated ads, . . . was balanced against the First Amendment rights of the press to the commercial speech. . . . And in that case, the ordinance won.[1] The discrimination interest that was furthered by the local ordinance was held to be more important than the commercial speech interest that was recognized as existing under the First Amendment. But other than in that case, cases and theories talk about how the Supreme Court might balance the interests, but this particular one has never been confronted.

So what I am going to be doing is arguing to you that a new form of governmental interest is what you are recognizing. You are saying the government has recognized an interest in sex equality, and you now see that pornography harms the equality of the sexes, and you're going to create a civil action for people who are harmed to further the equality of the sexes, which is something you already have a law that recognizes.

The fundamental argument about how pornography is sex discrimination is that it is central in maintaining sex as a basis for discrimination. What that means, concretely, is that pornography in, by, through, because of, and in an entire cycle of abuse . . . defines [and treats] women as sexually subordinate beings. It defines our subordination as our sexuality and equates that with our gender. This is something that, as a life status, no woman completely escapes, although many women are victimized much more specifically and intensely by it. It is also sex discrimination because all of its victims, including men, are singled out for the ways they are victimized on the basis of their gender. In other words, the way men are harmed by pornography is always done to them, through their gender. It's not the same as women, but it is sex-specific . . . The abuse is always a gender abuse. This law is sex-specific in the way it addresses how women are specifically harmed by pornography, and gender-neutral in its design, which allows men to sue for injuries as well.

[Discussion of specific amendments offered to the ordinance.]

I'll now say a couple of words about existing law and why [this ordinance] is consistent with the way the First Amendment has been interpreted. Many people believe that the First Amendment is absolute. This is an advocacy position taken by people who wish it was. At this point, it isn't. There are many harms, in fact, that have been found to outweigh what is otherwise, and should be, a highly stringent guarantee of freedom of speech.

---

1. Pittsburgh Press Co. v. Pittsburgh Comm'n on Human Relations 413 U.S. 376 (1973).

Contrasting this ordinance with existing exceptions to First Amendment law, one finds that our definitions are a good deal more concrete and closed-ended than numbers of definitions that have been found not vague under the First Amendment—for example, the word indecent. In many cases, existing sanctions are more severe than the ones we provide. That is, they are criminal, they provide for incarceration. This does not. Almost no existing First Amendment exception has the quantity or quality of demonstration of concrete harm that this one does. Obscenity law, for example, virtually assumes the harm in the face of the finding that obscenity does not cause harm. We have here studies that show pornography by this definition, which is not an obscenity definition, causes concrete harms. There's an entire array of evidence that is more substantial than virtually any demonstration that the Supreme Court has ever had. And actually, no existing First Amendment exception recognizes a harm of this scope, that is to say, the status of 53 percent of the population. Or the magnitude, . . . the rape, battery, sexual harassment, forced prostitution and sexual abuse of children which can be documented to flow from and be part of and be required in and by the pornography. And none of it shows an industry of the size of existing adult traffic in women, eight billion dollars, a figure that I think is both low and old, and none of it shows anything of such wide-spread legitimacy.

You may be thinking that because pornography is so legitimate, that's a reason why the Supreme Court won't see it as an exception to the First Amendment. If you instead see that . . . because it is so accepted, we are treated and seen in these ways, its legitimacy becomes a demonstration of harm, not a reason why there is no harm. . . .

[Account of data and Minneapolis testimony.]

A likely legal standard for measuring . . . the trafficking provision may not be whether it is scientifically valid, although, in fact, it is. But . . . whether a group like you could conclude that there is a relationship between the evidence of all kinds and the harms that you are trying to prevent, by allowing people to move civilly against the people who do this. The trafficking provision, if you compare it, for instance, with the *Miller* test of obscenity, what harm did they find there? They found a danger of offending the sensibilities of unwilling recipients or exposure to juveniles. What we have here is not just a danger. We have here an actuality. And we have not just sensibilities being offended, but physical bodies being systematically violated. We have not just a danger of exposure to juveniles, we have the use of adult pornography to coerce young people into performing both for pornography and prostitution. Anyone who is serious about doing anything about either child pornography or the sexual abuse of children will find that you cannot do it without also addressing adult pornography, because women are infantilized in pornography and adult pornography is used on children. It is not a separable abuse.

There are also other legal areas which provide partial support. They include the provisions for that speech, as they said, which by its very utterance inflicts injury. That's called the so-called "fighting words." Unfortunately, to date, women have not fought for the most part, so the things that pornography calls us have not literally been "fighting words." . . . But words which, by their very utterance inflict injury have been seen to be regulable. The group libel area provides some support, and I have mentioned where the Supreme Court balanced a discrimination interest against commercial speech, as precedent.

The Supreme Court has recognized that, in some cases, a regulation of expression furthers the purposes of the First Amendment. That may seem paradoxical unless you consider the ways that women have been systematically deprived of credibility, of the ability to speak, the way we have been silenced by pornography. Justice Stewart, in one case, said, "when expression occurs in a setting where the capacity to make a choice is absent, government regulation of that expression may co-exist with, and even implement, First Amendment guarantees."[2] What we are showing is a pattern of abuse where women have no choice but to live in a world in which pornography is systematically forced on us. Even Justice Douglas, who is an architect of the absolutist position on the First Amendment, has stated a test which I think we have met here. He said, "freedom of expression can be suppressed if, and to the extent that, it is so closely brigaded with illegal action as to be an inseparable part of it."[3]

What we are showing here, and what is documented even more concretely in the [Minneapolis] hearings, . . . is a way in which pornography, as we have defined it only, is central in a cycle of abuse from which it is inseparable. Those abuses are all actions, about which we have not been able to do anything effective. We have not been able to guarantee equality of the sexes. . . . We have not been able to do anything about rape, very little actually about sexual harassment. What we have is women seen [and treated] as sexually inferior beings. And the question, I think

2. Ginsberg v. State of New York, 390 U.S. 629, 649 (1968) (Stewart, J., concurring).
3. Roth v. U.S., 354 U.S. 476, 514 (1957) (Douglas, J., dissenting).

for the First Amendment, is going to be whether the fact that it is words and pictures that are at the center of this cycle of abuse, is going to mean that the pornographers' speech is going to be more important than women's lives. Have I taken all my time?

CHAIRWOMAN: Perhaps if you could wrap it up we could go forward and then I'll give you a chance at the end to summarize on the ordinance.

MacKINNON: Okay. You will hear people talking about this [ordinance] and one of the things that they will do is attempt to apply this to a million examples that are not sexually explicit. If the sex is not explicit, we are not talking about this law. Very few grand masters, old classics, all the things that everyone's going to try to tell you are so legitimate yet would be covered by this law—on the whole, they are not sexually explicit. What this is an attempt to do, is to make sure that the pornography appears to you indistinguishable from everything else. Obscenity is very difficult to distinguish from everything else. Pornography, as defined here, is concrete and is defined in such a way that it is not hard to distinguish from other things. So that's an objection from obscenity law.

People will also seek to evade what pornography does by saying it doesn't do everything. Well, I haven't said it does everything. People will say, "there was rape before the printing press." Well, what I am saying to you is that pornography is documented to cause the harm that it causes. It causes a major part of these harms. I want those people to say why we shouldn't do this, which is something we *can* do about rape, in addition to everything else we can do about rape, rather than telling us it doesn't do everything. I think they should respond to what it *does* do.

You will also hear people say, "this happens just the same to other groups. What are you making a special case about women and sex discrimination for?" I've never understood whether they mean you shouldn't do the right thing now because you might have to do the right thing later, or you shouldn't do the right thing now because you might have to do the wrong thing later. Well, courts are rather good at not doing the wrong thing later. And in fact we're finding, with this, that it's rather hard to do the right thing later, since there are in fact group libel laws in some places and other laws where harms—for instance, in the child pornography case—are seen to justify doing something about what are otherwise people's First Amendment rights. . . .

Pornography does to women, because it is sexual, something that is unlike what other literatures do to other groups of people. But . . . there are other practices that are central to the abuse of other groups of people.

For instance, in this country segregation is central to what defines people of color as different therefore subordinate in a way that makes it impossible to see that it's there, unless you see it and you understand about racism. What I think pornography does is occupies a similarly central place in the subordination of women. It defines our status as different therefore inferior in a way that makes our subordination just seen as our sex characteristics, just our differences. And that is the way I think that should be analyzed.

You will also hear people saying, conceding the harm, "we understand this causes harm. That's why speech is so important. It makes people do things." But essentially the speech is more important. . . . They are willing to have women pay the cost for the pornographers and their consumers' so-called freedom—which is to say, their freedom to enjoy and profit from sexual bigotry. The fact that it can be called speech has obscured the fact that it is not our speech. It is not women's speech. It is the silence of women. So I'll end there.[4]

CHAIRWOMAN: Thank you, Ms. MacKinnon. We'll hear from you a bit later. I would like to call to the podium a person who I will call Mary to keep anonymity for her. She's a victim of incest and pornography and she's giving voluntary testimony on the issue. She's a client and resource person of a noted behavioral scientist and I would like her to come forward at this time. I think you should hold the microphone, it's a little easier to hear.

MARY: My name is Mary and I came here today because I was a victim of child pornography at the age, that I can remember, from three years old to fourteen. But I know I was as a baby, because I caught my father with my two younger brothers and two younger sisters from their first day of birth. He had two suitcases full of pornography. One of them was like a large trunk size suitcase full, and the other was, there was like a set of luggage with three suitcases. He used the biggest one and when he would go to close the suitcase, it was like he, he had to close them just like you would an over-stuffed suitcase, the pictures stuffed inside so he would close it without them falling out.

I come from three generations of incest. My mother was a victim of it also. There were four boys and three girls in her family. She was raised Catholic. My father's father was a Seven[th]-Day Adventist minister. My father also went on to sexually molest, in the same way he did my sisters

---

4. Andrea Dworkin's brief *amicus curiae* in the subsequent litigation over this ordinance provides a fuller articulation of the argument for its constitutionality. See Appendix B, pp. 310–320.

and brothers and myself, seven out of eleven of his own grandchildren. My two, I wouldn't let him around them with a ten-foot pole, the other two was born after he died.

There was sodomy, there was bondage. Everything that Ms. MacKinnon has said is true. I won't have to go into all this to save time, but I am going to go into some very graphic details . . .

To start off with, I'll be 48 years old in July. My father had tied my, I've had my feet tied, at the age of three years old, I've hung upside down on an old coat hook, at the same time, my father has inserted foreign objects, heated and non-heated, in me and at the same time forced me to have oral sex with him. These people are professionals. [It] was not heated to the extent to where it left any scars on the outside, but the mental scars are with me the rest of my life. I have been, at three years old, I've had anal intercourse, vaginal intercourse with my father. I have been given complete ejaculations in my mouth, all of my body, with his ejaculation into the bowels. I've had my hands and feet tied, depending on which position my father wanted me in. I have had my mouth taped to teach me that big girls don't cry because everybody isn't as fortunate to have a father that will teach them the facts of life. My father also, at the age of four years old, shared his pornography with my babysitter across the street, and allowed me to be used in her and her boyfriend's orgies.

At ten years old, we lived across the street from a family that had a boy and a girl. The girl and I became friends and my father was out of town at the time. When my father was home, you're a very isolated family, and I don't mean that you live out on the farm. You live in the city and that, and you have houses on both sides of you. But you're a lot more isolated than if you are living out in the country. But at the time, I went over there and I only stayed a couple of nights. I couldn't stay anymore because that was also an incestuous situation. There were the father and the mother, there was pornographic magazines all over all of the house, the girl was about my age, the boy was about a year or two younger. And he had the same aggressive actions that his father did towards his sister, that his father did toward his mother, and that his father also had toward his sister and him. . . . I couldn't tell nobody, because he had tried with me, and things like this. But there was nobody to tell because you're programmed, you're programmed very well, to know that if you say anything, or if anybody finds out, everybody's going to know that it was your fault, that you were the enticer.

Now, logically, at 47 years old, I know a three-year-old child could not be responsible. But in dealing with, in living with this, logic has nothing to do with the therapy, with the overcoming, the mental anguish, the mental everything that you have to live with. I have to this day, I have video flashbacks of things that have happened to me. I can just be doing normal everyday things. I don't even think about it, my father or anything, they just come. You can't go to a phone because they don't come at eight o'clock, twelve o'clock, and the same time every day or they don't do this. When you have these nightmares at night and you wake yourself up just catching yourself in time for your scream—I woke my family up, my husband up about three times since we've been married, screaming, because I didn't wake up in time before I did. There is no way that society in general could excuse this.

My main deal right now is that I have not been victimized as an adult, not physically, but it's been an on-going thing mentally. It's a life-long, traumatizing thing that never goes away. I don't [have] my childhood, I don't [have] different stages of growing up, I couldn't tell you the first thing about what it's like to grow up. Adulthood, it makes it very hard for me because, I'm very blunt, I will tell you, that it's been over five years since I have been able to have any sexual things with my husband. I can't handle it. There never has been that much contact. My sisters and brothers have all been, they've been prostitutes, drug addicts, alcoholics, my nieces and nephews, they're messed up. I've never been able to turn to drugs or alcohol or prostitution or anything. I don't know why. It don't make me any better, any stronger, or anything. I just never could.

But this last four years I've been [fortunate] coming into contact with a Dr. Frank O'Sanka—he's a behavioral consultant of Napierville, Illinois—and fortunate to be a very small part of what he does in traveling around and doing seminars and things like this. And it backfired, because I thought I would be able to give more than I receive. Well, it backfired, because this has been the only good therapy I've ever had in my life. And I tend to receive more than I give.

Now even though any one of you out here have never been direct victims, don't mean you aren't victims. All of you in society are indirect victims. . . .

CHAIRWOMAN: Thank you, Mary, I think we'll have to go forward now because we have to get done within some kind of time limit. Thank you very much.

MARY: But I want to thank you all for coming and I hope you get out there and do something and stop the pornography because otherwise—I want to say one thing. They keep saying that you can't legislate morality. Well, I don't know why not, because they have been legislating immorality for years and look where it's got us. Thank you all very much.

CHAIRWOMAN: I would like to call a lady called Judy, who's the mother of a twelve-year-old girl who was repeatedly victimized over a four year period by a man who was using pornography extensively.

JUDY: I don't how much weight I can add to this for you other than the fact that I would like to let you know that I am a concerned parent. Our daughter was a victim of sexual assault for a period of four-and-a-half years. And when this man was arrested in our home, found in his car, in the trunk of his car, was a considerable amount of pornographic material. Our child is not in our home. This was so traumatic for her that she had to be hospitalized and probably will not be in our home for another year, which means that, as a victim, she was removed from our home for a period of over two years. The perpetrator—we did press charges—he spent one year in jail, and is now out, while our child is still not at home. I am a concerned parent and I would like you to look at this real closely.

CHAIRWOMAN: Thank you very much. I would next like to call to testify Detective Terry Hall, an IPD detective with sex offenses unit.

TERRY HALL: Good evening, my name is Detective Terry Hall with the Indianapolis Police Department. I was asked to come here today to give you a little bit of insight into my investigations as a sex crimes investigator. . . . I'll try my best to give you some examples [of] how pornography has come under my investigations. Quite a few rape investigations that I have conducted, especially where there was violence, upon arresting the suspect, I find that there were hard-core pornography in the suspect's house or in the suspect's car. I've had several rape victims, especially, it seems, to always be the more violent rapes, where the rape victim was made to look at pornography while the rape was occurring. I think I'm not qualified to say whether this started the rape or whether the rape would have been done without the pornography. I'm just telling you that when I make my investigation, especially on the more brutal ones, usually there's pornography, hard-core pornography, there showing something like sado-masochist or bestiality. . . . I've had a large amount of pornography used by adults to school young girls in the sexual acts. I have recently investigated a case where a ten-year-old boy was being sexually abused by seventeen-year-old boys who used pornography and expecting certain sexual acts that they wanted him to do. I've also had a family, complete family, that used pornography and I started working on a molestation that was with a father and went all the way down through the children where extensive pornography was used, even over into uncles and cousins.

The lady that was just up here previously is one of the most devastating cases to my estimation that I have ever had to investigate. It took a personal toll on my life as fourteen years as a police officer. I would like to expand on that case a little bit. The person that did this molestation was not a crumb bum, which most people think people who deal in pornography are low-stature-type people. This man was a prominent Indianapolis attorney who used the pornography to school and indoctrinate this child into thinking that everything she done was okay. And when I got to the child, she did think everything she done was okay, because, as she stated, that it was in the books, and children are taught to read and taught to pay attention to books from a very early age. Because this man was a very educated man, he was an attorney, it was very easy for him, with the help of visual aids—and we all know that lecture is probably the worst way to convey any type of educational material and that visual aids is one of the best—this visual aid that was used was pornography. I'm not talking about just a little bit of pornography, meaning hard-core magazines. Films were used, the child was made to have a type of sex with an animal, and a lot of other things that I'm sure that I don't need to go into here. All of it was copied from or directly out of a book, just like they was depicted in the book. It wasn't anything innovative or anything he made up. It was directly by the book. When I arrested the man, in the people's home, he had cameras and instamatic pictures of the girl committing sex acts on him. This girl was eight years old when this started and when I opened the trunk of his car, he had around three hundred hard-core magazines with pornographic pictures in them.

I just would like to think that this probably wouldn't have happened with this or maybe the girl would've caught on if he couldn't point out that everyone was doing this and this was a natural thing to do. I guess I'm not qualified to say that. However, it makes one think, especially when I keep running into these cases where I arrest the suspect and I find so much pornography, hard-core pornography, around, especially showing abuse and pain to the victim of the sexual attack. That's about all I had to say unless there's any questions.

CHAIRWOMAN: Are there any questions of the Committee? Thank you very much. As a final witness for this or to testify for the ordinance, Deborah Daniels from the Prosecutors' Office.

DEBORAH DANIELS: Thank you, Madam Chairman, Members of the Committee. I appreciate the opportunity to talk to you. My testimony is really two-fold. I'll begin by presenting the testimony of T. V., who is a local counselor to persons in the community. She had to be out of town and could not be present. . . . She titles it "Women in Pornography."

In ten years of counseling with men and women, I have had several incidents with clients where pornography played a great part in the violence that ensued in their lives. It would seem that the need to be violent, to get retribution for whatever pain and anguish is going on in these men's lives, is often enhanced by pornographic literature. I am reminded of a case in particular in which a woman had been married for fourteen years, during the last ten years of which, pornographic literature had been a large part of her husband's sexual arousement. He would look at the pornographic literature, then come to her, wake her up, beat her, then demand she perform acts depicted in the literature. There were times when this behavior was as violent as cutting her with a razor, slapping, hitting and kicking her, tying her to the end of the bed and requiring her to do demeaning sexual acts involving other people, as well as her mate. It may seem unusual that this woman stayed with this man, but those of us who have worked with women who have been involved [in] violent sexual encounters understand that fear becomes the main element in such a woman's life that demeaning responses that she has had to give make her very fear filled and very much afraid to leave a relationship. There are always threats along with this, such as the "if you don't do this, I will . . ." kind of thing. As a result, she becomes the typical battered woman, only more so. Fear takes over as the primary element of her life, and she can't find a way to get loose from the relationship. Another incident that recently came to my attention was a woman who came to me because she was to marry a man who had been a Viet Nam war veteran. She was quite terrified because this man had performed violent acts of sex with her. He told her that the only [way] he could be sexually active with her was to read pornographic material and get his anger up again. When his anger was up, through violence and pornographic material (books and other written material, not movies), then he could perform. Otherwise, he couldn't. He would bring home pornographic literature, make her read it with him, then perform acts of violence.

She then mentions that the whole Vietnam issue needs to be looked at closely and that those men have had a terrible experience.

The third incident that recently happened was a woman who became a rape victim. Before the rapist involved himself, he put her through demeaning, sexual, violent actions, twisted her body in unbelievable shapes and tied her legs and hands together. He forced her to have sex with an animal. He marked X's on her back, shaved her, then showed her pictures from pornographic magazines, all the time performing sex acts upon himself, then raped her. He placed her in disfiguring positions, such that she found it impossible to free herself. He laughed a great deal and pointed to the pictures, say[ing], "this is how it ought to be with women." In another incident, a man said to me when I confronted him with his sexual behavior, that the only way to take care of a woman (which he learned through reading books in shopping centers and then throwing them away) is to beat her up one side and down the other, to make her get dressed up in black stockings and high heels, to make her wear men's clothing, all kinds of deviant behavior. "I read these magazines, then throw them in the trash in shopping centers." As I said before, the effect of this kind of behavior on women is pathetic in that it begins the strong, battered woman complex, and she finds it virtually impossible to break herself from the relationship. I have worked with three women coerced into prostitution at a "respectable" level. By that I mean prostitution for private men's clubs. In each of these three cases, the woman entered a relationship with a man, believing that it was a stable relationship, only to find after a month or two that the man engaged in unacceptable sexual behavior. Each of the three women was demeaned by this behavior to the extent that she was unable to free herself. The man in each case acted as a pimp. He took the woman to men's clubs, provided pornographic literature, then required the woman to dance and perform acts to satisfy the desires of other men. Each of the women was made to do the kinds of things described in pornographic magazines. Each of these women is now free of these relationships and prostitution. It is erroneous to think that pornographic literature is simply erotic. More than the sexual act, it raises the level of violence in an individual.

The remainder of my testimony will deal with basically the harm issue. A lot of people are asking why the Marion County Prosecutor's Office is involved in furthering this amendment at all. It is not, as Professor MacKinnon indicated, a law enforcement tool. It is not something in which the Prosecutor's Office will be involved directly at all. It provides for a civil action in which people can go to court. . . . The reason that we are very interested in the dialogue on this issue is that there's been a lot of talk for a long time about the general issues involving pornography or obscenity, and the idea that what people interested in limiting this material are doing is trying to force their morality onto other people. What we are very interested in, with this approach, is that it focuses the discussion on the real harm that results to women from this kind of material. . . . [discussion of empirical effects of pornography] I would say that Dr. Donnerstein, to whom I keep referring, who is a Ph.D. in Psychology with the University of Wisconsin, is a leading authority in the area. He unfortunately could not be with us today. He is at this time planning on being available next Monday to answer any questions if in fact this proceeds out of committee today and goes to the Council. He will be present at the meeting in case anyone has any questions and he will be available that day to answer any questions. . . .[5]

To bring this a little closer to home, there was a recent case in which Deborah Weaver returned home to find a burglar in her house. I'm sure you all read about this in the papers. It was only last week. The fellow who was arrested as her alleged killer gave a confession to the police in which he stated that on the day of the killing, he visited several adult bookstores. Now . . . [I can't say that] [break in soundtrack] what he carried over with him into the house directly caused this act. I will say that he went into the house, unscrewed, according to his statement to the police, unscrewed the light bulbs in the house so that it would be totally dark, and waited for the victim to return home. When she did, he sexually assaulted her, tortured her, according to his statement, and brutally murdered her. I make reference to this simply to give you an idea, I can't say for sure what the correlation is, but he, in his own statement, indicated that he had been reading pornographic material.

I would like to make reference to some of the material we're talking about. Frankly, I didn't know until fairly recently what we're talking about, because I'm not a consumer of pornography myself. I felt that it was necessary, in order to prepare my testimony, to look at some of the materials that had been purchased by the Indianapolis Police Department Vice Branch recently, this year, in Indianapolis. I'd like to read you

---

5. Dr. Donnerstein was present and answered questions from Council members on June 4, 1984. No transcript of this hearing is available. Professor MacKinnon was not present. At that time, lawyers for Indianapolis introduced into the Administrative Committee record a transcript of a telephone interview that Catharine MacKinnon had previously conducted with Dr. Donnerstein. It is reproduced in Appendix A.

some of the titles of the magazines and their stories. One magazine is called "Bound to Tease." I think that's self-explanatory. One is called "Bondage Fever," and two of the stories in it are called "Unwilling Submission" and "Raging Restraint." Another magazine is called "Tied Up Tarts," with a subtitle, "Girls Who Love to Submit." One of the story titles is "Alma's Secret Fantasy." Basically the story-line has to do with a woman who hated to "admit it" but she learned that she enjoyed bondage and discipline, as they call it. Another story in that particular magazine is called "Bound and Beautiful." Another magazine is called "Restraint."

The stories involve "Tanya Learns the Ropes," "Tanya's Initiation into the Exotic Joys of Bondage." I read this story, and those who say that we should perhaps limit the ordinance to visual depictions, perhaps I should address this story. This particular story, though most of the magazine had graphic pictures of women, nude women, tied up in obvious expressions of pain, now this particular story didn't have any pictures, but it was all about a woman who had described herself, supposedly, at the outset of the story as an avid women's-libber, and she said that she'd never had a good sexual relationship with anyone because she was accustomed to going out with what she called wimps who respected her. She went to apply for a job one day, this is billed as a true story, written in the first person, supposedly, by this woman. She went to apply for a job one day, and who should appear at the door but Dirk, who appeared to be an obvious large, hairy, masculine, ferocious-looking man. Basically, he took her into his study for the job interview, bound her up, though she screamed and was frightened to death, and began to torture her. The whole story line indicates that she told him she was scared, and she told him she didn't want to do any of this, and she told him it hurt, and she asked him and begged him to stop and yet, the storyline indicates that secretly she loved it. Secretly, she was aroused and it was the most wonderful experience of her life. This tends to be the story that is retold and retold in this literature. And at the end of the story, of course, she describes herself as the man's willing slave. All she wants is to do any humiliating tasks he assigns to her. She has learned her lesson.

Another story in the same magazine is called "The Rich Bitch," and it was about teaching a snobbish female who, this man had felt, put him down in the past, a lesson, by binding her to the wall with chains and inflicting physical pain upon her. The last sentence indicated that, rather than Sally is now going to go the Prosecutor's Office and file charges against Frank, it said, Sally, from now on, will treat Frank more special because he's taught her a lesson.

Finally, two more magazines. One is entitled "Tied Up." And there's a story in it called "Bound Bitch," and there's a lot of reference to bitches, tarts, whores, women who deserve this sort of treatment. Another is titled "Black Bondage." The two stories featured in the magazine, in this particular issue, were called "Black Bitches: Bound, Gagged, and Loving It." And the second was "Roped and Raped." . . .

Some . . . suggest that perhaps education, public education, may be the cure. Many other civil libertarians also suggest that [what will cure] the problem is "more speech,"—you know, you can solve this problem by talking to it. We would suggest that there is no effective way—unlike in a laboratory situation where you can debrief your subjects—to reach all those persons who are exposed to pornography and convince them that the justification for the violence presented in those films, magazines, and other materials, is not real or valid. And that is why we support the ordinance as an innovative way to approach a real problem. Thank you for your attention.

CHAIRWOMAN: Thank you, Miss Daniels. And now we have those who would like to testify against the proposed amendment. Representing the ACLU, Mr. Bill Marsh.

BILL MARSH: Thank you, Madam Chairman. . . . The Indiana Civil Liberties Union emphatically endorses the policy declaration of this proposal which states that discrimination on the basis of sex is contrary to the principles of freedom and equality of opportunity. For many, many years, the Indiana Civil Liberties Union has been a vocal advocate of freedom and equal opportunity for women. In a recent article in the September 1983 issue of *Judicature* magazine, two Emory University professors presented a study which concluded that the American Civil Liberties Union, our national organization, emerged as the representative of women before the United States Supreme Court. The efforts of the ACLU have been successful on behalf of women. This study also found that the ACLU's presence in a case increased the chances of success for a gender-based claim by sixteen percent.

However, despite our continued strong support of new initiatives to bring real equality to women, the Indiana Civil Liberties Union urges you to reject Proposal 228 because the Proposal presents too great a danger to the free expression of ideas. The ICLU does not support pornography, and I personally loathe pornography, but we must be ever-vigilant to the protection of ideas, not only those ideas we support, but those that we loathe as well.

This proposal would result in the suppression of ideas, not just pornography, but constitutionally protected ideas, in several ways. Several aspects of this proposal would lend to significant self-censorship by bookstore operators, not only adult bookstores, but all bookstores in Marion County. Those provisions in the ordinance which would have that effect are as follows.

One, the definition of pornography is so vague that the individual bookstore operators will not be able to make an accurate assessment of whether a particular item is pornographic or not. And Ms. MacKinnon made strong reference to the point that there are specifics in the definition of pornography, but I would point out to you that I am referring to the portion of the definition which describes pornography as the sexually explicit subordination of women. A bookstore operator who's deciding what to sell and what not to sell will have to decide what that means, and I suggest to you that it's going to be extremely difficult for them to do that and they will opt in favor of self-censorship rather than run the risks of this ordinance.

Number two, the ordinance specifically provides that the bookseller is strictly liable for the contents of everything she sells. The prudent bookstore owner will only sell those items about which she has personal knowledge.

Number three, the definition of pornography can be applied to isolated passages in written material, whether pictures or words. This means that the bookstore operator will not be secure simply knowing the general theme or general tenor of a piece. She will be at peril anytime she sells an item which she has not read thoroughly.

Number four, any person believing that any isolated passage found in a publication in a bookstore in Marion County can first file a complaint with the Office of Equal Opportunity of the Indianapolis Corporation Council and number two, file a cause of action for damages in a court in Marion County. And I would add to emphasize the point, members of the Committee, that we are not concerned about the kind of material which Ms. Daniels just graphically described to you.

We are concerned about the impact which this ordinance would have on legitimate constitutionally-protected material in legitimate bookstores in Marion County. The manager of the bookstore at the university where I teach told me that there are several titles in his bookstore which he would remove if this ordinance was passed, not because he knows that they're illegal under this ordinance but because he doesn't know and he's not willing to run the risk. And those were textbooks which are used in university courses. George Orwell would likely perceive, if this ordinance is passed, swarms of Marion County residents, motivated by money or morality, descending upon the bookstores of Marion County in search of pornography. Every time this search proves successful to the satisfaction of the individual citizen, the bookstore owner, manager and cash register clerk will be called into court and/or called before the Indianapolis Corporation Council to defend the material. The outcome of the litigation, I suggest to you, will be largely irrelevant, because the time and expense involved in defending such a charge will consume any profit which the bookstore operator might realize. The cautious bookstore operator, in a traditional establishment bookstore, will likely opt to significantly restrict her inventory to decrease the risk of liability. Her action will also severely restrict free expression of ideas in this county.

Now the cover page of your proposal indicates that your attorney has not yet rendered an opinion as to the constitutionality of this proposal. Since you have each taken an oath to support and defend the Constitution, you should ask your attorney for an opinion of the constitutionality, because this ordinance is, without question, unconstitutional. When you request this opinion, specifically ask your attorney these questions. First, isn't this proposal contrary to the teachings of Marbury against Madison? *Marbury* has been an integral part of our system of government since 1803 and has been reaffirmed by the current United States Supreme Court in Nixon against the United States in 1974. *Marbury* provides that the Supreme Court of the United States is the ultimate interpreter of the Constitution and government at all levels is bound by that interpretation. The Supreme Court has drawn a line between constitutionally protected sexually explicit material and material which is not protected. The definition of pornography in the proposal is much different and is more restrictive than that provided by the Supreme Court.

Secondly, ask your attorney, doesn't this proposal violate Smith against California? In this case, the United States Supreme Court held that strict liability or eliminating the knowledge element violates the First Amendment because, and I quote, "[it] tends to impose a severe limitation on the public's access to constitutionally protected matter." Not pornography, it tends to restrict access to constitutionally protected matter.

Thirdly, ask your attorney this question: isn't this proposal contrary to Chief Justice Burger's admonition that the material must be taken as a whole and that it can be censored only if it does not have serious literary, artistic, political or scientific value? Next, ask your attorney this: doesn't the empowering of a censorship board, which is now known as the Office of Equal Opportunity, doesn't the empowering of this board to issue cease and desist orders and show cause orders violate the constitutional procedural requirements established by Friedman against Maryland?

And fifth, please ask your attorney this: isn't it true that the United States Supreme Court has held that civil remedies, which this proposal contains, as well as criminal sanctions are subject to the limitations of the First Amendment? And my written statement cites three cases in which the Supreme Court has done exactly that. After months of study, the Minneapolis City Attorney concluded that the ordinance proposed there, which is basically the same ordinance you're considering, is unconstitutional, and I am confident that your attorney will reach the same conclusion.

In closing, let me say this, and emphasize this point. Regardless of the fate of this proposal, the Indiana Civil Liberties Union will continue to be in the forefront of the crusade for the eradication of sex discrimination from our society. In our zeal to achieve this essential goal, however, we must, and we will, maintain our commitment to the free expression of ideas which is the cornerstone of our democracy. All of our liberties, I respectfully submit to you, are dependent on the diligent protection of free expression. Thank you.

CHAIRWOMAN: I would now like to call John Wood, an attorney with the firm of Bamburger and Fibelman.

JOHN WOOD: Members of the Committee and Council, my name is John Wood and I am an attorney in private practice. . . . My interest in this, primarily I'm appearing in a capacity as a former chairman and member of the Human Rights Commission. I was involved in the drafting of the First UNIGOV Ordinance which created the Commission in 1970. I worked with Harriet Kahn at that time, the late Harriet Kahn, who was a member of the city legal staff. And that was the first ordinance which actually created the Commission which had some enforcement powers to deal with the whole range of discriminatory practices which were covered under the Indiana Civil Rights Act. And Mayor Luger then appointed me as the first chairman of that Commission. It consisted of twenty-five members, appointed by both the Mayor and the City Council, and I served as a member of the Commission for . . . [break in soundtrack during which John Wood continued and Sheila Seuss Kennedy spoke].

[Discussion among Councilmembers of amendments and procedural matters.]

McGRATH: I move we continue studying this proposal and would move to table this for further study.

CHAIRWOMAN: Does that, do you mean, are you sending this back to Committee, is that what you're saying?

McGRATH: Well, I believe it is still in Committee, so my motion would be to continue to study in Committee.

CHAIRWOMAN: All right, and did you second that, Mr. Hawkins? It's been moved and seconded. Any discussion? All in favor say aye.

STRAITER: Miss Chairman, I really need to ask the counselor an opinion. I think that this needs to go before the full Council and I would be the last to want to be destroyed by the news media in terms of being wishy-washy or what have you, so I would hate to ask that it go to—and the only way that I know of to get it to the full Council is to recommend it to the full Council with a "do pass." And I'm not ready at this point to vote yes. But I am ready for it to get, you know, we've been talking about juries and I think it needs its day in court, and in order for it to have its day in court, it's got to go before our entire body. Now what other way do we have, or do I just have to sit up and say, sitting with a "do pass," when Monday I might not want to vote for it and then everybody say, well why did you send it out with a "do pass"?

McGRATH: I suppose one answer to that question is, this Committee is scheduled to meet again on Thursday. If Mr. McGrath's motion carries, it could be taken off the table at that Committee.

CHAIRWOMAN: It's possible. There is other business that we had hopefully scheduled that day. However, I understand how Mr. Straiter feels. I think I've heard a lot of people, maybe not too often, but many times, after more discussion and more evidence is presented, people have voted differently in the full Council than they have in Committee. I don't think our Committee votes are binding. I understand your intent and I certainly would understand where you were coming from. I feel that it deserves its day in court and I think that we probably, as a Committee, are not going to hear that much more different testimony. And perhaps the whole Council does deserve the right to give it their support or dis-support. . . .

[further discussion among Councilmembers with no result recorded on tape] . . .

Indianapolis: Appendices

Appendix A [Exhibit P]: Interview of Dr. Edward Donnerstein (by phone) by Catharine A. MacKinnon, January 10, 1984

MacKINNON: Dr. Donnerstein, this is Catharine MacKinnon. If you are there could you speak up.

DONNERSTEIN: Hello.

MacKINNON: Hi, this is Kitty MacKinnon.

DONNERSTEIN: Yes.

MacKINNON: I'm calling you about some materials that have surfaced in the debate surrounding the pornography ordinance since you were here.[1]

DONNERSTEIN: Okay.

MacKINNON: What I would like to do, if it's all right with you, is ask you a few questions about some of the specifics of them, particularly as they bear on your research, including not only the research you presented while you were here, but some of the other things that people have raised since you were here.

DONNERSTEIN: Okay, no problem at all. I would be happy to.

MacKINNON: Okay. One document that was a letter that was used by the Mayor—he referred to it as a partial basis for his veto of the ordinance—is a letter from an Ira L. Reiss, Professor of Sociology here at the University of Minnesota. Do you know Mr. Reiss? Are you familiar with his work?

DONNERSTEIN: Not familiar with his work. He has corresponded with me over the years, basically in terms of asking for reprints of certain articles which we have done, which I obviously have sent him like we send everybody else. And I also met him at the testimony there, the day I testified and spoke to him briefly afterwards about some of our newer research which he did not have a copy of at that point.

MacKINNON: So, he—your impression is that he was at the hearing such that he heard you testify?

1. Dr. Donnerstein's testimony in Minneapolis is on pp. 44–60.

DONNERSTEIN: Oh, I'm pretty sure, yes.

MacKINNON: Because after you spoke, he asked you—

DONNERSTEIN: Yes, he had come up and introduced himself and then of course the name rang a bell because he had communicated with me, you know, really over the years asking for reprints and other types of things.

MacKINNON: Well, one of the things he says in this letter is that he is familiar with the research by you, Malamuth, and others in the area of pornography and says "I feel that it was not clearly presented at the hearing. The key point that was omitted from the hearing was the basic support the current research gives to the findings of the President's Commission on Obscenity and Pornography presented in 1970. That Commission reported that pornography was not shown in the various research they had reviewed to lead to criminal sexual conduct. Donnerstein also basically agrees with that finding." And then he quotes from you. He says, "The quote from Donnerstein in his 1983 chapter 'Erotica and Human Aggression' from R. Dean and E. Donnerstein, editors, *Aggression: Theoretical and Empirical Reviews* [Academic Press, 1983], p. 138," and then he quotes from you, "Once again then, there is no evidence that exposure to nonviolent erotica will increase aggression against women." Could you comment on that characterization of your work in general?

DONNERSTEIN: Well, there's a couple things. One, even though it's a 1983 chapter, which might sound like yesterday, I think one has to realize that in the academic community most things are written four or five years before. So in terms of that particular quote, a couple of things: (1) we did say that exposure to nonviolent erotica will not increase aggression against women. I think there is two things important to bring out. One, what we mean by nonviolent erotica. I mean, there has been a lot of misunderstanding of what we're doing. We specifically create films which are sexually explicit but do not contain coercion, differential power, subordination, degradation—anything of that nature against women. They are sexually explicit. We do that to bring out the point that at least in the research that we were doing with short-term exposure, it is the violent element which leads to the effects in the short-term. Now, there are a number of important things here. One if we talk about nonviolent erotica in terms of the types of material we used—it is an artificial material. It is specifically created for experimental purposes. It is not the type of material which one would, let's say, normally find in an adult bookstore. It might be the type of material which perhaps [one] would use as a sex therapist, or in a sex education class, perhaps.

MacKINNON: So might that be more likely to be the materials which he as a sexologist would be familiar with?

DONNERSTEIN: Oh, of course, yes. And it is material which we pretty much created for experimental purposes. Now if one begins, however, in that particular chapter we mention that what needs to be looked at is of course long-term exposure to material which is not explicitly violent, in other words no graphic physical violence against women but which begins to deal with the trivialization of women, the objectification of women. And of course since this chapter has appeared, or really since it was written, which was around 1980—and it takes two, three years for the publishers to publish them—there has obviously been a lot of other research done on long-term exposure to nonviolent material but material which basically places women in submissive roles, unequal power roles, basically which trivializes women and that's in some of our newer work and newer chapters, which by the way are already published, and also in some of the work by Dolf Zillmann. What that research shows—

MacKINNON: Isn't it also the case that that research is based on actual films rather than experimentally made films?

DONNERSTEIN: Oh, yeah. In fact,—

MacKINNON: Could you discuss the differences between films made with the express purpose of removing force and films that are actually available films now on the market?

DONNERSTEIN: In the research which we have been doing now, and the research which Zillmann has been doing, films are taken off the general market and used as they are. There is no editing. In the initial experimental research which Reiss refers to we took those same films but completely cut them apart and re-edited them with scenes which would only be sexually explicit without any of these dynamics in it involved. You can't, you can't find the films, okay, in the adult bookstore which meets the criteria of just simply sexually explicit without creating any changes in attitudes and so forth and so on—it's something we create. I think that must be clearly understood. But if you get to the commercially released material, even though it might not be explicitly violent, that is physical violence, what you find is that with long-term exposure, yes you don't get changes necessarily in aggressive behavior but what you get are changes in people's attitudes about women, the perception of rape, perceptions of violence in general. You get a trivialization of women, you get a change toward an increase in callous attitudes towards women. And I think it's important to mention the Pornography Commission which I think you mentioned he referred to, did a study in which subjects were exposed to this type of material—I think ten minutes worth—and then their attitudes towards women were tested on a scale called the Sex-Callousness Scale, which is some fairly degrading statements regarding women, and they found no effect. However, in recent research by Zillmann in Indiana which is now out and is fairly well-known—even though it came out a year ago in the scientific journals—shows that with six weeks of exposure to this material, with really only a couple of hours a week which really isn't that much, by the way, you do find an increase in the Sex-Callousness Scale attitudes. In the research that we have been doing now for the National Science Foundation, which was just released, a preliminary report in the January issue of Psychology Today and which is now being written up for scientific journals, we also find with long-term exposure, changes of attitudes towards women, a trivialization of rape, seeing women as more worthless if they've been the victim of rape, so forth and so on. The issue here doesn't have to be an issue of does exposure to this material lead to aggressive behavior. The violent material leads to aggressive behavior. The nonviolent but commercially released type of material tends to affect people's attitudes about women, perceptions of women. Now whether or not that eventually spills over to aggressive behavior, one will have to determine from additional research. But, I think it's wrong to say that what we have said is that material which is not violent, physically violent, has no effect. That isn't the case at all. We have created, again, a very specific type of material to demonstrate to the scientific community that it is not the sexual explicitness in aggressive pornography which is the issue. It is one, in our early research, the aggressiveness against women, and now in our newer research and that by Dolf Zillmann, the role of women in the particular films. I think everybody has tried to point out sexual explicitness is not the issue. In that sense I agree with Reiss. It is not the issue.

MacKINNON: Right.

DONNERSTEIN: But, if I remember correctly—as I mentioned to you I had not read your bill beforehand, okay, because I try to stay out of the legal issues and try to stay neutral in this, but I did take a look at it afterwards and correct me if I'm wrong I don't think sexually explicitness was your issue either in any of this.

MacKINNON: No, [not by itself].

DONNERSTEIN: So, I think there is a little misunderstanding in what the research shows. Okay. And I think now it is quite obvious that the newer research demonstrates with even nonviolent material, but material which subordinates women or makes women submissive or strictly sexual objects, you do get changes in attitudes—attitudes which, by the way, the Pornography Commission looked for but did not find and the reason they didn't find it is that with that type of material, it is not going to happen overnight. I think it's ludicrous for us to think you change somebody after 18 years with ten minutes of exposure. It takes a little longer.

MacKINNON: In terms of the relationship between the attitude changes you have just been discussing and possible propensities for say rape—

DONNERSTEIN: Yes.

MacKINNON: Could you talk about the work of Neil Malamuth and the rape propensity predictions from the Rape Scale?

DONNERSTEIN: Yes. In fact, one thing one can do with known rapists, and again known rapists are a difficult population to deal with—I'm going to even criticize myself at this point, because I think in a sense it points to a lot of research that other people have brought up suggesting rapists have no exposure to the material, it doesn't have an effect. The problem is that they are a very unique population and a convicted rapist whom you have studied represents one out of every 500 rapes committed. So I think we have to keep that in mind. But even among those rapists, you can predict, for instance, recidivism based on their attitudes towards rape, and their sexual arousal to certain types of material. Now what Malamuth has shown is that in normal subjects, that is non-rapists as far as we know, if you know their attitudes towards rape, towards women, and their sexual arousal to certain types of pornography you can predict quite good statistically their aggressive behavior against women in laboratory type situations. So, if certain material, whether it is violent or nonviolent material increases or changes people's attitudes about women, about rape, then that can lead to aggressive behavior. What that suggests, I think very strongly, is that with the nonviolent material, the non-physically violent material, there are individual differences, meaning yes, it doesn't affect 100 percent of the people—Nobody has ever said that, okay?—but for instance we know, in the general male population, this is from the research of Malamuth and I think I discussed this at the hearing, that anywhere between 25 and 30 percent of normal males have the propensity to rape to begin with. That's a lot. That's an incredible amount, okay? Those people are very much affected by this type of material. And it tends to reinforce their attitudes and conceptions of women. The material doesn't have to be graphically violent, it can be material which plays into the common stereotypes we have about women.

MacKINNON: Which they perhaps may have already gotten from, is it fair to say, from exposure to previous pornography?

DONNERSTEIN: Exposure to previous pornography, I think exposure to the media in general. I think the problem of course is what the material is doing is definitely not catharting those attitudes away. Okay. If it is not causing and creating it, it is without question maintaining and reinforcing and for a certain percentage it might be that particular stimulus which activates violent behavior. I think we are always a bit—and I hate to use the word misguided—but in a sense we are by thinking unless [we have] hundreds and hundreds of thousands of people there is no problem. I think one has to think that if it is even one or two percent who are affected to commit violent crime and a certain material has a distribution of a couple of million, I don't think you have to be a statistician to figure out what's going on, not only to the victim, which in this case would be women primarily, but to the society in general. And we know there are certain people who are very much predisposed who the material drastically affects.

MacKINNON: Right. But it's also true, isn't it, that your recent experiments are principally on normals?

DONNERSTEIN: Oh, yes. And I think there again, a lot of this research is quite new and I wouldn't expect Professor Reiss and the others to be aware of it. It has just been published in a preliminary form, although the National Science Foundation has access to it because it is funded by them.

MacKINNON: But you did present it at the hearing.

DONNERSTEIN: We did present it at the hearing. That research of course shows that even with the most normal individuals who we could possibly find who are screened because they are classified as normal as possible, show changes in their perceptions of women, their perceptions of rape. That doesn't mean, again, that they are going to go out and commit a rape. Nobody can do that research. But it definitely shows their attitude about women, their attitudes about rape, are being changed.

MacKINNON: And that also included, if I recall correctly, that they were radically less likely to see as rape an account—[of a rape]?

DONNERSTEIN: Oh, yes, yes. And in fact they sit in the University of Wisconsin Law School courtroom in a jury box and watch a reenactment of an actual case and see less violence occurring to the woman, are less likely to convict, see the woman as more responsible for her rape, see her as more worthless, etc., etc.

MacKINNON: And that's with what you call X-only material?

DONNERSTEIN: X-only material, yes. And again the X-only material in this research that we are doing now is different from the "nonviolent erotica" we've used before. Unfortunately, we have used the same terms and that's a problem I think in the academic community in terms of how we operationalize things. But the material we use in the newer research is commercially released unedited material. We did not do anything with it.

MacKINNON: I would like to read you a sentence from Mr. Reiss' letter because I think what you just said, if you state it in terms of what he said, would clarify something.

DONNERSTEIN: Okay.

MacKINNON: He said, "Donnerstein uses films depicting rape in much of his experiments on violent pornography. In one of his most recent experiments, he used mostly college males and exposed some of them to non-violent erotica, some to violent erotica, some to a violent nonerotic film and some to a neutral film. Then he looked for differences in the willingness of each group of subjects to administer electric shocks to a woman confederate in the experiment who had previously deliberately angered the subjects. He found that the violent nonerotic film increases the willingness to administer shocks to a woman and that the nonviolent erotic film does not show such an increase. It is true that when you add the erotic and the violent in one film there is an even greater willingness to administer shock but it is clear to him that 'the more crucial factor' is the aggression shown in the film." And then he goes on to say, "The key findings here is that the nonviolent erotic films does not increase shocks and that only with the addition of violence is there any increase in shocks administered to females. Despite these findings, Donnerstein's testimony is used to promote the new pornography law which would put in jeopardy precisely those types of films he found not to increase aggression towards women."

DONNERSTEIN: Okay, a couple things. Again, one, we are researchers and theoreticians, the initial research we did was on what we labeled aggressive pornography, that is, films in which women are sexually assaulted which are not that uncommon, by the way. Okay. Now what we tried to do as I mentioned earlier was to demonstrate that it was not the sexual explicitness in that material, aggressive pornography, which leads to increases in aggression, it is the aggression or a combination. Consequently, as I mentioned earlier, we created films which were strictly sexually explicit, okay. Now in that sense I agree with Reiss. For aggressive pornography it is the aggression okay, not the sexual explicitness and the juxtaposition of the two is worse. But everybody would agree with that. Now what we've been doing as other researchers have been doing is say, now let's move away from the "aggressive pornography" into the more commercially released type of material which is sexually explicit but goes beyond that. It gets away from what would normally be defined as erotica and that is an equal relationship, no submissiveness, domination, degradation, etc., etc., okay, in the material, but is the common type of fare which is out there. And basically what you find there is what I mentioned before is changes in people's attitudes about women okay, with long-term exposure, that research, again, is new. And I should also mention by the way, that yes, we anger subjects but if one takes a good close look, by the way, also at that study in which he is talking about or that particular chapter, at least with the aggressive material, aggressive pornography, you don't have to anger subjects to get increases in aggressive behavior against them. And particularly now with our newer research, we have subjects again who are not only not angered, they are void clinically of any hostile feelings whatsoever, yet you find changes in their perceptions of violence, changes in their perceptions of women as a function of one, yes, aggressive pornography, two, R-rated sexually violent films, but also commercially released standard X-rated films. Those again are not films which we have called nonviolent erotica in this experimental research. And I think that that point really has to be emphasized.

MacKINNON: Right, there is another point made by Dr. Reiss, where he characterizes the relationship between the films that you used in your study and films that exist in the world. His phrasing on it is, "The new element that Donnerstein adds concerning whether one type of pornography, i.e., violent pornography, would produce increases in sexually aggressive behavior. The point that needs emphasis here at the outset is that this is but one type of pornography and the majority of pornographic films would not fit the label of violent pornography." Could you discuss that?

DONNERSTEIN: Well, okay. I assume he is going to define violent as sexual assault or rape. Let's talk about that first. In the more recent accounts you find probably on the covers of, there has been some studies by some Harvard physicians of the adult bookstore fare. And even without reading the material, or going into seeing what is in the material, just from covers alone around 30 percent of the material is graphically violent. Okay. Now of course we know that even some of the—inside the covers, there is some violent material. For instance, there is some recent research by Malamuth and Spinner, taking the more popular types of magazines like *Playboy* and *Penthouse* which on the cover obviously have nothing to do with violence yet, they have found that over the last six, seven years, there has been an increase in the amount of violent depictions in those magazines, with *Penthouse,* I think, accounting for about 15 percent of their pictorials, cartoons, and so forth and so on, have violent overtones. So it's hard here to deal with what is violent and what isn't. Also there is some recent research by Jim Check, up in Ontario, showing that of the commercially released, 25 percent of those which contain any sex scenes also contain scenes of violence, explicit violence. Now, if we are talking about what is 25–30 percent, that's a lot. That's commercially produced. In fact in our own research [when] we go looking for X-rated films we find pretty close, at least in the video cassette market, pretty close to 50 percent contain some scenes of violence in them. Okay.

MacKINNON: How did you select the X-rated films that you used?

DONNERSTEIN: In our own research?

MacKINNON: In your own research.

DONNERSTEIN: They are selected because they are, one, commercially available, very popular and have played in theaters, on campus and so on and are the commercially released variety and are well known, a lot of them as it turns out. The interesting thing about the X-rated commercially released market is how the violence is displayed, which I think is the most important thing. While maybe only 25 or 30 percent of them contain overt violence, I think we probably all find that 90–95 percent of the time when a woman is sexually assaulted or raped or aggressed against someway in these films, she is turned on and shows pleasure, enjoyment and so on and so on. And of course, I doubt if anyone would disagree in the academic community about what that does in terms of people's aggressive behavior and attitudes and so forth and so on because there is a little too much research on that. But I think when one talks about 25 percent or 30 percent we are talking about explicit, overt, physical violence. We are not talking about the types of material which Zillmann used, which is the other 70 percent. Which is the general commercial fare. Yes that might not lead directly, this other 70 percent, to immediate increases in aggressive behavior. But there's no question now from the newer research coming out that long-term exposure begins to change people's perception and attitudes about women and also about rape. Now what that eventually spills over into is hard to tell as you, I think, asked me before, can one predict aggressive behavior from attitudes? Yes, one can. So I think one can make some general speculation about what would be going on. Thirty percent is a lot, by the way. Particularly when you don't know you are going to be confronted with it. We, in our own research, have chosen films sometimes based upon titles and descriptions hoping they wouldn't contain overt physical aggression, okay, and lo and behold they do. So it's really hard to tell what the true percentages are.

MacKINNON: Right. There is an additional comment that bears on that in Mr. Reiss' letter. He says that one important question is whether the males—here he refers to the males in the experiment in which there was anger and then shocks were far more likely toward women—"An important question is whether those males who administered shocks to females in the experiment were thereby more likely to commit rape, etc., etc." He says that this is a very difficult question and then says, "In addition, the possibility of that pornography reducing aggression towards women is not even measured. For example, how many of these men gained a sense of sexual relief from these films which reduced their likelihood of aggressing against females."

DONNERSTEIN: None. But there has been research on that. I mean there is no research which demonstrates that the type of typical fare reduces aggressive behavior. In fact what the research has shown, okay, is that mildly erotic material, and that probably isn't the adult bookstore material, okay, but mildly erotic material and sometimes material which we create in the laboratory, does have a tendency to reduce aggressive behavior, mainly because it isn't arousing, it doesn't do anything. As soon as you move toward any material which becomes arousing, and we're not talking about violent material by the way, we're talking about sort of the standard fare, a film like "Debbie Does Dallas" which we use in our own research, would be considered arousing, okay. It increases aggressive behavior, if only because arousal increases aggressive behavior and that has been known for twenty years already. So to say that it reduces aggression, I'm not sure where that data really is when you are talking about the standard fare of material because the only way it could reduce aggression is to reduce arousal and we know it doesn't do that. In fact we know it increases general physiological arousal, it increases sexual arousal, so that there is no way that that can basically happen. And I think that often gets into [a] sort of a myth which also presents a lot of problems because I think one could also argue that if you have someone who is predisposed towards violence against women, a potential rapist, that if they view women being raped and then masturbate to the material that it's going to act as a safety valve. The problem is that what you are doing is conditioning sexual release, or relief, which is a very positive thing in men, to violence or to rape. One doesn't have to be a scientist to understand what conditioning does. It only takes a few trials and then you run into problems. I think I mentioned in the hearings some of the more recent research by Neil Malamuth which is now out in a number of book chapters which shows that you can get this conditioning very quick to the point that now men, normal males, will become sexually aroused just to scenes of women being raped because of this whole long-term conditioning process. I think the whole idea of catharsis really has to be put aside. It was a theoretical idea which was talked about years ago and I think that if somebody is going to address the issue, let them cite the data. It's not going to be there, by the way. What will be there is that mild erotica, erotica okay, can go ahead in some cases reduce aggressive behavior. That isn't standard fare, okay, that we're talking about. I think that's important to point out here.

MacKINNON: In the paragraph that follows that one and maybe what Professor Reiss is considering possible data for the catharsis hypothesis, although that may not be why he put there what he says, is that, he is talking about his conception of the causal role of pornography in our culture as the key question and then goes on to say that as he reads the data on human sexuality, "The type of pornography we have is a reflection of our basic society, not a cause of aggression against women." He then cites work by a Danish [author] Kuchinsky, called "The Effect of Availability . . ."

DONNERSTEIN: Oh, yeah.

MacKINNON: From the *Journal of Social Issues* 1973 indicating no increases in sexual crimes and a drop from 220 to 87 in the annual rate of child molestation. Could you comment on that data?

DONNERSTEIN: Yeah, well a couple of things, one it's a correlation which means you cannot determine any causality at all, and that's been known for a long time. Secondly,—

MacKINNON: Unlike your study?

DONNERSTEIN: Oh, yeah, you don't know what comes first here the chicken or the egg compared to experimental research where independent of subjects' predispositions, we determine what they see. So you see, you can talk about cause and effect. With correlational studies you cannot, which Kuchinsky's work is. Secondly, which I think is also important regarding this is, one, if you find a reduction in child molestation which he does—I know Berl Kuchinsky well—is that one, he talks about catharsis which of course becomes totally impossible on the grounds that if there wouldn't be child pornography, you can't get catharsis. So that's sort of an inconsistency right there. More important, of course, a number of things. One, the data is correlational and there are a number of people who have reanalyzed it and find differences and I think the problem is criticisms of both sides, those who find increases and those who find decreases. Secondly, it's unique to Copenhagen. I mean here we have a society which has certain attitudes about children which are a little different than ours. Secondly, we have a culture which by the way is very anti-violence in the media period. Okay. So to go ahead and generalize from what transpires in Copenhagen to what might transpire in New York City or Madison or Minneapolis, is impossible to do because for instance if I wanted to go ahead and look at the correlations, I could take the city of Madison which I think showed about a 40 percent increase this year in sexual assaults okay—

MacKINNON: Reported sexual assaults?

DONNERSTEIN: Reported sexual assaults, correct. I would also know that there has been an increase, we have data on that, in the amount of sexual violence in films. Now I could easily put together correlations which show that as sexual violence in films has gone up, Madison has shown an increase in reported instances of rape. Well, that doesn't tell us anything at all. Again you don't know what is coming first. I think that one can find any type of data one wants; that doesn't mean that in Copenhagen there hasn't been a decrease, there may well have been a decrease. But you don't know what it's due to and in fact again if you look at the whole culture you would find that there is a whole host of factors operating here which probably without any changes in the legislation probably would have found exactly the same thing. But you are never going to—the only way you can determine causality, by the way, is through experimental research. Secondly, the only way to determine what happens in our own culture with this type of material is to do studies here. There have been some, some stuff by Murray Strauss which is very recent by the way, I don't think that Professor Reiss would be quite familiar with this, it has just come out, that is also correlational which has just the opposite effect.

MacKINNON: What does that show?

DONNERSTEIN: Well, it basically shows that as the readership of certain types of magazines which would be classified as pornography goes up so does the incidence of rape and sexual assault. Well that's just the opposite of Kuchinsky.

MacKINNON: Right.

DONNERSTEIN: My feeling is though that it is all correlational study and the problem is that you can't make any definitive statements and I think we have to be fair to all the data. If we want to cite the Copenhagen stuff, fine, but I think we are going to have to look at the Strauss data. People like [John] Court, even though there is criticisms of it, but people who have done correlations in other countries really find the opposite effect. It's not really a fair test and I think we can't—by the way, I don't think we can constantly keep going back to 1973, 1972 data which is older than that, by the way, to the Pornography Commission data which is talked about here which is 1968, 1969.

MacKINNON: So, you are saying that the 1973 issue of the *Journal of Social Issues* is a republication of the Pornography—[Commission]?

DONNERSTEIN: Oh, that is exactly what it is. Oh, yeah. And basically we just can't keep bringing up data of 14, 15 years ago. Times have changed, the materials have changed, the questions we ask are changed. As an example, some of the classic data—and I don't disagree with it, I think that one can still find it today—is that rapists or convicted sexual assault individuals have less exposure to pornography and this was the '68, '69 data by Goldstein and other people. That might be true. They might have less exposure to what we normally would have called back in the late sixties "pornography." What we know, however, is that they have less exposure mainly because they are often not aroused by that material. What a pedophile or child molester is aroused by is kiddie porn. How much kiddie porn was around in the late sixties? That's what they would search out. What a rapist is turned on to, we learn now from the research of Abel and Malamuth, is that they are turned on to violence against women. How much violent material was there in the late sixties? They are not searching out normal fare, because normal fare is not a sexual turn-on to them. Today, however, you find particularly with very violent rapists, and here I'm talking about those who maybe commit murder, mutilation, something of that nature, there is a lot of anecdotal data now that those individuals had in their possession materials depicting very similar types of crimes. Okay. That type of material was fairly underground in the sixties. And basically we were also asking in the sixties the question that rape would be strictly a crime of sexual motivation only. Okay, that if somebody views pornography they become sexually aroused that pushes them out to commit a rape. So since rapists don't expose themselves to sexually explicit material consequently there can be no relationship. Well, first of all that is contradictory, number one, with more recent data. Secondly, it goes through the issue through the back door and, more important, given all the new research it strongly suggests that they seek out different types of material.

MacKINNON: Thus, the issue is not so much how much pornography people who become sexual offenders were exposed to, as what kind of pornography they were exposed to?

DONNERSTEIN: What kind, yes.

MacKINNON: And was available?

DONNERSTEIN: And was available at that time. And secondly, if you take a good close look, not at the final Commission report, but the actual data, okay, you find a substantial minority indicate that the material did have an effect, about 40 percent. Now—

MacKINNON: A minority of 40 percent?

DONNERSTEIN: A minority of 40 percent. But, you see, it's very easy to say the majority do not. So I think one must take a very, very close look at the data but also realize that you can't talk about the material and studies done in the late sixties. I think, a lot of people would argue that some of the slides and even some of the films shown really aren't that representative of what's out there today and they definitely aren't representative of what's out there today. They definitely aren't representative, by the way, [of material] which has violent overtones. The Commission made it their policy to stay away from violent material except in one article by Percy Tannenbaum which did use violent material and did find, by the way, an increase in aggressive behavior. But since that type of material was nonexistent, no mention was made and no real data was collected from rapists about particular types of materials they were dealing with, I think that you would even find people like Goldstein and others, who are now aware of the newer data, who wouldn't agree with some of the statements and research years ago. In fact, even Kuchinsky argues that, for crying out loud, you have the most violent material in the states I've ever seen. Okay? That you're dealing with totally different types of things here in totally different cultures.

MacKINNON: He says that the material in the United States is more violent than that in Denmark?

DONNERSTEIN: Yes, yes. And that—you know, he himself would admit you can't make comparisons between Copenhagen and anyplace else. Copenhagen [is] Copenhagen just like Minneapolis is Minneapolis.

MacKINNON: Right. I think that you've touched on most of the research that was also referred to in the article in the *Tribune* about—I mean, it quotes Mr. Goldstein from 1973, it quotes Mr. Kuchinsky from 1973—

DONNERSTEIN: Yeah, in fact, I'm glad—somebody did by the way, I do have a copy of that. And in fact Mr. Newlen actually, I had spoken to him—he tried to get ahold of me when I was on vacation. I got back to work a little too late. And he had mentioned that he did put it in the Saturday day paper of the *Minneapolis Star.* So I did get a copy of the article.

MacKINNON: Is there anything else, then, from that article that you would like to respond to?

DONNERSTEIN: I think that it's sort of the traditional type of thing. One, again, I don't think you can keep bringing up 1973 *Journal of Social Issues* out of the old Pornography Commission data. Number two, of course when you speak to sex therapists or people in human sexuality, it's very interesting, they all say, there is some problems with the violent material. I mean, there is really agreement there. But the types of material that they deal with in sex education courses or in materials which they cite as having a therapeutic effect, is not the material which is the standard fare of adult bookstores. It's like it's the material we use in some of our earlier research. There are companies which make films specifically for sex education. Okay? For the most part, you aren't going to find these gross power differentials, submissive, degradation occurring. I don't think any sex therapist would go ahead and try to instill that. I mean, I might be wrong, but I don't think that might be the case. I think the material is quite different.

MacKINNON: So what you are saying is that the material that they are using when they say "erotica" or "nonviolent erotica" is not what you're studying when you study what you call pornography?

DONNERSTEIN: Oh, no, no, not at all. It's totally different. In one sense, I think in any academic discipline there is a long time between the time certain articles get out—in one discipline, my own field of psychology, till it gradually gets filtered down into the sociological community, the human sexuality community, the legal community. Unfortunately, there are years and years before a lot of these definitions are really cleared up. And I think basically there is some misunderstanding of what we and other researchers have meant by our material. We are not saying at all that something that a sex therapist or human sexuality class at maybe the University of Minnesota might show, has an effect. It might be very therapeutic, but those are different types of materials made specifically for that purpose, just like we made it for ours. That is not what you are going to go to and randomly find in your local adult bookstore.

MacKINNON: What I would like to do now is ask you a couple of questions about the definition in the ordinance itself in relation to the research that you've been talking about, and the definitions that you've been talking about.

DONNERSTEIN: Okay.

MacKINNON: Do you have a copy of it there?

DONNERSTEIN: Yes.

MacKINNON: Okay, on page 3 the definition of pornography section (gg) subsection (1) it says, "Pornography is the sexually explicit subordination of women." It goes on to say other things, but I'd just like to ask you about that part, "sexually explicit subordination of women" and how that phrase fits with the lines that you have drawn and the definitions that you have made in your research?

DONNERSTEIN: Yeah. I think it is the subordination, degradation, dehumanizing of women, the unequal power relationship which is the issue. Okay. Sexual explicitness, no.

MacKINNON: But all your research is about sexually explicit—[materials]

DONNERSTEIN: All our research is about sexually explicitness, yes, yes exactly.

MacKINNON: So that when this says "sexually explicit subordination of women," is it fair to say that the combination of the violence that you study in some of the materials with the coercion and force and degradation that you study in other materials are the kinds of things that could also be encompassed by the term, "sexually explicit subordination of women"?

DONNERSTEIN: Yes, yes, oh, yes. Sexually explicit erotica does not include subordination of women, okay? So when I talk about non-violent erotica in our research we do not mean material, okay, which in any way objectifies, degrades, subordinates women. In fact, our material was put together with the help of our rape crisis center, women's support center and so on. Primarily by women who had their definition of what should be purely erotic and recreated [in] the film. Again, that has to be strongly emphasized. Just like, by the way in a sort of aside, when we had to do research on negative reactions of women to being raped in films, we had to create that film, too, because we couldn't find a standard ten-minute loop film in an adult bookstore which didn't show a woman being sexually attacked or assaulted without her being turned on. Okay? That's a common type of scenario. So a lot of the stuff we created is artificial in nature.

MacKINNON: Right, right. But you do include something other than violence in your definition of pornography. That is, to say, what you study when you say nonviolent erotica, that not only excludes any form of subordination but if there is the presence of anything like force or coercion or dehumanization then it's gone.

DONNERSTEIN: It's gone, yeah, yeah. Now that would not be the case of the new research we're doing with what we call X-rated material, okay? That is material as it is and some of that material is going to contain without question mild forms of violence. What we try to take out is explicit graphic violence.

MacKINNON: Then you leave in forms of force, coercion—

DONNERSTEIN: Yeah. In fact, I mean, the notion "no, no, no, no—now yes," okay, is the common theme and that is of course the way the films just are. That we mean non-violent in this newer research meaning somebody's not attacked or cut with a knife.

MacKINNON: Okay. Now I'd like you to look at the one through nine characteristics there that are additional characteristics that have to be present before something is pornography. Could you just read through those in order and say what you know about the current research on each of those descriptions?

DONNERSTEIN: Okay. Women are presented dehumanized as sexual objects, things or commodities. Of course, the new research by Dolf Zillmann shows that long term exposure to exactly that type of material (he would use the word "trivialize"—but it's really the same thing here) leads to [an] increase in callous attitudes, a reduction in sensitivity to rape. Our own new research shows exactly the same thing, okay? The thing is it's a little longer for the effects to occur.

MacKINNON: And your studies are the first long term studies of that material?

DONNERSTEIN: Yeah, truly long term. The Commission did long term studies, by the way, but all they did was to look at sexual arousal and interest in sex and what Zillmann argues is yes, people do become habituated. They become less sexually aroused. But what's happening is at the same time they are becoming desensitized to women in general and we do the same thing in our own research. Yes, people are less bothered about it but that doesn't mean there aren't changes which are now occurring in their own attitudes and that's the thing that the Commission, by the way, just didn't ask. Mainly because it just wasn't theoretically an issue at that point, where it is today.

Two, women are presented as sexual objects who enjoy pain and humiliation. Well, as I mentioned, a lot of the research that we've done and Malamuth does deals with sexually violent material in which the common scenario is that women get turned on to aggression and that it's a sexual thing for women and that tends to not only reinforce attitudes in males who have those attitudes to begin with, but tends to change subjects who might be a little ambiguous about these issues and increases their willingness to say they would commit rape. It increases their acceptance of myths about rape and acceptance of interpersonal violence. There is just tons of research on that.

Number three, women are presented as sexual objects who experience sexual pleasure in being raped. That is the common aggressive pornography. Okay? In fact, if one takes a look at, of course, any S/M magazine, that is the scenario and just about all the films—well, 95 percent of the films we use—that also occurs. That rape, sexual violence, is a turn-on.

Women are presented as sexual objects tied up, or cut up, or mutilated, or bruised—again, yes. That type of material—and I think it's interesting to say, that even if you present material that is graphic, in which the victim doesn't get turned on but let's say is mutilated, raped and experiences a great deal of pain—again, the research by Malamuth shows that there are about 25 percent or 30 percent of the "normal" male population who gets turned on off of that material. Okay? Now the vast majority get turned on to the material in which the woman shows a positive reaction. But even if you take that out and show some of the most graphic forms of violence like in the research we are doing now, by the way, that is a turn-on to a strong minority and I think there is no question about that and also, by the way, a turn-on to known convicted rapists.

Women are presented in postures of sexual submission. Again, that is sort of the trivialization and women strictly as objects and the newer research shows that that has an effect with long term exposure on attitudes.

Women's body parts including but not limited to vaginas, breasts and buttocks are exhibited such that women are reduced exactly to those parts. In fact, in the X-rated material, part of our de-briefing to re-sensitize subjects to the issue of women and try to eliminate some of the stereotypes and their changes in the perception of rape, is to go back and say what these films have done is literally treated women as parts rather than as a whole person. In fact, we make it very specific that one of the reasons these X-rated non-violent films, okay, are affecting them is because women are seen strictly as sexual objects and long term exposure to that trivializes women, makes them seem promiscuous, always asking for it, consequently when they now serve as jurors in rape trials they get the usual "oh, she was there for a particular reason, she was really asking for it." And that leads to a less sensitive attitude about rape and about women.

MacKINNON: Is that also true, typically, for the materials that persistently show women in postures of sexual submission?

DONNERSTEIN: Oh, yeah, yeah. It's just basically treating women as strictly objects period. Subordinate, submissive to men, being there really to do one thing and that is to serve men's sexual need. That is not, again, what we have defined as erotica in our research, okay. There is an equal relationship going on in our particular view.

Women are presented as whores by nature. Well, basically if you look at the new Zillmann research and read some of the items from the Sex Callousness Scale not only—it's hard to tell whether the material depicts that as much as that is the perception subjects get from it. In fact, the Sex Callousness Scale is about as blatant as one can get, I think. And you find with normal fare, nonviolent material, you get it.

Women are presented as being penetrated by objects or animals—yes. Particularly in the violent material. Zillmann also argues in a *Journal of Communication* article and in one of his new books, is that what happens is that after people become desensitized to normal fare, they now began to search out what he calls more bizarre material—could be aggressive, could be bestiality which they now become sexually aroused to. So they are now becoming aroused and turned on to women having intercourse with animals or women being hung up, raped, etc. because the other material was no longer, by the way, creating any effect. In fact, material such as bestiality did lead to increases in aggressive behavior, by the way. Because it was so arousing, in that research.

Women are presented in scenarios of degradation, injury, abasement, torture, shown as filthy or inferior, bleeding, bruised, etc.—yes. To me, that's basically the standard aggressive pornography fare and again in the vast majority of that material, women get turned on by all of this and that affects most of the subjects in the research which we have looked at, and other people. But even if they don't get turned on you find a good strong percentage of subjects who are already pre-hostile who get turned on to that. So it's really very much of a Catch-22 in a lot of that. In that sense, I think, with all of these there is now research on the effects. And basically, I think one of the problems is, that the type of material we've talked about again, and we've been going through this for the last hour on sexually explicit non-violent erotica, is not one of these.

MacKINNON: Could you also talk a little bit, briefly, about the kinds of materials that have been used by the researchers, in that the statute talks about pictures, it talks about the written word, and so on? Could you just characterize the type of materials that people use, as to the validity of this definition and its effects?

DONNERSTEIN: I think the interesting thing about the research is that a lot of people are doing it quite independently of each other, not knowing what other people were doing. Some people were using audio tapes, some were using written passages, some were using just slides, some were using films—everybody was finding the same thing. It tended to make little or no difference what essentially was the modality which was being used here. And that was interesting because it did add a lot of external validity to the research. It suggested that it is not specific to a ten-minute film clip. In fact, most of Neil Malamuth's research which I addressed at the hearing dealt with either audio tapes or written passages which subjects read. The research by the way of Gene Abel which I addressed, with rapists, are written passages. Taken from novels, magazines, etc., etc. It makes really literally no difference. I think one can get into a little nit-picking about whether one's going to be more arousing than the other, but in the long run there seems to be no difference that anybody has found between it—nor should there be. People can fill in the gaps.

MacKINNON: Okay. Those are all the questions that I have. What I would like to do is call you back and work out the physical arrangements here.

DONNERSTEIN: Okay, will do. Bye-bye.

Appendix B: Brief *Amicus Curiae* of Andrea Dworkin, American Booksellers v. Hudnut, Indianapolis, Indiana (Excerpt)

ARGUMENT

I. Pornography Is a Central Element in the Oppression of Women

Judge Barker says that pornography as defined in the Ordinance is constitutionally protected speech.[1] This means that the abuse of women in pornography, the trafficking in women that constitutes the bulk of pornography, the coercion of women required to make pornography, the abuses of women inevitably resulting from pornography, and the inequality created by pornography all have constitutional protection. Women cannot function as citizens in this world of social and sexual predation.

The Ordinance characterizes pornography as "a discriminatory practice based on sex." Speech and action are meshed in this discrimination, which is a system of sexual exploitation constructed on sex-based powerlessness and which generates sex-based abuse. The presence of speech cannot be used to immunize discrimination and sexual abuse from legal remedy.

When pornography is photographic, it is indisputably action. It gets perceived as speech because the woman in the photograph is effectively rendered an object or commodity by the pornography; the perception of the photograph as speech in itself denies the human status of the woman in it. The so-called speech belongs to whomever took or sold the photograph—the pornographer—not to the woman used in it, to whom things were done as if she were an object or commodity, and who indeed continues to be sold as an object or commodity. The woman is excluded from recognizably human dialogue by the uses to which she is put. The courts reify this injustice when they take the photograph to be real speech and

---

1. See *American Booksellers Assoc'n v. Hudnut*, 598 F. Supp. 1316 (D. Ind. 1984) (Barker, J.) for the district court opinion being discussed here.

do not recognize the woman in it as a real person who, by virtue of being human, is necessarily being used in ways antagonistic to full human status. The court accepts the pornographers' misogyny as its own if it holds that the pornographers' exploitation of a woman's body is an appropriate use of her: that what she is entitled to as a human being is properly expressed in these uses to which she is put.

The actions immortalized in pornography are not ideas, thoughts, or fantasies. The vocabulary of "sexual fantasy," often applied to pornography as a genre, is in fact the language of prostitution, where the act that the man wants done and pays to get done is consistently referred to as his "fantasy," as if it never happens in the real world. He goes to a prostitute and pays her money so that she will do what he tells her to do, and it is this *act* that is called "fantasy."

Similarly, in pornography, *acts* done to or by women are called "speech," even though the woman is doing an act dictated by what is required to sexually gratify men. Her body is a commodity in itself. Her body is also the literal language of the so-called publisher, who in reality is a pimp trafficking in women. Because the pimp introduces a camera into the trafficking, his whole process of exploiting the woman's body is protected as "speech."

The First Amendment predated the invention of the camera. The founding fathers could never have considered that there might be physical rights of people trampled on by rights of speech: that in protecting a photograph, for instance, one might be protecting an actual act of torture. In pornography, photographs are made with real women. These photographs are then used on real women, to get them to do the acts the real women in the photographs are doing.

The hostility and discrimination produced by written pornography is just as real. In written pornography, the vocabularies of sex and violence are inextricably combined, so that erection and orgasm are produced as pleasurable responses to sexual abuse. This behaviorally conditions men to sex as dominance over and violence against women. The nature of written pornography is definable and distinct enough from all other written material that it can be isolated as well as recognized. Sexually explicit and abusive male dominance, conveyed in repeated acts of rape, torture, and humiliation, is the entire substance of written pornography. *See* Smith, "The Social Content of Pornography," 26 *J. Communication* 16 (1976). It is impossible, however, to separate the effects of written pornography from the effects of photographic pornography.

Obscenity law recognizes the incredible physical impact of this kind of sexually explicit material, written and photographic, on men—an impact so different from the impact of any known form of "speech" that the Supreme Court has repeatedly held that obscenity is not speech, even though it is words and pictures. *See, e.g., Roth v. United States,* 354 U.S. 476, 485 (1957).[2][2] The standard of "prurient interest" suggests the kind of line that the court wants to draw between "speech" and "not speech" even with regard to words and pictures. "Prurient" means "itch" or "itching"; it is derived from the Sanscrit "he burns." If he itches, let alone burns, the power and urgency of his response is not socially innocuous. Pornography creates the physiologically real conviction in men that women want abuse; that women are whores by nature; that women want to be raped and humiliated; that women get sexual pleasure from pain; even that women get sexual pleasure from being maimed or killed. *See* Minneapolis City Council, Public Hearings on Ordinance to Add Pornography as Discrimination Against Women (hereinafter, "Minneapolis Hearings"), Sess. III (Dec. 13, 1983), 5 P.M. session at 34 (testimony of Barbara Chester); Malamuth and Check, "Penile Tumescence and Perceptual Responses to Rape as a Function of Victims' Perceived Reactions," 10 *J. Applied Social Psych.* 528 (1980). Obscenity law is premised on the inevitability of male sexual response to sexually explicit verbal and visual stimuli; it occurs in a world of concrete male dominance, obscenity law itself originating in a context of legalized male ownership of women.

Judicial decisions reflect and perpetuate the focus on male response, by wholly ignoring women, both in and outside the pornography. The statutory definition of pornography in the Ordinance articulates for the first time in the law how pornography both uses and impacts on women in particular, which is what distinguishes it as a uniquely destructive phenomenon. Pornography is appropriately recognized as an energetic agent of male domination over women. Pornography creates a devastating relationship between the status of some women, who are particularly powerless and vulnerable to abuse, and the status of all women. The vicious exploitation through sex of some women in pornography as entertainment establishes a sexual imperative in which forcing sex on any woman

2. [2.] Obscenity laws and standards themselves are based on values of male domination and sexual inequality. Obscenity laws are woman-hating, incorporating antiwoman strains in early Judeo-Christian theology that hold women to be carnal, provocative, evil, dirty, sinful, and lewd. The prohibitions on nudity implicitly assume that a woman's body unclothed is a sexual provocation, and that sexual expressiveness by a woman is necessarily lewd and lascivious.

is justified. The bad treatment of some women in pornography justifies the second-class status of all women in society, because the bad treatment is presented as an appropriate response to the human worthlessness of women as such. Only *some* Christians had to be slaughtered as public entertainment in Roman circuses for all Christians and all Romans to understand who could be hurt, harassed, and persecuted with *de facto* impunity.

Pornographers draw on and benefit from particularly cruel aspects of women's vulnerability. Incest and child sexual abuse produce between two-thirds and three-quarters of the women who get exploited in pornography. *See* James and Meyerding, "Early Sexual Experiences and Prostitution," 134 *Am. J. Psychiatry* 1381 (1977); Silbert and Pines, "Pornography and Sexual Abuse of Women," 10 *Sex Roles* 857 (1984); Senate Committee on the Judiciary, Subcommittee on Juvenile Justice, "A Hearing to Consider the Effects of Pornography on Children and Women" (Aug. 8, 1984) (Testimony of Katherine Brady). The ownership of a girl by her father or other adult male, including sexual ownership of her, is deeply implicated in the continuing vulnerability of adult women to the sexual abuse of pornography. It is not possible to draw a firm line between the uses of children in pornography, recognized in *New York v. Ferber,* 458 U.S. 747 (1982), and the uses of women in pornography, since so many of the women are habituated to sexual abuse, even first used in pornography, as children. The court must not accept the pornographers' propaganda, which insists that these women have made a career choice as free and equal adults for pornographic exploitation. The ownership of women and children by adult men is historically linked (for example, in the power of the Roman *paterfamilias*); and it is empirically and sociologically linked in the abuse of women and children in pornography.

Pornography is deeply implicated in rape, *see* Minneapolis Hearings, Sess. III (Dec. 13, 1983) at 11 (testimony of Bill Neiman), 14 (testimony of S. G.), 18 *et seq.* (testimony of Carole laFavor); in battery, see *id.* at 21 (testimony of Wanda Richardson), 27 *et seq.* (testimony of Donna Dunn) in incest, *see id.* at 67 *et seq.* (testimony of Charlotte Kasl); in forced prostitution, *see id.* at 75 *et seq.* (testimony of Sue Santa). Pornography is also a consistent phenomenon in the lives of serial killers. *See* S. Michaud and J. Aynesworth, *The Only Living Witness* 104, 105, 115, 118, 130 (1983) (Ted Bundy); T. Schwarz, *The Hillside Strangler* 152–153 (1982); T. Sullivan and P. Maiken, *Killer Clown: The John Wayne Gacy Mur-*

ders 28, 29, 218, 223; P. Johnson, *On Iniquity* 39, 52, 80, 81 (1967) (Moors murders); E. Williams, *Beyond Belief* 135, 143, 148–156 (1968) (Moors murders); G. Burn, *". . . somebody's husband, somebody's son:" The Story of Peter Sutcliffe* 113–116, 123 (1984) (Yorkshire Ripper).[3][3]

Pornography presents the rape and torture of women as entertainment. This is surely the nadir of social worthlessness.

II. Pornographers' Rights of Expression are Outweighed by Women's Rights to Equality

A. *The Expression of Ideas Through Injurious Acts Is Not Constitutionally Protected*

It is wrong to say, as Judge Barker did, that pornography as defined in the Ordinance expresses ideas and is therefore protected speech, unless one is prepared to say that murder or rape or torture with an ideology behind it also expresses ideas and might well be protected on that account. Most acts express ideas. Most systems of exploitation or inequality express ideas. Segregation expressed an idea more eloquently than any book about the inferiority of black people ever did. Yet the Supreme Court overturned segregation—after protecting it for a very long time—because the Court finally grasped its harm to people. The difference between the Court's view in *Plessy v. Ferguson,* 163 U.S. 537, 551 (1896), that segregation harmed blacks "solely because the colored race chooses to put that construction upon it," and its view in *Brown v. Bd. of Education of Topeka,* 347 U.S. 483, 494 (1954) that segregation "generates a feeling of inferiority as to their status in the community that may affect their hearts and minds in a way unlikely ever to be undone," is dramatic and instructive. The fact that the idea that segregation expressed would suffer because the idea required the practice for much of its persuasive power did not afford segregation constitutional protection: attempts to invoke First Amendment justifications have been thoroughly repudiated. *See, e.g., Norwood v. Harrison,* 413 U.S. 455 (1973), where the attempt was made to invoke rights of association and free exercise of religion; *Bob Jones University v. United States,* —— U.S. ——, 103 S.Ct. 2017 (1983) (upholding state prohibition on sex discrimination in public ac-

---

3. [3.] Ted Bundy described a hypothetical killer like himself in this way: "Then he got sucked into the more sinister doctrines that are implicit in pornography—the use, the abuse, the possession of women as objects." Michaud and Aynesworth, *supra,* at 105.

commodations against freedom of association challenge); *Hishon v. King & Spalding,* —— U.S. ——, 104 S.Ct. 2229 (1984) (upholding application of Title VII against freedom of association challenge).

An effort to claim that segregation was protected as first amendment "speech" because it has a point of view and an ideology would be a transparent use of the First Amendment to shield a practice of inequality; and such a claim for pornography is similarly transparent. Exploitation cannot be protected because it expresses the idea that the people being exploited are inferior or worthless as human beings or deserve to be exploited. All exploitation fundamentally expresses precisely that idea.

B. *The Sexual Exploitation of Women Perpetuated by Pornography Negates Women's Rights to Equality*

In her decision, Judge Barker says that "[a]dult women generally have the capacity to protect themselves from participating in and being personally victimized by pornography." Slip op. at 38. The fault, she suggests, is with the individual who is hurt, and no legal remedy is justified. Adult men generally have the capacity to protect themselves from being murdered; yet murderers are not excused because they only succeed in murdering men who are dumb enough, weak enough, or provocative enough to get killed. Indeed, no one ever thinks of male victims of violence in those terms at all. Yet that valuation of women hurt by pornography is implicit in Judge Barker's misogynistic logic.

It is not true that women can protect ourselves from being victimized by pornography. Pornography's effect on our civil status—the way it creates attitudes and behaviors of discrimination against us—is beyond personal remedy. Pornography's role in generating sexual abuse is beyond our capacities as individuals to stop or moderate, especially with no legal recourse against its production, sale, exhibition, or distribution. Sexual abuse is endemic in this country. One-fifth to one-third of all women have an unwanted sexual encounter with an adult male as children; one woman in a hundred has had a sexual experience as a child with her father or step-father; it is estimated that 16,000 new cases of father-daughter incest are initiated each year. *See* J. Herman, *Father-Daughter Incest* 12–14 (1982). Studies and police and hospital records in different localities suggest that battery occurs in one-third to one-half of all marriages. *See* R. Langley and R. Levy, *Wife Beating* 4–11 (1977); D. Russell, *Rape in Marriage* 98–100 (1982). A documented forcible rape occurs every seven minutes; and rape remains one of the most under-reported violent crimes. *See* Federal Bureau of Investigation, *Uniform Crime Reports for the United States* at 5, 14 (1983). Studies continue to be done in all areas of sexual abuse, including sexual harassment, marital rape, and prostitution; and the figures showing frequency of abuse increase as the descriptions of violence become more precise and the political efforts of feminists provide a context in which to comprehend the abuse.

The place of pornography in actually producing the scenarios and behaviors that constitute that mass of sexual abuse is increasingly documented, especially by victims. Coercion of women into pornography is expanding as the market for live women expands, especially in video pornography. Women in homes do not have the real social and economic power to keep men from using pornography on them or making them participate in it. There has been an increased use of cameras in actual rapes, with the subsequent appearance of the photographs on the commercial pornography market. Pornography itself is also being used as a form of sexual assault: the public violation of a woman—photographs made against her will or by fraud or without her knowledge, then published as public rape. Her forced exposure, like rape, is an act of hostility and humiliation. With the normalization of pornography, women who have pictures of themselves used against them as sexual abuse have no social or legal credibility to assert that rights of privacy were violated, because they appear indistinguishable from other women in similar photographs whose active compliance is presumed.

The statutory definition of pornography in the Ordinance, far from being "vague," delineates the structure of actual, concrete material produced and sold as pornography by the $8-billion-a-year pornography industry. *See U.S. News and World Report,* June 4, 1984, at 84–85. No adult bookstore has any problem knowing what to stock. No consumer has any problem knowing what to buy. No pornography theatre has any trouble knowing what to show. The so-called books are produced by formula, and they do not vary ever in their nature, content, or impact. They cannot be confused with the language of any writer I have ever read, including Jean Genet and Jerzy Kosinski, who are particularly graphic about rape and hate women. It may be difficult to believe that the definition is accurate and clear, because it may be difficult to believe that we are actually living in a country where the material described in the statutory definition is being produced, especially with live people. Nevertheless, we do. Or perhaps one effect of using $8 billion of pornography a year is that the basic premise of this law appears bizarre by contrast with the pornography: that women are human beings with rights of equality; and that being hurt by pornography violates those rights.

C. The Elimination of Sex Discrimination Is a Compelling State Interest that Is Furthered by the Ordinance

Sex discrimination keeps more than half the population from being able to enjoy the full benefits of free speech, because they are too poor to buy speech, too silenced through sexual abuse to articulate in a credible way their own experiences, too despised because of their sex to be able to achieve the public significance required to exercise speech in a technologically advanced society. The First Amendment protects speech already articulated and published from state interference. It does nothing to empower those who have been systematically excluded—especially on the bases of sex and race—from pragmatic access to the means of speech.

The First Amendment is nearly as old as this country. The eradication of sex discrimination is new as a compelling state interest, perhaps causing Judge Barker to underestimate its importance. *Compare, e.g., Goesaert v. Cleary,* 335 U.S. 464 (1948) (upholding legal restrictions on women's occupational choices) *with Roberts v. United States Jaycees,* —— U.S. ——, 104 [S. Ct.] 3244 (1984) (upholding application of state antidiscrimination law to business and civic group). Without vigorous action [on] behalf of equality, women will never be able to exercise the speech that the First Amendment would then protect.

State governments were not held to the proscriptions on government in the First Amendment until the Supreme Court held that the due process clause of the Fourteenth Amendment incorporated first amendment standards. *See, e.g., Fiske v. Kansas,* 274 U.S. 380 (1927). Nevertheless, the simple reality is that the First Amendment and its values of free speech existed in harmony with both legal slavery and legal segregation. No effective legal challenge to those systems of racial subordination was mounted under the rubric of freedom of expression, even though in both systems reading and writing were at issue. In slavery, laws prohibited teaching slaves to read or write. *See* K. Stampp, *The Peculiar Institution* 208 (1956). In segregation, separate-but-equal education assured that blacks remained widely illiterate; then literacy tests were used to screen voters, so that blacks could not qualify to vote. *See Oregon v. Mitchell,* 400 U.S. 112, 132–33 (1970) (Black, J.); *Gaston County v. United States,* 395 U.S. 285 (1969). *Cf. Griggs v. Duke Power Company,* 401 U.S. 424, 430 (1971) (inferior segregated education hurts blacks where employer uses non-job-related educational criteria for employment decisions). Rights of speech, association, and religion (being kept out of certain churches, for instance, by state law), were simply denied blacks. The Civil War Amendments are an institutional acknowledgment that power-lessness is not cured simply by "more speech"; first amendment values alone could not fulfill constitutional ambitions for dignity and equity that reside in principles of justice not abrogated even by sadistic political institutions like slavery. The Fourteenth Amendment, however, purpose-fully used the word "male" in its guarantee of voting rights, U.S. Const. amend. XIV, §2, to rule out any possible application of equality rights to women's social and political condition. The right to vote, won in 1920, gave women the most mundane recognition of civil existence as citizens. U.S. Const., amend. XIX. The equality principles underlying the Four-teenth Amendment were even then not applied to women until 1971. *Reed v. Reed,* 404 U.S. 71 (1971).

The absolute, fixed, towering importance of the First Amendment and the absolute, fixed insignificance of sex discrimination and of equality interests in Judge Barker's decision is a direct consequence of how late women came into this legal system as real citizens. Equality must be the legal priority for any group excluded from constitutional protections for so long and stigmatized as inferior. Yet the historical worthlessness of women—which is why our interests are not as old as this country—un-dermines any claim we make to having rights that must be taken as fundamental: equality for women is seen as trivial, faddish. The First Amendment, by contrast, is fundamental—a behemoth characterized by longevity, constancy, and familiarity. Because women have been silenced, and because women have been second-class, our equality claims are seen as intrinsically inferior. The opposite should be the case. Those whom the law has helped to keep out by enforcing conditions of inferiority, servi-tude, and debasement should, by virtue of that involuntary but intensely destructive exclusion, have the court's full attention when asserting any equality claim.

This must certainly be true when speech rights are asserted in behalf of pornographers, since the speech of the pornographers is exercised largely through sexual abuse and is intricately interwoven with physical assault and injury. The First Amendment here is clearly being used to shield those who are not only powerful but also cruel and cynical. The victims, targeted on the basis of sex, must ask for relief from systematic sexual predation through a recognition of equality rights, because only equality stands up against the injury of longstanding exclusion from constitutional protections. Judge Barker holds that only expression matters, even when the expression is trafficking in women; equality does not matter, and the systematic harms of inequality and abuse suffered by women on a massive scale do not matter. This view of the First Amendment relies on historical inequities to establish modern constitutional priorities.

The courts must, instead, give real weight to equality interests, because of their historical exclusion from the original Bill of Rights. The deformities of the social system caused by that exclusion destroy justice, which requires symmetry, equity, and balance. By refusing to give equality values any weight when in conflict with free speech values, Judge Barker allows speech to function as if it were a military arsenal: hoarded by men for over two centuries, it is now used to bludgeon women, who have been without it and have none in reserve; we do not even have slingshots against Goliath. If equality interests can never matter against first amendment challenges, then speech becomes a weapon used by the haves against the have-nots; and the First Amendment, not balanced against equality rights of the have-nots, becomes an intolerable instrument of dispossession, not a safeguard of human liberty. The real exclusion of women from public discourse has allowed men to accumulate speech as a resource of power; and with that power, men have articulated values and furthered practices that have continued to debase women and to justify that debasement. The First Amendment, then, in reality, operates to the extreme detriment of those who do not have the power of socially and politically real speech. In this case, Judge Barker is saying that real people being tortured are properly not persons with rights of equality that are being violated; but, because a picture has been taken, are the abstract speech of those who exploit them. She is saying that the victim in the photograph is properly silent, even if gagged; that the victim's historical exclusion from speech need not, cannot, and should not be changed by vigorous legislative and judicial commitments to equality. She is saying that the woman's body is properly seen as the man's speech; and, in this corrupt logic, that the picture that in fact documents the abuse of a human being is to be dignified as an idea that warrants legal protection. Equality is indeed meaningless in this arrangement of power; and speech is a nightmare with a victim whose humanity is degraded by both the pornographers and the court.

D. *The Pornographers Degrade the First Amendment*

The pornographers also degrade the First Amendment by using it as a shield to protect sexual abuse and sexual trafficking. If the court allows these parasites an impenetrable shield of absolute protection because they use pictures and words as part of the sexual abuse they perpetrate and promote, there is really no end to the possible manipulations of the First Amendment to protect like forms of exploitation. All any exploiter has to do is to interject speech into any practice of exploitation, however malignant, and hide the whole practice behind the First Amendment. By isolating the speech elements in other practices of discrimination and asserting their absolute protection, the discrimination could be made to disappear. Consider, for example, a common situation in sexual harassment in employment, where a "speech" element—a sexual proposition from a supervisor—is part of a chain of events leading to an adverse employment consequence. *See, e.g., Tomkins v. Public Serv. Elec. & Gas Co.,* 568 F.2d 1044, 1045 (3d Cir. 1977), in which a conversation over lunch was a crucial component of the Title VII violation. No court has held that the mere presence of words in the process of discrimination turns the discrimination into protected activity. The speech is part of the discrimination. The Constitution places no value on discrimination. *See Norwood v. Harrison,* 413 U.S. 455 (1973); *Palmore v. Sidoti,* —— U.S. ——, 104 S.Ct. 1879 (1984).

If the First Amendment is not to protect those who have power against the just claims of those who need equality; if pornography is sexual exploitation and produces sexual abuse and discrimination; then the Ordinance is more than justified. It saves our constitutional system from the indignity of protecting sex-based abuse. It exonerates principles of equity by allowing them vitality and potency. It shows that law can actively help the powerless and not be paralyzed by the cynical manipulations of sadists and profiteers. It is an appropriate and carefully balanced response to a social harm of staggering magnitude.

CONCLUSION

For the foregoing reasons, the judgment of the District Court should be reversed.

Respectfully submitted,
Andrea Dworkin

Appendix C: Brief of the Neighborhood Pornography Task Force, *Amicus Curiae*, in Support of Appellant Hudnut v. American Booksellers Association, Inc.

INTRODUCTION

The neighborhoods bordering on East Lake Street in South Minneapolis have been fighting the encroachment of pornography into their community since Ferris Alexander opened his first bookstore and theater on Chicago Avenue and Lake Street in 1974.[1][2] Concerned residents picketed theaters, conducted tours of bookstores and waged a media campaign to alert the public about the brutalization, violence and crime that pornography was causing in their neighborhood. But, by 1976, Ferris Alexander owned three adult bookstores on Lake Street and other pornographers owned two more. Public pressure clearly had not succeeded. Speech, as exercised by neighborhood groups, could not fight the money and power of the pornographers.

In 1976, residents approached the Minneapolis City Council and asked it to pass a zoning law which would slow the growth of pornography in their neighborhoods. They thought that "controlling" pornography through zoning was their only legal option. The City Council passed a zoning ordinance in 1976 which provided two restrictions on "adult uses."[2][3] First, no adult use could be operated within 500 feet of a residentially zoned or office zoned district, a church, a licensed day care facility, elementary or high schools, and public educational facilities serving persons 17 or younger. §540.410(c). Second, no adult use could operate within 500 feet of another adult use. §540.410(d). The Eighth

---

1. [2.] By 1975, Ferris Alexander and his brother owned or controlled 21 adult bookstores and 8 theaters in the Twin Cities, Rochester, and Duluth. Ferris Alexander was found guilty in 1973 of "criminal conspiracy to transport obscene material across state lines." He was indicted in 1969. He served eight months and paid a $20,000 fine. *Twin Cities Reader,* September, 1980. The Internal Revenue Service is seeking more than $3.4 million in back taxes and penalties from Ferris Alexander, who the agency says has earned more than $2 million a year from businesses that include pornographic bookstores and movie theaters in the Twin Cities. The IRS asserts that Alexander's businesses had a combined gross income of $5.3 million for the years 1978 and 1979, including nearly $2 million from movie theater tickets alone. In its case against Ferris Alexander, the IRS says that he reported only $364,000 in 1979. *Minneapolis Star and Tribune,* February 12, 1984.

2. [3.] The ordinance identifies the following uses subject to control: adults only bookstores, adults only picture theaters, massage parlors, rap parlors, and saunas. Minneapolis Code of Ordinances § 540.410(a); hereafter referred to as § 540.410.

Circuit Court of Appeals found the ordinance unconstitutional because it would have diminished the number of pornographic bookstores and theaters. *Alexander v. City of Minneapolis,* 698 F.2d 936 (8th Circuit; 1983). Quoting from the lower court opinion, the Court said "[E]nforcement of §540.410 would have the effect of substantially reducing the number of adult bookstores and theaters in Minneapolis, and no new adult bookstores and theaters would be able to open." *Alexander v. City of Minneapolis,* 531 F.Supp. 1162, 1171 (D. Minn. 1982). The decision implied that pornography must remain in some neighborhoods because it was already there. Indeed, the Court assumed the burden of insuring that adult bookstores and theaters have optimum economic advantage. Acknowledging the plaintiff's argument that there were as few as three sites open for relocation if the ordinance were passed and that these three sites were not economically suitable for relocation, the Court said, "Because we find that the twelve legally permissible relocation sites do not supply sufficient access to the constitutionally protected adult uses in question we need not look to their actual availability or economic feasibility or how these factors would affect the constitutionality of the ordinance." 698 F.2d at 939, ftn. 7. The Eighth Circuit opinion confirmed what neighborhood residents had begun to suspect: if zoning was the best the legal system could offer, neighborhoods would never be able to rid themselves of the blight and crime brought into their area of the city by pornography.

From 1978 to 1983, while residents of South Minneapolis awaited a court decision on the zoning law, conditions in the neighborhood worsened. The harassment and intimidation experienced by women who live in neighborhoods with a high concentration of pornography was documented before the Minneapolis City Council during public hearings on the civil rights ordinance on pornography.[3][4] A woman from St. Paul who lived in a neighborhood with two adult movie theaters and bookstores and one adults only "club" testified that she had been propositioned several times by men who were looking for prostitutes. She said that parents fear for their children's safety and women who live in the neighborhood feel unsafe, constantly vulnerable to harassment and rape by the customers of the adult establishments.

Residents of the neighborhoods bordering on East Lake Street in Min-

3. [4.] *Minneapolis City Council Government Operations Committee Public Hearings on Ordinances to Add Pornography As Discrimination Against Women,* December 12–13, Session II, 90-100 (1983).

neapolis experience the same harassment and fear. The presence of two adult theaters, three adult bookstores and three saunas on a thirteen block span by 1983 left them no choice but to be aware of the pornography and of the harassment, intimidation and blight that is associated with it. The crime rates, especially for prostitution related offenses, are higher in the neighborhoods bordering on East Lake Street than in other areas of the city (see Appendix A). The presence of adult establishments has created a hostile and aggressive zone for women and children. Women who live and work in the neighborhood are harassed and propositioned by men who come into the neighborhoods to buy pornography or to pay for sex. One woman who lives in the neighborhood stated: "I get to work every day using the bus. The men who come out of this store [at 4th and Lake] look you up and down in a very lewd gaze. It's insulting to be treated like a prostitute when you're just waiting for a bus."4[5] Women live in constant fear of rape because women are the victims in areas with high crime and violence. Women who live in the neighborhoods are not safe on their own streets at night. They cannot shop, visit friends, wait for buses or buy groceries in peace. Women who live outside the neighborhood also do not feel safe in coming there. The aggression and violence around the adult establishments limits their freedom to visit friends or to shop in the area. The fear, intimidation and violence created by the saturation of pornography on East Lake Street has had a concrete impact upon every woman in the neighborhood and upon many women who live outside of it.

The adult establishments also affect the lives of children in the neighborhood. They are forced to view the posters advertising such movies as *Hot Dallas Nights,* and often can find abandoned pornographic materials in the alleys behind adult bookstores. Parents find it impossible to protect their children from the influence of pornography and from the aggression of strangers.

The adult bookstores and theaters which now line Lake Street have indelibly marked the character of the business community. Once a prosperous commercial area, East Lake Street now is characterized by decline and deterioration. Many legitimate businesses have moved out of the neighborhood and new ones have not replaced them. Business owners are frightened by the real possibility of business failure. When women do not feel safe on the streets, they will not come to the stores to shop.

4. [5.] *Whittier Globe,* December 1980.

Legitimate businesses do not want to subject their employees, especially women employees, to harassment from the customers of the adult bookstores and theaters.

People in this neighborhood are demoralized and increasingly cynical about the fairness of the political process and of the legal system itself. From 1976 to 1983, a group of over two hundred residents, including single women, women with children, and men continued to meet and discuss the problem of pornography in their neighborhood. When Ferris Alexander began construction of another massage parlor on Lake Street in the fall of 1983, they responded. Seven members of the group—a health administrator at a local hospital, a community school director, a local business person, the director of a neighborhood organization, a school teacher, a law student, and a University of Minnesota professor—formed the Neighborhood Pornography Task Force and asked the City Council to reintroduce a zoning law which they hoped would prevent the opening of another "adults only" business on Lake Street. Once again, they saw zoning law as their only option.

The second Minneapolis experience with zoning was as unsuccessful as the first. The citizens of South Minneapolis learned that political clout and wealth determine who must bear the burden of pornography to secure the "rights" of all. A city planner familiar with the history of zoning in Minneapolis and with the legal standards required of zoning plans proposed that seven commercial areas be zoned to allow adult establishments. Four of the seven areas were on East Lake Street. One was located in a predominantly white, wealthy area of the city. Residents of that neighborhood vehemently opposed the ordinance. The neighborhood around East Lake Street, because of its high concentration of black, Native American, Southeast Asian and poor people, was presumptively an acceptable target.

The city council continued to work on a zoning strategy amidst heated political controversy. None of the members of the city council wanted pornography in their ward, but the initial zoning proposal would have zoned part of *each* inner city ward for "adult" establishments while protecting the more affluent, white districts of the city. The city council could not ignore the problem. They scheduled a public hearing on September 29, 1983, to give members of the community a chance to express their opinion on the newly proposed zoning ordinance. The Neighborhood Pornography Task Force asked Catharine MacKinnon, a University of Minnesota law professor, and Andrea Dworkin, a feminist writer, to testify at the public hearings on zoning. At the time, MacKinnon and Dworkin were jointly teaching a class on pornography at the University of Minnesota Law School. They suggested to the city council that zoning strategies were the wrong approach to pornography and that the city council should recognize that pornography is a form of sex discrimination and a violation of women's civil rights.

The testimony of MacKinnon and Dworkin at the public hearings on zoning clarified for Amici that women and children were the real direct victims of pornography. They had seen and experienced the abuse of women in their neighborhood and witnessed the increased aggression and hostility around them. They had looked at the pornographic magazines and books that were as devastating as the decline in the quality of neighborhood life around them: women were hung from light fixtures, whipped, chained, mutilated and shit upon. Amici now recognized that the fundamental issue is the right of all women to equality and freedom and that women are denied exercise of those rights because of pornography.

The Minneapolis City Council hired MacKinnon and Dworkin to draft a civil rights ordinance on pornography. The ordinance describes exactly what the members of the Neighborhood Pornography Task Force had seen in the actual pornography that had been forced on them for years. Pornography is: "the sexually explicit subordination of women, graphically depicted whether in pictures or in words, that also includes one or more of the following: (i) women are presented dehumanized as sexual objects, things or commodities; or (ii) women are presented as sexual objects who enjoy pain or humiliation; or (iii) women are presented as sexual objects who experience sexual pleasure in being raped; or (iv) women are presented as sexual objects tied up or cut up or mutilated or bruised or physically hurt; or (v) women are presented in postures of sexual submission or sexual servility, including by inviting penetration; or (vi) women's body parts—including but not limited to vaginas, breasts, or buttocks—are exhibited, such that women are reduced to those parts; or (vii) women are presented as whores by nature; or (viii) women are presented being penetrated by objects or animals; or (ix) women are presented in scenarios of degradation, injury, or torture, shown as filthy or inferior, bleeding, bruised, or hurt in a context that makes these conditions sexual."

The Minneapolis City Council passed the ordinance on December 30, 1983. Mayor Donald Fraser vetoed it on January 5, 1984. It was immediately reintroduced and the city council passed an amended version on July 13, 1984 which Mayor Fraser vetoed the same day. The Amendment passed by the Indianapolis City Council on April 23, 1984 and amended on June 11, 1984 is substantially similar to the Minneapolis ordinance. The definition of pornography in the Indianapolis ordinance, however, does not cover all of the injuries of pornography as the Neighborhood Pornography Task Force came to recognize them. In particular, the Amendment does not contain the following subparts of the definition of pornography that the Minneapolis ordinance contained: (i) women are presented dehumanized as sexual objects, things or commodities; (v) women are presented in postures of sexual submission or sexual servility, including by inviting penetration; or (vi) women's body parts—including but not limited to vaginas, breasts, or buttocks—are exhibited, such that women are reduced to those parts; or (vii) women are presented as whores by nature. The definition in the Amendment is narrower than the actual injuries of pornography that the Neighborhood Pornography Task Force has been fighting to combat and that the Minneapolis City Council recognized as real when it covered them in its civil rights ordinance on pornography. We say this to emphasize the extremely narrow nature of the definition of the Indianapolis ordinance when measured against Amici's actual experience with pornography.

ARGUMENT

I. Neighborhoods Are Not Protected by Zoning Laws

Cities have a legitimate interest in preserving the character of their neighborhoods and the quality of life for citizens who live in those neighborhoods. In upholding a Detroit zoning ordinance addressing pornography, the Court noted that the city's interest in attempting to preserve the quality of urban life "is one that must be accorded high respect. Moreover, the city must be allowed a reasonable opportunity to experiment with solutions to admittedly serious problems." *Young v. American Mini Theaters,* 427 U.S. 50, 71 (1976). In the area of zoning law, the Court was even ready to allow regulations which admittedly used the *content* of the material as a basis for placing them in a different classification from other motion pictures and books. They found that "society's interest in protecting this type of expression is of a wholly different, and lesser, magnitude than the interest in untrammeled political debate that inspired Voltaire's immortal comment ('I disapprove of what you say, but

I will defend to the death your right to say it.')." *Young,* 427 U.S. at 70. In the context of protection of neighborhoods, the Court recognized that pornography, defined more broadly than obscenity and more broadly than this Amendment, does not serve the underlying First Amendment value of protecting political debate in the marketplace of ideas. The Court's recognition that the State has a legitimate interest in the preservation of neighborhoods was correct. Their support of zoning as a means to achieve that end has not proved adequate.

Zoning is not a neutral tool. Whenever a city zones pornography out of one neighborhood, they must zone it *into* another neighborhood. Some neighborhoods are thus protected at the expense of other neighborhoods. In *Young,* the Court condemns some neighborhoods to endure blight and deterioration for material that they recognized as worthless.

The decision about where adult bookstores and theaters are located is deeply rooted in already existing social and political inequalities. Those without power, especially racially and ethnically disenfranchised portions of the population, are consistently victimized. Those with power and money insist that the material be protected, yet refuse to allow it in their neighborhoods. Many come to the pornography districts, buy pornography and live women, and then return to the more affluent areas of the city where they live. Those who live in the pornography districts cannot escape. In Minneapolis, these citizens are primarily poor people and people of color . . . They do not have the power or the resources to keep the pornography that the law protects out of their neighborhoods. The pornography is protected, but they are not.

Under present interpretation of the Constitution, certain individuals must be bombarded with pornography, harassed on the street, and forced to live in a disreputable part of town, because other people claim the right to view material that they will fight to keep out of their own neighborhoods. Zoning supports pornography. Any zoning law must be interpreted as an affirmative statement by city leaders that they want pornography in poor and minority neighborhoods.

The language in court decisions on zoning indicating a desire to protect neighborhoods must therefore be regarded as inaccurate at best, as deliberately misleading at worst. Zoning laws hurt neighborhoods far more than they help. They create an illusion that the legal system is addressing the problem of pornography, when in truth, it does not. Urban citizens, like those of South Minneapolis, are led to believe that zoning laws and obscenity laws are the only options open to them. When those tools prove ineffective, they have been told that nothing else can be done. This undermines faith in government and contributes to the cynical perception that the law can pretend to recognize a harm and provide a remedy while actually covering up the harm and providing no relief at all.

As long as the material itself remains free from judicial scrutiny, any laws which limit the availability of presumably protected materials will be unconstitutional. The courts must decide whether pornography serves the underlying values of the First Amendment and is entitled to full First Amendment protection. Skirting the issue through zoning laws or obscenity laws is not acceptable when individuals and entire communities are daily being injured because of pornography.

II. The State Has a Legitimate Interest in Protecting Residents of Neighborhoods with a High Concentration of Pornography Through a Civil Rights Ordinance on Pornography

The defense of pornography rests upon principles that are antithetical to the premises of democratic government. The Fourteenth Amendment to the Constitution says that a state may not "deprive any person of life, liberty, or property, without due process of law; nor deny to any person within its jurisdiction the equal protection of the law." It is a statement by our government that equal treatment of all citizens ranks as a high priority and that the state may not constitutionally enforce laws which classify certain individuals for treatment that denies them life, liberty or property.

The enforcement of zoning laws which force pornography upon poor and minority neighborhoods denies the residents of those neighborhoods their right to equal protection under the law. When the State insists that pornography must remain in certain neighborhoods, it denies liberty to the women who live there, yet are afraid to walk on the streets at night to visit friends or neighborhood stores. It denies liberty to women outside the neighborhood who are afraid to come into a hostile and crime-ridden area after dusk. Women become second class citizens who cannot exercise freedom of association because of the conditions of pornography. The State also denies a decent quality of life to residents who must daily confront the urban blight, crime and violence that have entered their neighborhood with the adult bookstores and theaters. The individuals who live in these neighborhoods are singled out for special treatment because they live in certain neighborhoods which city officials have decided are unworthy of protection from the harms of pornography that they actively seek to eliminate from wealthy, politically powerful neighborhoods. The residents of South Minneapolis who cannot afford to move are individually and collectively hurt because of their residential status.

Indianapolis City-Council General Ordinance No. 35, 1984 might be interpreted to provide a remedy for the individuals who have pornography forced on them because of the discriminatory application of zoning laws. An individual who was forced to look at pornography could sue the perpetrator and/or the institution who was forcing pornography on them under Section 1. Sec. 16-3(g)(6) which provides a cause of action for the forcing of pornography on any woman, man, child or transsexual in any place of employment, in education, in a home, or in any public place. The individual would have to prove that the material in question met the definition of pornography set forth in the Amendment and that force was included. An injunction against the further forcing of the pornography could be obtained if all the elements of the case were proven.

Residents of South Minneapolis could also use the trafficking provision of the Amendment to sue the sellers and exhibitors of pornography who are denying neighborhood residents privacy and safety and profiting from trafficking in women. If a citizen could prove that something met the definition of pornography in the Amendment and that it was not an isolated passage or an isolated part of the work as a whole, they could get an injunction against the further sale or exhibition of the material, as well as damages from sellers and/or exhibitors. There is presently no other way to make the sellers and exhibitors responsible for the harm that they are causing to neighborhoods. This Amendment, rather than leaving neighborhood residents with legal remedies that have no effect upon the problems that plague them, empowers citizens to take action in a socially responsible and legal way to improve the condition of their lives. Good laws create legal remedies that closely match the injuries being addressed. The Amendment provides a more effective remedy than either zoning or obscenity laws because it directly meets the needs of neighborhood residents in deteriorating, crime-ridden neighborhoods without any other current possibility of legal relief.

The Amendment is also more effective because it acknowledges that the government has the *right* and the *power* to provide legal remedies for actual injuries under a narrow and carefully drawn definition of pornography and to draft local legislation which it believes will move us toward achieving equality for all citizens, including women and neighborhood residents who live in the zones surrounding "adult" establishments. Defenders of pornography often argue that there are no grounds upon which pornography can be distinguished from other forms of speech. Justice Brennan, in dissent in *Paris Adult Theaters v. Slaton*, 413 U.S. 49, 84 (1973) stated that "[a]ny effect to draw a constitutionally acceptable boundary of state power must resort to such indefinite concepts as 'prurient interest,' 'patent offensiveness,' 'serious literary value' and the like. The meaning of these concepts necessarily varies with the experience, outlook and idiosyncrasies of the person defining them." Judges assume there [are] an infinite number of standards, which is the same as saying there *are* no standards. The defenders of pornography accordingly argued that all forms of expression, whether in politics, art or pornography are equally legitimate. In this view, the only principle acceptable in a democratic government is that there *are no principles* on which to say that one publication is more damaging or dangerous than any other.

This view is incorrect. We have never assumed that the law cannot intrude to protect the life, health and safety of its citizens. "What is government itself," asked Madison, "but the greatest of all reflections of human nature? If men were angels, no government would be necessary." *The Federalist,* #51 (New York: Modern Library, n.d.), p. 37. A government that sought to abolish any consideration of principles would not be worthy of being called a government. Elected and appointed officials are invested with an obligation to do far more than preserve the security of citizens, although pornography does threaten that. They are also charged with insuring justice and equality.

The Neighborhood Pornography Task Force wants its government to insure justice and equality for all citizens, especially women, because it believes that no one will be free until we all are free. It wants this court to recognize the injustice of pornography and to uphold an Amendment which provides legal recourse to its victims. Many of those who deny the government's power to recognize the injustice of pornography or its ability to rectify those injustices are the same people who want statutes prohibiting discrimination in housing or education, or criminalizing the selling of children and wife battering. As Justice Burger noted in *Paris Adult Theaters,* "[s]tates are told by some that they must await a 'laissez-faire' market solution to the obscenity-pornography problem, paradoxically by people who have never otherwise had a kind word to say for 'laissez-faire' particularly in solving urban, commercial and environmental pollution problems. *Idea in America* 37 (1972)." One must ask why material that graphically, brutally and systematically subordinates women sexually must remain forever beyond the bounds of legal remedy?

Releasing controls over pornography will not cause it to diminish in quantity or in violence toward women. As long as small producers can make a film like *Deep Throat* for $25,000 and bring in a return of $50 million in the first few years,[5][6] there will be a strong incentive to make them. As long as pictures can be taken of a wom[a]n while she is being raped, and sold on the commercial pornography market as protected free speech, men will continue to rape women and sell the pictures of the rape to pornographers. And as long as the pornography industry is as large as it is, women will be coerced into making it. The industry could not exist without coercion.[6][7]

By refusing to act, the legal system assents to the brutal torture of women and children in pornography. It assents to the forced deterioration of neighborhoods. It assents to the denial of a decent quality of life for the poor and non-white who must live in neighborhoods with a high concentration of pornography. It assents to the legitimization of rape, battery and sexual abuse of women. It assents to and encourages the proliferation of pornography in a culture that is already highly pornographic.[7][8] Allowing pornographers the right to express themselves through trafficking in women means that the state has *chosen* to protect pornographers' individual rights over women's rights to dignity, equality and freedom and over the rights of citizens in neighborhoods like South Minneapolis to a decent quality of life.

5. [6.] J. Cook, "The X-Rated Economy," 1978 *Forbes* 18.

6. [7.] See Cong. Rec. S13191-13197 (daily ed., October 3, 1984). Senator Specter, introducing the Pornography Victims Protection Act, stated: "People are coerced into performing in pornography largely because a huge national market exists for such materials. Consumers have spent hundreds of millions of dollars to see these magazines, films and videos. Given the enormous profit of such productions, elimination of this type of coercion will require Government action to reduce demand." Ibid., p. S13192.

7. [8.] The pornography industry is an $8 billion a year business. See Galloway and Thornton, "Crackdown on Pornography—A No-Win Battle," *U.S. News and World Report,* June 4, 1984, pp. 84–85.

The Los Angeles Hearing

LOS ANGELES COUNTY COMMISSION FOR WOMEN
APRIL 22, 1985
ROOM 374, HALL OF ADMINISTRATION
500 W. TEMPLE, LOS ANGELES, CALIFORNIA

Commissioners:
Edna J. Aliewine
Maria F. Avila
Gloria Carpenter
June Dunbar
Celeste H. Greig
Miya Iwataki
Anita L. King
Sandra Klasky
Susan C. McMillan
Stella Ohanesian
Helen Paster
Colleen Z. Petty
Myra Riddell
Betty Rosenstein
Maria Contreras Sweet

Board of Supervisors:
Pete Schabarum
Kenneth Hahn
Edmund Edelman
Deane Dana
Mike Antonovich

CHAIR STELLA OHANESIAN: And now I'd like to go on to the set item that is at 11:00 o'clock. And as you know, we have had public hearings before, and as many of you know we have been studying this issue for the past 8 months. Now there are those here today that have not had the opportunity, or were not aware of the impact of this proposed ordinance, and have requested an opportunity to testify. For that reason, and because we want to hear all points of view, and be fair to all, we scheduled this item on our agenda again. Now our concern is that this ordinance be legal and enforceable, and we know that our issue is legitimate and needed. Therefore, as I said before, for those of you who have not signed in, if you will please sign in and identify yourself and your affiliation, and restrict your presentation to three minutes so that everyone will have an opportunity to be heard. And also, in the interest of time, I will ask that the commissioners hold their questions until all have testified. And again, in order to make it move perhaps a little more evenly, I would like to suggest that we have three that are in favor of the ordinance speak, and then three that are opposed to the ordinance speak, if there is no objection to that. All right.

COMMISSIONER 2: Also, as a public commission, your testimony is being recorded and is a matter of public record.

COMMISSIONER 3: I would like to suggest that it be reversed, and start out with three who are opposed to the ordinance and then three who are in favor.

CHAIR: All right.

COMMISSIONER 3: Because I think there are so many people who have expressed dissatisfaction, and I'd like to hear them first.

CHAIR: All right, . . . if there is no objection . . . We are going to have one opposing speaker and one speaker in favor of until we have gone through all of them. And as time permits, of course. You will state your name and your affiliation.

SYLVIA GENTILLY: My name is Sylvia Gentilly. I am from the Wages for House [Work] Campaign, and I have been asked by U.S. Prostitutes Collective to read a statement, and it is within your time frame, I hope. . . . This statement has been endorsed by Black Women for Wages for Housework, Rape Action Project, North American Network of Women Runners, Eighties Ladies, Wages to Lesbians, No Bad Women—Just Bad Laws. USPO is opposed to the Los Angeles County Anti-Pornography Ordinance. We are not proposing a change in the wording of the ordinance. We think the entire concept is going in the wrong direction. We know that even without passage of the ordinance, sex industry workers are already feeling an increased violence against them by men who think they've got society's approval to "hunt down hookers." Women who have worked very hard to get away from pimps are being forced back into dependence on pimps, hoping for some form of protection against these attacks. Women are being brutalized and raped at the hands of some abusive police who operate as though they had the approval of society, including some feminists. The debate alone on the ordinance has caused sex industry workers the price of increased violence and increased dependence on pimps. Surely the County Commission and Board of Supervisors cannot be for giving more business to pimps. If the ordinance is passed, some of the places where sex industry workers are employed will be forced underground, and the workers will be forced underground along with the businesses. It is unrealistic to expect that if sex industry businesses are closed, their workers will automatically find other jobs. USPO has found that the majority of sex industry workers are single mothers with families to support. Some are working regular jobs, but that's not enough to make ends meet. Juveniles who run away from home, where many are being raped and physically or psychologically abused, have nowhere to go.

The anti-porn ordinance won't solve the problems these kids face but will compound them. We often hear the sex industry workers bring crime into the neighborhood, that they are hooked on drugs, that they spread VD. First of all, the U.S. Department of Health has found that only 5% of VD can be traced to prostitutes. Secondly, drug dependence among sex industry workers is no higher than among other sectors of society. Thirdly, most of the sex industry workers, according to the U.S. Attorney General's office, is not controlled by organized crime. In fact, the anti-porn ordinance's creation of another underground industry will pave the way for organized crime to move in.

Women work in the sex industry because they need the money, not because they like the sex. If they are forced to work underground, they will be forced to do more work, use their bodies more, and be required to work in prostitution. They could be forced to do porn shows that they are currently refusing, because that's the way for owners of these businesses to make it worthwhile for them to operate an illegal business.

If it is an anti-pornography ordinance that sends sex workers underground in the first place, it's absurd to think that they will soon be [suing] if they object to the working conditions. The porn ordinance will force the closure of some indoor sex industry operations. What happens when these closures take place, as has happened in Sacramento, is an automatic increase in street prostitution, because women have to find a way to eat, pay the rent, feed and clothe their children. Increases in street prostitution mean more police crackdowns that are usually ineffective, as well as costly to the taxpayer, and more pimps. In fact, the statistics point to the enforcement of prostitution laws as selective and racist, with the majority of those jailed for prostitution being Black women. Therefore these crackdowns can immediately be seen as an attack on the Black communities, where unemployment is high, and few options are available for young Black people.

Many women in USPROS network are Black, and are particularly concerned about the use of "enforcing the porn ordinance" to further harass the Black community. Feminists who support the porn ordinance say they are not attacking prostitutes, yet the ordinance explicitly calls for the enforcement of the prostitution laws.[1] They can't have it both ways.

The anti-porn ordinance blames porn for problems we face as women—discrimination, violence, rape, harassment. We disagree. Poverty causes these problems. The present cuts in welfare, food stamps, health and other human services are increasing the number of sex industry workers, while other women are forced to take low-paying, dead-end jobs. Many of us are forced to put up with sexually and physically abusive husbands, to tolerate lecherous bosses, to keep quiet about rape and sexual assaults.

Instead of spending so much time and money on an ordinance that will harm those most vulnerable among us, why not put the resources instead into establishing homes for juvenile runaways, tuition decreases so that women aren't forced into the sex industry to put themselves through school, as they are currently doing; increased welfare payments so that prostitution doesn't have to pick up the slack for inadequate payments; funding more low or no-cost child care programs, so that women aren't forced into the sex industry to pay for the kind of quality child care they want for their children; increased availability of decent low-income housing; elimination of wage differentials among men and women. As long as women are earning 47 cents to every dollar that a man earns, as is true in California, you will find women in the sex industry. Support the inclusion of women's financial contribution to the economy in the gross national product, so that we aren't always viewed as scroungers when we win payments for services.

In other words, get to the roots of the problem that creates the situation where women are vulnerable and therefore exploited in the porn industry. Some who support the ordinance try to get support for their claim by listing how difficult and dangerous it is to be in the sex industry. It is difficult and dangerous, however, the anti-porn ordinance will not

---

1. The ordinance does not call for enforcement of prostitution laws.

solve these problems, but compound them. Band-aid solutions like the anti-porn ordinance just won't work. Worse yet, it will increase the violence, coercion and oppression of women who are the first affected by such an ordinance: sex industry workers.

Thank you. . . .

CHAIR: If you'll state your name and your affiliation.

JEFFREY MASSON: My name is Jeffrey Masson, and I'm a psychoanalyst [who taught] at the University of California at Berkeley, [and was] former Projects Director of the Sigmund Freud Archives.

I'd like to commend you first for your stance and the courage it took to take that stance. One defense of pornography maintains that it is only a form of fantasy, not of action. Like other forms of speech then, it must be protected against encroachment on inner freedom. People should be allowed the freedom of their thoughts and fantasies. The perspective from which this is defended is a Freudian one, and Freud's discoveries about the nature of fantasy are often called upon in conjunction with Freudian thinking about women and sexuality. But if we subject Freud's thinking about the nature of sexual fantasies to a more searching examination, particularly in the light of the new documents that have recently become available—I'm referring to my edition of the Freud-Fliess letters which was published this month by Harvard University Press[2]—what is most striking is how far removed Freud's views were from the true state of affairs.

Freud argued that almost all of his women patients' lives were dominated by the fantasy that their father had sexually abused them. At first Freud thought this fantasy was a historical reality: a traumatic memory from childhood. But later he decided he had been misled by the women, who had been impelled to create these fantasies because of the nature of female sexuality. Let us listen briefly to Freud on the question directly, writing in 1925 in his autobiographical study:

> Before going further into the question of infantile sexuality, I must mention an error into which I fell for a while, and which might well have had fatal consequences for the whole of my work. Under the influence of the technical procedure which I used at that time, the majority of my patients reproduce from their childhood, scenes in which they were sexually seduced by some grown up person. With female patients, the part of the

2. *The Complete Letters of Sigmund Freud to Wilhelm Fliess, 1887–1904*, trans. and ed. Jeffrey Moussaieff Masson (Harvard University Press, 1985).

seducer was almost always assigned to their father. I believed these stories, and consequently supposed that I had discovered the roots of the subsequent neurosis and these experiences of sexual seduction in childhood. If the reader feels inclined to shake his head at my credulity, I cannot altogether blame him. When, however, I was at last obliged to recognize that these scenes of seduction had never taken place, that they were only fantasies which my patients had made up, which I myself had perhaps forced on them, I was for some time completely at a loss.[3]

Freud's view expressed in this passage—that women invent, out of sexual needs, memories of sexual seduction—has dominated psychiatric and psychological thinking for eighty years. It has dominated as well most major defenses of pornography. It is only in the last few years that women have begun questioning Freud's reasoning. Their criticisms have escalated as we achieve an ever-greater awareness of the reality of sexual abuse in the childhood of many women. On top of this growing knowledge of the reality of abuse came the discovery from the Freud Archives, many of which I published in *The Assault on Truth,* that Freud himself knew that sexual abuse was extremely pervasive in his day, and that it was not fantasy, but reality. However, the theory of fantasy was far more acceptable to the male-dominated medical society of his day. Had Freud stood by his women patients, he would have been totally isolated from his male colleagues, for he would have been criticizing not only their blindness, but also the society they lived in. And in those days, it was simply unthinkable for women who had survived incest to come together and support one another. It was too shameful and deep a secret. But thanks to the women's movement in this country, women are getting together for the first time and saying that it really does happen, and in numbers that make it apparent that we are dealing with one of the most serious problems of current society.

Freud's views about fantasy have been, for the women who know about the reality of abuse, totally discredited. While we may not entirely understand Freud's motivation for his about-face, there can be no doubt that sexual abuse was a reality in his day, as it is in ours, and that the women who came to Freud were not inventing stories, as he claims, but telling him about a painful reality.

Pornography is a record of that same reality, of those very acts that Freud claimed did not exist. By shifting the blame for the reality of incest

3. Sigmund Freud, *An Autobiographical Study* (The Hogarth Press, 1959), pp. 33–34.

on the inventive power of the woman, saying that it was her wish, her fantasy, Freud provided many men with a convenient explanation for the occasions that from time to time surfaced. They could be dismissed as the accusations of "hysterical" women, women who were—[4]

CHAIR: Mr. Masson, it is time. If you could make it brief, please.

MASSON: OK, I'm sorry. All right, I'll end by simply saying that pornography in my opinion is the expression of sexual abuse, no more a fantasy than sexual abuse is a fantasy. Thank you very much.

CHAIR: And for the opposing point of view.

BETTY BROOKS: Our statement [is] from FACT. I also have a statement from the National Task Force on Prostitution. As the representative from the Feminist Anti-Censorship Task Force, Los Angeles, I wish to register publicly and clearly our opposition to the anti-pornography civil rights law proposed by the Los Angeles Commission on the Status of Women to the Board of Supervisors. Such a law would create a private cause of action for a violation of civil rights, allowing an individual to bring a civil suit if that individual was offended by pornography as defined in the law.

Individually and collectively, we stand committed to the principles of feminism and progressive social reform. We are activists dedicated to eradicating sexism and violence against women, ending the physical and psychological victimization of children, and achieving true sex equity and the freedom of choice in the pursuit and enjoyment of alternative lifestyles and sexual preferences which do not do violence to others. It is in fact precisely this commitment we share that compels us to oppose this

---

4. [The remainder of the statement reads] ". . . sexually needy, and turned for satisfaction to a perverted imagination. Now that we know, today, that this is not so, what has happened to Freud's theories about fantasy? They have not been discarded, they have simply shifted ground. Now, we are told, they are helpful in understanding the nature of pornography. But I entreat you to consider that we may be faced with yet another example of men who exploit and harm women attempting to cover up what they really do by calling it something else. It is not surprising that the philosophy of sexual liberation would call upon Freud's ideas about fantasy, by pretending to protect the rights of women and children to their sexual fantasies. But these were never, according to the historical record, the fantasies of women and children, rather they are the acts of men imposed in reality upon protesting but powerless women and children. I would go further than the feminists who say pornography is the theory, rape the practice, and say that pornography is already the practice. Pornography, in my opinion, is the expression of sexual abuse. It is no more a fantasy than sexual abuse is a fantasy. It is a problem of male psychology, and while women may have an obligation to explain it, they are surely under no obligation to tolerate its persistence. Pornography is an act, and one that abuses women by its very existence. To tolerate pornography under the guise of protecting freedom of expression, or freedom of thought, or freedom of fantasy, is to subscribe to a view of fantasy that has no basis in reality, and has simply served as yet another instrument of women's subjugation. I urge you to think about it more deeply than the Freudians have."

proposed law, for in its enactment lies the frightening possibility that the very goals of feminism to which we are committed may themselves become the victim of retaliation through the unintended but entirely allowable use of such a law and its concept by those who hold the attitudes it seeks to repudiate.

Evidence of this unsettling prospect can be found in the support for this approach and these ordinances by forces who do not seek sex equity for women. These forces assisted in the passage of the Minneapolis and the Indianapolis ordinances and totally changed the concept of the ordinance in Suffolk County, New York. We acknowledge that this approach on its face does not ban pornography, however it is defined, from public availability and view. Nonetheless, this law treads on the dangerous ground of specifying what material is appropriate for people in a democratic society to view.

We concur with the assessment by County Council, LA Women Lawyers' Association, and other competent legal experts that the legality and constitutionality of this type of law are highly suspect. This issue will probably only be decided with any certainty by a review and ruling by the U.S. Supreme Court, but such a prospect causes us concern, given the distinctly conservative bent of the Court's rulings in recent years. With the likelihood of vacancies in the near future, we are concerned that those vacancies may be filled by justices who satisfy the current fundamentalist urge to redefine, in a sweeping manner, what is moral and immoral, pure and obscene, decent and pornographic, and right for women to be in this society.

We do not seek to stifle public debate of this issue. In fact it has been our effort to respond to those who had presented feminists as favoring this law. All feminists do not favor this law. We were not asked to submit formal evidence in opposition to this proposed law by the County Commission on the Status of Women, nor have we been invited to submit alternative proposals to the Council for ending violence against women. Therefore, we request that this proposed law be defeated, and before any such proposals be reworked or redefined, that a vigorous public debate be supported by the Board and the Commission considering economic feasibility, community support, and constitutionality.

We also recommend, and this is not in the statement, that in fact the Commission in fact do further work on the health manual, which is a positive point of view of human sexuality, and begin to work on some positive measures, rather than—

CHAIR: Dr. Brooks, can you make it brief, please. . . .

BROOKS: Community education is essential to the health of our society and its citizens. Recognizing this, we acknowledge that few resources have been devoted to bringing about individual and social change as it relates to the issues surrounding pornography. But while we see the need to expand these efforts, we cannot accept such approaches as this one, one which allows individuals to use their personal preference to decide for all others what we should say, should read, or be seen, one which provides an official government standard of what would be permitted to exist in our minds, one which attempts to empower one group to silence another simply as a matter of personal choice, one which seeks to regulate thought, expression and ideas. . . . Thank you . . .

CHAIR: And in favor of the ordinance, [Anonymous].

UNIDENTIFIED COMMISSIONER: What are these that you are passing out?

ANONYMOUS: I am appearing before the Commission as a private citizen, and would ask that my name be deleted from the public record to protect my privacy and the privacy of other innocent victims.

CHAIR: You do realize this is being taped.

ANONYMOUS: I do realize that it's being taped. I would like my name deleted from the record.

CHAIR: All right.

ANONYMOUS: I'm here today to tell you that it shouldn't hurt to be a woman.

I'm here today to tell you that pornography is a problem that is not a problem that is restricted to those in poverty. The trafficking in pornography is so pervasive that it extends to victims that live in hundred-thousand-dollar homes, in the suburbs, in nice neighborhoods, the nice families, people that are married to minister's sons.

It's been my personal experience that I had to find the collection that you're looking at. It's been my personal experience that I've had to look into the faces of those women and know that someone that I care about has cut me out of his life because of reliance on his five-fingered lover and the centerfolds in those books. Anyone that tells me that pornography is not desensitizing, so that a man would choose a unidimensional, glossy, ten-and-a-half by twenty-four-and-a-half-inch centerfold with a staple in her navel over a real live, flesh-and-blood wife, who would do anything in her power to please him, doesn't understand the depth of the despair of those that are victimized by this.

Victims of this are cut off by society—nobody wants to hear what our secret is. I think a bill like this gives victims in our society, a society that protects those that are harmed by having actionable recourse to courts, should be protected by the type of legislation that you're putting forward. We [need] to be able to protect ourselves, and also the innocent children who can also become party to this terrible, terrible tragedy. . . . Thank you.

ROSEMARY PAGOSLEV: My name is Rosemary Pagoslev, and I speak on behalf of Bread and Roses Bookstore, where I have been employed throughout some of the time I was in law school. . . .

As a long time feminist, I am pained by the tone of controversy among feminists over this issue, and I sympathize with the plight of the Commission in having to make a decision where there are strong women on both sides of the issue who are asking you to go for their side. As a woman, and the mother of a daughter, I am concerned about violence against women. I myself was raped when I was seventeen, and I'm sure that there are many violent forces in the society that could be stopped if the right form were found to stop them. But I think that pornography is a jellyfish. When we see it on the beach it looks shiny, when you get up close to it, it looks slimy, and when you try to touch your hands on it, it stings like hell.

We are opposed to the ordinance. As booksellers, we are especially concerned about the possible passage of an ordinance that would seriously impair the right of our citizens to read the literature of our choice, and those citizens that we are speaking of are the women of Los Angeles. If you enter any ordinary bookstore—Crown or Dalton's—you will see books filled with men's concerns and men's names. Women's entry into the world of publishing has been very recent, and with a few major exceptions, has been primarily of only the greatest, and among those, women who were using men's names in order to get published. Just as women's literature has been late coming into the mainstream, books about women's concerns have been absent from the bookshelves. Most bookstores, when they have a women's section, are talking about books to do with pregnancy and child care, and a lot of those are written by men.

We believe that this ordinance is vague and unconstitutional. When there was the hearing at the County Board of Supervisors, one of the supervisors said that he didn't care if it was unconstitutional, that they would fight it out in the courts. What we are concerned about is the effect that this ordinance will have on women if it goes through, while they fight it out in the courts, trying to find out if it's unconstitutional.

We are afraid that our civil liberties will be attacked. We are afraid that what happened to us in December at the bookstore, which is, we had a display of books on sexuality in the window, the window was broken and all those books were torn up. We are afraid that if this ordinance goes through, women's bookstores will become like the abortion clinics, a target for terrorism from people who think that they are fighting a holy war.

And finally, I would like to say, to remind you of the words of the poet Heinrich Heine, who said, "wherever they burn books, they will also in the end burn human beings." Thank you.

CHAIR: And in favor of the ordinance, we have Pauline Bart.

PAULINE BART: I'm Dr. Pauline Bart. I'm a visiting professor of sociology in women's studies at UCLA, the school from which I obtained my Ph.D., and a visiting scholar at the Law School at UCLA. In the fall, I was [a] visiting scholar at Harvard Law School. It is because I am a rape researcher—my last study was based on interviews with 94 women who had been raped, or whom somebody had tried to rape—as well as a woman, a mother, a grandmother, that I support this ordinance.

It is because I have been studying the law that I know the difference between obscenity law and this ordinance. And this is why I support the ordinance.

It is because many of the women who were raped [in my study] were told, some with a gun or a knife at their neck or their head, that they were going to enjoy it, and they were told that they had to tell their assailant how much they were enjoying it. One such woman who was a professor of philosophy was told to "have an orgasm" with a gun to her head. It is because these women told me that it was harder to tell their assailants that they enjoyed the rape than enduring the actual assault itself, it is because of these women who shared these experiences with me, that I support the ordinance.

It is because when a potential rapist tried to pull my 75-year-old mother into his car in Santa Barbara, telling her what a good time he was going to show her, and she was able to get away and memorize the license plate number of the car, and went to the police, and they didn't believe her, and they did pick up the man, and it was only when he skipped bail that even the people she knew, her friends, believed her, and because this is the message that pornography sends out, that I support the ordinance.

I have been talking with women who have been raped, or have been attacked and avoided rape, for approximately the past ten years, and it is to make their suffering meaningful, that it may be used so that other women will not have to endure this, that I support the ordinance.

It is because I am a researcher on pornography as well as on rape, and because having read pornography I have read many of the excellent studies on its effects, and knowing that pornography is pro-rape propaganda, that I support the ordinance.

It is because Diana Scully, a professor of sociology at Virginia Commonwealth University, who has been talking to rapists who are imprisoned, wrote the following that I support the ordinance. She wrote a letter to Gary Meltzer, the City Attorney of Los Angeles:

> Per your request, enclosed are copies of two papers presenting my research on convicted rapists which might be useful in your deliberation on the anti-pornography proposal. You will note that the relationship I draw between rape and pornography is indirect but powerful. That is, violent pornography trivializes rape and encourages men to think of violence as a part of normal sexual relations. It also provides the language which men can and do use to neutralize and justify their sexually violent behavior. When rapists I studied told me that despite the injuries they have been inflicting on their victims, "She enjoyed it," they were describing the same image projected in pornography. Essentially their culture had taught them to expect women to enjoy rape. I hope this city, and in this case the County of Los Angeles, decides to act in favor of this proposal.

It is because Professor Diana Russell found that 10 percent of the women in her sample drawn from San Francisco households who had been asked to do, or demanded to do, something that they did not want to do because the person asking them had read about it in pornography—and this is just the tip of the iceberg; there had been many women who had been pressured to do things that didn't know that it came from pornography—that I support the ordinance.

It is because of one of the rapists that they honored . . .

CHAIR: Dr. Bart, your time is . . .

BART: I am going to read you the last verse of a poem that I, too, wrote in response to, in this case, not being allowed to speak at Cal State at North Ridge in the symposium on pornography. . . .

> I may not speak to sex educators
> about pornography;

> I may not say that pornography
>   leads to desensitization
> Which leads to violence against women and children.
> Pornographers having protected speech
>   leads to women having unprotected lives.
> My speech is not protected
>   because my speech may lead
>   to censorship.

. . .

SANDRA HALE: I'm Sandra Hale. I teach women's studies at Cal. State, Long Beach, and I want to say . . . that I have taught against pornography for a very long time . . . . But since then, some events have changed my life and have turned me around with regard to anti-porn ordinances.

I'm speaking to you as the Director of Women's Studies at Cal. State, Long Beach, who was stripped of the directorship in 1982 for refusing to fire, or more correctly not rehire, part-time faculty under attack from right-wing fundamentalists. My opposition to the anti-pornography ordinance comes out of this experience of teaching women's studies at CSULB, a liberated program still under attack. Fundamentalists' objections to classroom ideas and texts precipitated an unprecedented purge of feminist faculty and created a demoralizing chill in our classrooms. Those of us who teach or taught at CSULB know who will be the first to lose basic freedoms if this ordinance or others like it are passed.

Pornography and the degradation of and violence against women must be stopped, but as I was quoted in the LA Times as saying, "The strategies we use must not abridge our freedoms." In February, 1982, a complaint by fundamentalists was lodged with me, then Director, against faculty teaching our Health, Bodies and Sexuality courses. Specifically, the complaint was directed at Professor Betty Brooks for her alleged use of pornographic material and her advocacy of lesbianism. And then, after viewing the African liberation posters on my office wall, they later broadened the complaint to include Marxist revolutionary thought. We later learned that members of the Grace Brethren Church of Long Beach and California Eagle Forum had been collecting the titles of our textbooks for over one year before that. Jessica Shaver, the spokeswoman of the time, indicated to me that she had taken two of Professor Brooks' texts to the police, to the Veterans' Administration, to the hospital across the way, and also had complained to the campus bookstore about carrying those books. She was attempting, she said, to have the books—which were *Our Bodies, Our Selves,* and *Sapphistry*—deemed pornographic and censored from sale from the bookstore. She was hoping to show that Professor Brooks was selling pornography to minors, that is, if anyone in her class was 17 years old. She also was attempting to show that by reading the books in question, students were being encouraged to do physically harmful things to themselves. After I informed Shaver and her committee that a teacher has the right to use any book or ideas in a university classroom, she and the committee took the complaint to the University president. The rest is academic history. The ACLU has taken our case, claiming it is one of the most significant free speech cases in decades.

Our program at CSULB was not unusually radical. In fact, we're nearly identical in curriculum and faculty styles to San Francisco State and Sacramento State. But we were considered in the vanguard of sexuality courses. Now, with all the changes, we offer fewer sections of Women and Their Bodies. We have had to cancel a course entitled Women's Sexuality. . . .

What I'm asking of you is that the ordinance, if passed, would make us very vulnerable to a suit. In fact, Schlafly's Eagle Forum, the chair of the California Eagle Forum is already suing the California state university system for allowing an illegal women's studies program to exist, citing some of our literature. And I have given you a list of those books that they are attempting to censor. We implore you therefore, not to give them any more weapons in which to file such suits against us. We are in favor of opposing pornography, but within a feminist framework. Thank you very much. . . .

TOBY SUMMER: . . . I was born and raised in Los Angeles. I've been a lesbian for twenty-five years. It cost me an education that I never got. And part of the result was that I wound up being a hooker. I did it on Sunset Boulevard in Santa Monica, in Venice, in Whittier, and this is the first time I have told anybody.

I would like to submit for you something that I bought today, so you know what I'm talking about. For you, my money, for your knowledge. I have flagged some pages. I want you to look at the rapists. This is what their speech looks like. I want you to look at the women bound in children's cribs. I want you to look at the transsexuals who are raped. The pages are stuck together because they use the pornography and re-sell it. I want you to look at the clothespins on women's breasts. I want you to look at the women who look like little children, with dolls, in the center-fold.

I want you to look and to study. I want you to see what they mean when they say they own women. I want you to look and see the gags in their mouths so they can't speak, and the bathing caps that they stick in their mouths, and then pull over the tops of their heads so they can't breathe. And I want you to look at what it's like to be a mother in this country: "Knocked Up Mamas." And defend it.

. . . Defend it. Thank you.

CHAIR: Pat Brown. All right.

PAT BROWN: [I am a] member of the National Organization for Women's National Board from the Southwest Region. In September, the National Board for the National Organization for Women formed a subcommittee to look at the issue of pornography and the proposed ordinances. After a great deal of study and a great deal of debate the National Organization for Women decided at this point in time to not support these ordinances.[5] Now that is not because we do not care about violence against women. It is not because we do not care about the sexist images that are portrayed in pornography. It's simply that we feel that this is perhaps not the best solution to the problem.

Some of the questions that we raised, and I raise them for you today, are: what would such an ordinance do to sex education in this country? What would it do to erotica? How do you define erotica, as opposed to pornography? And I don't believe anyone has done that to this point in time. What would it do to women's erotica? What would it do to lesbian erotica?

Having worked for many years as an ob-gyn nurse practitioner, I can share with you that the young women in this country have very little sex information and education, know very little about their bodies, have very little sense of identity of themselves as persons apart from men, who are still giving in to the lines that women of my generation, 35 years ago, gave in to then. If you love me, you will. Those kinds of lines. I submit to

5. In 1984, National NOW passed the following resolution: "Resolved, that NOW finds that pornography is a factor in creating and maintaining sex as a basis for discrimination. Pornography, as distinct from erotica, is a systematic practice of exploitation and subordination based on sex which differentially harms women and children. This harm includes dehumanization, sexual exploitation, forced sex, forced prostitution, physical injury, and social and sexual terrorism and inferiority presented as entertainment. Pornography violates the civil rights of women and children. Be it further resolved that NOW supports education and action by the chapters on this issue."

you that it's far more important at this point in our history, for us to support increased sex education for young people, both young women and young men. That we help young people learn how to parent, learn how to talk with one another so that they can share their feelings and not take out their anger in violent ways, as men currently do.

Combating sexism in the media has been a long, enduring battle that women still must fight. It is not just pornography that perpetuates violence, it is comic books, it is television, it is film. I would encourage you to look at another way of dealing with this problem. I would encourage us to fight to enforce the laws that are on the books; to encourage stiffer sentences for offenders, such as life in jail for rapists, or death, or castration.

I would encourage us to also look at ways of enacting new laws, such as putting a tax wherever violence is perpetuated, including in comic books, and using the revenue from such tax to support programs that help to retrain, reeducate and prepare women to enter a workforce where they're hireable so that they do not have to make a living off of their bodies unless they choose to do that knowingly. And that that revenue be further used to increase the number of shelters that are so sorely needed for battered women and to enact shelters for other women for whom no shelters exist, such as battered lesbians. Thank you.

CARL FABER: Dr. Carl Faber, in favor of the ordinance.

I am a clinical psychologist and teacher. I have been doing psychotherapy in this community for almost 25 years. I have been privileged to work with many, many dynamic and thoughtful women. An almost universal problem is a problem of damage to the self in the women I've known deeply. The self is silent, the self is broken, the self is numb. The self in our work is something like the religious notion of the soul, an inner form or sound or crystal structure that tells us what to do, who to be, what direction to go in. We need it to know who we are. The self is driven into seclusion and damaged by shame and humiliation. When it happens we pull back, we cover up, and when it happens a lot, we go deeply into ourselves.

Well documented, and I've listened to it for years, is the damage done by rape, emotional and sexual incest in families, battering, and almost every woman's story of having had sexual intimacy hundreds of times when they didn't want it, because they were afraid of a man's rage, or afraid of losing him in a privileged male society. Less documented is the damage done by the image-disrespectful attitude, inhuman attitude, attitude toward woman as only a sexual object that is now poured out of adult theaters and has become a face of mainstream movies. It's a part of marketing everywhere you go in every department store.

And it leaves women who are thoughtful and open in a desperate dilemma. If they are open to the humiliation that they deal with daily, they feel pain and impotent rage. The only way they get relief from that is by fragmenting themselves, dying inside and giving up—despair versus suicidal desperation.

I believe that this community should be a respectful place to live in for all of its members, and I urge you to support this legislation to give women a safe place to live. . . .

CHAIR: Welcome. This is Sally Fisk, and she represents the Stonewall Democratic Club.

SALLY FISK: I find the climate I'm sitting in here this morning one of the most frightening I have ever been subjected to. I feel like we are attempting to resurrect witchburning. I feel like there is an Oliver Cromwell in the shadows. I am appalled to find myself defending the literature put on your desks. It is repulsive, it is repugnant, and if it is repressed, I will see the poems of Auden and Rich, the drawings of Kate Millett, and the works of many of my friends suppressed.

I would like to read you a statement. As southern California's largest gay and lesbian political club, Stonewall has taken a clear and outspoken stance over the past decade on women's issues. As an individual, both politically and as a newsperson, I have worked to find ways to quell the increasing wave of violence against women. I see no solution to that problem in the proposed law. It is hard for me to imagine many women affected by violence utilizing the law. Conversely, it appears to me to be a clear threat to the civil liberties of writers, publishers and book sellers. While it is an inventive attempt to circumvent the First Amendment, it is a reprehensible one. It would create a chilling climate for all of us who write, who publish, who sell literature.

Most particularly I perceive it as a threat to gay men and lesbians who only recently have moved out of an oppression sufficiently to begin to fill the body of literature and to have their own bookstores. Almost as much as I abhor gratuitous violence and the objectifications of women, I abhor laws which tamper against our freedoms assured us in the Bill of Rights. Such laws do spiritual violence to us all. Every woman among us would be better served by a continuing effort to examine and change the texture of a society which fosters a rage against women and its individuals.

Stonewall Democratic Club as a body has voted its opposition to this law and made a commitment to oppose its passage with all possible efforts. Thank you very much.

CHAIR: And speaking in favor of the ordinance, Dr. Gail Stevenson.

GAIL STEVENSON: I'm a licensed clinical psychologist, and I've been in private practice in this community for approximately ten years. . . .

Mostly what I want to bring to your attention is the very negative destructive effect of pornography on women. As Dr. Faber so eloquently stated, pornography produces deep shame in the personality of women. Historically, women have been able to deny this shame simply by identifying with and acknowledging their inferiority in the culture. My impression of the last six or seven years, as women no longer accept the position of inferiority, is that they are also not able to defend against the shame that is part of their personality. . . .

From my clinical experience, I would say to you that there is no doubt in my mind that women as well as men are deeply harmed by pornography, and I think that this vehicle of the legislation that you are considering provides a much needed vehicle for those who would try to seek remedy against those who harm them with pornography, and I would strongly urge you to pass this resolution, or this ordinance.

CHAIR: And our last speaker against, opposing the ordinance would be Carol Soble. Are you ready to speak now, Carol? You would like to wait until all of the others have spoken? The others are all . . . well, I mean this is the last one for the opposing viewpoint. . . . [inaudible audience comment]. Pardon me, we have the procedure set up that we will have a fa-. . . [inaudible audience comment]. But Sylvia Gentilly has spoken before, and Betty Brooks has spoken before. You know our time is limited.

UNIDENTIFIED COMMISSIONER 2: Madam Chair, I would like to know who is running this hearing. I believe that we are running this hearing for the public to give their testimony, and a tit-for-tat was not what we had in mind. We are listening to testimony from the general public, and I believe we have called on Miss Soble several times. In the interest of time, I think we ought to get on with it, and not worry about how many people are for or against, speaking. I resent having someone from the audience try to run how this is going to be heard.

CHAIR: Would you like to speak at this time? . . . [inaudible audience comments]. Dr. Brooks, if they had one person to speak, and you had ten, would you feel comfortable if they had the last word? . . . You're out of order. . . .

All right. Carol.

CAROL SOBLE: Thank you. My name is Carol Soble. I'm the associate director of the American Civil Liberties Union, Southern California. . . .

I'd like to echo the opinion that this Commission has from the County Counsel as to the problems facing you. I find the preemption problem insuperable. But setting it aside for the moment, I'd like to go to some of the other issues that I think are problems.

One, of course, is the issue of vagueness. The other is the issue of overbreadth. I have heard people speaking for this ordinance in other forums say that when people raise the specter of the repression of women's literature, that that will not occur, because the EEOC, the Equal Employment Opportunity Commission generally, does not recognize same sex oppression. But this is an enormous difference between the law as it is presented here in Los Angeles and as it has been presented in Indianapolis, where it is now before the courts. And that is the fact that Los Angeles has nothing approximating a local Equal Employment Opportunity Commission. So there is nothing preventing people from doing what's now happening in Long Beach, and what has happened in Oakland, California where feminist books have been taken before the school boards in communities throughout this country. To move to have books by women, about women and for women brought into court by other women, who disagree with those books, to move to have books around gay and lesbian literature the subjects of litigation by other people who oppose gay and lesbian literature—

I think it's important in your debates to also recognize the impact of the First Amendment. It is not an anomaly, as it has been presented. It is a principle that is as relevant today as it is before in our history.

I think too, that there's been a confusion of terms. I have heard people say that obscenity and pornography are not the same thing, and I would agree with that, and that this is not obscenity they are talking with, this is pornography. I would disagree with some of that, and I think the confusion is best illustrated by the arguments that are being made about pornography and obscenity, using the example of Linda Marchiano. Linda Marchiano has been a victim of coercion in pornography; I don't want to debate that, but clearly, it is without doubt, a fact that the movie which she did, *Deep Throat,* has been one of the most widely publicized obscenity convictions in recent times.[6] I think there was a confusion of terms

---

6. Some prosecutions of *Deep Throat* for obscenity resulted in convictions. See, e.g., U.S. v. Battista, 646 F.2d 237 (6th Cir. 1981); U.S. v. One Reel of Film, 481 F.2d 206 (1st Cir.1973). Most did not. See, e.g., U.S. v. Various Articles of Obscene Merchandise, Schedule No. 2102, 709 F.2d 132, 13 Fed. R. Evid. Serv. 816 (2nd Cir. 1983).

there. It is obscenity. Catharine MacKinnon has said that obscenity does little harm. I would disagree with that. Nevertheless, I think that we have to be careful not to deal with those illusionary terms.

Pornography will not go away. I think women already have an opportunity to access the courts. But pornography will not go away, so what we should really concern ourselves with is how we will change the attitudes that foster inequality against women in this society, and I think that is best done through education.

No matter how many times we call pornography "conduct," it remains words and images. They are negative words and images. I don't disagree with that. I don't like pornography, but nevertheless they are attitudes deserving of First Amendment analysis. If they are not to have First Amendment protection, then they lose that protection through First Amendment analysis, and there is none of that applied here—no stringent tests to prevent the First Amendment from being given a blanket exception. Thank you.

CHAIR: Thank you, Carol. Peter Bogdanovich, speaking in favor of the ordinance.

PETER BOGDANOVICH: In the name of freedom of speech, a lot of people are being silenced in Los Angeles. In the name of sexual freedom, a lot of people are being sexually enslaved and abused. Most of them are women. Both those in pornography and those in legitimate entertainment are included.

Since Dorothy [Stratten] was killed,[7] a lot of women have written to me or told me what *Playboy* has done to them. It exploits them—their bodies, their minds, and their dreams. Even if they manage to avoid personal liaison within the sex factories, they spend the rest of their lives trying to forget it, or live it down, or cover it up, or get away from it. Other young women have been tricked, pressured, blackmailed into pornography, and they have trouble, there's trouble getting them out. Actresses who consented to some nudity in legitimate films, pictures of this have been put into pornography without their consent. Cybill Shepherd had that happen to her when, from a picture we did together—and believe me, if I had that scene to do over again, we'd just as soon not do it naked, because it wasn't really necessary.

There are lucky ones who won lawsuits. They could afford lawsuits, but didn't repair what happened to them. Since my last testimony, I've

---

7. See Peter Bogdanovich, *The Killing of the Unicorn* (New York: William Morrow, 1984), which was submitted to the Commission. Dorothy Stratten, who appeared in *Playboy*, was murdered by her pimp husband.

been in touch with many people in the entertainment field about this ordinance. They, along with the people that I'm mentioning, the silent people, they're all afraid to come down here and tell you exactly about their experiences, although they want the law, they think it would improve their lives professionally as well as personally. Women who were in pornography are afraid to speak out because it will call attention to their past, which will destroy the margin of legitimacy that they have been able to establish for themselves. These women live in fear of exposure, and there are a lot of them.

The pornographers and their supporters are so powerful, and the connection between the pornography industry and the legitimate entertainment industry is so intimate, that directors and producers and writers and creative people of all kinds do not feel able to take a stand against pornography because they're going to be blackmailed by legitimate studios, distribution houses, etc. Some say, "Just wait till I get this distributed, then I'll be free to go down and tell you what I know," or "I'm waiting to sell a TV show, and then I'll be able to come out publicly for the ordinance." The real story is that people are intimidated out of speaking by those in power over their lives—in this case, powerful corporations that control expression in this country, and sexual so-called expression is, first of all, very big business.

When feminists say that pornography is not speech, it is silence, they are speaking not only for all women, but for those in the entertainment industry as well, the ones that are silenced out of coming down here to tell you, this afternoon, that they want the pornographers stopped. Thank you.

CHAIR: Thank you very much. I am going to have to, we simply do not have, time to listen to all of the others, who are all in favor of the ordinance. We will have to do this at perhaps the next meeting. I would like to allow 15 minutes for commissioners to ask questions. If there is no objection.

UNIDENTIFIED COMMISSIONER: I object strongly to continuing this in the next meeting. . . .

CHAIR: Well, I will call upon them. . . .

PATRIC MAYERS: I'd rather stand. Good morning. Thank you for allowing me to speak. I'm speaking in favor, and I have several reasons that have not been touched upon this morning. I am president of one of Mayor Bradley's commissions, and through two years ago was a senior consultant for State Senate President David Roberti. At that time, while with Senator Roberti, we have throughout the state a terrible, rampant prostitution problem, particularly in the Hollywood area. And after considerable investigation, the entertaining of all kinds of expertise, we felt that one way to go about this heinous problem in the community was to go after the infrastructure of prostitution, which is the pimps. And through my work Senator Roberti authored, and was eventually passed in both houses, signed into law by Governor Jerry Brown, a mandatory first time conviction, one year prison sentence for pimping. And I would present to you and suggest that we have a parallel situation here. Going after the worst elements in publishing, proselytizing, the distributing is an apt way to go.

My interest in agreeing to Senator Roberti's instructions to make something of this, and let's see what we can do about prostitution, has to do with the fact that my wife, May Ann, married a man a year before I was married to her some six years ago, was at gunpoint forced to commit fellatio on a gentleman who eventually was sentenced to Atascadero. And when the police came to his home in the Hollywood area, his bedroom walls were just plastered with *Hustler* extracts, depicting women's breasts, he mutilated, sliced off, all kinds of strange instruments in their vaginas and rectums and baseball bats and pens and things like that. We had a very disturbed person here. And I would suggest that this kind of material that fans the flames of very disturbed minds, and with total respect to the First Amendment people here, the few among the several in opposition, I would suggest that we have a dreadful problem. And there are victims all the time, there are victims like my wife, who seven years ago was terribly violated and still sleeps badly as we approach this day.

Thank you very much for your time, and also I would urge that this be done with dispatch, that the quicker this is done, fine. And I don't see that we have to hear the eventual constitutionality of this ordinance. If Rosa Parks had feared the constitutionality of her sitting in the back of the bus, she never would have gotten on that bus. Thank you very much.

ELANA BOWMAN: I am a member of the WAVAW[8] Coordinating Committee [and] the National Lawyer's Guild. I want to tell you about three specific cases from my practice and from volunteer work at the Domestic Violence Project of the Los Angeles Free Clinic.

Currently, one of my divorce clients is a battered woman and is attempting to deny her husband the legal right to visit their children, since

8. Women Against Violence Against Women.

she recently discovered that he had molested both of the children. During their marriage, his pattern of abuse was to treat her especially kindly for several weeks, taking her to dinner and paying her compliments, then turning on her, picking a fight, and beating her. Then he would resume months of indifference and coolness. During one period of this very nice treatment she discovered hidden behind his bureau a number of Spanish-language pornography magazines. One was of bondage and whippings, and it was entitled, *Nasty Wife*. A few days later she found a knife and a rope under their bed. She had never seen a rope in their house before. The following day her husband began calling her a nasty wife for the first time in their marriage, and telling her that she needed to be punished for all the bad things she did to him. That night she took her children and moved to a battered women's shelter and started a divorce proceeding.

In a second case, a psychiatrist brought one of his patients, a woman in her sixties, to his home for several therapy sessions. During one of these sessions, he showed her a series of pornography slides telling her she was sexually inhibited, and this treatment was beneficial. He then raped her, and held her in his home for the entire night, and raped her throughout the night while pornographic slides were automatically shown in the same room. He released her in the morning, saying the experience was part of her treatment.

In the third case, I was working up the papers for a restraining order at the Domestic Violence Project, when a woman began telling me that her husband confessed to her that he had raped his daughter from his first marriage, and that he served time for it. She asked him how he could do that to his own blood. He answered that it was all right, that the little girl hadn't minded it, and that he had enjoyed it enough for both of them. He had seen the pictures of it, and when girls did it enough, they liked it, and that they really did like it or they wouldn't do it in the pictures he had seen. We talked more about that, and I asked her if she thought that the porn he read was any cause of what he had done. She said, "Of course," and he had those magazines now, and she had had enough. She had a little girl too, and she was doing all she could to stop him from getting to her daughter.

This debate has been focused, as with all progressive legislation, on the damage done to the rights of the oppressors. In 1964, the focus was on the rights of racist motel owners to refuse public accommodations to blacks. In the '70s, the focus was on the employer's free speech right to sexually insult women at the workplace. Now, the focus is on the rights of the makers and distributors of porn, not on the rights of the women who are its deliberate victims. Thank you. . . .

DANI ADAMS: I'm the director of Women Against Violence Against Women in Los Angeles. WAVAW is a feminist educational organization [that] does not have occasion to deal directly with women who are survivors of violence. However, those of us on the coordinating committee are activists who are also involved in other areas of the women's movement: self-defense classes for women, rape crisis services, battered women's shelters. We hear women's stories, and we have read feminist essays written by women who have talked with more women.

We have also read all of the scientific studies that I'm sure you're all familiar with. So we know that women are being raped, beaten and murdered at rates that are epidemic. Nearly 50 percent of us will be raped, over 60 percent of married women are physically abused by their husbands, and 25 percent of our children are sexually abused before the age of eighteen. We know that men read more pornographic literature than news magazines. We know that boys get their early sex education reading *Playboy, Penthouse* and other pornography, all of which shows women willingly submitting to everything from pseudo-rape situations made to look romantic to being tied or chained, to being whipped and cut and mutilated. We also know from studies that men who viewed sex-violent material tended to be more stimulated by the idea of rape and less sympathetic to the victim. And we have learned that anywhere from 30 to 70 percent of men in those studies admitted that they would rape if they could get away with it. We also know that people of all ages learn by reading books and looking at pictures. Otherwise, why do we have schools?

As feminists, we know that attacks on women take many forms. Job discrimination, sexual harassment on the job, harassment on the street, battering, rape, torture and murder. WAVAW knows as well the continuum from objectification of women to violence against women that the print and film media bombard us with continually. And we know that what we do in our lives affects what we see in these media. And beyond any doubt, what the media shows us affects what we do.

Those who oppose this ordinance, when pressed, usually admit they are against any such law, and it seems they are willing to do and say anything to stop this ordinance. Most of their arguments have been used before, in opposition to civil rights laws and consumer protection laws, to name just two. And some of their arguments are just plain insulting and off the subject. We feminists in favor of an ordinance are not talking about erotica or educational photos, or sex, or prostitution, or homosexuality, and we're certainly not talking about obscenity. Most of us are not sexually repressed, and we are aware of the possibility, as they say, that someone may try to use this ordinance against it, but I'm sure unsuccessfully. . . . I think this ordinance as it's written will confine itself to harmful material, and if there's anything in this ordinance that's illegal or unconstitutional, the courts will find it. That's not our job.

We've been told by some feminists that we should talk about this issue some more, and that we should be doing public education. They also say that this won't stop violence against women. Women have been talking and educating for years. It's time for something more. We know we can't stop all violence in one step, but it's defeatist to do nothing. This ordinance will give a woman who is harmed the individual power to sue for damages, no more and no less. . . . That's what we want to see. We must take the first step to break the circle of violence. Thank you.

CATHARINE MacKINNON: I would like to respond very briefly to a couple of the legal points that have been raised and to say something about the design of this ordinance in general.

We have heard numbers of attacks on this law this morning that are very wrong on the way it would work, and on who would be able to bring claims, and on what kinds of materials the law would most likely apply to. Most broadly, we have heard attacks on this proposed ordinance that are essentially based on the evils of existing law, some of the ways existing laws have been abused. Those laws are prone to that kind of abuse. And at the same time, the same people have suggested that we should enforce existing laws, which is a little ironic.

Most broadly, I have heard support for pornography in a way that suggests to me, putting it together with what the psychologists have mentioned, that very often people who are abused by a system respond by identifying with the abuser and by defending the source of the abuse. Women fear that any time we try to change the situation in which we are abused, it may be made worse. What we're attempting to do here is to change the existing situation so that there will be any chance that it will ever be better. And that's true both legally and on the level of direct action against violence.

I'd like to talk for a minute about how narrow the law is that we have proposed, particularly in light of the kinds of abuses that women have mentioned this morning.

Under our definition, it is entirely unlikely that the definition of pornography would apply to what is called mere nudity. It is also very unlikely that it would apply—it would not be legal if it were to apply—to all sexually explicit materials, whether or not women are subordinated in their making, distribution or use. That it doesn't apply either to the violence-only materials, it doesn't apply to ads, most media, or a great deal of violence in mass media.

In addition to that, we have the force provision, which would not apply directly to materials that are simply on the newsstands, that somebody simply comes on to, or that are on someone's wall. Under our assault provision, it is sufficiently narrow that it wouldn't apply to all the situations in which women don't know where the assault came from, aren't able to track it down to specific pornography.

The coercion provision, that is for women who are coerced into pornography, would not apply to things like simple pressure, and frankly, it would not apply to those circumstances in which women are coerced by poverty, by economic desperation. It would set a base for their working conditions, even those it does not apply to—as I'm sure you know, it does not apply to live sex.

So what we have, then, is the trafficking provision, which would permit women to address the evils of pornography that you have heard about this morning [that cannot be addressed] through those direct provisions. The trafficking provision however—it, itself—doesn't apply to possession. It doesn't apply to consumption. It applies to the people who push it. It applies to the pornographers: the makers, exhibiters, sellers, and distributors.

You've heard a lot of abuses today. Some of them would be actionable under this law, but those that would not be, are the ones that both point out how in fact narrow this law is, and how it could not be abused in the ways people have suggested to you that it could. But also that, through the trafficking provision—even though it does not address consumption, does not address possession, and in that sense does not go to free choice—it would address problems, including abuses that . . . are not actionable under [existing] law. Thank you.

B. J. CLING: My name is B. J. Cling. I am a clinical psychologist in private practice in Los Angeles. I recently had a throat operation, and I'm having a problem here for a moment. I'm also about to graduate from UCLA Law School, and I have done a post-doctoral fellowship at USC in the Department of Psychiatry and Law. Following that I was on the clinical faculty there for two years. In my part of practice, and more specifically, in my work at USC I worked with sex offenders, mostly child molesters and flashers, and I also evaluated a number of rapists. I feel that what should be considered here is balancing the First Amendment against what I think is a very greatly underestimated harm to women.

I would like to say that, as a psychologist, I was frankly unaware of the enormous part that pornography is playing and has played in the minds of the sex offenders who I evaluated. And this is because, at least for me, it was only when I went to UCLA and took a course in which this problem was addressed, that I began to think back to the use of pornography with these men who I had evaluated, because as a psychologist this was never discussed. We didn't even look for it. So it was only when it was told to us incidentally that we discovered it, and it wasn't until I recently started thinking back that I realized there was a lot of it, and that it's grossly underestimated.

For example, one of the many child molesters who I evaluated told me that his modus operandi was to have young girls, six and seven years old, he would befriend them. He was a man who was about forty. He would befriend them, and he would have them come over to his house and he would pay them to clean his house, you know, a quarter, a dollar. And he would casually put around pornography on the living room table, and then he would open it up for them, and then he would try to get them to pose for it, like they were in the movies. This I did not really piece together until recently as the use of pornography. It's a very clear use.

Another example, actually this comes from my private practice. There are several patients of mine who habitually use pornography and have severe sexual problems. One is, as a matter of fact, a homosexual who uses constant violent pornography to excite himself, and it is impossible for him to now make love with his lover, who he loves. It's only possible for him to have violent sex with people he doesn't know.

Another man who uses pornography at least twice daily, who's a fine upstanding citizen, finds it impossible to relate to women in any normal way. And it is my belief now that this has to do with the constant recurring of these sexual images in pornography that has taught him what sexuality is all about, which he finds impossible to have with a normal woman. And that is probably because he's not willing at this point, I hope, to force someone to do those things with him, and no one has voluntarily been willing to do those things.

Anyway, I guess I would just say in summary, that I feel that psychologists, and I plan to help educate them, [must] become aware of the part that pornography is playing in a sex offense. You will hear much more testimony as to its harm. It's just that, as psychologists, we have been in ignorance of this. Thank you.

SARAH SCHULTZ: My name is Sarah Schultz, and I'm a psychiatric nurse, and the only organization I've been involved in lately is Students Against Violence at Cal. State, Northridge. I work in a hospital where I had an instance happen that really made the whole issue of what I was supporting at school come into my life.

I overheard half of a phone conversation with one of the young housekeepers, and she was telling her friend, "I know it's pornography, is what they're trying to do." And it was like I didn't want to be in tune to what was going on, so I tried to turn off the conversation, and afterwards I asked her if she was all right. And she proceeded to tell me her friend, who's on welfare, has three children, saw an ad in the newspaper. It said "Girls, Girls, Girls." And she brought it in and showed it to me, and it's very typical in all the newspapers: Modeling, $300 a day. And she felt she could get money for her children for Christmas for presents. She didn't have money. And so this young lady that I know was trying to talk her out of it, and it went on. I would see her every once in a while. I don't see this particular person on a daily basis. It's more like every three weeks or so. And each time she began telling me the persuasion that was going on, and I could understand how easily a young woman could slip into this.

She began by going for the interview, and they made pictures of her, and paid her the money and told her they were going to make her a star. And it seemed all—everything seemed all right. So she proceeded to leave, and they said, by the way, we may have some lingerie ads you could do for us. We need you, just take your clothes off. I want to see if there's any marks on your body. She did that, put her clothes on and left. And all along this young woman that I know is trying to talk her out of it.

Well, it got to the point where they started at one location. Then they began to tell her she could become a star on cable television. They took her to another location that—all I know is Melrose near La Cienega, looks like a library, and this young lady I know was taken along one evening, hoping to recruit her. But she didn't get involved in it. She described it as looking like a library. It was run by an Asian man, a black man, and a white man, and an Indian man. And it was very sophisticated as far as [being] computerized and how the doors are very secure. Each room had names on 'em. It was sadomasochistic things that were going on.

She came home and when the woman I know did not get involved, the young woman who was involved in all of this was given "punishment" for not having the friend come along. She was then, began to be threatened. The young woman came home with welts on her arms and the young woman I know kept saying, "they're beating you." And she's saying, "No, no, it's all right. It's all right." She pulled her shirt up quickly and saw there's welts all over her back. There's track marks on her arm, and then she confessed to her that she was told there would be harm to her children if she didn't cooperate. And it's to the point of immobilization.

This young lady, I consoled her as much as I could. I talked with a police psychologist that I work with, and she said that the police wouldn't get involved because it is pornography. I felt totally helpless. I contacted Women Against Violence Against Women, and got the phone number, gave it to this young woman, and they've been supportive of her.

OK. And I just feel like this ordinance is so important because this is going on every day, especially here in Los Angeles. Real important. Thank you.

CHAIR: Thank you very much. And we have one more person, attorney Gloria Allred.

GLORIA ALLRED: Morning. I'm just going to take a few seconds rather than the three minutes, because I just was here this morning to give testimony, but I have been so impressed by the personal testimony of those people who came to speak in support of the ordinance, to speak in support of it from their own personal experiences—either they have had as victims of pornography, or as part of the family, or as a psychoanalyst or members of the psychological community who have treated such victims—that I think I would like to see their testimony in support of the ordinance given the most weight. And I just leave you with what Golda Meier said quoting Hillel, "If I am not for myself, who will be? If I am only for myself, what am I? And if not now, when?"

CHAIR: Thank you. And we thank all of you for being here, because we need all these different points of view in order to have a workable ordinance. . . .

The Massachusetts Hearing

BOSTON, MASSACHUSETTS
MARCH 16, 1992

REPRESENTATIVE BARBARA HILDT: Thank you, Mr. Chairman. Mr. Chairman and the Committee, thank you for hearing testimony on House Bill 5194, "An Act to Protect the Civil Rights of Women and Children."

I wish to begin my testimony with a statement of facts. Fact: Every twenty-two days a Massachusetts woman is murdered by her husband or male partner. Fact: In 1989, violence against women forced more than 21,000 women to seek shelter from batterers in Massachusetts. These women were caretakers of approximately 32,000 children at risk. Fact: The Massachusetts Department of Social Services substantiated that 22,532 women were physically or sexually abused last year, a 19% increase over the year before, an epidemic of violence that threatens our families, our schools, and our communities. Fact: Abused children are seven times more likely to commit suicide and twice as likely to abuse alcohol or drugs. Fact: Pornography is a $10 billion a year industry and it is growing. Fact: Pornography in the past two decades has increasingly depicted images of violence against women and children and deemphasized its sexual content. Fact: Each and every time a child is depicted in a pornographic image, that child is being sexually exploited and abused.

I appear before the Committee today to testify in favor of House Bill 5194, "An Act to Protect the Civil Rights of Women and Children." This legislation, as its title suggests, will permit individuals who can prove that they have been injured by pornography to seek civil damages through the courts. Opponents of this bill will claim that the First Amendment protects their right to portray women, men and children in any manner they see fit, regardless of how they damage the lives of others. But no one has the right to scream "fire" in a crowded theater, because of the injury they may cause. And the pornographer should not profit from human suffering and hide behind a veil of constitutional protection. Each of us is ultimately responsible for the injury we cause.

This bill defines pornography as the graphic sexually explicit subordination of women, men and children. Under this new law, it shall be considered sex discrimination to coerce, intimidate or fraudulently induce any person into performing in pornography. It shall be sex discrimination to force pornography on a person in any place of employment, education, home or public place. It shall be sex discrimination to assault, physically attack or injure any person in a way that is directly caused by specific pornography. It shall be sex discrimination to defame any person through the unauthorized use of pornography of their proper name, image or recognizable personal likeness. It shall be sex discrimination to produce, sell, exhibit or distribute pornography in such a way that it causes harm to another person. Libraries and academic institutions in which pornography is available for study are exempted from the provisions of this bill.

Let me emphasize that this proposed law will allow individuals, primarily women and children, to sue for damages if they can prove that their civil rights have been violated by the production, use or display of pornographic materials. This is not a bill about censorship. It is a civil rights bill—which is a critical distinction for this Committee.

The Committee will hear testimony today from a variety of people who came forward, sometimes at personal risk, to describe their personal experience with pornography or have studied this issue and have concluded that new law is needed to contend with some of the damaging consequences. The damage done to the lives of women and children is significant. It is long-lasting, and we can do something to restore the rights of those who have been so damaged. I urge the Committee to listen to this testimony carefully and to evaluate the merits of arguments in favor of this law and to issue a favorable recommendation on House Bill 5194.

. . .

REPRESENTATIVE SHIRLEY OWENS-HICKS: Thank you, Mr. Chairman, for taking me out of turn. I'm here to be recorded in favor of House 5194. . . .

REPRESENTATIVE MARY JEANETTE MURRAY: I do want to be recorded in favor of House 5194, a bill that I think is long overdue, and we ought to do something about it. . . . You're going to hear a lot of testimony on this issue today, and I hope that you will take a good look at this issue and give us a favorable on it. Thank you very much.

REPRESENTATIVE MARC DRAISEN: Thank you very much, Mr. Chairman, for allowing me to speak out of turn. I will be brief. I guess I'll just start out by saying that I'm here to speak in favor of House 5194.

I became involved in the matter of 5194 when my constituent Professor Gail Dines asked me to attend a screening of a slide show. . . . In the course of that profoundly disturbing slide show, I guess I became aware how either naive or sheltered my own existence had been prior to that time. . . . I would urge all members of the Committee, no matter how difficult it may be, to some time, in the course of deliberating on this bill, take a look at either all or a portion of the images of violence against women which have become routine—not only in pornographic literature, but, to a lesser degree, even in some of the more legitimate media within [this] state and in our country.

It seemed to me then, and at the time after that when I decided to cosponsor this bill, that no interpretation of the First Amendment, as I understand it, could possibly have been intended by the founders of the country to legitimize or make routinely available images which not only so clearly are exploitative and demeaning of women in our society, but whose obvious impact must be to encourage, to reward, or to sanction the behavior of such violence. It seems to me therefore that we must find some way legislatively to address this problem and to eliminate, to the best of our ability, the trade in such images.

Now, having said that, I would state that there are serious and legitimate concerns about this bill that will be aired by many very intelligent and capable people on both sides of the issue before you today. Rep. Hildt and I have had, with a number of people on both sides of this issue, I think a very good exchange several weeks ago, raising very critical questions, reasonable questions, about the definition of pornography from a sexual perspective versus a violent perspective, about whether or not it is most appropriate to approach this issue by eliminating production or eliminating distribution, by whether you want to have sanctions before the fact or after the fact, about whether or not this is best dealt with from a discrimination perspective or a criminal perspective—all of which are legitimate questions. I would urge you, Mr. Chairman, to use your leadership to try and bring forward a resolution and consideration of these questions. Any piece of legislation can be perfected and improved.

However, the central point which I would like to drive home today is that this is so serious an issue, an issue which cuts across simply liberal or conservative lines, that it is in my opinion incumbent upon this legislature to deal with it in some way. And I am confident that a way can be found which is reasonable, from the perspective of our constitutional restraints, as well as which will enable us to eliminate images which certainly encourage the violent treatment and the demeaning of women in our society. I think that House 5194 in its current draft points us along the direction of one possible road toward that objective.

And I would urge therefore the Judiciary Committee to consider it seriously, to take into account possibly amendments which might perfect it in its effort to withstand court challenges, and to report it favorably to the floor of the House. Thank you very much.

WILLIAM HUDNUT: Thank you very much, Mr. Chairman, members of the Committee, my name is Bill Hudnut. I was mayor of Indianapolis for sixteen years, two years a congressman before that, and am now a fellow at the Institute of Politics at the JFK School of Government and a resident of Massachusetts, along with members of my family who are buried out in Holyoke.

I was the mayor of Indianapolis and encouraged an ordinance similar to this to be passed by our City Council in 1984—which it was, by a vote of 25 to 4. Two hours after I signed the bill, there was a lawsuit filed against it and it was immediately thrown into the courts, and subsequently, in later 1984, the ordinance was declared unconstitutional. The reason given by the federal judge was that the language was too broad and vague. We appealed it, ultimately all the way up to the Supreme Court, where the original ruling was upheld.[1] Having some eight years having transpired since then, I am welcoming the opportunity to come to you to say that I don't regret what we did in Indianapolis, and I wish those who are supporting 5194 all success in their efforts here in Massachusetts.

I think that the United States of America is a society which values free speech very much, but not when it goes so far as to dehumanize or demean or degrade other human beings. There are limits that the Constitution and the Supreme Court have placed on free speech. It has already been mentioned. You cannot cry "fire" in a crowded building, because of the harm that may result from doing that, in terms of people getting stampeded at the door. Well, harm can be caused by words and pictures

---

1. The U.S. Supreme Court summarily affirmed American Booksellers Ass'n Inc. v. Hudnut, 475 U.S. 1001 (1986). The entire appellate opinion, with a brief introductory comment, is reproduced in the Appendix to this book on pp. 465–482.

that are pornographic and that in some way graphically and sexually depict, through the materials, subordination of women.

What we're trying to do here, it seems to me, is to connect the fight for civil rights for women to the fight against the blighting influences of pornography in a community, blighting influences that will deny women equal opportunity, which is a civil rights issue. We're not talking here, it seems to me, about an issue that has to do with freedom of speech, so much as we are talking here about an issue that has to do with protection of our community and of women against the poisonous influence of pornography that leads to vicious acts against them in many instances— and you will be hearing some testimony about that.

So, in sum, I appreciate the opportunity to be here. I hope the experience in Indianapolis is instructive. I know that the attorneys who argued the case against our city are in the room, and they won and I lost. But I think this is a battle worth fighting and worth coming around again on, and I would hope that in the enlightened wisdom of you and your colleagues in the Massachusetts legislature would pass this legislation. Thank you very much.

WALSH: [inaudible]

HUDNUT: Before I signed it, I said, "We're not going to put this into effect until we see how this court case is disposed of," because I knew the lawsuit was coming, so it never went into effect, because two hours after I signed it, the lawsuit was filed and it was in the courts, and ultimately the declaration of unconstitutionality was found. So what has happened here is, we're trying to tighten the language, refine the language, define things better, and make it more restrictive so that it can come within the framework of the First Amendment, which we all honor.

There are two or three things that are different. The main thing that's different is in the trafficking provisions. It is limited to that which is depicted—not to words, just to visuals. The second difference is that the Indianapolis ordinance required people to go with their complaint to our Equal Employment Office and then, if that office wanted to take it to a court, they could. Here, they are given the right to take it directly to court. The third difference is that this is a bill that does not restrict the definition just to violence like Indianapolis did.

DiMASI: Are there any attorneys on your side [who are familiar with the law]?

HUDNUT: I think there are some attorneys who are very familiar with it on my side. I'm sorry, I'm just a dumb preacher who fell from grace and went into politics. [Laughter.] Catharine MacKinnon is here and there are others.

This is a situation where reasonable, sincere people of good character and conscience will differ. And I know you have to sort it out, and it's not a black and white issue. There are indeterminate grays here. I think what we have to do is find out where the preponderance of right lies and then move in that direction, according to the dictates of our conscience. That's what we tried to do in Indianapolis. And our sincere opinion—even though it was opposed by much of the media in Indianapolis and even though, editorially, I took a lot of hits for it—it seems to me that somehow the framers of the Constitution did not intend free speech to make it possible for women to be demeaned and degraded and dehumanized in the United States of America.

DiMASI: Let's call from the opposing side. Michael Bamberger.

MICHAEL BAMBERGER: Good afternoon, Mr. Chairman. My name is Michael Bamberger. I'm here as general counsel for the Media Coalition, which is a group of some eight trade associations involved in mainstream publishing, bookselling, video, software, the recording industry, etc. But I'm here even more so as the counsel in the two prior successful challenges of the bill you have before you. Let me very briefly give you a history of the bill and suggest to you why it is futile to put it again to the courts.

Let me say that, to start off with, that the members of the Media Coalition are as concerned about the civil rights of the citizens of the Commonwealth of Massachusetts and desire to eliminate gender-based discrimination whenever and wherever it occurs. But that does not mean I suggest that this group should support an unconstitutional bill.

The bill was originally drafted by Professor MacKinnon together with others in Minneapolis in 1983. In late 1983, it was passed by the Minneapolis City Council and it was vetoed by Mayor Fraser early in 1984, on the ground that while the aims may be laudable, the means were patently unconstitutional. Later that year, the bill, as Mayor Hudnut suggested—slightly modified—was passed by the City-County Council of Indianapolis, Indiana. A lawsuit was promptly brought and each of the courts before whom the lawsuit was heard found it unconstitutional. It was found unconstitutional by the district court, it was affirmed by the Court of Appeals and—I beg to differ with Mayor Hudnut—it was affirmed by the U.S. Supreme Court in what is called a summary affirmance, and thus ended that ordinance.

Two years later, no, a little more than that, in 1988, the bill in substance once again appeared as a citizens' initiative in the city of Bellingham, Washington. It was passed. We [brought] a lawsuit there. The claim was made similar to the position that Mayor Hudnut was making here—the claim was made by many, including Professor MacKinnon at that time, that times were different, the bill was slightly different, the Supreme Court decision wasn't binding. That was all knocked down by the federal district judge there. Judge Dimmick held it unconstitutional, granted summary judgment, and that bill dies.

Thus, the only challenges have been these four challenges and it has been uniformly held unconstitutional. And I should mention, incidentally, that in both the *Hudnut* case and in the *Bellingham* case, plaintiffs' counsel were granted substantial attorneys fees against the cities involved for having to challenge a statute that was unconstitutional.

I urge this group that the Commonwealth of Massachusetts has better ways to spend its time and money than rehashing an unconstitutional bill, and that I urge it, seek some other way, if these harms [are] not already redressed or redressable under the laws of the Commonwealth. Thank you.

DiMASI: [inaudible question]

BAMBERGER: I believe you've all gotten copies of this and what I did is, I attached the various legal opinions. I don't suggest you read them now. The Seventh Circuit Court of Appeals, the federal Court of Appeals, held that the core definition of pornography—which is virtually identical in that ordinance with the one in the bill that you have before you—violated the First Amendment because it went beyond that which could be regulated by the state, basically on the ground that because a view is reprehensible does not permit one to ban it. Therefore Judge Easterbrook said that since the central definition fell, the entire statute, which relied on the definition, fell as well. In the lower court, the trial judge also found that the statute was unconstitutionally vague in many respects and spells it out there as well, and basically that it covers and would restrict the sale and permit the injunction of the sale of mainstream material which is protected by the First Amendment.

DiMASI: Is there anything different about this particular bill, or is it substantially the same as the one you argued [inaudible]?

BAMBERGER: It is substantially the same. I did not argue it before the Supreme Court. The Supreme Court affirmed on papers. The definition of pornography is the same. As mentioned by Mayor Hudnut, there is one difference here, with respect to one of the infractions, that apparently they limit the regulation to pictorial material rather than written material, and as Professor MacKinnon was quoted in the *Times* yesterday, that may make it *politically* more palatable, but it doesn't change the constitutional issue.

[Question concerning the coercion clause is inaudible]

BAMBERGER: My understanding, for example, is that as part of the criminal laws of the Commonwealth, there is a provision which prevents the taking away of one's civil rights by means of coercion. I'm told there is already one in the law. I do not know how it is applied. I have not examined it.

The bill has many parts. One is the coercion issue, which you have raised. Another one is what Mayor Hudnut referred to as the trafficking provision, which in effect permits any woman suing on behalf of women generally to go in and say, "this material harms women," and to try and get it banned throughout the whole state. That there is no present provision for, nor do I believe that can constitutionally be.

[Question on community standards and privacy is inaudible]

BAMBERGER: Certainly the Commonwealth of Massachusetts could give rights to persons whose rights of privacy have been invaded. New York, where I am from, has a rather broad provision that includes not only using a picture without authority but also misusing it—taking it for one purpose and using for another. That has been held constitutional in New York and I presume similar laws, if they are not already in place here, could be put in place here.

[Question inaudible]

BAMBERGER: I believe that the bill is unconstitutional for many reasons. I believe the two core reasons are the vagueness in trying to determine what is covered and the apparent breadth of the coverage.

[Question on whether coercion is already covered under Massachusetts laws]

BAMBERGER: I can't speak about the laws of the Commonwealth of Massachusetts. Many states have laws that say, for example, if you are coerced or duped into a sexual act that's a form of assault to which you have not consented. Therefore, you have a remedy in court and you may well have a remedy on the criminal side as well.

[Question about pornography and its relationship to discrimination against women in physical injury, or discrimination in employment and opportunity]

BAMBERGER: To the extent that I can discern it, the premise of the legislation is that a multitude of harms which have been suffered by women relate to published materials that depict women in a subordinate role, and then from that there follows a whole series of remedies.

DiMASI: Is it that you disagree that that doesn't happen, or do you disagree that it can be defined, what type of information gives rise to that particular kind of subordination—is that what you're saying?

BAMBERGER: I'm in no position to agree or disagree whether in a general sense all these ills can be traced to this source. I'm just a poor lawyer. [Inaudible]

BAMBERGER: I believe that most states have laws that could today be read as Judge Easterbrook set forth. The coercion provision in this bill goes further and says that the fact that the person signed a contract, the fact that the person knew what she was doing, or the fact that the person consented does not prove lack of coercion. One has a problem with that, because if you eliminate all the possible elements you can use to prove consent, it's very hard to deny coercion.

[Walsh question inaudible]

BAMBERGER: I think one of the problems—and that's not speaking as a lawyer but speaking from yourself—one of the problems in terms of analyzing this bill, and grappling with it, that the phrase "sex discrimination" sweeps in a range of harms going from rape at one extreme to humiliation to the having at large materials that one is uncomfortable with, and can I think of a word that can wrap it all up and solve the constitutional problem? No. I think you really have to separate the different concerns and the different rights granted and then see which of these rights are not presently appropriately handled and which can be handled in constitutional [inaudible].

[Question inaudible]

BAMBERGER: Part of them have already been achieved. I presume that the obscenity laws of the Commonwealth of Massachusetts prohibit the sale, distribution, etc. of material that is obscene on the one hand, and probably material that is harmful to minors in terms of minors on the other hand, so that what might be called the trafficking part of the bill here is presently covered fully and it's a question and I'm sure it's well enforced.

With respect to the rights of victims to sue, those who are harmed as a result of someone dealing with obscenity, there are several difficult questions. Number one is the causation question: how can one prove or know that someone did this because of that. There is the continuing danger that you don't want to divert your efforts towards hitting businesspeople because of a harm rather than trying to go criminally after the criminal actor who in fact himself did the harm. But leaving that aside, there have been arguments made at the local level once with certain types of issues, possibly violent obscenity, that if one could prove causation, that there might be a claim there. There are enormous problems with it: constitutional problems, problems of causation, problems of suing the deep pocket and not worrying about stopping the rapist, and so on. So, there are really problems everywhere you go.

I, unfortunately, cannot say, "I have a wonderful solution." One of the attractive things about this bill is it says, "If you get rid of this, a whole major problem of our society may be alleviated." I wish I could say [that], but unfortunately I can't.

[Question inaudible]

BAMBERGER: A statute of limitations—you have rights of the plaintiff and rights of the defendant, and you have to try to balance the two. One of the suggestions that has been made, and I'm not really in a position to speak to it because I haven't looked at it carefully, is to provide some appropriate tolling time during which there is no knowledge of the ability to bring the lawsuit. If this young woman did not know that her image had been retained and put in a video and appears some years later, possibly by a tolling device rather than a broad extension of the statute of limitations may be the way to go. But that is not an area that I have really examined closely.

PAT HAAS: My name is Pat Haas. I live in Brookline. I experienced from 1987 to 1989 in a two-year relationship with my batterer—from the very beginning, I was forced to provide videos for him. He found one particular one very appealing. It was of sadomasochism. He spent hours watching this movie and he then started forcing me to do the things that were in this movie. One night, I spent an evening with him. I had hot wax dripped on me. A couple of weeks later, I was forced to pierce my nipples, I was forced to have sex with other people, it didn't make any difference—men, women, groups. He had me playing watersports games, which is drinking urine. And every time I said no, he would find a way of beating me. Most of the time it was with a two-inch belt. He had knives at my throat; he tried strangling me on occasion. I'd been threatened with a .38. He put a gun at my son's head. At the end of the relationship, one of the things he wanted most was my death, either at his hands or at mine, and I was forced to take an overdose. I was clinically dead for between two and four minutes. I spent 21 days in the hospital. And at this point, two and a half years later, I am still trying to pick up the pieces.

It has been a long, hard road, and this law needs to be passed to stop this kind of man. He did what was in these movies. There are videos of me out there somewhere. There are Polaroids that supposedly were destroyed. I don't know. I was told by the police that if these things come to surface, I can face criminal prosecution for things I had no control over. And he needs to be stopped, and the people who make these kind of movies need to be stopped.

DiMASI: Was he arrested or charged for—

HAAS: He now will be charged. After two and a half years I now have a criminal complaint. I go to a support group for battered women. I have been in therapy for three years. I have a network of friends and family that haven't abandoned me. It has been a long road up.

DiMASI: Is this man in custody right now?

HAAS: No. He's at large, and I don't know if that hold that he had over me is still there. I have not faced that man in a long time. If he said to me, "come back," I would be dead within a matter of weeks. Because that's what he wants from me. . . . He took things straight out of the movies and used them on me. If he had seen a snuff film, I wouldn't be here at this moment. What he has done to me, he has attempted on his own children.

PEGGY CHARREN: I appreciate the opportunity to come talk in opposition to 5194. I'm president of Action for Children's Television which is a child advocacy group, national with members across the country and the support of maybe 50 major national organizations from the American Academy of Pediatrics to the National P.T.A. that have stood with ACT for more than two decades, as we said that censorship was not the way to deal with the problem of children's television and children's media. That you can turn off what's terrible, you can't turn on what's missing, so ACT has devoted its advocacy time to trying to create a market for what was missing.

We recently won a case when we took the FCC to court for its attempt to ban indecency 24 hours a day. We won at the Court of Appeals and we won recently when the FCC appealed it to the Supreme Court and the Supreme Court refused to hear it.

We are opposed to what we think is a misguided effort, although certainly anyone would sympathize with the previous testimony and with women who are abused and with children who are abused in this country. But we're opposed to this effort to increase the banning of speech by redefining pornography as a way of dealing with these problems. We think that censorship is a slippery slide and that what is obnoxious, what's perceived to be terrible speech to one person, may be somebody else's essential education.

I know that isn't in the minds of the people who designed the proposed legislation, but the problem is that censorship statutes can be used by people who have much narrower ideas about what is appropriate to ban. They want to ban, say, an hour show that could be perceived to be pornographic when really it's education about AIDS. And that's the problem with censorship generally. Legislation includes speech that I find important to have in a democracy, and I'm not willing to let this kind of legislation further limit what we can see and hear.

There are already laws on the books I think that can protect people who get into the kinds of conditions that the previous speaker was in, and there are others that we can promote. I think we can promote equal opportunity in employment so that you have people running communications systems, for example, of both sexes, where you are less likely to get programming that doesn't take the needs of women seriously.

Censorship legislation will not and never can take care of the problems of what children see and hear on television or on video or anywhere else, and the fact that the government is willing to step in and make the rules might cause some parents to think they don't have to pay attention, and that would be doing parents a tremendous disservice. Thank you.

KAREN HARRISON: I'm testifying under a pseudonym, Karen Harrison. I live in the New Bedford area. I've had many experiences with sex discrimination directly linked to pornography. Some of these were harmful to me physically, but all of them were harmful to me emotionally. I've had six abusive relationships and four of these six involved pornographic indignities. These are as follows. For each of the men I am going to refer to, I am using their real first names.

The first one was Carl, who was a bisexual child molester. He followed and collected child porn, gay porn and enema porn publications. He forced me to be photographed naked by him. He pressured me to come on to young teenage boys in the town. He'd try to get them home with me so he could get to them. When I would not do this, he would criticize my age, my looks, and would get violent. He also wanted me to come on to hitchhikers he would frequently pick up in the seat next to me. He wanted me [to] pick them up and bring them home and start a sexual session with them while he watched or could join in. When I would not do this, he got angry and violent. These were ideas he read about in gay and kiddie porn publications of how to get victims to come to your home. Porn materials were always kept on hand. He wanted me to do the kinky things that he read about in magazines. I remember one article in particular that he made me read. It was about a man who threatened to leave his wife if she didn't stop [inaudible]. So he began to retrain her. Every time he brought home a certain briefcase it would have a kinky surprise, a sexy surprise, that she would have to submit to. The first surprise was an enema. The surprises got more and more bizarre until the woman admitted that she started to like them and was disappointed if he didn't bring the briefcase home. One of the last surprises mentioned was putting chocolate Hershey's kisses—unwrapped—up the woman's rear end and then she would squat over his face and squeeze them all into his mouth with her bowel muscles. He asked me to do this and I refused.

I was forced to shave my pubic area to look like the little girls in the magazines. He made constant comments in public to peers and family about how much I put out and if it was performed to his standards. Some of the magazines kept in the house were *High Times, Hustler, National Lampoon, Penthouse, Playboy, Swedish Erotica*—Swedish porn and kiddie porn. He forced me to watch him perform oral sex on a [dog]. He molested several children in my care, unknown to me, and I found out [after he] left me. He [found out] and raped me with several of his friends.

The second relationship was with a man named Jim who worked in a bookstore warehouse supply company in the New Bedford area. . . . They had a poor inventory system. He stole porn magazines and books by the boxload. There were stacks and stacks of them on both sides of the bed and out in the rooms where guests, including my parents, could see them. He would refuse to move them and got violent when asked to. He forced me to spend hours and weeks on the beach getting painful sunburns so I would be tan and sexy like the girls in the pictures. He forced me to look at pictures of men and women defecating and puking on each other. He would have parties with his male friends. He would pass these magazines out and give some away as gifts. I was the only female in the room on these occasions. I was forced to wait on them, distributing beer and sandwiches while they openly commented sexually about the women in the pictures. They would get drunk and put me down for not having big boobs like the women in the pictures. If I tried to leave the room or got insulted during any of these times, he would get angry and hit me. I was stupid and oversensitive. Most girls don't care if men look at porn, I was told.

He made no secret of needing these magazines to get turned on enough to touch me. I was forced to participate in a bondage episode that he read about. He forced me to pose nude for a photographer, playing with myself, in Rhode Island for money, all of which he kept because he could not keep a job at this time. He collected these magazines religiously and hurt me if I moved, touched or acted wrongly in any way. I was beaten so severely while I was pregnant by this man that I miscarried and had internal damage and bleeding because I was no longer attractive like the girls in the pictures. They had flat stomachs, I was told. He read a story in a magazine about a woman who would take baths in ice cubes to be cold a half an hour before the husband would come home, and she would powder herself with white powder so she would look dead and [then they had] sex. I was asked to try this.

During all this, he began drinking and gambling heavily. When we broke up, I found an unpaid $500 telephone bill in my name to the 900 sex numbers found in the backs of these magazines.

My next relationship was with a man named Michael. He was a pornographic movie and pornographic magazine fanatic. He collected tapes of porn movies and kept them in our clothes drawers instead of our clothes. He was the most proud of the Traci Lords tapes from when she was underage. He forced me to watch these movies with him and suggested I watch them while he was at work. He would even quiz me when he came home to see if I had. He would force me to have sex with him during these movies in positions where he could still see the movies, or move me to one side so that he could still see them. If I got insulted about this, he got angry and violent and turned it around so that it became my fault and I had to apologize.

He forced me to go to VCR shops and pick out sex tapes with me openly. One movie in particular he forced me to watch and reenact was called *The Story of O*. He threatened to leave me if I didn't perform kinky or [inaudible] acts. During this time, he was drinking heavily and using pot and coke. Another one of the movies he wanted to act all the sex scenes out with me was $9\frac{1}{2}$ *Weeks*.

One of these kinky acts I was forced to do was to cut a hole in an army cot that lined up with his crotch. He would lay naked on his stomach and poke his penis through the hole and I would have to lay underneath and perform oral sex. He read this in the kinky column of a magazine that it was a wife's gift to her husband. He had our sex and lovemaking video-taped and showed it to all his friends the next day while I was at work. He said we could destroy it, but later that day I couldn't find it and he told me to forget about it.

He tied me up and blew strawfuls of cocaine up into my nose and then would rape me. He read this in a porn magazine that said that coke would turn women on and I would not take the coke willingly. He wanted me to do the things he saw the people in the movies do, like have sex with other people, other couples, and especially with other women. He wanted to come home and find me having sex with women like on the tapes. He told me that this was one of his biggest fantasies, and he tried to convince me that it was mine as well. He told me that if I felt guilty about it, he would tie me up and I could pretend it wasn't my fault. He forced me to have sex with sex toys bought through the back pages of the sex magazines. He commented openly about our sex lives in front of me to his friends while high on coke, pot, or [inaudible].

He read a story in a fantasy column of a magazine about a man and a woman acting out rape. He broke into my apartment and tried it on me. He waited until I came home from work and he attacked me from behind in the dark. He would tie me to the kitchen table and blindfold me and leave me in the dark for hours and come home with friends to touch me sexually. This was an idea he read in an article in a sex magazine about brainwashing techniques. He would get high on cocaine and come home and force me to have regular, anal and oral intercourse for hours and hours and hours until I was raw, dry and bleeding. When I couldn't stand the pain he would put cocaine on my vagina so he could keep going. He read this in a magazine that said it would numb me and turn me on. He would tie me up and put cigarettes out on my legs when I refused to have sex with other people like in the movies and threaten to leave me.

He put me in several situations with other people to sexually switch partners, but I always left. He would stay for hours. He would spank me and hit me frequently during sex like in the movies and the articles. He forced me to dress in certain ways, day and evening, like the women in the magazines and movies. He constantly criticized my weight and my figure. I was forced to diet continuously and reminded at the table in front of others what I was eating and how much.

I was forced to be in the room with his male friends and swinging cou-ples during sex videos and wait on them. During these episodes, I was forced to wear outfits and act certain ways at these times like the hostess in those sex movies. He forced me to go to strip bars with him and not get upset or he'd hurt me. One night, he even forced me to dance and strip at one particular club on amateur night. He kept the money that I made.

He would pick and choose collector issues of porn magazines and I was made to look and feel inferior to these women, especially blondes with big breasts and women who posed sexually with other women. I was made to feel inferior to the women on MTV constantly. Magazine pictures and posters were hung on the walls whether I liked it or not. He began touching me in public and wanting to have sex with me on a restaurant table like a scene in a video movie that he made me watch one night over and over and over and over.

My next and final relationship was with a man named Patrick, a police officer. He had a five-year-old son. His magazines were pornographic and mixed with gun and vigilante magazines, and he kept opening them in the bathroom and living room at all times, except when I first met him. I was repeatedly raped throughout every day and several nights with his handcuffs. I was forced to go to strip bars with him and eventually to work there. It was his fantasy for me to strip for others but to go home with him. He lost his job and kept the money I made working.

He would force me to watch porn videos with his son in the next room and then would rape me and use the language heard in the videos. For example, I can't forget, he told me was going to split me in half with his cock and I was a bitch and I was forced to admit I loved it and if I didn't say this, he would hit me and rape me harder. He always spanked me during sex and pulled my hair very hard like in the movies we watched. He would leave me at home with no clothes or blankets to cover up with while his five-year-old son was there so I couldn't leave him. He drank and did coke in secret and took prescription drugs like Valium, Percodan and codeine, and also fed them to me. He had several sex magazines and books on brainwash methods and methods of control. He raped me anally with handcuffs for hours one day while drunk because the magazines told him that a woman's anus is tighter than her vagina and I had refused to have anal sex with him. He touched me constantly in public and in front of his son because the magazine's Kinky Corner said that if you do it in public, it's more exciting. He bought many of these videos from vendors who sold them out of the backs of their vans and at flea markets.

About this time, I began to realize that sex is not love and money can't buy love, but maybe it can buy freedom. So I wanted to make enough money to escape these men and, in particular, the New Bedford area and the life I had led up until now. I went back to the strip bars to make money. I cannot tell you the lie and the fantasy that it is for men. Waitressing, I cleaned the floors and I own a box of men's wedding rings that I found on the floor. I have come to believe from these experiences that most men are scum.

The degradation and inferiority and humiliation of being presented as two tits and a hole for entertainment was not as bad as the sexual harassment I received from the management of these places. Customers are not allowed to touch you, but management can and does. You cannot complain to the Labor Board because they say you put yourself there willingly, and usually it's under the table. I felt worthless, but I need enough money to move and complete college and get a degree.

Because of these experiences I have been made to feel so inferior that I was saving and had planned for breast implants. I had dyed my hair blonde and ruined it at one point. I weighed 86 pounds. I now have severe emotional and medical issues, revolving around the stress, physical punishment and trauma I have gone through. I have come to realize that this pain will never go away. Thank you.

DiMASI: I want to know if any of these individuals have been prosecuted for what they did.

HARRISON: No. They're all walking around. The last one, the police weren't going to do anything about it because he was a police officer and his father was the chief of police for thirty-two years in that town.

DiMASI: Are you still receiving counseling?

HARRISON: Yes, I am. They're helping me emotionally and physically, but no prosecution has been pushed at this point. The battered women's society in New Bedford did try and push for a detective to come to my home and get samples of water and food and it was tested and found to have arsenic at the crime lab in Boston. And it's been a year and we have never heard another thing.

DiMASI: Are you still actively pursuing prosecution?

HARRISON: I'm terrified of these people, the last one in particular. The police officer has a history. He hurt several other women before me. And there's a history on all these men.

DiMASI: Had you ever filed a complaint in the police department where this police officer works?

HARRISON: Yes. They made me submit to having my blood taken and urinating to test the arsenic levels and they made a male detective go in a room with me while I urinated to see that I wasn't poisoning myself. So I was just so victimized by all of this that I moved and I'm just trying to pick up the pieces and try to be a whole person again.

[Question: How long were the relationships?]

HARRISON: . . . The first man, Carl, was five years. The second man, Jim, was five years. The third man was three and a half, and the police officer was between six and nine months.

[Question: What caused you to end each of them?]

HARRISON: The first incident, when I found he was molesting children in my care. I was hurt as a child and I couldn't condone that. The second incident, he was cheating on me, and she got pregnant, and he married her. The third incident, I said pick me or coke. I want a conventional life. No more of this. And he picked coke.

[Question: Was there a possibility of physical violence if you left?]

HARRISON: Yes. I was always told in several of these relationships that no other man would ever have me. It would be him or I'd be dead.

WENDY KAMINER: I'm a public policy fellow at Radcliffe College. I'm an attorney and a writer. I was also briefly of the women's movement against pornography in the late 1970s, and I have some sympathy for women's fears of pornography. Some of it is violently misogynist. I also worked on 42nd Street for several years as an attorney in the New York City Mayor's office and I am here to testify against H5194.

It violates the First Amendment, and I wouldn't worry too much about what the framers thought about pornography. The framers didn't think that women should have the right to vote. This bill is also bad for women. Censorship campaigns in this country, of which this is a part, have always targeted sex education, information about abortion and birth control. This is a bill that both Jerry Falwell and Phyllis Schlafly would love. It demonizes speech, it scapegoats speech, often a quick fix for undesirable behavior. Jerry Falwell, for example, has claimed that sex education makes teenagers pregnant, as some feminists claim that pornography makes men commit rape. In fact, human behavior is a bit more complicated and variable than that. Attempting to control antisocial speech overestimates the power of words as much as it undervalues the right to utter them. The relationship between violence in the media and violence in real life is complex and variable. Different people respond to the same images differently. And while the idealization of violence may have a cumulative effect on behavior, no single image isn't in any simple way the cause of any single act.

But this bill does more than assume, without foundation, that pornography is a clear and present call to sex discrimination. It's said that pornography *is* sex discrimination. Advocates of this bill deny that it constitutes censorship because they deny that pornography is speech—and that is simply Orwellian. The line between speech and behavior is sometimes blurred. Dancing nude down a public street is surely a way of expressing yourself. It may also be a form of disorderly conduct. But if pornography is a form of sex discrimination, then an editorial criticizing the president is a form of treason. If pornography is [a] form of sex discrimination, then by testifying before this Committee, defending people's rights to publish and read pornography, I am participating in the exploitation of women. You might as well make me liable for sex discrimination.

This bill will, in fact, do nothing to eliminate sex discrimination or sexual violence. At best, it is a distraction from the problems women face. At worst, it is a lie. If you want to combat the bad speech that you believe contributes to sexual violence, combat it with good speech of your own. Find a way to introduce programs on violence and changing gender roles in the public schools. If you want to do something for teenagers who are caught up in the pornography business, find a way to provide good schooling, drug treatment programs and foster care for children from broken homes or no homes at all. If you do want to do something about spouse abuse, find a way to increase employment for men and women so that husbands don't come home and kick their wives out of frustration, and wives don't have to stay in abusive marriages because they can't afford to support themselves. Focus on the underlying causes of violence and the actual—not the metaphoric—instruments of it. Remember that in Florida, where some consider rap music too lethal to be legal, almost anyone can buy a gun. Thank you.

[Question inaudible]

KAMINER: I'm an attorney. I practiced law for several years as a legal aid attorney and I worked in the Mayor's office in New York for several years in a special project on 42nd Street in part dealing with the pornography business. I'm also a writer.

[Question inaudible]

KAMINER: I think we should be honest about this, and if you want to make a legislative finding—and I don't know how you'll do this—that pornography causes violence, if you want to say that pornography is sex discrimination, don't pretend that you are doing this consistent with the First Amendment. We can call any kind of speech that we don't like "behavior," and if we do that, we might as well get rid of the First Amendment. There are people who think that feminist literature is an attack on the nuclear family, that it's not just speech, it's behavior. It's socially subversive behavior. It makes a mockery of the First Amendment. Without pornography, we would still have violence against women. The causes are much more complicated and much harder to deal with.

[Question inaudible about coercion]

KAMINER: I would categorize it as a crime. I think coercion and assaults are crimes and they are dealt with [by] the criminal law, to the extent that this bill would deal with coercing people to make pornographic movies. Coercing people sexually is redundant. To the extent that it deals with speech, it is unconstitutional.

We're entering a video age. We're entering what some people consider a post-literate age. A lot of communication is done through film and video images. There are people who think that the work of Robert Mapplethorpe is as dangerous as some feminists think that pornography is dangerous.

I don't deny that pornography may be a problem. We live in a very violent society and pornography is a part of that. It affects every one of us. But I view pornography as a social problem, not a legal problem, by which I mean that it is not a problem amenable to legal solutions. Not as long as we have the First Amendment.

[Question inaudible]

KAMINER: I don't believe the people simply copy what they see in the movies. A lot of us see the same movies and we don't go out and shoot people. I just don't think it's as simple as that. Maybe the acts wouldn't be the same, and people would have to use their own diseased imaginations to figure out what to do, but they would figure it out.

[Question inaudible]

KAMINER: There's a bill before the Senate Judiciary Committee now—the Violence Against Women Act—that is one good way to approach this problem. It makes gender-based violence a civil rights violation in the same way that acts of racial violence are civil rights violations. That is not an act that affects speech. It looks at violence—it looks at spouse abuse and rape and other sexual assaults. I think that's a much better way to approach the problem. It certainly sends a very important symbolic message to people that assaulting women, that assaulting anybody, because of their sex is a violation of their civil rights. I think that's a very important principle.

[Question inaudible]

KAMINER: [They're] calling speech "behavior." That doesn't change the fact that it is speech.

[Question inaudible]

KAMINER: I think the only way you can address the constitutional problems of this bill is to dispense with the bill. I have not addressed the details of it but the problems of it, and there are a lot of them because I think the basic concept of it is flawed. I think you cannot call pornography an act of sex discrimination. I think that is Orwellian.

[end of first tape]

L. B.: [portion not recorded] Once this videotape was on, he would make me submit to various sexual acts on the hardwood floors directly in front of a television set. Since we lived in an apartment building, he was very paranoid about neighbors finding out what he was doing, so he always threatened to "fuck me up" if I so much as whimpered or made any sound above a whisper. Even though the sound on the pornographic tape was off, he continually sent me to the door of the room to make sure the keyhole was covered, the door locked, and/or barricaded, and to listen for anyone walking down the hall. Meanwhile, I was to keep coming back to him to do whatever he wanted sexually. He wanted me to watch how the various women in the video performed oral sex on the men. And then he insisted that I do the same with him while he continued to watch that movie. If I didn't go down on him far enough or hard enough, he would put his hands on my head and push it up and down, sometimes so hard that I thought I would faint. If I gagged or choked, he would pull me up by my hair, throw me back onto the floor, hit and kick me, and verbally abuse me, calling me "worthless," "useless," and "a waste of his time." Then he would make me watch that video again, perform oral sex, and threaten to "break my jaw if I stopped."

Then he would make me turn around, get down on my hands and knees, and he would force intercourse, both vaginal and anal. While he did this, he insisted that I watch that video from whatever position I was in, so that I could learn more. He would not let me get up or change positions, even if I was in terrible pain. He'd ask me which men in that video I liked and whether they were as big or as good as he. Well, I quickly learned to say yes, that he was even better, otherwise the sex would become even more forceful and painful. Again, if I did not perform adequately in any position, he would threaten to go out and find a whore who knew what she was doing, like the women in that video. He said continually that he wanted to turn me out, which meant turn me into a prostitute, and then *we* could make a pornographic movie too. But I had to keep watching that video in order to learn the skills and the techniques.

A number of times after watching the video, he actually took me to some filthy places, often crack houses, telling me that he felt that I was ready, that I was his whore, and that he knew men who would pay big bucks for me. But I had to do it right, I had to please them, or else he and I would be in danger. In hallways, in stairwells, in basements, and bathrooms of crack houses, in seedy hotels, in apartments where sometimes there were small children in cribs, my partner offered me like a prize to numerous men and women. He would force me to strip and seduce them, all the while coaching me, instructing me, talking to me as if from that video, even when he was having sex with other women in the same room. He once traded me for cocaine to a man who forced me to have sex with him at knifepoint. After all this, we went home to the video, that pornographic video, and the abuse continued. My partner pointed out to me what I didn't do right, what I should have done, what I could have done much better. That video became my nightmare. Every time he made me turn it on, I became sick with fear for I knew that I was in for hours of verbal abuse, physical pain and sexual torture. And I was trapped. If I protested, if I tried to leave, if I made but a sound, he would threaten to break every bone in my body and put me in the hospital. And sometimes I wished I *had* gone to the hospital, just to get away from that video. Thank you.

KAREN HUDNER: Mr. Chairman, for the record, I'm Karen Hudner and I'm the lobbyist for the Civil Liberties Union of Massachusetts. We have been a defender of the First Amendment for over seventy years, and we are strongly opposed to House 5194.

This is not a civil rights bill as its title claims. It is an attempt at censorship. It is a resurrection of the infamous Indianapolis pornography statute, which the courts, as you have heard, have already struck down. The ACLU national office filed an *amicus* brief in the Indianapolis case.

I don't think this is a proposal to aid women and children or to prevent violence, but it's really just a justification for censorship measures. I'm someone who believes passionately in the First Amendment, and I'm truly appalled to see a whole generation of young women being taught that censorship is acceptable in a free society, and that creating the potential for ruinous money damages based on the supposedly harmful effects of pornography will not punish any other form of artistic expression.

And I really can speak from experience. When I was in college in the early '50s, you couldn't read *Lady Chatterley's Lover* in this country. We had strict censorship laws, and a friend of mine smuggled that book through customs, thereby risking arrest, and circulated [it] in our dormitory. English majors got put first on the top of the list. I think that what happens and what people always forget is that hard-core pornography exists quite happily underground even when you have very strict censorship laws. In Victorian times, which was the most prudish age that we know of, hard-core porn was widely circulated underground. What happens is that things of artistic merit, things that are on the cutting edge of artistic expression, are the things that always get censored. And I think that what will get censored first is feminist works. They will be the first ones to go under an ordinance like this.

I think also behind censorship drives is a hidden agenda. They mentioned the right wing, the Moral Majority. Two of the books most often banned from libraries [and] schools are *Slaughterhouse Five* by Kurt Vonnegut and *The Diary of Anne Frank*. Now, the Vonnegut book is always banned because it has sex and bad language in it—not too much different, I think, than his other books, which also have sex and bad language. That particular book contains a devastating picture of the fire bombing of Dresden by the American Air Force. The agenda for *The Diary of Anne Frank* is not so hidden. It was banned on the West Coast by a group which said, "It perpetuates the myth that the Holocaust really happened."

I would urge you to give this bill an unfavorable report, and to go forward with things that will really help women, some of the women that you have heard today. For instance, funds for battered women's shelters were cut in this year's budget. In the proposed budget for 1993, the governor removed all the funds for battered women's shelters. Drug and alcohol abuse is very often a symptom or a cause of violence and abuse. I think that if we're serious about it, we will put the funds back in the drug and alcohol abuse programs. Those were cut 16 percent in FY92. And that means that about 6,000 people are on the waiting list for drug and alcohol abuse programs. I think that if you are serious about helping women who have had violence in their lives, these are the kinds of things that you will do. Thank you.

DiMASI: Any questions? Thank you very much.

CATHARINE MacKINNON: Mr. Chairman, I've just given you a resume and a short book by me and Andrea Dworkin on the civil rights approach to pornography, of which this bill is an instance.

Your constituents, the women who have testified to you about their experiences, have told you something of what it has done to their lives to live in a society surrounded by pornography, a society saturated with pornography, in which the pornography currently has more protection than the women do. So long as it is available as it is now, these things they have told you about will continue to be done to them, as they are now being done, and to others like them, because they are women.

I wish I could tell you that this happens only in Massachusetts. But based on the experience that Andrea Dworkin and I have had with pornography worldwide, and in particular with this bill—which leads women to believe that if they come forward, they will be listened to for the first time—we've found that the reach of pornography is nationwide, indeed it is global. It is documented by scholars and researchers from studies, as well as by women like those you have listened to, from their lives.

This empire of organized crime—which is what it is—this practice of abuse, torture and slavery, is nothing other than a technologically sophisticated and highly profitable form of trafficking in women. It first exploits and abuses the women, children and sometimes men in it, in order to make the materials. Then when the materials are mass-produced, so is the abuse, as consumers—as you have heard—act it out and take it out on the women around them in all kinds of ways, from seeing women as less than human, using them as objects for sexual abuse, to rape and murder. By making inequality sexy—which is the very particular thing that pornography does—by making the denigration of women sexually pleasurable to the consumer, pornography generates these massive violations of civil and human rights that you have just begun to hear about today.

Should you need any further graphic testimony, the pornography itself will supply it to you. In there, you will see women and children being violated, being humiliated, tortured, whipped, chained, burned, bound, gagged, suffocated, on a continuum of use and abuse, beginning in objectification like *Playboy* and continuing through racist and misogynist vilification and sadomasochistic abuse, and sometimes ending in death as in snuff films, in which a woman or a child is actually murdered in order to make a sex film.

The proposed law that you're considering today faces that reality and calls it by its real name and would be effective in stopping it.

I have been asked by the Women's and Children's Civil Rights Campaign to speak to you a little about how this law would work. I would like to do that for a couple of minutes, and then I would like to address two of the questions that have been asked by you. One, why is this law needed? Why isn't existing law adequate to this? And the other is the Chairman's question about constitutionality.

This law would give those who are victimized through pornography access to court to prove their injuries and to seek relief. It defines pornography in law for the first time. It defines it as the graphic sexually explicit subordination of women, or anyone else, that also includes a range of abusive, subordinating and dehumanizing presentations. Only materials that are graphic, not simulated or implied, that are sexually explicit— that is, presenting sex acts or sexualized or fetishized body parts—and, in addition, that actually subordinate women, either those in the materials, or can be proven to subordinate other women in the world, are covered. And, of course, if men, children or transsexuals are used in these same ways, they would also be covered.

The first cause of action would give those who are coerced into pornography, through fraud, force or pressure, such as Linda "Lovelace" who was coerced into the film *Deep Throat,* the right to sue both those who did the coercion—what we think of as the lesser pimps—and those up the food chain, who feed off of them, the bigger pimps, those who dignify themselves as publishers, as distributors, those who make the really big money off of women's abuse. To reach these materials removes the main material incentive, the profit, the money—other than the sex itself, which is also an incentive—for doing this kind of coercion. No existing law addresses these materials based on the coercion in them. Anything less than stopping the coerced materials simply encourages the pornographers to violate women and run with the videotape.

The cause of action for forcing pornography on a person would give anyone who could prove pornography was aggressively thrust on them a claim against the person who forced it on them—in their home, in school, in doctors' offices, in employment.

The defamation claim would give women who are used in pornography against their will—who have often been feminists who oppose the pornographers, and have their heads spliced in over other women's bodies, or have pornographic lies written about their lives—it would give them a form of relief where currently none exists.

The claim for assault would give anyone who can prove that specific pornography directly caused their attack or assault a claim against the pornography's makers, its sellers, and its distributors, as well as a claim against the direct attacker. What this part of the law does is it holds the pornographers responsible, under very limited and difficult-to-prove but possible-to-prove conditions, for the devastation they caused. Think about the testimony that you have been hearing today, and the possibilities of proving that each of these assaults were directly caused by specific pornography. They have the specific pornography, they have the assault, and they have what *they have to say* about that cause.

The trafficking provision, which covers, in this instance, *only* the visual materials, provides access to court to seek relief from this massive array of violation and violence, this subordination, and all these acts of second-class status in which pornography is instrumental, when it can be proven that it is instrumental.

Now I would like to talk about the several questions that have come up about whether there is existing legal relief for these kinds of abuses.

This law is needed, we think, because the legal system really is doing nothing effective to prevent or redress injuries like these, like a great many that the women have spoken about this morning. Lawyers . . . are very fond of fancy theories that will make existing law cover all existing problems. But the problems of inequality, that come from being a member of a socially disadvantaged group historically, are not yet very well understood by law. The law has not until very recently been designed with any of them in mind, so it doesn't tend to work well for them. For example, sexual harassment could in theory have been covered by tort law, by a law of assault, or by intentional infliction of emotional distress. But nothing effective was done about it by law until it was called the right name, which is discrimination based on sex. And I remind you that a substantial percentage of sexual harassment is words. Lynching is another example. It should have been illegal as murder, but nothing effective was done about it by law until it was called its right name: discrimination based on race.

"Obscenity" is the only legal name we have for anything like what we have heard here today. But nowhere in the legal definition of obscenity do you find the rape, sexual harassment, sexual abuse of children, or prostitution that we have heard about. In theory, films of rapes, snuff films in which people are murdered, are therefore protected speech. Child pornography could or should, in all of this creative legal theorizing, have been effectively addressed by obscenity law. We had obscenity law. But it was not until the state of New York called child pornography what it is, and legislated against it based on recognizing its harm to children—which is wholly apart from anything the obscenity definition addresses—that anything effective was done about it. That law was opposed by many, including by Mr. Bamberger, who testified earlier today, on grounds that the law against child pornography violated the First Amendment.[2]

The Media Coalition for which he spoke, and which he represents, it might be noted, exists to protect, in quotes, sexually explicit materials. Sexually explicit materials are [also] exactly those which existing child pornography laws prohibit and which the Supreme Court has found consistent with the First Amendment to criminalize. The real name of what we are here to discuss today is pornography, and it is a practice of discrimination, violence and bigotry on the basis of sex. In the face of its overwhelming reality, to say that existing law is adequate amounts to saying that the existing level of abuse of women is acceptable. This shows the worst kind of callousness, human disidentification, and complacency. And it also raises the question, if all these problems—the problem of Pat, the problem of Karen—if all of these problems can be solved by existing law—what L. B. just told you about—why are they not being solved? Why has the pornography industry quadrupled in the last twenty years, as these supposedly adequate laws are on the books?

As the Supreme Court of Canada recognized in its recent decision, finding harm to women and equality as the basis for regulating pornography in that country, it rejected appeals to education and victim assistance as exclusive approaches to the problem of pornography, and wisely noted that what we need are multiple approaches to this problem. We have learned that this problem is socially invisible until women make it visible. This particular law, this bill that you have before you today, which puts power in women's hands, instead of suppressing the pornography, and with it women's injuries, what it would do in reality is to bring them out in the open, as it has done here today. It would bring them

---

2. Michael A. Bamberger argues that New York's law recognizing child pornography as an act of child abuse violates the First Amendment in his Brief on behalf of American Booksellers Association, Inc., Association of American Publishers, Inc., Council for Periodical Distributors Associations, Freedom to Read Foundation, International Periodical Distributors Association, Inc., National Association of College Stores, Inc., American Civil Liberties Union, The Association of American University Presses, Inc., New York Civil Liberties Union, and St. Martin's Press, Inc., as *Amicus Curiae*, New York v. Ferber, 458 U.S. 747 (1982).

out into the light, by making it possible to actually do something effective about it for the first time.

Now with the Chairman's indulgence, I would address briefly the constitutionality question that he raised.

DiMASI: [inaudible]

MacKINNON: I appreciate the Chairman's indulgence. The only constitutional question that has been raised here, and I assume it's the one you want discussed, is the First Amendment. I think that is the only one that's ever been seriously raised.

The First Amendment test that exists in this country is that the harm that materials do is to be weighed against the value that the materials have. And under that test, a great many things have been found not to be First Amendment-protected speech. One of them is child pornography, on the theory that it does more harm than whatever good these materials do as speech—that the harm is too much, we do not tolerate that, whatever speech value these things may have. What the case that has been discussed by William Hudnut and Mr. Bamberger did, was turn that test on its head, and for that reason is simply legally wrong. What it did is, it conceded that pornography causes harm. Indeed, all this discussion about the causation issue—which I must say testimony such as Karen's makes mincemeat out of. I mean, you can only have causation between two things if you can separate them. How do you separate the pornography from her abuse? There is no such separation.

What that Court found in Indianapolis—that is, the Appeals Court—was that pornography *does* cause all the abuses that the women here today have been saying it causes. There is no dispute about it, and there is no dispute about it in the law. [The Court] found that pornography produces rape and sexual abuse. The Court found that it makes women be second-class citizens on the street. It found that it even contributes to unequal pay at work. However, what that Court said is, that *that* merely shows us how valuable pornography is as speech. In other words, the harm that it does is the measure of its value. That's exactly the opposite of the Supreme Court's approach. The Supreme Court's approach is, the harm that it does has to be measured *against* its value. So it's just simply wrong in law. The Supreme Court of the United States accepted it as a conclusion, but did not by its procedure endorse any of its reasons. That's what a summary affirmance does. There was no argument. There were three dissents, saying that they wanted to hear argument, and that was before all the recent changes in the composition of the Supreme Court, so what we have seen here is—

[interruption by DiMasi inaudible]

What [the judge] does is, he transforms what is being done to women into an idea about something being done to women. But in the process, the court accepts that the pornography does do these things to women. Unambiguously.

DiMASI: [inaudible discussion including reading an excerpt from the opinion in *American Booksellers v. Hudnut* by Judge Easterbrook]

MacKINNON: I do believe I'm in the state of Massachusetts where you have a group defamation law, just as a matter of note. As a result, the kinds of materials that he [Easterbrook] is using there as a defense—that is, why it is that this, too, should be protected—are kinds of materials that are already criminal in this state.

Now beyond that, the issue is that what he has done is take materials—see, he slips mentally. Sometimes Judge Easterbrook is able to focus on subordination as an act, and he understands that pornography subordinates women, and he accepts the legislative conclusion that it does. And he stated it in an excerpt that you didn't read—eloquently, vigorously, clearly, and accurately. Where he says, causes rape and injury, causes harm in the workplace, even contributes to inequality of pay, and so on. *He* said that. All I am saying is that, as to the causation question, that Court recognized that we have won that issue. The causation has been established.

DiMASI: OK, let's assume there's causation, what about the definition of pornography?

MacKINNON: Yes. Then Judge Easterbrook went on to disagree with the definition and say that what this does is, it establishes an "approved viewpoint" about women. Basically there are two things wrong with that, legally speaking. One thing is that, once again, he has taken what he had recognized as an abusive act and turned it back into an idea. He doesn't seem to be able to keep a grip on the fact that pornography is being addressed here for what it *does*. One can continue to say the things that are *said* in pornography. What you have to prove under this law is that they are being *done* through the materials.

Part of what Easterbrook was addressing, of course, is the words-only materials. . . . As the trafficking provision mobilizes the definition, what Judge Easterbrook was largely disagreeing with, if you check his examples, are almost all words-only materials. So it was harder for him to get a grip on the fact that we're talking about something being done. But if they're visual materials, it first of all has got to be done to somebody—*done,* or it isn't there. And then somebody has to prove what is done through it. This is a bill about getting access to court so we can try to prove what is being done—that's all. So he was thinking that it was a thought being thought. Now, if all it is is a thought being thought, that's a defense, because no woman can prove that an act was done. You can't prove subordination occurred. So, there are some confusions.

The other thing that's wrong with it, is that nothing requires the State of Massachusetts to be neutral between equality and inequality. And Judge Easterbrook seemed to be of the view that if we legislate against inequality, that's a viewpoint discrimination because we haven't equally legislated against equality, or something. But the state is permitted to take a viewpoint in its law. You're permitted to be against child pornography. You don't have to equally take the view that you can be for child pornography and therefore when you prohibit it, that's an impermissible viewpoint discrimination. So it's completely reversed logic. It is, to borrow a term, Orwellian. It calls things the opposite of what they are, and then says you can't [stop them].

DiMASI: [inaudible question]

MacKINNON: Actually, Judge Easterbrook did not find the ordinance vague. When you read the decision you will see him saying, indeed it is, as he put it, all too clear. It was very clear to him what was being addressed here. It was also, I would add, very clear to the real pornographers who intervened in this action and attempted to say, "Excuse us, but the American Booksellers, I don't know about what it is that they do, but we, the ISSI Theaters, are the real people against whom this is directed, and we would like to be heard as well." Now, presumably—and this is speculation on my part—there was some behind-the-scenes stuff, and [they said], "Wait a second, we the American Booksellers look an awful lot better defending this action than you people coming out from under a rock. You don't make a good presentation in public. You're the real thing. Stay out of this, just let us try to fudge the issue by making it seem as though we are you, and you are us, and anything that prohibits what you do, will prohibit what we do. We put a good face on your business." So, that's a certain way of addressing your question, which is to say, the pornographers know what they do.

DiMASI: [questions concerning the definition of pornography as unconstitutional]

MacKINNON: His resolution was that it discriminates on the basis of viewpoint, because, in our terms, it addresses only the inequality, and not the equality also. In other words, it takes a position by the state against an entire series of, what he called, ideas, which we are saying was a total misconstruction of what the law requires—it requires acts.

DiMASI: [inaudible question]

MacKINNON: What I'm saying is, we can legislate against inequality. For example, sexual harassment is a law against inequality. And it is words. And defendants don't come in and say, "I uttered protected speech, and you can't prohibit my speech based on its viewpoint," its viewpoint being what? Contempt for women, abuse of women, subordination of women, actuated through words. Now that's just to take an example that is overwhelmingly words-only.

There is no First Amendment that says that one cannot take a position against inequality. What we are dealing with here, is a need to do something beyond what has already been done in law, and that is, to take equality into account when we interpret protected speech.

At the same time, in this particular instance, it's important to take into account that women's speech is not protected by the First Amendment. The women you have been hearing from have been silenced under this supposed protection of speech. It is only this bill that makes it possible for their speech to come to be heard and to be free. So there are speech interests on both sides of this thing, but there are no equality interests on the pornographer's side. It's an industry of inequality.

DiMASI: Any questions from the panel? I thank you very much.

MacKINNON: I would be happy to be of whatever assistance I could to the Committee in the future, if you should wish it.

DiMASI: [inaudible question]

MacKINNON: Actually, Andrea Dworkin and I are both leading experts. She is here, yes, in the front row.

ANDREA DWORKIN: I was not going to [testify] because Catharine MacKinnon is really testifying on behalf of both of us. We felt that it was so important that you be able to hear from women who've actually had the experiences.

[Discussion inaudible]

SENATOR POLUMBO: [inaudible question about nude-only videos that are made consensually]

MacKINNON: Actually, they're not covered by this bill—but not because of whether they're consensually made, but because, the way you've described them, if it is nudity only, that wouldn't necessarily be sexually explicit, and it has to be sexually explicit. Nude only is not enough.

PANEL MEMBER: [question concerning desecration of the American flag]

MacKINNON: What [Judge Easterbrook] is talking about there is that one should be able to do something about materials that are produced through coercion. There is currently no coercion-based law that gives somebody who has been coerced into pornography any relation to those materials. That is, because it is her, they are hers. . . .

Okay, now I'll talk about the American flag. You would like me to, so I will. The American flag [raises] a question of symbolic expression—that is to say, when you violate it, what you violate is what it means to you.

POLUMBO: What it means to us collectively.

MacKINNON: Yes, what it means to everyone. So that when it is defaced or violated or mutilated, what is being harmed is its meaning and its place in the collective community. With pornography, we are saying something different, and that is that a woman is not a symbol, a woman is a human being.

Certainly the meaning to all women of the fact that it is possible to violate, mutilate, deface women in these ways is very clear. And the clarity of it is that we are not full citizens, that we do not have full rights, that when these kinds of things are done to us, that our government does not stand up against that. Yes, it has that meaning to all of us that see it. But more concretely, and what this law is addressed to, is the actual injuries themselves, the mutilations, the violations, the abuse, the subordination . . . [end of tape] [gap in recording]

POLUMBO: That's a concern that I have, the plight of women that are indirectly being affected by this, by their boyfriends, or husbands or whatnot is as a result of women engaging in this activity consensually. That's where pornography came from.

MacKINNON: It's been our information that pornography comes from pimps who want to make it and consumers who want to consume it. That is, that it is both supply-and-demand-driven in that sense. It is the pimps—the pornographers—who procure women for use, because they can make money through manipulating the sexuality of men in this entire culture to want to experience their sexuality in this way. And then they do. And then that sexuality is acted out on other women, so that you don't have women in your freely-consenting model waking up one morning and saying, "Today is the day on which I make a free choice. Today is the day in which I'm going to decide whether I want to be a brain surgeon, or whether I want to go and find a man and spread my legs for a camera." That isn't how women get into pornography.

POLUMBO: Are you saying that women in the videos and magazines are all nonconsensual? It's all coercion?

MacKINNON: No. What I'm saying is that the women are in there because men will pay to see the things done to them that are done. That's why they're there.

And in addition to that, I'm trying to suggest that there is a larger social context in which women are valued as and for sex, and that most of these women were sexually abused as children. One of the major consequences of that, that women fight for the rest of their lives, is that it makes you experience that when you're being violated and abused, you're being loved and valued and approved. And so the appearance of consent, which is what they are highly prized for, is then what communicates to the consumer and is part of the sexual arousal and then, the world is to believe that the woman is "consenting" in some free way.

Now I want to be clear, as I attempted to initially here, that our law does not assume that all pornography is coerced. It does not. And indeed does not touch that question. Since there never has been a law that allows women who *are* coerced to bring an action for it, we don't know really how many there are, because there is nothing they can do about it. They are overwhelmingly poor, they are totally dispossessed, largely completely desperate. Many are actually underage. Most of them started as children, so the distinction between child and adult pornography is just the distinction between the same group of people at a later point in time, if they live that long. They are forcibly addicted to drugs, they are physically pimped to men for their own individual use as well as the pornographers for their use. We're talking about a massive group of exploited women here. The notion of consent suggests a form of freedom that is not factually accurate.

The law, as I said, does not assume that everyone is coerced. . . . At the same time, I would urge you to face the reality here, which is that these are not free women. These are not the women with the most choices in society. If it is a free choice, I would like to know why it is the women who have the fewest choices who are doing it.

POLUMBO: [inaudible question concerning payment to women in pornography]

MacKINNON: Yes, very little, most of it skimmed off by the pimp. I would suggest to you, with all respect, that it is the success of the pimps' perspective when one comes to believe that the women are overwhelmingly consenting to it. It's good for business that we think this. That's why the conclusion is so widely promulgated in society that women are doing it voluntarily or freely. . . .

GAYLE MARKELS: Mr. Chairman, members of the Committee, my name is Gayle Markels, and I'm vice president and counsel at the Motion Picture Association of America. And on behalf of the Motion Picture Association, which is a trade association representing many of the major producers and distributors of motion pictures in the United States today, such as Walt Disney, Columbia, Paramount, Twentieth Century Fox, Universal, Orion, and Warner Brothers, I'd like to thank you for this opportunity to appear before you in opposition to H5194.

I'd like to say from the beginning that the Motion Picture Association is not opposed to legitimate efforts to combat violence. As a former prosecutor in New York, I can state without equivocation that motion pictures, books and magazines do not cause crime. Violence and crime have their roots in poverty, drug and alcohol abuse, dysfunctional families, and inadequate schools. Violence existed long before the advent of motion pictures or even the written word. You could ban all motion pictures, you could close every book store and every video store tomorrow, and crime wouldn't go away. It's like so many quick fixes—it simply just won't work.

The Motion Picture Association believes that this legislation, which subjects nonobscene speech to a never-ending cycle of litigation, should be defeated for the following reasons:

First, the proposal is unconstitutional because it goes far beyond what the court has said can be used as a standard obscenity regulation. This extremely broad definition of pornography would subject mainstream filmmakers to civil litigation if a single party believes that the work degrades women or if they believe that they or someone else is harmed by the work. This standard is unworkable. The Supreme Court has repeatedly stated that courts may not regulate nonobscene speech, either by subjecting it to criminal or civil liability, and those points were covered earlier so I'm not going to go into the American Booksellers case.

The definition of pornography, the sexually explicit subordination of women, is so broad and so vague that mainstream producers of motion pictures, books and magazines will not be able to determine what falls within the statute's prohibitions. Under H5194, any woman may bring a complaint as "a woman acting against the subordination of women." Statutes that regulate speech must be drafted with precision. This bill fails to provide adequate notice of what is included. The chilling effect with such a vague definition of pornography will force mainstream producers and distributors to cease distributing their works to avoid threat of litigation.

The potential reach of this bill is endless. Academy Award-winning films such as *The Accused,* which starred Jodie Foster and depicted a rape and subsequent rape trial, could be included. The Academy Award-winning film, *Two Women,* starring Sophia Loren, which depicts the story of a mother and daughter in war-torn Italy, could be included. Shakespeare's *The Taming of the Shrew,* Pat Conroy's *The Prince of Tides, Gone with the Wind,* James Bond, news reports and news footage, paintings, *A Streetcar Named Desire,* I submit even the Bible would fall within the parameters of this bill. If enacted, motion picture theaters and video stores may be forced to close their doors, as filmmakers fearful of prosecution steer clear of the State of Massachusetts.

Moreover, H5194 is bad public policy because it permits criminals to point their fingers and blame their crime on anybody other than themselves. The legislation holds the wrong party accountable. Criminals should be accountable for their crimes, not writers or filmmakers. H5194 doesn't even require that a criminal complaint be filed, or that a conviction be obtained, before a victim may file a lawsuit suing a bookseller or filmmaker. If you want to stop violence against women and children, arrest those criminals responsible and punish them immediately. Ask any cop. Movies don't cause crimes. Bring in the prosecutors. Ask their opinion. Poverty, drug and alcohol abuse and guns do.

Finally, as a woman and a mother, I question whether women need additional protection from the spoken, written and visual media. Historically, women have been protected by society. We've been protected from voting, we've been protected from working outside the home, and we've been protected from higher education. Legislation which puts women on a pedestal rarely improves our status in society. Censorship will not improve the status of women. Protecting women through better legislation, through job protection, through laws against discrimination, through battered wife help—that would make a difference. Further, we all possess the power of the dollar. If you don't approve of a book or magazine, vote with your pocketbook. Go somewhere else. In a free society, we cannot allow one group to silence another. Censorship is a dangerous road. We urge the Committee to vote against H5194. . . .

DiMASI: [inaudible comment]

MARKELS: I would like to say that this bill isn't limited to pornography. The scope of this bill would address mainstream products that anybody finds offensive or degrading. It is not limited to the traditional, court-approved definition of pornography or obscenity. That's why the mainstream film companies are concerned.

FREDERICK SCHAUER: Mr. Chairman, my name is Frederick Schauer. I am a member of the Massachusetts Bar, and I am the Frank Stanton Professor of the First Amendment at the John F. Kennedy School of Government at Harvard University. In addition to serving in 1985 and 1986 as one of the eleven commissioners of the Attorney General's Commission on pornography, I am the author of *The Law of Obscenity, Free Speech: A Philosophical Inquiry* and numerous other writings on free speech, free press, and the legal and constitutional aspects of obscenity and pornography. Prior to coming to Harvard in 1990, I was professor of law at the University of Michigan, and have been a law professor since I left the private practice of law in 1974. Of course, not only do I not speak for the Kennedy School or for Harvard University, I do not speak here on behalf of any individual, corporation, institution, or organization—that being part of my own long-standing practice of never entering into a client or consulting relationship, whether paid or unpaid, believing that such a relationship is inconsistent with my own views about academic independence.

Speaking on behalf of myself, I find it a constant source of astonishment that a society that so easily and correctly accepts the possibility that a cute drawing of a camel can have such an effect on the number of people who take up smoking, has such difficulty accepting the proposition that endorsing images of rape or other forms of sexual violence can have an effect on the number of people who take up rape. We accept that movies glorifying advertisements for tobacco and alcohol may be part of a social problem. But when the social problem is the massive tolerance of sexual violence against women, we as a society are far less willing to see that what are, in effect, advertisements for rape may have a similar effect.

In light of the Chairman's questions of a few minutes ago, I would like to focus just on the constitutional questions, believing that my views about the issue of images and sexual violence are probably apparent from what I have just said.

There has been some—but in my view insufficient—attention to the focus or to the question of the meaning of the terms "graphic sexually explicit." Like many other legal terms, it is likely that that either is, or would in the near future become, a term of art. There is no reason to believe the term "graphic sexually explicit" is drastically different in scope from what exists now within existing obscenity law. Therefore, in light of existing understandings, pursuant to which, although these are controversial understandings, they are existing understandings in the caselaw nevertheless, pursuant to which highly sexually explicit material has historically been viewed as either outside the First Amendment or only on the periphery of the First Amendment. Under existing law, the view that the limitation to "graphic sexually explicit" is irrelevant is plainly erroneous.

Let me talk for just a minute, purely as a predictive matter. As Professor MacKinnon mentioned, three justices dissented in the *Hudnut* case from the decision of the court to summarily affirm. The Supreme Court had a year earlier, in a case called *Anderson v. Celebrese,* said that summary affirmances are not to be taken as having significant precedential effect. In addition, if one takes the views of some number of other justices, Justice Scalia's view—Scalia not having been on the court at the time—that existing obscenity law is problematic, Justice Stephens' view in *Young v. American Mini-Theaters,* that highly sexually explicit material is on the periphery at best of the First Amendment—purely as a predictive matter, it seems to me reasonably likely that the Supreme Court of the United States as currently constituted would uphold a law such as this, given its existing limitations of the graphic sexually explicit.

I do not mean to say that you may not exercise your own judgments about what you think the First Amendment should require or should not require. I do ask that you keep in mind the distinction between what some people are saying that the First Amendment should require, and what it does. In terms of what it, in fact, does require under existing interpretations by the Supreme Court of the United States, this law is in some respects substantially narrower than existing obscenity law. *Kaplan v. California* in 1973 allowed existing obscenity law to be applied to materials that were entirely verbal or linguistic, yet the limitation in section IIE here contains no such limitation.

DiMASI: [time limit]

SCHAUER: Certainly. I am happy to answer any questions you want. My 30-second summary would be quite simple. The issue here, whether the law can deal with material that both relates to the degree of sexual violence in this society and is part of the degree of sexual violence in this society, when limited to graphic sexually explicit material, is a matter that on existing law is substantially unclear, such that you should not take representations about its unconstitutionality under existing law seriously. It is an issue that is both in flux and unclear.

DiMASI: Thank you very much.

RICK KARPEL: My name is Rick Karpel. I'm a director of government relations for the Video Software Dealers Association. The Video Software Dealers Association is a national trade group for distributors and retailers of home video cassettes. We represent about 20,000 of the 30,000 video stores across the country. In Massachusetts, we have approximately 125 member companies, representing about 450 stores, and our members include large chains like Blockbuster Video, Strawberries, and Tower Video, regional chains like Videosmith and Endless Video, and nonspecialty outlets such as Stop & Shop, and Shaw's supermarkets.

I am here today to testify against House Bill 5194 for one simple reason. If it passes, most video stores in the state will be forced out of business. Why? Because the definition of pornography in this bill is so vague and so overbroad that it would impact most of the material found on the shelves of the family video stores in the state. For example, take the videotape *Thelma and Louise,* which last week was rated No. 1 in the country on the *Billboard* charts. *Thelma and Louise* contains sexually explicit scenes, in some of which women are portrayed in positions of sexual submission, which is language taken directly from the statute, and others in scenarios of degradation or humiliation—again, language from the statute. Therefore, one could argue that *Thelma and Louise* would be actionable under H5194, despite the fact that critics have generally praised the film. *Thelma and Louise* would be a problem under H5194 because movies in which women are treated in a disapproved manner, as sexually submissive, are unlawful no matter how significant the literary, artistic, or political value of the work taken as a whole.

Certainly the proponents of this legislation will argue that they do not intend that a movie like *Thelma and Louise* should fall in the net of works proscribed by this bill, but unfortunately if H5194 becomes law, video dealers in the state of Massachusetts will not be in the position to make fine distinctions. They will be faced with the prospect of huge liability judgments should it turn out that they mistakenly stocked an item that was later to be found an example of pornographic sex discrimination under the highly subjective standard of this bill. As a result, they will be forced to remove from their shelves all material containing sexually explicit scenes, including many mainstream Hollywood movies, as Ms. Markels just suggested. We do not believe that this is what members of the Committee had in mind, and we therefore urge you to oppose this radical, absurd and dangerous piece of legislation.

POLUMBO: [question concerning *Silence of the Lambs* and women's participation in such films]

KARPEL: The reality of this bill, when you look at the coercion segment of this bill, is it tortures the meaning of the word coercion. There are so many exceptions under the bill as to what constitutes coercion that there is absolutely no defense against someone who would be sued in this, that what they did was not coercion. There is no way to defend yourself under this bill against the charge that what you did was coercion. I mean there are so many exceptions to possible defenses. Although that part of the bill doesn't apply to video [stores]. We're more concerned with trafficking. We're more concerned with what happens if this bill passes, some of our members get sued, they're brought into court, and at that point, it's not going to be up to the proponents of this bill to define what the term "sexually explicit" means. It's going to be up to a judge. It's not going to be up to the proponents or this judge to bring action. It's going to be up to anyone, anyone who can claim damage on the part of another woman. Actually, one thing we haven't discussed in this bill—it also applies to men, children and transsexuals, so it applies to anyone, anywhere, who feels that someone somewhere was damaged by a videotape or a book or some other type of material that can be claimed to be sexually explicit. [inaudible discussion]

KARPEL: I think it is easy to go after the behavior, and not some kind of speech that is pretended to cause the behavior, or it is claimed it caused the behavior. I think there are laws that exist to go after that.

LIERRE KEITH: My name is Lierre Keith. I live in Northampton and I do educational slide shows about pornography and violence against women. I want to talk first about my own victimization, and the role of pornography in that, and then briefly about my educational work.

My brother started sexually abusing me when I was 4 or 5, and pornography was part of the abuse. To be specific, he would describe a certain pose that he'd seen in *Playboy* or *Penthouse,* and he'd make me do it. Often he would compare my body to the pictures in a very detailed and graphic and humiliating way. He also became obsessed with a feature they have in *Hustler.* He told me it was called The Beaver Hunt, and men could send in photographs of their wives and their girlfriends. And indeed *Hustler* still has The Beaver Hunt every month. I have an example of it in my slide show. He thought this was the greatest thing, that he could be a pornographer too, so he made me pose for The Beaver Hunt and took pictures.

Women who are sexually abused as children live through a certain kind of hell. We're forced, we're manipulated through shame and guilt, our bodies are used, we're humiliated and we're silenced. And then we're told we wanted this. Especially we're told by the pornographers. We're told that we were active participants somehow. We deserve Purple Hearts for what we've been through, and all we get is more pornography.

When I was 15, my boyfriend tried to kill me. He came to my house after we'd broken up and he tried to strangle me. I had bruises up and down my neck the next day. I'm alive because I fought for my life. He told me later that he wanted to kill me, that he brought a pair of scissors so he could stab out my eyes, that he wanted to have sex with my dead body, and then he was going to chop up my body and smear my blood on the walls. And he said that he'd seen it. At 15, I wasn't sure what he meant. Later, when I became a feminist, I came to learn that there are snuff films, where a woman is really killed for sexual pleasure. Now even in *Playboy* and *Penthouse* and *Hustler,* there are plenty of examples of death as an erotic experience, so I don't know specifically what it was that Dave saw—I didn't ask. The thing I hate most about this story is that if he had succeeded, my 10-year-old sister would have been the next one home.

Now, doing my slide show, I've heard enough stories to last a lifetime. An Asian-American woman who was raped, not once but twice. And both of her assailants told her about pornography they'd seen of Asian women. And lots of stories from incest survivors and battered women of being shown pornography and then forced to perform what was in it. The story of a teenage girl raped by one of her classmates, one of his friends made a video and then they had a party where they showed the video. I've also met a woman who was forced as a child to participate in making a snuff film, where another little girl was really murdered, and it was filmed. Now this happened in Massachusetts. This is happening in America right now. The murder of real women is being sold as sexual entertainment, and it could have been me. It could have been my body chopped to pieces, and it could have been my 10-year-old sister, with that horror formed forever in her brain.

Now either my life matters or it doesn't. You have the power to do something about this. I'm asking you to use it. Thank you.

NANCY RYAN: My name is Nancy Ryan. I am the executive director of the Women's Commission for the city of Cambridge, and I'm also one of the founding members of the Feminist Anti-Censorship Taskforce, which formed in Cambridge in 1985 because a bill almost identical to this was introduced in the city of Cambridge, and when the City Council decided not to pass it, it was placed on a referendum and it was defeated. I learned a lot from that effort, and I've learned a lot from the women who spoke here today, and I want to emphasize to you that I oppose this bill for reasons that are clearer to me than they ever were. The man who did these violent acts would have done them with or without pornography. Violence against women existed long before pornography. Exploitation of women is an economic fact of the society in which we live. Women's humiliation begins with our second-class citizenship in this society, and pornography is one of its symbols. I don't believe that in this case we can deal with the problem by going at the symbols.

I want to say just a few things about the facts of the situation we have with this bill. It distresses me that women's civil rights are being protected by people like former Mayor Hudnut, who when he was a member of Congress was against choice,[3] by representatives of the Meese Commission, when Edwin Meese has fought against everything that women have tried to achieve in this society, and other influences from the right wing.

It's very important to women that we have had a constitution which protected our right to free speech and our right to privacy. Those are the protections that have enabled us to gain what we have gained today. It is not possible for me to support an effort against violence against women which jeopardizes our capacity to continue to fight for women's rights.

I believe desperately in the fight against violence against women. Like the woman who spoke just before me, I do a slide show in Cambridge Public Schools on images of women. Next week, in Cambridge Rindge and Latin School, we're going to have a video on images of women which will be shown to the entire school. We have a Dating Violence Interven-

---

3. William Hudnut has always supported a woman's right to choose an abortion.

tion Project, which goes from classroom to classroom and talks with kids about respect between men and women. These are the efforts that I believe we have to take, along with picketing and screaming out loud about every violent image of women that's produced in our society, whether it's in mainstream movies or underground pornography. But I believe our responsibility is to scream and yell and to get our neighbors to scream and yell and tell people, march with your pocketbook and march with your mouths, but I don't think we can risk the assault that we're facing right now on our constitutional rights as women by aligning with a group of people who would limit those rights even more.

I urge you to find other ways to deal with violence against women. As a previous speaker said, our governor is taking away all of our monies for battered women's services. Our rape crisis centers have been cut dramatically in the last two years. Restore those funds, give us local capacity to fight violence against women. I urge you to take that route. Thank you for allowing me to speak.

DiMASI: Thank you. Any questions? Claudia Martínez?

CLAUDIA MARTINEZ: Thank you, Mr. Chairman. My name is Claudia Martínez and I'm a resident of Somerville. I'm in my last year as a graduate student at Harvard Divinity School and I will graduate in June with a Master's in Divinity. I also work part-time as an administrative assistant for the Dean's Office at Radcliffe College. Prior to my work as a graduate student, I was promotion manager for several radio and television stations in the country, as well as for a national publication. I come before the Committee today as a concerned citizen, anxious to stop the exploitation of women and young girls and young boys.

I am in a unique position to talk about the pain that being a part of pornography brings. Between 1959 and 1964, I lived a very schizophrenic existence. I was one of several stars, if you will, at a porno studio where live sex acts between children and women and animals were enjoyed by a largely male audience. Other times of my life were spent in my middle-class home, going to school, taking piano lessons and attending choir practice at my church.

The porno studio that I was subjected to was filled with evil and pain for me. I was humiliated and repeatedly raped. I was forced to perform fellatio on patrons in the bleachers in the audience. I was forced to smile as animals hurt my body. Other children were not as fortunate as I was. After a night of ridicule, my father would take me home. I knew many children who lived in a trailer behind the studio. Many of them had been runaways and they were locked into the trailer to prevent their running again. Their search for something better in this life ended in a smoky tavern filled with drunken laughter.

I understand that pornography has changed with the advent of video, but the intent and the pain that it causes has not. Children do not usually pose for long periods in front of crowds of screaming men anymore, but the transmission of their self and their image has haunting effects that last forever. The coercion that is perpetrated on them, the brainwashing—children with diminished self-esteem usually grow into prostitutes, drug abusers, alcoholics, child abusers. They hate themselves and many times turn that hatred out toward society. Pornography kills the souls of so many, not only the soul of the child, but the soul of those who would exploit others in order to feel more powerful.

The effects of this child abuse upon me was devastating. I remember being a little eight-year-old girl with no need for a training bra. My nipples and my genitalia were often rouged to copy the styles of older women in porno magazines. The dogs I was subjected to were the inspiration of the owners who had read about the animals in pornographic novels. I saw very little boys and girls who were handcuffed to posts. In my early twenties, I was extremely promiscuous and frequented porno parlors for fun.

And I'd be silent about the abuse I lived with. Although my abuse happened in another state, over thirty years ago, it does not mean that the degradation of pornography does not continue. Children are still forced into the same positions that I was. I was not only a victim of extreme assault upon my body, but I was occasionally subjected to viewing the violence perpetrated on other children. I was raped by men, I was raped by animals, and I was raped by other children who were coerced into raping me. I speak not only for myself, but I want to remember the children who died in these conditions—children whose parents never cared, children who are buried across this country that we'll never know about. [end of tape; break in recording]

DANIEL CHARTRAND: I'm Daniel Chartrand. I'm the former executive director of the New England Booksellers Association and I am currently a board member of the American Bookseller's Foundation for Free Expression. I'm also currently a bookseller and I'm a resident of the Brighton district of Boston, Massachusetts.

I'm urging you to reject House Bill 5194 because H5194 would force the suppression of books that are protected by the First Amendment.

This bill would punish publishers and booksellers for producing and distributing works that they have a constitutional right to disseminate. The U.S. Supreme Court has ruled that the states may regulate only material that is obscene or child pornography, according to its guidelines. The definition of pornography in this bill clearly applies to a wide range of mainstream works, including art and photography books and novels by mainstream authors whose general and local acceptance is proved by their appearance on national and regional bestseller lists. In order to protect themselves from suits, publishers and booksellers would need to discontinue the sale of nearly all materials with any sexual content.

I'd just like to go a little further and mention that, in response to Ms. MacKinnon's testimony, booksellers are not in league with pornographers in appealing legislation like the Indianapolis bill. Booksellers are not in favor of sexual violence in pornography. They are, however, against the chilling effects that legislation such as this bill would effect.

I'm also going to quote from an editorial that appeared in the *Rocky Mountain News* by the president of the American Booksellers Association. This was in response to national legislation on this issue, but it applies to this as well. She ends her editorial by saying, "The Pornography Victims Compensation Act turns upside down the relationship between the booksellers and their customers that has been established by the First Amendment. It is not the booksellers' job to tell people what books they may buy. The First Amendment protects the right of the reader to make those choices for him or herself."

DiMASI: Is Jackson Katz here?

JACKSON KATZ: Thank you, Mr. Chairman. My name is Jackson Katz, and I'm the founder of a group called Real Men, which is an anti-sexist men's group. The purpose of our group is to get men to start taking responsibility for the outrageous level of sexism and sexual harassment and sexual violence and all forms of violence against women in society. I'm also a graduate student at the Harvard Graduate School of Education.

I'm supporting this bill because I think, as Professor MacKinnon said earlier, one of the effects of this bill would be to bring this subject into the light. What I think we've heard today from numerous women, some really compelling testimony about how pornography has harmed them.

One thing that we really haven't delved into is how men are affected by pornography, that is, men who are the consumers of pornography and what that does to the way that we deal with women. I think our generation has grown up with more pornography than any generation in human history, and it's an absolutely central aspect of the conditioning of young boys. It's hard to overstate how important pornography has been in the past twenty-five years in terms of my generation and young boys who are growing up today. That's where they're learning about sex, and that's where they're learning about women, in many ways through pornography.

There's a professor of psychology at UMass Boston who has done his doctoral dissertation and subsequent research on sexual aggression among young college males, and he's found that in dozens and dozens of interviews that young guys will sit there in a room with him, and they'll admit to or just talk matter-of-factly about, "I did this to her, I did that, and then we did this and that," and they never once refer to themselves as rapists, of course, and they never once refer to the behavior that they've engaged in as raping behavior, or in any way criminal. But this psychologist will tell you that he knows that if they were under oath in the court of law, they would be admitting to first degree felonies, but they think it's normal, perfectly natural heterosexual relations.

I travel around the country and speak to college audiences, both male and female, and mixed audiences, and one thing I find over and over again, in frank discussions, is that pornography is extremely influential in the lives of young boys growing up today, and girls, but specifically I speak to guys. Again, I can't overstate how important it is in conditioning young boys. This blizzard of images of women in degrading and humiliating positions, guys just come to think of that as normal.

There was an article in the *New York Times* last week about sexual harassment in schools, how there's a whole new area of litigation that's opening up with young girls who are sexually harassed. If you read that article on the front page of the *Times* last week, you'll find that guys are saying that they don't know what to do, what they can do and what they can't do, what's acceptable and what isn't acceptable. As I read that, I said to myself, it's obvious where they're learning on one level what is and what isn't acceptable. In other words, you could take some of the dialogue out of these kids' mouths right out of a discussion of pornography that I've had on numerous occasions.

Pornography is a subtext to relations between the sexes, young boys and young girls today. That's why my group supports this bill.

There's another group in Boston called Men to End Sexual Assault, and they support this bill. Many men who work in this field, who work with young boys and who work with men to try to work against sexism and violence against women, will tell you that pornography is an extremely important issue. And that's why I'm supporting the bill.

BOB CHATELLE: Hi, I'm Bob Chatelle. I'm a fiction writer. I won't say poor fiction writer, that would be redundant. I live near Central Square in Cambridge, I'm a delegate of UAW Local 1981, the National Writer's Union, and a Boston local steering committee member.

I oppose H5194, misnamed An Act to Protect the Civil Rights of Women and Children. Pornography comprises expressive work wherein depictions of sexual activity predominate, and whose primary intent is to arouse sexually the readers or viewers. Some pornography, as we've heard, is ugly, vile and offensive. Some pornography is imaginative and beautiful. No clear boundary separates pornography from art. The notion that pornography causes crime contradicts the premises of a free and democratic society. That is, adults have free will, actions are based on information, error should be challenged in the free market of ideas.

Citizens are free to make their own decisions, even terrible decisions, and those who commit violence shall be held fully responsible before the law. I can think of no idea that more opposes the ideals of our nation's founders than the notion that it's all right to suppress a book because someone reading it might commit a crime. Why not ban the books of Dr. James Dobson—he's the leading anti-porn crusader who claims that pornography motivated Ted Bundy. Why not ban Agatha Christie? What about the Bible, which sick minds have used for centuries to justify countless atrocities?

As a writer, I insist upon my right to explore the entire realm of human experience, including sexuality. As a gay writer, I am especially concerned. In Canada, where there is no First Amendment, and where Professor MacKinnon has advanced her procensorship agenda, the usual censorship victims are gay and lesbian writers, journalists, bookstores.

Sexual abuse and harassment must not be tolerated, women must achieve their fair share of freedom and power. But H5194 does nothing for women, children or anyone else. I ask you to give it an adverse report. Thank you for your time and consideration.

SUZANNE FULLER: My name is Suzanne Fuller. I live in Northampton, Massachusetts.

The first incident I'd like to talk about is representative of many incidents that I experienced by the man that abused me for years. This man was an avid user of pornography: *Penthouse, Playboy,* pornographic videos, strip bars, and 1-900 sex calls. He came home after being out all night at strip bars, and he wanted intercourse. I was very frightened from past times that he had forced me. As he was on top of me and inside of me, he called me a "cunt, a whore." He repeated over and over again as he grabbed at me and slapped me, "Come on, you fucking cunt, I know you love my cock." I was crying and pleading for him to stop. I tried to get away from him. He beat me as he tried to tie me up to the bed with sheets. "I'm going to fuck you to death," he would say. He had me face down and forced his penis in my anus. I escaped for a moment to the corner of the room, scrunched down, naked, beaten. Fearing for my life, I screamed for help. Beating and kicking me, he forced his penis in my face, saying that if I did not suck on him, he would kill me.

He forced me to watch porn flicks, insisting that I should like them, learn from them, and be like those women, so I could please him. He would always be forceful during intercourse after viewing these porn videos. He insisted that I repeat what the women did, as he repeated what the man did. He would hit me as he forced me. I felt humiliated, terrified. I was his sex slave. He showed me a picture of a woman, it was either from *Penthouse* or *Playboy,* and he said that he believed that she was me. Later, he told me that his deepest fantasy was to rape me, which he did repeatedly. After an unwanted visit from him, when he was abusive and once again insistent on sexual acts, I discovered later when receiving my phone bill, that prior to the abuse, he had made many phone calls to the 1-900 sex calls that he had [seen] in the *Valley Advocate.*

In addition, this man has also been harassing other women. One night, after watching a porn video at his friend's house, he called the woman next door, and insisted that she go outside the house naked and perform sexual acts so he could watch. He told her that if she did not do this, he would kill her and her children. He was eventually found guilty for this incident.

It is very apparent to me the direct correlation of the use of pornography and the abuse that I survived. Today I am grateful to be alive. The extreme abuse I suffered was exaggerated and learned through the use of pornography.

JOHN SWOMLEY: Good afternoon, my name is John Swomley. I've submitted some testimony as a co-chair of the Boston Coalition for Freedom of Expression, an artists organization that is opposed to censorship. I'm also a criminal defense lawyer.

Much of what I have to say . . . has already been spoken to and addressed. But what I would like to point out, what has been systematically going on here in this Committee, is that you've heard from Ms. MacKinnon and you've heard from even Representative Hildt about certain statistics that show that there is a rising amount of pornography and there's a rising percentage of violent crime against women. They leave the statistical realm at that point in time and rely on empirical evidence which they have paraded here. One witness after another after another. They talk about the wealth of statistical analysis that can support their theories, and yet they don't provide any here before the Committee. Now, one of the few statistics that I've seen on the percentage of violent pornography comes from the Meese Commission, and their own study showed .6 percent of the major sexually explicit material contained acts of violence. And they relied upon a Canadian study, which said 10 percent. Now, the definition that the proponents of this bill have relied upon is a definition exclusively of violence. And, at best, they have a 10 percent figure for that. Now, what they try and do then is go from that figure to a causal link to violence against women generally.

Now, I can only testify as to my empirical history and that is as a criminal defense lawyer in Brooklyn, New York, for the last four years, and I've represented hundreds of abusers, people who have committed horrible acts against women, from rape all the way down to verbal assault, and none of that involved pornography. What that doesn't do is tell you that there is or isn't a link. It just shows that you can produce anyone to say anything.

Essentially, when you get to the issue of causation, you have to decide, is the violent act predicated upon the pornography? That is, without the pornography, would there be a violent act? And I think it's preposterous to think that it wouldn't be. I mean, when you use Ted Bundy as an example, would he have committed the acts against women that he ultimately was executed for doing without the pornography? And I think you'd have to say, yes, he would. None of the evidence that has been shown here today counters that, and there's no evidence offered to you—scientific, sociological or otherwise—to say there is a link between violent pornography and violence against women. There are far more effective ways to address that problem: social programs. Thank you.

ANN RUSSO: My name is Ann Russo, and I've been teaching at the Massachusetts Institute of Technology for the last five years. I teach a course on violence against women in contemporary U.S. society. I have

researched and written extensively on issues particularly of sexual violence, and particularly in terms of the connection between the production
of that violence and the production and consumption of pornography. I
wrote my doctoral dissertation on pornography and the linkages with
sexual violence, particularly exploring this civil rights approach to pornography embodied in the bill that is before you today.

From my research and investigation, I believe this civil rights approach
most directly addresses the specific harms of pornography to women and
children, and men where applicable. That is, it addresses how pornography actively discriminates against women, in its production, consumption and distribution.

For my testimony here today, I would like to specifically talk about the
information that I have as a teacher of a course on violence at M.I.T.
of the extensive use and functioning of pornography at M.I.T. Many of
the students in my class have come to me and told me about the role
of pornography in their particular abuse, many stories similar to what
you've heard today, but they also talk to me a lot about how pornography is used in the particular educational environment at M.I.T. as a result
of it being shown in the common living spaces in the coed dormitories,
also, secondly, the way it is used in different labs and worksites at M.I.T.,
and, thirdly, in terms of computer pornographic harassment. I want to
give a couple examples of these so you can see how pornography functions to discriminate against women.

But first I would like to say briefly what happens to women as a result
of these abuses—that women feel very diminished. It's already a difficult
environment to be at M.I.T. as a woman because traditionally women
have not been accepted there as legitimate scholars and students. The
existence of pornography further diminishes their self-esteem and self-
confidence. Some students I know have had to take time off, have had to
take a year off, have had to take two years off, because of issues of sexual
harassment and abuse at M.I.T. Many of them have had great difficulty
in concentrating on their school work and jobs. Many have been silenced
in talking about it because they are immediately harassed for speaking
out against it.

One example is in the dorms, where despite requests by women students that pornographic films not be shown in common living rooms,
some male students insisted on their right to show the films. In two cases,
a male student insisted on showing *Deep Throat*, a film which presents
Linda "Lovelace" Marchiano, who we talked about earlier today, despite

women students in the dorm telling this particular man that it was offensive to show *Deep Throat* since it has been documented in her books—*Ordeal* and *Out of Bondage*—that she was tortured and terrorized into. Secondly, they told him that at least one of the students who was a resident of that dormitory had been throat-raped in that particular way, and she felt particularly traumatized by the showing of that film. Despite her efforts and other women's trying to talk to him about showing the film, he showed it anyway to a whole group of students from the dorm. As a result, she and other students lost sleep, she lost a lot of school time. The one student was a doctoral student, and felt extremely harassed. She tried to address this through the M.I.T. administration and got nowhere because they still refuse to take an active stance around pornography. And then she was further harassed in that dormitory through threatening notes, etc., for trying to stop the showing of that film.

I would like to talk briefly about two other instances because I think they're important. These apply to the forcing provision. A number of instances have occurred at M.I.T. in labs where pornographic pictures are displayed, and there are only one or two women in the lab. When the women complain about it, instead of taking the pornography down, the response has often been defensiveness, anger and more pornography has been put up. That's an example of force. Another example is the computer pornography where the students are trying to write their papers in computer networks and they'll have pornography right next to them being shown on the screen, and again making it difficult for them to do their work.

I want to end by saying I really believe that pornography silences women and that this bill gives women a voice to seek redress.

POLUMBO: [inaudible question regarding MIT's response to this]

RUSSO: Right. There were attempts to deal with it. In the case of the *Deep Throat* situation, what they did was they sort of railroaded the student, even though they had a policy.

POLUMBO: They allow X-rated films to be shown in the dormitories?

RUSSO: They supposedly had a policy against it, but they don't enforce it because they're afraid that they're going to get a lawsuit against them. So they shuttled the student from one office to the next.

POLUMBO: Who is they? The administration?

RUSSO: The administration, yes. It's been an ongoing issue at M.I.T. because there was a tradition at M.I.T. to show pornography as part of registration and orientation day, until about ten years ago, and it's because of protests, which have been met with other protests saying that it's a breach of freedom of speech that they have a right to show pornography on that particular day.

POLUMBO: So they allow it to be shown?

RUSSO: They don't allow it but they don't totally enforce their policy against it. They'll encourage it. . . .

BETSY WARRIOR: My name is Betsy Warrior, and I'm founder of the Battered Women's Directory, which is a national and international resource for battered women describing services that they can get all over the world. I'm also the author of *Battered Women's Directory*. But more importantly, for the last fifteen years, I've run a support group for battered women and have trained many others to facilitate support groups for battered women to escape abusive situations or help resolve the relationships that they are in.

I'm here today to tell you that out of the hundreds and hundreds of women that have come through these groups over the last fifteen years, many have had partners who were pornography consumers and who used pornography as a mere instruction manual, in some cases to dictate the kinds of abuse inflicted on their wives and their girlfriends. For others, it seemed to be a goad to initiate or intensify abusive patterns of behavior against women. This includes all degrees of abuse, from disparaging, demeaning and degrading attitudes to outright attempts at murder, and that is just a small part of it. I've heard of many, many cases of attempted murder, and in some cases the completion of murder, that has been enacted through using pornography.

I think pornography needs to be considered as hate literature, and hate literature with criminal intent to deprive women of their civil and their legal rights to cause discrimination and harassment. Pornography is not an instrument of free speech, but an instrument employed to abuse women and humiliate them into silence. Therefore, I think laws should be designed to curb the appalling impact this hate material has on the lives of women. Therefore, I support the legislation being proposed here. Thank you. If you have any questions—

[inaudible]

WARRIOR: Yes, some of the women, in fact, that have come through my group, testified here today.

[UNIDENTIFIED REPRESENTATIVE]: [inaudible]

WARRIOR: Many cases the police won't take seriously because there are no laws on the books like the law that is being proposed here today.

[UNIDENTIFIED REPRESENTATIVE]: [What about murder?]

WARRIOR: In some cases yes, and in some cases no. They will just let the thing lapse until they say there isn't enough evidence to pursue any perpetrator.

[Question on whether any of the women sought restraining orders.]

WARRIOR: Many, many of them have gotten restraining orders—a good number of them, probably over 50 percent, maybe 60 percent, I would say. A man who testified earlier today who defended people who were rapists, etc., said that nobody gave any statistics here. It might be anecdotal, but coming through the support group, I'd say probably 60 percent or more women explicitly state that their abusive relationships and lives were affected in some way by pornography—to heighten or intensify or to initiate.

[UNIDENTIFIED REPRESENTATIVE]: [inaudible]

WARRIOR: Oh, all relationships, even in some cases where stepfathers or boyfriends or husbands also abused the children, pornography was sometimes a factor in those cases as well.

JEAN M. MORAN: My name is Jean Moran. I'm currently a graduate student in nuclear engineering at the Massachusetts Institute of Technology. During my sophomore year living at a dormitory at M.I.T., I was forced to deal with not only how pornography affected women's lives in general, but how it affected my life as well. In December of 1988, some residents decided to throw a bachelor's party for one of the residents. This included beer and pornography videos being shown in one of the common areas of the dormitory. For the pornography viewing, a door was pulled closed and secured. No signs were posted. Doors to the lounge from the stairwell were also closed. Again, no signs were posted. Despite the closed doors, women on the third floor were able to hear the video. When I found out right after, I became outraged. I felt violated. I felt unsafe. I went to the third floor and was even more disturbed to find one of the three graduate residents of the dorm still in the lounge. This magnified all of my earlier feelings of outrage and distress. Whom could I trust? The showing of pornography had been at the very least condoned and viewed by a figure of authority in the dorm. After this, the group decided to continue showing the pornography in one of the resident's rooms.

I was one of the few women who spoke out and attempted to explain to men and women why pornography hurt me. Rumors spread quickly throughout the dorm about me, and people I once considered friends gave me nasty looks. While visiting a friend, I was verbally harassed by three men. The same graduate resident who had been present at the pornography showing silently watched me being driven to tears, reaffirming the men's stance and their abusive treatment of me. A friend of mine was threatened by the house president that she would have the lab partner from hell if she did not quiet down and silence me. For about two weeks, I was followed around the dorm by one of the men. He would be at most two steps behind me, encroaching upon my feeling of personal space and my sense of safety. He would wait for me outside of people's bedrooms trying to listen to conversations, in places he was known not to frequent. When the housemaster was made aware of the situation by a friend, all of the proposed actions seemed unreasonable. It felt as if I was only setting myself up for retaliation. After feeling the anger from people while speaking out against pornography, I did not feel strong enough to face more intimidation and harassment from my peers.

The whole experience created a lot of pain, anger, fear, and tears in me. It affected my schoolwork, and it's amazing I made it through the semester and still made it through M.I.T. I can still feel all of this. No one should feel uncomfortable in their own home. For these reasons, I support the bill.

BARRY SHUCHTER: My name is Barry Shuchter. I'm representing a group, Men to End Sexual Assault, in this area. We are writing in support of Bill 5194, an Act to Protect the Civil Rights of Women and Children.

Our group, Men to End Sexual Assault, has worked in the anti-rape movement for six years as a project of the Boston Area Rape Crisis Center. Through speaking engagements, workshops and public forums, we encourage men to take responsibility toward ending violence against women. We believe this responsibility includes learning to recognize the harm that pornography causes to women, both in its production and its consumption.

While we encourage men to become more responsible in their personal lives and relationships, that alone is not enough. It is also crucially important to address the larger social and political realities of the pornography industry that affect women as a group. We believe this bill represents an important and necessary step toward correcting a major imbalance in our society in which the rights of men to produce and view pornography often diminish the rights of women to be free and safe on the streets and in their homes. Attempts to just legislate or censor pornography would not address this imbalance, it would just regulate it.

Only a civil rights approach such as this bill provides can give women the legal tools they need to gain the power and self-protection that men take for granted.

We realize this issue is very complex, and we've given alternate points of view due and lengthy consideration. Our conclusion is to strongly urge you to adopt this bill as proposed. And it's signed by eleven men from our group. Thank you.

DiMASI: Anyone else in favor or opposed to this legislation 5194? Anyone else?

JAYE MORRA: Yes. I wanted to say I'm a senior at Wheelock College in Boston, and I'm in favor of this bill.

I was taking a class with Gail Dines, a professor at Wheelock College, who has introduced me to feminism. And outside of that class, I have done a lot of research on my own. I was very interested in the pornography issue because I never realized how much it does affect me. Like a woman who testified before, her boyfriend had said to her, when I see this woman in the pictures, it's you. And I've realized that I'm no different from any of these women in these magazines, and these guys who are looking at these magazines, they don't know who these women are any more than they know who I am.

And when I have to walk down these streets in Boston, I have to be scared for my life, because I know that the rape rate is so high. I've been raped once before. I don't want to be raped again. I was raped at a university, knowing that pornography runs rampant at that university.

I studied pornography for approximately 17 hours in two days, so that I could do a lecture at Simmons College on the effects of pornography. I titled it, "What Pornography Really Is," because I feel that women do not know what pornography really is because we're not meant to. Pornography is meant for men. So it's about time that I went out and saw what pornography really is, and informed women of what it really is. So I did just that, and I found articles giving directions of how a guy should take his girlfriend away for the weekend and all these things he should do to her while they are away. I was reading through this, and these things were absolutely torturous, giving men all kinds of ideas of what they can do to their girlfriends, and how they can hit them where the bruises won't be obvious to people, and torturous things such as not letting her go to the bathroom and making her hold it for hours, and hours, and hours, and when she finally can go, to make her go in a litter box, and all these kinds of things.

Then I decided to protest Video Expo, which is a pornography store that opened up right near my college, and three women's colleges are surrounding the store. A radio station, very popular with college men, was giving away free adult videos to only fraternities in this area, which really scared me, because I know that there are lots of rapes in colleges and I know that there are lots of rapes filmed in colleges. So I went on to protest, and I got a great response. And I feel like I have to speak for a lot of women and a lot of college women to say that this pornography that's surrounding me is really frightening. I think a bill like this would give us the right to speak.

Like someone said earlier, this bill shouldn't be passed because a man *might* do danger to a woman, or might hurt a woman. I think we have to realize, and it's been said before, that it's not "might hurt a woman." You have to hurt these women in order to make this pornography. To have a woman hanging from a tree, like I've seen, you have to actually hang her from a tree. So it's not what they might be doing, it's what they *are* doing. And I think it's about time that women get the right to speak.

DiMASI: Thank you very much. Any questions? Anybody else want to testify on this bill?

DORIAN GREGORY: I don't know whether you'd call me a statistic or an instance of empirical evidence, but I know I was hurt because of pornography.

My name is Dorian Gregory. I live in Northampton. When I was a child, five or six years old, the boys in the neighborhood had pornography and they sexually abused me. I do not know whether they found it in the woods, or whether they got it from their homes. There were four or five, sometimes six of them, and they ranged in age from 8 to 13. They did to me what they saw in the pornography. The pornography told us what to do. Mostly they saw naked women, *Playboy* or *Penthouse* stuff, so they stripped me or convinced me to strip myself. They also saw pictures of sexual intercourse, so this is what they did to me. One after another, they took turns being the man in the picture, and I was to lay there and be the woman.

The cause of my abuse was pornography. The pictures that they had gave them the ideas and told them what to do, and if it was in the picture, it was the truth. And I thought that's what it meant to be a woman. And I believe that with this law, we can begin to change what it means to be a woman. Thank you.

DiMASI: Anyone else?

JAMES D'ENTREMONT: My name is James D'Entremont. I'm a member of the Dramatists Guild. I'm a playwright. I'm also a member of the National Campaign for Freedom of Expression and the National Coalition Against Censorship.

I just want to say briefly that I oppose this bill uncategorically for three reasons. It's unconstitutional. It doesn't begin to address real serious abuses in our society that need to be addressed. And, finally, this bill is an egregious gift from the political left to the political right, which is pursuing censorship nationwide.

DiMASI: Anyone else? Hearings closed on H5194.

Massachusetts: Written Submissions

Submission of Julie White, Boston, Massachusetts

The following testimony contains descriptions of incidents which occurred over a period of eight years in which I worked as a prostitute, dancer and nude model. I choose to remain anonymous because the negative stigma of being a prostitute could harm my present career, family and friends.

As a prostitute I worked in massage parlours, peep shows, private apartments, street corners, bars and for escort services. I worked in most major cities across the country. In all of these cities, wherever pornography is being sold, that is where prostitutes work. We did not choose to work in these places but would get arrested or thrown out of hotels or bars if they were not in the so called red light district. The prostitutes I knew who were African American or Latin[a] had even less options because many places would not hire them and police would bust them if they strayed out of a certain area. Once I had been arrested for prostitution and nudity and obscenity I had no more civil rights. When I was mistreated by a customer, club owner or hotel security, I could not go to the police because they would arrest me or ignore me.

At the age of seventeen I began dancing in topless and bottomless bars. I was working for a pimp and was under a lot of pressure from him and the club owners to make a lot of money. In these bars they had pornographic videos playing constantly which contained graphic scenes of various sexual acts. The women in the videos were usually naked and the men were often clothed except for their penis. One movie showed a woman with three men, one on top of her having intercourse, one pushing his penis in her mouth and one rubbing his penis on her breast. I had never seen pornographic movies before. I soon found out that in order to make tips I had to lay on the dance floor, spread my legs and expose my genitals to the customers, just like in the videos. I had to simulate postures such as being on my hands and knees and arching my back as if being entered from behind by a penis. I had to look at the customers and stick out my tongue as if performing oral sex. This was all extremely degrading.

A co-worker talked me into doing a photo session with a photographer she knew. She showed me a spread she had done for Penthouse magazine which she said he had shot. I later found out she got a finders fee for bringing me to him. I had to sign a release form which said I would only be paid a certain amount if a photo was sold to a magazine. I was told to wear red nail polish and cover my genitals with red lipstick. The photographer told me to suck in my stomach even though I was very slim. The most humiliating part was when the photographer told me to spread my legs as wide as I could and look right at the camera making facial expressions depicting arousal while masturbating with a pearl necklace or pushing my breasts together with my hands. One photograph that I know of from this shoot was sold to a magazine. It was a shot of me on my hands and knees, my buttocks facing the camera and spread so that my genitals were exposed while I peeked over my shoulder so that my face was very recognizable. This appeared on the back of High Society magazine as an ad for back issues for twelve months straight. I do not know what happened to the other photographs. I remember being afraid that a relative would see that picture.

The first massage parlour I ever worked in I had to dance topless in the lounge which I did not get paid for, as well as service customers. I was still seventeen and very naive. One day someone was taking pictures of me. The next thing I knew, a picture of me clothed only in a G string, was on a flyer advertising this massage parlour and being handed out on every corner. I did not give permission for that photo to be used but could not do anything about it. Shortly afterwards I got into an argument with the owner over a racist comment he made and he punched me in the face, took all my money and threw me down some stairs.

The massage parlours and private houses I worked in all had pornographic videos available for the customers, either in the bedrooms or in the waiting room. A lot of my work consisted of acting out particular scenes for the customer which caused him to become aroused. If a customer was into real hard core movies in which women were tied up, whipped, raped, urinated on etc., then he would want me to act out that kind of scene. On several occasions a customer requested that I act like I was his daughter and he would then rape me while I screamed "No Daddy, please don't, I'm so scared" and so on. I had several life threatening experiences with customers who were into violent fantasies. A very wealthy man lured me into his private house by offering me a large sum of money which I needed at the time. He locked me into his bedroom and after throwing some money at me he threw me face down on the bed and tore off my clothes. He choked me until I almost passed out and said he would kill me if I didn't do what he said. He jammed his fist up my rectum and smeared my own feces all over my body while he masturbated and made me say things like my cunt was hot for him. When he achieved orgasm he ejaculated in my hair and all over my body. When I got back out on the street I had no one to go to for help even though I had been raped and violated in the worst way.

Some of the most violent pornography that I saw was in the houses of customers that I saw through escort services. Sometimes they had magazines with women being gang raped, urinated on, defecated on and being penetrated with inhuman objects like scissors. A lot of times these men were high on cocaine or other drugs and would watch pornographic films for hours and hours while having sex with one woman after another. I considered the men who were into pornography to be the most dangerous and potentially violent since that is what aroused them. One time a customer took out a heavy leather belt and started beating me across the stomach and breasts. He was into pornography which showed young girls tying each other up and whipping each other. I tried to remain calm and keep it like a game even though I was in a great deal of pain. I convinced him to reverse roles and let me whip him instead. I had large purple bruises on my body the next day.

At least fifty percent of the men that I saw professionally were into fantasies and pornography such as I have described. They were men from all over the world and all types of professions. Every prostitute I know has had similar experiences. Often we keep it to ourselves because it is very painful to remember. I have been scarred for life both mentally and physically. I have violent nightmares on a regular basis which replay my worst experiences of sexual violence over and over. I have difficulty relating to people in normal social situations. I cannot make love with someone without having flashbacks of being a prostitute. I have very little self confidence. I especially support this bill because it includes a set of conditions including prostitution which cannot disprove coercion and therefore gives me rights which I did not have before.

Letter of Mary R. Harvey, Ph.D., and Judith L. Herman, M.D.

March 16, 1992

Representative Sal DiMasi
Committee on the Judiciary
The Commonwealth of Massachusetts State House
Boston, 02133

Dear Representative DiMasi:

This letter is to lend our strongest possible support to HB5194, an act designed to ensure and protect the civil rights of women and children in this Commonwealth. At the Cambridge Hospital Victims of Violence Program, and in our private clinical practices, we see an alarming number of women whose victimization by physical and sexual violence was preceded in childhood and/or accompanied in adolescence and adulthood by the violent, exploitive and anti-erotic images being proffered on the American public by a pornography industry that knows no bounds and accepts no responsibility. Please give Massachusetts women and children the right to claim and prove harm.

Sincerely,

Mary R. Harvey, Ph.D., Director, and Judith L. Herman, M.D., Director of Training
Victims of Violence Program
Department of Psychiatry

Submission of Mary Ann Cloherty, March 12, 1992, Boston, Massachusetts

Working as a woman in a non-traditional job (union carpentry) I have encountered many covert and overt aggressions. Pornography on a job site is one of the more blatant ways a woman is told that "this is a male domain;" "Go Away."

Sometimes I am sent to a job and (gratefully!) the men have been advised *beforehand* to remove the porno shots from the elevator or the tool shack or whatever common areas we may share. Sometimes not.

When I was working on the Mass. Avenue Bridge (the *only* female on the bridge) I was in an environment which was exceptionally hostile. All the crew shared a common table saw which was placed in a central location. Periodically one or more of the carpenters would use the saw and then return to the area on the bridge where they were working. When I approached the table saw one day the whole crew became quiet and watched me. Nailed to the table directly in front of the saw was a playing card. The "playing card" was an explicit close up of female genitalia with a large 16 penny nail (this is basically a SPIKE) nailed into the vagina. When I saw it some of my coworkers started snickering and laughing.

After viewing this, I found myself feeling depressed. Did I set myself up for this humiliation? *Why* was I working in this field?, etc. Questions which provoked a sense of *personal* responsibility for *their* hostility.

Ultimately, I seized the porno card and ripped it into pieces and dropped it into the river. What would tomorrow be like, I wondered.

The hostile environment is real, damaging and effective in repelling women. I fully support passage of legislation which would protect workers from such blatant harassment.

Submission of Kathleen O'Neill Alexander, March 16, 1992, Boston, Massachusetts

Members of the Judiciary Committee:

My name is Kathleen O'Neill Alexander. I reside . . . in Northampton. I have been a rape crisis program coordinator and counselor at the University of Massachusetts at Amherst. I also taught a course there for six years entitled: Violence Against Women: A Multi-cultural, Multiracial Perspective. I have been program coordinator of Daybreak, Inc., a shelter for battered women and children in Worcester. I have been involved with the National Coalition Against Sexual Assault since 1983. And I am the author of *Reclaiming Our Lives: A Handbook for Rape Crisis Counselors and Educators in Massachusetts.* Over the last ten years I have committed myself to working on behalf of victims of violence. Presently, I am the Director of the Victim Witness Assistance Program in the Northwestern District Attorney's Office. I have had the privilege to work with District Attorney Judd J. Carhart for the last three years serving the people of Hampshire and Franklin counties.

I regret that due to court responsibilities I must have someone else read my testimony.

I know the impact and violence of pornography first hand. I am a strong and confident woman who is still haunted by the violent images and degradation that pornography has had on my life. I was a serious Irish-Catholic-school fifth grader. One afternoon after school some of my chums and I were on 239th Street in the Bronx in a vacant lot. This was next to the apartment building I lived in. About seven or eight kids were playing in the lot and we found a tattered brown paper bag. Of course as children we were hoping for some wonderful treasure inside. But the bag was filled only with magazines. They were all of women who were naked and some of them looked like they were in pain. Several kids were shocked. Some laughed. There were comments on how disgusting this material was. People tried to guess who left the bag. While the conversation went on it seemed like an eternity. I was sick inside. It could have been my father. These were the kinds of books my father looked at. In my house there were films, photographs and magazines. They were all over. There was one item so abhorrent and violent that it is difficult to describe to you.

It was a handkerchief. I was putting the ironing away for my mother. We ironed everything—sheets, pillow cases, towels, underwear, etc. I was in my Dad's dresser, as I had permission to be. There was a hankie with images of women imprinted on it. They were all bleeding from the vagina. They looked to be in such awful pain. I had seen his magazines before but nothing like this. I recall women with dark hair and some with Asian features. I wanted to crawl up in a ball and die. Was this what my father did to women? Was this what he thought should happen to women? Did this happen to my mother? Was this going to happen to me? Why would he keep this in our house? Was he going to go to hell for this? Was I because I had seen it?

Parties among adults in our house involved pornography. It was used to get people to strip and "play games" particularly the Skyes and the people from Lake George. I always made sure I cried into my pillow so no one could hear me. I kept watch so no one would come into my younger brother['s] and my bedroom. I would try to get up for the six o'clock Mass, especially on a day after these parties. Sometimes I was so tired I overslept and just made it to school. I could hear the haunting laughter and screaming that went on for days.

What I couldn't have known as a child, I have come to realize as an adult who has worked with victims of violent crimes. And that is, that I just wasn't looking at pictures—I was looking at women's lives. The influence of pornography is not a literary or artistic influence but a violent influence at the expense of women and children['s] lives. My own healing process was very painful. I have worked with women who have had pornography used while they were being beaten by their husbands. I have heard from women that while they were being raped a perpetrator referred to pornography. Sometimes women have told me they were forced to imitate whatever was in the picture. One woman told me that her entire incest victimization, by her older brother always included pornography. Collectively, women have suffered humiliation, degradation and violence at the hands of pornography. It has taken years to deal with the turmoil of my own experience. One of my most painful struggles even now at 43 years old is having a sense of my body size and physical appearance. I have suffered eating disorders and had to overcome a great deal of pain that I directly attribute to the barrage of sexually explicit images and the activities that took place in my home.

There is no pleasure in violence for the victim of pornography. The private and public humiliation we feel at the hands of men and boys who consume this woman-hating material cannot be understood by any representation of government unless you have the insight and empathy to understand that we speak of fear for our daily personal safety. The integrity of our very existence is being jeopardized by men's consumption and activities due to pornography.

Thank you for your attention. Please support the Antipornography Civil Rights Law. Through this you will acknowledge the harms of pornography and provide relief to all women and children who seek its protection.

Submission of Gail Kielson, Boston, Massachusetts

My name is Gail Kielson and I work at Necessities/Necesidades, an organization in Northampton, Massachusetts that provides services to battered women. I am a Licensed MSW, and for 17 years have worked with women and children who were living with abuse. I am unable to testify in person today because we at Necessities/Necesidades are short-staffed and it is essential that I be there to work with the women using our services, many of whom are living in life-threatening situations.

We have recently begun to formally ask the battered women who call us whether the abuser uses pornography and from this we *conservatively* estimate that at least $\frac{1}{2}$ of the abusers use pornography as a part of the abuse. Battering is based on an issue of power and control, with the abuser using all kinds of methods to continually assert his power and control over the woman. Throughout, he is persistently working to deny her of her ability to make informed decisions about her life and through threats, coercion, and continual terror succeeds at clearly establishing himself as "in control". We frequently hear a woman say that she feels like a prisoner in her own home, and in fact, she is.

The use of pornography is but one means that an abuser uses to degrade and humiliate the woman. The stories that I hear are horrific and just when I think I've heard it all, I hear another horrifying story that sends me reeling. Women frequently state that abusers bring home pornographic videos and make them perform the acts depicted in the video. One woman described endless days and nights of this, with her husband demanding that she leave her place of business, a shop that she owned, and come home and enact the sexual tortures depicted on the videos; or he would demand that she leave the caretaking of her children and come into the locked bedroom and he would rape her. She attempted to protect her children from the knowledge of what transpired behind these locked doors, but their wide, terrified eyes indicated that they knew that she was being abused and they were helpless to protect her. Another woman said that she would come home from work, begin to make dinner for her children, and would hear her husband come in, turn the television on and know that he would then demand that she perform the acts shown on the pornographic videos. She had no choice but to submit, because if she did not he would threaten to beat her, or would beat her into submission. Another woman described how her husband brought home the videos and when she tried to withstand his sexual demands he put a gun inside her vagina and thus forced her to submit to his acts of abuse. Another woman said that her partner used pornographic books and read portions to her and then made her perform the degrading sexual acts described therein. Another woman said, tearfully, that her husband brought home pornographic videos and made her have sex with other men as he watched her and the videos simultaneously. Another woman said that her partner, while watching pornographic videos, raped her with all kinds of objects—pipes, sticks, knives. Perhaps the most horrifying story of sexual abuse, linked to pornographic use I heard was from a woman who was repeatedly raped, handcuffed to the bed, raped with all kinds of objects by her husband who continually used pornographic material. After years of terrifying abuse she managed to flee her husband

and come into our shelter. He pursued her, terrified her and her children, threatened to kill her. When he was finally arrested and incarcerated her children began to disclose sexual abuse. As the children began to feel safer and safer their disclosures became more and more horrifying, for their father, paternal grandparents and paternal uncle had persistently and consistently, sexually abused them, using pornographic videos as a constant part of the abuse. Not only had the children been forced to have sex with each other and several playmates, but the adults had used objects in their genitals, had killed animals in their presence, had made them engage sexually with animals, had hung them from rafters, had threatened to throw them off a cliff, all acts depicted in the pornographic videos. The result was that after several years of these disclosures, we were able to get the Commonwealth to bring him to trial and he was given 80–100 years in prison. However, these children are all in psychiatric treatment, one child had to be placed in a residential facility because he was actively suicidal, one child rarely talks, and walks through life with a haunted look, one child acts out in school. The mother has flashbacks of her own sexual abuse and lives, not only with her own terror, but with her self-imposed guilt that she had not protected her children. She cannot hear me say to her—"but he did this to them when you were off working, working to support the family and he maintained the secrecy by threatening that if they disclosed this horror he would kill them and you, their mother."

Had I more time I could continue to regale you with stories that I have heard women tell me about the connection of pornography and sexual abuse. They have told me their stories with shame, with tears, with resignation. As the words pour out of their mouths, sometimes hesitantly, sometimes in a flood, I can see that they are reexperiencing the horror of the acts, the horror of the degradation, the terror of the moment. I share their tears, I share their horror, but I rage and I seethe. Pornography is but one example of the underlying societal sanctions of violence against women that is endemic and epidemic in our country. I am working, daily, minute by minute, to arrest this epidemic. You, as legislators, have an opportunity through this act, to make a statement that says we are *all* ready to do something to stop violence against women.

The Ordinances

<hr>

Minneapolis Ordinance, 1983

83-Or AN ORDINANCE of the CITY OF MINNEAPOLIS

1st Reading: 11-23-83
Ref. to: Govt Ops Comm.
Public Hearing: 12-12; 12-13-83

Council Members Hoyt, White, and Scallon present the following ordinance:

Amending Title 7, Chapter 139 of the Minneapolis Code of Ordinances relating to Civil Rights: In General.

The City Council of the City of Minneapolis do ordain as follows:

Section 1. That Section 139.10 of the above-entitled ordinance be amended to read as follows:

139.10 <u>Findings, declaration of policy and purpose.</u>

(a) <u>Findings.</u> The council finds that discrimination in employment, labor union membership, housing accommodations, property rights, education, public accommodations and public services based on race, color, creed, religion, ancestry, national origin, sex, including sexual harassment AND PORNOGRAPHY, affectional preference, disability, age[,] marital status, status with regard to public assistance or in housing accommodations based on familial status adversely affects the health, welfare, peace and safety of the community. Such discriminatory practices degrade individuals, foster intolerance and hate, and create and intensify unemployment, sub-standard housing, under-education, ill health, lawlessness and poverty, thereby injuring the public welfare.

(1) SPECIAL FINDINGS ON PORNOGRAPHY: THE COUNCIL FINDS THAT PORNOGRAPHY IS CENTRAL IN CREATING AND MAINTAINING THE CIVIL INEQUALITY OF THE SEXES. PORNOGRAPHY IS A SYSTEMATIC PRACTICE OF EXPLOITATION AND SUBORDINATION BASED ON SEX WHICH DIFFERENTIALLY HARMS WOMEN. THE BIG-OTRY AND CONTEMPT IT PROMOTES, WITH THE ACTS OF AGGRESSION IT FOSTERS, HARM WOMEN'S OPPOR-TUNITIES FOR EQUALITY OF RIGHTS IN EMPLOYMENT, EDUCATION, PROPERTY RIGHTS, PUBLIC ACCOMMODA-TIONS AND PUBLIC SERVICES; CREATE PUBLIC HARASS-MENT AND PRIVATE DENIGRATION; PROMOTE INJURY AND DEGRADATION SUCH AS RAPE, BATTERY AND PROSTITUTION AND INHIBIT JUST ENFORCEMENT OF LAWS AGAINST THESE ACTS; CONTRIBUTE SIGNIFI-CANTLY TO RESTRICTING WOMEN FROM FULL EXER-CISE OF CITIZENSHIP AND PARTICIPATION IN PUBLIC LIFE, INCLUDING IN NEIGHBORHOODS; DAMAGE RELA-TIONS BETWEEN THE SEXES; AND UNDERMINE WOMEN'S EQUAL EXERCISE OF RIGHTS TO SPEECH AND ACTION GUARANTEED TO ALL CITIZENS UNDER THE CONSTITUTIONS AND LAWS OF THE UNITED STATES AND THE STATE OF MINNESOTA.

(b) Declaration of policy and purpose. It is the public policy of the City of Minneapolis and the purpose of this title:

(1) To recognize and declare that the opportunity to obtain employment, labor union membership, housing accommodations, property rights, education, public accommodations and public services without discrimination based on race, color, creed, religion, ancestry, national origin, sex, including sexual harassment AND PORNOGRAPHY, affectional preference, disability, age, marital status, or status with regard to public assistance or to obtain housing accommodations without discrimination based on familial status is a civil right;

(2) To prevent and prohibit all discriminatory practices based on race, color, creed, religion, ancestry, national origin, sex, including sexual harassment AND PORNOGRAPHY, affectional preference, disability, age, marital status, or status with regard to public assis-

tance with respect to employment, labor union membership, housing accommodations, property rights, education, public accommodations or public services;

(3) To prevent and prohibit all discriminatory practices based on familial status with respect to housing accommodations;

(4) TO PREVENT AND PROHIBIT ALL DISCRIMINATORY PRACTICES OF SEXUAL SUBORDINATION OR INEQUALITY THROUGH PORNOGRAPHY;

(5) To protect all persons from unfounded charges of discriminatory practices;

(6) To eliminate existing and development of any ghettos in the community; and

(7) To effectuate the foregoing policy by means of public information and education, mediation and conciliation, and enforcement.

Section 3. That Section 139.20 of the above-entitled ordinance be amended by adding thereto a new subsection (gg) to read as follows:

(gg) Pornography. Pornography is a form of discrimination on the basis of sex.

(1) Pornography is the sexually explicit subordination of women, graphically depicted, whether in pictures or in words, that also includes one or more of the following:

  (i) women are presented dehumanized as sexual objects, things or commodities; or

  (ii) women are presented as sexual objects who enjoy pain or humiliation; or

  (iii) women are presented as sexual objects who experience sexual pleasure in being raped; or

  (iv) women are presented as sexual objects tied up or cut up or mutilated or bruised or physically hurt; or

  (v) women are presented in postures of sexual submission; or

  (vi) women's body parts—including but not limited to vaginas, breasts, and buttocks—are exhibited, such that women are reduced to those parts; or

  (vii) women are presented as whores by nature; or

  (viii) women are presented being penetrated by objects or animals; or

  (ix) women are presented in scenarios of degradation, injury, abasement, torture, shown as filthy or inferior, bleeding, bruised, or hurt in a context that makes these conditions sexual.

(2) The use of men, children, or transsexuals in the place of women in (1) (i–ix) above is pornography for purposes of subsections (l)–(p) of this statute.

Section 4. That Section 139.40 of the above-entitled ordinance be amended by adding thereto new subsections (l), (m), (n), (o), (p), (q), (r) and (s) to read as follows:

(l) Discrimination by trafficking in pornography. The production, sale, exhibition, or distribution of pornography is discrimination against women by means of trafficking in pornography:

(1) City, state, and federally funded public libraries or private and public university and college libraries in which pornography is available for study, including on open shelves, shall not be construed to be trafficking in pornography but special display presentations of pornography in said places is sex discrimination.

(2) The formation of private clubs or associations for purposes of trafficking in pornography is illegal and shall be considered a conspiracy to violate the civil rights of women.

(3) Any woman has a cause of action hereunder as a woman acting against the subordination of women. Any man or transsexual who alleges injury by pornography in the way women are injured by it shall also have a cause of action.

(m) Coercion into pornographic performances. Any person, including transsexual, who is coerced, intimidated, or fraudulently induced (hereafter, "coerced") into performing for pornography shall have a cause of action against the maker(s), seller(s), exhibitor(s), or distributor(s) of said pornography for damages and for the elimination of the products of the performance(s) from the public view.

(1) Limitation of action. This claim shall not expire before five years have elapsed from the date of the coerced performance(s) or from the last appearance or sale of any product of the performance(s), whichever date is later;

(2) Proof of one or more of the following facts or conditions shall not, without more, negate a finding of coercion;

    (i) that the person is a woman; or

    (ii) that the person is or has been a prostitute; or

    (iii) that the person has attained the age of majority; or

(iv) that the person is connected by blood or marriage to anyone involved in or related to the making of the pornography; or

(v) that the person has previously had, or been thought to have had, sexual relations with anyone, including anyone involved in or related to the making of the pornography; or

(vi) that the person has previously posed for sexually explicit pictures for or with anyone, including anyone involved in or related to the making of the pornography at issue; or

(vii) that anyone else, including a spouse or other relative, has given permission on the person's behalf; or

(viii) that the person actually consented to a use of the performance that is changed into pornography; or

(ix) that the person knew that the purpose of the acts or events in question was to make pornography; or

(x) that the person showed no resistance or appeared to cooperate actively in the photographic sessions or in the sexual events that produced the pornography; or

(xi) that the person signed a contract, or made statements affirming a willingness to cooperate in the production of pornography; or

(xii) that no physical force, threats or weapons were used in the making of the pornography; or

(xiii) that the person was paid or otherwise compensated.

(n) <u>Forcing pornography on a person.</u> Any woman, man, child, or transsexual who has pornography forced on him/her in any place of employment, in education, in a home, or in any public place has a cause of action against the perpetrator and/or institution.

(o) <u>Assault or physical attack due to pornography.</u> Any woman, man, child, or transsexual who is assaulted, physically attacked or injured in a way that is directly caused by specific pornography has a claim for damages against the perpetrator, the maker(s), distributor(s), seller(s), and/or exhibitor(s), and for an injunction against the specific pornography's further exhibition, distribution, or sale. No damages shall be assessed (A) against maker(s) for pornography made, (B) against distributor(s) for pornography distributed, (C) against seller(s) for pornography sold, or (D) against exhibitors for pornography exhibited prior to the ENFORCEMENT date of this act.

(p) <u>Defenses.</u> Where the materials which are the subject matter of a cause of action under subsections (l), (m), (n), or (o) of this section are pornography, it shall not be a defense that the defendant did not know or intend that the materials were pornography or sex discrimination.

(q) Severability. Should any part(s) of this ordinance be found legally invalid, the remaining part(s) remain valid.

(r) Subsections (l), (m), (n), and (o) of this section are exceptions to the second clause of section 141.90 of this title.

(s) Effective date. Enforcement of this ordinance of December 30, 1983, shall be suspended for six months from the date of enactment to facilitate training, education and voluntary compliance. Liability under subsections (m), (n) and (o), except as provided specifically in (o), shall be retroactive to the date of passage.

83-Or AN ORDINANCE of the CITY OF MINNEAPOLIS

1st Reading: 11-23-83
Ref. to: Govt Ops Comm.
Public Hearing: 12-12; 12-13-83

Aldermen Hoyt, White and Scallon present the following ordinance:

Amending Title 7, Chapter 141 of the Minneapolis Code of Ordinances relating to Civil Rights: Administration and Enforcement.

The City Council of the City of Minneapolis do ordain as follows:

Section 1. That Section 141.50 (1) of the above-entitled ordinance be amended by adding thereto a new subsection (3) to read as follows:

(3) Pornography: The hearing committee or court may order relief, including the removal of violative material, permanent injunction against the sale, exhibition or distribution of violative material, or any other relief deemed just and equitable, including reasonable attorney's fees.

Section 2. That Section 141.60 of the above-entitled ordinance be amended as follows:

141.60 Civil action, judicial review and enforcement.

(a) Civil actions.

(1) AN INDIVIDUAL ALLEGING A VIOLATION OF THIS ORDINANCE MAY BRING A CIVIL ACTION DIRECTLY IN COURT.

(2) A complainant may bring a civil action at the following times:

(i) Within forty-five (45) days after the director, a review committee or a hearing committee has dismissed a complaint for reasons other than a conciliation agreement to which the complainant is a signator; or

(ii) After forty-five (45) days from the filing of a verified complaint if a hearing has not been held pursuant to section 141.50 or the department has not entered into a conciliation agreement to which the complainant is a signator. The complainant shall notify the department of his/her intention to bring a civil action, which shall be commenced within ninety (90) days of giving the notice. A complainant bringing a civil action shall mail, by registered or certified mail, a copy of the summons and complaint to the department and upon receipt of same, the director shall terminate all proceedings before the department relating to the complaint and shall dismiss the complaint.

No complaint shall be filed or reinstituted with the department after a civil action relating to the same unfair discriminatory practice has been brought unless the civil action has been dismissed without prejudice.

RECORD OF COUNCIL VOTE

Council Member	Aye	Nay	Council Member	Aye	Nay
Dziedzic	X		Scallon	X	
O'Brien		X	Howard	X	
Daugherty		X	Rockenstein	X	
White	X		Schulstad		X
Slater	X		Hoyt	X	
Carlson		X	Pres. Rainville		X
Kaplan		X			

PASSED: DEC. 30, 1983

Minneapolis Ordinance, 1984

AN ORDINANCE of the CITY OF MINNEAPOLIS

1st Reading: 1-27-84
Ref. to: Task Force on Pornography & GOVT OPS Comm.
Public Hearing: 6-20-84

Council Members Hoyt, Sayles Belton, White, and Scallon present the following ordinance:

Amending Title 7, Chapter 139 of the Minneapolis Code of Ordinances relating to Civil Rights: In General.

The City Council of the City of Minneapolis do ordain as follows:

Section 1. That Section 139.10 of the above-entitled ordinance be amended to read as follows:

139.10 Findings, declaration of policy and purpose.

(a) Findings. The council finds that discrimination in employment, labor union membership, housing accommodations, property rights, education, public accommodations and public services based on race, color, creed, religion, ancestry, national origin, sex, including sexual harassment AND PORNOGRAPHY, affectional preference, disability, age, marital status, or status with regard to public assistance or in housing accommodations based on familial status adversely affects the health, welfare, peace and safety of the community. Such discriminatory practices degrade individuals, foster intolerance and hate, and create and intensify unemployment, sub-standard housing, under-education, ill health, lawlessness and poverty, thereby injuring the public welfare.

(1) SPECIAL FINDINGS ON PORNOGRAPHY: THE COUNCIL FINDS THAT PORNOGRAPHY CONTRIBUTES TO CREATING AND MAINTAINING SEX AS A BASIS FOR DISCRIMINATION. PORNOGRAPHY IS A SYSTEMATIC PRACTICE OF EXPLOITATION AND SUBORDINATION BASED ON SEX WHICH DIFFERENTIALLY HARMS WOMEN. THIS HARM INCLUDES DEHUMANIZATION, SEXUAL EXPLOITATION, PHYSICAL INJURY, INTIMIDATION, AND INFERIORITY PRESENTED AS ENTERTAINMENT. THE BIGOTRY AND

CONTEMPT IT ENCOURAGES, WITH THE ACTS OF AG-
GRESSION IT PROMOTES, DIMINISH OPPORTUNITIES
FOR EQUALITY OF RIGHTS IN EMPLOYMENT, EDUCA-
TION, PROPERTY, PUBLIC ACCOMMODATIONS AND PUB-
LIC SERVICES; PROMOTE RAPE, BATTERY AND PROSTITU-
TION AND INHIBIT JUST ENFORCEMENT OF LAWS
AGAINST THESE ACTS; CONTRIBUTE SIGNIFICANTLY TO
RESTRICTING WOMEN IN PARTICULAR FROM FULL EX-
ERCISE OF CITIZENSHIP AND PARTICIPATION IN NEIGH-
BORHOODS AND OTHER CIVIL LIFE, DAMAGE RELA-
TIONS BETWEEN THE SEXES; AND UNDERMINE
WOMEN'S EQUAL EXERCISE OF RIGHTS TO SPEECH AND
ACTION GUARANTEED TO ALL CITIZENS UNDER THE
CONSTITUTIONS AND LAWS OF THE UNITED STATES
AND THE STATE OF MINNESOTA.

(b) Declaration of policy and purpose. It is the public policy of the City
of Minneapolis and the purpose of this title:

(1) To recognize and declare that the opportunity to obtain employment, labor union membership, housing accommodations, property rights, education, public accommodations and public services without discrimination based on race, color, creed, religion,
ancestry, national origin, sex, including sexual harassment AND
PORNOGRAPHY, affectional preference, disability, age, marital status, or status with regard to public assistance or to obtain
housing accommodations without discrimination based on familial status is a civil right;

(2) To prevent and prohibit all discriminatory practices based on race,
color, creed, religion, ancestry, national origin, sex, including sexual harassment AND PORNOGRAPHY, affectional preference,
disability, age, marital status, or status with regard to public assistance with respect to employment, labor union membership, housing accommodations, property rights, education, public accommodations or public services;

(3) To prevent and prohibit all discriminatory practices based on familial status with respect to housing accommodations;

(4) TO PREVENT AND PROHIBIT ALL DISCRIMINATORY
PRACTICES OF SEXUAL SUBORDINATION OR INEQUAL-
ITY THROUGH PORNOGRAPHY;

(5) To protect all persons from unfounded charges of discriminatory practices;

(6) To eliminate existing and the development of any ghettos in the community; and

(7) To effectuate the foregoing policy by means of public information and education, mediation and conciliation, and enforcement.

Section 2. That Section 139.20 of the above-entitled ordinance be amended by adding thereto a new subsection (gg) to read as follows:

(gg) Pornography. Pornography is a form of discrimination on the basis of sex.

(1) Pornography is the graphic sexually explicit subordination of women, whether in pictures or in words, that also includes one or more of the following:

    (i) women are presented as sexual objects who enjoy pain or humiliation; or

    (ii) women are presented as sexual objects who experience sexual pleasure in being raped; or

    (iii) women are presented as sexual objects tied up or cut up or mutilated or bruised or physically hurt; or

    (iv) women are presented as sexual objects for domination, conquest, violation, exploitation, possession or use, through postures or positions of submission or servility or display; or

    (v) women are presented being penetrated by inanimate objects or animals; or

    (vi) women are presented in scenarios of degradation, injury, torture, dismembered or truncated or severed or fragmented into body parts, shown as filthy or inferior, bleeding, bruised, or hurt in a context that makes these conditions sexual.

(2) The use of men, children, or transsexuals in the place of women in (1) (i–vi) above is pornography for purposes of subsections (l)–(p) of this statute.

Section 3. That Section 139.40 of the above-entitled ordinance be amended by adding thereto new subsections (l), (m), (n), (o), (p), (q), and (r) to read as follows:

(l) Coercion into pornographic performances. Any person, including transsexual, who is coerced, intimidated, or fraudulently induced (hereinafter "coerced") into performing for pornography shall have a claim against the maker(s), seller(s), exhibitor(s) or distributor(s) of said pornography which may date from any appearance or sale of any product(s) of such performance(s), for damages and for the elimination of the products of the performance(s) from the public view.

Proof of one or more of the following facts or conditions may or may not be admissible but shall not, without more, conclusively negate a finding of coercion:

    (i) that the person is a woman; or

   (ii) that the person is or has been a prostitute; or

  (iii) that the person has attained the age of majority; or

  (iv) that the person is connected by blood or marriage to anyone involved in or related to the making of the pornography; or

   (v) that the person has previously had, or been thought to have had, sexual relations with anyone, including anyone involved in or related to the making of the pornography; or

  (vi) that the person has previously posed for sexually explicit pictures for or with anyone, including anyone involved in or related to the making of the pornography at issue; or

 (vii) that anyone else, including a spouse or other relative, has given permission on the person's behalf; or

(viii) that the person actually consented to a use of the performance that is altered into pornography; or

  (ix) that the person knew that the purpose of the acts or events in question was to make pornography; or

   (x) that the person showed no resistance or appeared to cooperate actively in the photographic sessions or in the sexual events that produced the pornography; or

  (xi) that the person signed a contract, or made statements affirming a willingness to cooperate in the production of pornography; or

 (xii) that no physical force, threats, or weapons were used in the pornographic sessions or in the sexual events recorded in the pornography; or

(xiii) that the person was paid or otherwise compensated.

(m) <u>Discrimination by trafficking in pornography.</u> The production, sale, exhibition, or distribution of pornography is sex discrimination by means of trafficking in pornography. Any woman has a claim hereunder as a woman acting against the subordination of women. Any man or transsexual who alleges injury by pornography in the way women are injured by it shall also have a claim.

(1) City, state, and federally funded public libraries or private and public university and college libraries shall not be construed to be trafficking in pornography.

(2) The formation of private clubs or associations for purposes of trafficking in pornography shall be considered a conspiracy to violate civil rights.

(3) This section shall not be construed to make isolated passage(s) or isolated part(s) actionable.

(n) Forcing pornography on a person. Any woman, man, child, or transsexual who has pornography forced on him/her in any place of employment, in education, in a home, or in any public place has a claim against the perpetrator and/or institution.

(o) Assault or physical attack due to pornography. Any woman, man, child, or transsexual who is assaulted, physically attacked or injured in a way that is directly caused by specific pornography has a claim for damages against the perpetrator(s), maker(s), distributor(s), seller(s), and/or exhibitor(s), and for an injunction against the specific pornography's further exhibition, distribution, or sale. No damages shall be assessed (A) against maker(s) for pornography made, (B) against distributor(s) for pornography distributed, (C) against seller(s) for pornography sold, or (D) against exhibitors for pornography exhibited prior to the enforcement date of this act.

(p) Defenses.

(1) Where the materials which are the subject matter of a claim under subsections (l), (m), (n), or (o) of this section are pornography, it shall not be a defense that the defendant did not know or intend that the materials were pornography or sex discrimination.

(2) It shall be a defense to a claim for damages under subsections (m) & (l), or the sale, distribution, or exhibition part of (o), that the respondent did not know, or should not reasonably have known, that the materials are pornography.

(3) It shall be a defense to a claim under section (m) that the materials complained of are those covered only by section 139.20(gg)(1)(iv).

(q) Severability. Should any part(s) of this ordinance be found legally invalid, the remaining part(s) remain valid. Should any part(s) of this ordinance be found legally invalid as applied in a particular way or to a particular case or category of cases, that part(s) remains valid as applied in other ways or to other cases or categories of cases, unless the remaining application would clearly frustrate the Council's intent in adopting this ordinance.

(r) Enforcement dates.

(1) Enforcement under (m) or the second sentence of (o) shall be suspended until January 1, 1985, to permit training, public education and voluntary compliance.

(2) No liability shall attach under (m) or as provided in the second sentence of (o) until January 1, 1985. Liability under all other sections of this act shall attach as of the date of passage.

RECORD OF COUNCIL VOTE

Council Member	Aye	Nay	Council Member	Aye	Nay
Dziedzic	X		Scallon	X	
O'Brien		X	Niemiec		X
Hilary	X		Cramer		X
White	X		Schulstad		X
Coyle	X		Hoyt	X	
Carlson		X	Pres. Rainville		X
Sayles Belton	X				

PASSED: July 13, 1984
VETOED: July 13, 1984

Indianapolis Ordinance, 1984

CODE OF INDIANAPOLIS AND MARION COUNTY, INDIANA
Chapter 16
HUMAN RELATIONS; EQUAL OPPORTUNITY[1]

Sec. 16-1. Findings, policies and purposes.

(a) *Findings.* The city-county council hereby makes the following findings:

(1) The council finds that the practice of denying equal opportunities in employment, education, access to and use of public accom-

1. This is an edited version of the civil-rights law of the City of Indianapolis and Marion County. All language relating specifically to pornography is underlined. Spelling has been corrected.

modations, and acquisition of real estate based on race, color, religion, ancestry, national origin, handicap, or sex is contrary to the principles of freedom and equality of opportunity and is a burden to the objectives of the policies contained herein and shall be considered discriminatory practices.

(2) Pornography is a discriminatory practice based on sex which denies women equal opportunities in society. Pornography is central in creating and maintaining sex as a basis for discrimination. Pornography is a systematic practice of exploitation and subordination based on sex which differentially harms women. The bigotry and contempt it promotes, with the acts of aggression it fosters, harm women's opportunities for equality of rights in employment, education, access to and use of public accommodations, and acquisition of real property; promote rape, battery, child abuse, kidnaping and prostitution and inhibit just enforcement of laws against such acts; and contribute significantly to restricting women in particular from full exercise of citizenship and participation in public life, including in neighborhoods.

(b) It is the purpose of this chapter to carry out the following policies of the City of Indianapolis and Marion County:

(1) To provide equal employment opportunity in all city and county jobs without regard to race, color, religion, handicap, national origin, ancestry, age, sex, disabled veteran, or Vietnam era veteran status;

(2) To encourage the hiring of the handicapped in both the public and the private sectors and to provide equal access to the handicapped to public accommodations;

(3) To utilize minority-owned businesses, securing goods and services for the city and county in a dollar amount equal to at least ten (10) per cent of monies spent by the City of Indianapolis and Marion County;

(4) To utilize women-owned businesses and encourage the utilization of women in construction and industry;

(5) To protect employers, labor organizations, employment agencies, property owners, real estate brokers, builders, lending institutions, governmental and educational agencies and other persons from unfounded charges of discrimination;

(6) To provide all citizens of the City of Indianapolis and Marion County equal opportunity for education, employment, access to

public accommodations without regard to race, religion, color, handicap, sex, national origin, ancestry, age, or disabled veteran or Vietnam era veteran status;

(7) To provide all citizens of the City of Indianapolis and Marion County equal opportunity for acquisition through purchase or rental of real property including, but not limited to, housing without regard to race, sex, religion or national origin; and

(8) To prevent and prohibit all discriminatory practices of sexual subordination or inequality through pornography.

Sec. 16-2. Nondiscrimination clauses.

(1) Every contract to which one of the parties is the city or the county, or any board, department or office of either the city or county, including franchises granted to public utilities, shall contain a provision requiring the governmental contractor and subcontractors not to discriminate against any employee or applicant for employment in the performance of the contract, with respect to hire, tenure, terms, conditions or privileges of employment, or any matter directly or indirectly related to employment, because of race, sex, religion, color, national origin, ancestry, age, handicap, disabled veteran status and Vietnam era veteran status. Breach of this provision may be regarded as a material breach of the contract.

(2) All applications, postings, announcements, and advertisements recruiting applicants for employment with the city or county shall conspicuously post in the bottom margin of such recruiting bids a clause as follows: "An Affirmative Action Equal Employment Opportunity Employer."

Sec. 16-3. Definitions.

As used in this chapter, the following terms shall have the meanings ascribed to them in this section:

. . .

(d) *Board* shall mean the equal opportunity advisory board.

(e) *Complainant* shall mean any person who signs a complaint on his/her own behalf alleging that he/she has been aggrieved by a discriminatory practice.

(f) *Complaint* shall mean a written grievance filed with the office of equal opportunity, either by a complainant or by the board or office, which meets all the requirements of sections 16-18 and 16-19.

(g) *Discriminatory practice* shall mean and include the following:

(1) The exclusion from or failure or refusal to extend to any person equal opportunities or any difference in the treatment of any person by reason of race, sex, religion, color, national origin or ancestry, handicap, age, disabled veteran or Vietnam era veteran status.

(2) The exclusion from or failure or refusal to extend to any person equal opportunities or any difference in the treatment of any person, because the person filed a complaint alleging a violation of this chapter, testified in a hearing before any members of the board or otherwise cooperated with the office or board in the performance of its duties and functions under this chapter, or requested assistance from the board in connection with any alleged discriminatory practice, whether or not such discriminatory practice was in violation of this chapter.

(3) In the case of a real estate broker or real estate salesperson or agent, acting in such a capacity in the ordinary course of his/her business or occupation, who does any of the following:

a. Any attempt to prevent, dissuade or discourage any prospective purchaser, lessee or tenant of real estate from viewing, buying, leasing or renting the real estate because of the race, sex, religion or national origin of:

1. Students, pupils or faculty of any school or school district;

2. Owners or occupants, or prospective owners or occupants, of real estate in any neighborhood or on any street or block; provided, however, this clause shall not be construed to prohibit disclosure in response to inquiry by any prospective purchaser, lessee or tenant of:

(i) Information reasonably believed to be accurate regarding such race, sex, religion or national origin; or

(ii) The honest professional opinion or belief of the broker, salesperson or agent regarding factors which may affect the value or desirability of property available for purchase or lease.

b. Any solicitation, promotion or attempt to influence or induce any owner to sell, lease or list for sale or lease any real estate, which solicitation, promotion or attempted inducement includes representations concerning:

1. Race, sex, religion or national origin or present, prospective or possible purchasers or occupants of real estate in any area, neighborhoods or particular street or block;

2. Present, prospective or possible neighborhood unrest, tension or change in the race, sex, religion or national origin of occupants or prospective occupants of real estate in any neighborhood or any street or block;

3. Present, prospective or possible decline in market value of any real estate by reason of the present, prospective or possible entry into any neighborhood, street or block or persons of a particular race, sex, religion or national origin;

4. Present, prospective or possible decline in the quality of education offered in any school or school district by reason of any change in the race, sex, religion or national origin of the students, pupils or faculty of such school or district.

(4) Trafficking in pornography: The production, sale, exhibition, or distribution of pornography.

a. City, state, and federally funded public libraries or private and public university and college libraries in which pornography is available for study, including on open shelves, shall not be construed to be trafficking in pornography, but special display presentations of pornography in said places is sex discrimination.

b. The formation of private clubs or associations for purposes of trafficking in pornography is illegal and shall be considered a conspiracy to violate the civil rights of women.

c. This paragraph (4) shall not be construed to make isolated passages or isolated parts actionable.

(5) Coercion into pornographic performance: Coercing, intimidating or fraudulently inducing any person, including a man, child or transsexual into performing for pornography, which injury may date from any appearance or sale of any products of such performance.

a. Proof of the following facts or conditions shall not constitute a defense:

1. That the person is a woman; or

2. That the person is or has been a prostitute; or

3. That the person has attained the age of majority; or

4. That the person is connected by blood or marriage to anyone involved in or related to the making of the pornography; or

5. That the person has previously had, or been thought to have had, sexual relations with anyone, including anyone involved in or related to the making of the pornography; or

6. That the person has previously posed for sexually explicit pictures for or with anyone, including anyone involved in or related to the making of the pornography at issue; or

7. That anyone else, including a spouse or other relative, has given permission on the person's behalf; or

8. That the person actually consented to a use of the performance that is changed into pornography; or

9. That the person knew that the purpose of the acts or events in question was to make pornography; or

10. That the person demonstrated no resistance or appeared to cooperate actively in the photographic sessions or in the sexual events that produced the pornography; or

11. That the person signed a contract, or made statements affirming a willingness to cooperate in the production of pornography; or

12. That no physical force, threats, or weapons were used in the making of the pornography; or

13. That the person was paid or otherwise compensated.

(6) Forcing pornography on a person: The forcing of pornography on any woman, man, child or transsexual in any place of employment, in education, in a home, or in any public place.

(7) Assault or physical attack due to pornography: The assault, physical attack, or injury of any woman, man, child, or transsexual in a way that is directly caused by specific pornography.

(8) Defenses: Where the materials which are the subject matter of a complaint under paragraphs (4), (5), or (7) of this subsection (g)

are pornography, it shall not be a defense that the respondent did not know or intend that the materials were pornography or sex discrimination; provided, however, that in the cases under paragraph (g)(4) of section 16-3 or against a seller, exhibitor or distributor under paragraph (g)(7) of section 16-3, no damages or compensation for losses shall be recoverable unless the complainant proves that the respondent knew or had reason to know that the materials were pornography. Provided, further, that it shall be a defense to a complaint under paragraph (g)(4) of section 16-3 that the materials complained of are those covered only by paragraph (q)(6) of section 16-3.

. . .

(n) *Office* shall mean the office of equal opportunity created by this chapter.

. . .

(p) *Person* shall mean and include one or more individuals, partnerships, associations, organizations, cooperatives, legal representatives, trustees, trustees in bankruptcy, receivers, governmental agencies and other organized groups of persons.

(q) *Pornography* shall mean the graphic sexually explicit subordination of women, whether in pictures or in words, that also includes one or more of the following:

(1) Women are presented as sexual objects who enjoy pain or humiliation; or

(2) Women are presented as sexual objects who experience sexual pleasure in being raped; or

(3) Women are presented as sexual objects tied up or cut up or mutilated or bruised or physically hurt, or as dismembered or truncated or fragmented or severed into body parts; or

(4) Women are presented being penetrated by objects or animals; or

(5) Women are presented in scenarios of degradation, injury, abasement, torture, shown as filthy or inferior, bleeding, bruised, or hurt in a context that makes these conditions sexual; [or]

(6) Women are presented as sexual objects for domination, conquest, violation, exploitation, possession, or use, or through postures or positions of servility or submission or display.

The use of men, children, or transsexuals in the place of women in paragraphs (1) through (6) above shall also constitute pornography under this section.

. . .

(v) *Respondent* shall mean one or more persons against whom a complaint is filed under this chapter, and who the complaint alleges has committed or is committing a discriminatory practice.

Sec. 16-4. Office of equal opportunity—Created; purpose.

There is hereby created a section of the legal division of the department of administration entitled the office of equal opportunity. This office and its board are empowered as provided in this chapter to carry out the public policy of the state as stated in section 2 of the Indiana Civil Rights Act, within the territorial boundaries of Marion County.

Sec. 16-5. Same—Composition of office; functions.

The office shall be directed by a chief officer who shall also be the affirmative action officer for the city and county. The chief officer shall be appointed by and serve at the pleasure of the mayor and shall be responsible for performing the following functions:

(1) To monitor internal employment practices [specified] . . .

(2) To monitor contract compliance as follows: [specified] . . .

(3) To receive, investigate and adjudicate community complaints as specified in sections 16-18 through 16-28.

Section 16-6. Same—General powers and duties.

In addition to the functions previously mentioned in section 16-5, the office shall have the following powers and duties.

(1) To gather and distribute information for the purpose of improving human relations and removing inequities to protected groups in the areas of housing, recreation, education, employment, law enforcement, vocational guidance and related matters.

(2) To assist other governmental and private agencies, groups and individuals in reducing community tensions and preventing conflicts between persons of different racial, ethnic and religious groups.

(3) To discourage persons from engaging in discriminatory practices through informal methods of persuasion and conciliation and through programs of public information and education.

(4) To furnish technical assistance upon request to persons to assist them in eliminating discriminatory practices or otherwise implementing the policy and purposes of the Indiana Civil Rights Act.

(5) To make such general investigations, studies and surveys as the office shall deem necessary for the performance of its duties.

(6) To prepare and submit at least annually a report of its activities to the mayor and to the public, which report shall describe the investigations and proceedings conducted by the office, the outcome thereof and the progress and the achievements of the office and the community toward elimination of discriminatory practices.

(7) To cooperate with the Indiana State Civil Rights Commission, any appropriate federal, state or local agencies, and with private organizations, individuals and neighborhood associations in order to effectuate the purposes of this chapter and to further compliance with federal, state and local laws and ordinances prohibiting discriminatory practices.

(8) To perform any other duties assigned by ordinance or the mayor.

Sec. 16-7. Equal opportunity advisory board—Created; purpose.

There is hereby created an equal opportunity advisory board empowered as provided in this chapter to carry out the public policy of the state as stated in section 2 of the Indiana Civil Rights Act, within the territorial boundaries of Marion County.

Sec. 16-8. Same—Composition of board; appointment and terms of members.

. . .

Sec. 16-13. Complaint adjudication; territorial application.

This chapter shall apply within the territorial limits of the consolidated city and within the territorial limits of the county, with respect to any discriminatory practice occurring within such territorial limits and which relates to:

(1) Acquisition of real estate; or

(2) Employment; or

(3) Education controlled by any public board or agency; or

(4) Public accommodations; or

(5) Pornography.

Sec. 16-14. Unlawful acts other than discriminatory practices; penalty.

(a) It shall be unlawful for any person to discharge, expel or otherwise discriminate against any other person because that person:

(1) Has filed a complaint alleging a violation of section 16-15;

(2) Has testified in a hearing before the board or any committee thereof;

(3) Has otherwise cooperated with the board or office in the performance of their duties and functions;

(4) Has requested assistance from the board or office in connection with any alleged discriminatory practice, whether or not the discriminatory practice was in violation of section 16-15.

(b) It shall be unlawful for any person willfully to file a complaint alleging a violation of section 16-15 with knowledge that the complaint is false in any material respect.

(c) Any person who violates any of the provisions of this section shall, upon conviction, be subject to fine in an amount not less than ten dollars ($10.00) nor more than three hundred dollars ($300.00); provided, however, no such fine shall be imposed upon any person against whom the board or office has proceedings under this chapter with respect to any violation of subsection (a), which violation is also a discriminatory practice. Any proceeding to impose a penalty under this section shall be commenced within six (6) months after the date the violation occurred.

Sec. 16-15. Discriminatory practices declared unlawful.

Each discriminatory practice as defined in section 16-3 shall be considered unlawful unless it is specifically exempted by this chapter.

Sec. 16-16. Persons and activities to which sections 16-14 and 16-15 do not apply.

(a) Sections 16-14 and 16-15 shall not apply to employment performed for the consolidated city and department or agency thereof, or any employment performed for the county or agency thereof which is represented by the corporation counsel pursuant to IC 18-4-7-5.

(b) Subject to the provision of section 16-3(g)(4), the provisions of sections 16-14 and 16-15 shall not include any not-for-profit corporation or association organized exclusively for fraternal or religious purposes, nor any school, education, charitable or religious institution owned or conducted by, or affiliated with, a church or religious institution, nor any exclusively social club, corporation or association that is not organized for profit and is not in fact open to the general public.

(c) Sections 16-14 and 16-15 shall not apply to the rental of rooms in a boardinghouse or rooming house or single-family residential unit; provided, however, the owner of the building unit actually maintains and occupies a unit or room in the building as his/her residence and, at the time of the rental the owner intends to continue to so occupy the unit or room therein for an indefinite period subsequent to the rental.

(d) The following shall not be discrimination on the basis of sex:

(1) For any person to maintain separate restrooms or dressing rooms for the exclusive use of either sex;

(2) For an employer to hire and employ employees; for an employment agency to classify or refer for employment any individual; for a labor organization to classify its membership or to classify or refer for employment any individual; or for an employer, labor organization or joint labor-management committee, controlling apprenticeship or other training or retraining programs, to admit or employ any individual in any such program; on the basis of sex in those certain instances where sex is a bona fide occupational qualification reasonably necessary to the normal operation of that particular business or enterprise.

Sec. 16-17. Grounds for complaint; persons who may file; persons against whom complaint may be made.

(a) A complaint charging that any person has engaged in or is engaging in a discriminatory practice prohibited by sections 16-14 and/or 16-15 may be filed with the office by any person claiming to be aggrieved by the practice, or by one or more members of the board of employees of the office who have reasonable cause to believe that a violation of sections 16-14 and 16-15 has occurred, in any of the following circumstances:

(1) In the case of the acquisition of real estate, against the owner of the real estate, a real estate broker, real estate salesperson or agent, or a lending institution or appraiser;

(2) In the case of education, against the governing board of any public school district which operates schools within the territorial limits of the consolidated city or of the county;

(3) In the case of a public accommodation, against the owner or person in charge of any such establishment, or both;

(4) In the case of a public facility, against the governmental body which operates or has jurisdiction over the facility;

(5) In the case of employment, against any employer, employment agency or labor organization;

(6) In the cases of trafficking in pornography, coercion into pornographic performances, and assaults or physical attack due to

pornography (as provided in section 16-3(g)(7) against the perpe-
trator(s), maker(s), seller(s), exhibitor(s), or distributor(s).[)]

(7) In the case of forcing pornography on a person, against the
perpetrator(s) and/or institution.

(b) In the case of trafficking in pornography, any woman may file a
complaint as a woman acting against the subordination of women and
any man, child, or transsexual may file a complaint but must prove
injury in the same way that a woman is injured in order to obtain relief
under this chapter.

(c) In the case of assault or physical attack due to pornography, compensation for losses or an award of damages shall not be assessed
against:

(1) Maker(s), for pornography made,

(2) Distributor(s), for pornography distributed,

(3) Seller(s), for pornography sold, or

(4) Exhibitor(s) for pornography exhibited, prior to the effective
date of this act.

Sec. 16-18. Contents of complaint.

To be acceptable by the office, a complaint shall be sufficiently complete so as to reflect properly the full name and address of the complainant or other aggrieved person or persons; the full name and address of
the person against whom the complaint is made; the alleged discriminatory practice and a statement of particulars thereof; the date or dates
of the alleged discriminatory practice; if the alleged discriminatory practice is of a continuing nature, the dates between which the continuing discriminatory practices are alleged to have occurred; a statement as
to any other action, civil or criminal, instituted before any other administrative agency, commission, department or court, whether state or federal, based upon the same grievance alleged in the complaint, with a
statement as to the status or disposition of any such other action; and in
the case of alleged employment discrimination a statement that the employer employs six (6) or more employees in the territorial jurisdiction of
the office.

Sec. 16-19. Execution and verification of complaint.

The original complaint shall be signed and verified before a notary public
or other person duly authorized by law to administer oaths and take
acknowledgments. Notarial services shall be furnished by the office without charge.

Sec. 16-20. Timeliness of complaint.

No complaint shall be valid unless filed within ninety (90) calendar days from the date of occurrence of the alleged discriminatory practice or, in the case of a continuing discriminatory practice, during the time of the occurrence of the alleged practice; but not more than ninety (90) calendar days from the date of the most recent alleged discriminatory act.

Sec. 16-21. Referral of complaint to Indiana State Civil Rights Commission.

The chief officer may, in his/her discretion, prior to scheduling of the complaint for hearing under section 16-26, refer any complaint to the Indiana State Civil Rights Commission for proceedings in accordance with the Indiana Civil Rights Act.

Sec. 16-22. Receipt of complaint from Indiana State Civil Rights Commission.

The office is hereby authorized to receive any complaint referred to it by the Indiana State Civil Rights Commission pursuant to section 11a of the Indiana State Civil Rights Act, and to take such action with respect to any such complaint as is authorized or required in the case of a complaint filed under section 16-17.

Sec. 16-23. Service of complaint on respondent; answer.

The chief officer shall cause a copy of the complaint to be served by certified mail upon the respondent, who may file a written response to the complaint at any time prior to the close of proceedings with respect thereto, except as otherwise provided in section 16-26. The complaint and any response received shall not be made public by the chief officer, the board or any member thereof or any agent or employee of the office, unless and until a public hearing is scheduled thereon as provided in section 16-26.

Sec. 16-24. Investigation and conciliation.

(1) *Investigation.* Within ten (10) working days after the receipt of a complaint filed pursuant to this chapter, the chief officer shall initiate an investigation of the alleged discriminatory practice charged in the complaint. All such investigations shall be made by the office at the direction of the chief officer and may include informal conferences or discussions with any party to the complaint for the purpose of obtaining additional information or attempting to resolve or eliminate the alleged discriminatory practice by conciliation or persuasion. The office shall have the authority to initiate discovery, including but not

limited to interrogatories, request for production of documents and subpoenas, on approval of the chief officer at any time within ten (10) working days after filing of a complaint. Any request by the office to compel discovery may be by appropriate petition to the Marion County circuit or superior courts.

(2) *Report of investigation; determination by panel.* Unless the complaint has been satisfactorily resolved prior thereto, the chief officer shall, within thirty (30) working days after the date of filing of a complaint pursuant to section 16-17, report the results of the investigation made pursuant to subsection (1) to a panel of three (3) members of the board designated by the chairperson or vice-chairperson or pursuant to the rules of the board, which panel shall not include any member of the board who initiated the complaint, who might have participated in the investigation of the complaint, or who is a member of the complaint adjudication committee. The chief officer shall make a recommendation as to whether there is reasonable cause to believe that the respondent has violated sections 16-14 and/or 16-15. The chairperson, vice-chairperson or such other member of the panel so designated may, for good cause shown, extend the time for making such report. Such extension thereof shall be evidenced in writing, and the office shall serve a copy of the extension on both the complainant and the respondent. The panel shall then determine by majority vote whether reasonable cause exists to believe that any respondent has violated sections 16-14 and/or 16-15. In making such a determination, the panel shall consider only the complaint, the response, if any, and the chief officer's report; provided, however, the panel may request the chief officer to make a supplemental investigation and report with respect to any matter which it deems material to such determination.

(3) *Action when violation found.* If the panel, pursuant to subsection (2), determines that reasonable cause exists to believe that any respondent has violated sections 16-14 and/or 16-15, it may direct the chief officer to endeavor to eliminate the alleged discriminatory practice through a conciliation conference. At least one panel member shall be present at any conciliation conference at which both the complainant and respondent are present or represented. If the complaint is satisfactorily resolved through conciliation, the terms of any agreement reached or undertaking given by any party shall be reduced to writing and signed by the complainant, respondent and the chief officer. Any disagreement between the respondent and the chief officer in regard to the terms or conditions of a proposed conciliation agreement may

be referred to the panel which considered the complaint, and the decision of the panel with respect to such terms or conditions shall be final for purposes of conciliation proceedings under this subsection, but shall not be binding upon the respondent without his written consent thereto. No action taken or statement made in connection with any proceedings under this subsection, and no written conciliation agreement or any of the terms thereof, shall be made public by the board or any member thereof, or any agent or employee of the officer, without the written consent of the parties, nor shall any such action, statement or agreement be admissible in evidence in any subsequent proceedings; provided, however, the board or officer may institute legal proceedings under this chapter for enforcement of any written agreement or undertaking executed in accordance with this subsection.

Sec. 16-25. Complaint adjudication committee; duties.

A complaint adjudication committee is hereby established. The committee shall be composed of seven (7) members of the board. The committee shall meet for the purpose of holding public hearings on citizen's complaints, which shall be at such times as its members deem necessary.

Sec. 16-26. Hearings, findings and recommendations when conciliation not effected.

(a) *Hearing to be held; notice.* If a complaint filed pursuant to this article has not been satisfactorily resolved within a reasonable time through informal proceedings pursuant to section 16-24, or if the panel investigating the complaint determines that a conciliation conference is inappropriate under the circumstances surrounding the complaint, the complaint adjudication committee may hold a public hearing thereon upon not less than ten (10) working days' written notice to the complainant or other aggrieved person, and to the respondent. If the respondent has not previously filed a written response to the complaint, he/she may file such response and serve a copy thereof upon the complainant and the office not later than five (5) working days prior to the date of the hearing.

(b) *Powers; rights of parties at hearing.* In connection with a hearing held pursuant to subsection (a), the complaint adjudication committee shall have power, upon any matter pertinent to the complaint or response thereto, to subpoena witnesses and compel their attendance; to require the production of pertinent books, papers or other documents; and to administer oaths. The complainant shall have the right to be represented by the chief officer or any attorney of his/her choice. The respondent shall have the right to be represented by an attorney or any other person of his/her choice. The complainant and respondent shall have the right to appear in person at the hearing, to be represented by an attorney or any other person, to subpoena and compel the attendance of witnesses, and to examine and cross-examine witnesses. The complaint adjudication committee may adopt appropriate rules for the issuance of subpoenas and the conduct of hearings under this section. The complaint adjudication committee and the board shall have the power to enforce discovery and subpoenas by appropriate petition to the Marion County circuit or superior courts.

(c) *Statement of evidence; exceptions; arguments.* Within thirty (30) working days from the close of the hearing, the complaint adjudication committee shall prepare a report containing written recommended findings of fact and conclusions and file such report with the office. A copy of the report shall be furnished to the complainant and respondent, each of whom shall have an opportunity to submit written exceptions within such time as the rules of the complaint adjudication committee shall permit. The complaint adjudication committee may, in its discretion, upon notice to each interested party hear further evidence or argument upon the issues presented by the report and exceptions, if any.

(d) *Findings of fact; sustaining or dismissing complaint.* If, upon the preponderance of the evidence, the committee shall be of the opinion that any respondent has engaged or is engaging in a discriminatory practice in violation of the chapter, it shall state its findings of fact and conclusions and serve a copy thereof upon the complainant and the respondent. In addition, the committee may cause to be served on the respondent an order requiring the respondent to cease and desist from the unlawful discriminatory practice and requiring such person to take further affirmative action as will effectuate the purposes of this chapter, including but not limited to the power to restore complainant's losses incurred as a result of discriminatory treatment, as the committee may deem necessary to assure justice; to require the posting of notice setting forth the public policy of Marion County concerning equal opportunity and respondent's compliance with said policy in places of public accommodations; to require proof of compliance to be filed by respondent at periodic intervals; to require a person who has been found to be in violation of this chapter and who is licensed by a city or county agency authorized to grant a license, to show cause to the licensing agency why his license should not be revoked or suspended. If, upon the preponderance of the evidence, the committee shall be of the opinion that any respondent has not engaged in a discriminatory practice in violation of this chapter it shall state its findings of fact and conclusions and serve a copy thereof upon the complainant and the respondent, and dismiss the complaint. Findings and conclusions made by the committee shall be based solely upon the record of the evidence presented at the hearing.

(e) *Appeal to the board.* Within thirty (30) working days after the issuance of findings and conclusions by the committee, either the complainant or the respondent may file a written appeal of the decision of the committee to the board; however, in the event that the committee requires the respondent to correct or eliminate a discriminatory practice within a time period less than thirty (30) working days, then that respondent must file his/her appeal within that time period. After considering the record of the evidence presented at the hearing and the findings and conclusions of the committee, the board may affirm the decision of the committee and adopt the findings and conclusions of the committee, or it may affirm the decision of the committee and make supplemental findings and conclusions of its own, or it may reverse the decision of the committee and make findings of fact and conclusions to support its decision. The board may also adopt, modify or reverse any relief ordered by the committee. The board must take any of the above actions within thirty (30) working days after the appeal is filed.

(f) *Members of Board who are ineligible to participate.* No member of the board who initiated a complaint under this chapter or who participated in the investigation thereof shall participate in any hearing or determination under this section as a member of either a hearing panel, the complaint adjudication committee or of the board.

(g) *Applicability of state law; judicial review.* Except as otherwise specifically provided in this section or in rules adopted by the board or the complaint adjudication committee under this chapter, the applicable provisions of the Administrative Adjudication Act, IC 4-22-1, shall govern the conduct of hearings and determinations under this section, and findings of the board hereunder shall be subject to judicial review as provided in that act.

Sec. 16-27. Court Enforcement.

(a) *Institution of action.* In any case where the board or the committee has found that a respondent has engaged in or is engaging in a discriminatory practice in violation of sections 16-14 and/or 16-15, and such respondent has failed to correct or eliminate such discriminatory practice within the time limit prescribed by the board or the committee and the time limit for appeal to the board has elapsed, the board may file in its own name in the Marion County circuit or superior courts a complaint against the respondent for the enforcement of section 16-26. Such complaint may request such temporary or permanent injunctive relief as may be appropriate and such additional affirmative relief or orders as will effectuate the purposes of this chapter and as may be equitable, within the powers and jurisdiction of the court.

(b) *Record of hearing; evidentiary value.* In any action filed pursuant to this section, the board may file with the court a record of the hearing held by the complaint adjudication committee pursuant to section 16-26, which record shall be certified by the secretary of the board as a true, correct and complete record of the proceedings upon which the findings of the complaint adjudication committee and/or the board were based. The court may, in its discretion, admit any evidence contained in the record as evidence in the action filed under subsection (a), to the extent such evidence would be admissible in court under the rules of evidence if the witness or witnesses were present in court, without limitation upon the right of any party to offer such additional evidence as may be pertinent to the issues and as the court shall, in its discretion, permit.

(c) *Temporary judicial relief upon filing of complaint.* Upon the filing of a complaint pursuant to section 16-17 by a person claiming to be aggrieved, the chief officer, in the name of the board and in accordance with such procedures as the board shall establish by rule, may seek temporary orders for injunctions in the Marion County circuit or superior courts to prevent irreparable harm to the complainant, pending resolution of the complaint by the office, complaint adjudication committee and the board.

(d) *Enforcement of conciliating agreements.* If the board determines that any party to a conciliation agreement approved by the chief officer under section 16-24 has failed or refused to comply with the terms of the agreement, it may file a complaint in the name of the board in the Marion County circuit or superior courts seeking an appropriate decree for the enforcement of the agreement.

(e) *Trial de novo upon finding of sex discrimination related to pornography.* In complaints involving discrimination through pornography, judicial review shall be de novo. Notwithstanding any other provision to the contrary, whenever the board or committee has found that a respondent has engaged in or is engaging in one of the discriminatory practices set forth in paragraph (g)(4) of section 16-3 or as against a seller, exhibitor or distributor under paragraph (g)(7) of section 16-3, the board shall, within ten (10) days after making such finding, file in its own name in the Marion County circuit or superior court an action for declaratory and/or injunctive relief. The board shall have the burden of proving that the actions of the respondent were in violation of this chapter.

Provided, however, that in any complaint under paragraph (g)(4) of section 16-3 or against a seller, exhibitor or distributor under paragraph (g)(7) of section 16-3 no temporary or permanent injunction shall issue prior to a final judicial determination that said activities of respondent do constitute a discriminatory practice under this chapter.

Provided further, that no temporary or permanent injunction under paragraph (g)(4) of section 16-3 or against a seller, exhibitor or distributor under paragraph (g)(7) of section 16-3 shall extend beyond such material(s) that, having been described with reasonable specificity by the injunction, have been determined to be validly proscribed under the chapter.

Sec. 16-28. Other remedies.

Nothing in this chapter shall affect any person's right to pursue any and all rights and remedies available in any other local, state or federal forum.

INDIANAPOLIS CITY-COUNTY COUNCIL
GENERAL ORDINANCE NO. 35, 1984,
SECTION 7 & SECTION 8[2]

SECTION 7. (a) Because this ordinance amends certain provisions adopted in General Ordinance No. 24, 1984, the effective date of that ordinance is postponed until the effective date of this ordinance. (b) The expressed or implied repeal or amendment, by General Ordinance No. 24, 1984, or by this ordinance, of any other ordinance or part of any other ordinance does not affect any rights or liabilities accrued, penalties incurred, or proceedings begun prior to the effective date of this ordi-

2. These sections were not included in the codification of Indianapolis City-County General Ordinance No. 35, 1984 in the Code of Indianapolis and Marion County, Indiana, Chapter 16. It is a policy of the Indianapolis City-County Council not to codify sections of ordinances regulating effective dates and severability.

nance. Those rights, liabilities, and proceedings are continued, and penalties shall be imposed and enforced under the repealed or amended ordinance as if this ordinance or General Ordinance No. 24, 1984, had not been adopted. (c) An offense, committed before the effective date of this ordinance, under any ordinance expressly or impliedly repealed or amended by this ordinance shall be prosecuted and remains punishable under the repealed or amended ordinance as if this ordinance had not been adopted.

SECTION 8. Should any provision (section, paragraph, sentence, clause, or any other portion) of this ordinance be declared by a court of competent jurisdiction to be invalid for any reason, the remaining provisions shall not be affected unless such remaining provisions clearly cannot, without the invalid provision or provisions, be given the effect intended by the council in adopting this ordinance. It is further declared to be the intent of the City-County Council that the ordinance be upheld as applied to the graphic depiction of actual sexual subordination whether or not upheld as applied to material produced without the participation of human subjects nor shall a judicial declaration that any provision (section, paragraph, sentence, clause or any other portion) of this ordinance cannot validly be applied in a particular manner or to a particular case or category of cases affect the validity of that provision (section, paragraph, sentence, clause or any other portion) as applied in other ways or to other categories of cases unless such remaining application would clearly frustrate the Council's intent in adopting this ordinance. To this end, the provisions of this ordinance are severable.

Massachusetts Ordinance, 1992

HOUSE . . . . No. 5194

By Ms. Hildt of Amesbury, petition of Barbara Hildt, Mary Jeanette Murray, Nancy H. Evans, Marc D. Draisen, Barbara Gardner and Sally P. Kerans for legislation to protect the civil rights of women and children from pornography and sex discrimination. The Judiciary.

The Commonwealth of Massachusetts
In the Year One Thousand Nine Hundred and Ninety-Two.

AN ACT TO PROTECT THE CIVIL RIGHTS OF WOMEN AND CHILDREN.

Be it enacted by the Senate and House of Representatives in General Court assembled, and by the authority of the same, as follows:

SECTION 1. It is hereby found and declared that pornography is a practice of sex discrimination which exists in the commonwealth and threatens the health, safety, peace, welfare and equality of its citizens. Pornography is a systematic practice of exploitation and subordination based on sex that differentially harms and disadvantages women through dehumanization, psychic assault, sexual exploitation, forced sex and prostitution, physical injury and social and sexual terrorism and inferiority presented as entertainment and existing laws have proven inadequate to solve such problem. It is further found that the bigotry and contempt which pornography promotes and the acts of aggression which it fosters:

(a) diminish opportunities for equality of rights in employment, education, property, public accommodations, and public services; (b) create public and private harassment, persecution, and denigration; promote injury and degradation such as rape, battery, sexual abuse of children, and prostitution, and inhibit just enforcement of laws against these acts; (c) demean the reputations and diminish the occupational opportunities of individuals and groups on the basis of sex; (d) expose individuals who appear in pornography against their will to contempt, ridicule, hatred, humiliation, and embarrassment and target them for abuse and physical aggression; (e) lower the human dignity, worth, and civil status of women and damage mutual respect between the sexes; (f) contribute significantly to restricting women in particular from full exercise of citizenship and participation in the life of the community; and (g) undermine women's equal exercise of rights to speech and action guaranteed to all citizens under the laws and constitution of the commonwealth.

SECTION 2. The General Laws are hereby amended by inserting after chapter 151E the following chapter:

CHAPTER 151F.
PROHIBITION OF CERTAIN SEX DISCRIMINATION.

Section 1. As used in this chapter, the term "pornography" shall mean the graphic sexually explicit subordination of women through pictures or words, including by electronic or other data retrieval systems, and shall further include the presentation of women's body parts, including but not limited to, vaginas, breasts or buttocks, such that women are reduced to such parts or the presentation of women:

(a) as dehumanized sexual objects, things or commodities;

(b) as sexual objects who enjoy humiliation or pain;

(c) as sexual objects experiencing sexual pleasure in rape, incest or other sexual assault;

(d) as sexual objects tied up or cut up or mutilated, bruised or physically hurt;

(e) in postures or positions of sexual submission, servility or display;

(f) being penetrated by objects or animals; or

(g) in scenarios of degradation, humiliation, injury, torture, shown as filthy or inferior, bleeding, bruised or hurt in a context that makes these conditions sexual.

The use of men, children or transsexuals in the place of women shall also be deemed to be pornography for purposes of this definition.

Section 2. (a). It shall be sex discrimination to coerce, intimidate or fraudulently induce any person into performing for pornography. The injury incurred hereunder may occur upon any appearance or sale of any product resulting from such performance. The maker, seller, exhibitor or distributor of said pornography may be liable for damages and subject to an injunction to prohibit or eliminate such product from the public view. For purposes of this subsection proof of the following facts shall not, singly or in combination, disprove coercion:

(1) the person is a woman or a girl;

(2) the person is or has been a prostitute;

(3) the person has attained the age of majority;

(4) the person is connected by blood or marriage to anyone involved in or related to the making of the pornography;

(5) the person has previously had, or been thought to have had, sexual relations with anyone, including anyone involved in or related to the making of the pornography;

(6) the person has previously posed for sexually explicit pictures with or for anyone, including anyone involved in or related to the making of the pornography;

(7) anyone else, including a spouse or other relative, has given permission on the person's behalf;

(8) the person actually consented to a use of a performance that is then changed into pornography;

(9) the person knew that the purpose of the acts or events in question was to make pornography;

(10) the person showed no resistance or appeared to cooperate actively in the photographic sessions or events that produced the pornography;

(11) the person signed a contract, or made statements affirming a willingness to cooperate in the production of the pornography;

(12) no physical force, threats, or weapons were used in the making of the pornography; or

(13) the person was paid or otherwise compensated.

(b) It shall be sex discrimination to force pornography on a person in any place of employment, education, home, or any public place. Complaints may be brought only against the perpetrator of the force or the entity or institution responsible for the force.

(c) It shall be sex discrimination to assault, physically attack, or injure any person in a way that is directly caused by specific pornography. Complaints may be brought against the perpetrator of the assault or attack, or against the maker, distributor, seller, or exhibitor of the specific pornography.

(d) It shall be sex discrimination to defame any person through the unauthorized use in pornography of their proper name, image, or recognizable personal likeness. For purposes of this subsection, public figures shall be treated as private persons. Authorization once given may be revoked in writing any time prior to any publication.

(e) It shall be sex discrimination to produce, sell, exhibit, or distribute pornography, including through private clubs. This subsection applies only to pornography made using live or dead human beings or animals. Isolated parts shall not be the sole basis for complaints under this subsection.

City, state, and federally funded public libraries or private and public university and college libraries in which pornography is available for study, including on open shelves but excluding special display presentations, shall not be construed to be trafficking in pornography.

Any woman may bring a complaint hereunder as a woman acting against the subordination of women. Any man, child, or transsexual who alleges injury by pornography in the way women are injured by it may also complain.

Section 3. It shall not be a defense to a complaint brought under this chapter that the respondent did not know or intend that the materials at issue were pornography or sex discrimination.

No damages or compensation for losses shall be recoverable under subsection (e) of section two, or other than against the perpetrator of the assault or attack under subsection (c) of section two, unless the defendant knew or had reason to know that the materials were pornography.

Section 4. Any person who has a cause of action under this chapter, or their estate, may complain directly to a court of competent jurisdiction for relief.

Any person who has a cause of action under this chapter, or their estate, may seek nominal, compensatory, punitive damages without limitation, including for loss, pain, suffering, reduced enjoyment of life, and special damages, as well as for reasonable costs, including attorneys' fees and costs of investigation.

In claims under subsection (e) of section two, or other than against the perpetrator of the assault or attack under subsection (c) of section two, no damages or compensation for losses shall be recoverable against the maker for pornography made, against a distributor for pornography distributed, against a seller for pornography sold, or against an exhibitor for pornography exhibited, prior to the effective date of this chapter.

Any person who violates this law may be enjoined except that:

(a) In actions under subsection (e) of section two, and other than against the perpetrator of the assault or attack under subsection (c) of section two, no temporary or permanent injunction shall issue prior to a final judicial determination that the challenged activities constitute a violation of this law.

(b) No temporary or permanent injunction shall extend beyond such pornography that, having been described with reasonable specificity by said order, is determined to be validly proscribed under this chapter.

Section 5. The availability of relief under this chapter is not intended to be exclusive and shall not preclude, or be precluded by, the seeking of any other relief, whether civil or criminal.

Section 6. Complaints pursuant to this chapter shall be brought within six years of the accrual of the cause of action or from when the complainant reaches the age of majority, whichever is later.

Appendix: American Booksellers Ass'n. Inc. v. Hudnut

Editors' Note

On May 1, 1984, shortly after the Indianapolis ordinance was passed by the City-County Council and signed into law by Mayor William Hudnut, the City was sued before anyone had a chance to use it. Plaintiffs American Booksellers Association, Inc. with other media groups (including those that make up the Media Coalition)[1] claimed that the existence of the ordinance violated the First Amendment. Federal District Judge Sarah Evans Barker agreed (*American Booksellers Ass'n. Inc. v. Hudnut*, 598 F. Supp. 1316 [S.D. Ind. 1984]). In the course of the District Court proceedings, pornographers I.S.S.I. Theater, Inc., describing their business as "specializ[ing] in the sale and exhibition to the adult public of books, magazines, periodicals, newspapers, films and video tapes describing and depicting the various aspects of human sexual behavior,"[2] intervened to assert that they were far more appropriate than American Booksellers to represent the interests against the ordinance:

> None of the plaintiffs identified in the complaint of American Booksellers Associations, Inc., and others alleges that it sells or exhibits materials dealing with sex, much less specializes in the sale or exhibition of such materials as do intervenors. Consequently, intervenors have a greater and more immediate interest in the litigation of the constitutionality of this

1. Those who sued are: American Booksellers, Inc., Association of American Publishers, Inc., Council for Periodical Distributors Associations, Freedom to Read Foundation, International Periodical Distributors Association, Inc., Koch News Company, National Association of College Stores, Inc., Omega Satellite Products Co., Video Shack, Inc., and Kelly Bentley, resident of Indianapolis.

2. Motion to Intervene as Plaintiffs, Cause No. IP 84-791C, U.S. Dist. Ct., S.D. Ind. (May, 1984), §1.

ordinance than any of the existing plaintiffs as described in their complaint.[3]

Clearly, the pornographers know the difference between what they sell
and the stock in trade of American Booksellers. These pornographers
then disappeared from the proceedings, taking no further visible part.
Presumably, the appearance of real pornographers was a momentary embarrassment to the Media Coalition's First Amendment strategy of hiding pornography behind their legitimate front, of erasing the line drawn
by the ordinance between pornography and other verbal and visual materials, to their defense that pornography is indistinguishable from art
and literature.

Indianapolis appealed to the Court of Appeals for the Seventh Circuit.
The attorneys for Indianapolis were Mark Dall and Kathryn A. Watson.
Appearances filed for American Booksellers, Inc. were Sheila Seuss Kennedy, Michael A. Bamberger, lawyer for the Media Coalition who presented oral argument, Richard W. Cardwell, and Burton Joseph, also a
lawyer for *Playboy*.

Indianapolis's record before the Seventh Circuit included substantial
excerpts from the Minneapolis Hearings. In support of the ordinance,
briefs *amici curiae* were filed by many grass-roots and survivor groups
against violence against women, by survivors, and by activists. They
were: Women Against Pornography, Pornography Resource Center, Men
Against Pornography, Pornography Awareness, Alpha Human Services,
Citizens Against Pornography, Lincoln Women Against Pornography,
Men's Task Force on Pornography, Minnesota Coalition for Battered
Women, Northwest Women's Services, Pornography Education Center,
Task Force on Prostitution and Pornography, Washington County Sexual
Assault Center, and La Raza Centro Legal, Inc. (Ralph A. Hummell);
Minneapolis City Council Members Charlee Hoyt and Van White
with Region II of the Minnesota Coalition for Battered Women (Fred
Ojile); Feminists Against Pornography (Deborah M. Chalfie); Linda
Marchiano and the Estate of Dorothy Stratten (Catharine A. MacKin-
non); Andrea Dworkin (*Pro Se*) (see Appendix A to Indianapolis Hear-
ing, pp. 310–320 above); The Neighborhood Pornography Task Force
(Janella Miller) (see Appendix B to Indianapolis Hearing, pp. 321–331
above).

In support of American Booksellers, two briefs *amici curiae* were

3. Ibid., §3.

filed, one by the American Civil Liberties Union, the Indiana Civil Liberties Union, and the Illinois Civil Liberties Union (James A. Klenk, Dale M. Cohen, John Wood, Burt Neuborne, Charles S. Sims), the other by the Feminist Anti-Censorship Task Force (Nan D. Hunter).[4] Nan D. Hunter was employed as a staff lawyer for the American Civil Liberties Union at the time, although this was not indicated on the brief. John Wood, who testified in the Indianapolis Hearing, was with Bamberger and Feibleman (Mr. Bamberger represented the Media Coalition).

The Seventh Circuit affirmed, finding that the ordinance violated the First Amendment, in a decision set out in full below (*American Booksellers, Inc. v. Hudnut,* 771 F.2d 323 [7th Cir. 1985]). Subsequently, Indianapolis took a direct appeal to the U.S. Supreme Court, which affirmed summarily, 106 S. Ct. 1172 (1986). A summary affirmance, now largely obsolete, is a device through which the U.S. Supreme Court, without reading briefs or hearing oral argument, upholds an appellate result without expressing any views on the reasoning used in the opinion that reached that result. While summary affirmances are formally rulings on the merits, the reasoning in the appellate opinions affirmed—in this instance, the decision written by Judge Easterbrook below—is binding only in the circuit in which it was written. This leaves substantial latitude, for example, for another ordinance to be introduced, to be found constitutional in another circuit, and to be reviewed and upheld by the Supreme Court. The likelihood of a finding of constitutionality is improved if the ordinance is revised or if the law of the subject has changed in the interim.

Three justices dissented from the summary affirmance in *Hudnut,* saying they wanted to hear argument,[5] often a sign that legal reconsideration may be favorably viewed. Summary affirmances need not bind later Supreme Courts.[6] Nothing in its legal history prevents the civil rights approach to pornography from being found constitutional. All the arguments in support of its constitutionality retain legal validity. The future of the ordinance remains open.

4. See Brief *Amici Curiae* of Feminist Anti-Censorship Task Force, 21 *Michigan Journal of Law Reform* 69 (1988).

5. Hudnut v. American Booksellers Ass'n, Inc., 475 U.S. 1001 (1986). (The Chief Justice [Burger], Justice Rehnquist, and Justice O'Connor would note probable jurisdiction and set the case for oral argument.)

6. Robert Stern et al., *Supreme Court Practice,* 7th ed. (1993), pp. 215–221.

AMERICAN BOOKSELLERS ASSOCIATION, INC., Association of American Publishers, Inc.; Council for Periodical Distributors Associations; Freedom to Read Foundation; International Periodical Distributors Association, Inc.; Koch News Company; National Association of College Stores, Inc.; Omega Satellite Products Co.; Video Shack, Inc.; and Kelly Bentley, Plaintiffs-Appellees, v. William H. HUDNUT, III, Mayor, City of Indianapolis; The City of Indianapolis; The County of Marion; The Department of Administration of the City of Indianapolis; Office of Equal Opportunity of the City of Indianapolis; Equal Opportunity Advisory Board of the City of Indianapolis; and Joseph McAtee, Chief of Police; Stephen Goldsmith, Marion County Prosecutor; and Jame Wells, Marion County Sheriff, Defendants-Appellants. 771 F.2d 323 (7th Cir. 1985).

Before CUDAHY and EASTERBROOK, Circuit Judges, and SWYGERT, Senior Circuit Judge.

EASTERBROOK, Circuit Judge.

Indianapolis enacted an ordinance defining "pornography" as a practice that discriminates against women. "Pornography" is to be redressed through the administrative and judicial methods used for other discrimination. The City's definition of "pornography" is considerably different from "obscenity," which the Supreme Court has held is not protected by the First Amendment.

To be "obscene" under Miller v. California, 413 U.S. 15, 93 S.Ct. 2607, 37 L.Ed.2d 419 (1973), "a publication must, taken as a whole, appeal to the prurient interest, must contain patently offensive depictions or descriptions of specified sexual conduct, and on the whole have no serious literary, artistic, political, or scientific value." Brockett v. Spokane Arcades, Inc.,——U.S.——, 105 S.Ct. 2794, 2800, 86 L.Ed.2d 394 (1985). Offensiveness must be assessed under the standards of the community. Both offensiveness and an appeal to something other than "normal, healthy sexual desires" (Brockett, supra, 105 S.Ct. at 2799) are essential elements of "obscenity."

"Pornography" under the ordinance is "the graphic sexually explicit subordination of women, whether in pictures or in words, that also includes one or more of the following: (1) Women are presented as sexual objects who enjoy pain or humiliation; or (2) Women are presented as sexual objects who experience sexual pleasure in being raped; or (3)

Women are presented as sexual objects tied up or cut up or mutilated or bruised or physically hurt, or as dismembered or truncated or fragmented or severed into body parts; or (4) Women are presented as being penetrated by objects or animals; or (5) Women are presented in scenarios of degradation, injury, abasement, torture, shown as filthy or inferior, bleeding, bruised, or hurt in a context that makes these conditions sexual; or (6) Women are presented as sexual objects for domination, conquest, violation, exploitation, possession, or use, or through postures or positions of servility or submission or display." Indianapolis Code s 16-3(q). The statute provides that the "use of men, children, or transsexuals in the place of women in paragraphs (1) through (6) above shall also constitute pornography under this section." The ordinance as passed in April 1984 defined "sexually explicit" to mean actual or simulated intercourse or the uncovered exhibition of the genitals, buttocks or anus. An amendment in June 1984 deleted this provision, leaving the term undefined.

The Indianapolis ordinance does not refer to the prurient interest, to offensiveness, or to the standards of the community. It demands attention to particular depictions, not to the work judged as a whole. It is irrelevant under the ordinance whether the work has literary, artistic, political, or scientific value. The City and many amici point to these omissions as virtues. They maintain that pornography influences attitudes, and the statute is a way to alter the socialization of men and women rather than to vindicate community standards of offensiveness. And as one of the principal drafters of the ordinance has asserted, "if a woman is subjected, why should it matter that the work has other value?" Catharine A. MacKinnon, Pornography, Civil Rights, and Speech, 20 Harv.Civ.Rts.—Civ.Lib.L.Rev. 1, 21 (1985).

Civil rights groups and feminists have entered this case as amici on both sides. Those supporting the ordinance say that it will play an important role in reducing the tendency of men to view women as sexual objects, a tendency that leads to both unacceptable attitudes and discrimination in the workplace and violence away from it. Those opposing the ordinance point out that much radical feminist literature is explicit and depicts women in ways forbidden by the ordinance and that the ordinance would reopen old battles. It is unclear how Indianapolis would treat works from James Joyce's *Ulysses* to Homer's *Iliad;* both depict women as submissive objects for conquest and domination.

We do not try to balance the arguments for and against an ordinance such as this. The ordinance discriminates on the ground of the content of the speech. Speech treating women in the approved way—in sexual encounters "premised on equality" (MacKinnon, supra, at 22)—is lawful no matter how sexually explicit. Speech treating women in the disapproved way—as submissive in matters sexual or as enjoying humiliation—is unlawful no matter how significant the literary, artistic, or political qualities of the work taken as a whole. The state may not ordain preferred viewpoints in this way. The Constitution forbids the state to declare one perspective right and silence opponents.

I

The ordinance contains four prohibitions. People may not "traffic" in pornography, "coerce" others into performing in pornographic works, or "force" pornography on anyone. Anyone injured by someone who has seen or read pornography has a right of action against the maker or seller.

Trafficking is defined in s 16-3(g)(4) as the "production, sale, exhibition, or distribution of pornography." The offense excludes exhibition in a public or educational library, but a "special display" in a library may be sex discrimination. Section 16-3(g)(4)(C) provides that the trafficking paragraph "shall not be construed to make isolated passages or isolated parts actionable."

"Coercion into pornographic performance" is defined in s 16-3(g)(5) as "[c]oercing, intimidating or fraudulently inducing any person . . . into performing for pornography. . . ." The ordinance specifies that proof of any of the following "shall not constitute a defense: I. That the person is a woman; . . . VI. That the person has previously posed for sexually explicit pictures . . . with anyone . . .; . . . VIII. That the person actually consented to a use of the performance that is changed into pornography; . . . IX. That the person knew that the purpose of the acts or events in question was to make pornography; . . . XI. That the person signed a contract, or made statements affirming a willingness to cooperate in the production of pornography; XII. That no physical force, threats, or weapons were used in the making of the pornography; or XIII. That the person was paid or otherwise compensated."

"Forcing pornography on a person," according to s 16-3(g)(5), is the "forcing of pornography on any woman, man, child, or transsexual in any place of employment, in education, in a home, or in any public place." The statute does not define forcing, but one of its authors states that the definition reaches pornography shown to medical students as part of their education or given to language students for translation. MacKinnon, supra, at 40–41.

Section 16-3(g)(7) defines as a prohibited practice the "assault, physical attack, or injury of any woman, man, child, or transsexual in a way that is directly caused by specific pornography."

For purposes of all four offenses, it is generally "not . . . a defense that the respondent did not know or intend that the materials were pornography. . . ." Section 16-3(g)(8). But the ordinance provides that damages are unavailable in trafficking cases unless the complainant proves "that the respondent knew or had reason to know that the materials were pornography." It is a complete defense to a trafficking case that all of the materials in question were pornography only by virtue of category (6) of the definition of pornography. In cases of assault caused by pornography, those who seek damages from "a seller, exhibitor or distributor" must show that the defendant knew or had reason to know of the material's status as pornography. By implication, those who seek damages from an author need not show this.

A woman aggrieved by trafficking in pornography may file a complaint "as a woman acting against the subordination of women" with the office of equal opportunity. Section 16-17(b). A man, child, or transsexual also may protest trafficking "but must prove injury in the same way that a woman is injured. . . ." Ibid. Subsection (a) also provides, however, that "any person claiming to be aggrieved" by trafficking, coercion, forcing, or assault may complain against the "perpetrators." We need not decide whether s 16-17(b) qualifies the right of action in s 16-17(a).

The office investigates and within 30 days makes a recommendation to a panel of the equal opportunity advisory board. The panel then decides whether there is reasonable cause to proceed (s 16-24(2)) and may refer the dispute to a conciliation conference or to a complaint adjudication committee for a hearing (ss 16-24(3), 16-26(a)). The committee uses the same procedures ordinarily associated with civil rights litigation. It may make findings and enter orders, including both orders to cease and desist and orders "to take further affirmative action . . . including but not limited to the power to restore complainant's losses. . . ." Section 16-26(d). Either party may appeal the committee's decision to the board, which reviews the record before the committee and may modify its decision.

Under Indiana law an administrative decision takes effect when rendered, unless a court issues a stay. Ind.Stat. s 4-22-1-13. The board's decisions are subject to review in the ordinary course. Ind.Stat. s 4-22-1-14. Judicial review in pornography cases is to be de novo, Indianapolis Code s 16-27(e), which provides a second complete hearing. When the board finds that a person has engaged in trafficking or that a seller, exhibitor, or distributor is responsible for an assault, it must initiate judicial review of its own decision, ibid., and the statute prohibits injunctive relief in these cases in advance of the court's final decision. (This is unlike the usual procedure under state law, which permits summary enforcement. Ind.Stat. ss 4-22-1-18 and 4-22-1-27.)

The district court held the ordinance unconstitutional. 598 F.Supp. 1316 (S.D.Ind.1984). The court concluded that the ordinance regulates speech rather than the conduct involved in making pornography. The regulation of speech could be justified, the court thought, only by a compelling interest in reducing sex discrimination, an interest Indianapolis had not established. The ordinance is also vague and overbroad, the court believed, and establishes a prior restraint of speech.

II

The plaintiffs are a congeries of distributors and readers of books, magazines, and films. The American Booksellers Association comprises about 5,200 bookstores and chains. The Association for American Publishers includes most of the country's publishers. Video Shack, Inc., sells and rents video cassettes in Indianapolis. Kelly Bentley, a resident of Indianapolis, reads books and watches films. There are many more plaintiffs. Collectively the plaintiffs (or their members, whose interests they represent) make, sell, or read just about every kind of material that could be affected by the ordinance, from hard-core films to W. B. Yeats's poem "Leda and the Swan" (from the myth of Zeus in the form of a swan impregnating an apparently subordinate Leda), to the collected works of James Joyce, D. H. Lawrence, and John Cleland.

[2] The interests of Bentley and many of the members of the organizational plaintiffs are directly affected by the ordinance, which gives them standing to attack it. Buckley v. Valeo, 424 U.S. 1, 11–12 & n. 10, 96 S.Ct. 612, 630–31 & n. 10, 46 L.Ed.2d 659 (1976). There is no need to invoke the special standing rules applicable to overbroad laws that affect

speech, see Schad v. Borough of Mount Ephraim, 452 U.S. 61, 101 S.Ct. 2176, 68 L.Ed.2d 671 (1981); Henry P. Monaghan, Overbreadth, 1981 Sup.Ct.Rev. 1.

[3][4] The district court prevented the ordinance from taking effect. The expedition with which this suit was filed raises questions of ripeness and abstention. Ripeness is a prudential question, see Buckley, supra, 424 U.S. at 13–18, 96 S.Ct. at 631–34; Thomas v. Union Carbide Agricultural Products Co.,——U.S.——, 105 S.Ct. 3325, 3332–34, 87 L.Ed.2d 409 (1985). A case is not ripe if the issues are still poorly formed or the application of the statute is uncertain. A challenge may be ripe, however, even when the statute is not yet effective. Entertainment Concepts, Inc. v. Maciejewski, 631 F.2d 497, 500 (7th Cir.1980), cert. denied, 450 U.S. 919, 101 S.Ct. 1366, 67 L.Ed.2d 346 (1981). The statute challenged in Pierce v. Society of Sisters, 268 U.S. 510, 45 S.Ct. 571, 69 L.Ed. 1070 (1925), had an effective date two years in the future, yet the Court found the suit ripe. Here, as in Pierce, the dispute may be resolved without reference to the administration of the statute. We gain nothing by waiting. Time would take a toll, however, on the speech of the parties subject to the act. They must take special care not to release material that might be deemed pornographic, for that material could lead to awards of damages. Deferred adjudication would produce tempered speech without assisting in resolution of the controversy.

It is also inappropriate to abstain under Railroad Commission v. Pullman Co., 312 U.S. 496, 61 S.Ct. 643, 85 L.Ed. 971 (1941). Abstention is appropriate when state courts may clarify the meaning of a statute, thus sharpening the constitutional dispute and perhaps preventing an unnecessary constitutional adjudication. This statute, however, is all too clear. Cf. Mazanec v. North Judson—San Pierre School Corp., 763 F.2d 845, 848 (7th Cir. 1985). A state court could not construe this ordinance as an "ordinary" obscenity law; another law serves that function. Ind.Stat. s 35-49-1-1 et seq. It is designed to be distinctively different, to prohibit explicitly sexual speech that "subordinates" women in specified ways. If abstention was unnecessary in Brockett, despite the argument (which convinced the Chief Justice and Justices Rehnquist and O'Connor, see 105 S.Ct. at 2804–05) that a state court could save the statute by excising or construing a single element of the definition of obscenity, it surely is unnecessary here, for it is the structure of the statute rather than the meaning of any one of its terms that leads to the constitutional problem.

III

[5] "If there is any fixed star in our constitutional constellation, it is that no official, high or petty, can prescribe what shall be orthodox in politics, nationalism, religion, or other matters of opinion or force citizens to confess by word or act their faith therein." West Virginia State Board of Education v. Barnette, 319 U.S. 624, 642, 63 S.Ct. 1178, 1187, 87 L.Ed. 1628 (1943). Under the First Amendment the government must leave to the people the evaluation of ideas. Bald or subtle, an idea is as powerful as the audience allows it to be. A belief may be pernicious—the beliefs of Nazis led to the death of millions, those of the Klan to the repression of millions. A pernicious belief may prevail. Totalitarian governments today rule much of the planet, practicing suppression of billions and spreading dogma that may enslave others. One of the things that separates our society from theirs is our absolute right to propagate opinions that the government finds wrong or even hateful.

The ideas of the Klan may be propagated. Brandenburg v. Ohio, 395 U.S. 444, 89 S.Ct. 1827, 23 L.Ed.2d 430 (1969). Communists may speak freely and run for office. DeJonge v. Oregon, 299 U.S. 353, 57 S.Ct. 255, 81 L.Ed. 278 (1937). The Nazi Party may march through a city with a large Jewish population. Collin v. Smith, 578 F.2d 1197 (7th Cir.), cert. denied, 439 U.S. 916, 99 S.Ct. 291, 58 L.Ed.2d 264 (1978). People may criticize the President by misrepresenting his positions, and they have a right to post their misrepresentations on public property. Lebron v. Washington Metropolitan Area Transit Authority, 749 F.2d 893 (D.C.Cir.1984) (Bork, J.). People may teach religions that others despise. People may seek to repeal laws guaranteeing equal opportunity in employment or to revoke the constitutional amendments granting the vote to blacks and women. They may do this because "above all else, the First Amendment means that government has no power to restrict expression because of its message [or] its ideas. . . ." Police Department v. Mosley, 408 U.S. 92, 95, 92 S.Ct. 2286, 2290, 33 L.Ed.2d 212 (1972). See also Geoffrey R. Stone, Content Regulation and the First Amendment, 25 William & Mary L.Rev. 189 (1983); Paul B. Stephan, The First Amendment and Content Discrimination, 68 Va.L.Rev. 203, 233–36 (1982).

Under the ordinance graphic sexually explicit speech is "pornography" or not depending on the perspective the author adopts. Speech that "subordinates" women and also, for example, presents women as enjoying pain, humiliation, or rape, or even simply presents women in "positions of servility or submission or display" is forbidden, no matter how great the literary or political value of the work taken as a whole. Speech that portrays women in positions of equality is lawful, no matter how graphic the sexual content. This is thought control. It establishes an "approved" view of women, of how they may react to sexual encounters, of how the sexes may relate to each other. Those who espouse the approved view may use sexual images; those who do not, may not.

Indianapolis justifies the ordinance on the ground that pornography affects thoughts. Men who see women depicted as subordinate are more likely to treat them so. Pornography is an aspect of dominance. [1] It does not persuade people so much as change them. It works by socializing, by establishing the expected and the permissible. In this view pornography is not an idea; pornography is the injury.

There is much to this perspective. Beliefs are also facts. People often act in accordance with the images and patterns they find around them. People raised in a religion tend to accept the tenets of that religion, often without independent examination. People taught from birth that black people are fit only for slavery rarely rebelled against that creed; beliefs coupled with the self-interest of the masters established a social structure that inflicted great harm while enduring for centuries. Words and images act at the level of the subconscious before they persuade at the level of the conscious. Even the truth has little chance unless a statement fits within the framework of beliefs that may never have been subjected to rational study.

Therefore we accept the premises of this legislation. Depictions of subordination tend to perpetuate subordination. The subordinate status of women in turn leads to affront and lower pay at work, insult and injury at home, battery and rape on the streets. [2] In the language of the legislature, "[p]ornography is central in creating and maintaining sex as a basis of discrimination. Pornography is a systematic practice of exploitation and subordination based on sex which differentially harms women. The bigotry and contempt it produces, with the acts of aggression it fosters, harm women's opportunities for equality and rights [of all kinds]." Indianapolis Code s 16-1(a)(2).

Yet this simply demonstrates the power of pornography as speech. All of these unhappy effects depend on mental intermediation. Pornography affects how people see the world, their fellows, and social relations. If pornography is what pornography does, so is other speech. Hitler's orations affected how some Germans saw Jews. Communism is a world view, not simply a Manifesto by Marx and Engels or a set of speeches. Efforts to suppress communist speech in the United States were based on the belief that the public acceptability of such ideas would increase the likelihood of totalitarian government. Religions affect socialization in the most pervasive way. The opinion in Wisconsin v. Yoder, 406 U.S. 205, 92 S.Ct. 1526, 32 L.Ed.2d 15 (1972), shows how a religion can dominate an entire approach to life, governing much more than the relation between the sexes. Many people believe that the existence of television, apart from the content of specific programs, leads to intellectual laziness, to a penchant for violence, to many other ills. The Alien and Sedition Acts passed during the administration of John Adams rested on a sincerely held belief that disrespect for the government leads to social collapse and revolution—a belief with support in the history of many nations. Most governments of the world act on this empirical regularity, suppressing critical speech. In the United States, however, the strength of the support for this belief is irrelevant. Seditious libel is protected speech unless the danger is not only grave but also imminent. See New York Times Co. v. Sullivan, 376 U.S. 254, 84 S.Ct. 710, 11 L.Ed.2d 686 (1964); cf. Brandenburg v. Ohio, supra; New York Times Co. v. United States, 403 U.S. 713, 91 S.Ct. 2140, 29 L.Ed.2d 822 (1971).

Racial bigotry, anti-semitism, violence on television, reporters' biases —these and many more influence the culture and shape our socialization. None is directly answerable by more speech, unless that speech too finds its place in the popular culture. Yet all is protected as speech, however insidious. Any other answer leaves the government in control of all of the institutions of culture, the great censor and director of which thoughts are good for us.

Sexual responses often are unthinking responses, and the association of sexual arousal with the subordination of women therefore may have a substantial effect. But almost all cultural stimuli provoke unconscious responses. Religious ceremonies condition their participants. Teachers convey messages by selecting what not to cover; the implicit message about what is off limits or unthinkable may be more powerful than the messages for which they present rational argument. Television scripts contain unarticulated assumptions. People may be conditioned in subtle ways. If the fact that speech plays a role in a process of conditioning were enough to permit governmental regulation, that would be the end of freedom of speech.

It is possible to interpret the claim that the pornography is the harm in a different way. Indianapolis emphasizes the injury that models in pornographic films and pictures may suffer. The record contains materials depicting sexual torture, penetration of women by red-hot irons and the like. These concerns have nothing to do with written materials subject to the statute, and physical injury can occur with or without the "subordination" of women. As we discuss in Part IV, a state may make injury in the course of producing a film unlawful independent of the viewpoint expressed in the film.

The more immediate point, however, is that the image of pain is not necessarily pain. In *Body Double*, a suspense film directed by Brian DePalma, a woman who has disrobed and presented a sexually explicit display is murdered by an intruder with a drill. The drill runs through the woman's body. The film is sexually explicit and a murder occurs—yet no one believes that the actress suffered pain or died. In *Barbarella* a character played by Jane Fonda is at times displayed in sexually explicit ways and at times shown "bleeding, bruised, [and] hurt in a context that makes these conditions sexual"—and again no one believes that Fonda was actually tortured to make the film. In *Carnal Knowledge* a woman grovels to please the sexual whims of a character played by Jack Nicholson; no one believes that there was a real sexual submission, and the Supreme Court held the film protected by the First Amendment. Jenkins v. Georgia, 418 U.S. 153, 94 S.Ct. 2750, 41 L.Ed.2d 642 (1974). And this works both ways. The description of women's sexual domination of men in *Lysistrata* was not real dominance. Depictions may affect slavery, war, or sexual roles, but a book about slavery is not itself slavery, or a book about death by poison a murder.

Much of Indianapolis's argument rests on the belief that when speech is "unanswerable," and the metaphor that there is a "marketplace of ideas" does not apply, the First Amendment does not apply either. The metaphor is honored; Milton's *Areopagitica* and John Stuart Mill's *On Liberty* defend freedom of speech on the ground that the truth will prevail, and many of the most important cases under the First Amendment recite this position. The Framers undoubtedly believed it. As a general matter it is true. But the Constitution does not make the dominance of truth a necessary condition of freedom of speech. To say that it does would be to confuse an outcome of free speech with a necessary condition for the application of the amendment.

A power to limit speech on the ground that truth has not yet prevailed and is not likely to prevail implies the power to declare truth. At some point the government must be able to say (as Indianapolis has said): "We know what the truth is, yet a free exchange of speech has not driven out falsity, so that we must now prohibit falsity." If the government may declare the truth, why wait for the failure of speech? Under the First Amendment, however, there is no such thing as a false idea, Gertz v. Robert Welch, Inc., 418 U.S. 323, 339, 94 S.Ct. 2997, 3006, 41 L.Ed.2d 789 (1974), so the government may not restrict speech on the ground that in a free exchange truth is not yet dominant.

At any time, some speech is ahead in the game; the more numerous speakers prevail. Supporters of minority candidates may be forever "excluded" from the political process because their candidates never win, because few people believe their positions. This does not mean that freedom of speech has failed.

The Supreme Court has rejected the position that speech must be "effectively answerable" to be protected by the Constitution. For example, in Buckley v. Valeo, supra, 424 U.S. at 39-54, 96 S.Ct. at 644-51, the Court held unconstitutional limitations on expenditures that were neutral with regard to the speakers' opinions and designed to make it easier for one person to answer another's speech. See also FEC v. National Conservative PAC,——U.S.——, 105 S.Ct. 1459, 84 L.Ed.2d 455 (1985). In Mills v. Alabama, 384 U.S. 214, 86 S.Ct. 1434, 16 L.Ed.2d 484 (1966), the Court held unconstitutional a statute prohibiting editorials on election day—a statute the state had designed to prevent speech that came too late for answer. In cases from Eastern Railroad Presidents Conference v. Noerr Motor Freight, Inc., 365 U.S. 127, 81 S.Ct. 523, 5 L.Ed.2d 464 (1961), through NAACP v. Claiborne Hardware Co., 458 U.S. 886, 102 S.Ct. 3409, 73 L.Ed.2d 1215 (1982), the Court has held that the First Amendment protects political stratagems—obtaining legislation through underhanded ploys and outright fraud in Noerr, obtaining political and economic ends through boycotts in Claiborne Hardware—that may be beyond effective correction through more speech.

We come, finally, to the argument that pornography is "low value" speech, that it is enough like obscenity that Indianapolis may prohibit it. Some cases hold that speech far removed from politics and other subjects at the core of the Framers' concerns may be subjected to special regulation. E.g., FCC v. Pacifica Foundation, 438 U.S. 726, 98 S.Ct. 3026, 57 L.Ed.2d 1073 (1978); Young v. American Mini Theatres, Inc., 427 U.S. 50, 67-70, 96 S.Ct. 2440, 2450-52, 49 L.Ed.2d 310 (1976) (plurality opinion); Chaplinsky v. New Hampshire, 315 U.S. 568, 571-72, 62 S.Ct. 766, 768-69, 86 L.Ed. 1031 (1942). These cases do not sustain statutes that select among viewpoints, however. In Pacifica the FCC sought to keep vile language off the air during certain times. The Court held that it may; but the Court would not have sustained a regulation prohibiting scatological descriptions of Republicans but not scatological descriptions of Democrats, or any other form of selection among viewpoints. See Planned Parenthood Ass'n v. Chicago Transit Authority, 767 F.2d 1225, 1232-33 (7th Cir.1985).

At all events, "pornography" is not low value speech within the meaning of these cases. Indianapolis seeks to prohibit certain speech because it believes this speech influences social relations and politics on a grand scale, that it controls attitudes at home and in the legislature. This precludes a characterization of the speech as low value. True, pornography and obscenity have sex in common. But Indianapolis left out of its definition any reference to literary, artistic, political, or scientific value. The ordinance applies to graphic sexually explicit subordination in works great and small. [3] The Court sometimes balances the value of speech against the costs of its restriction, but it does this by category of speech and not by the content of particular works. See John Hart Ely, "Flag Desecration: A Case Study in the Roles of Categorization and Balancing in First Amendment Analysis," 88 *Harv.L.Rev.* 1482 (1975); Geoffrey R. Stone, "Restrictions of Speech Because of its Content: The Strange Case of Subject-Matter Restrictions," 46 *U.Chi.L.Rev.* 81 (1978). Indianapolis has created an approved point of view and so loses the support of these cases.

Any rationale we could imagine in support of this ordinance could not be limited to sex discrimination. Free speech has been on balance an ally of those seeking change. Governments that want stasis start by restricting speech. Culture is a powerful force of continuity; Indianapolis paints pornography as part of the culture of power. Change in any complex system ultimately depends on the ability of outsiders to challenge accepted views and the reigning institutions. Without a strong guarantee of freedom of speech, there is no effective right to challenge what is.

IV

The definition of "pornography" is unconstitutional. No construction or excision of particular terms could save it. The offense of trafficking in pornography necessarily falls with the definition. We express no view on the district court's conclusions that the ordinance is vague and that it establishes a prior restraint. Neither is necessary to our judgment. We also express no view on the argument presented by several amici that the ordinance is itself a form of discrimination on account of sex.

Section 8 of the ordinance is a strong severability clause, and Indianapolis asks that we parse the ordinance to save what we can. If a court could do this by surgical excision, this might be possible. Zbaraz v. Hartigan, 763 F.2d 1532, 1545 (7th Cir. 1985). But a federal court may not completely reconstruct a local ordinance, and we conclude that nothing short of rewriting could save anything.

The offense of coercion to engage in a pornographic performance, for example, has elements that might be constitutional. Without question a state may prohibit fraud, trickery, or the use of force to induce people to perform—in pornographic films or in any other films. Such a statute may be written without regard to the viewpoint depicted in the work. New York v. Ferber, 458 U.S. 747, 102 S.Ct. 3348, 73 L.Ed.2d 1113 (1982), suggests that when a state has a strong interest in forbidding the conduct that makes up a film (in Ferber sexual acts involving minors), it may restrict or forbid dissemination of the film in order to reinforce the prohibition of the conduct. A state may apply such a rule to non-sexual coercion (although it need not). We suppose that if someone forced a prominent political figure, at gunpoint, to endorse a candidate for office, a state could forbid the commercial sale of the film containing that coerced endorsement. The same principle allows a court to enjoin the publication of stolen trade secrets and award damages for the publication of copyrighted matter without permission. See Harper & Row, Publishers, Inc. v. Nation Enterprises,——U.S.——, 105 S.Ct., 2218, 85 L.Ed.2d 588 (1985). Cf. Snepp v. United States, 444 U.S. 507, 509 & n. 3, 100 S.Ct. 763, 765 & n. 3, 62 L.Ed.2d 704 (1980).

But the Indianapolis ordinance, unlike our hypothetical statute, is not neutral with respect to viewpoint. The ban on distribution of works containing coerced performances is limited to pornography; coercion is irrelevant if the work is not "pornography," and we have held the definition of "pornography" to be defective root and branch. A legislature might replace "pornography" in s 16-3(g)(4) with "any film containing explicit sex" or some similar expression, but even the broadest severability clause does not permit a federal court to rewrite as opposed to excise. Rewriting is work for the legislature of Indianapolis. Cf. Stanton v. Stanton, 421 U.S. 7, 95 S.Ct. 1373, 43 L.Ed.2d 688 (1975); Califano v. Westcott, 443 U.S. 76, 99 S.Ct. 2655, 61 L.Ed.2d 382 (1979).

The offense of forcing pornography on unwilling recipients is harder to assess. Many kinds of forcing (such as giving texts to students for translation) may themselves be protected speech. Rowan v. Post Office, 397 U.S. 728, 90 S.Ct. 1484, 25 L.Ed.2d 736 (1970), shows that a state may permit people to insulate themselves from categories of speech—in Rowan sexual mail—but that the government must leave the decision about what items are forbidden in the hands of the potentially offended recipients. See Bolger v. Youngs Drug Products Corp., 463 U.S. 60, 103 S.Ct. 2875, 77 L.Ed.2d 469 (1983) (the government may not define for itself a category of constitutionally protected but sexual speech that may not be mailed). Exposure to sex is not something the government may prevent, see Erznoznik v. City of Jacksonville, 422 U.S. 205, 95 S.Ct. 2268, 45 L.Ed.2d 125 (1975). We therefore could not save the offense of "forcing" by redefining "pornography" as all sexually-offensive speech or some related category. The statute needs a definition of "forcing" that removes the government from the role of censor. See also Planned Parenthood Ass'n, supra, holding that the "captive audience" problem does not permit a government to discriminate on account of the speaker's message.

The section creating remedies for injuries and assaults attributable to pornography also is salvageable in principle, although not by us. The First Amendment does not prohibit redress of all injuries caused by speech. Injury to reputation is redressed through the law of libel, which is constitutional subject to strict limitations. Cases such as Brandenburg v. Ohio and NAACP v. Claiborne Hardware hold that a state may not penalize speech that does not cause immediate injury. But we do not doubt that if, immediately after the Klan's rally in Brandenburg, a mob had burned to the ground the house of a nearby black person, that person could have recovered damages from the speaker who whipped the crowd into a frenzy. All of the Justices assumed in Claiborne Hardware that if the threats in Charles Evers's incendiary speech had been a little less veiled and had led directly to an assault against a person shopping in a store owned by a white merchant, the victim of the assault and even the merchant could have recovered damages from the speaker.

The law of libel has the potential to muzzle the press, which led to New York Times v. Sullivan. See also Ollman v. Evans, 750 F.2d 970, 994-98 (D.C.Cir.1984) (en banc) (Bork, J., concurring). A law awarding damages for assaults caused by speech also has the power to muzzle the press, and again courts would place careful limits on the scope of the right. Certainly no damages could be awarded unless the harm flowed directly from the speech and there was an element of intent on the part of the speaker, as in Sullivan and Brandenburg.

Much speech is dangerous. Chemists whose work might help someone build a bomb, political theorists whose papers might start political movements that lead to riots, speakers whose ideas attract violent protesters, all these and more leave loss in their wake. Unless the remedy is very closely confined, it could be more dangerous to speech than all the libel judgments in history. The constitutional requirements for a valid recovery for assault caused by speech might turn out to be too rigorous for any plaintiff to meet. [4] But the Indianapolis ordinance requires the complainant to show that the attack was "directly caused by specific pornography" (s 16-3(g)(7)), and it is not beyond the realm of possibility that a state court could construe this limitation in a way that would make the statute constitutional. We are not authorized to prevent the state from trying.

Again, however, the assault statute is tied to "pornography," and we cannot find a sensible way to repair the defect without seizing power that belongs elsewhere. Indianapolis might choose to have no ordinance if it cannot be limited to viewpoint-specific harms, or it might choose to extend the scope to all speech, just as the law of libel applies to all speech. An attempt to repair this ordinance would be nothing but a blind guess.

No amount of struggle with particular words and phrases in this ordinance can leave anything in effect. The district court came to the same conclusion. Its judgment is therefore

AFFIRMED.

SWYGERT, Senior Circuit Judge, concurring.

I concur in Parts I, II, and III of the court's opinion except for the following strictures. Although raised in the district court, neither ripeness nor abstention was made an issue on appeal. Given that fact, I believe both are pseudo-issues and this court need not treat them sua sponte. True, some of the intervenors have discussed abstention in their briefs; but we are without the benefit of the views of the real parties at interest in this case on either issue. More importantly, a discussion and resolution of these issues are quite unnecessary to the disposition of this appeal.

I also believe that the majority's questionable and broad assertions regarding how human behavior can be conditioned by certain teachings and beliefs (see ante at 328–329, 330) are unnecessary. For even if this court accepts the City of Indianapolis' basic contention that pornography does condition unfavorable responses to women, the ordinance is still unconstitutional.

As to Part IV of the opinion, I agree that the ordinance is unconstitutional on first amendment grounds and that there is no need to discuss vagueness or prior restraint. I do, however, disassociate myself from the extensive statements with respect to how the Indianapolis City Council could fashion an ordinance dealing with pornography that might pass constitutional muster. Indianapolis has asked us to sever the ordinance and save those parts that are not unconstitutional, if we can. All then that this court is required to do is to rule that the ordinance is not severable. Statements regarding which portions of the ordinance may be constitutional are merely advisory and are not the function of this court.

Footnotes

1. "Pornography constructs what a woman is in terms of its view of what men want sexually. . . . Pornography's world of equality is a harmonious and balanced place. Men and women are perfectly complementary and perfectly bipolar. . . . All the ways men love to take and violate women, women love to be taken and violated. . . . What pornography does goes beyond its content: It eroticizes hierarchy, it sexualizes inequality. It makes dominance and submission sex. Inequality is its central dynamic; the illusion of freedom coming together with the reality of force is central to its working. . . . [P]ornography is neither harmless fantasy nor a corrupt and confused misrepresentation of an otherwise neutral and healthy sexual situation. It institutionalizes the sexuality of male supremacy, fusing the erotization of dominance and submission with the social construction of male and female. . . . Men treat women as who they see women as being. Pornography constructs who that is. Men's power over women means that the way men see women defines who women can be. Pornography . . . is a sexual reality." MacKinnon, supra, at 17-18 (note omitted, emphasis in original). See also Andrea Dworkin, *Pornography: Men Possessing Women* (1981). A national commission in Canada recently adopted a similar rationale for controlling pornography. Special Commission on Pornography and Prostitution, 1 *Pornography*

and Prostitution in Canada 49-59 (Canadian Government Publishing Centre 1985).

2. MacKinnon's article collects empirical work that supports this proposition. The social science studies are very difficult to interpret, however, and they conflict. Because much of the effect of speech comes through a process of socialization, it is difficult to measure incremental benefits and injuries caused by particular speech. Several psychologists have found, for example, that those who see violent, sexually explicit films tend to have more violent thoughts. But how often does this lead to actual violence? National commissions on obscenity here, in the United Kingdom, and in Canada have found that it is not possible to demonstrate a direct link between obscenity and rape or exhibitionism. The several opinions in Miller v. California discuss the U.S. commission. See also Report of the Committee on Obscenity and Film Censorship 61-95 (Home Office, Her Majesty's Stationery Office, 1979); Special Committee on Pornography and Prostitution, 1 *Pornography and Prostitution in Canada* 71–73, 95–103 (Canadian Government Publishing Centre, 1985). In saying that we accept the finding that pornography as the ordinance defines it leads to unhappy consequences, we mean only that there is evidence to this effect, that this evidence is consistent with much human experience, and that as judges we must accept the legislative resolution of such disputed empirical questions. See Gregg v. Georgia, 428 U.S. 153, 184-87, 96 S.Ct. 2909, 2930-31, 49 L.Ed.2d 859 (1976) (opinion of Stewart, Powell, and Stevens, JJ.).

3. Indianapolis briefly argues that Beauharnais v. Illinois, 343 U.S. 250, 72 S.Ct. 725, 96 L.Ed. 919 (1952), which allowed a state to penalize "group libel," supports the ordinance. In Collin v. Smith, supra, 578 F.2d at 1205, we concluded that cases such as New York Times v. Sullivan had so washed away the foundations of Beauharnais that it could not be considered authoritative. If we are wrong in this, however, the case still does not support the ordinance. It is not clear that depicting women as subordinate in sexually explicit ways, even combined with a depiction of pleasure in rape, would fit within the definition of a group libel. The well received film *Swept Away* used explicit sex, plus taking pleasure in rape, to make a political statement, not to defame. Work must be an insult or slur for its own sake to come within the ambit of Beauharnais, and a work need not be scurrilous at all to be "pornography" under the ordinance.

4. See, e.g., Zamora v. CBS, 480 F.Supp. 199 (S.D.Fla.1979),

among the many cases concluding that particular plaintiffs could not show a connection sufficiently direct to permit liability consistent with the First Amendment.

*   *   *

William H. HUDNUT, III, Mayor, City of Indianapolis, Indiana, et al. v. AMERICAN BOOKSELLERS ASSOCIATION, INC., et al., 475 U.S. 1001, 106 S.Ct. 1172 (1986).

The judgment is affirmed.

THE CHIEF JUSTICE, Justice REHNQUIST and Justice O'CONNOR would note probable jurisdiction and set the case for oral argument.

Index